DIMENSIONS OF HUMAN SEXUALITY

DIMENSIONS OF HUMAN SEXUALITY

Kenneth L. Jones
Louis W. Shainberg
Curtis O. Byer

Mt. San Antonio College

wcb
Wm. C. Brown Publishers
Dubuque, Iowa

wcb group

Wm. C. Brown   *Chairman of the Board*
Mark C. Falb   *President and Chief Executive Officer*

wcb

WM. C. BROWN PUBLISHERS, College Division
Lawrence E. Cremer   *President*
James L. Romig   *Vice-President, Product Development*
David A. Corona   *Vice-President, Production and Design*
E. F. Jogerst   *Vice-President, Cost Analyst*
Bob McLaughlin   *National Sales Manager*
Marcia H. Stout   *Marketing Manager*
Craig S. Marty   *Director of Marketing Research*
Marilyn A. Phelps   *Manager of Design*
Eugenia M. Collins   *Production Editorial Manager*
Mary M. Heller   *Photo Research Manager*

BOOK TEAM
Edward G. Jaffe   *Executive Editor*
Brenda Fleming Roesch   *Editor*
Lynne M. Meyers   *Associate Editor*
Mary M. Monner   *Developmental Editor*
Marilyn A. Phelps   *Designer*
Laura Beaudoin   *Senior Production Editor*
Faye M. Schilling   *Photo Research Editor*
Mavis M. Oeth   *Permissions Editor*

Cover and chapter opening illustrations are reproduced from a series of monoprints by Michele Scott, Claremont Graduate School, Claremont, California.

Library of Congress Catalog Card Number: 84–72845

ISBN 0-697-08243-1 (cloth)
        0-697-00561-5 (paper)

Printed in the United States of America
10   9   8   7   6   5   4   3   2   1

CONTENTS

PREFACE

Dimensions of Human Sexuality is a basic text for college human sexuality courses that include both the behavioral and biological aspects of sexuality. Although many good texts are available for such courses, this book differs from other college human sexuality texts in its balance between behavioral and biological material, its readability and clarity, and its attention to the many ethical considerations in the expression of human sexuality.

Many steps have been taken to ensure that this text is appropriate for its intended audience. Before the first word was written, numerous people who teach human sexuality were surveyed for their ideas regarding the ideal text. The content and organization of *Dimensions of Human Sexuality* reflect the excellent suggestions of these colleagues. As the text was written, extensive reviews were obtained from professors in all areas of the United States and in all types of colleges. Finally, the manuscript was thoroughly edited to guarantee reading ease and interest.

Organization

The authors considered many alternative plans of organization for this text. The plan adopted has been extensively classroom-tested and has proven effective in actual use. However, the five parts of the text are free-standing and can be used in any sequence desired.

Part 1 introduces the subject of human sexuality and then explores methods of sexual research to provide students with a basis for judging the validity of what they read here and elsewhere. Because today's students are deeply interested in the *context* in which sexual interaction occurs, part 1 also includes a unique chapter on sexual values and concludes with a chapter on love and intimacy.

Many of the important concerns of a human sexuality course involve the biological aspects of sexuality, the subject of part 2. After three chapters survey sexual anatomy and physiology and biological sexual development, separate chapters consider patterns of sexual response and sexual pleasuring. A chapter on sexual difficulties and therapies completes part 2.

Part 3 examines the psychosexual life cycle from birth to death. The special interests, needs, and challenges of each age group are presented in a sequence of four chapters that emphasize the positive aspects of sexuality.

Topics relating to reproductive biology are grouped in part 4. A chapter on fertility control is followed by a discussion of conception, pregnancy, and birth. Part 4 concludes with a study of sexually transmitted diseases, including their impact on our fertility and offspring.

Part 5, the final section of *Dimensions of Human Sexuality,* explores important behavioral aspects of sexuality. Chapter topics include homosexuality, variations in sexual behavior, the commercialization of sex, and power and violence in sexuality.

Approach

Throughout this text, special emphasis is given to topics of pressing interest to today's college students and society in general. Just a few of the important subjects covered include gender roles, love and sexuality, sexual decision making, sexual techniques, sex therapy, abortion, AIDS, homosexuality, prostitution, pornography, rape, and sexual harassment.

Dimensions of Human Sexuality reflects our diverse society with its wide range of ethnic affiliations, religious beliefs and nonbeliefs, sexual orientations, socioeconomic backgrounds, and political persuasions. The authors understand that, for many of the issues discussed in this text, there are no universally acceptable conclusions to be reached. They have tried to give a balanced presentation of a diversity of viewpoints, allowing the reader to draw his or her own conclusions. The approach to personal expressions of sexuality is nonjudgmental, although the authors do not hesitate to take a stand in cases where the expression of one person's sexuality infringes upon the rights or well-being of another person.

Learning Aids

Many learning aids have been built into *Dimensions of Human Sexuality*. These aids eliminate the need for students to purchase a separate study guide, as is necessary with so many of the human sexuality texts currently on the market.

Each chapter opens and closes with an attention-getting vignette. Boxed informational features present topics of special interest to the reader. These boxes allow coverage of a topic in greater depth without interrupting the flow of the chapter and help to sustain reader interest. The phonetic pronunciation of any difficult term is given where the term first appears in the text. Thought-provoking questions, often of a personal nature, appear at key points in each chapter. Illustrations have been carefully selected for maximum learning value. Each chapter ends with a review summary to reemphasize and reinforce the most important points in that chapter. Finally, a glossary at the end of the book clearly defines all terms used in the text.

Instructor's Resource Materials

Dimensions of Human Sexuality is accompanied by a very complete instructor's resource manual. For every chapter, the *Instructor's Manual* presents learning objectives, suggested teaching strategies and classroom activities, a complete outline of the text with supplemental lecture material, and examination questions. A total of 1,731 examination questions, including discussion, true-false, multiple-choice, and matching, are offered. These questions are also available on complimentary Wm. C. Brown TestPak computer diskettes for instructors adopting the book. Each adopting instructor will also receive 56 acetate transparencies for projection, featuring diagrams derived from those in the text and specially adapted for overhead projection. The authors' goal has been to provide a rewarding experience for both students and instructor using this book.

Acknowledgments

The authors wish to thank the following people for their reviews of this book: Beverly B. Palmer, California State University, Dominguez Hills; Geri Ann Johnson, University of Nebraska, Lincoln; Warren L. McNab, University of Nevada, Las Vegas; John Leach, Western Illinois University; Peter F. Maneno, Normandale Community College; James N. Burdine, Seton Medical Center, Austin, TX; Anna Beth Culver, University of Wisconsin, La Crosse; Patricia Reagan, University of Utah; B. E. Pruitt, Association for the Advancement of Health Education; Stuart Fors, University of Georgia.
We are very grateful to the fine staff of Wm. C. Brown Publishers for their invaluable assistance in the preparation and production of this book.

1

SEXUAL
DIMENSIONS

1

What Is Sexuality?
Biological Factors/Psychological Factors/Cultural Factors

Why Study Human Sexuality?
*To Obtain Factual Knowledge/To Develop a Positive
Sexual Self-Concept/To Clarify Sexual Values and Ethics/
To Improve Communication/To Maximize Sexual Pleasure/
To Recognize Destructive Elements in Relationships/To
Manage Personal Fertility/To Prevent, Recognize, and
Deal with Sexually Transmitted Diseases/To Understand
and Cope with Problems in Sexual Response/To Critically
Evaluate Sexual Research*

"What is sexuality?" asked the professor the first day of class. I thought back to when I was growing up. . . . I remember my mom telling me not to touch myself, my dad telling me not to cry . . . to act like a man. I remember, when I was just a kid, sneaking up to my brother's tent and listening to the older boys tell funny stories about girls with bad reputations. I learned sexual plumbing in junior high Biology, what not to do in Health, what to try to do with my first girlfriend, and how to prevent a broken heart from my last lover. It was then that I decided that it was about time to stop the treadmill and take a look at what sex, and for that matter, life, was all about. This course on human sexuality just might be the right place to start.

I hope this course isn't going to be another plumbing handbook. I had enough of that in high school. Still, I wish I knew more about a woman's body. . . . They seem to have so many problems. I never know what they really want.

What *I* want is a little honesty. Why do men and women who know so little about sex spend all their time thinking about it? Why do we hurt each other without thinking? When is sex good? When bad?

I'm not sure if sexuality is about sex or being sexy, but I hope it means something positive, because up to now it's been anything but!

---

celibacy   holistic
(sel'ĭ-bah-se)*   (ho-lis'tik)

Just what is sexuality? Is there any difference between sex and sexuality? Are all of us sexual? Are we always sexual? What can one expect of a course in human sexuality? These are just a few of the questions this chapter attempts to resolve.

What Is Sexuality?

When the word *sexual* became part of the English language several hundred years ago, it was no more than a narrow, technical term that simply referred to being either male or female. In the eighteenth century, the meaning of sexual was broadened somewhat to refer also to the process of reproduction. It wasn't until the nineteenth century that the noun *sexuality* came into use. Although the definition of sexuality was originally limited only to the quality of being male or female, it was gradually expanded during the 1800s to include people's feelings. By the late 1800s, even nonreproductive processes such as **masturbation** (self-stimulation for sexual pleasure) were perceived as expressions of sexuality.

Today, we use the term *sex* when referring to the biological aspects of reproduction, which encompass the **anatomy** (structure) and **physiology** (function) of the two sexes. We also use this term when discussing the biological mechanisms of sperm and egg production, sexual arousal, mating, and pregnancy.

We use the term **sexuality** to refer not only to reproduction and the pursuit of sexual pleasure but also to our need for love and personal fulfillment. The term incorporates the many psychological and cultural factors in human sexual behavior. Sexuality includes our awareness of and reaction to our own maleness or femaleness and that of everyone with whom we interact. The term encompasses such feelings as femininity, masculinity, desire, satisfaction, love, loss, hurt, intimacy, loneliness, caring, sharing, touching, jealousy, rejection, self-esteem, and joy.

We are all sexual. While we all have our own particular styles of sexuality, even those of us who choose a life of **celibacy** (sexual abstinence) remain sexual beings. Furthermore, our sexuality extends from birth until death. It doesn't begin at age eighteen and end when we turn fifty. Today, our sexuality is regarded as an important part of our personality, a fundamental and all-pervasive characteristic of our humanity. Right or wrong, we see a sexual element in nearly all human activity, regardless of how nonsexual the activity might be.

Sexuality incorporates the many psychological and cultural factors in our sexual behavior.

Because sexuality is truly holistic (the whole is greater than the sum of its parts), it is thus best studied through a multi-disciplinary approach. Perhaps more

*The accent marks used in the pronunciation guides are derived from a simplified system of phonetics standard in medical usage. The single accent (') denotes the major stress. Emphasis is placed on the most heavily pronounced syllable in the word. The double accent (") indicates secondary stress. A syllable marked with a double accent receives less emphasis than the syllable that carries the main stress, but more emphasis than neighboring unstressed syllables.

than any other aspect of our lives, sexuality reflects and integrates biological, psychological, and cultural factors. Every sexual feeling, every sexual behavior is influenced by all of these forces and can be understood only through considering each of them.

Biological Factors

Since humans are biological organisms, biology is involved in most discussions of sexual behavior and functioning.

Biological factors in sexuality begin exerting their influence early in embryonic development as the sex organs differentiate into either a male or a female form. Many authorities now also believe that the human brain undergoes sexual differentiation prior to birth (see chapter 7), which means that, to some degree, our ultimate sexuality is influenced even before we are born.

Throughout the life cycle, our sexuality continues to be molded by biological forces. Even as infants and children, we experience physical sexual arousal, as evidenced by vaginal lubrication or penile erection. During puberty, the biological changes we undergo profoundly influence how we perceive ourselves as sexual beings. As adults, our hormones and general physical health are ongoing biological forces that influence our sexuality.

Psychological Factors

Our sexuality is also influenced by complex psychological factors. First, there is our concept of ourselves as either male or female and our notions of what forms of behavior are appropriate for our particular sex or **gender.***

Second, our sexual feelings and behaviors are influenced by a lifetime of experiences, stored away in both the conscious and unconscious portions of our minds. To which persons we feel sexually attracted, on the basis of their gender and other physical and behavioral characteristics, is conditioned by our prior experiences. Our immediate positive or negative feelings about someone, even before we know that person as an individual, are influenced by the kinds of experiences we have had previously with similar-appearing or -behaving persons. How we will feel or behave in any particular situation is again conditioned by our prior experiences.

Third, self-esteem, our sense of personal value or worth, has a major influence over our sexual feelings and behavior. People who feel good about themselves usu-

---

*Some authorities make a clear distinction between the terms *sex* and *gender,* viewing sex as the physical fact of being male or female and gender as the social and behavioral aspects of sex—how we behave as males or females. Other authorities make less distinction, using the two terms interchangeably. In this text, we use the terms *gender* and sex interchangeably when dealing with biological male and female characteristics but use the term *gender* when discussing the psychological aspects of being female or male.

milieu
(me-lyuh′)

ally feel positive about their sexuality, are able to form intimate relationships with others, and, when they have sexual relationships, find these relationships fulfilling. Self-esteem will be a recurring theme throughout this book because it is so deeply involved in our sexuality.

Cultural Factors

Over all of the biological and psychological forces shaping our sexuality lies a significant cultural overlay. Since most of us are exposed to only one culture as we grow up, we naturally tend to assume that whatever our culture accepts as being sexual, or as appropriate sexual behavior, must be perceived similarly everywhere. This, however, is far from the case.

Not only do concepts of sexuality vary from place to place, but they vary from era to era in the same place. The same portion of our anatomy—for example, the legs, earlobes, shoulders, or neck—might be perceived as extremely sexual at one time or place yet carry no sexual connotations at another time or place. Similarly, the same body decoration—for example, clothing, tatooing, or cosmetics—might or might not be perceived as sexual. The same behavior, such as kissing or embracing, can carry entirely different connotations in different cultures. Acceptable behavior in one culture may be totally unacceptable behavior in another culture.

It is meaningless to explore sexuality without reference to its cultural milieu (environment) because our feelings and perceptions are strongly influenced by our culture, and, as we have said, sexuality is a matter of feelings.

Our immediate positive or negative feelings about someone are conditioned by our previous experiences with similar looking or behaving people, plus our cultural concept of what features are considered to be sexually attractive.

1. How would you define your sex? How would you define your sexuality?
2. Why is a multi-disciplinary approach best suited to the study of human sexuality?

Why Study Human Sexuality?

Most of us have grown up in a society that holds extremely ambivalent (having simultaneous attraction and repulsion) attitudes about sexuality. On the one hand, we learn (from such sources as family, friends, school, and the media) that sexual attractiveness is considered important in our society. But at the same time, often from the same sources, we pick up undertones of anxiety and/or guilt about actually acting out our sexuality.

The fact that our sexuality influences almost every aspect of our lives, including how we relate to people of both sexes in all kinds of situations, and how we perceive our roles in family relationships, in our careers, and in society, further confuses the situation.

The sections that follow describe how studying human sexuality can help to clarify this ambivalent sexual atmosphere and reinforce positive feelings about our sexuality.

To Obtain Factual Knowledge

Perhaps the most obvious goal of the study of human sexuality is to gain a solid, factual understanding of its many aspects. Human sexuality is an academic discipline and includes a large body of factual, measurable information. This information can expand our perspective on sexuality beyond the limited confines of our own experiences to include other times, places, and cultures. It can provide a basis for judging the validity of what we hear and read relating to sexuality and can help us recognize the myths and prejudices to which we are so commonly exposed. We can see that the way people are culturally "supposed to be" is not always the way they are.

To Develop a Positive Sexual Self-Concept

Another reason for studying human sexuality is the positive sexual self-concept that will likely result. Our sexual self-concept (how we perceive ourselves sexually) is an important part of our total self-concept. Feeling good about our sexuality is part of feeling good about ourselves. And feeling good about ourselves is basic to emotional health.

People who hold positive attitudes about sexuality find that their personal sense of sexuality enhances their self-esteem. People whose feelings of sexuality give rise to a sense of guilt or anxiety, however, may find that awareness of their inherent sexuality can detract from their self-esteem. And poor self-esteem is a major emotional health problem in our society today.

Part of a positive sexual self-concept is a feeling of being sexually adequate. In our culture, which places so much emphasis on the performance aspects of sex (for example, the number of orgasms attained), someone who feels sexually inadequate is likely to feel inadequate as a total person. Actually, a vicious circle exists, in which poor self-esteem enhances feelings of sexual inadequacy. (A vicious circle is a sequence of events or processes in which the first influences the second, which, in turn, reinforces the first.) The resulting sexual problems can lead to even poorer self-esteem. Fortunately, the converse is also true. A high sense of self-esteem enhances feelings of sexual adequacy.

The concept of self-fulfilling prophecy is also strongly related to our sexual self-concept. Self-fulfilling prophecies, in general, are expectations that influence our behavior in such ways that our expectations are fulfilled. Thus, if our sexual self-concept is healthy, we tend to expect sexual success, and we tend to find it. If our sexual self-concept is poor, we tend to expect sexual failure and thus tend to fail.

A course in human sexuality, while no guarantee for sexual success, can make us feel better about our sexuality, which then makes us feel better about ourselves.

To Clarify Sexual Values and Ethics

Many of us are uncertain about our sexual values and ethics. Under what circumstances is a sexual relationship appropriate? Is **monogamy** (being married to only one person at a time) desirable? Is masturbation a sin? We are exposed to a barrage of conflicting values from our family, friends, religion, and the media. Somehow, from all of this, each of us must develop a personally meaningful and workable set of values and ethics to guide our own lives.

It is not the role of a human sexuality course to lay down specific guidelines for behavior. Sexual ethics are a highly personal matter for each individual to work out according to his or her value system. A course in human sexuality can assist in this process, however, by bringing our values into sharper focus, by helping us to distinguish our personal values from those of our parents or our culture. Once we understand our values and where these values came from, then the ethical decisions by which we guide our behavior can be made on a more conscious basis.

To Improve Communication

On an impersonal level, people today talk about sexual topics much more freely than they did in the past. Yet, most people are still quite reluctant to discuss their personal sexual feelings and experiences. Poor sexual communication can be a significant problem affecting many aspects of our lives.

Since communication is often hindered by an inadequate vocabulary, one way in which a human sexuality course can improve sexual communication is by helping us to know and feel comfortable with the proper terminology for various aspects of the sexual anatomy and physiology. Many sexual words are loaded with emotional connotations—merely hearing or using certain terms causes anxiety. Becoming more familiar with such words and their origins and true meanings helps to diminish our anxiety.

A course in human sexuality can also make it easier to communicate sexual facts and positive attitudes about sexuality to our children. Most of us find very little in our educational experiences to prepare us for parenthood, and the sexual education of children is one of the most commonly mismanaged aspects of parenthood. Too many parents feel uncomfortable with their own sexuality or may lack either the factual knowledge or the ability to communicate that knowledge to their children. Sexual anxieties are thus perpetuated from generation to generation. And, of course, much of what our children perceive is communicated nonverbally. In thousands of subtle ways, we communicate to them whether we feel comfortable with sexuality—both ours and theirs—or whether we feel threatened by it.

Finally, a human sexuality course can help us to develop the ability and confidence to express our most personal sexual feelings, ideas, and experiences. Improved sexual communication can resolve many of the sexual problems each of us has to deal with from time to time. In addition, becoming better sexual communicators can also teach us about being good, nonjudgmental listeners when others are trying to communicate with us.

To Maximize Sexual Pleasure

Sex is an important source of pleasure for most people. A human sexuality course can help us to maximize our sexual pleasure in many ways: The course can help us to understand our own sexual responses and needs as well as those of our partner. It can help us to overcome the inhibitions that so commonly block sexual pleasure. It can help us to communicate our needs and preferences. A course in human sexuality can also relieve some of our anxieties about the normality of certain sexual activities we might want to try, thereby increasing the variety of sexual activities we can enjoy.

To Recognize Destructive Elements in Relationships

Sexuality can be a very positive force in our lives. However, some interpersonal expressions of sexuality are potentially destructive. A human sexuality course can help to make us aware of these destructive elements and alert to their development in ourselves or in our partners. Exploitation, excessive dependency, and jealousy are three of the negative forces that threaten a positive sexual relationship.

Exploitation involves using someone to our advantage. Sexual exploitation, then, involves using a partner to our sexual advantage. Deception (tricking or misleading someone), for example, is exploitative. An example of sexual deception would be making false promises to persuade a reluctant person to become a sex partner (this is called **seduction**). Any situation in which one person holds more power than another and takes advantage of that power without concern for the well-being of the other is also exploitative. An imbalance of power can result from differences in age, physical or emotional strength, wealth, or position. **Incest** (sex involving close relatives) is often viewed as this kind of power-based sexual exploitation. So is **sexual harassment** (an employer making sexual demands of an employee).

Excessive dependency is another potentially destructive factor in a relationship. While any close relationship involves some element of dependency, many relationships include a degree of dependency that is destructive to one or both persons involved. Excessive dependency limits the growth of the dependent person. It also causes anxiety, depression, and reduced self-esteem. The person who is the object of the dependency may find that his or her own personal growth is restricted by the relationship.

Effective communication contributes to a rewarding sex life. A human sexuality course helps to develop communication skills.

Finally, **jealousy** (excessive possessiveness) is a destructive element in many relationships. Jealousy is a reflection of insecurity or a lack of self-confidence, not of intense love. It often drives away the person who is so desperately needed.

A study of human sexuality can help us not only to recognize but also to deal with these and other destructive elements should they ever appear in our own personal relationships.

To Manage Personal Fertility

A course in human sexuality provides basic, factual information about fertility management—how to maximize the chances for the conception and birth of a healthy baby and, if pregnancy is not desired, how to select the safest, most effective, and best method of fertility management for each of us.

To Prevent, Recognize, and Deal with Sexually Transmitted Diseases

Sexually transmitted diseases (STDs) are at epidemic proportions today. The incidence of gonorrhea, for example, stands at about three times the per-capita rate of the 1950s. Some STDs seriously threaten the health of an infected person or his or her offspring. A study of human sexuality includes vital information on preventing sexually transmitted diseases, recognizing the symptoms of STDs, and what to do should symptoms appear.

To Understand and Cope with Problems in Sexual Response

Most of us can expect to encounter at least some difficulty in sexual response at some time in our lives. Often, these difficulties are only temporary responses to fleeting life situations. For many people, however, such sexual problems can seem frightening and overwhelming. A course in human sexuality can help us to understand the causes of many sexual difficulties, how to effectively deal with the problem, and how to find qualified help if necessary.

To Critically Evaluate Sexual Research

The mass media often report the findings of new sexual research. But how do we evaluate this information? Sexual research widely ranges in quality, as does most research. Some sexual research is carefully done by highly qualified individuals. However, some investigations suffer from basic flaws in experimental design, or valid data may be subject to faulty interpretation. And accurate research is sometimes distorted and sensationalized by the media, either to increase sales or to prove a point.

A course in human sexuality can familiarize us with the methods of contemporary sexual research and provide us with a basis for personally evaluating that research.

1. How does what we feel about our sexuality relate to our total self-esteem?
2. How comfortable do you feel about discussing your sexual feelings? Have you been in situations in which better communication might have improved a relationship?
3. Have you identified any areas in which your study of human sexuality will be personally useful?

This course is going to be much more than I thought it would be. I guess I hadn't given much thought to the role that communication plays in my own sexuality. To really love someone, you need to know them inside and out, as well as know yourself. Sex isn't love—I guess I really knew that all along—but I can see now that really learning about and understanding my sexuality isn't going to be as easy as I thought.

Summary

1. The concept of sexuality incorporates the biological, psychological, and cultural factors in human sexual behavior.

2. Sexuality is holistic: The whole is greater than the sum of its biological, psychological, and cultural components.

3. A study of human sexuality can help us to obtain a factual understanding of the many aspects of sexuality; to feel more comfortable with our own sexuality and that of others; to clarify our sexual values and ethics; to develop our ability to communicate sexual ideas and feelings; to maximize our sexual pleasure; to recognize destructive elements in our relationships; to deal with potential problem areas in sexuality, such as unwanted pregnancies, sexually transmitted diseases, and problems in sexual response; and to critically evaluate sexual research.

2

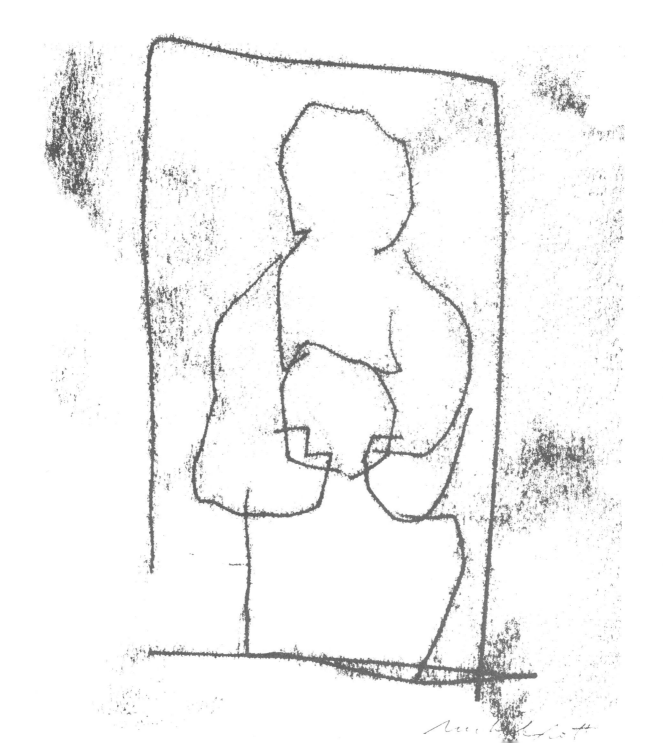

The Research Process
*Stating a Hypothesis/Testing the Hypothesis and
Collecting the Data/Analyzing Research Data/Evaluating
the Research Results*

Milestones in the History of Sexual Research
*Sigmund Freud/Havelock Ellis/Alfred Kinsey/William
Masters and Virginia Johnson*

Review of "Popular" Sex Research
Hunt's *Playboy* Survey/Magazine Surveys/The Hite
Reports

"Sexual research methods! I bet my Business Stats prof would love to help count their scores!"

"Bill, don't be so crude. Haven't you ever wondered where some of the magazines that discuss sexual trends get their information that we take as gospel? How in the world can they say that women like to perform oral sex more than they like to receive it? Who did they ask??? I mean, here we are, normal, red-blooded college students who end up believing all this garbage that's written on sex and we never even try to find out where they get their so-called facts!"

"Carol, who cares? They know what they're doing. They're sex experts, aren't they? I mean, *Playboy* isn't going to hire anyone who doesn't know about sex!"

"Yeah, but where do they get their information? Who does the experimenting? Who acts as a control? How is it kept valid? How many people are interviewed? What kind of people? Do they really represent everybody, or are they a bunch of sickos that volunteer for weird sex experiments?"

"What are you, some kind of an expert all of a sudden?"

"No. I looked at the chapter ahead of time. You know, it wouldn't hurt you if you tried studying ahead of time for a change, instead of always jumping to conclusions."

"Carol, sex is sex. Those guys who write the books and the magazines are doing all the paperwork so we can benefit from their expertise. Why bother worrying about where the info comes from? Just enjoy!"

"Look, I want to know how some of these so-called experts go about knowing what they know. I'm not going to blindly accept anything. You do what you want, you usually do."

Research is a method of obtaining information and answering questions. In this chapter, we discuss the research process and various sexual research methods, including clinical research, experimental research, survey research, and observational research. We learn how sexual research is conducted and become familiar with the terminology and tools of this research.

Our goal is to become capable not only of understanding the findings of sexual research but also of placing these findings in the proper personal perspective. We need to be able to critically evaluate sexual research and to decide for ourselves the validity of the research conclusions for each of us.

The Research Process

Sexual researchers, like all scientific researchers, must go through a series of four steps to obtain their information. These steps are (1) stating a hypothesis, (2) testing the hypothesis and collecting the data, (3) analyzing the research data, and (4) evaluating the research results.

Stating a Hypothesis

The first step in any research process is deciding what we want to learn from the research. Suppose sexual researchers are trying to find out how many times a week married couples have sexual intercourse. First, they review and evaluate all previous research in this area. This will establish if the question has been answered in the past. If there have been previous studies, the researchers may change the question to find out the relationship between the number of times a week couples have intercourse today and the number of times couples had sexual intercourse in a past study or past studies. Previous studies also serve as guidelines in establishing patterns of research and the best type of sampling (interviews, questionnaires, case studies, etc.) to use to produce the desired results. A review of previous research may also help to reduce errors since researchers can see where changes can be made to make the current study more accurate.

Then researchers formulate a **hypothesis,** a tentative, written assumption to be tested by their research. In this case, the researchers' hypothesis might be: "The average married couple has sexual intercourse three times a week."

Testing the Hypothesis and Collecting the Data

The researchers must now test their hypothesis and collect the research data, while strictly adhering to a **research design** (prescribed standards for planning and conducting the research). The four primary research designs in sexual research are clinical research, experimental research, survey research, and observational research.

Each of these methods has its own strengths and weaknesses, and researchers must decide which research design will most conclusively test their hypothesis.

The research designs are not necessarily independent of each other—in fact, they often overlap. Researchers may decide, for example, to combine observational research with experimental research.

We now look at each of these research designs in detail.

Clinical Research

Clinical research involves studying people who are suffering from physical or mental disorders in an attempt to discover more about the disorder and to assess the value of the current treatment for that disorder. Individuals go to see a physician, psychologist, or therapist when they feel something is wrong. While treating the individual, the clinical researcher accumulates information in an attempt to understand more fully the individual's problems and to assess current treatment. To a certain extent, clinical research is going on whenever anyone is being treated by any medical professional.

Clinical research in human sexuality has not always been well accepted. In the past, any deviation from heterosexual sex for the purpose of reproduction was considered unhealthy, abnormal, or sinful, and, thus, people who sought treatment for sexual problems were often considered sexual deviates or criminals. Early clinical researchers in human sexuality were considered to be "pathology-seeking" individuals, meaning that they were looking for abnormalities, and information gathered by these professionals usually was never released or never accepted by others if released. Actually, reviews of this research has added significantly to our current knowledge.

Today, there is a greater tolerance for and understanding of sexual behavior that deviates from "normal" heterosexual reproductive intercourse, and clinical research in human sexuality usually is well received. Much of our current information concerning rape, incest, sexual abuse, transsexuality, and sexual difficulties has been obtained from clinical evaluation of individuals who sought treatment for these problems.

Most clinical research in human sexuality results from evaluations of **case studies,** which are intensive analyses of single individuals or small groups of individuals. Physicians, psychologists, and sociologists release anonymous case studies of their patients or clients, usually after the individual has completed treatment. Researchers then compile, evaluate, and compare these case studies to find similarities and to establish trends.

Much of the current clinical research in human sexuality deals with treating gender identity problems and sexual dysfunctions. For example, the single most common sexual dysfunction that occurs in men is *erectile dysfunction* (impotence), the inability of a man to produce an erection. Many physicians, psychologists, and therapists are treating individuals with this problem throughout the country. Some professionals treat as few as one patient, while others (usually clinics specializing in the disorder) are treating dozens. Each professional, in keeping detailed medical records, recording effective therapies, and publishing this information, adds to the clinical research into erectile dysfunction and its treatment.

Case studies, however, explain specific conditions being treated and can only be considered absolutely true for those individuals under therapy. Information from case studies can be applied, with relative certainty, to others with similar problems, but, without collaborating research by more general methods (surveys or questionnaires), case studies are usually not applicable to the general population.

On the positive side, many case studies of a specific problem, from widely separated areas of the country over a period of time, show who are representative cases. Also, as positive results of treatment become more widely known, more people come forward for treatment, and the actual extent of the problem becomes better known.

Isolated case studies of unusual conditions are usually not relevant research and are often reported only as curiosities. But it is important that these cases be reported since their review by other researchers may be helpful some time in the future.

Experimental Research

Experiments in human sexuality are a relatively recent phenomena. Before the 1960s, for example, it was taboo to show people sexually stimulating material and to obtain the physiological measurements required in certain types of experimental sexual research. Today, researchers generally can conduct human sexual experiments without a powerful reaction from the public. But the nature and rigid design of experimental research, while providing conclusive and precise results, often limits its applicability in human sexuality.

In experimental sexual research, individuals are confronted with specific stimuli, under laboratory conditions, and their reactions are measured. First, the researchers assemble a group of people who are basically identical with regard to such characteristics as age and social background. The researchers then randomly assign each individual to one of two groups—a control group and a research or experimental group. **Random assignment** means that each subject in the experiment has the same probability of being picked for either group. During the experiment, the researchers introduce a unique experimental condition (such as a specific treatment or question) to the experimental group but not to the control group. By measuring the subsequent differences in reaction between the two groups, the researchers can ascertain the effects of the experimental condition with great precision. In some cases, these experiments are conducted in specially designed rooms that are equipped with television cameras, tape recorders, one-way mirrors, and other methods of observing and recording sexual behavior.

Such experimental research is best suited for studies in which the researcher has specific, definable, and limited questions to test. Experiment results are precise because researchers can control the majority of extraneous factors that commonly affect the results of clinical and survey research.

Experiments in human sexuality, however, are difficult to design. Not only must researchers assemble a matched group of subjects (a difficult feat at best), they must also create an experimental sexual situation that is the same as the real-life situation under study. Some researchers, for example, have attempted to experimentally measure sexual arousal by presenting subjects with movies, pictures, or slang words depicting sexual acts while measuring the blood flow to the subjects' genital organs. These researchers argue that their measurements reveal the same differences in reaction as real-world sexual situations. Other researchers argue, however, that in a real-world sexual situation, a person is active, involved, and receiving information from all five senses—sight, hearing, smell, taste, and touch. They question whether the measurements obtained by the researchers affect the subjects' responses, whether the subjects' responses would be fundamentally different outside the experimental environment, and to what degree the subjects' responses depend upon the subjects' cultural background. These researchers feel that the best sexual research is conducted in nonlaboratory surroundings and presented in nonlaboratory terms.

In addition to the problems involved in designing experimental sexual research, another problem is that experimental research can test for only one variable at a time (or a very limited number of variables). It is not efficient for studies that explore numerous aspects of sexuality at the same time.

Because of these limitations, survey methods of research are usually more useful in studying human sexuality, even though they yield results that are less conclusive and precise than the results obtainable from experimental research.

Survey Research

The most common method of obtaining data about human sexuality is through sex sampling surveys. Survey research in human sexuality consists of asking selected groups of people carefully prepared questions about their sexual behavior and attitudes. Identifying the "selected groups of people" to be surveyed is a major part of survey research. Before asking any questions, researchers must identify the population to be studied and the best method of sampling that population.

Population A **population** is any recognizable group to be studied in survey research. For example, a population could be all adult human beings in the world, all men between the ages of twenty-five and thirty in the United States, or all female adolescents in Los Angeles County.

Suppose, as we mentioned earlier, that researchers wanted to find out how many times a week married couples have intercourse. The researchers would be interested only in a population of married couples but would need to specify whether the research would involve, for example, married couples throughout the world, married couples in the United States, or, perhaps, only married couples in California.

Sampling The validity of survey research often depends upon the **sample group** (a smaller, representative group taken from the population) that the researchers identify.

For example, suppose the researchers in our example defined their population as all of the married couples in the United States. Obviously, the researchers have neither the time, money, or personal resources to question every married couple in the country about their intercourse frequency. If they could question one married couple chosen at random out of every fifty married couples in the United States, however, the results would probably be valid for all of the married couples in the United States.

Researchers must be careful that their samples are both random and representative. For the sample in our example to be random, every married couple in the United States would have to have the same probability of being chosen for the research.

For the sample in our example to be representative, the married couples chosen for the research would have to come from all parts of the country. If all the couples came only from Missouri, Kansas, Nebraska, and Iowa, for example, the sample would not be representative of married couples in the United States, but of married couples in the Midwest.

Once survey researchers have identified the population and the sample group to be surveyed, the questioning process can begin. The questioning can take the form of either a personal interview or a questionnaire.

Interviews and Questionnaires Interviews can be conducted either face-to-face or over the telephone. One advantage to this type of encounter is that the interviewer can establish a rapport (a harmonious relationship) with the person being interviewed, which may result in the interviewee giving answers that are more open and more honest. Interviewers are trained, however, to keep the interview on a professional basis so as to avoid what Kaplan (1964) calls **shared humanity,** where both the interviewer and the interviewee are influenced by the reactions of the other to the questions and the questioning process.

A random sample of the population is interviewed to produce valid results.

Another advantage is the flexibility of an interview. An alert interviewer can change the direction of an interview according to the interviewee's responses. For example, if a person responds affirmatively to a question about whether or not he or she has engaged in extramarital intercourse, the interviewer can introduce a series of questions about extramarital intercourse that the interviewer would not have asked had the initial response been negative. Another aspect of this flexibility is that interviewers have the opportunity to clarify and restate any questions that the interviewee appears to find confusing.

Finally, interviews allow interviewers to obtain responses from people who, because of low reading levels, blindness, etc., would not be able to respond to a questionnaire.

Written questionnaires, on the other hand, may produce responses that are more honest than they would have been had the questions been asked in a face-to-face interview because respondents to questionnaires usually feel more assured of their anonymity. Another advantage of questionnaires is that they tend to be less costly than personal interviews because they require fewer people to administer. In addition, far greater numbers of individuals can be sampled through questionnaires than personal interviews, and the questionnaire can often be structured so that it can be computer tabulated, allowing for the sampling to be completed much more rapidly.

Problems with Sex Sampling Surveys   Although sex sampling surveys are a relatively inexpensive, highly flexible, and fast way of gathering data from a large number of people, they do have two major disadvantages.

The first is the problem of nonresponse. After carefully identifying a sample population to be questioned, researchers may be frustrated to find that only a fraction of that sample population is willing to participate in the research. Especially in surveys of human sexuality, large numbers of individuals choose not to respond. This nonresponse may introduce what is called a **"volunteer bias"** into the research, since it seems likely that the characteristics of those individuals who volunteered to respond are different from those who chose not to respond. Research on volunteer bias to determine how volunteers differ from nonvolunteers is not yet conclusive. Exactly how much nonresponse actually biases survey results is also unknown at this time.

A second disadvantage of sex sampling surveys is inaccuracy. Survey researchers must rely upon respondents' self-reports of sexual behavior and attitudes. But how accurate are these self-reports?

It is often difficult to remember specific facts, and many sexual surveys require individuals to recall sexual behavior from many years earlier. People's recall may be in error. More recent feelings and events tend to obscure and change the interpretations of previous feelings and events.

Another basic concern related to inaccuracy is whether or not people are truthful. Some respondents to sex surveys may consciously or unconsciously distort or conceal the reality of their sexual activities. Some may exaggerate their sexual activity to make themselves appear more sexually active or liberated; others may minimize their sexual activity so that they don't appear oversexed or abnormal. Some may conceal or deny aspects of their sexuality altogether because these aspects may seem abnormal or be too painful to recall. One way to offset this distortion is to ask the same question in several ways and to watch the consistency of the respondents' answers. Also, assuring respondents of complete anonymity and impressing upon them the necessity for accurate information in scientific research such as this may help to minimize the problem.

Another source of inaccuracy in sexual surveys are the estimates respondents give regarding the amount of time they spend in specific sexual activities. Most people have trouble estimating time in the first place but find it especially difficult when they are engaged in an activity such as sex. Questions that require estimates, then, may be introducing inaccuracies into the survey.

Finally, inaccuracies in survey research may result from the way in which questions on the questionnaire or during the interview are worded. Skillful researchers are able to word questions to elicit almost any desired response. And, thus, research results may reflect, either intentionally or unintentionally, the personal biases of the researcher.

Observational Research

Observational research consists, in essence, of a human observer or an instrument observing and recording the activities of individuals in either a natural setting or a laboratory setting. In human sexuality studies, observational research is usually conducted within a laboratory setting.

As is discussed later in the chapter, Masters and Johnson were the first to conduct observational research in human sexuality. They observed—both directly and with the use of photographic equipment—the sexual activities of men and women in a laboratory setting to obtain data on the anatomy and physiology of sexual response.

Observational research in human sexuality has its own set of problems. The first is finding individuals who are willing to volunteer as subjects for the research. While most people would probably be willing to complete an anonymous questionnaire, few are willing to be observed while engaging in sexual intercourse.

Another problem is that often no control groups are used in observational research. Some people question whether sexual behavior observed in the laboratory is the same as private sexual behavior. For example, in 1974, G. A. Lincoln attempted to show changes in male sex hormone levels before and after exposure to an erotic film. Blood was taken from a group of men every ten to forty minutes for several hours before and after the men viewed a thirty-minute erotic film, and the men's hormone levels were calculated. Lincoln concluded that male hormone levels do not change in response to erotic films. Athanasiou (1980), however, feels that it is more possible that the needle punctures and blood drawing required in Lincoln's laboratory test could override a thirty-minute film in controlling hormone levels in the blood. Thus, the question remains: Can the results obtained in the laboratory be valid for the general population?

A third drawback to observational research is that it is expensive and time consuming. Consequently, a rather small sample of subjects is usually involved in such studies.

Finally, the informal nature of observational research can pose a problem. Two researchers observing a man and a woman in sexual intercourse, for example, may notice different things and perhaps reach contrary conclusions. Which observer is correct? Which observer do we believe? The lack of a formal research method can make the results of observational research difficult to validate.

Observational research in human sexuality, however, has one primary advantage over the "self-reports" often requested in survey research. We explained in the previous section that inaccuracies resulting from poor memory, dishonesty, distortion, and poor estimates were a major problem of sex sampling surveys. The observational research design can eliminate some, if not all, of these problems since the subject of the research does not "report" anything. His or her behavior and responses are simply observed.

---

1. What is a hypothesis? Choose an area of sexual behavior and formulate a hypothesis.
2. Which of the four research designs discussed do you think would be best to test your hypothesis from question 1? Why?
3. Why do you think that the most common method of obtaining data about human sexuality is through survey research and not clinical, experimental, or observational research?
4. What is a population? Give examples of several different populations. Do you fit into one specific population or a series of populations?

Analyzing Research Data

After the actual research has been performed, researchers usually have gathered a set of data (information) that needs to be analyzed and interpreted so that conclusive research results can be drawn. Most data analysis is statistical. Although the formulas and thought processes involved in statistical data analysis are beyond the scope of this text, we will briefly discuss several of the more common statistical terms.

Common Statistical Terms

Let's go back to the example mentioned earlier about the sexual researchers attempting to determine the number of times a married couple has sexual intercourse in a week. Suppose that, after sampling, the researchers obtain the data shown in table 2.1. The data show that the number of times married couples in the United States have intercourse every week varies from zero to fifteen. Zero to fifteen is called the **range** of the sample. Often, the range is too wide to be meaningful in a report and thus must be summarized in some manner.

One way to summarize a study such as this is to plot the data from table 2.1 on a graph, marking the **frequency** of intercourse on the horizontal axis and the number of married couples reporting this frequency (**incidence**) on the vertical axis (figure 2.1). Frequency is the number of times the event occurred and is the frequency of occurrence. Incidence, on the other hand, is the rate at which a certain event occurs. Consequently, the number of couples who engage in a particular frequency of sexual intercourse represent the incidence of occurrence.

The curve produced by plotting this hypothetical example shows that the greatest number of married couples (520 couples) in the survey group tend to have sexual intercourse, on the average, three times a week. This number (three times a week) is also called the **mode** (the maximum frequency that the event occurs) and is represented by the highest point on the curve.

Table 2.1 Hypothetical Data from Research to Determine the Frequency of Sexual Intercourse among Married Couples.

Frequency of Intercourse Per Week	Number of Couples Reporting This Frequency
0	10
1	30
2	500
3	520
4	400
5	300
6	250
7	200
8	150
9	120
10	100
11	80
12	60
13	50
14	30
15	10

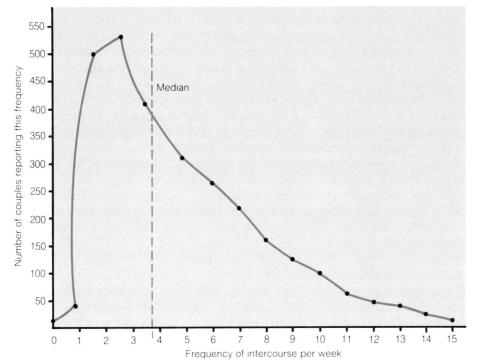

Figure 2.1 A graph of the hypothetical data (shown in table 2.1) of the frequency of sexual intercourse among married couples.

The **mean** is the average number of times there is intercourse during a week for all of the married couples. It is calculated by finding the total number of times that the married couples in the sample engaged in sexual intercourse during a week (14,690 times) and dividing by the total number of married couples (2,810 couples). The mean for this example is 5.23 or 5.

The term *median* is related to data placed on a curve, such as in figure 2.1. The **median** of a study is a perpendicular line (figure 2.1) that represents the number that splits the sample in half. Half of the sample subjects fall below the median, and half are above. In our example, the median would be close to four, since 1,060 of the subjects have sexual intercourse less frequently during the course of a week and 1,350 of the subjects have sexual intercourse more frequently than this number.

The median in this study is not an exact number because the study did not produce a "normal" curve; that is, one where exactly half of the subjects are above or below the center of the curve. In most research, researchers hope to obtain a normal curve because the symmetry of the curve allows a more exact interpretation of the data. But, too often what is obtained is a curve like figure 2.1, and this type of a curve requires more interpretation by researchers.

Statistically Normal Behavior Versus Humanly Normal Behavior

In statistical terms, normality is what is average or usual. By this definition, statistical abnormality, then, is all behavior that falls outside the usual or average. This definition of what is normal or abnormal requires no value judgments about the behavior in question. The researcher simply counts the number of individuals displaying the behavior, stipulates a normal range, and classifies the individuals in the sample (and all others that are similar in their behavior) as being either normal or abnormal.

The danger is our confusing statistically normal behavior with humanly normal behavior. If, for example, we read that sexual research shows that the average person has intercourse three times a week, we tend to compare our sexual behavior with the reported average and make conclusions about our normality or abnormality. Such conclusions can cause unnecessary emotional conflicts ("Am I undersexed?" "Am I oversexed?").

The concept of normality goes far beyond statistics. A reported statistical average is just a number and not a standard for judging normality. Normality and abnormality cannot be judged outside of the social, emotional, and physical context of the behavior in question.

Evaluating the Research Results

Once researchers have stated a hypothesis, tested that hypothesis using one or a combination of the four research designs, and analyzed the research data, just how valid are the results? Sexual researchers face some unique problems in determining the validity of their research because sexual research is not as exact as research into the natural or physical sciences, and it will never attain this precision. There are several reasons for this.

First, the subject matter of sexual research is people, and people are difficult to study. People, for example, are not likely to volunteer to have their sexual behavior observed or discussed. If researchers manage to persuade them to participate in the sexual research, people tend to overinterpret the questions and overevaluate and overscrutinize their responses before actually divulging any information to researchers. And, as we discussed earlier, there is what Kaplan (1964) calls shared humanity: whenever one person attempts to study another, both are influenced by the behavior of the other. Only a few results of sexual research are valid for all people. Most are fully valid for a few people, partially applicable to others, and invalid for many.

Another reason why sexual research is not exact is because introspection (the use of personal experience to explain or judge information) greatly influences sexual researchers' interpretations of data. All scientists tend to judge information according to their own biases, life-styles, and cultural perspectives, but this use of introspection is especially true in sexual research. The introspection of sexual researchers is grounded upon the researchers' accumulated knowledge of human sexual behavior and attitudes. For this reason, sexual researchers tend to be more aware of their personal biases, prejudices, and limitations than the average layperson and thus are more likely to arrive at accurate conclusions. But, in spite of these skills that add precision to observations, even recognized authorities in human sexuality research sometimes disagree.

Does this mean that sexual researchers cannot say anything without some measure of confidence? We hope not. Over the years, researchers have developed skills and tools that add precision to their observations and that correct for bias and personal prejudices in their interpretations of findings. For example, the science of statistics has refined the techniques of sampling to produce great accuracy. Microelectronics now allow people to participate in observational studies while in their own homes, and the data are collected remotely. By far the most important tool that adds precision to sexual research is the computer. The computer allows great numbers of individuals to be sampled, thereby increasing the variety of persons sampled in any survey. Computer evaluation of data also equalizes interpretations of data from many different researchers. In addition, modern communications among researchers allow more professionals to evaluate data before it is published.

The important point to remember is that the results of all sexual research are open to individual evaluation, and the personal validity of sexual research interpretations should always be questioned.

Sexual research is an ongoing process. We will never reach the point where everything about sexuality (or any subject for that matter) is definitely known. Many

libido
(lĭ-be′do)

of today's accepted "facts" will be replaced with new "facts" revealed through further research.

---

1. How does statistically normal behavior become confused with humanly normal behavior? Do you compare your sexual attitudes and actions with the statistics you read? Do you feel that your sexual attitudes and actions are normal?
2. Why is sexual research not exact?
3. The next time you read a report on some sexual research that has been conducted, what kinds of questions are you going to ask yourself about that research before you accept the research results?

Milestones in the History of Sexual Research

Early sexual research was the by-product of explanations for emotional problems. Freud's work to discover the causes of mental illness, for example, developed into sexual explanations for mental illness. Sex, up to and during Freud's time, was usually considered a means of reproduction, and the emotional satisfaction of sex was never considered. It is easy to see why, in such an atmosphere, there was no research into sexual philosophies or behavior. It was not until the research of Havelock Ellis and the sexual surveys of the 1920s that explanations of normal sexual behavior began to emerge.

Sigmund Freud

Sigmund Freud (1856–1939) was a pioneer in sexual research.

Sigmund Freud (1856–1939) was an Austrian neurologist, a physician who specialized in the diagnosis and treatment of the nervous system. Freud's theory about the causes of hysteria (senseless, wild emotionalism) was the first attempt to explain sexual behavior. In his *Selected Papers on Hysteria and Other Psychoneurosis* (1912), Freud concluded that hysteria developed from early sexual conflict. Freud theorized that an infant was born with a specific amount of sexual energy (called the **libido**) which when discharged was pleasurable, but when blocked from discharge caused tension resulting in hysteria. His cure for hysteria consisted of gradually uncovering any sexually traumatic memories of infancy, reenacting these memories, and then removing what Freud called the "emotional (sexual) energy" connected with these infantile sexual experiences. Release of this "emotional energy," according to Freud, relieved the symptoms of hysteria. Freud found a number of instances in which the exact recollection of such early sexually traumatic memories did, in fact, lead to the relief of the hysterical symptoms. His procedure for uncovering these memories is now known as psychoanalysis.

In his book *The Ego and the Id* (1927), Freud later hypothesized that the root of most neurosis, not just hysteria, was the sexual trauma of the infant and child, reexpressed in adult neurotic behavior. As explained in a book published several years after his death (*The Standard Edition of the Complete Psychological Works,* 1953), however, after several years of applying this sexual trauma theory to neurosis, Freud began to question this hypothesis. Not only was Freud unable to always find the traumatic sexual experience, but also so many people exhibited neurotic behavior that it was hard, even for Freud, to believe that every neurotic patient was suffering from such infantile sexual trauma.

During this period (the early 1900s), Freud embarked on an interesting self-experiment. He conducted a self-analysis and discovered the beginnings of his own sexual emotional development as a child. This experience led him to the realization that, for most individuals, the sexuality of the infant expresses itself later in life in sexual fantasies, not in actual experiences or in abnormal social behavior. Working from this theory, Freud found that some individuals develop neurotic behavior regardless of their sexual emotional development, while others develop normal behavior patterns. These findings disproved the theory that infantile sexual repression was the only cause of mental illness. This research resulted in the publication of *Three Essays on the Theory of Sexuality* (1905), in which Freud presented the first theories of psychosexual development. This was the first instance of concepts based upon the erotic life of the individual being published.

Freud did not conduct what would be considered research today. His research consisted of personal observations or personal feelings or experiences. He formulated a theory, then accumulated observations that confirmed his predictions. This is why, with time, many of his theories were changed, even by him. This type of research would be unacceptable today. However, during Freud's time, modern methods of clinical, experimental, survey, or observational research would have been unthinkable.

Havelock Ellis

Havelock Ellis (1859–1939) was a British psychologist who, in his seven-volume *Studies in the Psychology of Sex* (1942), was one of the first to publish data from sexual surveys.

At the same time that Freud was developing his vast sexual theories based upon his own feelings, Ellis was gathering data and working toward social-sexual reforms. Ellis's ideas were more acceptable to social reformers than were Freud's psychoanalytic theories of sexuality. Ellis recognized that a full understanding of sexuality depended upon surveys of normal, everyday people and not upon studies of criminals and the mentally ill. Ellis decided to survey fairly normal people about their sexual practices.

Havelock Ellis (1859–1939) was an early researcher in the social implications of sexuality.

From 1920 through 1938, Ellis's writings stimulated a number of small-scale sex surveys and inquiries about sexual behavior in many parts of Europe, including Scandinavia, Germany, Russia, and other northern European countries. These surveys were the basis for reforms in the sex education of children and in laws about homosexuals and eventually led to the formation of the World League of Sexual Reform after World War I.

Alfred Kinsey

Alfred Kinsey (1894–1956) was the first modern sexual survey pollster.

Alfred Kinsey (1894–1956) was a biologist at Indiana University whose specialty was evolutionary theory. In 1938, he was asked to teach the human sexuality part of a marriage and family course. When Kinsey discovered that there was very little information on normal sexual behavior, he developed a survey questionnaire for his students and then used the information from the questionnaires in the course.

Kinsey's questionnaires were the beginnings of his research into human sexual behavior. For the next ten years, he conducted the first major national sex survey in the United States and was the first to use scientific sampling techniques to obtain his information. The data was collected from very structured personal interviews. The information revealed what Gagnon (1975) called social bookkeeping: sexually, who does what with whom, how, and how often.

Kinsey's research culminated in two landmark volumes—*Sexual Behavior in the Human Male* (1948) and *Sexual Behavior in the Human Female* (1953). Because the information in these books was widely reported in newspapers and magazines, the books raised one of the most widely spread public and professional storms since Darwin, and Kinsey's work was both severely criticized and highly praised. Kinsey brought sex out of the bedroom and into the public eye and was instrumental in laying the foundation for the greater freedom in sexual behavior and understanding we have today. His work also stimulated the formation of the *Institute for Sex Research.*

William Masters and Virginia Johnson

While Kinsey used a survey research design to obtain information about sexual behavior and attitudes, Masters and Johnson approached human sexuality from a completely different perspective. They used a laboratory setting to conduct some of the first observational research into the anatomy and physiology of human sexual response.

Masters and Johnson's research consisted of using electronic sensors and photographic and direct observations of couples and individuals engaged in sexual activity in a laboratory setting. Initially, they sought out prostitutes as subjects because the researchers felt that people from the general population would never volunteer for such research. They later discovered that they were wrong when an appeal for volunteers brought an enthusiastic response. As a result, their later research relied on middle-class volunteers. The product of their research, *Human Sexual Response* (1966), was based on measurements from and observations of over ten thousand episodes of sexual activity by 382 women and 312 men.

Following their work on the anatomy and physiology of sexual response, Masters and Johnson turned their attentions to sexual problems and to the treatment of these problems. In 1970, they published *Human Sexual Inadequacy,* which described a variety of therapies for treating sexual difficulties.

The work of Masters and Johnson has been the basis for many of the therapies currently used in the treatment of sexual dysfunction throughout the world.

Masters and Johnson were the first researchers to directly observe sexual activity within a laboratory.

1. Explain how Freud conducted his research. Would his methods be acceptable today? Why or why not?
2. Would Ellis's methods of conducting research be more acceptable to contemporary researchers than Freud's methods of conducting research? Why?
3. Given the opportunity, would you feel comfortable volunteering to be a subject in a research project in which your sexual responses were going to be observed and measured? Do you think that the results of such research would reflect a certain amount of volunteer bias? Why or why not?

Review of "Popular" Sex Research

A visit to a local magazine shop or paperback book counter may reveal a number of titles whose literary emphasis is sexual fantasy, but which purport to be "scientific." The reason for this bombardment is simple: Sexuality sells. The market for sex-related materials is insatiable. Yet, much of this literature contains oversimplified, distorted information and very little in the way of substantialized, validated research results.

Careful, valid sexual research produces new information slowly. It takes time, often years. The researcher must design a study, gather information (over periods of months or years), analyze the data, verify the information with other researchers, and then prepare an article or book for publication. Often, the time from first idea to final publication of a research project may be five years or more.

In the next few pages, we examine some of the more popular sex surveys that have been published in recent years—not to discuss the results of these surveys but to evaluate the methods that were used to conduct the research. These kinds of surveys have only limited value because sampling and interpretation problems biased the results.

At the same time that we review this "popular" sex research, it is important that we remember that today there are a number of individuals, organizations, and institutions that are not as well known to the general public doing research in human sexuality. Many are conducting valid research that will result in accurate information. Melvin Zelnik and John F. Kantner of Johns Hopkins University, for example, have conducted several surveys (1971, 1976, 1979) of the sexual activities and attitudes of the United States teenage population. Ansley J. Coale has gathered research data on teenage pregnancy. This type of research is accurate, informative, and very well received by sex educators throughout the nation. Magazines and journals that publish valid information on human sexuality include *Medical Aspects of Human Sexuality, New England Journal of Medicine, Archives of Sexual Behavior, Sexology, Sexual Medicine Today,* and the journals of various biological, medical, and psychological disciplines.

Hunt's *Playboy Survey*

During the early 1970s, the Playboy Foundation, financed by *Playboy* magazine, commissioned Morton Hunt to undertake a large-scale sex survey. (Hunt is a professional journalist who specializes in writing popularized versions of scientific studies on sexuality.) There were two purposes to this survey—to find up-to-date information about sexual practices and to see if sexual practices had changed since the Kinsey survey done thirty years before.

The results of the 1972 survey were initially published in *Playboy* magazine. Later, Hunt compiled all of the information in his book entitled *Sexual Behavior in the 1970s* (1974).

The Research Guild, an independent market survey and behavioral research organization, designed the questionnaire and collected the information for the survey. Names were chosen at random from the telephone book in twenty-four cities in the United States. These people were contacted and asked to participate anonymously in private panel discussions of present trends in American sexual behavior. Twenty percent of the people contacted came to the discussions and were asked to fill out questionnaires.

This survey contained some basic sampling problems. First, choosing names from a telephone book is a form of selective sampling because not all segments of society have phones or listed phone numbers. Furthermore, phones are listed most often in male names, and more men than women are listed. Many women, fearing identification as single women, choose unlisted numbers. All of this means that more men than women are able to participate in surveys when names are chosen from a telephone book. A phone survey such as this is really a chance selection of an alphabet.

A second sampling problem was that the Research Guild concentrated its efforts in large urban areas so that large discussion groups could be arranged. Therefore, rural and suburban populations were excluded from participating. The Research Guild tried to overcome these problems by contacting large numbers of people. But this probably only increased the problem by further isolating the urban sample from all other segments of the population.

Another sampling problem of Hunt's *Playboy* survey was that this survey, like all other surveys, had to contend with volunteer bias. As explained earlier, this term is used to describe the fact that many of the people who volunteer for sexual surveys are those who like to talk about their sexual behavior. Individuals who are not very sexually active generally do not volunteer. Thus, as a result of volunteer bias, surveys tend to report increased sexual behavior, not reduced sexual behavior.

Hunt's sample was much smaller than Kinsey's. However, most researchers feel that Hunt's *Playboy* survey was at least as accurate as the Kinsey report.

Magazine Surveys

During the 1970s and early 1980s, large-scale sex surveys were conducted by three well-known magazines—*Psychology Today, Redbook,* and *Cosmopolitan.* The *Psychology Today* survey was conducted in 1969 and reported in 1970. *Redbook* published one questionnaire in 1974, the results in 1975, and then conducted another survey in 1981. *Cosmopolitan* conducted its survey in 1979 and published the results in 1980.

Statistics from magazine surveys are biased because of sampling problems. In the first place, magazines are designed by their publishers to appeal to select groups. There are men's magazines, women's magazines, auto magazines, fitness magazines, and so on. Only the readers of the magazine, then, can be surveyed. In the *Redbook* and *Cosmopolitan* surveys, for example, only women were surveyed. Ninety percent of the first *Redbook* sample were women in their middle thirties who were married, well-educated, and had incomes higher than the national average. In the *Cosmopolitan* survey, a younger, well-educated, more independent, unmarried, career-minded woman was surveyed. The *Psychology Today* survey elicited responses from both males and females. These people were also well-educated—mostly professionals or students—and rated themselves as being "sexually liberal."

The fact that magazine surveys eliminate as possible respondents all persons who cannot read, are not motivated to read, or cannot afford the cost of the magazine is another way in which the survey sample is biased.

One final sampling problem in magazine surveys is a form of volunteer bias. Researchers feel that the people who return the magazine questionnaires are the ones most comfortable with the questions being asked. People who are uncomfortable with the survey questions tend not to respond. For example, after the *Psychology Today* survey, a few people wrote to the magazine not to respond to the survey but to complain that the survey was pornographic.

The sampling problems of magazine surveys indicate that the respondents to these surveys are not typical of the general population. As a result, the conclusions of these surveys cannot be applied to the general population and have limited value.

Variations in the Kinsey and Hunt Survey Results

Two of the more important attempts to obtain a representative picture of sexual behavior in the United States were the classic studies of Kinsey (1948, 1953) and Hunt (1974). Hunt reported that he had found remarkable changes in the thirty years since Kinsey. A comparison of some of the results of these two studies can give us an idea of the degree of change in the last thirty years in such areas as frequency of intercourse, foreplay and intercourse, masturbation, orgasm, and satisfaction with marital sex.

The Kinsey studies consisted of structured interviews of 5,300 males and 5,940 females. These people represented a wide range of ages, educational levels, and geographical distribution. The Hunt study, *Sexual Behavior in the 1970s,* consisted of self-administered questionnaires of 982 males and 1,044 females. An additional 100 males and 100 females were interviewed in-depth for the book's narrative material. Hunt varied his sample according to race, marital status, education, occupation, and urban-rural distribution in an effort to collect data paralleling that of Kinsey's so as to compare the two generations.

Hunt found that, since Kinsey's studies, the frequency of intercourse had increased for all age groups, although the increases were greater for males than for females (see box table 2.1). Hunt observed that the smaller increase for females may have meant that women were reporting the frequency of their sexual intercourse more accurately in the 1970s than in the Kinsey studies.

Foreplay and Intercourse

In Hunt's survey, the duration of foreplay and intercourse had increased greatly over the durations reported by Kinsey.

Kinsey's findings indicated that precoital foreplay in marriage was often quite perfunctory, often consisting of just a kiss or two. Extending foreplay to as long as five minutes was uncommon. Hunt found that by the 1970s foreplay had become quite involved and averaged about fifteen minutes.

Box Table 2.1   Changes in Intercourse Frequency from Kinsey to Hunt.

Frequency Per Week As Estimated by Husbands

| 1938–1946 (Kinsey) | | | 1974 (Hunt) | | |
Age	Mean	Median	Age	Mean	Median
16–25	3.3	2.3	18–24	3.7	3.5
26–35	2.5	1.9	25–34	2.8	3.0
36–45	1.8	1.4	35–44	2.2	2.0
46–55	1.3	.8	45–54	1.5	1.0
56–60	.8	.6	55 and over	1.0	1.0

Frequency Per Week As Estimated by Wives

| 1938–1946 (Kinsey) | | | 1974 (Hunt) | | |
Age	Mean	Median	Age	Mean	Median
16–25	3.2	2.6	18–24	3.3	3.0
26–35	2.5	2.0	25–34	2.6	2.1
36–45	1.9	1.4	35–44	2.0	2.0
46–55	1.3	.9	45–54	1.5	1.0
56–60	.8	.4	55 and over	1.0	1.0

Source: Copyright © by Morton Hunt. From *Sexual Behavior in the 1970s,* by Morton Hunt, published by Playboy Press.

cunnilingus
(kun″i-ling′gus)

The duration of intercourse also increased across the years. Kinsey reported that 75 percent of the males in his survey reached orgasm within two minutes after intromission. Hunt's sample reported that the median duration of marital intercourse was ten minutes and that the prolongation of the sexual act was the goal of many.

Hunt also reported that people in the 1970s used a greater variety of sexual techniques in their sexual activities. In general, the increases in techniques were greatest for activities that had been strongly tabooed in the past, such as oral-genital acts. Kinsey found that 15 percent of high school males had engaged in cunnilingus (oral stimulation of the female's genitals), while Hunt found that 56 percent of high school males had experienced cunnilingus.

Hunt's people also used a greater variety of coital positions than did their counterparts in Kinsey's surveys. Kinsey reported that over 80 percent used the face-to-face sexual position, with the man on top. Seventy percent of males reported that this was the *only* position they had ever used. Hunt found that the male-above position was also most widely used, but that the female-above position was used by 75 percent of the couples some of the time while 40 percent used the rear-entry vaginal intercourse position for variety.

Masturbation
Kinsey found that 50 percent of married males (between the ages of twenty-six and thirty-five) masturbated occasionally and that 30 percent of their wives also masturbated. Hunt found that 72 percent of the males in this age group masturbated, while 75 percent of their wives masturbated. Men used masturbation as a sexual outlet when their wives were not available for intercourse. Wives reported that they masturbated for a variety of reasons, including the absence of the husband, relaxation of tensions, and as an enjoyable addition to intercourse with their husbands.

Orgasm
Kinsey reported that his research suggested that orgasm was not nearly as important to the female as it was to the male. Both Kinsey and Hunt reported that orgasm in married women either depended upon orgasmic sexual activity prior to marriage or regular sexual activity over the course of ten or fifteen years of marriage.

Kinsey reported that 36 percent of the married females in his sample had never experienced orgasm from any source before marriage. By contrast, over 99 percent of late adolescent males in his study were experiencing orgasm more than twice a week (mostly by masturbation). Almost all marital intercourse resulted in orgasm in the male, while the average Kinsey female reached orgasm only 70 to 77 percent of the time. Of the Kinsey wives, 45 percent reported having orgasm 90 to 100 percent of the time. Fifty-three percent of the Hunt wives reported orgasm all or almost all of the time.

Satisfaction with Marital Sex
Kinsey's studies did not report data on sexual satisfaction, but Hunt presented findings that indicated that the sexual aspect of significantly high percentages of people's marriages was positive. Among the youngest married males, 99 percent viewed their sex lives as "mostly" or "very" pleasurable. Ninety-four percent of the older males reported the same findings. Married women presented a somewhat different picture. The percentage rating their marital sex "very pleasurable" rose from 57 percent for the under twenty-five group to a high of 63 percent for the thirty-five to forty-five age group.

Shere Hite conducted surveys through popular magazines and turned information into scientific conclusions. Many researchers criticize the validity of such conclusions.

The Hite Reports

From 1972 through 1980, Shere Hite was the director of the Feminist Sexuality Project, a research group established to design and conduct sex surveys of both women and men. Hite's work resulted in two books: *The Hite Report* (1976) on female sexuality and *The Hite Report on Male Sexuality* (1981).

The questionnaire for *the Hite Report* on female sexuality consisted of approximately sixty essay-type questions. The questionnaires were sent to women's groups throughout the United States, including the National Organization for Women, abortion-rights groups, and the National Organization of University Women. Notices asking readers to send for the survey questionnaire were placed in *The Village Voice* (a liberal New York newspaper) and in *Mademoiselle, Brides,* and *Ms.* magazines. *Oui* magazine ran the questionnaire and requested readers to fill it out and return it.

Of the over 100,000 questionnaires that were distributed, only 3,019 were completed and returned. Approximately a third of the returned questionnaires came from readers of *Oui* magazine, a third from members of women's organizations, and a third from women who saw the notice in *The Village Voice*.

Hite's sample showed a greater variety than the samples from the *Redbook* or *Cosmopolitan* surveys. Respondents ranged from fourteen to seventy-eight years of age. The majority were single, described themselves as having had some college, but were not currently in college. Yet, the respondents comprised neither a random nor representative sample of women in the United States.

The questionnaires for *The Hite Report on Male Sexuality* consisted of 173 essay-type questions. Versions of the questionnaires were printed in magazines such as *Penthouse* and the questionnaires also could be obtained by writing for it.

Of the approximately 119,000 questionnaires that were distributed, only 7,239 were completed and returned. The respondents tended to have an educational level that was considerably higher than the national average and again comprised neither a random nor representative sample of men in the United States.

Hite's surveys on female and male sexuality exhibited many of the basic sampling problems discussed in the previous section on magazine surveys. In addition, many of the women questioned were reached through feminist publications and organizations, and, thus, a high percentage of the respondents were probably feminists, a detail that would obviously bias the sample. Also, what type of man would take time to fill out a 173-item questionnaire and write lengthy answers? Many experts suggest that these men are either angry about their sex lives or want to brag about them.

Hite says that her reports are not meant to be scientific or representative, but a review of sexuality. The nonscientific natures of the reports are shown by the constant use of the words *most, some, many,* and *a few* instead of statistical data. These kinds of vague statements can result in misleading conclusions, and many sex educators and therapists caution against uncritical acceptance of Hite's findings. However, Hite's reports do extensively quote the respondents. These quotations, while statistically meaningless, can offer some insights into the sexual behavior and attitudes of both men and women.

---

1. When you pick up a magazine, do any sexy headlines on the cover grab your attention before headlines about current events, business, sports, etc.? Can you explain your response?
2. What are some of the sampling problems typical of a phone survey? Can you think of any ways to avoid these problems?
3. Magazine surveys of human sexuality typically have sampling problems that tend to limit the value of their results. Would knowing this prevent you from reading the results of such surveys? What kinds of qualifiers would you want to keep in mind as you read the survey results?
4. The population samples for the Hite reports were neither random nor representative. If you had a chance to survey men and women in the United States about their sexuality, what ideas would you have about distributing the questionnaires that would tend to eliminate some of the bias evident in the Hite reports?

"Carol, you were right. That chapter on sex research makes it seem like sex can't be researched very well at all! Those magazines that discuss sexual trends can print anything they want and call it fact because no one can prove them wrong. Maybe there shouldn't be any research at all if they can't prove it."

"No, Bill, don't you see that the point is that research methods must be questioned and improved every step of the way? It's a good thing that people like Kinsey, Masters and Johnson, and Hite did do the work they did. Otherwise, we wouldn't have the chance to openly talk about sex the way we do now. We'd be back to the boring ways of old."

"Yeah, I suppose you're right, but I'm going to think twice before believing everything I read. I always did think something was screwy about that stuff. I mean, how can anyone have sex 5.2 times a week? The point two must be really lousy!"

Summary

1. Research is a method of obtaining information and answering questions. We need to be able to critically evaluate sexual research and to decide for ourselves the validity of the research conclusions for each of us.

2. The research process consists of four steps: (1) stating a hypothesis, (2) testing the hypothesis and collecting the data, (3) analyzing the research data, and (4) evaluating the research results.

3. A hypothesis is researchers' tentative, written assumption to be tested by their research, and forming a hypothesis is the first step in any research process.

4.　Once researchers have formulated a hypothesis, they must test their hypothesis and collect research data. To do this, the researchers select and adhere to one of four possible research designs: clinical research, experimental research, survey research, or observational research.

5.　Clinical research involves studying people who are suffering from physical or mental disorders in an attempt to discover more about the disorder and to assess the value of the current treatment for that disorder. Most clinical research in human sexuality results from researchers compiling, evaluating, and comparing case studies to find similarities and to establish trends.

6.　In experimental sexual research, individuals are confronted with specific stimuli, under laboratory conditions, and their reactions are measured. Experiment results are precise and conclusive, but the nature and rigid design of experimental research often limits its applicability in human sexuality.

7.　Survey research in human sexuality consists of asking selected groups of people carefully prepared questions about their sexual behavior and attitudes. Researchers first identify the population to be studied and the best method of sampling that population. Then researchers either conduct interviews with the sample group or ask the sample group to complete questionnaires. Sex sampling surveys are a relatively inexpensive, highly flexible, and fast way of gathering data from a large number of people, but they have two major disadvantages: nonresponse and inaccuracy.

8.　Observational research in human sexuality usually consists of a human observer or an instrument observing and recording the sexual activities of individuals—usually in a laboratory setting. One problem of observational research is finding individuals who are willing to volunteer as subjects. Also, observational research is expensive and time consuming, and some people question whether the results obtained in the laboratory can be valid for the general population. Finally, the lack of a formal research method can make the results of observational research difficult to validate.

9.　The third step in the research process is analyzing the research data. Most data analysis is statistical. Several of the more common statistical terms found in human sexuality research are range, frequency, incidence, mode, mean, and median.

10.　The fourth step in the research process is evaluating the research results. Sexual researchers face some unique problems in determining the validity of their research because sexual research is not precise. The reasons for this are, first, there are inherent problems when trying to conduct research on people, and second, the use of introspection greatly influences sexual researchers' interpretations of data. Over the years, however, researchers have developed skills and tools that add precision to their observations and that correct for bias and personal prejudices in their interpretations of findings. The important point to remember is that the results of all sexual research are open to individual evaluation, and the personal validity of sexual research interpretations should always be questioned.

11. Early sexual researchers included Sigmund Freud, whose research consisted of personal observations and personal feelings or experiences; Havelock Ellis, who was the first to publish data from sexual surveys; Alfred Kinsey, who was the first to use scientific sampling techniques to obtain information; and William Masters and Virginia Johnson, who used a laboratory setting to conduct some of the first observational research into the anatomy and physiology of human sexual response.

12. Some of the more popular sex surveys that have been published in recent years contain some basic problems in sampling and interpretation. Hunt's *Playboy* survey shows signs of selective sampling and volunteer bias. Magazine surveys are biased because only the readers of the magazine, usually a select group of people, are questioned. The Hite reports on sexuality exhibit many of the basic sampling problems that magazine surveys face and can only be considered reviews of sexuality, not scientific research.

13. It is important that we remember that there are a number of individuals, organizations, and institutions that are conducting valid sexual research that will result in accurate, informative, and well-received information.

3

Sex, sex, sex, sex, *SEX*. That's all anyone ever talks about anymore! Growing up, sex was the big *IT*. Have you done *it*? Did you get *it*? Was *it* good? Even my parents talk about *it*! You read about *it* in books, you see *it* on TV, we smell *it* in perfume, we wear *it* in jeans! I mean, how can I figure out what *it* is, if I'm drowning in *it*?

Sometimes I get confused. Why does it have to be so important? I have a fairly healthy respect for sex, at least I think I do. I've never abused my body, I even like it, but sometimes I just don't understand what all the fuss is about.

I grew up lucky, I guess. I learned about sex like everyone else—in health class, in the locker room, at slumber parties, behind the school—but more than that, my Mom and Dad talked about sex. They figured they'd better get in their side of it, too.

Not everyone is so fortunate. There's a girl in my psych class who's really hung up on Freud—she blames her parents for her sexual identity problems. My last boyfriend was always trying to get in my pants. Once he did, the challenge was over and so was the relationship.

The guy I'm dating now is really nice, but he hasn't made a move on me yet. I don't think he's gay—I can't tell if it's me, or him, or something else. John won't even discuss it when I bring it up. I like to touch and cuddle, which seems OK, but as soon as I start to really get going, he draws away. I sure wish he'd talk about it!

We can thoroughly discuss the biological structure and functions of sex organs, hormonal control of the reproductive processes, expected sexual responses, sexual difficulties, the range of behavioral variations in sexual practice, and so on. Somewhat more difficult for us to discuss and to grasp, however, are the moral questions of how we should *behave* in a given sexual situation.

For example, it is one thing to discuss premarital sex and how its incidence has changed from the 1950s until the 1980s but quite another thing to evaluate the rightness or wrongness of premarital sexual activity. Is premarital sex all right as long as both people feel affection for each other and feel happy about what they are doing? Do both partners understand and accept the extent of their commitment to each other? Does love always need to accompany sexual intercourse? Is a person's sense of trust and self-esteem enhanced or inhibited by his or her sexual activity? Have the partners discussed how they will handle a pregnancy in the event that it occurs?

Society's continuously changing attitude toward sexual values and morality influences the answers to these questions. Adults and young people, each from different generations, try to reconcile what is right or wrong, and the answers they arrive at are not always the same. The 1977 Yankelovich, Skelly, and White survey found that among people over fifty years old, 80 percent believed that it was morally wrong for unmarried teenagers to have sexual relations. Among those people thirty-five to forty-nine years old, 72 percent believed that teenage premarital sex was morally wrong. The same survey showed that only 34 percent of those people under twenty-five felt that teenage premarital sex was wrong (compared to over 60 percent who felt it was *not* morally wrong). These statistics indicate that the "rightness" or "wrongness" of teenage premarital sex is not a stagnant issue. Attitudes are constantly changing.

In this chapter, we discuss sexual morality and the unique sexual value system that each of us develops. How do we acquire our sexual values? Why do we adhere to our sexual values? How can we clarify our sexual values? All of these questions are addressed.

We also examine how our sexual values and sexual morality has been influenced by religion, people, and events throughout recorded history. The chapter concludes with some insights into our current sexual morality.

Moral Values and Sexuality

We humans are unique from other animal species in our development of something we call **values.** We are not controlled by instinctual needs alone. We grow and learn, and we have experiences; from these experiences come general guides to behavior. These guides, which give direction to all of life, are called values (Raths, Harmin, and Simon 1978).

Our values influence what we do with our time and energy. They reflect the worth we assign to something. We often assign a higher worth to items with "survival" value, such as food and shelter, than to items with "pleasure" value. As certain survival needs become less critical or become guaranteed, however, we reorder our value structure according to personal needs, likes, and wants. We may decide, for example, to assign worth to intellectual fulfillment, parenthood, prestige, wealth, or the creation of beautiful things.

As our experiences change, our values evolve and mature. Thus, unless our world stands still, our values are not fixed.

Moral Values

As social beings, some of our values relate to our conduct with, and treatment of, other people. These values are called **moral values.**

Moral values usually reflect more than the simple extremes of right and wrong, good and bad. Deciding how to behave typically involves conflicting demands, the weighing and balancing of different factors, and complicated judgments. How well we integrate moral values into our daily actions describes our character.

The highest moral values are those that focus on the personhood of the individual, both our own and that of others. **Personhood** relates to our *being,* our center of personal existence. Those actions that enhance growth within ourselves or other people, that build trust, and that help guarantee all of us the realization of our full potential are moral. Those actions that adversely affect our or other people's self-esteem, self-worth, and self-appreciation, or that demean or limit our or other people's realization of their full potential are immoral.

Sexual Moral Values

Sexual moral values (hereafter referred to as sexual values) relate to the rightness and wrongness of sexual conduct, and when and how sexuality should be expressed. As with other values, each of us must decide which sexual conduct, feelings, and actions are of greatest worth to us personally.

Sexuality is valued differently by different persons, groups, and the law. For example, most of us are repelled by the idea of sex with our own children (incest), but some people apparently aren't, as evidenced by the rate of reported incest in this country. Some of us may value sex outside of a legal marriage, while others of us may insist that any sexual intercourse must involve a legal spouse. Some of us may value anal intercourse as a sexual activity, while in some states this sexual act is illegal.

Probably the greatest tug-of-war between sexual value systems results from our decision to either place great importance on society and the preservation of its institutions (such as marriage)—even at the expense of the individual—or to view the individual as being more important than social traditions. For example, many people today (men as well as women) whose sexual value systems place greater importance on the individual feel that women, as sexual partners, have been dominated by men for men's selfish sexual interests. They point, for instance, to the double standard of premarital sexual behavior in which young men are excused for their sexual liberties, while young women are condemned for taking similar sexual privileges. People whose sexual value systems focus on society and its institutions might excuse such double standards as perhaps necessary for the preservation of an orderly, male-dominated society.

Sources of Sexual Values

Our sexual values are learned, and we each learn our sexual values in different ways, at different rates, and with different results. We acquire our sexual values from our social environment—our parents, our friends, the books we read, the television shows we watch, and any religious standards we might be exposed to. Much of this happens with little critical review on our part. We tend to go along with the tide, placing worth on those things that people around us value.

Parents are the earliest sources of our sex information. They may provide words for body parts but leave out the words relating to erotic activities. They may try at some time to share information on sexual issues, but not about lovemaking. Sometimes, parental information comes only after considerable peer input, and then the information may be mostly about what adolescents should *not* do and why they should not do it. These sessions are more likely directed toward females, because they are viewed as the guardians of morality and of the association of love to sex (Gagnon 1977).

Sex information from peers begins during early school years, but most of it comes during early teen years. Peer sex information is especially influential because peers are going through the same experiences, at about the same time. (This may be more true for males than females.) While such information may be wrong, peers value it highly. Some information is learned by actually engaging in sexual activity; other information results from discussions with peers before and after the peers engage in sexual activity.

Peer input is reinforced by media sources (television shows, movies, Ann Landers, *Redbook, Cosmopolitan, Playboy*), particularly those engineered for the youth culture. Many of these sources endorse teenage sexual activity (Gagnon 1977).

Organized religions also play a major role in setting standards of right and wrong for our sexual behavior. Many of the countries of the Western world have their cultural roots in the Judeo-Christian religions. Fundamental to these religions is the belief that human life has worth and is sacred, and that the personhood of the individual is to be respected and protected. As a consequence, those cultures with Judeo-Christian roots have based many of their laws governing the conduct of people, including sexual behavior, on teachings such as the Ten Commandments and

Sexual Mythology

Myths are beliefs without factual basis and of unknown source, and are handed down from person to person, generation to generation. Clouded by misinformation, myths serve to shelter us against the mysterious, the tabooed—but also insulate us against factual knowledge that may be frightening or uncomfortable. Through knowledge and information, these biases can be exposed, explored, and dispelled.

Especially common are sexual myths. Here are some sexual myths, along with an informed answer to each myth:

Myth: *Men have stronger sex drives than women.*

Facts: Masters and Johnson's data show that sexual arousal rates and the physiologic response cycles are virtually alike for both sexes. In fact, many men desire intercourse less often than their spouses.

Myth: *Athletes should not have sex the night before a big athletic event.*

Facts: The energy expended in an orgasm is about the same as that used in walking up a flight of stairs or running a block. Vital quantities of energy are not lost during climax.

Myth: *A man cannot have an orgasm without ejaculating.*

Facts: While ejaculation ordinarily accompanies orgasm in the male, a man can climax without the release of any ejaculate. This is especially common in prepubescent boys, old men, after prostatic surgery, and in cases of multiple orgasm.

Myth: *Sexually active teenage girls secretly want to get pregnant.*

Facts: According to one metropolitan survey, 95 percent of sexually active females did *not* want to become pregnant.

Myth: *Most cases of sexual molestation are committed by strangers.*

Facts: In at least 75 percent of cases of sexual molestation, the victim *knows* her or his assailant.

Myth: *Regardless of the rumors, few married people engage in extramarital sex.*

Facts: According to recent research data, perhaps as many as 60 percent of married men and 40 percent of married women engage in extramarital sex at some time.

Myth: *Sexual intercourse during pregnancy can cause a miscarriage.*

Facts: There is absolutely no evidence that intercourse can induce a miscarriage. If this were so, there would be no need for the millions of induced abortions performed in the United States each year.

Myth: *After menopause, a woman is no longer interested in (or capable of) sexual pleasure.*

Facts: The ending of childbearing capacity has no relationship to sexual pleasuring. After menopause, a woman is fully capable of sexual intercourse, orgasm, and pleasuring. In fact, because she no longer faces a risk of getting pregnant, she may enjoy sexual activity more.

Myth: *Nudity by parents overstimulates a child sexually.*

Facts: Seductiveness, not nudity, overstimulates children. Parents can be seductive without being nude and nude without being seductive. Parents transmit feelings of self-consciousness and self-assurance to children in many situations, including nudity.

Myth: *It's the man's place to initiate sex.*

Facts: Regardless of who initiates sex, it can be equally satisfying. In fact, always having to initiate sexual activity causes some men performance anxiety and affects erectile ability. The reluctant woman may become overly passive, and the male may withdraw—a form of behavioral paralysis in both.

A Woman's Sexual Values

I read *Anna Karenina* when I was sixteen. I didn't hear of Grace Slick until I was twenty-five. Somewhere between the two of them, my life and the life of my generation lies—with our expectations, beliefs, and behavior shaped by the nineteenth-century values of our parents, our sense of defensive necessities shaped by the clash of romanticism and vulgarity in the fifties, and our adult life (what there has been of it) lived out in the egalitarian antiromanticism of the sixties, when every pattern of existence that I had struggled to adapt to, promptly became obsolete and was replaced by its near opposite.

I am of that generation that was brought up to believe that women had very special emotional needs, that love was always, or almost always, a more significant or more encompassing experience for a woman than for a man, and that, because of the dichotomies between men and women, it was necessary to protect women against the ravishments of male sexuality. I was taught: women love, men screw; save yourself for marriage; taught: don't squander your inner resources on someone who will only smash them; taught: men have affairs, women don't (although it was never clear with whom those men were having affairs if not women, since no one assumed they were having them with men); taught: men respect women who can say no; men want to marry virgins; taught: if you do what Anna Karenina did, you'll wind up where she wound up, dead on the railroad tracks. The moral of the story was: don't let your passions (if you have passions) run away with you. It can only lead to a bad ending.

Source: From Bengis, Ingrid. *Combat in the Erogenous Zones*. New York: Alfred A. Knopf, 1972.

the Golden Rule. Thus, the standards of right and wrong as based on such religious codes affect our sexual values even though we may have received no formal religious education.

It is important for parents to realize that their teenagers may not relate all or any of the sexual information that they have acquired from other sources. For this reason, parents should urge their children to make as many sexual decisions as possible in terms of values that both the parents and the children see as important.

1. Define a moral value. Around what factors does such a definition center? Can you give a specific example of an act that would be considered immoral?
2. Try to identify some of your sexual values. Speculate as to how you probably acquired these values.
3. What might be some of the advantages and disadvantages of acquiring a major share of our sexual values from our peers?

Behavioral Scripts

We express our sexual values in rather organized and predictable ways. According to Gagnon (1977), our value systems provide a framework, or **script,** for ordering our behavior and conduct. An idea taken from the theater, scripts are behavioral scenarios that determine the who, what, when, where, and why of our behavior. They are devices for guiding our actions and for helping us to understand those actions. They are plans in our heads that describe what we have done in the past, what we are presently doing, and what we plan to do. We use scripts to justify actions that are in line with our expectations and to raise questions about actions that are not so in line. We also use scripts to determine courses of action and to check accomplished behavior against the plans.

Scripts prescribe standard ways of behaving in given settings. We have scripts for sitting through a lecture, for using the library, or for going to the theater. When people in a given setting have similar scripts, behavioral interaction flows smoothly. When people in a given situation have different scripts, however, there may be a conflict. The "class clown" script of a student, for example, often conflicts with the "lecture" script of the instructor.

Who, What, When, Where, and Why of Sexual Scripting

According to Gagnon (1977), all social behavior, including sexual, is scripted, and as with any other scripting, sexual scripts usually determine the who, what, when, where, and why of our sexual behavior.

For example, our sexual script closely defines *who,* with regard to gender, age, marital status, race, religion, social class, and relationship, we make love with. Our sexual script may approve of sexual intercourse between two consenting adults but forbid intercourse between an adult and a minor.

What we do sexually is also determined by our sexual script. We may feel comfortable engaging in certain sexual acts but feel apprehensive about doing others. A male's sexual script, for example, may allow him to kiss his partner's bare breasts but not her genitals.

The *when* of our sexual activity may refer to the time of day or week, or to a period in our life. For example, some people's sexual scripts may call for lovemaking in the morning; others may call for it only on Saturday nights; still other people's scripts may see lovemaking as a welcome activity anytime. If our sexual script dictates that sexual intercourse should be performed only for reproductive purposes, then perhaps we will engage in sexual intercourse only during the reproductive period of our life cycle.

The *where* of our sexual activity is also usually spelled out in our sexual script. Most people in our culture are scripted to engage in sexual activity in privacy, most often in the bedroom, where there is opportunity for disrobing and sleep.

We develop our sexual script slowly as we move from infancy to adulthood.

Our sexual script also gives clues as to *why* we engage in sexual activity. Sex may be used for self-affirmation, to relieve anxiety, for pleasure or excitement, to relieve loneliness, or to produce a child. It may also be used to obtain love, to dominate, to express anger, to fulfill a duty, or to obtain money.

Scripting Our Sexual Behavior

It is important that we consciously and deliberately script all of our sexual behavior in terms of our sexual values. If we do, the scripting helps to integrate our personality; if we don't, the result can be a "pulling apart" or fragmentation of our personality.

Our sexual script and the sexual conduct it produces is not bestowed fully formed upon us. We develop our sexual script slowly as we move from infancy through childhood and adolescence and into adulthood. We build our script from contacts with others and from teachings, both formal and informal, both intentional and accidental, both sexual and nonsexual.

Scripting can place pressures on a person who does not have the social opportunity to conform to expected behavior.

While much of our sexual script forms without our even being aware of it, we nonetheless have a measure of control over and responsibility for the scripting we accept. Unlike other animals, we are not scripted entirely by natural instinct and outside circumstances. We have the capacity to change our script if necessary.

Varying our script, however, requires energy. Since the script involves individual expectations and social norms, any rescripting interrupts these as well as interferes with some particular sequence of behavior. The reassessment required to fit a new type of behavior into a new sequence of interrelated events takes time, demands thought, and runs the risk of being misunderstood. Such occurs with the family in which the husband/father in a heterosexual marriage "discovers" homosexual desires and breaks off the heterosexual relations with his wife and family. Each of the family members faces readjustments and the need for a rescripting of that part of their lives.

1. Describe a sexual script, how it is acquired, and how it is used.
2. Analyze the who, what, when, where, and why of your personal sexual script. Does your sexual script reflect your sexual values?
3. Have you ever attempted to change your sexual script? If so, how? What happened?

Development of Moral Reasoning

Paralleling and interrelated to the development of our sexual script is our development of moral reasoning. Kohlberg (1964) suggests that we pass through three stages of moral reasoning (preconventional, conventional, and postconventional) that can be further subdivided into seven stages. (See table 3.1.)

These stages are more concerned with what we believe is morally correct than with what we would actually do if faced with a moral problem. In other words, the focus is on the development of an *understanding* of morality. A yardstick used to confirm this developing understanding is the worth we attach to human life.

The Preconventional Level
At Kohlberg's first, or preconventional, level, which encompasses infancy through early childhood, we make a distinction between right and wrong only in terms of the physical consequences related with the words. Our behavior is good when it results in a pleasurable experience; it is wrong when associated with punishment, pain, or parental disapproval. We obey the orders of authority figures without any awareness of principles or any sense of general moral order. Values at this level are purely pragmatic (practical) and hedonistic (that which provides pleasure) (Hettlinger 1974).

Table 3.1 Kohlberg's Stages of the Development of Moral Reasoning.

Levels	Stages of Development	Usual Age Group	Reasons for Conforming	Moral Stage
Preconventional	Stage 0	Infancy	None	Premoral
	Stage 1	Early childhood	To avoid pain and punishment	Obedience and punishment
	Stage 2	Early childhood	To satisfy personal needs; to seek personal advantage: obtaining rewards, having favors returned	Reciprocity
Conventional	Stage 3	Late childhood	To avoid disapproval and dislike by others	Good child
	Stage 4	Adolescence	Out of respect for the social order, thus avoiding censure by authorities and the resultant guilt	Law and order
Postconventional	Stage 5	Adulthood	Out of respect for the rights of others, thus maintaining community welfare	Social contact
	Stage 6	Adulthood	Out of respect for persons as human individuals, thus avoiding self-condemnation	Principled (universal)
	Stage 7	Adulthood	Out of respect for personhood as a part of the infinite, or cosmic, unity	Principled (cosmic)

Source: Compiled from Kohlberg, Laurence. "Development of Moral Character and Moral Ideology." In *Review of Child Development Research,* vol. I, edited by M. L. Hoffman and L. W. Hoffman. New York: Russel Sage Foundation, 1964.

Little or no sexual scripting could be occurring at this level. In fact, the child at this level is often viewed as nonsexual.

The Conventional Level

At Kohlberg's second, or conventional, level, which encompasses late childhood through adolescence, the expectations and approval of the group (initially the family) begin outweighing the value of personal pleasure. We obey rules for their own sake in the interests of the general good. We may subordinate our immediate personal advantage to our sense of loyalty to others and to the satisfaction we gain from social approval.

At this level, sexual scripting is developing. The sexual decisions we make during adolescence are based on whether we feel it is important to uphold a standard that some voice of authority (civil or church) views as right. For example, we might choose to practice premarital chastity (abstention from sexual intercourse before marriage), not out of concern for our partner (this type of concern would come later, at level three), but simply because we may respect the teaching of our parents on this subject and want to avoid their disapproval and our own feelings of guilt.

The Postconventional Level

At Kohlberg's third, or postconventional, level, which encompasses adulthood, we develop the ability to examine and challenge pervading social definitions of right and wrong in terms of our own understanding. We learn to define "right" in terms of the moral principles we ourselves choose. We exhibit a pattern of independent behavior that is based on ideals, reflection, and critical judgment.

Postconventional moral reasoning involves the development of the social self. The identifying of one's self enables us to answer the question "Who am I?" in terms of standards of right and wrong. We, for instance, may choose not to engage in sexual activities that violate the rights of another person. If and when we violate such standards, we question within our own minds who we are, and we risk self-condemnation. Our "conscience," then, represents our self-expectations in the central areas of social life, and it is this conscience that has us treat others the way we would like to be treated. Moral reasoning would not, for example, allow for the encouraging of a new sex partner to agree to intercourse under an illusion of intimacy and false promises of marriage, only to leave that person stranded without explanation.

1. Identify and contrast the three levels we pass through in the process of developing moral reasoning. At what stage of the three levels do you place yourself?
2. When we reach the third level of moral reasoning, we want to treat others the way we would like to be treated. Have you ever failed to uphold this standard in your sexual behavior? How did you feel afterwards?

Guilt

When our behavior does not follow our sexual script, when we violate the sexual moral standards that we have established for ourselves, the usual result is a sense of **guilt.**

A contemporary behavioral view of guilt is that guilt represents parental and social standards that we internalize and then use to develop feelings of responsibility and self-control for our own behavior. Guilt feelings develop as an inner sense of distress over having violated (either in what we have done or in our thoughts) these parental and social standards. Such feelings arise from an awareness that we have let ourselves down, that our performance has not matched our expectations. Guilt often becomes a useful motivator because it causes us to redirect our behavior (Brennecke and Amick 1971; Zimbardo 1980).

When we are directly or indirectly responsible for violating expected behavior, we should be prepared for feelings of guilt. A young man who forces "friendly" breast and genital caressings onto his young, inexperienced girlfriend, may feel guilty over having violated her rights. His girlfriend may feel fright, guilt, and fear over having been involved in something she has been taught is improper and for which she may rightly or wrongly feel some responsibility. Such uncomfortable guilt feelings for either the male or the female may be sufficient to modify future behavior so as to avoid the sense of inner distress.

We have several possible courses of action for avoiding future feelings of guilt. First, if upon examination, we realize that our behavior was something about which we should feel guilty, we can resolve to behave more acceptably next time. Second, if we realize that our feelings of guilt are residual from earlier standards, we need to decide whether this particular behavior still requires guilt feelings. The young man mentioned earlier who may have exploited his young girlfriend with his over-zealous caressings would not need to feel guilty in later years over similar caressings of his wife. Finally, the traditional theological viewpoint holds that violating our personal moral code leads to appropriate feelings of guilt, and that for such mis-behavior, we need to seek, and expect, forgiveness.

Guilt may become an extreme reaction when the response to a situation leads to self-defeating anxiety and fear, when a person feels unnecessarily guilty or ashamed about too many things and anxious in too many unnecessary situations. Such crip-pling guilt can be labeled neurotic. The woman who feels guilty or defensive about being female or about her normal biological processes (such as menstruation) may be experiencing neurotic guilt. The resolution of such deep-seated types of guilt may require professional counseling.

In most cases, however, guilt serves a useful function: it is an internal behavioral guide that helps us to take responsibility for and exercise self-control over our own actions.

---

1. What is the function of normal guilt in our behavior?
2. When was the last time you felt guilty about your sexual behavior? How did you resolve your guilt?

Clarifying Our Sexual Values

Throughout our lives, we must make moral judgments about issues in sexual be-havior. We have to decide what our positions are on such issues as nonmarital sexual intercourse (with or without the intent of marriage), extramarital affairs, abortion, the use of contraceptives to control fertility, a homosexual orientation, masturba-tion, sterilization, artificial insemination, and transsexual sex reassignment.

surrogate   *in vitro*
(sur'o-gāt)   (in ve'tro)

Because all of us hold a variety of philosophical bases (presuppositions, beliefs), there is no way we can take a stand on any of these issues and expect everyone to agree with us. Also, a moral judgment that uses today's most current information to answer a question may tomorrow be unsatisfactory because better information has become available. A further complication are the brand new issues not having moral precedence that periodically emerge, such as **surrogate motherhood** (when one woman carries a baby for another) and **in vitro fertilization** ("test-tube" fertilization).

Some of us may be unable to take a moral position consistent with our basic beliefs unless someone else, such as a religious leader or philosopher, provides us with a rationale. Yet, for many others of us, the most satisfying rationale is that which we arrive at on our own.

Making our own moral judgments about sexual issues requires that we understand the process we go through in establishing our personal sexual value systems. Each of our sexual value systems is unique and reflects our self-image, lifestyle, method of communication, and philosophy on how we interact with other people in sexual relationships. We can clarify our sexual values in three ways: (1) by applying value criteria, (2) by distinguishing between values and value indicators, and (3) by responding to specific behavioral questions.

Value Criteria

One method of clarifying our sexual values involves identifying a set of guidelines, or a process, by which we can decide which of our beliefs, attitudes, activities, and feelings are of sufficient significance to become values. Raths, Harmin, and Simon (1978) identified three major criteria for clarifying our values—choosing, prizing, and acting—and these criteria have seven sub-criteria. For a given choice or expression to be identified as a value, it must meet the test of all seven sub-criteria. We now look at each of these criteria and their respective sub-criteria in detail.

Choosing

1. ***Choosing freely.*** Anything that is to serve as a guide in directing our life must be freely chosen. We value such voluntary choices very highly. If we "choose" something out of fear of some authority or because of outside pressures, we may not stay with that choice once the authority or coercion is removed.

2. ***Choosing from among alternatives.*** For something to be valued over some other choice, there must be a process of selection; there must be alternatives from which to choose. Only when there is more than one choice available can a value result.

3. ***Choosing after thoughtful consideration of the consequences of each alternative.*** A choice has greatest value when we carefully and intelligently weigh the choice against all of the available alternatives. The full range of alternatives must

be examined and the consequences of each understood. (For this reason, impulsive or emotional choices would be excluded from a list of true values.) A young woman who is pregnant and single may need to choose between marriage and keeping the infant, remaining single and keeping the child, giving the baby up for adoption, or seeking an abortion. After careful consideration of the options, one of the choices may emerge as more valued.

Prizing

4. ***Cherishing, or being happy with the choice.*** To be a value, a choice must be something that we cherish, prize, or wish to hold on to. Obviously, we do not cherish all of the choices we have made. We may have made these choices because they represented the best bargain we were able to strike under the circumstances. A single woman who is becoming sexually active, for example, realizes that she must use some method of contraception to avert a pregnancy. She realizes that no method is absolutely certain to work effectively for all women, regardless of how consistently it is used. To gain the most protection she opts for the birth control pill, knowing that for some women the Pill creates unexpected and unwanted physical problems. While she is distrustful of the Pill, she is more apprehensive about the consequences of a pregnancy. While she selects the Pill, she does so wishing she wouldn't be faced with such a choice.

5. ***Willing to affirm the choice publicly.*** Those choices that we have freely selected from various alternatives and of which we are proud are the ones that we are most apt to affirm to others. For example, a husband and wife who have chosen to remain childless may feel that they have made the best choice for them and thus be willing to discuss it openly with others. If we are ashamed of or disappointed in a choice that we have made, we do not value the choice highly and are not likely to affirm the choice with others.

Couple being married (Public affirmation of valued behavior).

Acting

6. ***Doing something with the choice.*** Only when we are willing to act upon a choice does it become a value. Talking about something without being willing to act upon it indicates that we do not value it highly. A young man who talks endlessly about some young woman but never takes any steps to establish a relationship with her does not value that potential relationship highly.

7. ***Repeating the choice in some pattern of life.*** If we value a choice, then we will probably repeat that choice in other life situations. Values tend to be persistent and to become a part of our pattern of living. For example, if a man values his choice to remain celibate until marriage, he will be able to repeat that choice in different sexual situations.

Value Indicators

It should be apparent from analyzing the seven sub-criteria for values clarification in the preceding section that not all choices develop into actual values. In fact, many of our choices or expressions are only **value indicators**—they give clues as to where our true values are headed.

Certain value indicators are often confused with true values. A *goal* or *purpose* is a value indicator that indicates an intended course of action that may or may not be completed. *Aspirations* are remote goals that may have future possibilities. In certain matters, we have *interests*. We may actively seek more information on interests through reading or listening, yet if we do not act on these interests, they do not become values. We develop *attitudes* toward issues. Some attitudes are based on feelings (more than the usual level of emotional involvement), others on beliefs or convictions (strong feelings). While attitudes may provide us with direction, we need to examine them more carefully before confirming such attitudes as values. Actions are important, but *activities* in and of themselves are only value indicators; they do not confirm a value.

When analyzing our sexual values and those of others, it is important that we not confuse a sexual value with a sexual value indicator. "Saying" that a position on an issue is a value (something that can be depended upon to guide behavior) and confirming it as a true value in the way we act may, in fact, be two different things. Since sexual values, our own as well as our partner's, have an impact on the compatibility between partners, prospective partners need to clarify and accept each other's values *before* beginning a serious relationship.

Specific Behavioral Questions

Another technique in clarifying values is to ask questions that stimulate the person answering the questions to a further ordering of their thinking and behavior. Questions relating to our sexual behavior might be similar to the ones that follow. Each question is followed by some of the considerations we should keep in mind while answering these questions for ourselves.

1. **Does our sexual behavior build self-respect, self-esteem, and self-confidence?** Any action that adversely affects our self-view destroys our ability to relate as a whole, loving person. Rhymes (1964) wrote:

> He who is able to love himself is able to love others also, for he has understood his true value and does not need to bolster up his own value by snatching it from others. When I am unaware of what I truly am, I am incapable of giving myself value.

2. **Is our sexual behavior based on a concern for the welfare of the other person?** Do we appreciate and love the other person not merely for what he or she can *give* and share, but for what he or she *is*? Fromm (1956) wrote:

> The lover does not give in order to receive; giving is in itself exquisite joy. But in giving he cannot help bringing something to life in the other person, and this which is brought to life reflects back to him. . . .

Love between sexual partners finds expression in caring, respect, and admiration for each other. These expressions of love help partners to grow. Selfish love, on the other hand, can prevent us from accepting our partner as he or she is. If our love is selfish, we may attempt to constrain our partner's freedom and to force him or her to act in the way we desire. We may attempt to use the other person to satisfy our own needs.

3. **Is our sexual behavior based on integrity?** If we have sexual integrity, we are not deceptive. The first essential quality of love is the absence of make-believe or illusion. We give ourselves permission to enter into warm, close relationships with others without embarrassment. We don't pretend to have attributes that we don't. If we have sexual integrity, we are not coercive, exploitative, or manipulative. We don't need to try to *control* the situation for fear that all of our failings will be discovered, and we don't try to manipulate others into sexual behavior that is contrary to their wishes. Attempting to induce a partner to trade off sex for love with, "If you love me, you'll sleep with me" can be answered by, "If you love me, you wouldn't pressure me into behavior I don't really desire." An attempt at such manipulation betrays sexual integrity.

4. **Is our sexual behavior built on trust?** A fundamental trust is created when we feel no need to put up a false front with our partner and have no fears that our partner will ask for more than we are able to give. We recognize and respect our partner's hesitations, joys, fears, and hopes. In a trusting relationship, for example, the male can acknowledge a need for help in building sexual sensitivity, while the female can learn to openly express sexual needs. Both can confide their innermost feelings to each other. A lack of trust creates a sense of betrayal and prevents us from genuinely opening up to another.

5. **Does our sexual behavior emphasize performance or does it increase our feelings of worth as a whole person?** Sexuality that concentrates on the performance of the genitals and the speed of their response detaches the genitals from the body

as a whole and makes intercourse and orgasm an isolated goal. Such sexual behavior fosters fear, guilt, and embarrassment. By contrast, total body sexuality means that we accept and value the sexual nature of the whole body. It means that we can learn to know others in an intimate way—by touching their face, rubbing their body, or giving them a hug—without feeling that unless coitus has occurred, the relationship has been without meaning. It means that we give part of ourselves to the sexual encounter and don't simply make our sexual organs available.

6. *Is our sexual behavior socially desirable and responsible?* Socially responsible sexual behavior requires a constant evaluation of how our behavior affects others and the ability to handle the consequences of our behavior. For example, if we are enjoying the development of an intimate and mutually satisfying relationship with another, we and our partner must decide at what point we are ready to make commitments to each other. Such pledges help to guarantee that both partners' needs—sex, love, security, emotional support, and companionship—are met. If we are responsible, we can make meaningful decisions regarding increasing levels of physical intimacy—beginning sexual intercourse, marriage or living together, methods of contraception, and having or not having children. Dodging such decisions (either by denying the existence of the issue or by forcing the decision onto the other person) raises questions as to our ability to act in a socially desirable and responsible manner.

7. *Is our sexual behavior healthy and emotionally mature?* Healthy sexual behavior creates feelings of trust and confidence, while unhealthy sexual behavior creates feelings of anxiety and guilt. Healthy and emotionally mature sexuality means that we discriminate in the selection of our sexual partners, rather than being sexually intimate with just anyone, and that such factors as tenderness and personal relationship increasingly determine the value of the sexual experience. If we are emotionally mature, we have a greater capacity for warmth, intimacy, and bodily enjoyment. Emotional immaturity leads to sex being viewed in purely sensual terms, resulting in reduced satisfaction and the tendency to establish only superficial relationships. Lack of intimacy, sensitivity, and depth in personal sexual development may eventually breed alienation.

The question-response process just exemplified is especially useful for identifying value indicators since it prods us to apply more exact criteria to our decisions on sexual issues.

It is important to note here that not everything needs to be a value. Beliefs, convictions, aspirations, and interests are also part of life. Clarification of values, however, helps us to more accurately assess ourselves and others.

procreation
(pro"kre-a'shun)

---

1. Apply the seven sub-criteria for values classification to several of what you believe to be your sexual values. Do your values meet the test of all seven sub-criteria?
2. Can you identify any value indicators in your sexual behavior? Why are they value indicators and not values?
3. Answer for yourself the seven behavioral questions about sexuality. Does this technique help you to clarify your sexual values? Why or why not?

Religious and Cultural Roots of Our Sexual Morality

In spite of the broad range of sexual attitudes and behavior within our culture, a definite sexual climate can be attributed to influences of Judeo-Christian traditions, seventeenth-century Puritan ethics, and remnants of the Victorian era. Inasmuch as many of the early converts to Christianity were of Roman and Greek heritage, these cultures have also contributed to our potpourri of "modern" sexual customs. In the next few pages, we sketch some of the major historical views that have influenced our sexual morality.

Hebrew Roots (1900–1000 B.C.)

The early Hebrews ascribed to the philosophy that the purpose of sexual behavior was **procreation** (reproduction) and maintaining the family lineage. Procreation was seen as a primary obligation, and nonreproductive sex was discouraged. Men had the responsibility to carry on the family name because it was believed that the semen ("seed") carried the substance of life. Women were considered receptacles in which the seed grew and was nurtured until birth.

If a man died without having a child by his wife, it was his brother's duty to marry and impregnate the widow. The first son born of that union was considered a child of the dead man and was given his name. In the Old Testament, Onan was put to death for engaging in coitus interruptus (withdrawing the penis before ejaculation), thereby failing to fulfill his social duty to impregnate his brother's widow (Gen. 38:8–10).

The family line was passed down only through a Hebrew woman. If a Hebrew man impregnated a Gentile woman, the child was considered to belong to her clan. A man was thus free to marry and have sexual relations with a Gentile woman, father her child, and leave her with the responsibility for the child. This created a double standard for Hebrew men and women: A Hebrew man was not totally restricted to sex with his wife (although he was not allowed to have sex with other men's wives), but a Hebrew woman was limited to sexual activity with only her husband. For reasons of inheritance and biological immortality, it was important for the man to know that the children borne by his wife were really his own.

bestiality   infanticide
(bes-te-al′ĭ-te)   (in-fan′ti-sid)

Early Hebrews had a great deal of respect for the institution of marriage and looked down upon unmarried persons. In fact, a man who voluntarily chose to remain unmarried was considered immoral. Men who married were instructed to select wives carefully. A Hebrew man was forbidden to marry a woman until he had seen her—just the opposite of the injunctions of most Oriental cultures. The adjustment of the couple to each other was very important. Following the marriage ceremony, the husband was admonished to stay free of business affairs and war for a period of one year so that he could devote full time to his new wife (Deut. 24:5).

Hebrew women were respected as wives and mothers, but Hebrew men generally had authority over their wives, their children, and their property. Men alone were allowed to initiate divorce on various grounds (including barrenness); a woman could not divorce her husband without his consent. In spite of these restrictions, Hebrew women were treated with more respect than were most women in other cultures at this time.

Hebrew girls were expected to remain virgins until marriage since a father could demand more money when negotiating a marriage contract if his daughter was a virgin. A father could, in fact, claim compensation from a man who robbed his daughter of her virginity. Engaged persons were regarded as married with respect to intercourse, and children were considered illegitimate only if they resulted from acts of **adultery** (sexual infidelity of a married person) or incest.

All in all, Hebrew law strictly regulated sexual behavior. Sexual intercourse within marriage for reproductive purposes was viewed as being very good, but other sexual activities, such as adultery, incest, and **bestiality** (sexual relations with an animal), were forbidden. Male homosexuality was taboo because it was not procreative, and also because it was associated with tribes that worshipped pagan gods. Masturbation was forbidden for males because it was considered wasteful spillage of semen (Lev. 15:16–18). Both masturbation and homosexual acts were considered unnatural and indicative of uncontrolled (and thus morally evil) sexual desire (Epstein 1967). Abortion was also prohibited, as were contraceptive practices. Menstruating women were viewed as unclean, and sexual relations during this period were taboo (Lev. 20:18; Lev. 15:19–24). Penalties for violations of the laws ranged from ridicule to death.

Early Greek and Roman Civilizations (1000–200 B.C.)

Both Greek and Roman sexual morality had a more secular (nonreligious) basis than the Hebrew. In contrast to the Hebrews, who were primarily concerned with procreation and not wasting the "seed" out of respect for God, for example, the Greeks were interested in limiting population growth for economic reasons. Both Greek and Roman cultures practiced abortion and **infanticide** (killing babies or letting them die), particularly during times of food shortage.

monogamous	Hetairae	Pornae
(mo-nog'ah-mus)	(he-ta'ra)	(por'na)

Marriage in the early Greek and Roman civilizations was officially monogamous (an exclusive union between one man and one woman), and a double standard was apparent in terms of sexuality morality. Both Greek and Roman brides—but not bridegrooms—were expected to be virgins. Greek and Roman men were allowed to commit adultery as long as the act was not with another man's wife (Reich 1978).

Greek and Roman women were considered inferior to men, were expected to be subservient to men, and, in general, were accorded less freedom and respect than Hebrew women. The roles of Greek women were well defined into three distinct classes. **Wives** were expected to provide their husbands with legitimate offspring. They were normally not a part of their husband's social activities, nor were they respected as social companions. Under the domination of their husbands, wives could be ordered to have abortions and had no voice over a husband's decision to take a child's life by infanticide. **Hetairae,** a special class of prostitutes, were well educated, and men sought them for intellectual and social companionship as well as for sexual favors. The **pornae** (prostitutes) were hired specifically for entertainment and sexual gratification.

Homosexuality was accepted by both the Greek and Roman cultures. Plato and Aristotle, in fact, believed that the highest form of human friendship was possible only between men.

Greek and Roman philosophies indicated a distrust of sexual desire and a negative view of sexual pleasure. Greek thinking, in particular, advocated purity of body for the sake of the soul. While allowing for some sexual pleasure, Plato saw sexual pleasure as one of the lower pleasures. Sexual desire was viewed as disturbing and irrational. Sexual intercourse was seen as needing to be moderated, if not eliminated, and was never to be indulged in for its own sake unless for purposes of procreation—even in marriage. The Greeks and Romans were not able to integrate sexuality into human relationships. Their contribution to Western sexual ethics was that pleasurable human sexuality should be viewed with suspicion and severe restriction.

Early Christian Influences

Like other cultural and religious traditions, Christian teachings are complex and subject to various outside influences as well as to internal changes with succeeding generations of Christians. Christianity did not begin with a system of sexual ethics. The teachings of Jesus and his followers, as recorded in the New Testament, provide what became a central focus for Christians—to love God and neighbor. Within that ethic, the New Testament offers grounds for valuing marriage and procreation as well as **celibacy** (abstention from sexual activity), for giving as much or more emphasis to internal attitudes and thoughts as to external actions, and for a sacred meaning for sexual intercourse while subordinating it as a value to other human values.

Yet, even Christian thinking was affected by earlier Greek thinking that suspicioned sexual enjoyment, allowed for sexual intercourse only as long as it was procreative, and applauded celibacy. As we shall soon see, these early Christian teachings were to be subject to further modification and restriction.

As for Jesus, although he himself remained celibate throughout his life, the sexual ethics he required of his followers were more liberal. He did not demand sexual abstinence on the part of others and often showed concern for the welfare of sexually promiscuous persons—both prostitutes and adulterers. Forgiveness for any human error played a main role in his philosophy, and he often forgave people for their "sins of the flesh."

Jesus's views on marriage can be implied from the New Testament, which indicates that Jesus changed water into fine wine at a marriage ceremony where the host had run out of wine. Had Jesus taken a negative view of marriage and its implied sexuality, he likely would have chosen another type of festivity at which to perform his first miracle. Beyond endorsing marriage, Jesus taught that marriage partners should be faithful to each other. He allowed for divorce only for violations of the sexual code (Matt. 19:9). This was a stricter position than that of the Jewish rabbis.

Jesus held a high respect for women, and his teachings never denounced women as evil, even though some of his later followers did. Jesus also was against the double standard, especially with reference to adultery, and he believed that adultery should be forbidden for both men and women.

The later Church built upon and added to the sexual ethics of Jesus. One of the first followers of Christ to speak out on sexual behavior was St. Paul. Influenced by Greek teachings, he taught that chastity and celibacy represented a high degree of purity and were superior to marriage. But he did concede that if sexual urgencies could not be smothered, marriage would be better than **fornication** (sexual intercourse between unmarried persons).

St. Augustine (A.D. 354–430)

Prior to his conversion to Christianity, St. Augustine was married, fathered a child by a former mistress, and had a succession of love affairs. Because of his constant struggle to control his sexual desire, he was impressed by several different non-Christian philosophers who abhorred both marriage and sexual intercourse. At the age of thirty-two, he read the writings of St. Paul and converted to Christianity.

St. Augustine became convinced that the highest calling for him was total abstinence from sexual activity. Soon an influential leader and bishop of the Roman Catholic church, he associated guilt, rather than pleasure, with sex. To him, sexual desire had a place in the theology of original sin, which effect was passed on from one generation to another through procreation. He viewed sex as permissible *only* for the purpose of procreation and believed that it should be performed with as little gratification as possible.

The Roman Catholic Church's view of sexuality was strongly influenced by St. Augustine and his books (*City of God, Confessions*). According to Hettlinger (1974), "The subsequent elevation of permanent chastity as a good in itself and as a requirement for the priesthood in the Roman Catholic Church was an important indication of the Church's devaluation of sexuality."

Augustine's followers, more zealous than he in their sexual proscriptions, included in their lists of sins any behavior they felt were departures from the procreative norm—even certain positions for sexual intercourse. While a few voices began to argue that sexual desire did not make sexual pleasure evil in and of itself and that nonprocreative sexual intercourse was justifiable, Augustine's thinking in sexual ethics was a force in ethical teachings through much of the Middle Ages and into the sixteenth century.

The Middle Ages: St. Thomas Aquinas (A.D. 1225–1274)

In the thirteenth century, St. Thomas Aquinas spelled out the position of the Roman Catholic Church on just about all matters pertaining to sex and morality. While introducing little new to sexual ethics, Aquinas saw moral evil as tied up with conscious moral choices, rather than with spontaneous bodily tendencies or desires. He believed that misdirected emotions became evil when they were freely affirmed. In his *Summa Theologica,* he condemned coitus by an unmarried couple because of the possible adverse effects upon the child who might be conceived. He argued against divorce because the children of a marriage needed a stable home. Believing that sexual acts should be procreative, he opposed contraception.

At the same time, however, Aquinas saw love as a passion and allowed for sexual union as an aid to interpersonal love. He hinted at a view of marriage that included the possibility of maximum intimacy. Some scholars insist that Aquinas eventually rejected an only antiprocreational view of marital intercourse and fully justified marital intercourse as an expression of fidelity between partners.

Aquinas also spoke out on abortion. In contrast to earlier Church leaders who viewed abortion at any stage of pregnancy to be murder, Aquinas viewed it as permissible until the "soul" was infused into the fetus at the time of **quickening** (first perceived movements of the fetus around the fourth month of pregnancy).

Toward the end of the Middle Ages, scholars opposed to the ethics of Augustine and Aquinas argued that sexual coitus in marriage was justified for its own sake—that sexual pleasure could be sought as sexual pleasure and that so enjoyed it contributed to the well-being of the persons involved. While not fully reversing the Augustinian tradition, these new positions on sexual ethics were involved in the debates of the sixteenth-century reformation.

The Reformation (A.D. 1517–1558)

The sixteenth century brought the reformation of the Roman Catholic Church, which resulted in the establishment of Protestant churches. The Reformation was characteristically a period of emerging beliefs challenging established beliefs. The two major leaders of the Reformation, Martin Luther and John Calvin, challenged the prevailing statutes of the Catholic Church on chastity, celibacy, and marriage. Both reformers elevated the status of marriage and helped to remove the taint of sin from marital intercourse. Both accepted sex as an honorable act within marriage.

Luther also believed that marriage was not a strictly religious affair. He felt that it should fall under the jurisdiction of civil, as well as religious, authorities, and his marriage at home rather than in a church exemplified his belief. Luther condemned divorce and remarriage except for reasons of adultery and desertion. He also argued that required celibacy was an unnatural state for humans.

Calvin believed marriage to be a social-sexual relationship, with the companionship aspect of the marriage relationship as important as the sexual aspect. In addition, he viewed sex as something holy and honorable within the marriage relationship and not simply a means for procreation or for fulfilling the sexual desires of the husband.

Puritanism (A.D. 1620–1800)

Puritanism grew largely out of a desire of some of the followers of Calvin to break with the Church of England, which they saw as too political and still too closely tied to Catholic doctrines. After many years of persecution, the Puritans sought religious freedom in the New World.

The New World was harsh, and efforts at sheer survival were demanding. Because the Puritans saw the preservation of the family unit as essential to their survival as a group, they were uncompromising in their condemnation of practices, such as adultery, that they felt might threaten the **nuclear family** (the primary family unit that lives together).

Contrary to popular belief, the Puritans were quite realistic and open about sex. Their belief in the basic sinful nature of humans, however, gave rise to constant self-examination and primary concern with the need for self-discipline. Their strict dress codes and restrictions on enjoyable pastimes were aimed at limiting stimulation of the senses, but not necessarily at suppressing sexual thoughts. Such rigidity was simply a part of their whole attitude toward hard work and self-accountability.

Puritans viewed the marriage bonds as being ordained by God, and they were opposed to sexual activity outside of marriage. Within marriage, the sex act was considered good and natural, and there were few regulations regarding marital sex. Men, in fact, were obligated to have intercourse with their wives, and failure to do so was a punishable offense. The avoidance of sexual pleasure, *per se,* was typical of the Victorian rather than the Puritan era.

Compared with today's standards, Puritan women had little sexual equality. They were valued primarily for what they could produce, be it babies, farm produce, or textiles. The husband was head of the family; the wife was expected to occupy herself with duties related to the family. It was not considered proper for women to make themselves conspicuous socially. Yet, by prior standards, Puritan women were better off than were women in earlier centuries.

The Victorian Era (A.D. 1837–1910)

Chronologically, the Victorian era spanned the reign of the English queen Alexandrina Victoria (1837–1910). Attitudes characteristic of this period, however, were not strictly confined within these dates nor to England. Since England was a very powerful nation, its ideas influenced many other countries, especially those where English was spoken.

The sexual morality of this era contrasted with those of the Puritan period in two ways. First, the restrictions of the Puritans were based upon individually held religious convictions—they were concerned with *piety* (belief based upon a personal religious experience and responsibility). For the Puritan, for example, adultery was a *personal* sin against God, rather than a violation of a creed or of a societal standard. The Victorian restrictions were founded upon a secular morality revolving around an emerging interest in science and the development of intellectual character—they were concerned with health and the use of sex for loftier goals than pleasure. The Victorians assumed that sex interfered with achievement; therefore, sexual pursuits had to be controlled so that higher aims could be realized. Second, whereas the Puritans were primarily interested in curtailing sexual activity outside of marriage, the Victorians attempted to restrict sexual behavior within marriage as well.

The Semen Theory was a pivotal theme in Victorian values. Victorians considered semen to have some of the same characteristics as money. For example, semen, like money, was thought to be a substance essential to a man's well-being and health. In the same way, since the Victorians were highly conscious of saving and reinvesting money, they felt that it was wrong to waste semen on pleasure, whether the semen was spilled into one's wife, another woman, or in a darkened closet.

Many monetary metaphors were used to describe sexual activity. One who had an orgasm was "spent"; the process of ejaculation was called "spending"; people who were chaste were "saving themselves for marriage"; and women were encouraged to save their sexual "assets" until matrimony.

Victorian women who "wasted" their virginity prior to marriage often lost the opportunity to marry at all. According to Victorian thinking, it wasn't difficult for females to save their respectability, since good women were not supposed to have sexual desires. Men imposed their "animal instincts" upon genteel women who were

The Victorians and Too Much Sex

Since the Victorians viewed semen as a vital substance essential to a person's well-being and health, its loss was carefully measured. Sylvester Graham (1794–1851), known today for the graham cracker, believed that the loss of an ounce of semen was equal to the loss of several ounces of blood, and that by ejaculating a man lowered his life force and exposed his body to disease and early death. He advocated the use of certain foods, including graham flour (unsifted wheat flour), to reduce sexual desire. Graham solemnly warned that both husbands and wives who overindulged in sex could expect:

languor, lassitude, muscular relaxation, general debility and heaviness, depression of spirits, loss of appetite, indigestion, faintness and sinking at the pit of the stomach, increased susceptibilities of the skin and lungs to all the atmospheric changes, feebleness of all the senses, impaired vision, loss of sight, weakness of the lungs, nervous cough, pulmonary consumption, disorders of the liver and kidneys, urinary difficulties, disorders of the genital organs, spinal diseases, weakness of the brain, loss of memory, epilepsy, insanity, apoplexy, abortions, premature births, extreme feebleness, morbid predispositions, and early death of offspring. (Bullough 1976)

Victorian fashions ensured that no trace of a woman's legs would show.

obligated to put up with sexual intercourse. Under no circumstances were women supposed to encourage it or show pleasure while being "used."

Victorian women often brought breach-of-promise suits against men who had promised marriage but for one reason or another did not fulfill their end of the bargain. Such legal actions were valid during this era because women lost varying degrees of marriageability upon engagement, even though sexual assets had not been relinquished.

The prudery of the Victorians often teetered on the brink of absurdity. Women's legs were treated as if they did not exist. Anything even suggestive of the fact that legs were part of the anatomy was objectionable. Sometimes piano and table legs would be hidden inside frilly coverings. Art museums conducted separate tours for men and women, so as not to cause embarrassment when paintings of nudes were seen. Since it was indecent for women to undress and allow physicians to touch their bodies, physicians frequently could only question female patients while pointing out areas on a mannequin. Masturbation was considered pathological for both sexes, and cages were manufactured that could be fitted over the genitals at night. Some devices had spikes sticking out of them for added protection.

It is not too surprising that a large portion of the population did not adhere to such rigid standards. Even though publicly ascribing to these attitudes, in private life the rich and the poor tended to behave pretty much as they always had. It was in the rising middle class that Victorian attitudes were most frequently translated into behavior.

Early in this century, the influences of the Victorian era were coming under scrutiny. Economic and sexual inequalities were openly criticized, and social reformers were seeking the end of sexual exploitation as a part of their social programs. Then came World War I with its mobilization of women to fill the jobs of absent men. The newly-found independence of women began to express itself in an increase in the incidence of divorce. By 1920, the number of divorces in the United States was more than double the number in 1910, although the number of marriages during the same period had increased by only 34 percent. In the years immediately following World War I, the social change continued, with people continuing to shift from acting as though sex did not exist to openly embracing it.

Compare and contrast the differing views that have been held throughout recorded history on the following issues:

1. Marriage
2. Sexual intercourse outside of marriage
3. Sexual intercourse within marriage
4. Women's rights
5. Abortion
6. Celibacy

Influences on Current Sexual Morality

During the last half century, sex has been given a special status in our culture. During this time, scientists in the United States have led in research into human sexuality. Every few years, there has been a major sex report or survey released—the Kinsey reports, another book by Masters and Johnson, the Hite reports, or a SIECUS (Sex Information and Education Council of the United States) report— in addition to many lesser writings and perspectives. Within the last two decades, human sexuality courses have become popular on virtually every college campus in the United States. Also, the media have become an enthusiastic carrier of the changes in sexual mores.

The benefit of this enlightenment has been an increased sexual freedom for the individual. Many couples now openly discuss their sexual relationships and work toward making them mutually gratifying and meaningful. Many more people now see sexuality as relating to the rest of life and as a reasonable topic of conversation.

Yet all of these new data and discussions, while disproving old myths, may be generating new ones. Many people, young and old, still feel uncomfortable with their sexuality. While the external signs of anxiety and guilt have lessened, internal anxiety may still be present. Questions of going to bed together have shifted from "will she(he)" or "won't she(he)" to "can she(he)" or "can't she(he)." The question (and heavier burden) has shifted from whether *we want to* to whether *we're adequate,* calling our self-esteem into question.

A cause for reflection in this cultural shift on sexuality has been the emergence of a new sex ideology that unites a new expectation of easily attained sexual competence with a disregard for the undesirable effects of sexuality. Proponents of this new sex ideology use easier methods of contraception, surer methods of treating sexually transmitted diseases, and legalized abortion as arguments to make virginity irrelevant and unreasonable. This new sexual liberation allows for no choice; it does not include a freedom to say "no" (Hettlinger 1974). Further, it runs the risk of making sex into a duty. While the proper Victorian woman and man felt guilty if she or he experienced sex, today people may feel guilty if they don't.

An overemphasis on sex and on achieving orgasm (that is, whether or not we had one and what kind it was) makes lovemaking a technical preoccupation that robs it of spontaneity and profound satisfaction. The new sexual liberation runs the risk of becoming a new puritanism (not to be confused with historical Puritanism) that alienates the body, separates emotion from reason, and uses the body as a machine (May 1969).

The two major forces that have influenced our present-day sexual moral values are scientific and technological developments and the advent of the New Morality.

Development of Science and Technology

New scientific and technical developments have contributed greatly to the new sex ideology. The most conspicuous of these developments have been efforts to regulate pregnancy. The development of the new contraceptives has allowed women for the first time in human history to engage in sexual activity with virtually no fear of pregnancy; in other words, it separates gratification from procreation.

None of the contraceptive devices has been more dramatic in effect than the birth control pill. Since its introduction, the Pill has become the leading form of contraception in the United States, and the incidence of nonmarital intercourse has increased significantly (Djerassi 1979).

The refinements in methods of inducing abortion have been no less far-reaching in affecting sexual behavior. Induced abortion has allowed for those women whose contraceptive methods have failed or were not used. Today, there is more than one abortion for every three births, with a mortality risk factor only one-seventh that of natural childbirth (Centers for Disease Control 1982; Hatcher et al. 1982).

While we cannot say that the Pill and abortion have been the only causes of the rising rates of nonmarital intercourse, they have obviously been contributing factors.

This greater acceptance of nonmarital sex has led, in turn, to new values not shared by most people a generation ago. Are these value changes right or wrong? If an acceptance of sexual activity before marriage leads to a happier and healthier

parameters
(pah-ram′ē-terz)

acceptance of our sexuality, do we judge the change in values to be right? If it leads to loss of respect for ourselves and our partner, do we judge the change in values to be wrong?

Science cannot help us here. People today often turn to science as a means of finding truth. As a discipline, however, science is morally neutral. Science has nothing to say about what *should* be; it can only try to determine what *is*. Therefore, while science and its technologies may affect our *behavior,* it is still up to us to decide how we are going to allow these innovations to affect our *values*.

The New Morality

The advent of the New Morality has also contributed to the new sex ideology emerging today. In his book *Situation Ethics: The New Morality* (1966), Joseph Fletcher proposed a new fundamental basis for deciding the moral course in a dilemma: "Whatever is the most loving thing in the situation is the right and good thing." In other words, people's attitudes or intentions in a certain situation determine whether their behavior in that situation is right or wrong.

Fletcher saw the **New Morality** as displacing the traditional system of rules. His thesis was that rules and guidelines were neither workable nor helpful—regardless of whether the rules came from religion, philosophy, culture, or community standards. He insisted that the situational context and circumstances of ethical decisions were usually so exceptional and unique that the rules of past examples simply do not apply. According to Fletcher, each situation is sufficiently different that a fresh ethical calculation has to be made for every case.

The thesis of the New Morality states that the type of love involved in a given situation affects the behavioral motivation in that situation. That love that values the pleasure that comes to one's self may be called "self-oriented love." Self-oriented love can be passionate, or it can be selfish, but it is always a factor in human sexuality. We need not be ashamed of self-oriented love as long as it does not reduce our partner's sense of self-esteem or take unfair advantage of him or her. That love that values the welfare of the other may be called "other-oriented love." This type of love demonstrates an attitude of concern for other persons, with little or no expectation of receiving something in return. Human sexuality always needs this type of love if it is to be truly human.

Thus, the essence of the New Morality is that the appropriate response regarding any moral choice is that each of us must act according to informed reason and the loving intentions within the parameters (boundaries) of that unique situation. If in so acting traditional rules are broken, we need not feel regret or guilt.

The use of this New Morality in guiding our sexual behavior calls for rational, unemotional appraisal of each situation and of both its immediate and long-term implications. First, we need to carefully define for ourselves the kind of love being expressed in the situation. The kind of love a person brings to a sexual encounter might tend more to be self-oriented love than other-oriented love. Second, we must view with discernment our motivations and the motivations of other people involved in the situation. All of this may be too big an order if we are caught up in the emotions of a situation. The New Morality places great stress, then, on the subjective thought processes that occur *before* an act. Whether we believe our decision is right is the important factor.

But what if there are unresolved guilt feelings afterwards? Proponents of the New Morality believe that guilt feelings are a carryover from our heritage—a product of traditional moral values from childhood. They explain that sex in a self-oriented love context is good, that there need be no feelings of guilt, and that guilt feelings might be due to emotional problems that might respond to psychotherapy. The implication is that feelings of guilt are bad and thus need to be eliminated and that the behavior that may have caused those feelings of guilt does not need to be eliminated. By this reasoning, if guilt feelings can be handled, then perhaps we can act according to our reason, or intellect.

The hazard of the New Morality is that its theoretical principles may be indiscriminately violated in common practice, with the result being that anyone wishing to behave sexually as they please will either deny expected feelings of guilt or rationalize them away.

1. Why can't the scientific method be used as a means of determining our sexual values?
2. What effect do you think the new technology of in vitro fertilization will have on our sexual behavior? What sexual values might it cause us to re-analyze?
3. What is your position on the New Morality? Would you find it difficult to apply the New Morality to your sexual behavior?

John is starting to open up to me a little. He says he's never been able to talk about sex at home, and with him being so shy it makes it hard for him to talk about it with his male friends. I wish I could get John to really trust me. I think I know what he's going through, yet I can't push him into anything he can't handle. He really is great to be with—I just wish we could have more. I guess sex will have to wait. Right now, it's more important for us to learn to trust and be honest with each other.

Summary

1. We humans are unique from other animal species in our development of values. Values are behavioral guides and are prioritized as to importance of needs. Our values are not fixed; they evolve and mature.

2. Those values that deal with conduct are called moral values, the highest of which relate to the personhood of the individual. Actions enhancing a person's fullest potential are moral; those demeaning such potential are immoral. How well we integrate moral values into our daily actions describes our character.

3. Sexual moral values relate to the rightness and wrongness of our sexual conduct. Acquired largely during childhood and adolescence, our sexual values reflect the attitudes of our social environment (parents, peers, media, religion).

4. Sexual values are organized into predictable behavioral scenarios called scripts. Similar scripting between individuals leads to unity of action; differing scripts may lead to conflict. Sexual scripting defines the who, what, when, where, and why of sexual conduct during each period of life. We can vary our behavior from our sexual script with sufficient motivation and effort.

5. Kohlberg (1964) suggests that we pass through three stages of moral reasoning: preconventional, conventional, and postconventional. The development of such reasoning moves from the physical consequences of misbehavior, to the approval by our social group, to internal motives, such as acts of conscience.

6. Guilt represents parental and social standards that we internalize and then use to develop feelings of responsibility and self-control for our own behavior. To avoid feelings of guilt, we can resolve to change our future behavior, we can reexamine our behavior to determine if guilt feelings are warranted, or we can seek forgiveness.

7. We can clarify our sexual values in three ways: (1) by applying value criteria to determine which of our beliefs, attitudes, activities, and feelings are of sufficient significance to become values; (2) by distinguishing between values and value indicators, which are values that are not fully developed; and (3) by carefully and thoughtfully responding to specific behavioral questions about our sexuality.

8. Our sexual attitudes and behavior are deeply influenced by our religious and cultural heritage.

9. The early Hebrews related sexual behavior to marriage and family living. Procreation was seen as a primary obligation, and nonreproductive sex was discouraged. While the family line was passed only through women, the semen of the man was considered to carry the substance of life. Men had authority over wives and children.

10. For early Greeks and Romans, sexual morality had a more secular basis. While marriage was officially monogamous, men were allowed to visit prostitutes. Women were given less respect and freedom than Hebrew women. Both Greeks and Romans practiced abortion and infanticide. Their philosophies indicated a distrust of sexual desire and a negative view of sexual pleasure.

11.   Christ and his followers endorsed marriage and expected marital fidelity, yet sexual pleasure was not forbidden. Women were held in high respect, and the double standard was condemned. While divorce was allowed only for violations of the sexual code, forgiveness was advocated. St. Paul and some other early followers of Christianity saw chastity and celibacy as more meritorious than marriage.

12.   Led by St. Augustine, fourth-century Christians applauded total abstinence. While permissible for procreation, sex was seen as a necessary evil and a source of guilt, and was not to be practiced for personal gratification.

13.   During the Middle Ages, the Church idealized chastity and virginity and condemned sex outside of marriage. While controversial, abortion codes were relaxed to allow abortion early in pregnancy.

14.   During the Reformation of the 1500s, Luther and Calvin challenged teachings on chastity and celibacy, and elevated the status of marriage.

15.   Puritans restricted sex to marriage and believed in sexual self-discipline, yet saw sexual pleasure as good. Preservation of the nuclear family was prized.

16.   The Victorians' morality was more secular in nature than that of the Puritans. The Victorians saw sex as interfering with intellectual achievements and viewed the wasting of semen in masturbation and nonprocreative intercourse as unhealthy. Prudery over the exposure of the human body was carried to the point of absurdity.

17.   The new technologies of the twentieth century can and have had a part in altering our sexual practices. Yet, science is morally neutral; it is still up to us to decide how new technologies will affect our values.

18.   A New Morality views sexual choices as based on a sense of love rather than sets of rules, with little or no guilt to regulate misbehavior.

4

"I called last night, but your roommate said you were busy. Got a lot of homework, huh?"

"Well, actually, I had a friend over. . . . We did get some studying done. Then we went . . . well, we went downtown to the bars."

"Oh . . . did you meet him in class or is he an old friend?"

"Well, actually, he was a she. Her name is Carrie, and she needed help with her English paper so I invited her over."

"Bob! I thought we were . . . I mean . . . you told me . . . didn't you tell me that you loved me?"

"C'mon, Sue, that isn't fair. I do love you."

"Going out with another girl isn't the best way of showing it."

"Sue, I'm sorry, but our relationship has to be based on trust. You need to be secure in that. I can't stop having friends just because I'm dating you."

"Bob, when people really love each other, they don't need to have friends of the opposite sex, at least not the kind that you'd take out after studying, *if* you were studying. . . . Where did you go after drinking, her place?"

"Sue, that was uncalled for."

"You're guilty! It's written all over your face. Just because I want to hold off making love until we get married, you feel you should get it on the side, is that it?"

"Sue, I love you. I want to spend time with you, maybe even the rest of my life, but until you calm down and realize that love is not possession, maybe we should take a breather away from each other."

"Bob, don't go. I'll try not to be so jealous. I've never been in love before—I don't know what to expect."

"Who does?"

reciprocity
(res''i-pros'i-te)

Enjoyable sexual activity and rewarding interpersonal relationships are mutually reinforcing. Most of us find that our most satisfying relationships occur within a valued emotional relationship. Conversely, we also find that a mutually pleasant sexual relationship often serves to strengthen our emotional relationship with another person. In this chapter, we explore the context of our sexual relationships. Liking, intimacy, loving, infatuation, and destructive relationships are some of the topics we examine.

Liking

Is liking just a lesser degree of loving, or is it a totally different phenomenon? Behavioral scientists don't seem to agree on an answer (Berscheid and Walster 1978; Zimbardo 1980). However, we are seldom uncertain about whether or not we like someone, even though we may not understand *why* we feel as we do ("I really like Tina. I don't know why, but I really like her." "There's something about that guy that I just don't like. I'm not sure what it is."). As we shall see in the next several pages, recent research has revealed quite a bit about why we like or dislike people.

The Reciprocity-of-Liking Rule

Our desire for the esteem of others is one of the most powerful of our motivating forces. Our need for social approval influences almost everything we do (McConnell 1980). Advertising for every kind of product—from cars to toothpaste to laundry detergent—capitalizes upon our seemingly desperate drive for the recognition and approval of others.

Social approval is valuable to us for several reasons. Few of us are secure enough in our sense of self-esteem that the reaffirmation of our worth by others no longer matters. Also, we depend on others to help us satisfy many of our other needs. The approval of other people allows us to feel reasonably confident that these needs will be met.

As a result, one of the strongest reasons for us to like someone is our discovery that that person likes us. Our usual reaction to this knowledge is instant affection (liking) for the person who likes us (Zimbardo 1980). Another person's liking us constitutes an emotional reward, and we are attracted to people who reward us. Knowing that someone likes us allows us to expect emotional rewards from that person, so we feel very comfortable about relating to him or her. We feel rather certain that that person will "be nice" to us (give us emotional reinforcement). We reciprocate by returning emotional reward—demonstrating our approval of him or her.

One exception to this reciprocity-of-liking rule occurs with people who have very low self-esteem. Research by Deutsch and Solomon (1959) showed that people

with high self-esteem feel that they deserve to be liked and are quick to assume that others like them. They accept the affection of others at face value. People with low self-esteem don't. When others seem to like them, they feel uneasy. They're suspicious. They suspect their friends' motives in liking them or their friends' judgment in feeling that they are worthy of being liked. Thus, low self-esteem people deny themselves the very form of emotional reward that could help them to build self-esteem.

Similarity of Attitudes

Research indicates that discovering that we share similar attitudes with another person also generates an attraction to that person (Zimbardo 1980). Interaction with someone whose attitudes are similar to our own acts to reconfirm the validity of our beliefs. When someone else expresses the same attitudes and opinions we hold on an issue, our conviction that our own attitude is the correct one is supported. Since it is pleasant to feel that our view of the world is the reasonable and correct one, such validation of our beliefs is emotionally rewarding. And, once again, we are attracted to people who provide us with emotional rewards.

If someone supports us in our choice of school, car, clothing, career, or any other decision we make, we feel good about that person because he or she has made us feel better about ourselves. If we know that a person feels as we do about things, we can feel fairly confident that it will be rewarding to spend some time with that person. If a person seems to despise everything that is important to us, we usually feel apprehensive about associating with that person. It seems doubtful that he or she is going to provide us with much emotional reward. Of course, in restricting our friendships to those holding views similar to our own, we deny ourselves the opportunity to learn from those whose ideas might be different from ours, yet still be valid.

Other Similarities

Other types of similarities, in addition to similarity of attitudes, have been shown to attract people to each other.

Murstein (1967), for example, found a significant correlation in the degree of emotional health of people forming attachments. According to Murstein, people enjoying good emotional health tend to form friendships with each other. People experiencing emotional problems also seem to find each other.

Initial attraction also is often based on physical appearance (Zimbardo 1980). Although physical attractiveness is a rather subjective concept and ideas of attractiveness are culturally influenced, Berscheid and Walster (1974) found that people tend to date and marry partners who they perceive as being about equally attractive. The researchers concluded that most people would prefer as attractive a partner as possible, but as a practical matter, are content with partners thought to be about as attractive as themselves.

Many investigations have shown that we tend to like and love people who are similar to ourselves in intelligence. Part of this may be due to the tendency of people of similar intelligence to be thrown together through their choice of educational pathways and careers. Another strong possibility is that we enjoy the companionship of people of about the same intelligence as our own more than the companionship of people much smarter or duller than ourselves.

A related correlation (Garrison, Anderson, and Reed 1968) is that people of similar educational levels interact with each other more often than do those who are dissimilar. Again, this is probably the result of both mutual attraction and of being thrown together by having similar careers and life-styles.

Other similarities that various researchers have correlated with liking and loving include age, ethnic background, socioeconomic level, degree of social interaction preferred, religious affiliation, and drinking and smoking habits.

All in all, while some dissimilar friends or lovers are exceptions to the rule, the general conclusion is that *similarity attracts.*

1. Think of some people that you really like. Can you identify which of their traits are the basis for your liking them?
2. Think of some people that you intensely dislike. On what traits do you base your dislike of these people?
3. Do your likes and dislikes seem to have a rational basis?

Intimacy

Many of us misuse the word ***intimacy*** as if it were synonymous with sexual intercourse ("We were intimate a few times"). Perhaps this misunderstanding reveals how little emotional intimacy we allow ourselves to enjoy. Sexual intimacy certainly involves physical closeness, but it may or may not include any emotional intimacy or closeness. It is quite possible to have emotional intimacy without sexual interaction or to have sexual intercourse without any true emotional intimacy.

Any close relationship in which each person feels free to communicate innermost feelings to the other is an emotionally intimate relationship. Freedom of communication is an essential characteristic of an emotionally intimate relationship. Thoughts, needs, and feelings can be freely expressed without fear of a judgmental response.

Relationships without the ongoing reinforcement of effective, sensitive communication eventually disintegrate because the individuals' needs are not fulfilled. In some relationships, for example, communication may center around "safe" topics, such as who is going to take care of what (pick up the laundry, fix dinner, etc.).

Gut-Level Communication

When we speak of revealing our "true selves" (self-disclosure), we need to understand that our true nature is not a fixed or static reality but a dynamic process in a constant state of change. We are what we think, feel, judge, value, honor, esteem, love, hate, desire, hope for, believe in, and are committed to. When we see our friends today, we must not assume that they are exactly the same people we knew yesterday. Now they have experienced more of life—more love, pain, pleasure, and hurt—and now they are different. And, of course, we are different today ourselves.

We communicate with each other at many levels of self-disclosure. The least intimate form of communication is "cliche communication" in which we reveal nothing of our inner feelings. "How are you?" "Just fine, thank you." "Sure is warm today." "Sure is." From this level of noncommunication, we gradually proceed through levels of revelation culminating in the open expression of deepest, innermost feelings, which John Powell calls "gut-level communication." In his classic *Why Am I Afraid to Tell You Who I Am?* (1969), Powell lays down five "rules" for gut-level communication:

1. Gut-level communication never implies a judgment of the other. We can reveal our emotional reactions to the other's actions: "I feel really (hurt, angry, good, nervous, etc.) when you (whatever action it is)." Here we reveal our response to that specific action, but we do not judge the whole person on the basis of that action. We do not force the other into defending his or her whole being, but we do allow for discussion and possible modification of a specific behavior pattern.
2. Emotions are not moral—they are neither good nor bad. They are simply factual—they exist. Most of us have emotions to which we do not want to admit. We may feel ashamed of our fears or guilty about our anger or sexual desires. Before we can freely communicate our feelings, we need to accept that everyone experiences all of these same emotions and that they are neither good nor bad and that feeling them does not make us either good or bad persons.
3. Emotions need to be integrated with the intellect and the will. This means that while we must experience, recognize, and accept our emotions fully, we must not always act on those emotions. To

Rarely, if ever, are the individuals' feelings about their lives and each other a topic of discussion. Emotionally, the individuals gradually drift apart until, other than for convenience and security, there is little reason to continue the relationship.

Communicating Intimacy

Since we characterize intimacy largely in terms of communication, let's briefly consider what contributes to effective communication. Successful communication requires *two* participants: a speaker who honestly expresses an idea or feeling and a listener who truly wants and tries to understand that idea or feeling.

To be effective speakers, we must first be in touch with our emotions because only then can we communicate those emotions. Many of us, however, have been conditioned to deny either the reality or the importance of our emotions. Many males, for example, have been taught it is unmasculine to reveal sadness in tears, to reveal fear in any way, or to reveal love through gentle words or caresses. Both sexes hide

psychosomatic
(si''ko-so-mat'ik)

do so is to allow our emotions to control our lives. Thus, while we want to feel free to admit our fears, we need not be paralyzed by them. While we can freely admit our anger, we cannot feel free to punch out the person whose actions cause us to feel angry.

4. In gut-level communication, emotions are reported. For one thing, when we do not speak out our emotions, we act them out in temper tantrums, acts of violence, or our own psychosomatic health problems. But also, when we base our relationships on anything less than openness and honesty, they fail to stand the test of time. They soon crumble, leaving neither partner fulfilled by the experience.

5. With rare exceptions, emotions are best communicated at the time they are being experienced. It is much easier and feels much "safer" to report an emotion after it has become history. It is almost like talking about another person. And, in a sense, that was another person. As we have said, we each are a different person every day. But the emotions that are most meaningful with respect to our current relationships are those that we are feeling right now—and that is when they are most profitably communicated. (One exception to this rule is when the person to whom you would communicate your feelings is currently so disturbed with him- or herself that your report would be distorted by that person's emotional state. Another is when your interaction with that person is so transient (for example, a discourteous clerk) that it is hardly worth your time to tell him or her your emotional reaction.)

Honest disclosure of feelings has at least two major benefits. The more obvious reward is the type of intimate relationships it allows. But it also results in a more clearly defined sense of self-identity for each of the people in the relationship. For only by disclosing ourselves to others can we really know who we are. As we said earlier, we are what we think, feel, value, etc. And only through communicating these things to others can we really understand ourselves.

or deny feelings of hurt and rejection. Yet, nothing is more undeniably real than the feelings we experience.

If, as speakers, we do not openly express our feelings, our feelings may build into resentment and begin to be communicated as hostility. However, since the hostility expressed is not directly associated with its cause, it is difficult for a friend or lover to modify the offensive behavior. Perhaps we are feeling sexually rejected but criticize our lover's appearance rather than expressing our feelings of rejection. In a way, the friend or lover is being "punished" without knowing why. In addition, we have failed in our role as speaker to honestly communicate our feelings.

Many of us tend to view the speakers as taking an active role in the communication process while listeners are passive. But listeners are also active participants, of whom much is required for communication to be successful. Listeners must be alert to the nonverbal signals that all of us constantly communicate. Many of us fail as listeners because we are so wrapped up in ourselves that we are unable

Be aware of the nonverbal messages people are constantly sending out; they often reveal more than the words people say.

to direct our attention and concern to the needs of others. This is often characteristic of people with powerful, unfulfilled emotional needs. For example, someone experiencing a period of low self-esteem is not likely to feel much concern for the needs being expressed by someone else at that time. Unless as listeners we are sincerely attentive, we more than likely will not perceive the intended meaning of what is communicated.

Misinterpretation is a common listening problem. We often take messages as being critical when in fact they are not intended as such. Major misunderstandings can develop simply because we fail to ask for clarification of some ill-taken or vague statement.

Patterns of ineffective communication can become well established. One insensitive response is likely to be met with another. People often argue and fight without ever getting around to discussing what is really bothering them. In many fights between lovers, the real problem is something other than what the fight appears to be about. For example, a couple might be arguing about whose idea it was to go to such a lousy movie, while the real problem may be that one of them feels that the other is overly dependent.

To be good speakers and good listeners, then, we must be constantly attentive to our feelings and the feelings of those around us. Only in doing so are we able to successfully communicate our true selves to others and allow intimacy to develop.

Risking Intimacy
Intimacy is a risk-taking proposition—it means exposing our true emotions to another person. When our defenses are lowered, it is easy for someone else, as part of his or her own defensiveness, to aim a hurt directly at one of our vulnerable areas. But

without this lowering of defenses, without this risk taking, intimacy can never develop (Viscott 1979).

Risk taking is easier if both persons in a relationship remain as nonjudgmental as possible, have a mutual concern for the welfare and happiness of each other, and accept each other for what they are. Such an atmosphere allows for continued and growing honesty and provides assurance that the vulnerability inherent in openness will not be taken advantage of. Both people can thus feel free to present themselves as they truly are, not as they would like to be or would like others to perceive them as being.

Benefits of Intimacy

If we are unaccustomed to emotional intimacy, the thought of revealing so much of ourselves to another person may seem quite threatening. Many of us must *learn* to allow intimacy to develop. But intimacy is well worth the communicating and risk taking involved.

Intimate relationships with friends or lovers help to satisfy our needs to belong, to give and receive affection, and to develop self-esteem. Intimate friends help us to deal with anxiety by lending us their support. They also enable us to keep our problems in perspective by sharing their troubles with us. And sometimes, just by listening to us in a nonjudgmental manner, intimate friends help us to reduce our emotional stress level by allowing us to verbalize our internal conflicts and sort out possible solutions.

Intimacy brings a new dimension to our lives and to any of our relationships—sexual or otherwise—and we should strive to preserve the intimate relationships we already have and to develop new ones.

---

1. How many of your relationships would you call intimate? Why do you consider these relationships intimate?
2. Do you seem to be able to develop intimate relationships easily, or do you find it difficult? Can you explain why?
3. Do you know anyone who seems to actively block the formation of intimacy? Why might they do this?

Love

As a society, we can be said to be "in love with love," to quote an old song. Love is a frequent theme in the arts and entertainment media. Literature, movies, television, and the stage all rely heavily on love, and the public never seems to tire of the theme.

Love in Popular Music

"All You Need Is Love," The Beatles, 1967 (John Lennon and Paul McCartney)

"Love Is Just a Four-Letter Word," Joan Baez, 1968 (Bob Dylan)

"Love Is Surrender," Carpenters, 1970 (Ralph Carmichael)

"Love Has No Pride," Linda Ronstadt, 1973 (Eric Kaz and Libby Titus)

"Love Comes from Unexpected Places," Barbra Streisand, 1977 (Kim Carnes and Dave Ellingson)

"True Love Leaves No Traces," Leonard Cohen, 1977

"True Love Tends to Forget," Bob Dylan, 1978

"Love's Unkind," Donna Summer, 1978 (Donna Summer, Giorgio Moroder, and Pete Bellotte)

"Ain't Love a Bitch," Rod Stewart, 1978 (Rod Stewart and Gary Granger)

"Hard Times for Lovers," Judy Collins, 1979 (Hugh Prestwood)

"Crazy Little Thing Called Love," Queen, 1980 (Mercury)

"Love Stinks," J. Geils Band, 1980

"Love Is Pain," Joan Jett, 1981 (Jett Pack Music)

All of these conflicting sentiments regarding love seem amusing when viewed collectively and retrospectively. Many seem to reflect a rather cynical view of love—perhaps they are a reflection of their times.

Some authorities speculate that popular music may have a substantial influence on its primary consumers—adolescents and young adults. Many of these people are still forming their attitudes and values and often strongly identify with their favorite musicians, accepting whatever values the music expresses as their own. How much influence do you feel popular music exerts on people?

At the same time, few words in our language have so many different shades of meaning. The phrase "I love you" can mean one thing to the person saying it and something quite different to the person hearing it said. We use the same word to express how we feel about our sex partners, our parents, our children, our cars, our country, and our pets. Obviously, in each case the word *love* means something different. Yet all of these loves must share some common element or elements that cause us to use the same word to describe them.

The most obvious common factor is that we value all of these things. We want, in some way, to possess them, to be with them, and to protect them even if, at the moment, they are not needed by us in any practical way. This last phrase is especially significant. We do not wish to be with people we love only when they are serving our needs. That would not be love. For example, there may be many people whom we do not love but might at some point want to have sexual contact with. We might be rather indifferent to these people at other times. When we love someone, we value his or her company even when we are not sexually interested.

Some people have said that love defies explanation. Some have stated that the "mystery" of love should remain mysterious, that to explain love scientifically would destroy its beauty. Some even doubt that love really exists as a valid phenomenon.

psychoanalytic
(si''ko-an''ah-lit'ik)

Do You Love Me?

"I love you." While this certainly sounds like a statement, it often is actually a *question*. When we say "I love you" to someone, we generally expect a reply. When someone else says "I love you" to us, we usually feel that we should make an appropriate response. The statement "I love you" frequently translates into the question "Do you love me?" or "Do you still love me?" or "Just what are your feelings about me?"

While we may not recognize that our response is in reality an answer to a question, we do usually respond by answering the question. The response "I love you, *too*" clearly indicates the nature of the interchange. The *too* reduces the value of the response and implies that the original "I love you" was really a question.

Another bit of evidence that "I love you" can be a question is demonstrated when we make that statement and get *no* response. Our question has been answered, but it was not the answer we were looking for, was it? Perhaps we should recognize the true intent of our communication and more straightforwardly ask "What are your feelings about me?" or "What do you feel about our relationship?" This approach is much more likely to stimulate a meaningful exchange of feelings than the typical "I love you," and "I love you, too."

But most authorities feel that love is a reality and that it can be explained in scientifically acceptable terms. They further believe that the study of love is highly worthwhile, since a better understanding of love should be of value to people in developing more rewarding relationships.

Views on Love

The phenomenon of love has been interpreted from many perspectives, including behavioral, psychoanalytic, and humanistic views. We will look at how each of these contributes to our understanding of love.

Behavioral View of Love

One of the less romantic but highly functional views of love comes from the behavioral psychologists or learning theorists, who see behavior as conditioned by reward and punishment (Miller and Siegel 1972). In this context, love is viewed as a *learned response*. By learned, behavioral psychologists mean that love is largely a product of experience, that the ability to love is not something we are born with but something that we must learn (McConnell 1980).

In other words, behaviorists believe that we approach a loved person because we have learned to associate that person with many different kinds of rewarding or reinforcing experiences. Behaviorists stress that these rewarding or reinforcing experiences must occur in unpredictable *ways* and at unpredictable *times* for love to develop (Berscheid and Walster 1978). If we *know* what kind of reinforcement will come from a person, and when it will come, then we will seek that person's company only when we want whatever we know that person will deliver. On the other hand, if we have come to associate someone with a wide variety of pleasant experiences that can occur at many unpredictable times, then we will seek that person's company much of the time. That person signals the possibility of some kind of rewarding event at any time, and, thus, we enjoy a state of pleasant expectation just by being near that person.

It follows from this line of thinking that "true" love can develop only after a rather long period of experience with someone. We cannot develop a history of varied and unpredictable reinforcement from someone instantly. Does this preclude "Love at first sight?" We will see soon.

This behavioral concept of varied reinforcement covers all kinds of love relationships. We reinforce each other in many different ways, leading to many different kinds of love.

In sexually loving relationships, for example, the physical pleasure of sex is a powerful reward. But, surprisingly, a more important source of reinforcement in the development of sexual love is the interest exhibited in us by an attractive person.

Our culture, and especially the media, emphasize the importance of sexual attractiveness as part of our personal worth and adequacy. We are taught from infancy that the attention of a suitably attractive person makes us adequate and worth something. If a very attractive person seems to be attracted to us, it is flattering, it makes us feel good, and it helps to relieve any feelings of inferiority or inadequacy we may have. This encourages us to approach this person and to seek his or her company. The more strongly other people view this person as desirable, the more rewarding it is for us to "capture" him or her and the more this person's interest in us becomes a powerful reinforcing agent.

It might be appropriate to mention here the interesting phenomenon called the **halo effect.** We tend to judge a likeable or physically attractive or intelligent person as being "good" in other respects, too. It enables us to be "blind" to the minor or even major faults of an attractive person and works doubly in our relationships. First, an attractive (or intelligent or very likeable) person who shows an interest in us is perceived by us to be desirable in all respects. And also, the fact that this fantastic person shows interest in us makes us feel better about ourselves in every respect.

Psychoanalytic View of Love

Also called the analytic or psychodynamic approach to psychology, psychoanalysis was developed and popularized by Sigmund Freud. Freud regarded sex as a primary human motivating force and love as merely an expression of sexual desire—a mechanism in the service of sex. To Freud, love represented an effort to relieve a state of sexual tension, and thus all love derived from sex. Freud also saw love of self and love of others as incompatible. He believed that a person had only so much love available and that whatever was reserved for the self reduced the amount that was available for others.

Table 4.1 Comparison of Sigmund Freud and Erich Fromm's Views on Love.

Freud	Fromm
Love as an expression of sexual desire	Love as striving to overcome the basic state of human loneliness
Love as an effort to relieve sexual tension	People becoming human through loving
Love of self and love of others as incompatible	Impossible to love others if we do not first love ourselves
Love as a selfish process	Love as a caring and giving process.

Later analysts, sometimes called neo-Freudians, defined love much more broadly than Freud. Erich Fromm (1956), for example, explained love as a striving to overcome the basic state of human loneliness.

In his classic book, *The Art of Loving* (1956), Fromm proposed five different kinds of love: brotherly love (love of all humanity), parental love (love of parents for their child), erotic love (craving for sexual union with another person), self-love (love of one's own being), and love of God (religious love). Thus, unlike Freud, Fromm believed that sexual love was but one of many forms of love. To Fromm, people became human through loving and could not love others if they did not first love themselves. Fromm conceptualized love not just in terms of need gratification, but as a caring and giving process. According to Fromm, a loving person felt and demonstrated concern for the welfare of his or her partner, and acted in ways that fostered the growth of his or her partner toward **self-actualization** (achieving our full inherent potential as human beings). Fromm believed that a loving relationship, then, was based on giving as well as receiving.

Table 4.1 compares and contrasts both Freud and Fromm's views on love.

Humanistic View of Love
Humanistic psychology integrates physiological, behavioral, emotional, and intellectual aspects of psychology. In contrast to much research in other types of psychology, humanistic psychologists typically study emotionally healthy people, rather than people with problems.

Feelings and emotions are extremely important in humanistic psychology. Emotions are viewed as valid in and of themselves, regardless of how or whether they influence behavior. Individual happiness and personal fulfillment are highly valued by humanists.

Humanists value love for the emotional satisfaction and human growth it provides. They define love in much broader terms than just sexual and other need fulfillment and emphasize the giving aspects of love, rather than just the rewards. The concept of love is extended beyond lovers and family to encompass a love of all humanity.

Humanist Rollo May (1969) viewed love as the direct opposite of the depersonalized, dehumanized life in a modern technological society. He saw modern people as becoming just more machines in a machine age and thereby losing their identity. According to May, when people lose their identity, they deny the value of love, which results in a search for substitutes, all of which prove unworkable. This might characterize some of the people who haunt singles' bars. These people seek, but fail to find, fulfillment in superficial, depersonalized relationships.

Research on Love

Given the importance most people attach to loving and being loved, surprisingly little research has been conducted on how love develops. Part of this is no doubt due to the subjective nature of love and the difficulty in applying scientific measurements to love. But research on love has also been inhibited by the popular belief that to try to study love scientifically would strip love of its romance and, thus, ruin it. However, considering the millions of people whose love relationships are so unsatisfactory, it seems that a greater understanding of love would probably be quite beneficial to humanity.

Some interesting research on love has been done by Elaine and G. William Walster at the University of Wisconsin at Madison. In *A New Look at Love* (1978), they distinguish between two very different forms of love: passionate love and companionate love.

According to the Walsters, **passionate love** is a strong emotional state of confused feelings: tenderness and sexuality, elation and pain, anxiety and relief, altruism and jealousy. **Companionate love,** on the other hand, is less emotionally intensive and involves friendly affection and a deep attachment to someone.

The Walsters believe that most lover relationships start out as passionate love (which some people might call infatuation) and, later, *may* develop into companionate love (which some people might call "true love"). During the passionate stage, the loved person is idealized—any faults he or she might possess are overlooked. Everything about the loved person is sexually exciting, even characteristics that may later be viewed as undesirable. Being in the passionate stage of love is a genuine peak emotional experience, and measurable physiological changes occur during this time. Many people report feeling more "alive" when in the passionate stage of love than during more normal circumstances.

Just as it is easy to become addicted to the physical and emotional effects of certain drugs, it is easy to become addicted to the effects of passionate love. Peele (1976) and Hatterer (1980) point out that we sometimes turn to each other out of the same needs that drive some people to alcohol and others to heroin. And love addiction can be just as destructive as these other addictions. The love addict searches for an "easy fix" for deep emotional needs through superficial "love" relationships. Like a heroin fix, the effects of passionate love last for only a limited time. When these effects wear off, usually in about six to thirty months, according to the Wals-

Companionate love is the strong affection we feel for those with whom our lives are deeply intertwined.

ters (1978), the love addict must find another "fix" in the form of a new passionate love relationship. The need to be in the constant state of excitement attainable only through the passionate stage of love deprives these individuals of the emotional rewards that can come with the development of companionate love.

Companionate love is the strong affection we feel for those with whom our lives are deeply intertwined. It includes shared experiences, understandings, emotions, and habits, and is less immediately intense than passionate love. Though the companionate couple usually still maintain an active sexual relationship, their lovemaking probably is not as frequent or as consistently intensive as it was during the passionate stage. Also, by this time, each lover's imperfections are no longer being overlooked by the other, and some conflict situations are likely to arise. It is during the companionate stage that the love "addict" is going to be scurrying out for another "fix"—if not a total replacement for the companionate lover, then at least a side affair.

Love at First Sight?

Is there such a thing as love at first sight? Most of us carry some mental image of a desirable mate. The picture may be incomplete, vague, and may include characteristics that would make such a person a poor choice for a long-term partner. Regardless, this image forms a large part of our basis for judging the sexual attractiveness of the people we meet each day. Love at first sight is possibly nothing more than the immediate perception that a particular person fits our unconscious image of a desirable lover (Miller and Siegel 1972). If such a person shows an interest in us, we immediately feel more sexually attractive and adequate.

This is not necessarily a poor basis for the beginning of true love. It is, however, only a beginning. As we have learned, love takes time to develop. A couple must build up a substantial record of making each other happy, comfortable, and emotionally rewarded. Each partner must demonstrate the ability to provide many different reinforcements for the other. Eventually, through enjoying each other in a variety of shared activities, the couple may develop a genuine love for each other. They may then look back at the origin of their relationship as having been love at first sight. But a more accurate description of the early stage of such a relationship is probably mutual sexual attraction or infatuation, which we discuss in the next section.

---

1. How many times have you thought you were in love? Looking back, how many of those times was it really love?
2. Contrast passionate love and companionate love. Have any of your relationships fallen into either of these categories?
3. Have you ever felt that you fell in love with someone "at first sight"? Do you still feel that what you felt was really love? Why or why not?

Love Versus Infatuation

How can we tell the difference between love and infatuation? Is there a difference? The answers apparently depend on of whom we ask these questions.

One view of **infatuation** is that it is "a state of strong sexual attraction to another, based mainly on resemblance to an unreal lover fantasy" (Miller and Siegel 1972). According to proponents of this view, the origins of this unreal lover fantasy can be traced back to early love relationships and cultural influences.

For example, various physical and behavioral traits of the objects of our early love—usually our parents—can become a part of the mental picture that we have of a hoped-for lover. Appearances or characteristics of real lovers that we may have had are also seen as contributing to our fantasy of the ideal lover. In addition, the mass media, by telling us in books and movies and on television what kinds of persons should turn us on sexually, are viewed as shaping our lover fantasy.

According to proponents of this view, this unreal lover fantasy that each of us develops is the key to the big difference between love and infatuation. Love, they explain, is based on a long history of actual emotional reward or reinforcement that occurs *with* the specific loved person. With infatuation, however, our early love relationships and cultural influences that occurred *prior* to meeting the object of our infatuation are immediately related to that person. Before we even get to know this person, we already perceive him or her as fitting our fantasy of an ideal lover. Thus, love occurs over time and with the specific loved person, while infatuation is an immediate response to a newly known person.

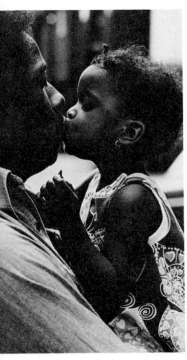

The characteristics of our early childhood love objects, usually our parents, play a big role in shaping our image of the ideal lover.

Can infatuation lead to love? It may be that some element of infatuation must be present at the beginning of a relationship or the relationship would never begin. In time, infatuation may lead to love. Perhaps the fantasy becomes reality, perhaps not. The exact time required to distinguish love from infatuation depends on the amount and variety of interaction. The wider the range of shared experiences, both pleasant and difficult, the sooner the true nature of the relationship is revealed.

Another view of infatuation, based on interviews with thousands of college students, is expressed by the Walsters (1978). This husband-wife research team states that there simply is no discernible difference between passionate love and infatuation: "Psychologists have become increasingly skeptical that passionate love and infatuation differ in any way—*at the time one is experiencing them.*" They further state that people use the term *love* to describe relationships that are still in progress and the term *infatuation* to describe once-loving relationships that, for whatever reason, were terminated.

One final interesting note on infatuation: If the difference between love and infatuation is so uncertain, how can some people, such as our mothers, distinguish between them when it comes to our relationships? Apparently, when people approve of a relationship, they are likely to call it love. When, for some reason, they disapprove, they tend to call it infatuation.

1.   Each of us holds a mental image of our ideal lover. Can you characterize your ideal lover? Do you know how your lover-fantasy developed?
2.   Have you been able to tell the difference between love and infatuation in your relationships? Have your evaluations of your relationships changed over time?

Inability to Love

Some unfortunate people are virtually incapable of sustaining a loving relationship. Time after time, relationships that initially seem to have the potential for being rewarding end before love really develops.

The most common cause of the inability to love is low self-esteem (Miller and Siegel 1972). A person with low self-esteem cannot accept the interest of an attractive potential lover. Rather than allowing this attention to build self-esteem, the low self-esteem person views the whole situation negatively. Instead of concluding that being desired affirms one's value, the low self-esteem person immediately devalues the person showing interest. The response is, "If she wants *me,* there must be something wrong with her."

People suffering from low self-esteem are constantly on the alert for any words or actions that might be interpreted as slighting them (Walster 1970). Even highly positive statements about them are devalued if there is any possible ambiguity, and interaction between people almost always involves some degree of ambiguity. People with high self-esteem take ambiguous statements to be flattering, while people with low self-esteem interpret the identical statements as derogatory.

For low self-esteem people, each new relationship is doomed to failure and leads only to the next unsatisfying relationship. These people often feel lonely, rejected, and isolated from others, even though they are the rejecting parties. Life may seem to lack meaning, at least in terms of interpersonal relationships.

Low self-esteem can be overcome, although seldom easily or quickly since these feelings often relate back to childhood and can be deeply ingrained. Zimbardo (1980) proposed a three-phase process of building self-esteem. The first phase involves developing an awareness of how we are thinking and reacting. Redefining our problems in terms of what causes and maintains the problems increases our feelings of control and provides us with a new perspective on what changes are possible. Phase two, according to Zimbardo, is trying out new responses, replacing, "She's probably just interested in me because she can't find anyone else," with, "She's interested in me because I'm an interesting person." Zimbardo's final phase of building self-esteem involves appraising the consequences of the new responses in positive ways that further build self-esteem. We should acknowledge that we have changed, appreciate the personal gains that have resulted from this change, and take full credit for a job well done.

The ability to love is based on these feelings of high self-esteem. In essence, we must value (love) ourselves at least a little before we can accept and value some-one else's love.

Love and Honesty

Love thrives on honesty—honesty regarding who and what we are and also honesty regarding our feelings about our partner.

Many of us have difficulty accepting the idea that someone can love us despite all of our inadequacies. This is why we sometimes find it difficult to disclose our-selves fully and honestly to another person. But pretending to be something that we are not is extremely difficult, and worrying that our dishonesty will be discovered results in uncomfortable anxiety and spent energy. Usually, we find that we are our own worst critics. What we perceive as personal weakness is usually not judged so harshly by others. When we fully reveal ourselves to others and find that they still approve of us, it is a great boost to our self-esteem, an extremely rewarding and comfortable feeling.

Similarly, honesty in revealing our true feelings about our partner is also es-sential to a loving relationship. Insincere compliments, even though well intended, soon become transparent, and the insincere complimentor quickly loses credibility. If someone knows that our compliments and expressed interest are not always gen-uine, he or she never knows when it is safe to believe us. So the only safe response is never to believe us. In behavioristic terms, we lose our power to reward that per-son. And since love is viewed in terms of reward, we have lost our ability to be loved by that person.

Honest reactions to our partner and his or her behavior gives our partner the ability to predict the circumstances in which we will be pleased or displeased. This knowledge may make it possible to avoid conflict-creating situations. At least, there is a sound basis for deciding whether or not the relationship should be maintained. If our partner does not know what behavior to avoid, it may be simpler just to avoid us.

Of course, two people may learn through their openness that they really have characteristics that make it very unlikely that they can ever love each other. But knowing and accepting this early can prevent years of destructive interaction.

Love and Sex

Sex offers many potential rewards capable of reinforcing a love relationship. First, a sexual orgasm is certainly among the greatest of human pleasures and seems likely to reinforce our approach behavior to the person who helps provide the orgasm. A second important reward in sexual intercourse is touching. Skin contact is a very

Sex offers many potential rewards capable of reinforcing a love relationship.

basic source of human pleasure dating clear back to infant-mother interaction. In addition, sex offers many psychological rewards. There may be the satisfaction of feeling wanted and accepted and reinforcement of feelings of personal worth. With so many rewards, sexual relations, especially those including orgasm, certainly contribute to the development of love for our sexual partner.

Does it matter in a sexual encounter whether or not the two people involved are in love with each other? Most of the people that the authors have surveyed feel that sexual pleasure is enhanced by a feeling of love for one's partner (see table 4.2). Remember that one characteristic of love is a strong desire to approach and be close to the loved person. If we love someone, we enjoy his or her company. Certainly, sexual interaction accomplishes this. The satisfaction of emotional needs associated with love thus adds to the physical pleasure of the sexual activity. In addition, since many people hold the belief that love justifies sex (again, see table 4.2), being in love relieves some of the guilt or anxiety that sexual activity might otherwise evoke in these people.

Table 4.2   Survey of Human Sexuality Classes: "How Closely Do You Think Love and Sex Are Related?"

Percent Females Agreeing	Percent Males Agreeing	
8.1	10.7	Sex and love are independent, and sex should be enjoyed for its own sake.
53.8	58.0	Love greatly enriches sexual relations but is not necessary for its enjoyment.
14.2	10.4	Sexual intercourse without love is not enjoyable.
25.1	20.0	Sexual intercourse is sacred and should be reserved for the expression of serious love.

Note: This is a survey of random human sexuality classes by an anonymous computer-tabulated questionnaire, Mt. San Antonio College, Walnut, California, 1978–1981. Respondees to the questionnaire were 403 females and 274 males. This survey represents a rather narrow range of people (college students in Southern California), and the results may not be representative for a broader range of people.

1. How do you feel when an attractive person indicates interest in you? Is your response usually positive or negative? Why?
2. Have you ever been dishonest with a lover? If so, why did you feel the dishonesty was necessary? What happened?
3. Have you ever been the recipient of an insincere compliment? How did you know the compliment was insincere? How did you handle the situation?
4. What are your own personal feelings and/or experiences concerning the relationship, if any, between love and sex?
5. Here's a tough one. If you had to choose between loveless sex and sexless love, which would you choose? Why?

Destructive Elements in Relationships

Unfortunately, not every relationship we form lives up to its potential for contributing to our emotional fulfillment. Some relationships, in fact, are destructive in that they limit our emotional or other growth and development, diminish our self-esteem, or restrict our self-actualization.

Destructive elements in relationships can originate from our own personality traits, those of our partners, or in the specific and often subtle ways our personalities interact with those of our partners. If the same type of problem seems to arise in each of our relationships, this tends to point to our own traits as the principal cause of trouble.

We explore two of the most common destructive patterns of interaction that appear in relationships: jealousy and excessive dependency.

Jealousy

One unpleasant aspect of loving is the potential for the development of unreasonable **jealousy.** Most people experience some degree of jealousy, and usually it is not disruptive of the love relationship. But there is a type of demanding, obsessive, and unrealistic jealousy that can severely damage or even destroy a relationship. As noted anthropologist Margaret Mead (1960) said:

> Jealousy is not a barometer by which the depth of love can be read. It merely records the degree of the lover's insecurity. It is a negative, miserable state of feeling, having its origin in the sense of insecurity and inferiority.

The common result of jealousy is the driving away of the one person that we want so desperately to hold.

Several psychological mechanisms may contribute to jealousy. Insecurity and feelings of inadequacy are thought to be the greatest causes of intense jealousy (Miller and Siegel 1972). Jealous people perceive their partner as being a highly desirable "possession," and they doubt that their own attractiveness or sexual adequacy is enough to hold onto such a person. They tend to idealize their partner (put him or her on a "pedestal") and underestimate their own worth.

Another mechanism producing jealousy is psychological **projection** (projecting our feelings or behavior onto others). Projection is the basis of much paranoia and produces jealousy in the following way: X finds the thought of having an outside love affair very exciting, which is a perfectly normal feeling. At the same time, however, the idea of an outside affair evokes anxiety, fear, and guilt because X has been taught that having an affair is wrong, evil, dangerous, or sinful. Therefore, X puts the anxiety-producing thought of having an affair out of X's conscious mind (and into the unconscious mind). It is not uncommon for X to then project X's own feelings about an affair onto Y, X's partner. Soon, X accuses Y of having an affair, believing that it is Y who is attracted to other partners, that it is Y who is the guilty one, and that it is Y's fault that the relationship is breaking up. This common source of jealousy can destroy an excellent relationship of mutual love.

Regardless of the irrational basis of jealousy, it seems very real to someone experiencing it. Not only does it drive away the loved person, but it can interfere with our effectiveness in all areas of living. Some people become so immobilized by jealousy that they are unable to carry out the responsibilities of their job or schooling.

One way to deal with jealousy is to build self-esteem, perhaps using Zimbardo's three-step process mentioned earlier. Another is to see relationships in a different light, to learn that our personal lives would be more satisfying and our professional lives more creative and productive if we and our partners felt free to interact (not necessarily sexually) with a great number of people.

Overcoming Jealousy

Jealousy is such a prevalent disorder that special "jealousy clinics" are held in many cities to help people deal with this destructive emotion. Here is a sample of the kind of advice they give (Walster and Walster 1978; Phillips 1980):

1. **Try to find out exactly what it is that is making you jealous.** Are you upset that other people find your partner attractive? Or is that OK? Are you upset that your partner is going out to lunch with someone else? Or is that OK too? Is it that your partner is having sexual relations with someone else? Is it that your partner might think this other person is a better lover than you? Or is it that the other person might think so? Is it that your partner might leave you? Are you so dependent on your partner that you could not make it if your partner left? Are you afraid you could never find someone else? Do you feel that you are no longer "number one" and that *everyone knows it*? Do you feel powerless because you realize that you cannot control your partner or your life? Do you feel emotionally, sexually, or intellectually deprived? Do you feel that your territory has been invaded? Do you feel that your property rights have been infringed? Do you feel that you want more time with

your partner? The first step, then, is to understand what you are feeling and why you feel that way.

2. **Try to put your feelings in perspective.** Ellis (1971) says that emotional problems are primarily caused by irrational attitudes and beliefs. People who suffer excessive jealousy may be childishly insisting on having the unattainable. Is it really so awful that your partner is interested in someone else? Don't you have such interests yourself? Is it true that you could not function without your current partner? Although you may never be able to eliminate all jealousy from your life, you can gain control over your emotions by viewing your situation more realistically.

3. **Maintain some separate friends and interests of your own.** Many counselors have found that it is easier for couples to maintain a close, while not excessively possessive, love relationship if they each maintain some separate friends and interests. It is much easier to have confidence in your desirability if you have an independent identity and if there are others who like and admire you. You are far less likely to fear being abandoned by your partner. And it will be a lot easier for you to cope if you are.

Excessive Dependency

Throughout this chapter, we have discussed love in terms of need fulfillment—each partner contributes to the fulfillment of one or more of the other's needs. However, partners do not necessarily fulfill the same needs for each other. In fact, each may be having very different needs fulfilled by the other. Sex for sex or companionship for companionship would be examples of trades fulfilling the same need for each partner. Sex for security, sex for ego reinforcement, or sex for companionship would be examples of situations where different needs are being fulfilled for each partner.

Zimbardo (1980) proposed the *equity theory,* which states that most people are quite comfortable with such trades as long as they feel that they are giving and receiving about equally. Most people, however, do not enjoy a relationship where the trade is perceived as unequal—*in either direction.*

Many relationships are very unequal and involve such an extreme degree of dependency on the part of one partner that the relationships may be viewed as destructive (Peele 1976). Our culture has encouraged women, in particular, to be dependent. For many people, the basic problem is a form of emotional immaturity. As children, we were of necessity highly dependent on others for most of our needs. Our welfare and happiness were largely at the mercy of others. As we grew up, most of us gradually assumed more and more responsibility for our own well-being. But some people never develop such autonomy. Even as adults, they delegate the responsibility for their emotional and/or physical well-being to others. These are the people who are likely to become overly dependent on those they love.

Dependency-prone individuals often experience a series of excessive dependency relationships. For, rather than strengthening the bond between lovers, excessive dependency usually acts to destroy relationships.

An excessively dependent partner is likely to be perceived by the other partner as a burden. While lovers normally enjoy doing things for each other, there is a limit to the amount of time and energy most people are willing to devote to even someone they love very much. If demands are made beyond that limit, resentment and hostility are almost certain to develop. Even if the true cause of the hostility is not communicated to the dependent partner, the hostility will still make itself felt—perhaps in fights, sexual problems, or the termination of the relationship.

Highly dependent people suffer from low self-esteem, and their feeling of dependency does nothing to boost their self-image. They usually feel a great deal of anxiety about the possible loss of the person upon whom they are so dependent. They may also be extremely jealous. Not uncommonly, a love-hate relationship develops. Dependent people can feel so bad about themselves and so miserable in their dependency that they actually grow to resent, even hate, the person upon whom they are so highly dependent. Conflict situations constantly arise in such relationships.

Excessive dependency can be overcome. The basic steps in the process are (1) recognizing or admitting to the nature of the problem, (2) developing an understanding of *why* one feels so dependent, and (3) initiating a program leading to the goal of increased independence.

In a series of excellent books (*Your Erroneous Zones,* 1976; *Pulling Your Own Strings,* 1978; *The Sky's the Limit,* 1980), Dr. Wayne W. Dyer presents a workable approach to overcoming dependency. His basic premise is that, as adults, we must assume responsibility for our own well-being and not let other people determine whether or not we can be happy. We must see ourselves as capable of charting the course of our own lives, of making plans and carrying them out. Dyer believes that while it is certainly desirable to enjoy the love and companionship of others as we go through life, we must relate to each other as equal adults, not as children relating to parents. The responsibility for our happiness, he says, is too important to delegate to anyone else.

1. Do you think that jealousy is a good measure of love? Why or why not?
2. Have you ever felt unrealistic jealousy in a relationship? How did you handle it?
3. Have you ever had a relationship with an overly dependent person? How did the relationship make you feel? Has the relationship ended? If so, why did it end?

Falling Out of Love

Love, the source of some of our greatest joy, can also be the cause of much pain. There may be many occasions in life when our happiness depends upon "getting over" being in love. Some examples include:

1. We are obsessed with a married person who betrays our trust again and again.
2. We are entangled with someone who is draining us emotionally and financially.
3. We are thrown into the deepest depression when we think of our "ex" making love with someone new.
4. We are desperately in love with someone who obviously does not feel the same way about us.
5. Our lover died in an accident two years ago, and we still can't bring ourselves to start dating again.

Falling out of love is usually a natural, though painful, process. Most people fall out of love without help. Time passes, they meet other people, and their lives go on. But for some of us, the loss of a lover can be almost overwhelming—an intense, enduring, immobilizing pain. Being in love when it is not returned can lead to depression, obsessive thoughts, sexual dysfunction, inability to work, difficulty in making new friends, and even to self-destructiveness.

In her book *How to Fall Out of Love* (1980), Debora Phillips takes a behavioristic approach to breaking the bonds of love. She reasons that, since our love for someone is a learned response, we can relearn a new response to that person. Relearning, through methods developed by behavioral therapists, can enable us to change behavior that causes us pain. In other words, those of us who are unable to function normally because of obsessive thinking about a former lover can learn how to use competing thoughts to break our obsession with the old lover and go on to new relationships. We do not have to learn to hate the person. We simply have to stop loving that person.

According to Phillips, the first step in falling out of love is called *thought stopping*. The idea is to spend progressively less and less time thinking about the loved person. Allowing a thought to come back time and again reinforces that thought, making it grow stronger and often more painful.

Phillips suggests that we begin thought stopping by making a list of some of the most positive scenes and pleasures we can think of that do not involve "that person." Just the act of writing the list helps us to start becoming involved with pleasure without being involved with our former lover. The list can include the most outrageous fantasies and incorporate anyone we know or might like to know (except our former lover).

Phillips proposes that once we have our list, we purposely bring on a thought of the person we want to fall out of love with but say, "Stop" the instant that thought enters our mind. Then, in the next instant, we should bring on the thought of one of the best scenes from our list.

According to Phillips, we should practice thought stopping intentionally ten times a day in addition to as many times a day as we have to use it unintentionally when we start to think of our former lover.

Phillips's second step in falling out of love is called *silent ridicule.* The purpose of silent ridicule is to get over idealizing our ex-lover as perfect in every way and involves designing a scene in which our ex-lover looks ridiculous or acts or talks absurdly. The scene should be based on the exaggeration of some imperfect characteristic of the person, and it must not evoke pity—only humor. For example, if immaturity is one of our former lover's traits, a silent ridicule scene might involve our former lover dressed as a baby and lying in a crib. Phillips advocates practicing the scene three to five times a day. Then, whenever we think about our ex-lover, we should bring on the scene. The goal, according to Phillips, is to think of the person, not only less often, but also in a more realistic way.

Phillips's third step in falling out of love is to aggressively work on *building self-esteem.* Ideally, a love relationship serves to reinforce our sense of self-esteem. However, being rejected or involved in a destructive relationship may be devastating to our feelings of personal value.

To build self-esteem, Phillips proposes keeping a stack of index cards and every day, on one card, writing down at least two positive things about ourselves. These positive things might be some of our basic characteristics or some good things we have done that day or at some time in the past. Phillips suggests that whenever we find ourselves thinking negatively about ourselves, we should say, "Stop" and immediately think a good thought about ourselves. As in all behavior therapy, it is just a matter of learning a more desirable response. How we think about ourselves has been learned, and we can learn to think about ourselves more positively.

Phillips's fourth and probably best way to fall out of love is to fall in love with someone new—*when we are emotionally ready.* This does not mean an immediate "rebound" romance, which is often as destructive as the love it replaces. But there does come a time when living in the memory of a past love is also destructive. Then, even if we have to force ourselves, we should get out and meet someone. Later, we will look back and be glad we did.

1. Have you ever found yourself "hung-up" on someone who did not feel the same way about you? How did you handle it?
2. Do you think that Debora Phillips's techniques for falling out of love would be effective? Do you plan to use them in the future? Why or why not?

"Bob, do you remember back to when we were in college, how jealous I used to get?"

"Yeah, it almost killed me! We were young. Love was different back then. It was hell walking around with butterflies in my stomach all the time."

"You felt like that? I thought girls were the only ones to go through love pains."

"Guys get 'em too. I was so in love with you back then. I still am—only I think I love you more, now that we've been through so much together."

"Love is safe now, more comfortable. Bob, I was so afraid I was going to lose you, I thought I'd die. I think of all that wasted energy spent worrying about how to keep you."

"Well, we're still together, aren't we?"

"Ever have any regrets?"

"No, not a one."

Summary

1. We like people who like us and who share our attitudes and whose other characteristics are similar to ours in such areas as emotional health, physical attractiveness, intelligence, and educational level.

2. Intimacy is a caring, loving, or liking relationship in which both persons feel free to communicate their innermost feelings to each other. The development of intimate relationships requires good communication skills, both from a speaking and a listening vantage point. Intimate relationships also require risk taking, mutual concern, mutual acceptance, and nonjudgmental attitudes. Intimate relationships help to satisfy our needs to belong, to give and receive affection, and to develop self-esteem.

3. Love can be interpreted from many perspectives. The behavioral view is that love is a learned response, reinforced by the rewards provided by the loved person. Freud viewed love as merely an expression of sexual desire; later psychoanalysts took a broader view. Humanists stress the giving aspects of love and extend the concept of love beyond lovers and family to encompass a love of all humanity.

4. Passionate love is the strongly emotional state characteristic of the early months of a relationship, while companionate love is the strong affection we feel for those with whom our lives are deeply intertwined.

5. Most of us carry a mental image of a desirable mate, and when someone fits that image, we feel sexually attracted and may believe that it is love at first sight. Love, however, takes time to develop, and a better description of the early stage of such a relationship is probably mutual sexual attraction or infatuation.

6. One view of infatuation is that it is a strong sexual attraction to another that is based mainly on the other's resemblance to an unreal lover fantasy that we have developed through early love relationships and cultural influences. Another view is that passionate love and infatuation are virtually indiscernible at the time that we experience them. Infatuation may or may not develop into love over time.

7. The inability to love is often associated with low self-esteem. A person with low self-esteem cannot accept the interest of an attractive potential partner and responds to this interest both negatively and defensively. The process of building self-esteem involves becoming aware of how we are thinking and acting, trying out new response behaviors, and appraising the consequences of the new responses in positive ways.

8. Love thrives on honesty—honesty regarding who and what we are and also honesty regarding our feelings about our partner.

9. Sex offers many potential rewards capable of reinforcing a love relationship. Conversely, most people feel that their sexual pleasure is enhanced when they feel love for their sex partner.

10. Relationships are destructive when they limit growth, diminish self-esteem, or restrict self-actualization. Demanding, obsessive, and unrealistic jealousy can destroy a relationship. Jealousy is not a measure of love, but of insecurity. Excessive dependency is unpleasant for both partners in a relationship. The excessively dependent partner is perceived by the other partner as a burden and suffers from low self-esteem and feelings of anxiety.

11. Sometimes our happiness depends on falling out of love. If time alone does not help us, there are definite steps we can take, ranging from thought stopping and silent ridicule to building up self-esteem and falling in love with someone new.

2

PHYSICAL SEXUALITY

5

External Sex Organs
Penis/Scrotum

Internal Sex Organs
Testes/Epididymis/Vas Deferens/Fluid-Producing Glands

Hormones
How Hormones Act/Control of Hormonal Secretions

Hormonal Control of Male Reproductive Processes
*The Hypothalamus-Pituitary-Testes "Connection"/
Hormonal Control of Testosterone Production/Hormonal
Control of Sperm Production/Hormonal Control of Sperm
Capacitation*

Hormones and Sexual Behavior

I never really understood what it takes to be a man until my wife gave birth to our son. As I watched Billy grow, I marveled at the way he would pick up little characteristics that were mirror images of me. I am proud that he is growing the way he is, but what happens when he grows up? I don't want him learning about sexuality the way I did.

When I was a kid, there were all the jokes about "flashlights" and "bats and balls." The word *penis* was never used, and when it was referred to, it was the center of a dirty joke. In grade school, teachers talked about hygiene, and we laughed about it behind the schoolhouse.

I was totally ignorant about my body back then. I don't want Billy to go through the same thing. I want to explain to him the importance of knowing his body. I want Billy to know the words *penis, scrotum, testes,* and *sperm* without being uncomfortable saying them. But when do I tell him? What will I say? Will it really make any difference?

In this chapter and in chapter 6, we explore the structure and functions of the reproductive systems of both men and women. Increasing our knowledge of our own bodies and that of our sexual partners does not necessarily increase our sexual satisfaction. However, such knowledge may help us to become more comfortable with our bodies, and that *does* increase sexual satisfaction.

This chapter concentrates on male sexual anatomy and physiology. We examine the external and internal structures of the male sex organs and develop some understanding of how the male reproductive system functions. A brief introduction to hormones and a discussion of hormonal control over male reproductive processes concludes the chapter.

Although the male genitals are quite visible, many people are essentially unfamiliar with the structures and functions of the male sexual anatomy. We encourage male readers in particular to use the information presented in this chapter as the basis for a detailed self-examination.

People of each sex are encouraged to thoroughly examine their genitals.

prepuce
(pre'pūs)

circumcision
(ser"kum-sizh'un)

frenulum
(fren'u-lum)

External Sex Organs

The external sex organs, or genitals, of the male consist of the penis and the scrotum.

Penis

The **penis** is the male organ for urination and sexual intercourse, and it varies in size and shape from one male to another as any part of the human body varies from one person to another.

Penis Size

The average penis is three to four inches long when flaccid (soft, nonerect) and about six inches long when erect. Its diameter when flaccid is about 1¼ inches and increases another quarter of an inch when erect. Normally sized penises, however, can be smaller or larger.

The size and shape of the penis are not related to a man's build, race, or ability to give or receive sexual satisfaction. And, a penis does not grow through frequent use or decrease in size because of lack of use in sexual intercourse.

Our society generally believes that a "big" penis provides more sexual satisfaction to a woman during intercourse. A woman's vagina, however, enlarges during intercourse to accommodate the size of the penis within it. It accommodates a smaller or larger circumference and a longer or shorter length. The length of the penis mainly determines the depth of vaginal penetration, which is relatively unimportant since the majority of vaginal nerve endings are located in the outer third of the vagina. As a result, penile size has very little to do with female sexual satisfaction. Because of the generally common (although inaccurate) belief that "bigger is better," however, a larger penis may have psychological significance to some people.

Outer Structures

The end of the penis is an enlarged region called the **penile glans** or head (see figure 5.1). (The word *glans* means "shaped like an acorn.") The urethral opening is at the center of the glans. Covering the glans is a loosely fitting **prepuce,** or **foreskin.** The surgical removal of the foreskin is known as **circumcision.** The shaft of the penis extends from the glans to the body wall.

While the entire penis is sensitive to physical stimulation, the greatest concentration of nerve endings is in the glans. Two specific areas on the glans are particularly responsive to stimulation. One sensitive area is the ridge where the glans arises abruptly from the shaft. This distinct ridge is called the **corona.** The second sensitive area is on the underside of the corona, where the glans is connected to the foreskin by a thin strip of skin called the **frenulum** or **frenum.** See figure 5.2.

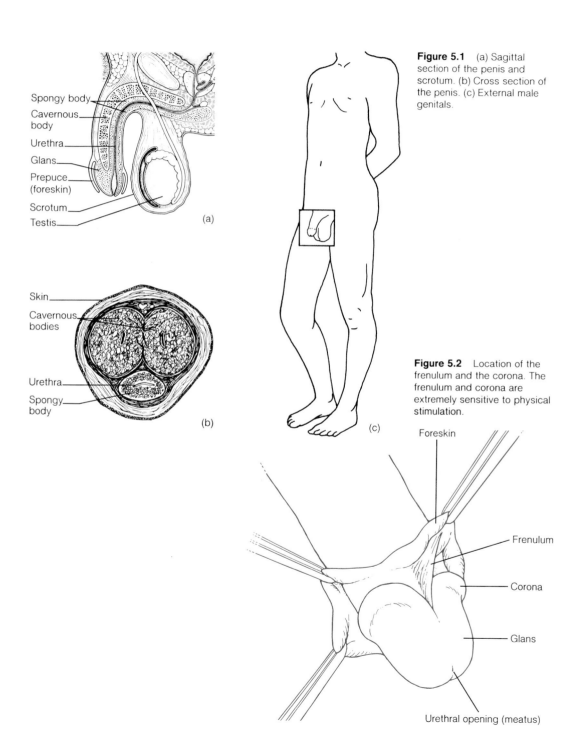

Spongy body
Cavernous body
Urethra
Glans
Prepuce (foreskin)
Scrotum
Testis

(a)

Skin
Cavernous bodies
Urethra
Spongy body

(b)

(c)

Figure 5.1 (a) Sagittal section of the penis and scrotum. (b) Cross section of the penis. (c) External male genitals.

Figure 5.2 Location of the frenulum and the corona. The frenulum and corona are extremely sensitive to physical stimulation.

Foreskin
Frenulum
Corona
Glans
Urethral opening (meatus)

Circumcision

Circumcision is the surgical removal of part of the foreskin (prepuce) of the penis. There are two methods of performing circumcision. In one method, a specially shaped piece of plastic is placed over the glans and the foreskin is stretched over the plastic and then trimmed off (box figure 5.1a). In the second procedure, as shown in box figure 5.1b, the foreskin is carefully cut "freehand" and then stitched. An anesthetic is not used for circumcision of babies, but it is used for a child or an adult.

In infancy, circumcision is usually performed for hygienic or religious reasons. Later in life, it may be performed for cultural or medical reasons.

The hygienic reasons for circumcision center around the relative ease with which a circumcised penis can be kept clean and free from odor. In uncircumcised males, secretions from glands in the foreskin may accumulate under the foreskin and combine with dead skin cells to form a cheesy substance known as **smegma.** If the foreskin of the uncircumcised male is not retracted and the glans cleaned thoroughly and regularly, smegma can build up and become odorous and an irritant.

Some research has indicated that women whose sexual partners are uncircumcised males may run an increased risk of cancer of the cervix. There is

Box Figure 5.1
Methods of performing circumcision. (a) In this method, a piece of plastic is placed over the glans and the foreskin is stretched over the plastic and trimmed off. (b) In this method, the foreskin is carefully cut "freehand" and then stitched.

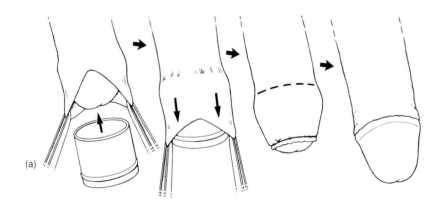

(a)

Internal Structures

Internally, the shaft and glans of the penis are composed of three cylinders of **erectile tissue** and the **urethra,** the duct through which urine passes from the bladder through the penis to the outside of the body. The three cylinders consist of irregular cavities and spaces (much like a dense sponge) known as **vascular** (able to contain blood) **spaces.**

Two of the cylinders are called the **cavernous bodies** (*corpora cavernosa*), and the third cylinder is called the **spongy body** (*corpus spongiosum*). The cavernous bodies are the upper cylinders and extend the length of the shaft of the penis. The spongy body is the lower cylinder of the penis and extends the length of the shaft and forms the glans. See figure 5.1.

also some evidence that cancer of the penis is more common in the uncircumcised male. This research, however, is far from conclusive at this time.

The cultural reasons for circumcision differ the world over. Often, circumcision is part of a religious rite, as with the Jewish and Moslem faiths. In certain cultures, circumcision heralds the onset of male adolescence and is performed as an initiation rite into adulthood.

Occasionally, there are medical indications for circumcision. The foreskin, for example, may be unusually long, and the foreskin opening may be unusually narrow. Or the glans, inside the foreskin, may become infected by bacteria or from diaper rash, and the infection may cause the foreskin to become scarred and abnormally tight. Or the foreskin may become "stuck" in a retracted position. All of these conditions are corrected by circumcision.

Routine circumcision is being challenged. According to the American Pediatric Society, there are no strong medical reasons that justify it (Paige 1978). As a consequence of such advice, fewer infant boys are being routinely circumcised.

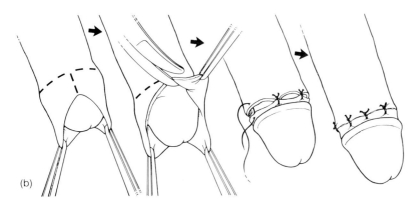

(b)

When the penis is flaccid, the cylinders of erectile tissue cannot be seen or felt as distinct structures. However, when the penis is erect, the spongy body stands out as a distinct ridge along the underside of the penis.

Erection and Ejaculation

Penile **erection** can be produced by direct stimulation of the external genitals or by stimulation from the brain.

Direct stimulation, such as light touching of the penis and rubbing of the penile skin, for example, causes nerve impulses to be transmitted through the pudendal nerve to an erection control center in the spinal cord. Pressures within the erectile tissues and the pelvic organs produce nerve impulses within the pelvic nerve, which are also transmitted to the erection control center in the spinal cord.

Retrograde Ejaculation

Some men experience what is known as **retrograde ejaculation.** As shown in box figure 5.2, retrograde ejaculation occurs when semen is expelled into the bladder rather than through the penis.

Retrograde ejaculation results from a reversed functioning of the two urethral sphincters, tiny rings of muscle surrounding the urethra. Usually, the internal urethral sphincter, located between the prostate and the bladder, contracts during penile erection and ejaculation, which prevents sperm from entering the bladder upon ejaculation, and the external urethral sphincter, located at the anterior of the prostate gland, relaxes just before ejaculation, which allows semen to be ejaculated through the urethra. In retrograde ejaculation, the reverse occurs. The internal urethral sphincter relaxes, and the external urethral sphincter contracts. This results in the semen being ejaculated into the bladder instead of out through the urethra.

Retrograde ejaculation is not harmful since the semen is later eliminated with the urine. A man who frequently experiences retrograde ejaculation, however, probably should consult a physician to ascertain whether there is an underlying health problem. This condition is common in men who have had the prostate gland removed. Also, illness, congenital anomaly (abnormalities existing at birth), and certain drugs (notably tranquilizers) can cause retrograde ejaculation.

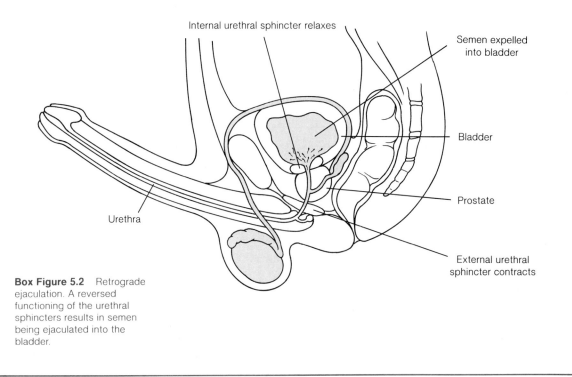

Internal urethral sphincter relaxes

Semen expelled into bladder

Bladder

Prostate

External urethral sphincter contracts

Urethra

Box Figure 5.2 Retrograde ejaculation. A reversed functioning of the urethral sphincters results in semen being ejaculated into the bladder.

vas deferens   epididymis
(vas def'er-enz)   (ep''ĭ-did'ĭ-mis)

A second erection control center higher in the spinal cord can cause an erection by stimulation from the brain. Erotic thoughts or visuals, for example, can trigger an erection without physical stimulation of the genitals.

After receiving nerve impulses from the genitals and/or the brain, the two erection control centers in the spinal cord initiate the two physiological processes necessary for penile erection: The smooth muscle (the muscle found in the walls of all hollow organs of the body except the heart) of the penis must relax, enlarging the vascular spaces in the three cylinders, and the arteries leading into the penis must dilate. When this happens, arterial blood, under relatively high blood pressure, floods the vascular spaces of the erectile tissue. The accumulation of blood in the erectile columns causes the penis to swell, elongate (lengthen), and become erect. There are no bones in the human penis, and erection is solely a function of the cavernous bodies and the spongy body filling with blood.

Ejaculation is the sudden expulsion of semen from the erect penis. Ejaculation is usually preceded by **emission,** which is a discharge of seminal fluid from the fluid-producing glands of the reproductive system. Ejaculation and emission are two separate physiological processes that are triggered by dual control centers in the spinal cord. Nerve impulses from the emission control center in the spinal cord are transmitted through the pelvic and hypogastric nerves to the fluid-producing glands of the reproductive system, causing emission. Then, nerve impulses from the ejaculatory control center in the spinal cord travel through the pudendal nerve to the muscles of the pelvic area, causing ejaculation.

After ejaculation, the arteries that supply blood to the vascular spaces of the penile erectile tissue constrict, reducing the flow of blood into the erectile tissue. The smooth muscle within the walls of the vascular spaces partially contracts, and the veins of the penis enlarge. These actions force the blood out of the erectile tissue and into the venous system (the veins that carry blood away from the organs) of the body. The penis gradually returns to its former flaccid condition. Usually, another erection and ejaculation cannot be triggered for a period of ten to thirty minutes or longer.

Scrotum

The **scrotum** (or scrotal sac) is a thin, loose pouch of sensitive skin in the groin area below the penis. The skin color of the scrotum is usually darker than the skin color of other parts of the body.

The scrotum contains the two **testes** (or testicles). Each testis is suspended within the scrotal sac by the **spermatic cord** (a structure that contains blood vessels, nerves, and sperm-carrying tubes called the **vas deferens**) and the **epididymis** (a structure lying between the testis and the vas deferens that is important in the maturing process of sperm).

The anatomy of the scrotum and also its placement outside of the abdominal cavity allows the scrotum to maintain the testes at about three to four degrees Fahrenheit below body temperature. This is extremely important since sperm production by the testes requires a temperature that is lower than normal body temperature. Colder air temperatures cause muscle fibers in the scrotum to contract, which moves the scrotum closer to the pelvic cavity and elevates each testis within the scrotum. Warmer air temperatures cause scrotal muscle fibers to relax, moving the scrotum away from the pelvic cavity and cooling the testes.

As shown in figure 5.3, the spermatic cord, testes, and epididymis can be located by feeling the scrotal sac. The spermatic cord is a firm, rubbery tube that can be found with thumb and forefinger above a testis. The epididymis feels like a small elevation on the testis at the base of the spermatic cord.

Figure 5.3 The spermatic cord, testis, and epididymis can be located with thumb and forefinger.

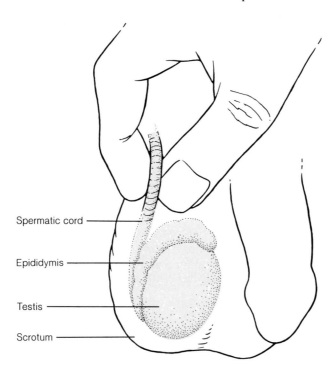

Spermatic cord

Epididymis

Testis

Scrotum

testosterone
(tes-tos′tĕ-rōn)

Kegel-Like Exercises for Males

Kegel exercises were developed by Arnold Kegel in 1952 to help new mothers to redevelop muscle tone in the muscles surrounding the vaginal opening (see chapter 6). A man's control over the muscles on the floor of the pelvis is not so dramatic as a woman's. However, the root of the male penis in the tissues of the pelvis is surrounded by muscles that are comparable to those surrounding the vaginal opening of the female. Kegel-like exercises can strengthen these muscles and may increase a male's sexual sensations during intercourse and at orgasm in the same way that Kegel exercises have been shown to work for women.

Men can gradually work their way into a Kegel-like exercise program by first locating the muscles at the root of the penis and stopping the flow of urine several times while urinating. Squeezing and relaxing these muscles fifteen times, twice daily, is a good start, but the repetitions should be gradually increased to sixty, twice a day. The contractions at this stage should be short.

Once sixty short contractions can be done twice a day with relative ease, the exercise can be intensified by holding each contraction for a count of three. The goal is to work up to sixty short contractions and sixty long contractions twice a day.

Men who have practiced a Kegel-like exercise program for several months have reported more pleasurable orgasms, better ejaculatory control, and increased pelvic sensation during sexual arousal. Because these exercises reduce muscle tension in the pelvic area, they may also help prevent prostate problems, such as enlargement of the prostate (hypertrophy) or inflammation of the prostate (prostatitis).

---

1. What are your feelings about the "bigger is better" theory of penis size? Do you believe that penis size plays an important part in female sexual satisfaction?
2. Explain the two physiological processes necessary for penile erection.
3. Men who work near hot objects (ovens, foundries, blast furnaces, hot engines) are sometimes sterile. What might cause this?

Internal Sex Organs

Male internal sex organs include the two testes, the epididymis, the vas deferens, and several fluid-producing glands.

Testes

The two **testes,** testicles, or male gonads are located in the scrotum and serve the dual function of producing sperm and the male sex hormone **testosterone.**

seminiferous
(se''mĭ-nif'er-us)

spermatogenesis
(sper''mah-to-jen'ĕ-sis)

rete
(re'te)

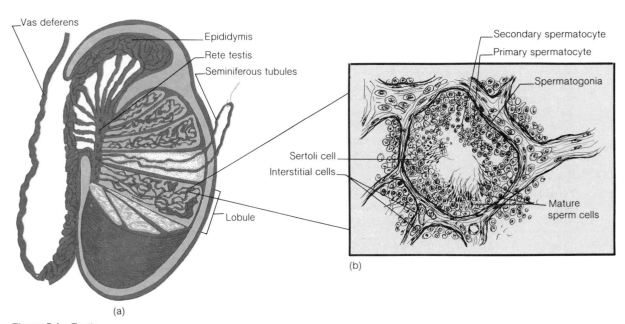

(a)

(b)

Figure 5.4 Testis.
(a) Sectional view of a testis showing its tubal system.
(b) Cross section of a seminiferous tubule showing the stages of spermatogenesis as described in the text. The Sertoli cells nourish the developing sperm. The interstitial (or Leydig) cells produce the major male hormone, testosterone.

Sperm Production

Each testis contains a number of highly coiled **seminiferous tubules** (figure 5.4a), which produce the male sex cells, **sperm.** Figure 5.4b is a cross section of a seminiferous tubule and shows the stages of **spermatogenesis** (the process for producing sperm).

In the first stage, spermatogonia, which are primitive sperm cells, enlarge and become primary spermatocytes. Primary spermatocytes then undergo meiosis (a special type of cell division) to become secondary spermatocytes. Secondary spermatocytes then develop into spermatids, which finally are transformed into mature sperm cells. Figure 5.5 illustrates the physical transformation of a spermatid into a mature sperm cell.

Spermatogenesis is a complex process and takes a number of weeks (sixty-six to seventy-four days). As mentioned earlier, the maturing of sperm can only occur at a temperature slightly below that of the body.

As sperm mature, they are moved through the seminiferous tubules to a network of ducts in the testis (the **rete testis**). As shown in figure 5.4a, the rete testis collects the sperm and effects their transfer out of the testis and into a single tube called the epididymis. As sperm move out of the epididymis and into the vas deferens, they are morphologically mature and capable of fertilizing an ovum. Once

acrosome
(ak′ro-sōm)

mitochondria
(mi″to-kon′dre-ah)

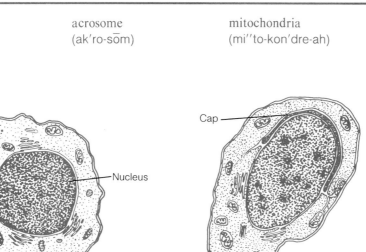

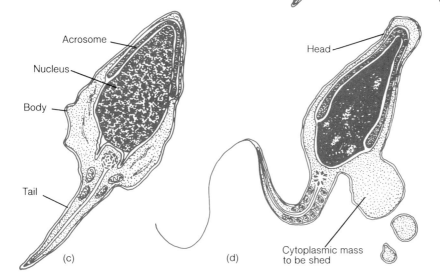

Figure 5.5 Development of a sperm from a spermatid. (a) The spermatid initially bears no physical resemblance to a sperm. (b) A tail starts to form from the cytoplasm of the cell, and a cap develops over one section of the nucleus. (c) The tail lengthens, a head forms, and the nucleus takes shape. The nuclear cap develops into an acrosome. Mitochondria migrate into the body. (d) Excess cytoplasm of the cell forms on one side and is cast off.

ejaculated, they have a life expectancy of from forty-eight to seventy-two hours within the female reproductive tract.

A mature sperm is a cell highly adapted for reaching and penetrating the female ovum (egg). It is composed of a head, body, and tail (figure 5.6). The head contains the chromosomes vital to life and an **acrosome,** a structure that contains chemicals that actually "digest" a hole into the ovum, allowing penetration by the sperm. The body contains **mitochondria,** structures that produce the energy needed for the movement of the sperm. The tail propels the sperm on its way to the ovum.

interstitial   Leydig's
(in''ter-stish'al)   (li'digz)

Figure 5.6 Sperm. A sperm is a cell highly adapted for reaching and penetrating a female ovum.

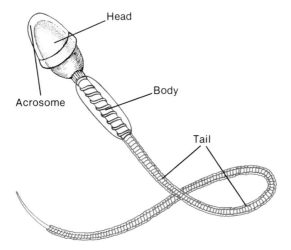

Testosterone Production

In addition to producing sperm, the testes manufacture the male sex hormone testosterone. As shown in figure 5.4b, specialized cells, called **interstitial** or **Leydig cells** line the spaces between the seminiferous tubules in the testes. Interstitial cells produce and secrete testosterone.

Testosterone production begins during puberty (age twelve or thirteen) and initiates and maintains the development of male secondary sex characteristics, the physical changes that lead to male sexual maturity. Hole (1981) lists these characteristics as follows:

1. Enlargement of the penis, scrotum, prostate gland, seminal vesicles, and Cowper's glands
2. Increased growth of body hair, particularly on the face, chest, axillary region, and pubic region, but sometimes accompanied by decreased growth of hair on the scalp
3. Enlargement of the larynx and thickening of the vocal folds, accompanied by the development of a lower-pitched voice
4. Thickening of the skin
5. Increased muscular growth accompanied by the development of broader shoulders and a relatively narrow waist
6. Thickening and strengthening of the bones

Testosterone also influences male sexual interest and motivation. Hormonal control of testosterone production is discussed later in this chapter.

seminal
(sem′ī-nal)

Epididymis

The **epididymis** lies along the posterior (back) border of each testis (see figures 5.4a and 5.7). It is a twenty-foot long, tightly coiled, threadlike tube that forms a continuous link between each testis and the vas deferens.

The epididymis is the site of sperm maturation and disintegration. The sperm slowly mature and are stored in the epididymis until released into the vas deferens for ejaculation or until they disintegrate or are reabsorbed.

Vas Deferens

As shown in figure 5.7, the **vas deferens** is a small, muscular tube that carries sperm upward from each epididymis to a widened portion of the tube known as the ejaculatory duct. Each ejaculatory duct is connected with a duct of a seminal vesicle, one of the male fluid-producing glands. While in the ejaculatory duct, sperm are mixed with the fluid from the seminal vesicle.

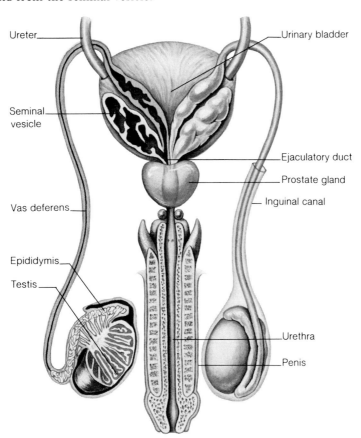

Figure 5.7 Ducts and glands of the male reproductive system.

Testicular Cancer

Testicular cancer accounts for the majority of cancers in males under thirty years of age, and it has more than tripled in incidence since 1972. The reasons for this increase are still uncertain. Some researchers believe that there may be a connection between the increase in testicular cancer and the treatment over twenty years ago of the victims' mothers with the synthetic estrogen DES while they were pregnant.

The most common symptom of testicular cancer is a scrotal lump that progressively increases in size. At times, there is pain, but this is not a usual symptom.

For this reason, a regular monthly self-examination of the testes is a wise preventative measure for all males. Most doctors recommend that a man examine himself when the skin of the scrotum is relaxed, as it is during a hot shower. A normal testis is smooth, egg-shaped, and firm, and the epididymis can be felt as a raised area at the rear of the testis. During a self-examination, the man should feel over the complete surface area of each testis and throughout the scrotum for any hard lump that feels like a marble or a BB. Such a lump is a sign of testicular cancer and should be reported immediately to a physician.

Advances in therapy have made testicular cancer among the most curable of all cancers. Treatment involves removal of the cancerous testis, followed by chemotherapy and radiation. Sexual function is not lost because the noncancerous testis is retained. Cure rates of 95 percent or even higher are possible when the cancer is detected early.

Fluid-Producing Glands

The fluid-producing glands—the seminal vesicles, the prostate gland, and the Cowper's glands—all produce a secretion collectively known as **seminal fluid.** Seminal fluid provides sperm with the liquid they need to swim in, the nutrients they need to stay alive, and the liquid medium needed for fertilization. When mixed with sperm, seminal fluid forms a grayish-white, sticky mixture called **semen.** Semen contains 60 to 120 million sperm per milliliter, and usually a male releases from two to six milliliters of semen at each ejaculation.

Seminal Vesicles

The paired **seminal vesicles** (figure 5.7) are pouchlike structures lying posterior to and at the base of the urinary bladder. They secrete fluid directly into the ejaculatory ducts at the ends of the vasa efferentia. While in the ejaculatory ducts, the fluid from the seminal vesicles mixes with the sperm brought up by the vasa efferentia. Upon ejaculation, this semen is ejected directly into the urethra, which conveys it to the outside of the body. The seminal vesicles contribute about 60 percent of the total volume of semen.

| prostaglandin (pros''tah-glan'din) | prostate (pros'tāt) | Cowper's (kow'perz) |
| | prostatectomy (pros''tah-tek'to-me) | bulbourethral (bul''bo-u-re'thral) |

The fluid from the seminal vesicles is very important to the sperm because its high fructose (sugar) content provides the sperm with an energy source. This fluid also contains a hormonelike chemical (**prostaglandin**) that seems to stimulate muscular contractions within the female reproductive tract. These contractions aid the sperm in moving to fertilize the female ovum.

Prostate Gland

The **prostate gland** is a single, doughnut-shaped gland about the size of a chestnut that surrounds the urethra (see figure 5.7). It is beneath the bladder and directly in front of the rectum. The ejaculatory ducts enter the urethra within the prostate gland.

Fluid from the prostate gland contributes about 30 percent of the total volume of semen and initiates the movement of sperm, which have been relatively immobile up until ejaculation. Also, this fluid, like the fluid from the seminal vesicles, is very high in fructose and helps to nutritionally sustain sperm cells for their trip through the female reproductive tract.

The prostate gland is relatively small in male children. It begins to grow during adolescence and reaches adult size at about twenty years of age. It stays relatively unchanged until about fifty years of age, when it often starts to enlarge again. In some older men, it can enlarge to the point where it squeezes the urethra and interferes with urination. All or part of the prostate must then be removed (**prostatectomy**). The prostate gland is also a common site of cancer in males.

Cowper's Glands

The paired **Cowper's glands** (also called **bulbourethral glands**) are each about the size of a pea and are located beneath the prostate gland on either side of the urethra. Fluid from the Cowper's glands is released into the urethra in response to sexual stimulation and often appears at the tip of the penis prior to ejaculation. This preejaculatory fluid occasionally contains live sperm from the last ejaculation, which means that a pregnancy is possible even if the male withdraws his penis from the female before ejaculation.

Some believe that the function of this fluid is lubrication of the end of the penis before sexual penetration of the female. It is more likely, however, that this fluid neutralizes the acidity of any urine present in the urethra in preparation for the passage of semen at ejaculation.

Table 5.1 summarizes the functions of the male reproductive organs.

Table 5.1   Structures and Functions of the Male Reproductive System.

Organ	Function
External	
Penis	Male organ for urination and sexual intercourse; richly supplied with nerve endings; associated with feelings of pleasure during sexual stimulation
Scrotum	Encloses the two testes; maintains the testes at a temperature suitable for sperm production
Internal	
Testes	
Seminiferous tubules	Produce sperm
Interstitial (Leydig) cells	Produce and secrete the male hormone testosterone
Epididymis	Stores slowly maturing sperm until sperm are released into the vas deferens for ejaculation or until they disintegrate or are reabsorbed
Vas deferens	Carries sperm upward from epididymis to ejaculatory duct
Fluid-producing glands	
Seminal vesicles	Secrete fluid with a high fructose content to nourish sperm; fluid also contains a prostaglandin to stimulate muscular contractions in the female that assist in sperm movement
Prostate gland	Secretes fluid that initiates the movement of sperm and nutritionally sustains sperm
Cowper's (bulbourethral) glands	Secrete fluid that neutralizes the acidity of any urine in the urethra prior to the passage of semen

1. What are the two primary functions of the testes? What parts of the testes are involved in each of these functions?
2. Describe the body parts of a mature sperm and explain how these body parts highly adapt a sperm for reaching and penetrating the female ovum.
3. If you are a male, do you remember when you began to develop male secondary sexual characteristics? Which of these physical changes were you actually aware of?
4. Can you explain why the relatively large amount of fluid a male produces at ejaculation is important?
5. Older men suffering from swollen prostate glands may have trouble urinating. Why would there be such a relationship?

endocrine
(en'do-krin)

Hormones

All processes of the body, including the reproductive processes, are controlled by a group of body chemicals known as **hormones.** In this chapter, we examine the nature of hormones, how they act upon cells in the body, and how hormonal secretions are controlled. Then we discuss hormonal control of the male reproductive system. In chapter 6, we will see how hormones affect the female reproductive processes.

How Hormones Act

Hormones are chemicals produced by the **endocrine glands** of the body (see figure 5.8). Endocrine glands secrete their hormones into the extracellular spaces surrounding endocrine gland cells. From here, the hormones are absorbed into the bloodstream and carried to all parts of the body. Because of their presence throughout the body, hormones are able to affect every process of the body.

A specific hormone only affects specific tissues of the body, known as the hormone's **target tissues.** The cells of a target tissue contain structures called **receptor sites** that "bind" to specific hormones and "allow" the hormones to enter the cell

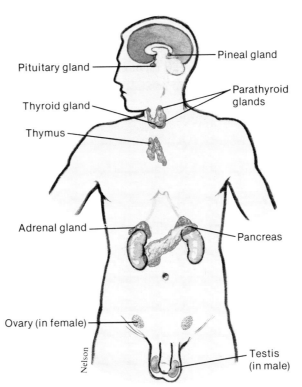

Figure 5.8 Endocrine glands.

Pituitary gland

Pineal gland

Thyroid gland

Parathyroid glands

Thymus

Adrenal gland

Pancreas

Ovary (in female)

Testis (in male)

Nelson

to perform their functions. Without receptor sites, hormones cannot gain entrance into a cell and do not function. Thus, the receptor sites control where, and which, hormones function in the body. Also, the "sensitivity" of a tissue to a hormone can be modified by the number of receptor sites available on the tissue's cells for binding to a hormone.

Control of Hormonal Secretions

The amount of any hormone in the body remains relatively stable because hormonal secretions are regulated by several types of control mechanisms.

One method of hormonal control is called a "feedback" mechanism. A common example of a feedback mechanism is the way in which a thermostat-controlled furnace works. We set the thermostat of a furnace to a desirable temperature. When the air in the room is warmed to that temperature, the thermostat is stimulated, and it "feeds back" to the furnace, which shuts off (this is called negative feedback). Then, when the temperature drops below the desired level, the thermostat again "feeds back" to the furnace, and the furnace turns on, reheating the room (this is called positive feedback). Thus, the furnace-thermostat system is controlled by a temperature imbalance, and the system works to correct this imbalance.

In the same way, the secretion of a hormone is activated by an imbalance between the rate of hormone production and the rate of the hormone's use or destruction in the body. When there is an imbalance, information is "fed back" to the secreting endocrine gland, often by signals from its target tissues, and the secretion of the hormone is regulated (see figure 5.9). As shown in figure 5.10, hormone con-

Figure 5.9 A negative feedback system. (1) Gland A secretes a hormone that stimulates Gland B to release another hormone. (2) The hormone from Gland B inhibits the action of Gland A.

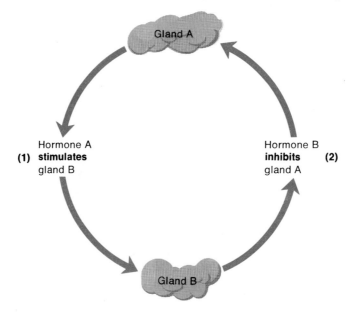

Hormone A
(1) stimulates
gland B

Hormone B
inhibits (2)
gland A

pituitary   hypothalamus
(pi-tu'i-tar''e)   (hi''po-thal'ah-mus)

centrations fluctuate slightly above and below their optimal level but remain relatively stable.

Another kind of hormonal control mechanism involves the nervous system. A
few endocrine glands are connected by nerves to the nervous system and secrete
their hormones in response to stimulation by nerve impulses (see figure 5.11).

A third type of hormonal control mechanism involves interaction between the
pituitary gland (an endocrine gland that secretes a number of hormones) and a part
of the brain called the **hypothalamus.** The pituitary gland is located directly below
the hypothalamus, and the pituitary and the hypothalamus are physically linked
through specialized blood vessels, nerves, and a system of tubes.

The hypothalamus secretes a series of substances known as hypothalamic releasing and inhibiting factors, whose target tissues are in the pituitary gland. These
factors cause the pituitary gland to adjust its secretion of its hormones. For example,
the pituitary gland responds to a specific releasing factor from the hypothalamus
by secreting a specific hormone. When this hormone reaches its optimum concentration in the body, a feedback signal is sent to the hypothalamus, and the hypothalamus discontinues secretion of the releasing factor.

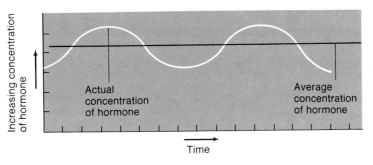

Figure 5.10 Hormone
concentration levels fluctuate
slightly above and below their
optimal level but remain
relatively stable.

Figure 5.11 Nerve control of
hormones. Some endocrine
glands secrete their hormones
in response to nervous
stimulation.

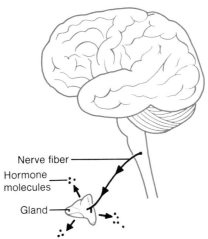

gonadotropic	gonad	luteinizing
(gon''ah-do-trōp'ik)	(go'nad)	(loo'te-in-i''zing)

---

1. What is a hormone? Have you used the word *hormone* in the past without really understanding what it meant? In what context have you used the word *hormone*?
2. Explain the hypothalamus-pituitary hormonal control mechanism.

Hormonal Control of Male Reproductive Processes

Male reproductive processes are the result of coordinated physiological events in the hypothalamus of the brain, the pituitary gland, and the testes. The hypothalamus, however, is the main control center.

The Hypothalamus-Pituitary-Testes "Connection"

The hypothalamus continually releases a steady level of a hormone called **gonadotropin-releasing factor (GnRF).** This substance stimulates the pituitary gland to secrete two **gonadotropins,** which are hormones that affect only the **gonads** (the testes in the male and the ovaries in the female).

The two gonadotropins released by the pituitary gland are **follicle-stimulating hormone (FSH)** and **luteinizing hormone (LH).** In the male, LH is often referred to as **interstitial cell-stimulating hormone (ICSH),** since its action on the interstitial (or Leydig) cells in the testes results in the production of the male hormone testosterone. ICSH is chemically identical to LH.

The pituitary's secretion of these two gonadotropins does not cyclically fluctuate from day to day in the male like it does in the female (see chapter 6). FSH and ICSH remain at relatively constant concentrations in the male body.

The release of FSH and ICSH by the pituitary directly affects the testes, which, as we discussed earlier in the chapter, are responsible for manufacturing and secreting the male hormone testosterone and also for producing sperm.

Hormonal Control of Testosterone Production

Testosterone secretion by the testes is apparently controlled by the amount of ICSH secreted by the pituitary gland. ICSH stimulates development of the interstitial (Leydig) cells of the testes. The interstitial cells then manufacture and secrete testosterone.

An optimum level of testosterone in the blood serves as a feedback mechanism to the hypothalamus, which then inhibits its secretion of GnRF, which, in turn, causes the pituitary to inhibit its secretion of ICSH. When the level of testosterone in the blood drops below the optimum level, the hypothalamus is no longer inhibited in its secretion of GnRF to the pituitary, and the cycle starts anew.

Sertoli's   inhibin
(ser-to'lēz)   (in-hib'in)

Hormonal Control of Sperm Production

As we learned earlier in the chapter, testosterone stimulates the development and maintenance of male secondary sex characteristics and also influences male sexual interest and motivation. In addition, however, testosterone, along with the ICSH and FSH released by the pituitary, influences sperm production in the testes.

FSH stimulates the seminiferous tubules in the testes to produce sperm cells. Then, under the direction of ICSH and testosterone, cells located within the seminiferous tubules, called **Sertoli cells,** promote the maturation of developing sperm cells and control the rate of sperm production.

A protein that may be a hormone and that has provisionally been called **inhibin** seems to be released by Sertoli cells as a feedback mechanism to the hypothalamus and/or pituitary. The theory is that increasing numbers of maturing sperm cause Sertoli cells to secrete increasing levels of inhibin. The higher level of inhibin is believed to have a negative feedback on the hypothalamus and pituitary, thereby decreasing production of FSH. A high concentration of inhibin, then, reduces the amount of FSH in circulation, thus reducing sperm production. A low concentration of inhibin allows the pituitary to release more FSH, thereby increasing sperm production.

It is important to remember that in all of this activity, the hypothalamus is the primary controlling mechanism. By releasing GnRF, the hypothalamus initiates a cycle of sperm and testosterone production that is essential to male reproductive processes. (Table 5.2 and figure 5.12 summarize this process.)

Table 5.2   Outline of Hormones That Affect Male Reproductive Processes.

Hormone	Source	Action
GnRF	Hypothalamus	Stimulates pituitary gland to secrete relatively constant levels of FSH and ICSH
FSH	Pituitary	Stimulates seminiferous tubules in testes to produce sperm
ICSH	Pituitary	Stimulates interstitial (Leydig) cells in testes to produce testosterone and helps to regulate sperm production
Testosterone	Testes (interstitial cells)	Stimulates development of male primary and secondary sex characteristics and maintains male characteristics and behavior; testosterone level in the blood affects GnRF, FSH, and ICSH production; helps to regulate sperm production
Inhibin	Testes (Sertoli cells)	Increasing number of maturing sperm cause Sertoli cells in seminiferous tubules of testes to secrete increasing levels of inhibin; inhibin effects a negative feedback on the hypothalamus and pituitary, decreasing production of FSH

Figure 5.12 Control of male reproduction. ICSH alone is required to stimulate secretion of testosterone by interstitial (Leydig) cells. ICSH, FSH, and testosterone are all needed for spermatogenesis. Sperm are also enhanced by the Sertoli cells of the testes. The level of sperm production may modulate the secretion of FSH by the release of some chemical provisionally named inhibin.

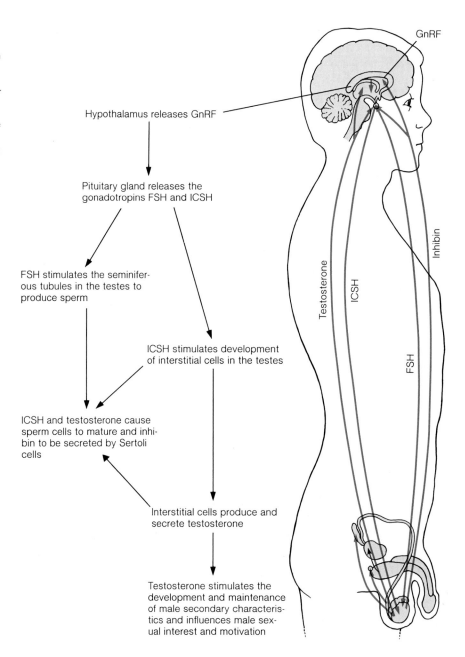

Hypothalamus releases GnRF

Pituitary gland releases the gonadotropins FSH and ICSH

FSH stimulates the seminifer-ous tubules in the testes to produce sperm

ICSH stimulates development of interstitial cells in the testes

ICSH and testosterone cause sperm cells to mature and inhi-bin to be secreted by Sertoli cells

Interstitial cells produce and secrete testosterone

Testosterone stimulates the development and maintenance of male secondary characteris-tics and influences male sex-ual interest and motivation

GnRF

Testosterone

ICSH

FSH

Inhibin

capacitation
(kah-pas''ĭ-ta'shun)

Hormonal Control of Sperm Capacitation

Mature sperm recovered at ejaculation are able to swim vigorously but cannot fertilize an ovum immediately. Sperm recovered from the uterus or fallopian tube of a female a few hours after sexual intercourse *are* capable of immediate fertilization of an ovum. This observation has led to the concept that sperm require a **capacitation period** (a period in which they attain the ability to fertilize) in the female reproductive tract.

Capacitation of sperm appears to require the female hormone estrogen. Thus, sperm need to be in an "estrogen-primed" uterus to be able to fertilize an ovum. This concept is now being used in the development of some new types of contraceptives.

Hormones and Sexual Behavior

The hypothalamus is a part of the brain, and the brain plays an important role in our sexual responses. Our thoughts, emotions, and memories along with visual, oral, and tactile stimuli are all communicated to the brain and thus to the hypothalamus. The hypothalamus sometimes acts upon such information by signaling the pituitary gland to release appropriate hormones. But how much do hormones actually affect our sexual behavior?

Demonstrating sexual behavior changes due to changing hormonal levels in humans is extremely complex, while showing hormonal and sexual behavior changes in other animals is much simpler. For example, when male and female castrated (testes or ovaries have been removed) rats, dogs, or other mammals are placed together, they do not display sexual behavior. But when these animals are treated with the appropriate sex hormones, sexual behavior is activated, and the sexual stimuli of the opposite sex become effective. Thus, in these animals, hormones allow an appropriate set of sexual stimuli to induce sexual activity. And basic hormonal mechanisms undergo considerable modification when attractiveness, partner preferences, the presence of young, and other variables express themselves in the social setting.

As another example, in talapoin monkey groups, consisting of four males and four or five females, only the dominant male is sexually active. When all of the males are inactive, their blood-testosterone levels are equal. During the periods the dominant male becomes sexually active and is aggressive to subordinate males, his blood-testosterone levels rise significantly while those in the subordinate males stay at low levels. If each male is isolated from the other males and put with the females, each male becomes a dominant, sexually active male, and his testosterone levels rise dramatically.

Even though such examples emphasize the interactions of hormones and sexual behavior, and the far-reaching consequences of social interactions determining sexual activity and reproductive status among some animals, human experimental evidence is still quite rudimentary.

1. Trace the hypothalamus-pituitary-testes "connection." Which hormones are released from which source? What effect does each hormone have? What is the primary controlling mechanism in this process?
2. Marijuana use can reduce the amount of testosterone in a male. Explain how marijuana use could affect sperm production.
3. If sperm need to be exposed to the female reproductive system before they are able to fertilize an ovum, how do you think in-vitro ("test-tube") fertilization takes place?

"Dad?"

"Yes, Bill."

"Do you remember when I was a kid, and you had one of those father-son type talks with me?"

"Which one? The one when we talked about your voice changing or our talk about your strange dreams?"

"You remember, when I was a little kid and you explained to me all about my body. Remember? You tried to explain my plumbing?"

"Oh, that talk! That was a long time ago. I remember being a little nervous on that one. But I think I got better as time went on. What made you bring it up?"

"Well, in our health class, I was really surprised at how dumb some of the guys were. They didn't know anything. The worst ones were the guys who are always bragging about being such studs!"

"Those who know the least usually talk the loudest."

"It was nice to be able to know what the teacher was talking about. I don't know where those other kids have been. Don't they get told anything? I mean, this may sound really corny, but I'm glad I've got you for a father."

"Oh, why?"

"If I didn't, I might be a real jerk, like some people I know."

Summary

1. The external sex organs, or genitals, of the male consist of the penis and the scrotum.

2. The penis is the male organ for urination and sexual intercourse. The average penis is three to four inches long when flaccid and about six inches long when erect, and penile size has very little to do with female sexual satisfaction. The enlarged region at the end of the penis is the penile glans, which is loosely covered by the prepuce or foreskin. The shaft or body of the penis extends from the glans to the body wall. Two areas of the glans—the corona and the frenulum—are particularly sensitive to physical stimulation. Internally, the penis is composed of three cylinders of erectile tissue and the urethra.

3. Penile erection can be produced by direct stimulation of the external genitals or by stimulation from the brain. Ejaculation is the sudden expulsion of semen from the erect penis and is usually preceded by emission, which is a discharge of seminal fluid from the fluid-producing glands of the reproductive system.

4. The scrotum is the thin, loose pouch of sensitive skin in the groin area below the penis and contains the testes, the spermatic cord, and the epididymis. The scrotum maintains the testes at a temperature slightly below body temperature, which is required for sperm production.

5. Male internal sex organs include the two testes, the epididymis, the vas deferens, and several fluid-producing glands.

6. The testes serve the dual function of producing sperm and the male sex hormone testosterone. Seminiferous tubules in the testes produce sperm, which are highly adapted for reaching and fertilizing the female ovum. The interstitial (Leydig) cells in the testes manufacture and secrete testosterone. Testosterone initiates and maintains the development of male secondary sex characteristics and also influences male sexual interest and motivation.

7. The epididymis is a tightly coiled tube, located along the posterior border of each testis, and forms a continuous link between the testis and the vas deferens. The epididymis is the site of sperm maturation and degeneration.

8. The vas deferens is a small tube that conveys sperm upward from the epididymis of each testis to the urethra through an ejaculatory duct within the prostate gland.

9. The fluid-producing glands consist of the seminal vesicles, the prostate gland, and the Cowper's glands. These glands produce seminal fluid, which when mixed with sperm, is called semen.

10. Hormones are chemicals produced by the endocrine glands of the body, and they affect all processes of the body, including the reproductive processes. The amount of any hormone in the body remains relatively stable because hormonal secretions are regulated by three types of control mechanisms: (1) a feedback mechanism, (2) a mechanism that involves the nervous system, and (3) a mechanism that involves interaction between the pituitary gland and the hypothalamus of the brain.

11.   Male reproductive processes result from coordinated physiological events in the hypothalamus, the pituitary gland, and the testes. The hypothalamus releases GnRF, which stimulates the pituitary to secrete ICSH and FSH. ICSH stimulates the interstitial cells in the testes to produce and secrete testosterone. FSH stimulates the seminiferous tubules in the testes to produce sperm cells, and then ICSH and testosterone promote the maturation of the developing sperm cells.

12.   Sperm appear to require a capacitation period in an estrogen-primed female reproductive tract before they are able to fertilize an ovum.

13.   Although we can demonstrate the interactions of hormones and sexual behavior, and the far-reaching consequences of social interactions determining sexual activity and reproductive status among some animals, human experimental evidence is still quite rudimentary.

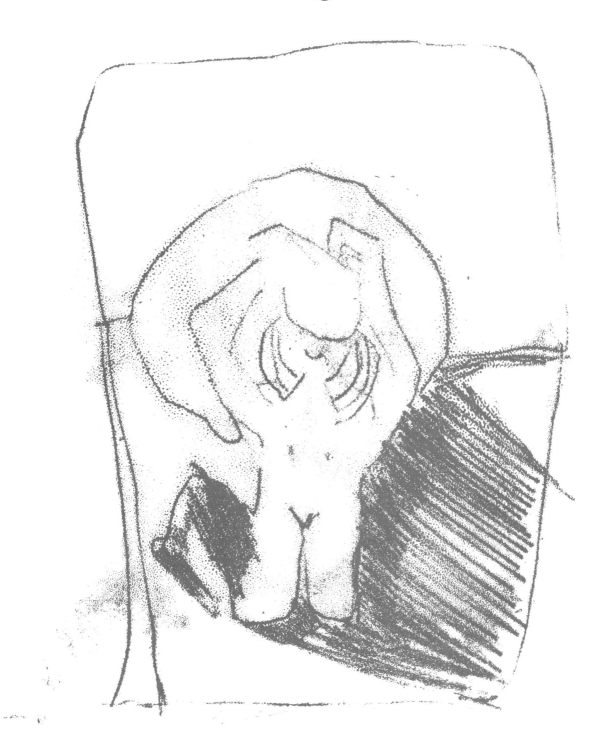

External Sex Organs
Mons Veneris/Labia Majora/Labia Minora/Vestibule/
Perineum/Clitoris

Internal Sex Organs
Vagina/Uterus/Fallopian Tubes/Ovaries

The Breasts

The Menstrual Cycle
Menstrual Cycle Length/Moods and Emotions of the
Menstrual Cycle/Premenstrual Syndrome/Menstrual
Cramps/Dysmenorrhea

Hormones Important to Female Sexual Development
Androgens/Estrogen/Progesterone/Prostaglandins

Hormonal Control of the Menstrual Cycle

Hormonal Control of Milk Production in the Breasts

Here I am, a twenty-one-year-old college senior, looking forward to a career in business and a life full of, I hope, happiness. Last night, my mother called to tell me how proud and happy she is that I have become a success. She also called to say she has cancer of the uterus. No, I thought. Not Mom, not cancer, it isn't fair! She was very calm about it, but then she's very calm about most every crisis that comes up. She is the most "womanly" woman that I know, and it angers me that the cancer has struck right at the heart of her femininity. She who has helped me through my growing to be a woman now needs my help.

Mom and I have always been close. When I first started menstruating, Mom was there to explain everything that was happening. She knew my mood swings, understood my anxiety, and always encouraged me to look on the bright side. I remember when I was a senior in high school and my boyfriend and I started getting a little too involved. I was really scared about getting pregnant. He said I couldn't, if we timed it right. I think his idea of timing was any time he wanted. It was Mom who sat me down and explained to me all of the details involved in getting pregnant, especially how *easy* it is. I could tell that it was hard for her to talk about sexual activity. I really respect her for being so open with me.

We used to laugh at the douche commercials on television—the mother and daughter scenes always seemed so phony. Our relationship isn't phony or sappy—it's one of love and respect. She has always taught me how to be at peace with my womanhood. She has been there every time I needed her. Now she needs me, and I'm not sure what I can do.

vulva
(vul'vah)

mons veneris
(monz ven'er-is)

labia majora
(la'be-ah mah-jor'ah)

To develop a sense of sexual well-being, both men and women must acquire knowledge and understanding of their bodies. In the last chapter, we examined male sexual anatomy and physiology. In this chapter, we focus on the female.

Our study of the female body begins with descriptions of the physical characteristics and functions of the female external and internal genitals. We also discuss the female breasts, which although not considered reproductive structures, are important to female sexuality. The female reproductive cycle—the menstrual cycle—is the next topic of discussion, and we first look at the menstrual cycle from the perspective of how it affects women's physical and emotional well-being. A detailed analysis of hormonal control of the menstrual cycle and also breast milk production concludes the chapter.

As in chapter 5, we encourage female readers in particular to use the information presented in this chapter as the basis for a detailed self-examination of their sexual organs. The external structures are the easiest to examine, and some of the internal structures can be viewed with the aid of a mirror. These self-examinations should be performed while bearing in mind that the reproductive structures are highly variable in their appearance, just as are other body parts.

Most external reproductive structures may be examined by just looking or through touch.

External Sex Organs

The external sex organs, or, genitals of the female are often referred to collectively as the **vulva.** The structures of the vulva include the mons veneris, the labia majora, the labia minora, the vestibule, the perineum, and the clitoris and are shown in figure 6.1.

Mons Veneris

The **mons veneris** (Latin for "the mound of Venus") is the area over the pubic bone that is covered by pubic hair in the adult female (figure 6.1). The mounded softness of the mons consists of a pad of fat lying between the skin and the pubic bone. The numerous nerve endings in the mons make caressing this area a pleasurable experience for most women.

Labia Majora

The **labia majora** (outer lips) lie closely together and extend back from either side of the mons (figure 6.1). Toward the rear, they taper and merge into the perineum (the space between the vagina and the anus).

The labia enclose and protect the other external reproductive structures and are formed from the same tissue as the male scrotum. The outer skin of the labia majora is covered with pubic hair and contains sweat glands, oil glands, and nu-

labia minora   clitoris   introitus
(la'be·ah mĭ·nor'ah)   (clit'o·ris)   (in·tro'ĭ·tus)

                                perineum   imperforate
                                (per''i·ne'um)   (im·per'fo·rat)

merous nerve endings. The inner surface of the labia majora is thin, sensitive, and hairless.

Touch or pressure to the labia majora produces sensations in the female that are similar to sensations the male feels upon stimulation of the scrotum.

Labia Minora

The **labia minora** (inner lips) are longitudinal folds of tissue located beneath the labia majora (figure 6.1). The labia minora begin as the hoodlike covering over the clitoris known as the clitoral hood, or prepuce. They then extend back until they merge with the labia majora at the perineum. These folds of tissue are thin and hairless and contain sweat glands, oil glands, and numerous blood vessels and nerve endings. The labia minora protect the vaginal and urethral openings.

Vestibule

The area between the labia minora is called the **vestibule** (figure 6.1). The urethra, vagina, and two sets of glands open into the vestibule.

In the female, the **urethra** is a short tube connecting the urinary bladder to the urethral opening located between the clitoris and the vaginal opening (figure 6.1). Urine passes out of the body through the urethra.

Posteriorly and on either side of the urethral opening are ducts of the **Skene's glands.** These glands develop from the same structures as the male prostate gland and secrete mucus to keep the vestibule moist.

The vaginal opening (called the **vaginal introitus**) is located between the urinary opening and the anus (figure 6.1). At birth, the vaginal opening is usually partially covered by a membrane called the **hymen.** The hymen remains intact until reduced through vigorous physical exercise, sports, play, or coitus. Usually, the hymen does not cover enough of the vaginal opening to interfere with menstrual flow. In rare cases, however, the hymen completely covers the vaginal opening and is known as an **imperforate hymen.** An imperforate hymen impedes menstrual flow and interferes with sexual intercourse but can be opened with a small incision by a physician.

On either side of the vaginal opening are two small glands known as the **Bartholin's glands.** These glands are the same as the Cowper's glands in the male and secrete a fluid that is either used as a lubricant during sexual intercourse or that serves to neutralize any urine in the area so that it cannot kill sperm during ejaculation.

Perineum

The **perineum** is the smooth skin that extends from the vaginal opening to the anus (figure 6.1). The perineal tissue contains numerous nerve endings and is sensitive to touch and pressure.

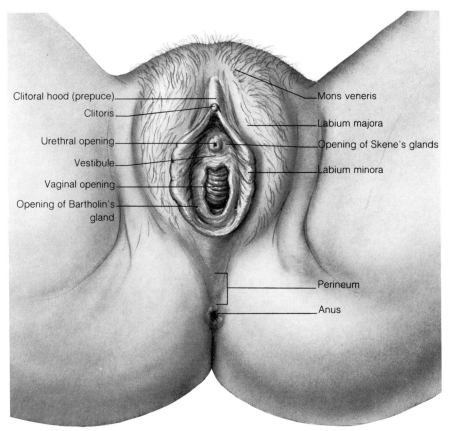

Figure 6.1 External reproductive structures of the vulva.

Clitoral hood (prepuce)

Clitoris

Urethral opening

Vestibule

Vaginal opening

Opening of Bartholin's gland

Mons veneris

Labium majora

Opening of Skene's glands

Labium minora

Perineum

Anus

Clitoris

The **clitoris** is a small projection at the anterior end of the vestibule, where the labia merge together (figure 6.1). The labia minora fold into a covering over the clitoris known as the **clitoral hood** or **prepuce.**

The clitoris is composed of a small mass of erectal tissue that is richly supplied with nerve endings. Although much smaller than the male penis, the clitoris has as many nerve endings as the penis and is formed from the same tissues as the glans, or head, of the penis.

Erectile tissues of the female, like those of the male, respond to sexual stimulation. Sexual stimulation of the clitoris and the nearby labia causes arteries leading to these structures to dilate. The resulting inflow of blood causes erection of the clitoris and swelling of the labia. Continued stimulation usually culminates in orgasm.

Female Circumcision

While male circumcision consists of surgical removal of part of the foreskin of the penis, female circumcision in different parts of the world can consist of the surgical removal or manipulation of several of the female genitals.

The least severe form of female circumcision consists of the surgical removal of the hood of the clitoris. This type of female circumcision was performed in the past because it was believed that removal of the clitoral hood improved female sexual responsivity in two ways. First, it exposed the clitoral glans to more direct stimulation, and, second, it allowed for the removal of lumps of accumulated smegma, which some specialists believed could cause severe pain during sexual intercourse.

Female circumcision of the clitoral hood is not a common practice today, however, since it has been found that direct stimulation of the clitoris can become painful or irritating and that the clitoral hood "protects" the clitoris from this kind of stimulation. Also, accumulated smegma under the clitoral hood is now often removed with a probe.

In primitive tribes in Australia, Asia, and Africa, female circumcision can consist of more radical procedures than simple removal of the clitoral hood. Female circumcision may also consist of removal of part or most of the external genitals (clitoris and labia minora). Removal of the clitoris and labia minora ensures that a woman will not find much pleasure in sexual intercourse and thus will not be likely to be unfaithful to her husband.

Another form of female circumcision involves closing the vagina by sewing together the labia majora, leaving only a small opening for the menstrual flow. Closure of the vagina is intended to ensure a woman's virginity at marriage, and the procedure is reversed after marriage.

Potential side effects of these procedures include severe hemorrhage, infection, and blood poisoning. Gruesome as they may sound, however, such forms of female circumcision are part of long-standing attitudes about sex, virginity, and marriage in these areas of the world.

The clitoris can be seen if the labia are gently parted and the prepuce is pushed back. It may be easier for a woman to find her clitoris the first time by touch, however, rather than by sight, because the nerve endings on the clitoris are very sensitive to touch.

The clitoris and the area around it need to be kept clean because bacteria and the secretions from the glands of the vestibule and vagina combine to form a material known as **smegma**. (We learned in chapter 5 that smegma also forms under the prepuce of the male penis.) Smegma may accumulate under the clitoral hood and occasionally hardens into lumps, which can cause pain during sexual arousal. A woman can prevent a buildup of smegma by drawing back the clitoral hood and cleaning the area whenever bathing or showering.

1. Name the external female sex organs and the functions of each.
2. Many people see the female external sex organs as beautiful and sensuous structures. Others find them ugly and shameful. How do you view them? Why do you think you feel this way?
3. Compare the female clitoris and the male penis. In which ways are they similar? In which ways are they different?

Internal Sex Organs

The internal genitals of the female consist of the vagina, the uterus, the fallopian tubes, and the ovaries. These structures are shown in figures 6.2 and 6.3.

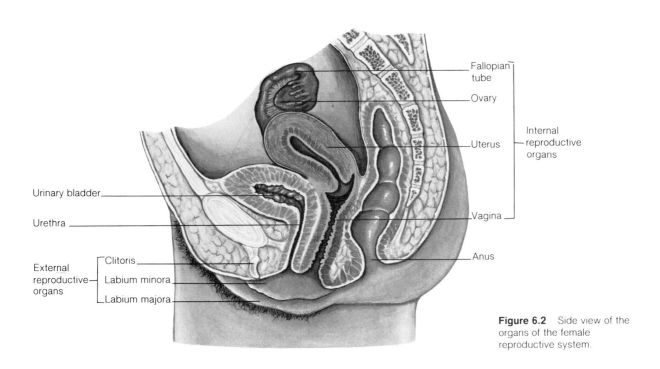

Figure 6.2 Side view of the organs of the female reproductive system.

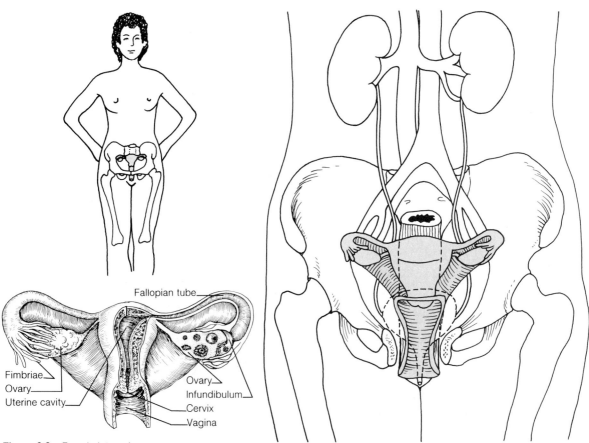

Fallopian tube

Fimbriae

Ovary

Uterine cavity

Ovary

Infundibulum

Cervix

Vagina

Figure 6.3 Female internal reproductive organs and their relationship to the body.

Vagina

The **vagina** is a tubular, muscular organ that extends upward and inward from the vestibule toward the small of the back. As shown in figure 6.2, the vagina is located posterior to the urinary bladder and urethra and anterior to the anus and rectum. In a nonsexually aroused woman, the vagina is approximately three to five inches in length. But the walls of the vagina lie in a series of folds that allow it a good deal of distension. It can expand in size and shape during sexual arousal to accommodate the male penis for sexual intercourse. Its walls also are able to expand enough to serve as a birth passage (birth canal) during childbirth. The monthly menstrual flow exits the body through the vagina as well. Only the outer third of the vagina is innervated.

immunoglobulins
(im″u-no-glob′u-linz)

Kegel Exercises for Women

Following the physical stress of childbirth, many women find that they have lost muscle tone in the muscles beneath the perineum and surrounding the vaginal opening. Loss of muscle tone in this area makes it more difficult for these women to control urination, and they often lose urine when they cough or sneeze.

In 1952, Arnold Kegel developed a series of exercises that were designed to restore this lost muscle tone and thereby help women to redevelop control of urination after childbirth.

To perform these exercises, a woman must first locate the pelvic muscles that support the vagina by voluntarily stopping and starting the flow of urine during urination. The muscles that stop the flow of urine also tighten the vagina around an inserted object, such as a finger or penis. These are the muscles to be strengthened by the Kegel exercises.

Once a woman has learned which muscles to concentrate on, she should contract those muscles, hold the contraction for two or three seconds, and then release. She should perform this exercise for ten repetitions five or six times a day, gradually working up to more.

Women who practice Kegel exercises on a daily basis should have much improved control of these muscles (and their urination) in six weeks. But it has also been found that Kegel exercises have some interesting advantages other than mere urinary control. Many of the women who strengthen these pelvic muscles also discover an increasing sensitivity of the vaginal area, which they find can result in increased sensations during intercourse and at orgasm. In addition, some women report that performing Kegel exercises makes it possible for them to stimulate their sex partners more because of the increased vaginal pressure they can apply to an inserted penis.

The lining of the vagina and the cervix (the narrow, outer end of the uterus located at the back of the vagina) produce secretions that are high in glycogen (animal starch) and that are broken down by bacteria into organic acids. This produces a vaginal fluid that is slightly acidic (pH 4.0 to 5.0), white to yellow in color, and supportive of yeast infections. During sexual arousal, the vaginal walls also produce a lubricating fluid that is important during sexual intercourse to help prevent irritation to the vagina. The secretions of the vagina vary in appearance, pH, and viscosity (stickiness) as hormone levels change during the menstrual month. (Keeping track of these variations in vaginal secretions is the basis of one method of contraception—see chapter 15.)

The vagina has three physical characteristics that make it relatively resistant to bacterial infections. First, the acidity of the vaginal fluid tends to kill harmful bacteria. Second, vaginal fluids contain **immunoglobulins,** which are bacteria-destroying chemicals, commonly called antibodies. And third, cells in the wall of the vagina have the ability to secrete bacteria-destroying antibodies, if needed.

douching
(doosh′ing)

Altering this natural chemical and bacterial balance in the vagina can result in vaginal problems from infection by microorganisms. Ways in which the chemical and bacterial balance of the vagina can be altered include:

1. Poor nutrition
2. Excessive **douching** (use of a liquid to flush the vagina) or the use of chemicals in the vagina
3. Antibiotic therapy
4. Hormone therapy, including the use of oral contraceptives
5. A moist vaginal environment, which comes from spending hours in a wet swimsuit or in clothing that does not "breathe" freely, such as tight nylon underwear or noncotton-lined pantyhose

Uterus

The **uterus** is a hollow, thick, pear-shaped organ whose function is to receive the embryo and nurture it until the time of the child's birth (figure 6.3). Although the size of the uterus changes greatly during and after a pregnancy, in its nonpregnant state, it is about three inches long and two inches wide (at its broadest point). The uterus is located above the vagina and is usually bent forward over the urinary bladder (figure 6.2).

The uterine walls are thick and composed of three layers (figure 6.4). The outer layer, the perimetrium, covers the uterus and holds it together and in place. The middle layer, the myometrium, is composed of muscle that contracts during

Figure 6.4   The three tissue layers of the uterine wall. The endometrium is the layer that is partially shed during menstruation.

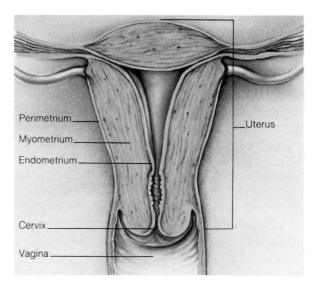

endometrium   fallopian   infundibulum
(en-do-me'tre-um)   (fal-lo'pe-an)   (in''fun-dib'u-lum)

childbirth, orgasm, and expulsion of the menses during the menstrual flow. The in-nermost layer of the uterus (the **endometrium**) is the layer that is partially shed during menstruation, as we discuss later in this chapter.

The narrow lower third of the uterus consists of the tubular **cervix,** which extends down into the vagina (figures 6.3 and 6.4). Just prior to ovulation, the mouth of the cervix is open so that sperm cells can pass through the cervix and into the uterus on their journey from the vagina to the female ovum. At other times of the month, mucus in the mouth of the cervix acts as an effective plug that prevents bacterial penetration into the uterus and beyond. A woman can feel her cervix by inserting one or two fingers into the vagina and reaching until she feels the firm, round projection at the end of the vaginal tube.

A **Pap smear,** which is a screening test for cancer developing in the tissues of the uterus or cervix, is obtained from the cervix. An instrument called a speculum is inserted into the vagina and holds the vaginal walls open. Then a tiny sample of tissue is scraped from two or three places on the cervix. This tissue is then smeared on a glass slide, stained, and examined for the presence of any abnormal cells.

The Pap smear can detect early cancerous changes in the cells of the cervix and for that reason should be a part of all women's regular preventative health care routine. The procedure is simple, painless (there are very few nerve endings on the cervix), highly effective, and lifesaving. The Pap test has reduced deaths from cervical cancer by more than 50 percent because of the early recognition and treatment of preinvasive cancer.

Fallopian Tubes

The two **fallopian tubes** are about four inches in length and extend from both sides of the uterus. One end of each tube opens into the uterine cavity, while the other end is funnel-shaped (called the **infundibulum**) and lies very close to an ovary. The infundibulum is surrounded by a fringe of fingerlike projections called the **fimbriae.** See figures 6.2 and 6.3.

Once in about every twenty-eight days in a sexually mature female, a mature ovum (egg) erupts from the surface of an ovary near the infundibulum of a fallopian tube. This eruption of the ovum is called **ovulation.** It is believed that the ovum is drawn into the fallopian tube by the rhythmic movement of the fingerlike projections surrounding the infundibulum. Once the ovum is inside the tube, tiny, hairlike cilia and rhythmic muscular contractions of the walls of the fallopian tube move the ovum down toward the uterus. If sperm are present within the fallopian tube, fertilization of the ovum may occur—usually in the upper two inches (upper third) of the fallopian tube.

estrogen   progesterone
(es′tro-jen)   (pro-jes′tē-rōn)

Ovaries

The two **ovaries** are almond-sized and almond-shaped. Each ovary is located at the end of a fallopian tube; thus, there is one ovary on each side of the uterus (figures 6.2 and 6.3). Each ovary is attached to several ligaments that help to hold it in position.

The ovaries, like the testes in the male, have dual functions. They produce and release **ova** (eggs) and female sex hormones.

Ova Production and Release

Ova production in females begins in the ovaries before birth. When a female infant is born, her ovaries already contain all of the potential ova that she will ovulate (release from her ovary) throughout her reproductive lifetime. Each of these immature ovums is enclosed within a thin tissue sac called a **follicle.**

The approximately 500,000 potential ova in the ovaries at birth are reduced to about 250,000 by puberty (Hole 1981). At puberty, the female becomes sexually mature, and her ovaries begin to mature and release the ova. Each reproductive month (approximately every twenty-eight days) a number of follicles in one of the two ovaries begin to grow. Only one of the follicles, however, matures to the point where it releases an ovum. The other developing follicles and the potential ova within them degenerate.

This process continues each month until all of the ova have either dissolved or been ovulated (usually when the woman is between the ages of forty-five and fifty), at which time the woman passes through **menopause** and becomes sterile. Thus, the postmenopausal woman has used up or dissolved all of the ova in her ovaries, and the ovaries have ceased to function.

Female Sex Hormone Production

In addition to producing and releasing ova, the ovaries secrete the two major types of female sex hormones: **estrogen** (which is actually a group of hormones) and **progesterone.** Estrogen and progesterone are of key importance in maintaining both the ovarian and uterine cycles of the female, and we discuss them in more detail later in the chapter.

Table 6.1 summarizes the external and internal female reproductive structures and their functions.

Table 6.1 Female Reproductive Structures.

Organ	Function
External	
Mons veneris	Physical stimulation associated with feeling of pleasure during sexual arousal and orgasm
Labia majora	Enclose and protect other external genitals
Labia minora	Protect the vaginal and urethral openings; react by swelling during sexual arousal
Vestibule	Space between labia minora; includes vaginal and urethral openings and two sets of glands
Vestibular glands	Secrete fluids that moisten and lubricate vestibule and outer portion of vagina
Perineum	Contains numerous nerve endings and is sensitive to touch and pressure
Clitoris	Richly supplied with nerve endings; when stimulated, becomes erect; continued stimulation usually culminates in orgasm
Internal	
Vagina	Receives the male penis during sexual intercourse; conveys menstrual flow to the outside of the body; serves as the birth canal for the fetus
Uterus	Receives and nurtures the embryo during development
Fallopian tubes	Convey ovulated ovum to uterus
Ovaries	Produce and release ova and female sex hormones

1. What are the three functions of the vagina? What characteristic of the vagina allows it to fulfill these three functions?
2. What is the danger of changing the internal chemistry of the vagina?
3. If you are a woman, have you ever had a Pap smear? Describe the procedure. What were the results? Have your Pap smear results ever been abnormal?
4. If a woman is born with hundreds of thousands of potential ova, why does she usually run out of ova by the time she is in her late forties?
5. Compare the dual functions of the female ovaries with the dual functions of the male testes (see chapter 5).

areola   sebaceous
(ah-re'o-lah)   (se-ba'shus)

The Breasts

The female breasts are not considered to be organs of the female reproductive system. Instead, they are labelled as female secondary sex characteristics, which are female adult physical characteristics that distinguish females from males. Yet, the breasts clearly play a part in female sexuality, and, for that reason, we discuss them here.

Figure 6.5 shows the structures of the breast and the stages of breast development throughout the life of a female.

The **nipple** is the structure in the center of the breast. The darker-colored area surrounding the nipple is called the **areola.** (During pregnancy, the areola becomes even darker.) The nipple may stick out from the areola, it may be flush with the areola, or it may seem to sink into the areola. The openings of the **mammary glands** (milk-producing glands) are in the nipples, and an adult woman may occasionally notice a slight nipple secretion. This secretion is coming from the **milk ducts** inside the breast and is normal. When a nipple is exposed to cold temperatures or is sexually aroused, small muscles around the nipple contract, causing the nipple to become more erect than usual.

The areola may have small bumps on its surface. These are **sebaceous** or oil glands that help lubricate the nipples during breast-feeding. It is also quite common for hairs to grow around the areola. These may appear suddenly, due to normal hormonal changes that take place during aging. Some women may notice an increase in hair growth during or following their use of birth control pills; this is also normal.

The inside of the breast consists of mammary glands, gland milk ducts, and fatty tissue. The milk-producing glandular tissue is very sensitive to hormonal changes throughout life—during adolescence, during the menstrual cycle, with the starting and stopping of birth control pills, and during pregnancy—with the result that there can be variations in the amount of glandular tissue in the breast at different times and thus variations in any one woman's breast size and shape at different points in her life (figure 6.5). For example, a woman's breast size may double during pregnancy.

Generally, however, when hormonal changes are not underway, the amount of milk-producing glandular tissue in the breast varies little from woman to woman. Thus, the usual size of a woman's breast has little or nothing to do with the amount of milk that a woman is capable of producing after childbirth. Small-breasted women can produce as much milk as large-breasted women. (We discuss how hormones control breastmilk production later in the chapter.)

Variations in the size and shape of the breasts from one woman to another are due primarily to the amount of fatty tissue that lies over, under, and between the glandular tissue. The amount of fatty tissue present in a breast is determined partly by a woman's body weight and partly by her heredity.

Figure 6.5 External and internal structures of the female breast. Internal structures and developmental stages of the female breast: (1) child, (2) adolescent, (3) adult (breast shape may be more droopy for many women), (4) pregnant adult, (5) lactating adult, (6) postmenopausal adult (note the small size of the mammary glands).

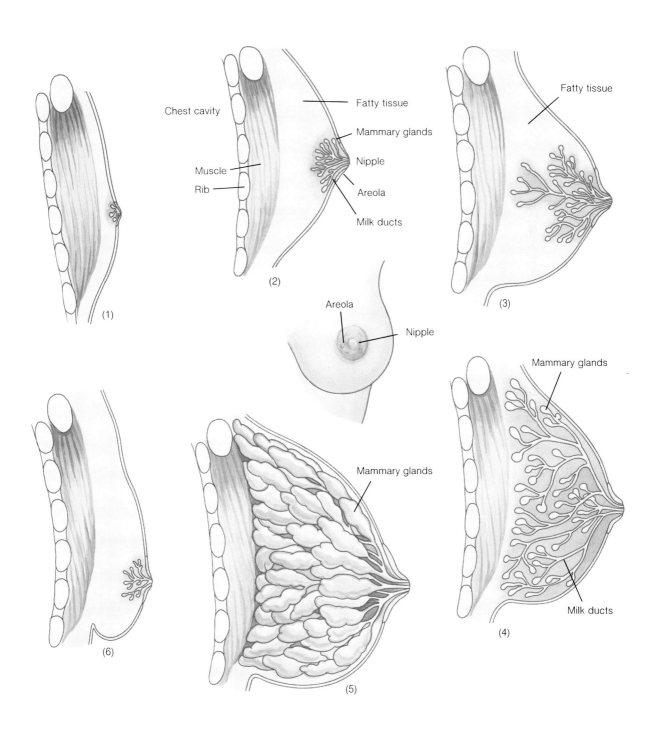

(1)

Chest cavity

Fatty tissue

Mammary glands

Nipple

Muscle

Areola

Rib

Milk ducts

(2)

Fatty tissue

(3)

Areola

Nipple

Mammary glands

Mammary glands

Milk ducts

(4)

(6)

Mammary glands

(5)

Stages of Breast Self-Examination

A woman should examine her breasts in two stages. In the first stage, the woman sits before a mirror. With her arms at her sides and her posture erect, she examines her breasts for symmetry in size and shape, noting any changes in *dimpling of the skin or depression of the nipple*. Then, with her arms overhead, she repeats this procedure (box figure 6.1a).

The second stage of breast self-examination is performed while the woman is reclining on a bed. During this portion of the examination, the woman places a flat pillow or folded towel under her left shoulder. This prop raises this side of the body and distributes the weight evenly over the chest wall.

Now, with her left arm at her side, the woman uses her right hand to systematically examine the flat, sensitive portions of the left breast, extending her examination well into the armpit area (box figure 6.1b). Then she proceeds to inspect the upper and lower outer portions of the breast (box figure 6.1c). She uses the sensitive flats of her fingers instead of their tips, and she gives this portion of her breast special attention. Again, any lump or thickening is noted. Having covered the armpit region and the upper and lower outer portions, the woman now goes over the remainder of the outer half of the left breast, feeling in successive stages from the outer margin to the nipple (box figure 6.1d).

Box Figure 6.1 Steps for the systematic self-examination of the breasts.

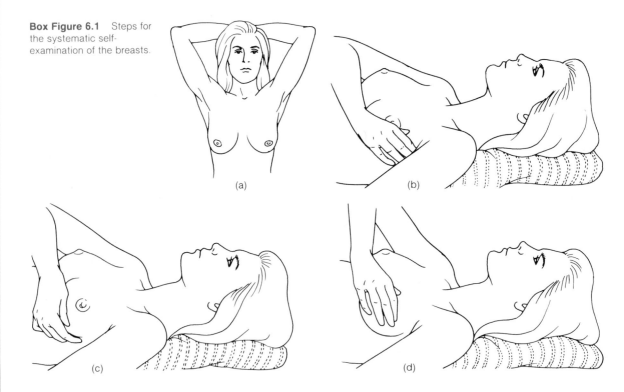

(a)

(b)

(c)

(d)

When the entire outer half of the left breast has been examined, the woman now raises her left arm over her head (box figure 6.1e). This spreads and thins the tissue of the left breast for the remaining steps. Beginning at the breastbone, the woman uses her right hand to press the tissue of the inner half of the left breast against the chest wall, moving in a series of steps from the breastbone to the middie of the breast (box figure 6.1f). At this point, she carefully palpates the nipple area and the tissues lying beneath it (box figure 6.1g). Still using the flats of her fingers, she notes the normal structures of her breast and any new lumps. Finally, she completes her examination of this breast by feeling the rest of the inner half of the breast systematically (box figure 6.1h). Along the lower margin, she will find a ridge of firm tissue, which is normal and should not alarm her.

Now the *second stage* of the breast self-examination procedure should be repeated on the other breast. Any new lumps or thickenings the woman has not noted in the past should be reported to her physician.

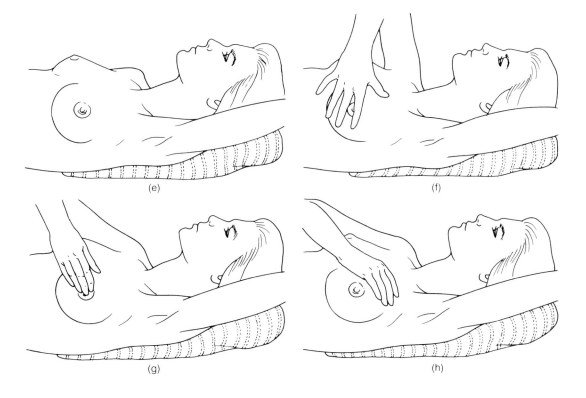

(e)

(f)

(g)

(h)

menarche
(mē-nar′ke)

It is very important that a woman examine her breasts for changes that could indicate breast tumors, growths, or cancer. Many breasts normally feel lumpy, and few of these lumps are dangerous when they persist throughout life. Thus, if a woman starts examining her breasts in her teens and becomes familiar with them, she can notice changes as she becomes older. Any change should be reported to a physician. Every woman should inspect her breasts monthly, immediately after the end of her menstrual period. Examination during the menstrual period is unsatisfactory because of the temporary changes and tenderness that normally may occur in the breasts at that time.

1.   What part do you feel that breasts play in female sexuality?
2.   Some people still try to discourage small-breasted women from attempting to breast-feed their babies. On what misinformation are these people basing their advice? Can small-breasted women supply enough milk for their babies? Why?

The Menstrual Cycle

The **menstrual cycle** is the female reproductive cycle that is characterized by regularly reoccurring changes in the uterus and the ovaries. These changes involve the maturation and ovulation of an ovum each reproductive month (approximately every twenty-eight days) and the preparation of the uterus to receive a fertilized ovum. If the ovum is not fertilized, the menstrual cycle concludes with the onset of **menstruation,** the monthly flow of bloody fluid from the uterus through the vagina.

The first day of menstrual flow is called day 1 of the menstrual cycle. The final day of the menstrual cycle is the day before the next menstrual flow.

Menarche, or the first menstruation, usually occurs at twelve or thirteen years of age, although the normal range of its occurrence is from ten to eighteen years of age (Gersh and Gersh 1981).

After menarche, menstrual cycles are usually irregular for one to two years, and ovulation may not occur regularly or at all. During this time, the secondary sex characteristics are developing, hormones are rising to adult levels, growth is taking place, and a large amount of body fat (15 to 25 percent of body weight) is accumulating in the female. This stored fat is important in maintaining a body level sufficient to trigger regular menstrual cycles. When this fat is lacking in a very thin woman or is depleted through excessive exercise or active sports (jogging, running, swimming, or aerobic exercises), the menstrual cycles may become irregular or stop completely until adequate fat deposits are rebuilt.

Menstrual cycles usually end when a woman is between the ages of forty-five and fifty, at which time the woman is said to be experiencing **menopause.**

Menstrual Cycle Length

The menstrual cycle is, on the average, twenty-eight days long, but this "average" is uncommonly encountered by most women. The menstrual cycle varies considerably from woman to woman and from one reproductive month to the next. Some cycles may be twenty-eight days; others may be twenty-four or thirty or thirty-two days; all are considered perfectly normal. Medically, the menstrual cycle may be as short as twenty or twenty-one days and as long as forty or forty-five days and still be considered normal.

One study of 2,300 women over more than thirty thousand menstrual cycles found that menstrual cycles varied from fifteen to twenty-five days within this group and that 13 percent of the women surveyed had menstrual cycles that varied by less than six days over a one-year period. Eighty-seven percent of the women experienced cycles that varied by more than seven days over a one-year period (Schrotenboer and Subak-Sharpe 1981).

Many conditions, such as emotional stress, dieting, and physical fitness activities, can alter or temporarily stop the menstrual cycle. As more women try to keep their bodies thinner than the recommended weight and participate in very strenuous physical fitness programs and sports, the average menstrual cycle will become longer and longer; that is, the number of days between menstrual flows will increase.

If a menstrual flow occurs more often than every twenty-one days, a woman should consult her physician. While many activities will lengthen menstrual cycles, very few will shorten them without being dangerous to the individual (Schrotenboer and Subak-Sharpe 1981).

Moods and Emotions of the Menstrual Cycle

A number of mood and emotional changes seem to be closely related to the different days of the menstrual cycle. Some changes appear to be linked to known physiological factors. Others have been linked to speculation or theories that have grown out of animal studies but that have not always been verified in human studies. The great majority of these mood and emotional changes, when they occur, probably result from a combination of the physical makeup of the woman involved; hormonal, prostaglandal, and other cyclic chemical changes; social attitudes and childhood training; and emotional stability.

During days 5 through 13 of the menstrual cycle, the endometrium of the uterus is growing from a thin, smooth layer into a thick, dense, tissue layer. This growth may take much of a woman's energy, and often a woman will not show a high energy level in her everyday activity during this time. She may not like to physically overexert herself during these days.

Estrogen rises and peaks in the bloodstream on day 12 or 13. Estrogen is the "feminine" hormone, and besides exerting control over the secondary sex characteristics, estrogen also seems to influence moods and behavior. During the days of

Toxic Shock Syndrome

In 1979, Dr. Andrew G. Dean, preventive medicine specialist of the Minnesota Department of Health, informed the Center for Disease Control (CDC) in Atlanta, Georgia, that an unusual illness had recently struck five previously healthy young women in Minnesota. He reported that the disease's symptoms were similar to those associated with a disease caused by the bacterium *Staphylococcus aureus,* which was first described in 1978. The CDC released the Minnesota report in early 1980, and new cases from all parts of the country were rapidly identified.

University of Wisconsin epidermiologist Jeffrey P. Davis and his associates described a strict set of diagnostic criteria for the disease, which they called *toxic shock syndrome (TSS)* in December 1980. A TSS patient shows a temperature above 102°F; low blood pressure, or a drop in blood pressure after standing up suddenly; a red rash on the palms; redness of the lining membrane (mucous membrane) of the throat or vagina; vomiting or diarrhea; impaired kidney or liver function; decreased calcium and phosphorus levels in the blood; and in severe infections, shock (collapse of the circulatory system due to the loss of circulatory fluid to the tissues of the body). The diagnosis is confirmed after laboratory tests rule out other causes of the symptoms.

The condition occurs almost exclusively in menstruating women, and 80 percent of the cases are in women under age thirty. Most TSS victims are using tampons when the disease strikes. Initially, one brand of tampon—Rely—was implicated in many TSS cases. The removal of *Rely* from the market reduced the incidence of TSS, but it did not stop the disease completely. More recently, cases of TSS have been associated with other tampon brands and with the use of contraceptive sponges.

How the disease occurs is not fully understood, but data suggest that *S. aureus* is carried into the vagina by tampons or contraceptive sponges and that victims keep the tampons or sponges in the vagina too long, allowing an unusual growth of *S. aureus. S. aureus*-contaminated blood can then enter the peritoneal cavity through the uterus and fallopian tubes. Certain strains of *S. aureus* have been shown to produce two toxins (poisons produced by bacteria)—*enterotoxin F* and a yet unknown fever-producing (pyrogenic) toxin—that are quickly absorbed into the bloodstream through the peritoneal walls and cause the illness.

Consequently, women who use either tampons or contraceptive sponges should never allow the devices to remain in the vagina for too long a time. These women also should be aware of the symptoms of TSS and should report any symptoms to their physician immediately.

high estrogen (days 12 through 14), many women seem to exhibit what is thought of as "feminine" behavior to a high degree. They may wear very feminine clothes, and color also seems to be very important to them at this time. The woman's energy levels may be heightened now, too.

At the time of ovulation (days 14 to 16), estrogen levels drop drastically. During this drop in estrogen, some women feel a stronger than usual sex drive. Since this is the time of ovulation, these feelings may increase a woman's chance of conceiving.

From ovulation through days 15 through 22, heightened energy levels may persist. This often is the time for physical activity and "projects." A woman may do something she has been putting off through the first part of the menstrual month, such as painting, refinishing a piece of furniture, or setting everything in order. There may be increased feelings of self-esteem, well-being, and happiness, and heightened emotional levels during this middle part of the cycle when estrogen, progesterone, and androgen levels are high.

At about day 22, the estrogen and progesterone levels begin to drop to their lowest levels of the menstrual cycle. The rapidly declining levels of estrogen and progesterone are believed to influence the emotional anxiety, depression, and irritability that seems to be the start of *premenstrual syndrome,* which we discuss in detail a little later in the chapter. When premenstrual syndrome exists, it seems to reach its height about two days before the menstrual flow (days 26 through 28).

This is also a time when the androgen hormones ("male" hormones) are higher than the female hormones (estrogen and progesterone), and the heightened androgen levels may be responsible for the heightened sexual feelings many women experience during this time and throughout the menstrual flow (days 1 through 5), when the female hormones continue to be at a low ebb in the body.

Premenstrual Syndrome

The physical discomforts and emotional mood swings that many women experience just prior to menstruation are all gathered under the label **premenstrual syndrome (PMS)**. There are a number of theories regarding the causes of premenstrual syndrome, but, as yet, none has been proven.

The symptoms of premenstrual syndrome usually occur on about day twenty-five of the menstrual cycle, reach their height on about day twenty-eight, and disappear when the menstrual flow appears. Symptoms may include mild to severe abdominal or back pain, upper leg cramps, tenderness and swelling of the breasts, skin eruptions (such as pimples or blotches), migraine and sinus headaches, swollen glands, nausea, sinus pain, drastic mood swings (crying, withdrawal, depression, irritability, and precipitation of arguments), a craving for sweet or salty foods, loss of appetite, and inability to "handle" alcoholic beverages (Schrotenboer and Subak-Sharpe 1981). Most women suffer at least one symptom of premenstrual syndrome every month. Some gynecologists believe that as many as 40 percent of all women experience the mood swings associated with PMS (Schrotenboer and Subak-Sharpe 1981).

The first step toward control of PMS is to establish whether or not the symptoms are indeed related to the menstrual cycle. Women who suspect that they may be affected by PMS should keep a careful calendar or diary of their symptoms and menstrual periods for a few months. If, month after month, for example, a woman experiences a migraine headache, drastic mood swings, crying spells, skin eruptions, or other symptoms just before the menstrual flow, she can usually safely assume

prolactin   diuretic
(pro-lak'tin)   (di''u-ret'ik)

PMS may include headaches,
mood swings, crying spells,
skin eruptions, and other
symptoms.

that she is affected by premenstrual syndrome. Recognizing the relationship between the body and mind in producing the wide range of PMS symptoms is needed
to cope with premenstrual syndrome.

Since there is no single treatment or therapy for PMS that has been proven
universally effective, the approaches for treating its symptoms vary greatly from
physician to physician and woman to woman. Dr. Katherina Dalton (1977) feels
that PMS is caused by a deficiency in the hormone progesterone. She, and others,
have had success in alleviating PMS symptoms by giving women progesterone during
the days that they would have suffered from PMS.

The U.S. Food and Drug Administration has approved the drug bromocyptine
for the treatment of PMS. Bromocyptine is a drug that blocks the production of a
hormone called prolactin. The rationale for using this drug is based on research that
has shown that some women have elevated levels of prolactin during the latter part
of the menstrual cycle. Physicians using bromocyptine, however, have found that
only about one in six women actually lose their PMS symptoms when using the
drug.

For years, some physicians have also prescribed the use of vitamin B_6 during
the PMS days to help relieve many PMS symptoms (Schrotenboer and Subak-Sharpe
1981). How vitamin B_6 (and other vitamins, such as C and A) act to relieve premenstrual syndrome is unknown, and their effectiveness has never been proven in
scientific studies.

Several PMS symptoms, such as swelling, bloating, and temporary weight gain,
result from water retention. Thus, women experiencing these symptoms often find
relief by using a diuretic (a substance or drug that removes water from the body
by increasing the flow of urine) and reducing their sodium (table salt and other
sodium-containing foods) intake during the PMS time. This reduces fluid retention
by releasing excess water through the kidneys.

Recurring skin problems, such as blotchy skin and pimples, can be caused by
an allergic reaction to some of the normal hormones present in a woman. An allergic
reaction to progesterone is the most common. For such allergic reactions, the woman
can use oral contraceptive pills, which will keep her from ovulating. If ovulation
does not occur, no natural progesterone is produced, and the allergic blotches or
skin eruptions will not appear.

All of this means that no one treatment is effective for PMS in all women. A
number of treatment possibilities are plausible, and a woman must persevere until
she finds a treatment, or series of treatments, that work for her. Table 6.2 outlines
some common remedies and behavioral modifications that have helped some women.
These, along with proper medical advice, may help to alleviate premenstrual syndrome until a more definite treatment is obtainable through research.

Table 6.2 Common Remedies for PMS.

Remedy	
Caffeine	May help or may make it worse. Caffeine is a diuretic and reduces body water content, thus helping the bloating, breast tenderness, and weight gain. But caffeine can also produce or amplify feelings of irritability and cause insomnia and headaches. Caffeine products include coffee, tea, chocolate, and many soft drinks.
Over-the-counter medicines	Contain very common ingredients. Midol and Pamprin are most commonly used. Midol contains aspirin (prostaglandin blocker) for pain and caffeine for water retention. Pamprin contains acetaminophen (Tylenol) and pamatrom, a diuretic, for water retention.
Potassium	Diuretics flush potassium out of the body. Potassium is needed for healthy nerves and muscles. Potassium-rich foods (bananas, apricots, dairy products) increase potassium levels and help in reducing cramps.
Vitamins	Vitamins B_6, C, and E may help in combating menstrual cramps. Supplemental vitamin B_6 seems to be needed by women using oral contraceptives.
Minerals	A good balance of minerals is needed for normal body functioning. Thus, a mineral supplement or plant source foods, which are high in minerals, may help some women to alleviate menstrual cramps.
Low-sodium	Reducing sodium (table salt and other sodium-containing foods) will reduce water retention and decrease bloating and weight gains due to water retention.
Sleep	An adequate amount of sleep is important. Fatigue just makes pain seem worse.
Exercise	Perspiration removes excess water. Exercise increases blood flow to muscles' increasing the amount of oxygen they obtain. This increases the muscles' ability to function without producing cramps and pain.

Menstrual Cramps

Women afflicted with severe menstrual cramps that are not relieved by aspirin or other over-the-counter pain-reducing medications may need to see a physician. Since any effective treatment is based on the physician establishing a correct diagnosis, the physician's questions should be answered frankly and honestly. The answers may hold important clues to possible causes of the menstrual pain.

For example, if the cramps began with the very first menstrual period, the problems may be due to a congenital narrowing of the cervix, a very rare condition that can be corrected with simple surgery. If the problem dates from a complicated miscarriage or abortion, it may have been caused by the abortion or the surgical procedures used. If the cramps started only recently and if there may have been

dysmenorrhea
(dis"men-o-re'ah)

possible exposure to a sexually transmitted disease, the physician will want to investigate this possibility further. Untreated gonorrhea can lead to a serious condition known as pelvic inflammatory disease (PID), which may cause menstrual cramps or abdominal pain. Other infections of the reproductive system also can produce PID. In most cases, however, no physical cause for the menstrual cramps and pain can be found.

Until recently, there was no satisfactory treatment for menstrual cramps, but now there are a number of prostaglandin-inhibiting drugs that can eliminate menstrual cramps and pain for the vast majority of women. (**Prostaglandins** are hormone-like substances that can cause specific actions to occur, such as relaxation or contraction of smooth muscle.)

In the early 1950s, British physicians reported that a drug being used to treat arthritis and other inflammatory disorders appeared to have the remarkable ability to totally eliminate severe menstrual cramps in women taking the drug for other conditions. The drug was phenylbutazone. At the time, little was known about how the drug worked. As more became known about prostaglandins, however, it was found that phenylbutazone was a prostaglandin-inhibiting drug. It has now been determined that most of the symptoms associated with menstrual cramps are caused by prostaglandins and that these symptoms can be eliminated or minimized by drugs that inhibit the synthesis, or block the actions, of prostaglandins.

During the 1970s, a number of prostaglandin inhibitors were developed. Also, in 1980, the Food and Drug Administration approved the use of mefenamic acid for the relief of menstrual cramps. This drug is believed to both inhibit the production of prostaglandins and to interfere with the action of the prostaglandins that are produced. By 1982, there were a number of such drugs on the market, and they had proved to be effective in about 80 percent of all women suffering from menstrual cramps (Schrotenboer and Subak-Sharpe 1981).

Dysmenorrhea

The physically painful menstrual flows that some women experience are known as **dysmenorrhea.** In recent years, the classical symptoms of dysmenorrhea have been intertwined with PMS. Consequently, today there is no clear distinction between dysmenorrhea and premenstrual syndrome. In the past, however, dysmenorrhea was divided into *spasmodic dysmenorrhea* or *congestive dysmenorrhea*.

Spasmodic dysmenorrhea occurs during the menstrual flow and is most often associated with younger women or with postpartum women (women who have just experienced childbirth). Symptoms include mild to severe low back pain, uterine cramps, tenderness of the breasts, and/or skin eruptions, such as pimples or blotches. This type of dysmenorrhea is due to a high ratio of progesterone to estrogen. Spasmodic dysmenorrhea may be treated by using birth-control pills (preventing ovulation also prevents the high amounts of natural progesterone during menstruation), pain-killing drugs, or muscle relaxants. Increased exercise and physical activity that decreases muscle tension also seems to relieve many of the symptoms.

Congestive dysmenorrhea and its symptoms parallel those of what is now known as premenstrual syndrome (PMS).

---

1. If you are a woman, by how much do the lengths of your menstrual cycles vary from month to month? Can you pinpoint any activity or emotional stress that might have contributed to making one cycle considerably longer than another?
2. Do you or someone you know experience premenstrual syndrome? What are the symptoms? How do you or this person you know feel about having the symptoms linked to the menstrual cycle?

Hormones Important to Female Sexual Development

Prenatally (before birth), the embryo develops spontaneously into a female in the absence of the male hormone testosterone. This is almost a "neutral" pattern of sexual development when compared to that of the male. However, after birth, female sex hormones must be present if full sexual development is to occur.

A female child's body remains reproductively immature until gonadotropic-releasing factor (GnRF) is secreted from the hypothalamus of the brain (figure 6.6). As we discussed in chapter 5, GnRF drains into the pituitary gland and stimulates the pituitary gland into releasing the gonadotropins follicle-stimulating hormone (FSH) and luteinizing hormone (LH). FSH and LH, in turn, stimulate the female's body to secrete several different sex hormones that produce the changes that lead to the development and maintenance of female secondary sex characteristics and menarche. These hormones include the malelike androgens (the most important of which is testosterone) and the female sex hormones estrogen and progesterone. Also involved are the prostaglandins, a group of hormonelike chemicals produced by individual cells throughout the reproductive tract.

Androgens

The concentration of malelike **androgens** in females is very low. Some of the androgens are secreted by the ovaries and adrenal glands, but more than half of the androgens in the female come from unknown sources.

In the female, the low levels of androgens are responsible for the female patterns of body hair development, especially the hair in the pubic and axillary (armpit) regions. For example, figure 6.7 shows that when high levels of androgens are present, as they are in males, the pubic hair tapers toward the navel. When only low levels of androgens are present, as in females, however, the upper border of the pubic hair

Figure 6.6 Hormones important to female sexual development and their functions.

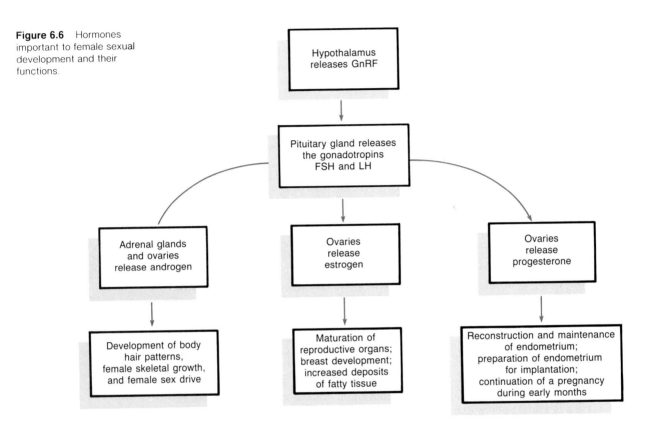

Figure 6.7 Pubic hair growth patterns in females and males. In females, the upper border of pubic hair is usually horizontal, while in males, pubic hair tapers toward the navel.

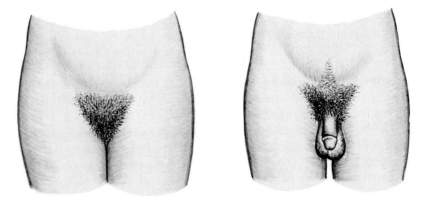

is usually horizontal. The development of the female skeletal growth pattern, which is characterized by the narrower shoulders and broader hips of the female, also seems to be related to a presence of only low levels of androgens. Androgens are also responsible for the sex drive of females as well as males. See figure 6.6.

Estrogen

Estrogen is the name applied to a group of hormones (estradiol, estrone, estriole, and others) that are secreted by the ovaries, the adrenal glands, and the placenta (the organ formed on the wall of the uterus during pregnancy that sustains the fetus). Estrogen's effects in the female parallel the effects of testosterone in the male, since estrogen stimulates the development of the secondary sex characteristics of the female and maintains these characteristics during the female's reproductive lifetime.

The female secondary sex characteristics include (Hole 1981):

1. Enlargement of the vagina, uterus, fallopian tubes, ovaries, and external reproductive organs
2. Development of the breasts and the ductile system of the mammary glands within the breasts
3. Increased deposits of fatty tissue in the breasts, thighs, and buttocks
4. Increased vascularization (development of blood vessels) of the skin

See figure 6.6.

Progesterone

Progesterone, like estrogen, is secreted by the ovaries, the adrenal glands, and the placenta during pregnancy. Progesterone plays a role in ovulation, reconstructive growth of the uterine endometrium after menstruation, preparation of the endometrium for implantation of the fertilized ovum, and continuation of a pregnancy during its early months. See figure 6.6.

Prostaglandins

Prostaglandins are a diverse group of hormonelike substances that are produced throughout the body. The prostaglandins involved in the reproductive processes cause the relaxation or contraction of smooth muscle. Different prostaglandins seem to be instrumental in ovulation, movement of sperm and ovum through the fallopian tubes, contraction of the smooth muscle of the uterus, and the expelling of the menstrual flow during menstruation. The ability of prostaglandins to cause spastic contractions of the smooth muscle of the uterus explains their use in inducing therapeutic abortions (see chapter 15).

Prostaglandins often work in pairs. For example, a specific pair seem to work on the uterus. One member of the pair relaxes the muscular layer, while the other allows this layer to constrict (causing menstruation, inducing labor, or producing abortion). The actions work during different times of the menstrual cycle. Early in the cycle, one of the pair relaxes the muscular layers, while later in the cycle, the opposing prostaglandin causes muscular contractions, cramping, and the menstrual flow.

---

1. Outline the chain of events that occurs once GnRF is secreted by the hypothalamus in a young female.
2. What are the functions of the various sex hormones present in the female body?

Hormonal Control of the Menstrual Cycle

During a typical menstrual cycle, changes take place in both the ovaries and the uterus. These ovarian and uterine changes both begin on day one of the menstrual cycle, occur simultaneously, and are cyclic, that is, they reoccur on a regular basis—in this case, usually about every twenty-eight days, the length of the average menstrual cycle. Both the uterine and ovarian cycles are under hormonal control. In the next few paragraphs, we outline a typical menstrual cycle and discuss which hormones are responsible for initiating and controlling uterine and ovarian changes. We also examine how the timing of the uterine and ovarian cycles correspond to each other. Figures 6.8 and 6.9 are good references in this regard.

Figure 6.8 The ovarian cycle. At no one time are all the structures illustrated present. At the beginning of the ovarian cycle, several follicles start to develop. One of these matures into a graafian follicle, while the others regress. Near the middle of the cycle (day 14 to 16), the mature follicle releases its ovum (ovulation). The follicle then becomes a corpus luteum. If there is no fertilization, the corpus luteum starts to regress in about ten days (day 24 to 26) and ends the cycle as a scar called the corpus albicans.

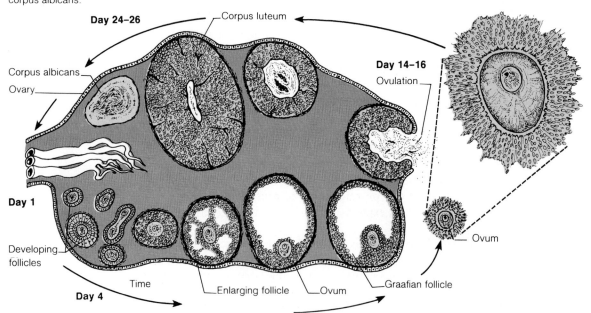

proliferative
(pro·lif′er·a·tiv)

Researchers now believe that a prostaglandin signals the hypothalamus each month to begin the menstrual cycle. How this is accomplished is not yet known (Schrotenboer and Subak-Sharpe 1981). The hypothalamus then secretes the gonadotropin-releasing factor (GnRF). GnRF flows into the pituitary gland, which responds by increasing the level of FSH and LH in circulation. FSH is primarily responsible for triggering follicular development in the ovaries (figure 6.8).

Under the influence of FSH, several follicles, each containing at least one potential ovum, start to enlarge. After two or three days, all of the enlarging follicles except one stop enlarging, regress, and are dissolved. The one remaining follicle, called the **Graafian follicle,** continues to enlarge until day twelve to fourteen of the cycle, at which time it is ready to release its ovum from the ovary through ovulation.

All of the developing follicles and the one follicle that continues to grow secrete an ever-increasing amount of estrogen into the bloodstream, which influences the body in three ways.

First, it causes the endometrium of the uterus to grow. As explained earlier, the uterus is composed of three layers (see figure 6.4), a thin outer layer, a middle muscular layer, and an inner layer, called the endometrium, bounding the uterine cavity. During the first five days of the menstrual cycle, the endometrium and a small amount of blood are shed from the body as the menstrual flow. Starting on day six of the cycle and continuing until around day fourteen or fifteen, the increasing levels of estrogen cause the endometrium to grow back to its normal thickness. This is called the **proliferative phase** of the uterine cycle (figure 6.9).

Second, during the days just prior to the menstrual flow, many women experience swelling, fullness, and sensitivity of the breasts. This is produced by an increased blood flow through the breasts and the influence of prostaglandins in circulation at this time. The increasing levels of estrogen in the bloodstream cause the swelling, fullness, and sensitivity of the breasts to disappear. The breasts reach their minimum size at five to seven days after the menstrual flow and remain unchanged until just before the next menstrual flow. Self-examination of the breasts for cancer is best performed five days after the cessation of the menstrual flow since it is easiest to feel any lumps or abnormalities when the breasts are smallest.

Figure 6.9 Uterine cycle. The first day of the menstrual flow is considered the first day of the uterine cycle. After the menstrual flow, the uterine endometrium rapidly thickens as a result of cellular growth (proliferative phase). In the second half of the cycle, glands in the endometrium start to secrete mucus and glycogen (secretory phase). Finally, the endometrium breaks down (menstrual phase), and a new cycle has begun.

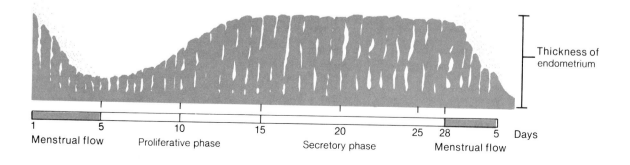

Thickness of endometrium

| 1 | 5 | 10 | 15 | 20 | 25 | 28 | 5 | Days |

Menstrual flow   Proliferative phase   Secretory phase   Menstrual flow

mittelschmerz
(mit'el-schmārts)

corpus luteum
(kor'pus loo'te-um)

corpus albicans
(kor'pus al'bi-kanz)

Finally, the increasing levels of estrogen act as a feedback to control hormones of the menstrual cycle. As the level of estrogen goes up, it inhibits the secretion of FSH and LH until the thirteenth day of the cycle. This is a negative feedback effect. On day thirteen, the effect of estrogen on the brain and pituitary gland changes to a positive feedback effect, causing a drastic surge of FSH and LH into the bloodstream. The surge of LH allows the release of prostaglandins that cause stretching of the wall of the ovary in the area of the "ripe" follicle, which restricts local blood flow and weakens the ovarian wall. As the ovarian wall breaks, it allows the ovum to escape from the ovary. Ovulation usually occurs on, or about, the fourteenth day of the menstrual cycle.

Most women never know when they ovulate. But some women experience pain, ranging from a few mild tinges to severe lower abdominal cramps, when they ovulate. This pain can occur every menstrual cycle or periodically throughout their reproductive life. This ovulation pain is referred to as **"mittelschmerz,"** from a German term meaning *middle pain,* and is caused by the ovum breaking out of the follicle during ovulation. According to Schrotenboer and Subak-Sharpe (1981), mittelschmerz is a side effect of the release of the prostaglandins that cause rupture of the follicle.

The ovulated ovum is drawn into a fallopian tube by the waving motion of the fallopian tube's fingerlike projections (fimbria). After entering the fallopian tube, cilia and muscular contractions of the fallopian tube move the ovum toward the uterus at a rate of about one inch every twenty-four hours. All of this movement is probably caused by prostaglandins being secreted in the area in response to the high LH level.

After ovulation, the opening in the ovary caused by ovulation heals over. The cells of the internal walls of the follicle proliferate and fill the old follicle. These cells become a structure known as the **corpus luteum** (figure 6.8). The corpus luteum is an endocrine gland and produces progesterone and estrogen during the period it is active.

If the ovulated ovum, which is now traveling down a fallopian tube, is not fertilized (an infertile cycle), the corpus luteum functions for about eleven days (until day twenty-five of the cycle). It then regresses, becomes a nonfunctional scar (the **corpus albicans,** figure 6.8), and ceases to secrete progesterone and estrogen. But, if the ovum is fertilized and a pregnancy occurs, the corpus luteum continues to function and produces progesterone for the first twelve to fourteen weeks of the pregnancy before regressing and becoming a corpus albicans. The proper amounts of progesterone and estrogen to maintain the pregnancy are then secreted by the placenta for the remaining twenty-four to twenty-six weeks of the pregnancy.

Following ovulation, the progesterone secreted by the corpus luteum causes the endometrial wall of the uterus to become soft, spongy, and moist with mucus and glycogen, which is called the **secretory phase** of the uterine cycle (figure 6.9). The mucus provides a fluid medium for the ovum, and glycogen provides a food supply for the ovum until it can become implanted. From day fourteen through day twenty-four, the endometrium is ready for implantation should an ovum be fertilized during this time.

If there is no fertilization, the progesterone released by the corpus luteum has a negative feedback effect on the pituitary, causing a drop in LH production. As LH supply drops, the corpus luteum degenerates and can no longer produce progesterone and estrogen. In the absence of progesterone, the endometrium dries and becomes loose and unstable. By the twenty-eighth day of the cycle, the endometrium is unable to be contained within the uterus, and the menstrual flow begins, which marks the beginning of the next menstrual month.

Table 6.3 summarizes and correlates the timing of the uterine, ovarian, and other changes occurring during the menstrual cycle. Table 6.4 looks at the menstrual cycle from the perspective of the hormones that control the cycle and their effects at different points during the cycle.

Table 6.3 Uterine, Ovarian, and Other Changes and Their Timing during the Menstrual Cycle.

Day 1–5	Uterus:	Menstrual flow; shedding of endometrium and small amount of blood
	Breasts:	Reduction in swelling, feelings of fullness, sensitivity, and tenderness; Day 5 is good time to do breast self-examination for cancer
Day 1–7	Brain:	GnRF from hypothalamus stimulates secretion of FSH and LH by pituitary
	Ovary:	FSH stimulates development of follicle and secretion of estrogen
	Uterus:	Menstrual flow, days 1–5; Day 6 begins repair and regrowth of endometrium
	Breasts:	By day 7, breasts reach their minimum size
Day 8–12	Ovary:	Increasing estrogen secretion
	Brain:	Decline in FSH and LH secretion because of negative feedback of estrogen
	Uterus:	Growth in endometrium is stimulated by estrogen
Day 13–14	Brain:	Surge in levels of LH and FSH secretion as result of positive feedback of estrogen
	Ovary:	LH surge on day 14 causes ovulation
Day 15–24	Ovary:	Corpus luteum secretes increasing amounts of progesterone and estrogen
	Brain:	Decline in level of LH caused by negative feedback of progesterone
	Uterus:	Progesterone produces changes making uterus ready to accept a fertilized ovum (if fertilization takes place)
Day 25–28	Ovary:	Degeneration of corpus luteum and decline in progesterone and estrogen
	Uterus:	Because of lower levels of progesterone, degenerative changes start taking place in endometrium, which will lead to menstrual flow
	Breasts:	Increasing feelings of fullness and swelling and sensitive to touch

Table 6.4 Hormonal Actions during the Menstrual Cycle.

Hormone	Source	Actions of Hormone
GnRF	Hypothalamus	Stimulates pituitary to secrete FSH and LH above a basal level
FSH	Pituitary	Stimulates ovary to develop mature follicle (with ovum); follicle produces increasingly high levels of estrogen
Estrogen	Ovary (follicle)	Causes rapid growth of endometrium of uterus; causes the breast sensitivity that often accompanies menstrual flow to disappear; rising level of estrogen has negative feedback (inhibiting) effect on hypothalamus and GnRF; GnRF output reduced, and secretion of FSH and LH inhibited; very high level of estrogen *reverses* effect on hypothalamus, stimulating it to suddenly release large dose of GnRF; GnRF causes pituitary to release sudden enormous surge of FSH and LH
LH	Pituitary	Surge of LH stimulates follicle to break open and discharge ovum and follicular fluid (containing estrogen); follicle converted into corpus luteum, which secretes estrogen and gradually increasing amounts of progesterone
Progesterone	Ovary (corpus luteum)	Causes endometrium to become thick, spongy, glandular, and receptive to a fertilized ovum (zygote); causes breast engorgement (may be sensitive or painful); has a *negative* feedback on pituitary, causing a drop in LH production, which results in the degeneration of the corpus luteum and a drop in progesterone and estrogen production; lack of progesterone initiates menstrual flow

1. Summarize the events of the uterine and ovarian cycles and explain how these events correspond to each other.
2. Outline the hormonal effects that control the menstrual cycle. Which hormones are released from which source? What effect does each hormone have?

Hormonal Control of Milk Production in the Breasts

Under normal circumstances, the breasts of an adult woman do not produce milk because the hormone **prolactin,** which is needed to stimulate the mammary glands to produce milk, is not being secreted by the pituitary. As we discussed in chapter 5, the hypothalamus of the brain is usually responsible for whatever the pituitary secretes or does not secrete. In this case, the hypothalamus releases a substance called **prolactin-inhibiting factor (PIF),** which inhibits the pituitary gland's secretion of prolactin.

lactation
(lak-ta'shun)

colostrum
(kō-los'trum)

oxytocin
(ok"se-to'sin)

During pregnancy, the high levels of estrogen and progesterone that the placenta produces further inhibit (via PIF) the release of prolactin. Placental estrogen and progesterone also stimulate further development of the breasts and mammary glands. During this period, the breasts often double in size, and the mammary glands become capable of secreting milk (**lactation**).

Following childbirth and the expulsion of the placenta, the maternal blood levels of estrogen and progesterone decline very rapidly. The rapid decrease in progesterone levels stops the secretion of PIF by the hypothalamus, which then makes it possible for the pituitary to secrete prolactin.

Prolactin stimulates the mammary glands of a new mother to secrete large quantities of milk. This hormonal effect does not occur until two to three days after childbirth. In the meantime, the mammary glands secrete a fluid called **colostrum,** which flows from the breast. Colostrum is similar to milk except that it lacks the fat found in milk. The mechanics of colostrum secretion are not fully understood.

The milk produced under the influence of prolactin does not flow readily from the mammary glands. It must be "ejected" by contraction of specialized cells surrounding the milk ducts. This ejection of milk is caused by the hormone **oxytocin.** Oxytocin is released during the delivery process (it produces contraction of the uterine muscles, which cause delivery) and is present in the bloodstream for a few days following delivery. After delivery, an infant's sucking of the nipple or areola signals the hypothalamus to secrete, and the pituitary gland to release, oxytocin into the bloodstream. The oxytocin travels to the breasts and stimulates the ductile system to contract. Consequently, milk is ejected into a suckling infant's mouth in about thirty seconds. This is called the milk "letdown." Some women have found that their emotions, such as their feelings when they hear their baby crying, can also signal the hypothalamus to release oxytocin and cause milk letdown.

As long as milk is sucked from the breasts, prolactin and oxytocin continue to be released, and milk continues to be produced and let down. If milk is not removed from the breasts regularly, the hypothalamus stops the secretion of prolactin, and within about one week, the mammary glands lose their capacity to produce milk. Oxytocin production ceases, and PIF levels increase, stopping the production of prolactin.

While the mammary glands are actively producing milk, the breast-feeding mother's menstrual cycle seems to be inhibited. Although it is possible for a woman to become pregnant while breast-feeding, usually she will not become pregnant during the period she is supplying all of the infant's nutritional needs. The mechanisms responsible for this effect are not completely understood, but it is thought that prolactin suppresses the release of FSH and LH from the pituitary gland. In any event, menstrual cycles may not begin for some time following the birth of an infant who is breast-fed.

In addition to delaying menstrual cycles, breast-feeding usually assists the uterus in returning to its normal size. Oxytocin, which as we've already discussed stimulates milk letdown, also causes contractions of uterine muscles while the mother is breast-feeding. These contractions aid the uterus in returning to its pre-pregnancy size and condition.

Table 6.5 outlines hormonal control of breastmilk production.

Table 6.5   Hormonal Control of Breastmilk Production.

Hormones	Hormonal Actions
Estrogen	Responsible for development of nipples, areolae, and ducts within the breast
Progesterone	Involved in development of mammary glands where milk is produced
Prolactin	Stimulates mammary glands of breasts to produce milk after childbirth
Oxytocin	Causes contraction of cells around milk-producing glands which "squeeze" milk into ducts and out of nipples (termed milk letdown); also causes contractions of uterine muscles
Prolactin-inhibiting factor (PIF)	Inhibits pituitary gland from releasing prolactin; normally present in the body

Sequence of Events

1. Toward the end of pregnancy, the levels of estrogen, progesterone, and PIF are *very* high. The placenta is responsible for most of the estrogen and progesterone levels.

2. Very high levels of progesterone inhibit actual milk production. The level of progesterone *falls very rapidly* after the placenta is expelled; thus the inhibition of milk production is gone. Prolactin from the pituitary then causes the breasts to fill with milk.

3. Infant suckling of the nipple signals the hypothalamus to secrete, and the pituitary to release, oxytocin. Oxytocin stimulates milk letdown.

4. Regular suckling signals the hypothalamus to reduce its usual output of PIF, thus causing increased flow of prolactin and enhancing regular milk production. Milk production stops if milk is not removed regularly from the breasts.

1. If a breast-feeding mother is separated from her baby for two weeks, is it likely that at the end of the two weeks she will still be able to breast-feed her baby? Why or why not? What would your answer be if the mother had regularly removed milk from her breasts with a breast pump during those two weeks?

2. Researchers believe that during the months that a woman breast-feeds her baby, prolactin suppresses the release of FSH and LH from the pituitary gland. What effect does this have on the woman's reproductive processes?

3. Alcohol inhibits oxytocin release by the pituitary. What problem might a breast-feeding mother expect if she drinks to excess?

The thought of being stripped of all of my female organs would destroy me, but Mom is handling it fairly well. She figures it's better to live healthy without 'em than to allow the cancer to spread. I know that without surgery Mom could have died, and we talked about the fact that this type of surgery is now done only when absolutely necessary. She feels confident that they got all of her cancer with the operation.

I realize how important it is for her to have me support her during this time. We've been going for long walks, talking about the future. I know she would like to see me marry and have children. I would like that, too, someday. I like to think that my girls will have the opportunity to know their grandmother, because, without her, I probably never would have made it.

Summary

1.   The external sex organs or genitals of the female are often referred to collectively as the vulva. The mons veneris is the pad of fat over the pubic bone and is covered by pubic hair in the adult female. The labia majora are longitudinal folds of tissue that extend back from either side of the mons and enclose and protect the other external reproductive structures. The labia minora are located beneath the labia majora and protect the vaginal and urethral openings. The area between the labia minora is the vestibule. The vagina and urethra open into the vestibule. The perineum is the smooth skin that extends from the vaginal opening to the anus. The clitoris is a small, sensitive projection at the anterior end of the vestibule, where the labia merge together.

2.   The internal sex organs or genitals of the female consist of the vagina, the uterus, the fallopian tubes, and the ovaries. The vagina is a tubular, muscular organ that extends upward and inward from the vestibule toward the small of the back. The vagina receives the male penis during sexual intercourse, conveys the menstrual flow to the outside of the body, and serves as a birth canal for the fetus. The uterus is a hollow, thick, pear-shaped organ whose function is to receive the embryo and nurture it until the time of the child's birth. The narrow lower third of the uterus consists of the tubular cervix, which extends down into the vagina. The two fallopian tubes are each about four inches in length and extend from both sides of the uterus. Fertilization of the ovum usually takes place in a fallopian tube. Each of the two ovaries is located at the end of a fallopian tube. The ovaries have the dual functions of producing and releasing ova and the female sex hormones.

3.   The female breasts are secondary sex characteristics and not organs of the female reproductive system. Breast structures include the nipple, the areola, mammary glands, milk ducts, and fatty tissues. Variations in the size and shape of the breasts among women are due primarily to the amount of fatty tissue in the breasts.

4.   The menstrual cycle is the female reproductive cycle that is characterized by the maturation and ovulation of an ovum each reproductive month and the prepa-

ration of the uterus to receive a fertilized ovum. If the ovum is not fertilized, the menstrual cycle concludes with the onset of menstruation. The first menstruation signals menarche; the cessation of menstruation, usually between the ages of forty-five and fifty, signals menopause.

5.   The menstrual cycle averages twenty-eight days in length, although most women's cycles vary considerably from one month to the next.

6.   Many mood and emotional changes seem to be closely related to the different days of the menstrual cycle, although they have not always been verified in human studies. Most of these changes probably result from a combination of the physical makeup of the woman involved; hormonal, prostaglandal, and other cyclic chemical changes; social attitudes and childhood training; and emotional stability.

7.   The physical discomforts and emotional mood swings that many women experience just prior to menstruation are all gathered under the label premenstrual syndrome (PMS). Most women suffer at least one symptom of PMS every month. No one treatment is effective for all women.

8.   Many women are afflicted by severe menstrual cramps each month. A number of prostaglandin-inhibiting drugs can now eliminate menstrual cramps for the vast majority of women suffering such pain.

9.   A female child's body remains sexually immature until GnRF is secreted from the hypothalamus of the brain. GnRF drains into the pituitary gland and stimulates the pituitary to release FSH and LH. FSH and LH, in turn, stimulate the female's body to secrete several different sex hormones, including androgens, the female sex hormones estrogen and progesterone, and a number of different prostaglandins.

10.   A prostaglandin signals the hypothalamus each month to begin the menstrual cycle. GnRF flows into the pituitary gland, and the pituitary increases the level of FSH and LH in circulation. FSH triggers follicular development in the ovary. The developing follicles secrete estrogen into the bloodstream. On day twelve to fourteen, a mature follicle releases its ovum through ovulation. After ovulation, the ovary begins secreting progesterone, which prepares the uterus for implantation if fertilization occurs. If there is no fertilization, the progesterone has a negative feedback effect on the pituitary, causing a drop in LH production. When the LH supply drops, the corpus luteum can no longer produce progesterone and estrogen. The lack of progesterone causes the endometrium to become unstable, and the menstrual flow begins.

11.   Under normal circumstances, the breasts of an adult woman do not produce milk. Following childbirth, however, the rapid decrease in progesterone levels stops the secretion of prolactin-inhibiting factor (PIF) by the hypothalamus. The pituitary then secretes prolactin, which stimulates the mammary glands in the female breasts to secrete large quantities of milk. The hormone oxytocin stimulates milk letdown.

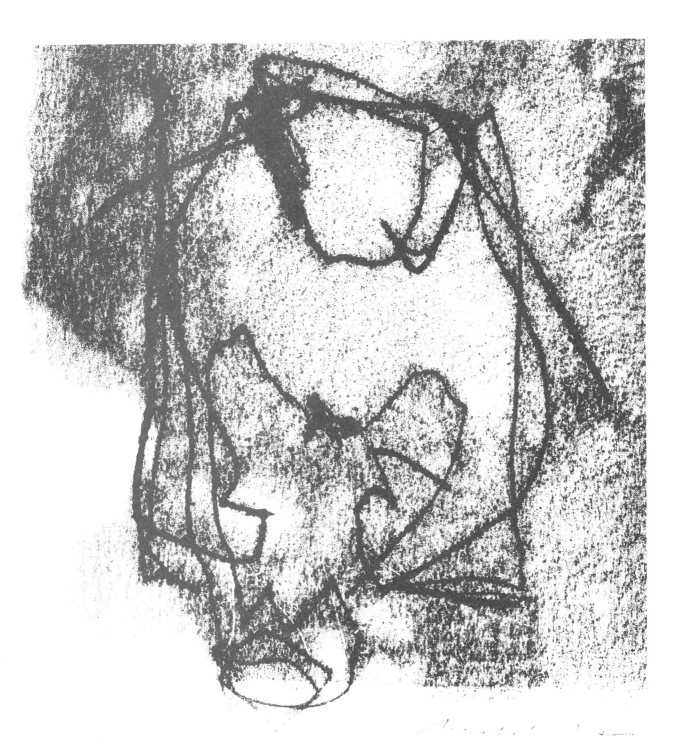

Cells
DNA/Cell Mitosis/Chromosomes/Meiosis

Inheritance of Sexuality
*Genetic Determination of Sexuality/Sex Chromosome
Abnormalities*

Embryonic Gonadal Development
Testicular Development/Ovarian Development

Prenatal Development of Sex Organs and Structures
*Development of Internal Genitals/Development of External
Genitals/Development of Abnormal Genitals*

Tests to Determine Sexual Status

Breast (Mammary Gland) Development

Prenatal Sexual Development of the Brain

"All right, Mrs. Jones, take a deep breath and . . . *push!* Good, slowly and push! C'mon, push hard! Keep coming, good, the baby's coming . . . one more good push . . . I've got the head, let's bring out the shoulders. Fine!"

"Oh, honey, she's beautiful! You did terrific. She's got lots of hair and is she ever looking around! Welcome to the world, Mary Lynne!"

"Er . . . wait a minute, Mr. Jones. I wouldn't jump so quickly to call the child a girl."

"What do you mean? She *is* a girl, I can see that! She doesn't have the equipment that it takes for a boy. What else would I call her?"

"Yes, doctor, what do you mean? I just got done carrying her for nine months and pushing her out for fourteen hours, how can *you* not know what sex she is? I don't think we're asking too much. We just want to know what she is. Is there something wrong? Is she deformed?"

"Mrs. Jones, there is nothing wrong with your baby. It's fine. Right at the moment, however, the genitals are swollen, and it is difficult to tell for sure which sex your baby is. We'll do a couple of tests, and we should be certain very soon. . . ."

deoxyribonucleic
(de-ok''se-ri''bo-nu-kle'ik)

mitosis
(mi-to'sis)

Our maleness or femaleness is strongly influenced by two very different forces, commonly referred to as *nature* and *nurture*. Nature includes biological and genetic factors, while nurture involves our learning experiences and the environment in which we live. The extent to which each of these forces determines our maleness or femaleness is an unresolved controversy (known as the nature versus nurture controversy), but it does seem that the two cannot be mutually exclusive.

In this chapter, we explore the "nature" aspect of our sexual development, including the genetic determination of our sexuality and the prenatal (before birth) development of our sex organs and structures. We also look at the prenatal sexual development of the brain and how this can affect us during and after puberty. Some of the "nurturing" aspects of our maleness and femaleness are examined in chapters 11 through 14.

Cells

A **cell** is the basic unit of life. Each single cell is an individual living structure, and each of us is an organized accumulation of cells. We are able to function because every one of our cells "knows" what it is and what function it is to perform for us.

DNA

Of the many compounds present in cells, the most important is **DNA (deoxyribonucleic acid)** (see figure 7.1). DNA molecules store genetic (inheritable) information in chemical "codes," called **genes**. The genes in DNA molecules "tell" our cells how to construct the many chemicals needed for all of the functions that occur in our cells and our body. DNA molecules also have the unique ability to duplicate themselves during cell mitosis.

Figure 7.1 DNA, the chemical molecule that stores genetic information. "Genes" are DNA.

Cell Mitosis

Mitosis, or cell reproduction, involves the dividing of one cell into two new cells. During mitosis, all of the DNA molecules within the parent cell are duplicated, and each of the two newly formed cells receives one exact copy of the parent cell's DNA molecules. Each of the two new cells must have copies of all of the original DNA molecules of the parent cell to survive, mature, and function. These duplicated DNA molecules contain the same genes as the original molecules in the parent cell, and thus the two offspring cells are genetically identical to each other and to their single parent cell. In this way, inheritance is passed from one cell to another.

The newly formed cells proceed to grow, mature, and differentiate (form into the type of cell they will be in the body, such as skin cell, muscle cell, and so on). Or, these new cells prepare to repeat mitosis to form new generations of cells as they are needed for repair and replacement.

karyotype
(kar′e-o-tĭp)

All of the cells that make up our body come about through the cellular reproduction of mitosis, and mitosis occurs continuously within the tissues of our body.

Chromosomes

During cell mitosis, the DNA molecules of the parent cell are contained within rod-like structures called **chromosomes.** The body cells of normal human males and females contain forty-six chromosomes (two sets of twenty-three chromosomes). Chromosomes act as "messengers" during mitosis and carry duplicated DNA molecules from the parent cell to the two new cells. Therefore, if the parent cell is a human cell, each of the two new cells will end up with forty-six chromosomes.

Figure 7.2a is a photograph taken during mitosis that shows the forty-six chromosomes of a human cell. Figures 7.2b and 7.2c are charts, called **karyotypes,** of the chromosomes of a male cell and a female cell. In karyotypes, the chromosomes are arranged and classified according to the size and shape of the chromosomes.

Figure 7.2 Human chromosomes. (a) The forty-six chromosomes at random. (b) Chromosomes of a male—note X and Y at lower right. (c) Chromosomes of a female—note two X chromosomes at lower right.

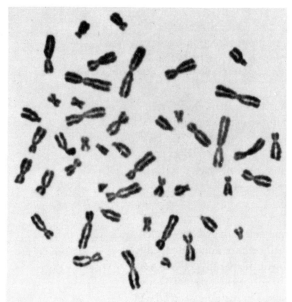

(a)

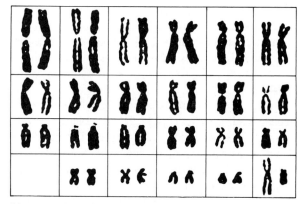

(b)

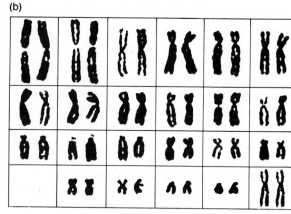

(c)

gamete
(gam'et)

meiosis
(mi-o'sis)

zygote
(zi'gōt)

oogenesis
(o''o-jen'ē-sis)

As we can see by the karyotypes in figures 7.2b and 7.2c, the chromosomes of human males and females are basically similar. All of the numbered chromosomes (called **autosomes**) in the male and female karyotypes are identical. The **sex chromosomes,** however, are distinguishable by size from males to females. The male cell contains an X chromosome and a smaller Y chromosome (XY), while the female cell contains two large X chromosomes (XX).

Meiosis

Human reproduction involves the fusion (merger) of two *sex* cells known as **gametes;** thus, it is known as **sexual reproduction.** In sexually reproducing animals, such as humans, a special population of cells produces the two gametes. In the male, the gamete is the sperm; in the female, it is the ovum.

Gamete-forming cells are found only in the **gonads**—the testes of the male and the ovaries of the female—and undergo a reduction in the number of their chromosomes through a process known as **meiosis.** During meiosis, the DNA content of the cell is *halved.* Meiosis occurs only during **spermatogenesis** (formation of sperm) and **oogenesis** (formation of ova).

In humans, meiosis results in the formation of four cells. Each of these cells contains twenty-three chromosomes. In a male, these four cells develop into four sperm. In a female, these four cells develop into three polar bodies (which die and dissolve) and one ovum.

Whereas the original parent cell contained two of each type of chromosome (see figure 7.2), each sperm or ovum contains a set of single-stranded chromosomes consisting of one of each type (see figure 7.3). These single-stranded chromosomes of the sperm or ovum contain only one of the two sets of genes needed to direct the inheritance of the individual. For development to take place, a sperm and an ovum must fuse together so that the cell contains a complete set of genes.

The gametes fuse together through fertilization. A human sperm containing twenty-three chromosomes penetrates a human ovum containing twenty-three chromosomes. The cell resulting from the union of these two gametes contains forty-six chromosomes and is called the **zygote.** All other cells of this new individual develop by mitosis from the zygote.

A simple example illustrating the results of meiosis involves the color of our eyes. The sperm or ovum that results from meiosis carries only one gene for each trait, such as eye color. When the sperm and ovum unite through fertilization, the two genes necessary for the development of each trait are then usually present. People with green eyes inherited one gene for green eyes from each parent. Similarly, people with blue eyes received one gene for blue eye color from each parent. People with brown eyes, however, received one gene for brown eye color from *either* parent. The other gene (either for green, blue, or gray eye color) only influenced the amount of brown pigment produced and the shade of brown.

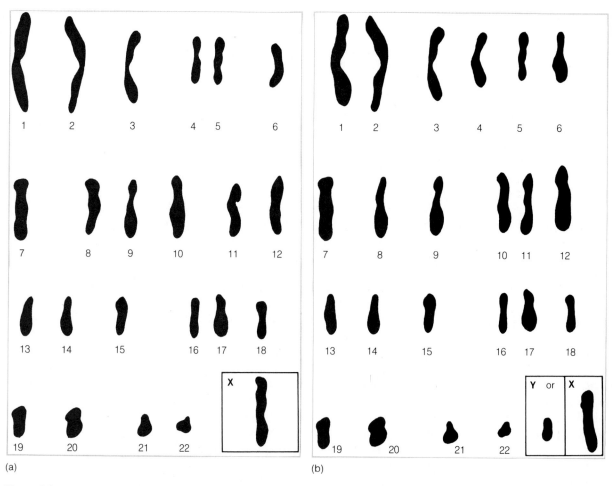

Figure 7.3 Karyotypes of single-stranded chromosomes as they would appear in an ovum or sperm after meiosis. (a) Chromosomes in an ovum. (b) Chromosomes in a sperm.

The process of meiosis assures us that each new generation will be genetically varied from previous generations. Because the sperm and the ovum each contribute only half of their genes, the individual that results from fertilization of the ovum by the sperm has a genetic combination that is different from both of the parents.

1. Explain how inheritance is passed from one cell to another.
2. Where does mitosis take place in the body? What does mitosis produce?
3. Where does meiosis take place in the body? What does meiosis produce?
4. Can you explain how inheritance was passed from your parents to you?

embryo
(em'bre-o)

Inheritance of Sexuality

We have seen how all humans receive their inheritance in two equal portions—half from the male via the sperm and half from the female via the ovum. These two cells fuse together through fertilization to form the first cell (zygote) of the new individual. Thus, the male and female have "reproduced" themselves in a new person.

During the remainder of this chapter, we examine how maleness and femaleness are inherited and how the tissues of the body are modified into male and female types.

Genetic Determination of Sexuality

As discussed earlier in the chapter, the sex chromosomes in a female cell are two relatively large X chromosomes (XX). The sex chromosomes in a male cell consist of one large X chromosome and a smaller Y chromosome (XY). Meiosis ensures that each ovum or sperm has only *one* sex chromosome—the ovum contains one X chromosome while a sperm can contain *either* an X chromosome or a Y chromosome.

The sex of an offspring is determined by the sperm that fertilizes the ovum. If the sperm is carrying an X chromosome, the fusing of the sperm (X) and the ovum (X) produces an XX combination that results in the development of a female. If the sperm is carrying a Y chromosome, the fusing of the sperm (Y) and the ovum (X) produces an XY combination that results in the development of a male.

What causes this differentiation in development? Research has shown that if all, or part, of a Y chromosome is present in the cells of a developing **embryo** (the unborn child during the first eight weeks of development after conception), the embryo develops testes. If the Y chromosome is absent from the cells of the developing embryo, the embryo develops ovaries. Thus, the *presence* of a Y chromosome causes a male to be produced, while the *absence* of a Y chromosome causes a female to be produced. The X chromosome appears to have no effect on initial sexual determination.

The Y chromosome is small (see figure 7.3b) and contains very little DNA to pass on heredity. For that reason, scientists believe that it is unlikely that all of the genes needed to develop organs as complex as the testes are located on the Y chromosome. The genes that cause the testes to be produced may actually lie on one, or more, of the autosomal chromosomes or on the X chromosomes. The Y chromosome probably contains a "switching" or "controller" gene that regulates the expression of some other chromosome, or chromosomes, needed to produce the testes.

The precise mechanisms by which the Y chromosome coordinates the development of the testes are far from clear but it has been established that the sex hormones are *not* involved. Injecting male hormones into a female mammalian fetus will not produce testes. Similarly, injection of female hormones into a male mammalian fetus will not suppress testes formation or produce ovaries.

Sex Chromosome Abnormalities

Occasionally, the union of ovum and sperm does not result in the usual combination of forty-six chromosomes, including two sex chromosomes (XX or XY). An individual may be born with one sex chromosome missing or with extra sex chromosomes, genetic combinations that result in congenital sexual disorders.

Table 7.1 catalogs the various sex chromosome disorders and provides descriptions of the characteristics of the individuals born with these abnormalities. Turner's syndrome and Klinefelter's syndrome are among the most widely recognized of such chromosomal disorders.

Turner's Syndrome

Turner's syndrome individuals have only forty-five chromosomes in each cell instead of the normal forty-six (figure 7.4). They have a normal number of autosomes (numbered chromosomes) but only one sex chromosome—an X. Thus, individuals with Turner's syndrome are said to have an XO karyotype (the "O" represents zero).

Figure 7.4 Turner's syndrome. (a) Appearance. (b) Karyotype—note single X chromosome.

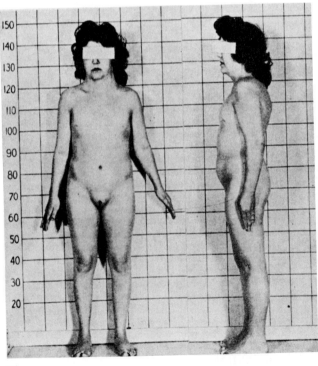

(a)

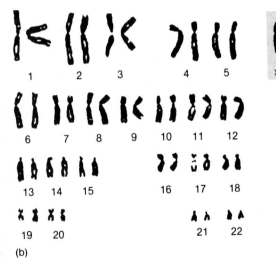

(b)

Table 7.1 Effect of Human Sex Chromosomes on Development of the Gonad and Sexual Differentiation.

Total Number of Chromosomes	Auto-somes	Number of Sex Chromosomes	Gonad Produced	Sex of Individual	Abnormality Produced	Description
45	44	+ X	Ovary	Female	Turner's syndrome	Individuals have no ovaries, are sterile, and external female genitals remain infantile; no pubertal development; no menstrual cycle; rarely attain adult height of more than five feet.
46	44	+ XX	Ovary	Female	Normal	
47	44	+ XXX	Ovary	Female	Triple X syndrome or Super-female	Individuals are not exceptionally feminine, have no sexual abnormalities, and many have children; most are mentally retarded.
48 and 49	44	+ XXXX and XXXXX	Ovary	Female		These females are known to exist; no known consistent pattern of traits; mental retardation seems to increase markedly as number of X chromosomes increases.
69	66	+ XXX	Ovary	Female	Lethal	Individuals do not live.

Total Number of Chromosomes	Auto-somes	Number of Sex Chromosomes	Gonad Produced	Sex of Individual	Abnormality Produced	Description
46	44	+ XY	Testis	Male	Normal	
47	44	+ XXY	Testis	Male	Klinefelter's syndrome	Internal and external genitals are male but testes are very small and do not produce sperm; underdeveloped pubic, facial, and body hair; enlarged breasts; reduced sexual drive; possible mental retardation.
48 and 49	44	+ XXXY and XXXXY	Testis	Male	Variations of Klinefelter's syndrome	Same clinical conditions as Klinefelter's syndrome, but individuals are more severely affected, and severe mental retardation is common.
47	44	+ XYY	Testis	Male	XYY syndrome	Individuals are tall (six feet and over); may have unusual sexual preferences, often homosexual; sperm production often reduced (may be sterile).
69	66	+ XXY	Testis	Male	Lethal	Individuals do not live.

Turner's syndrome can arise in several possible ways. The most common possibility is that the fertilized ovum never contained more than one X chromosome (Moody 1975). Another possibility is that the fertilized ovum "lost" an X or Y chromosome at the beginning of embryonic development. Also, some Turner's syndrome individuals have two X (XX) chromosomes in their cells, but one of the Xs is defective and nonfunctional.

Persons with Turner's syndrome have normal female external genitals, but they lack functional ovaries. Their ovaries are either missing entirely or are reduced to what are called "streak ovaries," which are bits of tissue almost completely lacking in oocytes, ova, or gland cells. Interestingly, XO fetuses have normal ovaries until the third month of gestation, at which time the number of potential ova begins to decrease until at puberty all have disappeared. Apparently, one X is sufficient to determine the sex (a female) and that the gonads will be ovaries, but a second X is necessary for normal functioning of the ovaries.

Without functional ovaries, there is no stimulation of normal female growth of the body, no development of the female sex organs and secondary sex characteristics, and no menstrual cycle. Individuals with Turner's syndrome are short in stature (seldom over 4 feet, 9 inches) and also exhibit a variety of other bodily peculiarities throughout life, but they are usually normal in their intellectual development.

Hormonal therapy in a Turner's syndrome individual can induce breast development and menstruation and also can assure maximal height, but is not successful in producing fertility.

Klinefelter's Syndrome

Individuals with **Klinefelter's syndrome** have forty-seven chromosomes in each cell (figure 7.5). There are two X chromosomes (XX) and a Y, producing an XXY configuration in the cells. The commonest manner of origin of XXY cells is an ovum containing two X chromosomes being fertilized by a normal sperm containing a Y chromosome, but this condition also can occur when a sperm containing both X and Y chromosomes fertilizes a normal ovum.

Since the Y is the male-determining chromosome, XXY individuals are males and have male internal and external genitals. Yet, the two Xs are not without effect. Males with Klinefelter's syndrome have very small testes that do not produce sperm. Many have femininelike enlarged breasts and reduced sexual drive. Impotence is common, as is underdeveloped pubic, facial, and body hair. Approximately 25 percent have some degree of mental retardation.

(a)

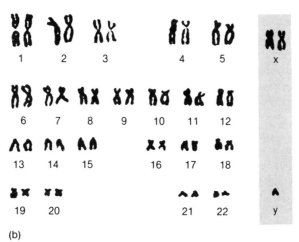

(b)

Figure 7.5 Klinefelter's syndrome. (a) Appearance. (b) Karyotype—note extra X chromosome (XXY).

1. What are the far-reaching consequences of the presence or absence of a Y chromosome in the cells of a developing embryo?
2. What effect does the X chromosome have on initial sexual determination?
3. A normal human cell contains forty-six chromosomes. Describe the chromosomal disorders that result when the total number of chromosomes in a human cell is forty-five or forty-seven.

primordial
(pri-mor′de-al)

Embryonic Gonadal Development

A baby takes about thirty-eight weeks to develop from one cell to a complete individual ready to be born. The development of the complete individual is discussed in chapter 16. In this chapter, we are concerned with the development of the sexual structures.

Up until the third to fourth week of pregnancy, there is no development of the tissues that lead to sexual differentiation (the development of the different sex organs). From the fourth to the sixth week, tissues that can become either testes or ovaries develop within the embryo. The changes necessary for this primordial (primitive or beginning) gonad to become either testes or ovaries do not begin until the sixth week of embryonic growth.

Testicular Development

If a Y chromosome is present in the cells of the developing embryo, its male-determining genes produce and/or control the H-Y antigen, which then initiates the organization and growth of the gonad into the male testes during the sixth week of embryonic development. Some cells organize into the seminiferous cords, which become the seminiferous (sperm-producing) tubules of the adult testes. Some of the cells within these cords will become sperm-producing cells, while others will become Sertoli cells, which influence the formation and development of sperm. Other cells lying between the seminiferous cords develop into the tissues that form and hold the testes together and into hormone-producing cells known as the interstitial (or Leydig) cells.

Ovarian Development

If a Y chromosome is not present in the cells of the developing embryo, then H-Y antigen also is not present, and the cells of the primitive gonad continue to go through mitosis and proliferate until the seventh week of development. Some of these cells then form into small clusters and become primordial follicles of the ovaries. These cells give rise to oocytes (immature ova) later in development. Other cells become the hormone-producing cells of the follicle. Cells that form around the primordial follicles develop into the tissues forming the ovaries.

While *initial* formation of the ovaries is dependent upon the *lack* of a Y chromosome, *complete* ovarian development requires the presence of the two X chromosomes found in most normal women. If the two X chromosomes are not present, a normal number of primordial cells is not produced, and the ovaries do not fully develop. A female with only one X chromosome develops "streak" gonads, which do not function as ovaries.

Müllerian   Wolffian
(mil-e're-an)   (woolf'e-an)

Prenatal Development of Sex Organs and Structures

The main role of the sex chromosomes in sexual development is completed with the establishment of the male testes or the female ovaries in the **fetus** (the unborn child from the ninth week of development until birth). From this point on, the fetus itself directs the rest of the sexual differentiation. In the male, the testes take over and direct the further development of the male body. In the female, the *absence* of male testes allows the development of the reproductive structures of the female.

Hormones from the ovaries are not necessary for the development of female sex organs. But the testes secretes two hormones that are essential for the development of male sex organs. Within the testes, the interstitial cells start to secrete testosterone, and the Sertoli cells begin secreting a hormone called **Müllerian inhibiting hormone.** The presence of these two hormones ensures the development of male sex organs. In the absence of these two hormones, feminine sex organs develop.

Development of Internal Genitals

The internal sex organs of the male or female develop from one of two distinct groups of fetal tissues. One group of cells is called the **Wolffian** (or male) **ducts.** The other group of cells forms the **Müllerian** (or female) **ducts.** As shown in figure 7.6, both of these genital ducts are initially present in all embryos and have the potential to develop into the internal reproductive structures of either sex.

Male Development

The testosterone secreted by the interstitial (Leydig) cells of the testes induces the Wolffian ducts to develop into some of the internal male sex organs—the epididymis, vas deferens, and seminal vesicles. The second testicular hormone, Müllerian inhibiting hormone, secreted by the Sertoli cells, causes the Müllerian ducts (which would produce female sexual organs) to regress and disappear (see figure 7.6).

Female Development

In a female fetus, the lack of testosterone and Müllerian inhibiting hormone causes the Wolffian ducts to regress and disappear. The Müllerian ducts persist, develop, and give rise to the fallopian tubes, uterus, cervix, and possibly the upper part of the vagina (see figure 7.6).

If a male or female mammalian embryo is castrated (gonads surgically removed), the internal sex organs develop in a normal female pattern. This demonstrates that ovarian hormonal activity is not required for development of the internal female sex organs. Female cells seem to have a built-in mechanism for development of the female internal genitals (Johnson and Everitt 1980).

homologous
(ho-mol'o-gus)

Figure 7.6 Prenatal development of internal reproductive structures. During the first week of development, the genital ducts of the embryo are identical and have the potential to develop into the internal reproductive structures of either sex. If both testosterone and Müllerian inhibiting hormone (MIH) are secreted by the fetal testes during the sixth week of development, the Wolffian ducts grow into male structures. If neither hormone is secreted during the sixth week, the Müllerian ducts form female structures.

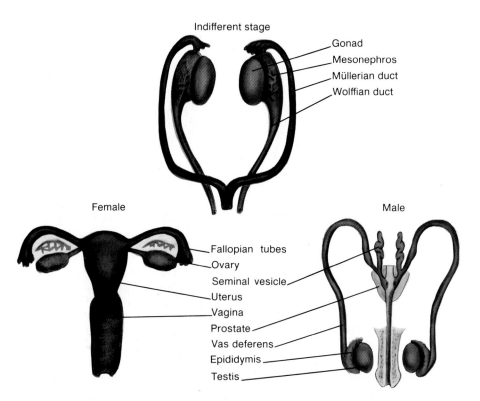

Indifferent stage

Gonad
Mesonephros
Müllerian duct
Wolffian duct

Female

Male

Fallopian tubes
Ovary
Seminal vesicle
Uterus
Vagina
Prostate
Vas deferens
Epididymis
Testis

Development of External Genitals

Unlike the development of the internal genitals, the external genitals of both males and females develop from the same embryonic tissues. These embryonic tissues take the form of folds and swellings and develop into female structures, male structures, and structures common to both males and females, such as the bladder, the perineum, and the folds surrounding the anus. Differentiation begins at about the sixth week after conception and is completed by the twelfth week.

Because the female and male external genitals develop from similar embryonic tissues, some structures of each sex are said to have homologous (corresponding) counterparts in the opposite sex. That is, the female clitoris is considered to be homologous to the male penis. Table 7.2 shows the female and male structures that are homologous.

Table 7.2 Homologous Sex Organs.

Female Organs	Male Organs
Glans of clitoris	Glans of penis
Shaft of clitoris	Shaft of penis
Hood of clitoris	Foreskin of penis
Labia majora	Scrotal sac
Labia minora	Underside of penile shaft
Skene's glands	Prostate gland
Bartholin's glands	Cowper's glands
Ovaries	Testes

Male Development

Testosterone from the testes in the male fetus causes the folds and swellings of the embryonic tissues to form into the prostate gland, the Cowper's (bulbourethral) glands, the scrotum, the penis, and the urethral tube within the penis (see figure 7.7).

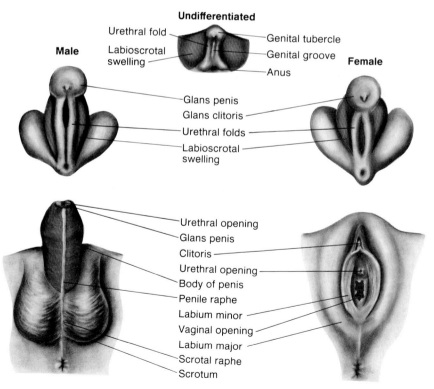

Figure 7.7 Prenatal development of male and female external genitals. Differentiation begins at about the sixth week and is completed by the twelfth week.

Female Development

In the female, the folds and swellings of the embryonic tissues form the Skene's glands, the Bartholin's glands, the vagina, the labia majora and minora, and the clitoris. This development is shown in figure 7.7. If the ovaries of a female mammal are removed, these changes still occur, indicating that, as with the development of female internal genitals, no ovarian hormonal activity is required for the development of these female external sex organs (Johnson and Everitt 1980).

Development of Abnormal Genitals

Without the proper hormones, there may be abnormal sexual development of the fetus. Castration or experimental suppression of testosterone in a developing male mammalian fetus, for example, will result in feminized male external genitals, while exposure of a female mammalian fetus to testosterone will masculinize her external genitals.

Testicular Feminization

The syndrome of testicular feminization is more accurately known as the androgen-insensitivity syndrome and, popularly, as the syndrome of the XY woman (figure 7.8). Typically, the 46,XY chromosome configuration is found in the male. The 46,XY androgen-insensitive fetus differentiates gonads that are testicular except for failure of spermatogenesis. Prenatally, these gonads secrete Müllerian inhibiting

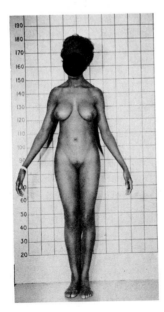

Figure 7.8 A case of the 46,XY androgen-insensitivity or testicular-feminizing syndrome in which the sex of assignment and rearing was as a girl. The syndrome is classified as a form of male hermaphroditism. In the 46,XY woman, or girl, the karyotype is the same as is normal in a male. In prenatal life, the gonads differentiate as testes, except for failure of spermatogenesis. Because all the cells of the body are insensitive to testosterone secreted by the testes, the internal reproductive organs are vestigially incomplete. By contrast, the external genitalia differentiate as those of a female. Under the influence of testicular estrogen, puberty is spontaneously feminizing.

adrenogenital
(ah-dre″no-jen′ĭ-tal)

hormone (MIH), which prevents development of female internal organs. They secrete also a normal male level of testosterone that cannot be used by androgen-dependent cells throughout the body, as they lack the requisite testosterone-binding sites. Hence the masculine differentiation of both the internal and external sexual structures is thwarted. Internally, the Wolffian duct development becomes vestigial. Externally, the genitalia differentiate as those of a female, as always happens when androgen is lacking. The internal genitalia do not undergo female differentiation. The uterus, responding to MIH by becoming vestigial, is represented as a cordlike structure. Menstruation cannot, therefore, be induced by cyclic hormonal treatment following puberty.

Otherwise, puberty is normally feminizing with respect to breast development and body contour. This feminization is caused by estrogen secreted from the testes at the level normal for a male, but without any competitive intracellular uptake of testosterone. Unable to use testosterone, hair follicles fail to grow facial or body hair. Axillary and pubic hair is either absent or sparse. The psychosexual status is female.

In many instances, XY girls pass diagnostically unnoticed until, in the teenage years, they are clinically evaluated for lack of menses. In former times, it used to be thought possible and desirable to conceal the diagnosis from the patient. That practice is now considered unethical. It is not feasible, as patients easily learn about their syndrome by eavesdropping, by having their own sex-chromatin test done in their school biology lab course, or through reading or television programs. Diagnostic self-knowledge enables a patient to consider marriage and adoptive or step-parenthood more pragmatically; and it also helps them to make a rational decision regarding gonadectomy as a precaution against the potential risk of gonadal malignancy later in life.

Adrenogenital Syndrome

The adrenogenital syndrome, also known as congenital virilizing adrenal hyperplasia (CVAH), is prenatal in onset and affects both the 46,XY and the 46,XX fetus. In the latter, the external genitalia are masculinized by the abnormal secretion of androgen, in the place of cortisol, from the adrenocortical glands, for which reason the condition is classified as a form of female hermaphroditism. The most extreme degree of masculinization produces a 46,XX boy (figure 7.9) for whom the genital tubercle has differentiated not into a clitoris, but a penis. The labial folds are fused into an empty scrotum.

When the degree of masculinization is less extreme, the clitoris is hypertrophied, but lacks a urethral tube; there is a mild to moderate degree of labial fusion; and the orifices of the urethra and vagina may not be externally separated, but concealed within a single opening or urogenital sinus. Regardless of whether the ex-

Figure 7.9 A case of the 46,XX adrenogenital syndrome in which the sex of assignment and rearing was as a boy. This syndrome is also known as congenital virilizing adrenal hyperplasia and is classified as a form of female hermaphroditism. In the 46,XX boy, or man, the karyotype is the same as is normal in a female. In prenatal life, the gonads differentiate as ovaries and the internal reproductive organs as female. By contrast, under the influence of abnormal secretion of androgen from the adrenocortical glands, the external genitals differentiate as male.

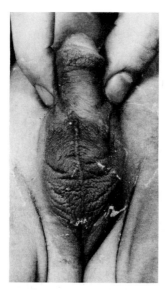

ternal genitalia are fully or partially masculinized, the internal reproductive structures are those of a female.

Failure to diagnose the adrenogenital syndrome neonatally may result in death, if there is an associated hormonal failure of salt-regulation. Diagnosis usually leads to assignment of the baby as a girl, for the genital abnormality can be feminized surgically, and the adrenocortical hormonal anomaly can be corrected by treatment, throughout life, by glucocorticoid (cortisol) replacement therapy. At adolescence, menstruation is usually late in onset, though otherwise normal. Pregnancy is possible, with delivery by Caesarian section. Sexual life and/or fantasy may be either heterosexual, homosexual, or both.

Prior to the discovery of effective hormonal therapy in 1950, individuals with the adrenogenital syndrome invariably had a virilizing puberty with onset as early as eighteen months of age. Today, in a case in which the sex of assignment and rearing is as a 46,XX boy, it is possible to regulate the proper timing of the onset of hormonal puberty, but to allow the body to develop as that of a male in adolescence and in adulthood. In such a case, the individual lives the life of a male, with a male role and identity, sexually, erotically, and otherwise, except for infertility.

1. Compare and contrast fetal testicular development with fetal ovarian development. What conditions must be present before testicular development begins? Before ovarian development begins?
2. Once the fetal testes have developed, the testes direct further sexual development of the male body. Do the fetal ovaries perform the same function in the female body? If not, how do female sex organs develop?
3. Explain how the Wolffian and Müllerian ducts develop into male and female internal reproductive structures. What two hormones are responsible for this development?
4. In chapter 6, we noted that the female clitoris and the male penis were similar in a number of ways. Now that you've learned how these organs develop, can you explain why they are similar?

Tests to Determine Sexual Status

A child's *genetic sex* may not always be the same as the sex indicated by the external genitals at birth. A physician may state with certainty when a baby is born: "It's a boy!" or "It's a girl!" But the physician is not always accurate. For example, if the testes have not descended into the scrotal sac, the scrotum may appear to be female labia. The penis may be diminutive and appear to be a clitoris. The baby may at first glance appear to be a female, while in fact, it is a male. When doubt exists as to the sex of a child, sex-status tests can clear up the confusion.

Simple sex-status tests can tell males from females before birth, at birth, and later on in life. Before birth, these tests can be dangerous to the mother and the child and should only be performed if there is a need greater than just determining the sexual status of the child. At birth and later in life, most of the tests for sexual status are the same and quite simple to perform.

One test involves checking for the presence of a *Y chromosome* in a cell. Cells from the child, or the umbilical cord, are stained with the fluorescent dye quinacrine. This stains the Y chromosome and produces a particularly bright fluorescent glow in the cell nuclei of a male.

Another test, the *sex-chromatin test,* determines the presence of the Barr body, a sizeable DNA-containing structure found almost exclusively in the cells of females. Cells are painlessly scraped from inside the cheek, stained, and examined under a microscope to determine the presence or absence of Barr bodies.

The *"drumstick" test* is another test used to establish sexual status. In this test, blood cells are examined, and an odd little "drumstick" formation projects from the nuclear mass in the type of female white blood cells called neutrophils. Neutrophils from males do not show a "drumstick."

Sex Testing at the Olympics

In 1949, it was observed that a sizeable, DNA-containing clump of material was visible in the nuclei of some cells from a human female but that this clump was absent from the cell nuclei of males. This material is variously called the *nuclear chromatin,* the *sex chromatin,* or the *Barr body.* It is visible in cells from most tissues of the female body and is defined by its plano-convex configuration and its location (just inside of the nuclear membrane). Barr bodies are found in 20 percent or more of the cell nuclei of every normal female and in none (or at most 1 or 2 percent) of the cell nuclei of normal males.

Although there has been a debate about the nature of Barr bodies, it now seems reasonably clear that a Barr body represents most or all of the second X chromosome of the female cell. Normal female cells contain two X chromosomes (XX), and one of these chromosomes is condensed into a form in which it is probably inert and forms the Barr body.

Detection of Barr bodies in cell nuclei is the procedure used at the Olympic Games to verify an athlete's sex. Since Barr bodies are most readily observed in cells lining the interior of the mouth, cells are scraped from the interior of the Olympic athlete's mouth, stained, and then examined under a light microscope. Feulgen stain for DNA is most commonly used, but many other stains are also satisfactory. One to two hundred cells are examined, and the number showing a Barr body are counted and expressed as a percentage. A person with no Barr bodies (or less than 5 percent) is said to be "chromatin negative" and is considered to be a male. A person with 5 percent or more Barr bodies is "chromatin positive" and is considered a female.

The presence or absence of Barr bodies is especially helpful in sexual determination at the Olympics because of the constancy of Barr bodies. They are first visible in the second week of fetal life and are uninfluenced by age, nutrition, disease, drugs, or hormonal status.

The sexual status of the newborn should be determined as soon as possible if the child's sex is not obvious at birth. Early and accurate sex assignment is crucial since it is the first step in the establishment of the child's identity or self-image as a male or female throughout life.

Breast (Mammary Gland) Development

The mammary glands of both sexes show equal development throughout fetal life. Only one functional mammary gland bud develops on each side of the chest wall in human embryos. These buds appear at about the sixth week and complete development by the eighth week of pregnancy. The internal milk ducts continue to proliferate and develop until, by the time of birth, fifteen to twenty-five branches are present in each breast. The nipples and areolae (including the areolar glands) arise during the fifth month of fetal development.

The breasts of boys and girls are identical prior to the onset of puberty. At puberty, however, the breast resumes its development.

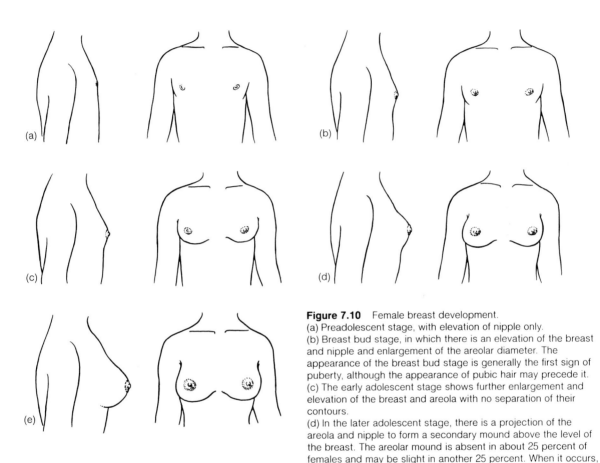

Figure 7.10 Female breast development.
(a) Preadolescent stage, with elevation of nipple only.
(b) Breast bud stage, in which there is an elevation of the breast and nipple and enlargement of the areolar diameter. The appearance of the breast bud stage is generally the first sign of puberty, although the appearance of pubic hair may precede it.
(c) The early adolescent stage shows further enlargement and elevation of the breast and areola with no separation of their contours.
(d) In the later adolescent stage, there is a projection of the areola and nipple to form a secondary mound above the level of the breast. The areolar mound is absent in about 25 percent of females and may be slight in another 25 percent. When it occurs, it often persists well into adulthood.
(e) The mature stage has projection of the nipple due only to recession of the areola to the general contour of the breast.

In the female, the areolar region and nipple start to elevate. During the pubertal and adolescent years, the breasts enlarge rapidly. This enlargement is caused by further internal branching of the milk-producing system and by the deposition of fat. By the late teens, the female breast appears as a hemisphere, with the areola and nipple at its apex. Figure 7.10 shows the different stages of female breast development.

The mammary glands of the male also resume development at puberty, reaching their full development when the male is about twenty years of age. At this time, the male mammary glands are about the same size as a ten or eleven-year-old female's glands.

Prenatal Sexual Development of the Brain

Sexual differences are not restricted to the sex organs. Just as the fetal genitals take on a masculine or feminine appearance, depending upon the presence or absence of testosterone, the fetal brain becomes masculinized if testosterone is present or remains feminized if testosterone is not present.

The masculinizing effect of testosterone in the developing embryo or fetus appears to be exerted upon the hypothalamus of the brain (Gersh and Gersh 1981). Certain areas of the hypothalamus, such as the preoptic area, show distinct anatomical differences between the sexes. Also, these differences can be altered by manipulation of testosterone.

The consequences of sexual differentiation in the fetal brain become evident during and after puberty. Physiologically, the brain differentiation influences cyclic sex hormone production, menstrual cycles, and cyclic fertility in the female, while it has a role in preserving the relatively constant level of sex hormone production and fertility in the male.

Psychologically and behaviorally, the brain differences may have some significance in gender identity (self-awareness of our identity or self-image as a male or female) and role identity (self-awareness of our behavior as a male or female) later in life but do not play as big a role in gender identity and role identity as the way in which we are reared (also see chapter 11).

If the correct hormones are present during and after puberty, the prenatal brain differentiation may not be at all important in gender and role identity. For example, individuals with female adrenogenital syndrome, commonly called the XX-male, have adrenal glands that produce excessive amounts of testosterone. The testosterone masculinizes the brain and also results in the appearance of male external genitals. But surgery, hormone therapy, and being treated as a female after birth will produce proper gender and role identity as a female.

Thus, prenatal development in the brain sets the stage for physiological and behavioral patterns that develop later in life, but proper hormones and cultural elements are influential throughout life.

---

1. If in the delivery room you were told that your newborn baby was a girl, how would you handle it six weeks later if your doctor now informed you that tests showed that your baby was actually a boy?
2. How much of our maleness or femaleness do you think is determined by nature (chromosomes, hormones, and brain differentiation) and how much is determined by nurture (learning and environment)?

"Mr. and Mrs. Jones, thank you for being so patient. I hope you weren't too set on the name Mary Lynne because you are now the proud parents of a very healthy baby boy. He gave us a bit of a surprise there at the beginning, but after checking the results of some sex identity tests that we ran, there is no doubt that your baby is a boy."

"Is he going to be normal? I mean, I didn't even see a penis."

"The male penis and the female clitoris are very similar sex organs. Sometimes, the clitoris may be swollen and look like a penis, or the penis may be rather small and sunk in at the beginning, looking as if it weren't even there."

"You're absolutely sure he's a boy? There's no mistake?"

"Don't worry, Mr. Jones. The boy will grow up fine. It will just take a few weeks for everything to settle into place. He'll have the same equipment as any other baby boy."

"I guess we should thank you, doctor. We could have called everyone and told them it was a girl. Then we would really have a problem to deal with. Thank you."

Summary

1. A cell is the basic unit of life. Each cell is an individual living structure, and each of us is an organized accumulation of cells.

2. DNA (deoxyribonucleic acid) molecules in cells store genetic information in chemical "codes" called genes. The genes in DNA molecules "tell" our cells how to construct the chemicals needed for life. DNA molecules duplicate themselves during cell mitosis.

3. Mitosis involves the dividing of one cell into two new cells. During mitosis, duplicate DNA is carried from the parent cell into the two new cells. Thus, the two offspring cells are genetically identical to each other and to their single parent cell.

4. Chromosomes are rodlike structures that act as "messengers" during mitosis and carry duplicated DNA molecules from the parent cell to the two new cells. The body cells of normal males and females contain forty-six chromosomes (two sets of twenty-three chromosomes). Karyotypes of male and female chromosomes differ only in that the cells of a male contain one X and one Y chromosome (XY) and the cells of a female contain two X chromosomes (XX).

5. Special cells within the gonads undergo meiosis and become gametes. The male gamete is the sperm; the female gamete is the ovum. During meiosis, the DNA content of the cell is halved so that the sperm and ovum each contain one set of twenty-three chromosomes. The sperm and ovum fuse during fertilization and form one cell (the zygote), which then contains the two sets of twenty-three chromosomes (forty-six total chromosomes). The zygote then undergoes mitosis to produce all future cells of the new individual.

6. The sex of an offspring is determined by the sperm that fertilizes the ovum. If the sperm is carrying an X chromosome, a female will develop. If the sperm is carrying a Y chromosome, a male will develop. The *presence* of a Y chromosome causes a male to be produced, while the *absence* of a Y chromosome causes a female to be produced. The X chromosome appears to have no effect on initial sexual determination. Precise mechanisms by which the Y chromosome coordinates the development of testes are far from clear.

7. Occasionally, the union of ovum and sperm results in an individual with one sex chromosome missing or with extra sex chromosomes. Turner's syndrome and Klinefelter's syndrome are among the most widely recognized of such chromosomal disorders.

8. During the sixth week of embryonic development, the Y chromosome's male-determining genes cause the developing gonad to form into male testes. Without a Y chromosome, the developing gonad continues to develop until the seventh week, at which time it starts to form female ovaries. Full ovarian development is dependent upon the cells of a female containing two X chromosomes (XX).

9. From this point on, the developing fetus itself directs the rest of the sexual differentiation. In the male, hormones from the testes direct development of both internal and external genitals. In the female, no hormones are needed for the development of either the internal or external genitals. Female cells seem to have a built-in mechanism for development.

10. Without the proper hormones, there may be abnormal sexual development of the fetus. Suppression of testosterone in a male fetus will result in feminized male external genitals (testicular feminization syndrome). Exposure of a female fetus to testosterone will masculinize her external genitals (female andrenogenital syndrome).

11. A child's genetic sex may not always be the same as the sex indicated by the external genitals at birth. Several sex status tests, however, can determine the sex of the individual relatively easily. Early and accurate sex assignment is important since it is the first step in establishing a child's sexual identity.

12. The mammary glands of both sexes show equal development throughout fetal life and remain identical until puberty, at which time they differentiate.

13. The fetal brain becomes masculinized if testosterone is present or remains feminized if testosterone is not present. Sexual differentiation in the fetal brain becomes evident during and after puberty when the brain differentiation influences cyclic sex hormone production, menstrual cycles, and cyclic fertility in the female, and has a role in preserving the relatively constant level of sex hormone production and fertility in the male. Brain differences also may have some significance in gender identity and role identity, which may be modified by hormones present during puberty. Thus, prenatal development in the brain sets the stage for physiological and behavioral patterns that develop later in life, but proper hormones are influential throughout life.

Sexual Desire

The Sexual Response Cycle

Excitement Phase/Plateau Phase/Orgasm Phase/ Resolution Phase

"Traps" in the Sexual Response Cycle

Differences in Response Patterns
The Male Refractory Period/Variability in Female Responses/Multiple Orgasm

---

"How do you feel?"

"OK, I guess."

"I'm sorry I came so fast. Sometimes, I guess I get . . . well . . . a little too excited."

"It's OK, really."

"But I want it to be good for you, too."

"Do we have to talk about it?"

"Yes, I think we should. Do you think it would help if we had a little more foreplay?"

"Look, it was just *fine*. I'm going to sleep. I'll reach orgasm next time, I promise. OK?"

"Don't be like that. I love you."

"Good night."

---

libido
(lī-be′do)

luteinizing
(loo′te-in-i′′zing)

Sexual response in humans is a process involving emotional, mental, and physical interaction. While very much an individual process, there are similar patterns in the way each body responds when sexually aroused. Research data indicate not only basic sexual response similarities among all females and among all males, but also fundamental response patterns that are similar in both females *and* males. The patterns are similar enough that we can outline a four-phase pattern of sexual response that applies to most people.

In this chapter, we discuss each of the four phases of sexual response, examining in detail the physiological (and sometimes psychological) components of each phase. While the fundamental similarities between male and female sexual response patterns are emphasized, we also look at how the response patterns differ between males and females. First, however, we discuss the development of sexual desire, without which the sexual response cycle would be irrelevant.

Sexual Desire

Sexual desire, or **libido,** is an appetite or drive. We experience it as specific sensations that cause us to seek out, or respond to, sexual stimuli. These sensations result from physical activation of a specific part of the brain. When this part is active, we may feel restless, open to sex, or vaguely sexy, or we may experience genital sensations (Kaplan 1979). After sexual gratification (orgasm), these feelings and sensations stop. When this system is inactive or inhibited, we have no interest in erotic matters and lose our appetite for sex.

The sexual centers of the brain are believed to have connections to the brain's pleasure centers. These pleasure centers are stimulated when we have sex, and for that reason erotic activity is interpreted as pleasurable.

There are also connections between the brain's sexual centers and the spinal reflex centers that regulate genital functioning. Stimulation from the brain's centers can arouse or inhibit genital reflexes. So when sexual desire is high, erection and lubrication occur easily and quickly, and orgasm is easily achieved. Without desire, the physical stimuli must be much more intense before the genitals will respond (Kaplan 1979).

A person who is attractive and receptive to us can stimulate our sexual desire. Smell, sight, sound, and touch can also be important stimuli. On the other hand, our brain centers can be turned off when we decide that it is not in our best interest to pursue sexual gratification.

While the female hormone estrogen does not enhance sexual desire, the male hormone **testosterone** controls sexual desire in both males and females. Without testosterone, there is little sexual desire in either sex (Kaplan 1979). A hormone secreted by the brain, **luteinizing hormone-releasing factor** (LH-RF), may also enhance sexual desire.

Music As an Erotic Stimulant

While music has less erotic effect than touching or visual stimuli and may not by itself bring on sexual arousal, it provides a vocabulary of emotion because of its power to create and reinforce fantasy. Like sex, it provides pleasure and emotional gratification.

Music can enhance erotic response in several ways. The lyrics to the music, for example, can be unmistakably erotic. Sexual words or phrases may stand out from the otherwise unintelligible lyrics of hard rock. Even romantic lyrics can be sexually exciting to an audience when performed by someone about whom the audience fantasizes.

The heavy beat or rhythm of music arouses us in dancing, in marching, in sports—as well as in sex. Such rhythm bears similarity to our physiological processes—breathing, heartbeat, and body movement. Sexual excitation usually involves rhythmic caressing and applying of pressure, and orgasm itself is an unmistakable rhythmic response of the muscles in and around the genitals and elsewhere in the body. Also, in dancing to the beat or rhythm of the music, the movement of the body, the closeness of the partners, and the visibility of erogenous body parts all bring dancing and music together in strong sexual suggestion.

The tone of the music can be sexually gratifying if it matches the arousal feelings of the person listening. As in sexual intercourse, the music can gradually build up in crescendo to climax and then fade away.

The audience's identification with the performer also can enhance sexual response. Closeness in age between the performer and the listeners may increase identification, especially if there is a sharing between performer and listener of social values and concerns.

While music may not, by itself, be sufficient to bring on sexual arousal and genital engorgement, if a person is susceptible to it, music can add to sexual pleasuring.

---

1. What types of stimuli tend to increase your sexual desire? What types of stimuli tend to inhibit your sexual desire?
2. What might be the problem if, during sexual activity, a male fails to obtain an erection or a female fails to lubricate?

The Sexual Response Cycle

The landmark work of William Masters and Virginia Johnson (1954–1966) detailed carefully observed and measured physical responses to sexual arousal and provided the first objective and detailed portrait of the human **sexual response cycle.**

Starting in 1954, Masters and Johnson investigated more than ten thousand sexual response cycles in 382 women and more than twenty-five hundred sexual response cycles in 312 men. Their female volunteers were between the ages of eighteen and seventy-eight, and their male volunteers were between the ages of twenty-one and eighty-nine. Although volunteers, the subjects were not selected randomly.

vasocongestion
(vas"o-kon-jest'yun)

The only requirement was that they be sexually responsive in a laboratory setting. While the group crossed social classes, they tended to be better educated than the general population.

Masters and Johnson wanted to observe, record, and sometimes film the responses of the genitals in particular, and the whole body in general, during the full cycle of sexual arousal, response, and resolution. Subjects were observed during both sexual intercourse and masturbation. Special devices were used to allow for observation inside the vagina.

The responses and general physiological conditions were observed in a typical laboratory setting that was outfitted with a bed and the necessary observing and recording equipment. The subjects were asked to perform sexually, initially without observation, then later with observers present.

Masters and Johnson's research procedures and findings, reported in *Human Sexual Response* (1966), have been widely accepted, and their work has become a standard against which other research is measured (Adams 1980). Their work also has provided a glossary of descriptive terms for sexual arousal that is now in near-universal usage.

Masters and Johnson divided the human sexual response cycle into four phases: excitement, plateau, orgasm, and resolution (see figures 8.1 and 8.2). Both in perceived feelings and in physical responses, there is no break or gap between the phases. They form a continuum.

In the discussion that follows, we outline the major physiological reactions occurring during each of the four phases of genital and extragenital arousal. The fundamental similarities in sexual response in both males and females are emphasized.

Figures 8.3, 8.4, and 8.5 show the changes in the female external genitals, vagina, uterus, and breasts during the sexual response cycle. Figure 8.6 shows the changes in the male genitals during the sexual response cycle.

Excitement Phase

The **excitement phase** (table 8.1) marks the beginning of erotic response. Depending on the nature of the sex play, the excitement phase may last from several minutes to several hours. The basic response in both sexes is pelvic vasocongestion and generalized myotonia.

Vasocongestion is the engorgement of blood vessels that results in an increased flow of blood into tissues. In normal blood circulation, the amount of blood flowing into the various organs is balanced by the amount of blood flowing out. Under certain conditions, blood flow into an area exceeds the capacity of the veins to drain the area, and the result is vasocongestion. Because of its greater blood content, congested tissue becomes swollen, red, and warm.

myotonia
(mi''-o-to'ne-ah)

Figure 8.1 Typical female sexual response patterns. Three basic patterns are possible in female sexual response. Pattern A somewhat resembles the male pattern (figure 8.2), except for the possibility of multiple orgasms without falling below the plateau level. Pattern B represents the nonorgasmic arousal. Pattern C represents intense female orgasm, which resembles the male pattern in its intensity and rapid resolution.

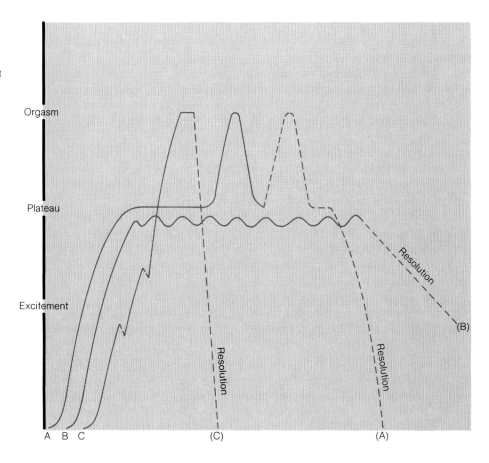

During the excitement phase, both physical and psychological stimuli can lead to widespread vasocongestion involving both superficial and deep tissues, especially those of the pelvic area. Most noticeable is the swelling of those organs containing erectile tissue—the clitoris, labia, vaginal opening, and penis (figures 8.3 and 8.6). Vasocongestion in the female will also lead to nipple erection and an increase in breast size (figure 8.5).

Myotonia is increased muscle tension. During sexual activity, myotonia becomes widespread, affecting both smooth and skeletal muscles. Myotonia develops somewhat slower than vasocongestion and may be both a voluntary and involuntary response.

The most obvious indications of response during the excitement phase are the erection of the penis (resulting from vasocongestion) in the male and the lubrication of the vagina in the female. This lubrication may range from very slight to copious.

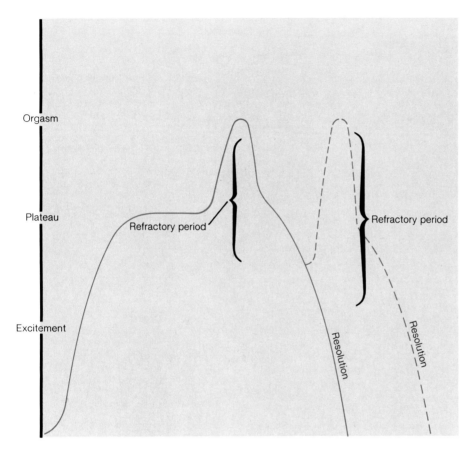

Orgasm

Plateau

Refractory period

Refractory period

Excitement

Resolution

Resolution

Figure 8.2 Typical male sexual response pattern. In their basic response pattern, males usually have a single orgasm. For a second orgasm to occur during the same arousal, a refractory period must separate the two orgasms.

In addition, both sexes begin to show increases in pulse rate, blood pressure, and breathing rate.

Both males and females may show variations in their degree of arousal during the excitement phase. Depending on the intensity of stimulation and the occurrence of interruptions that may interfere with the development of sexual excitement, there may be gains and losses in the degree of arousal.

Plateau Phase

The **plateau phase** (table 8.2) is a continuation or sustaining of the events that have occurred during the excitement phase, and for that reason it is often difficult to recognize when the excitement phase ends and the plateau phase begins. The plateau phase may last a few seconds, several minutes, or longer, depending on whether orgasm has been intentionally delayed.

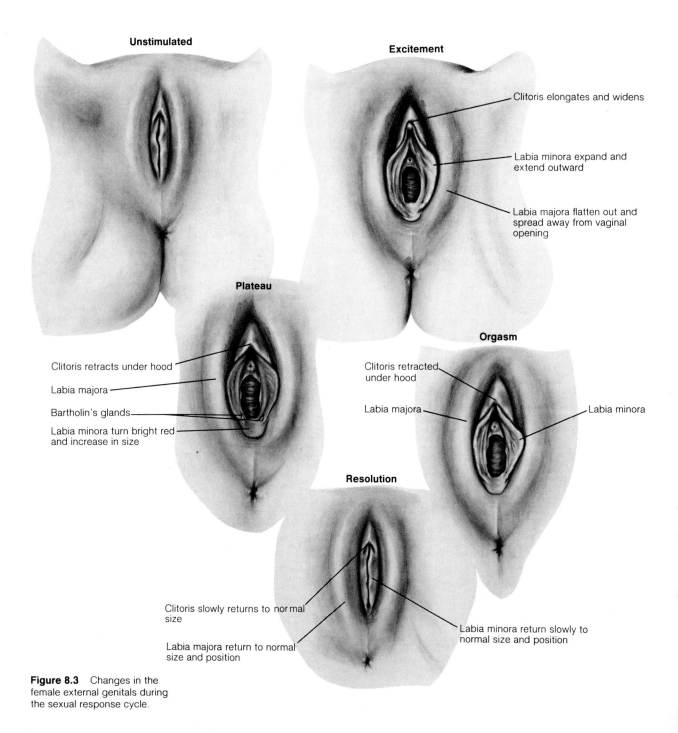

Unstimulated

Excitement

Clitoris elongates and widens

Labia minora expand and extend outward

Labia majora flatten out and spread away from vaginal opening

Plateau

Clitoris retracts under hood

Labia majora

Bartholin's glands

Labia minora turn bright red and increase in size

Orgasm

Clitoris retracted under hood

Labia majora

Labia minora

Resolution

Clitoris slowly returns to normal size

Labia majora return to normal size and position

Labia minora return slowly to normal size and position

Figure 8.3 Changes in the female external genitals during the sexual response cycle.

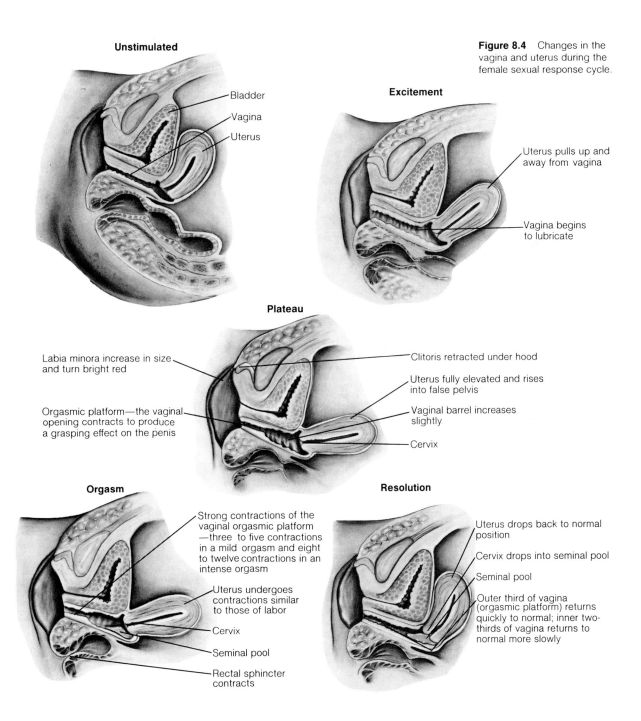

Unstimulated

Bladder
Vagina
Uterus

Figure 8.4 Changes in the vagina and uterus during the female sexual response cycle.

Excitement

Uterus pulls up and away from vagina

Vagina begins to lubricate

Plateau

Labia minora increase in size and turn bright red

Orgasmic platform—the vaginal opening contracts to produce a grasping effect on the penis

Clitoris retracted under hood

Uterus fully elevated and rises into false pelvis

Vaginal barrel increases slightly

Cervix

Orgasm

Strong contractions of the vaginal orgasmic platform —three to five contractions in a mild orgasm and eight to twelve contractions in an intense orgasm

Uterus undergoes contractions similar to those of labor

Cervix

Seminal pool

Rectal sphincter contracts

Resolution

Uterus drops back to normal position

Cervix drops into seminal pool

Seminal pool

Outer third of vagina (orgasmic platform) returns quickly to normal; inner two-thirds of vagina returns to normal more slowly

Vasocongestion continues to intensify during the plateau phase, resulting in further swelling of the genitals and breasts. It also causes a reddening of the labia minora in the female (figure 8.3) and the development of a sex flush in many females and some males. A **sex flush** is a reddened, rashlike discoloration spreading from the center of the lower chest out to the breasts, upper chest, neck, and head.

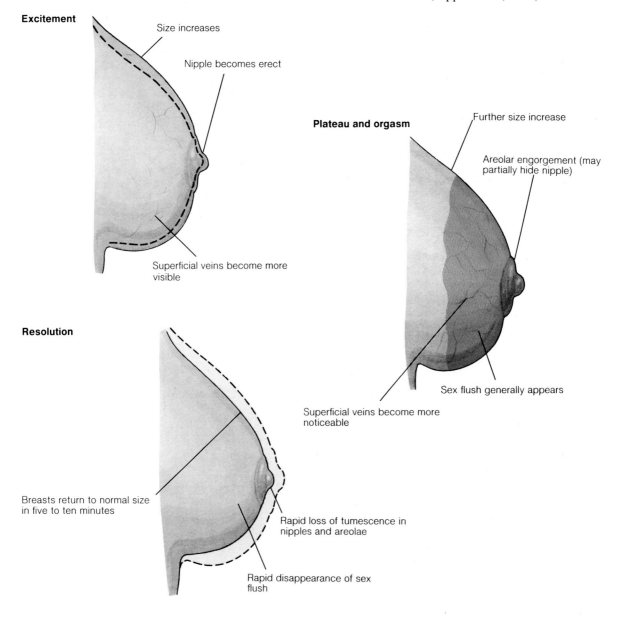

Figure 8.5 Breast response to sexual stimulation.

Excitement

Size increases

Nipple becomes erect

Superficial veins become more visible

Plateau and orgasm

Further size increase

Areolar engorgement (may partially hide nipple)

Sex flush generally appears

Superficial veins become more noticeable

Resolution

Breasts return to normal size in five to ten minutes

Rapid loss of tumescence in nipples and areolae

Rapid disappearance of sex flush

carpopedal
(kar″po-pe′dal)

Table 8.1 Female and Male Physiological Responses during the Excitement Phase.

Female Responses		**Male Responses**	
Vagina	Lubrication ("sweating") occurs within ten to thirty seconds with effective stimulation.	*Penis*	Becomes erect within three to eight seconds with effective stimulation. Erection may wax and wane during phase; may be easily impaired by nonsexual distractions. The smaller, flaccid penis may enlarge proportionately more in erection than the larger, flaccid penis.
Labia majora	Flatten out in nonmother and spread away from vaginal opening; in mother, become noticeably distended with blood.		
Labia minora	Expand noticeably in diameter as engorge with blood; extend outward.	*Scrotum*	Skin tenses, thickens, and elevates.
Clitoris	Shaft elongates two to three times and widens with blood engorgement. Head (glans) may expand up to twofold.	*Testes*	Elevate toward perineum; begin to increase in size and rotate. If phase is prolonged, may descend and reelevate several times.
Uterus	Begins to elevate (pulls up and away from vagina—becomes "tented").	*Breasts*	Nipples become erect (in about 60 percent of men studied) late in phase.
Breasts	Size increase late in phase; less size increase in suckled breast. Areolae noticeably engorge late in phase. Nipples become erect. Superficial veins become more visible.	*Sex flush*	Sex flush over chest, neck, face, and forehead may occur late in phase; occurs more frequently in warm rooms or in situations of extreme anticipation.
Sex flush	In 75 percent of women studied, a rashlike redness appears in the chest and upper abdominal area late in the phase.	*Other*	Generalized skeletal muscular tension; increased respiratory rate, pulse rate, and blood pressure.
Other	Generalized skeletal muscular tension; increased respiratory rate, pulse rate, and blood pressure.		

In the female, engorgement from vasocongestion also causes the formation of the **orgasmic platform,** a narrowing of the outer third of the vagina that intensifies contact with the erect, inserted penis (figure 8.4). Engorgement also results in the elevation of the clitoris, causing it to retract or draw up into the body (figure 8.3).

Myotonia also intensifies during the plateau phase and becomes quite marked throughout the body, especially in the face, neck, arms, and legs. **Carpopedal spasms,** which are spastic contractions of the muscles of the hands and feet, causing the hands and feet to appear clawlike, may be apparent. Pelvic thrusting becomes involuntary late in the plateau phase.

The continued arousal of the plateau phase results in a continued rise in pulse rate, blood pressure, and breathing rate.

Table 8.2   Female and Male Physiological Responses during the Plateau Phase.

Female Responses		**Male Responses**	
Vagina	Increased vasocongestion further reduces the opening to the outer third of the vagina. This engorgement, along with the engorged labia minora, creates the orgasmic platform to produce a grasping effect on the penis. Vaginal barrel increases slightly in width and depth ("ballooning").	*Penis*	Slight increase in coronal size due to engorgement. Glans may turn reddish-purple color in some men. Erection is more constant at this stage.
Labia majora	No further changes.	*Scrotum*	May thicken somewhat.
Labia minora	Increase in size and turn bright red in women with no children, bright red to deep wine in women with children. Orgasm occurs within a minute or two if stimulation continues after bright red color appears. Bartholin's glands may secrete one to three drops.	*Testes*	Fully elevated against perineum (orgasm never occurs without at least partial elevation of the testes). Marked increase in size of testes (from 50 to 100 percent).
Clitoris	Retracts from normal position late in the phase and withdraws under clitoral hood; so tender that efforts to touch it directly may cause discomfort.	*Cowper's glands*	Escape of two to three drops of Cowper's (preejaculatory) fluid late in phase.
Uterus	Fully elevated, it creates a "tented" effect with the upper vagina as the uterus rises into the false pelvis.	*Prostate gland*	As seminal fluid collects in prostatic urethra, there is a feeling of ejaculatory inevitability. Larger fluid volume is experienced as more pleasurable.
Breasts	Noticeable increase in areolar engorgement (may partially hide the nipple). Some further increase in breast size in nonmother. Superficial veins become more noticeable.	*Breasts*	No further response.
Sex flush	Generally appears late in excitement phase or during plateau phase on breasts in some women and may have widespread distribution over body.	*Sex flush*	May appear in late excitement phase or in plateau phase; indicates high levels of sexual tension.
Other	Overall increase in myotonia. Spastic contractions of facial, abdominal, and rib muscles may occur. Involuntary pelvic thrusting late in phase. Carpopedal spasms are apparent. Pulse rate, blood pressure, and breathing rate increase.	*Other*	Voluntary and involuntary muscle tensions increase. Involuntary facial contractions and involuntary pelvic thrusts late in phase may occur. Further elevation in pulse rate and blood pressure. Hyperventilation appears late in phase.

Orgasm Phase

Although a person experiencing it may feel that time is standing still, **orgasm** (also called **climax**) is the shortest phase of the sexual response cycle, typically lasting only three to fifteen seconds (table 8.3). In both males and females, orgasm is the explosive discharge of neuromuscular tensions brought on by intensive pelvic vasocongestion and skeletal myotonia. Rhythmic contractions of the orgasmic platform in the female and of the penile urethra in the male occur at 0.8 second intervals. Female orgasms frequently last slightly longer than male orgasms.

Table 8.3 Female and Male Physiological Responses during the Orgasm Phase.

Female Responses		Male Responses	
Vagina	Strong contractions of the orgasmic platform (three to five contractions in a mild orgasm, eight to twelve contractions in an intense one). Beginning at 0.8 second intervals, contractions gradually diminish in strength and duration. May be preceded by spastic contractions lasting two to four seconds.	*Penis*	Ejaculatory contractions along entire length of penile urethra. Expulsive contractions start at 0.8 second intervals, and after three to four contractions reduce in frequency and expulsive force. Final contractions several seconds apart.
Labia	No changes in the labia majora and labia minora.		Ejaculation occurs in two stages. (1) During emission stage, slight contractions of accessory organs (seminal vesicles, prostate, vas deferens, ejaculatory duct). Contractions last two to three seconds and give sensations of *inevitability* of coming ejaculation. Ejaculation cannot be stopped once this stage is reached. (2) In actual ejaculation, semen is propelled through penile urethra by muscles surrounding urethra.
Clitoris	No changes; stays retracted beneath the clitoral hood.		
Uterus	Undergoes contractions similar to those of labor. Contractions start in the fundus (dome) and spread downward.		
Anus	Rectal sphincter (anus) contracts rhythmically and involuntarily.		
Breasts	No further changes in breasts or nipples.		
Sex flush	Peaks.	*Scrotum/ testes/ Cowper's glands*	No observable changes in scrotum, testes, or Cowper's glands.
Other	Muscle spasms and involuntary contractions throughout body; loss of voluntary muscular control. Peak hyperventilation (40+ times per minute), peak pulse rate (100 to 180 beats per minute), and peak blood pressure occur.	*Sex flush*	If present, peaks.
		Other	Same as female responses.

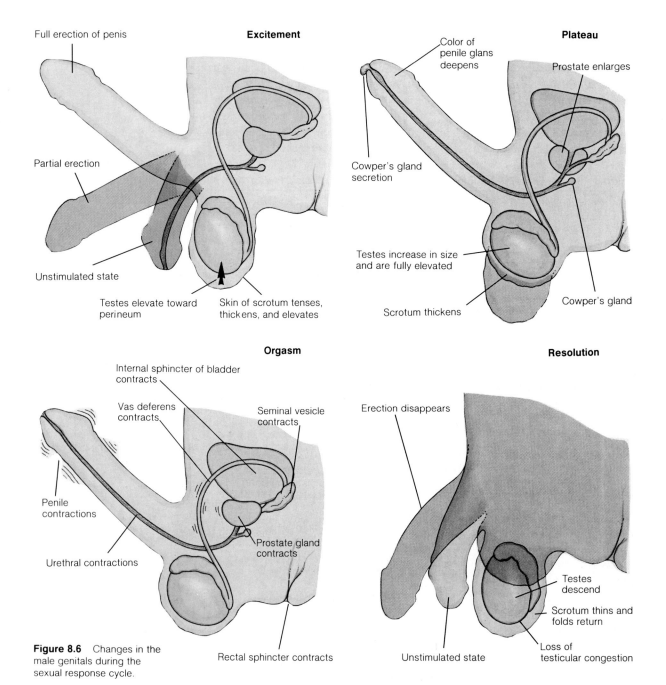

Excitement

Full erection of penis

Partial erection

Unstimulated state

Testes elevate toward perineum

Skin of scrotum tenses, thickens, and elevates

Plateau

Color of penile glans deepens

Prostate enlarges

Cowper's gland secretion

Testes increase in size and are fully elevated

Cowper's gland

Scrotum thickens

Orgasm

Internal sphincter of bladder contracts

Vas deferens contracts

Seminal vesicle contracts

Penile contractions

Urethral contractions

Prostate gland contracts

Rectal sphincter contracts

Resolution

Erection disappears

Testes descend

Scrotum thins and folds return

Unstimulated state

Loss of testicular congestion

Figure 8.6 Changes in the male genitals during the sexual response cycle.

tachycardia
(tak″e-kar′de-ah)

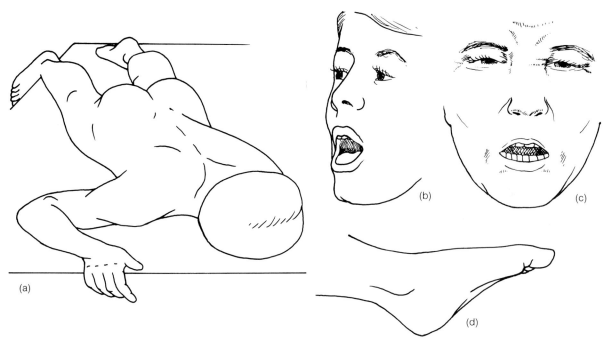

(a)

(b)

(c)

(d)

Figure 8.7   (a) During orgasm, there may be severe spastic contractions of the arms, legs, back, or lower abdomen. (b) The mouth may open involuntarily in a gasping reaction to hyperventilative demand. (c) As facial muscles contract involuntarily, the individual may frown, scowl, or grimace. (d) Carpopedal spasms result in hyperextension in the arch of the foot and clawlike contractions of the toes.

In both males and females, orgasm produces **tachycardia,** which is excessively rapid heart action. The pulse rate may be up to 100 to 180 beats per minute (compared with 70 to 80 beats per minute when unaroused). Partly as a result of this increased pulse rate, both males and females experience **hypertension,** which is an increase in blood pressure. Orgasm also causes breathing to become faster and deeper (forty breaths per minute—up from eighteen to twenty times per minute when unaroused). This is called **hyperventilation.**

Another physical manifestation of orgasm is intense myotonia in many body muscles (figure 8.7). The muscles of the hands and feet contract and grasp in carpopedal spasms. Muscle spasms and involuntary contractions occur throughout the body. The person may frown, scowl, or grimace as the facial muscles contract involuntarily. The mouth may open involuntarily in response to the body's need for more oxygen. Severe, spastic contractions of the arms, legs, back, and lower abdomen are sometimes apparent. Also, the sex flush peaks at this time.

Male Orgasm

Males experience orgasm in two stages: (1) a feeling of inevitability and (2) the ejaculation of semen. The first stage begins with a rising feeling of anxiety that something is soon to be happening inside the pelvic area. The rapid buildup of feelings has an imperative quality to it. The second stage begins with feelings of contractions deep within the pelvis as the prostate gland and the seminal vesicles contract in ejaculation, propelling the semen out of the urethra. When these feelings of contraction begin, there is no stopping the ejaculation, and the male "comes" in spurts of warm, milky semen (figure 8.6).

While men find orgasm from their own stimulation of the genitals to be stronger, many want something more from intercourse:

> I like intercourse more psychologically than physically. I get a lot of physical pleasure from intercourse, but I can also get that from masturbating. The physical feeling of moving my penis back and forth inside my lover is pleasurable, but probably not as intense as a good hand job or fellatio combined with hands. Psychologically, though, there's much to want—the anticipation of putting my penis inside my lover, knowing I'm going to be surrounded by her, warmed by the inside of her. Then when I first slowly enter her, I want the instant to last and last . . . (Hite 1981, p. 322)

Female Orgasm

Females experience orgasm with a feeling of suspension that is followed by a climax of intense sensation in the clitoris. The sensation then moves through the pelvis—some say a feeling of "falling," "opening up," or of "labor pains." A warmth spreading from the pelvis through the rest of the body may follow (figure 8.4). Some women feel sensations of throbbing in the pelvis:

> First, tension builds in my body and head, my heart beats, then I strain against my lover, and then there is a second or two of absolute stillness, nonbreathing, during which I know orgasm will come in the next second or two. Then waves, and I rock against my partner and cannot hold him tight enough. It's all over my body, but especially in my abdomen and gut. Afterwards, I feel suffused with warmth and love and absolute happiness. (Hite 1976, pp. 162–163)

Sigmund Freud was the first to propose that there were two types of female orgasm—clitoral and vaginal—and his theory was supported by other psychoanalysts. Freud held that a **clitoral orgasm** was attained exclusively through direct clitoral stimulation and that a **vaginal orgasm** was attained through vaginal stimulation.

Freud believed that female masturbation experiences in childhood resulted in orgasms attained by clitoral stimulation. He held that, as women grew older and matured, they transferred the primary site of erotic excitement from the clitoris to the vagina. Freud said that the significance of this transfer in erotic focus was that the vagina was the organ of reproduction and that sexual maturity was thus associated with the woman's role as a potential mother (Hettlinger 1974).

Freud's vaginal transfer theory was widely accepted by psychoanalysts and other professionals during the first half of this century. A mature woman was expected to achieve orgasm during vaginal penetration. Nonvaginal sources of erotic pleasuring were viewed as infantile and as a sign of incomplete psychosexual development. Many women spent years agonizing over why the vaginal orgasm was so "elusive" and the clitoral one so satisfying. Women who could have only clitoral orgasms were condemned as "vaginally frigid" or accused of being "fixated" at an infantile stage of development.

Various professionals were, during the first half of this century, beginning to criticize Freud's vaginal transfer theory, and during the last several decades many of them have been speaking out. Psychoanalysts such as Judd Marmor (1954) pointed out that the clitoris has a dense concentration of nerve endings that transmit pleasurable sensations. These nerve endings are largely absent in the vaginal walls.

These observations were confirmed with the data of Masters and Johnson (1966). According to Masters and Johnson, there is only one type of orgasm—clitoral orgasm.

The Masters and Johnson conclusion was based on two findings. The first was that all female orgasms are physiologically the same regardless of the location of the stimulation. In other words, an orgasm always consists of contractions of the orgasmic platform, whether the stimulation is clitoral or vaginal. Physiologically, an orgasm is an orgasm if the stimulation has been successful. This stimulation may come from masturbation, hand-genital or oral-genital stimulation, or from coitus. This in no way implies, however, that women may not psychologically perceive different types of orgasm.

The second Masters and Johnson finding was that the clitoris is the one female organ with the sole purpose of providing orgasmic pleasure and that clitoral stimulation is always involved in producing orgasm. During sexual intercourse, stimulation of the clitoris in its retracted and swollen state is achieved by pressing the penis against the labia minora, thus pulling on the clitoral hood. The clitoris is indirectly stimulated by the movement of the penis in the vagina. Thus, the "vaginal orgasm" actually involves clitoral stimulation (Federation of Feminist Women's Health Centers 1981).

Resolution Phase

Once orgasm is complete, the body enters the **resolution phase** (table 8.4) and returns physiologically to the unaroused state. Orgasm triggers the release of neuromuscular tension, which results in a state of deep body relaxation. Vasoconstriction of blood vessels gives way to **vasodilation,** so that blood flows out through the veins faster than it flows in through the arteries. The penis, labia, clitoris, nipples, and breasts rapidly lose their vasocongestion and return to normal (figures 8.3–8.6). Resolution, then, is the reversal of the arousal processes that occurred during the excitement and plateau stages. If there is no additional sexual stimulation, resolution begins immediately after orgasm.

Table 8.4   Female and Male Physiological Responses during the Resolution Phase.

Female Responses		Male Responses	
Vagina	The orgasmic platform, or the outer third of the vagina, returns quickly to normal; the inner two-thirds of the vagina returns to normal more slowly. The cervix and the upper walls of the vagina drop into the seminal pool on the vaginal floor.	*Penis*	Rapid loss of tumescence to about 50 percent larger than unstimulated size (may be slower if ejaculation purposely delayed); slower loss of remaining tumescence to prearousal level (especially if sexual stimulation continues).
Labia majora	Rapidly return to normal size and position; slower return if only plateau levels were reached.	*Scrotum/ Testes*	Rapid loss of congestion in some men; may take an hour or two in others. Slower if plateau phase was prolonged.
Labia minora	Return to unstimulated size and loss of coloration within five to fifteen seconds after orgasm.	*Breasts*	Slow loss of nipple erection, if present.
Clitoris	Returns to normal position within five to fifteen seconds (fifteen to thirty minutes for some women); may take several hours if no orgasm.	*Sex flush*	If present, rapidly disappears.
		Other	After a recovery (refractory) period (variable in different men) and with continued effective stimulation, a male may experience a second orgasm, but with the first orgasm being the more satisfying experience.
Uterus	The uterus returns to its unstimulated position and drops the cervix into the seminal pool on the vaginal floor.		
Breasts	Rapid loss of tumescence in nipples and areolae. Breasts return to normal size more slowly.		
Sex flush	Rapidly disappears.		
Other	With continued effective stimulation, the female may experience a second orgasm or more in rapid succession, with the second or third more sensorially pleasurable than the first one.		

Some of the changes of the resolution phase occur rapidly, others more slowly. Surface myotonia disappears within five minutes; deep myotonia disappears more rapidly. The carpopedal spasms cease almost immediately, and the fingers and toes relax. The rapid pulse, increased blood pressure, and fast breathing rapidly return to normal. The sex flush quickly disappears. Most vasocongested areas return to normal within seconds, although some, such as the penis and nipples, may take several minutes. Perspiration may appear on the palms of the hands and soles of the feet; it may also appear on the trunk, head, face, and neck.

During the resolution phase, idiosyncratic (one's own unique) reactions are common. Some people experience a profound need to rest and sleep. Others feel relaxed but energized. Some want solitude; others want closeness. Some want to talk; others don't. Some people want to eat, others want to drink, and still others may crave the stereotypical cigarette. Whatever the aftereffects, a vital person recovers in a short time.

---

1. Do you think that a prolonged candlelight dinner prior to sexual activity might be considered part of the excitement phase? Why or why not?
2. Describe the vasocongestion that occurs during sexual arousal. In what parts of the body does vasocongestion occur in males and in females?
3. Have you experienced myotonia during sexual arousal? What muscles did it affect? How long did it last?
4. Even though the physiological events at orgasm in both sexes are similar, do you think that males and females experience orgasm differently? Explain.
5. The resolution phase produces a number of different reactions in different people. If you are sexually active, how do you feel during this phase?
6. If you are sexually active, can you describe you and your partner's sexual response cycles? How closely do the cycles follow the four-phase model?

"Traps" in the Sexual Response Cycle

Now that each phase of the human sexual response cycle has been described, it is well to advise against certain traps we can fall into in subscribing to such a model stereotype.

The first trap is believing that everyone responds *exactly* alike. Some believe that even a little variation from the model implies a sexual problem. Actually, the model is the combined description of many study subjects, no two of whom were exactly alike. It is a composite, or average, of how the selected volunteers responded.

Second, while the model of the sexual response cycle may be the usual way we respond, our day-to-day response fluctuates depending on how we may be feeling on the inside and how we are seeing life on the outside. Our individual response patterns may be higher or lower, stronger or weaker, at various times. We may *never* match some aspects of the sexual response cycle model. We should neither be anxious nor fault ourselves as long as we are receiving the gratification we expect from sexual arousal and are relating well to our sexual partners. Again, at best, the model is a general guide to approximately how we might feel in any given response cycle.

A third trap of the sexual response cycle model is viewing the individual phases as separate events. The total response is a single *continuum* that, like an escalator, moves without interruption from phase to phase. The whole process has only been *arbitrarily* subdivided into four convenient phases, and no one phase of response should be taken out of context or detached from the other phases. The entire experience must be allowed to happen.

Fourth, sexual experiences vary considerably in intensity, both at a given age and over the many years of a person's life. To expect "mind-shattering" responses every time is both unnecessary and unrealistic.

One final precaution: Many believe that the measure of a good sexual relationship is the quantity and quality of orgasms sex partners experience whenever they make love. A report in *Redbook* by Philip and Lorna Sarrel (October 1980) reveals that achieving orgasm is not the determining factor of a satisfying sex life for either men or women. The survey showed that a more significant factor was how a person reacts to his or her sexual experience:

> The ability to share thoughts and feelings about sex with your partner is the single factor most highly correlated with a good sexual relationship. (p. 77)

Thus, the measure of a good sexual relationship is the ability of both partners to discover their sexual potentials, to communicate their feelings, and to give each other the opportunity to experience as full a range of sexual expressions as possible.

---

1. If you are sexually active and have had more than one sexual partner, did the sexual response cycles of your partners differ? If so, in what ways did they differ? How did you respond to these differences?
2. If you are sexually active, do your sexual experiences vary in intensity? If so, what do you think accounts for these variations?

Differences in Response Patterns

One of the most important conclusions of the Masters and Johnson data was that, disregarding anatomic differences, male and female sexual response patterns are fundamentally similar. In both sexes, arousal results in pelvic vasocongestion and muscular tension. In both sexes, vasocongestion reaches a crucial point. This is then followed by an explosive discharge of accumulated neuromuscular tensions called orgasm. In both sexes, the resulting muscular contractions occur in 0.8 second intervals. Yet, several significant differences between the male and female sexual responses also are apparent.

The Male Refractory Period

One basic distinction between male and female sexual response patterns is the male **refractory period.** Immediately after orgasm, a male enters a **refractory period,** during which time he cannot achieve another orgasm in spite of the type and intensity of sexual stimulation he may experience. This refractory period is maintained until the male's sexual tension has fallen to the early excitement level of response. Only after a certain amount of time, which may vary from several minutes to several hours, can the male respond again with full penile erection and orgasm.

There is no conclusive research on why males enter a refractory period. It may be due to the depletion of seminal fluids from the fluid-producing glands (prostate and seminal vesicles) or to some neurological inhibition. Physiologically, however, the process is like that in any tissue or organ of the body that will not respond to a second stimulation until a certain period of time has elapsed.

The female has no such genital refractory period and, in fact, may respond to repeated orgasmic experiences without a reduction of sexual tension to levels below the plateau phase of response.

The length of the male refractory period tends to increase with age. For some elderly men, regaining erection after orgasm is impossible for twenty-four hours or longer.

Variability in Female Responses

Another distinction between male and female sexual response patterns involves the variability of the female response pattern relative to the male response pattern (see figures 8.1 and 8.2). In general, the male sexual response cycle follows a fairly predictable pattern through the four phases. The female sexual response cycle may be more variable, depending on the site of arousal, arousability, and the psychological factors involved.

Site of Arousal

According to Masters and Johnson (1966), the site of genital stimulation in females has a strong bearing on the height of arousal attained. Clitoral stimulation is often more intense than vaginal stimulation and is more likely to induce multiple orgasms.

The female is in an interesting predicament anatomically. The vagina is where the penis enters and where the fusion between the woman's body and that of the man occurs. In a psychological sense, the vagina is where a woman perceives the relationships of sex.

The G Spot

Ever since the writings of Kinsey, Masters and Johnson, and Hite, the vagina has been viewed as an organ with few nerve endings beyond its outer third, thus having little sensitivity beyond this point. Vaginal orgasms have been seen as caused by indirect stimulation of the clitoris—that nerve-packed, highly erotic organ.

Yet, some women have claimed intense vaginal sensitivity and have insisted that orgasms from clitoral stimulation are not the same as those from intercourse.

Psychologist John Perry and sex counselor Beverly Whipple now say that there is a spot (called the **"G spot,"** after its discoverer, the German gynecologist Ernest Gräfenberg) on the front wall of the vagina that is especially sensitive in some women. The researchers also claim that some women expel an ejaculatelike fluid from their urethras during orgasm.

Their research has led Perry and Whipple, along with psychologist Alice Lada, to detail their "important newly discovered facts" in *The G Spot,* a book that some believe was prematurely conceived and is lacking in supportive documentation.

The G Spot has been criticized on several grounds. First, women are told that they can become vaginally orgasmic by stimulating their G spots, yet all of the women in the cited examples in the book were already vaginally orgasmic. Second, the composition of the female "ejaculate" is never clarified. Third, the book recommends pelvic muscle exercises not only for greater sexual enjoyment, but also for lessening of a list of female problems that includes cervical cancer. While many women do report increased sexual enjoyment after regular exercise of the pelvic muscles (see the information on Kegel exercises in chapter 6), any link between these exercises and prevention of such female concerns as cervical cancer has never been confirmed.

The authors of *The G Spot* promise a new arousal center, but this "finding" needs careful, anatomical correlation before it can be confirmed. The existence of an anatomical structure in all women must, after all, rest on more than some women's perception of their vaginal sensitivity.

At this point, the G spot is still a theory, and it is essential that G-spot theorizing not lead women who can't find their G spot, can't get a G-spot orgasmic response when stimulated, and can't ejaculate into sexual despair.

Yet, the vagina and the penis are not comparable organs. The erotic potential of the penis is much more comparable to that of the clitoris. The clitoris is exquisitely sensitive, while the vagina, the woman's organ for intercourse, is sensitive to touch only near its entrance (Kaplan 1974).

In other words, the major erotic site in a woman is the clitoris and not the vagina. During coitus, the clitoris, the lower vagina, and the labia minora (which tug on the clitoris as they are stretched by the penis moving in and out of the vagina) function as an integrated zone. While the penis (the male's most erotic organ) receives direct stimulation from rubbing against the vaginal walls, the clitoris is only *indirectly* stimulated by the tug of the labia minora.

A woman's sexual response pattern, then, depends to some degree on the type and intensity of stimulation she receives, while the male response pattern is more predictable. The male uses his most intensely sensitive organ (the penis) for intercourse and almost always reaches orgasm. The female, on the other hand, may receive only vaginal stimulation or indirect stimulation of the clitoris during intercourse and may or may not reach orgasm. While pure vaginal stimulation may be pleasurable, it does not usually lead to an orgasmic response unless it is accompanied by highly erotic fantasies. Indirect stimulation of the clitoris during intercourse may or may not result in orgasm, depending on the tension of the labia minora that tug on the clitoris. Direct clitoral stimulation, however, regularly produces orgasm (Kaplan 1974).

Arousability

The average female can reach orgasm through masturbation in less than four minutes; the average male needs between two and four minutes. The differences between the sexes in achieving orgasm are therefore not related to basic physiological variations, but to the mechanical and psychological factors of sexual arousal.

Some believe that **arousability** (the speed with which one can be aroused) is more slowly developed in women than in men:

> We know that the excitement phase for a woman must be significantly longer than for a man in order for her to achieve a high enough plateau phase to reach orgasm. [The need for a longer excitement phase *may* be due to] . . . a combination of infrequent masturbation, an unerotic vagina (with relatively few sense receptors), the absence of significant genital stimulation until middle or late adolescence, and the inhibitions resulting from the "good-girl" syndrome. (Bardwick 1971, p. 63)

These factors may combine to make female arousability *slower* and to make the usual levels of female arousal *lower* than those experienced by males.

Slower female arousability may be partially attributed to less masturbation experience. Most men gain an early knowledge of their erotic potential through masturbation. They learn the kinds of techniques and strokings that create the greatest amount of pleasure. Women, on the other hand, tend to be more ambivalent in their feelings toward masturbation. Their genitals are less visible and less accessible than those of males. Also, while females experience an increase in sexual interest at puberty, this increase is less intense than in adolescent males and thus the felt "need" for masturbation may not be as great. Hunt (1974) found that while 94 percent of males said that they had masturbated at some time, only 63 percent of females said that they had.

Cultural factors may also be partially responsible for slower female arousability. Many females attach less value to making themselves feel good; they have been taught to please others. Some do not even define themselves as sexual until they make love with someone (Gagnon and Simon 1973).

In addition, women may have difficulty in acknowledging their sexual sensations that come from clitoral arousal. The psychologically mature woman sees sex within a love relationship to a specific man. And while for all women the primary source of sexual excitation is the clitoris, the dominant organ of fusion with the man the woman loves is the vagina. So while the woman has pleasurable sensations from clitoral arousal, which is intense and reliable, she may fear that any sexual pleasure that does not come from, or involve, the vagina is not what the "healthy" and "normal" woman should feel.

The lack of a powerful sex motive in a woman may not only be the result of strong repressions and denials by her of her sexuality, but it may also be the result of how she sees her body and how that body functions in relationships. An important part of her sexuality is rooted in a need to feel loved, to be reinforced about that love, and to feel that she is creating an intimate and mutual love with a particular man.

In addition to *slower* female arousability, the usual levels of female arousal may also be *lower* than those of males, which means that, in general, the male sexual experience may tend to be more intense and satisfying.

Men, regardless of whether their sex lives are perceived as excellent or poor, report orgasms every time—or almost every time—they have intercourse. This orgasm is virtually always intense and satiating. It leaves the male at a lower level of sexual arousal than his original level.

On the other hand, sexual response patterns affecting orgasm differ among women and differ for the same woman at different times. After becoming sexually aroused, it is not at all uncommon for a woman to fail to achieve orgasm. Orgasmic difficulties are probably the most prevalent sexual complaints of women.

The differences in ease of achieving orgasm form a continuum, more or less a bell-shaped curve, reflecting a spectrum of erotic responsiveness (figure 8.8). At one end are those women who are totally nonorgasmic, regardless of how they are stimulated. Next are those women who can achieve orgasm with masturbation. At the middle of the curve are those, perhaps half of all women, who are potentially orgasmic if they receive clitoral stimulation from their partners, either before or after intercourse. Close to the other end of the spectrum is that minority of women who achieve orgasm by vaginal intercourse alone. Then at the extreme end of the spectrum are those women who are highly responsive, who can have orgasm even with breast stimulation, or who can have multiple orgasms during penile penetration without simultaneous clitoral stimulation (Kaplan 1974).

Some view high levels of arousal, which are relatively infrequent in some women, as comparable to the usual levels of arousal in the male. The "explosive" orgasm in the female that results in a lower level of arousal than before sexual excitement, represents the most desirable, yet, for many women, the most elusive sexual response pattern.

While it has been shown that women *can* achieve levels of arousal and orgasm that are similar in intensity and gratification to that of men, many women never do (Federation of Feminist Women's Health Centers 1981).

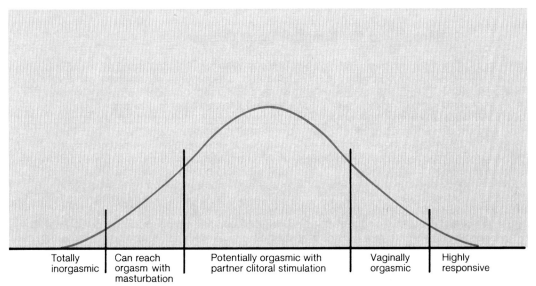

| Totally inorgasmic | Can reach orgasm with masturbation | Potentially orgasmic with partner clitoral stimulation | Vaginally orgasmic | Highly responsive |

Figure 8.8 Spectrum of female responsiveness.

Psychological Factors

Another reason why female sexual response patterns tend to be more varied than male sexual response patterns is that female sexuality is more susceptible to psychological influences than male sexuality. It is more easily suppressed and inhibited (Kaplan 1979).

Various images, perceptions, and associations can turn off sexual desire and arousability in a woman. If her partner draws attention to any of her unattractive physical features—her emerging stomach, her uncared for hair, her fat thighs—or if the woman has memories of past "injustices"—a birthday forgotten, a put-down by her husband in front of her friends—it can serve to shut down her sex centers. A woman can, in fact, "use" negative thoughts about herself to shield herself from feeling sexy. She may say to herself, "My breasts are too flat," "My nose is too large," or "I'm too short." Or she can control her erotic mood by bringing up memories of nonerotic situations—her work, too little money, or the demands of her children—to "turn off" sexual situations. She may, in fact, unconsciously focus on negatives and thereby contribute to her own inhibitions.

While inhibited sexual desire can be produced in both men and women of all ages, the sexual desire of women is more suppressed by harsher punishment, more severe warnings, and more intense negative factors than it is with males. While there is speculation about the relative effects of biological and cultural factors in such gender differences in sexual desire, much is still inconclusive at this time (Kaplan 1979).

Struggling for Simultaneous Orgasm

People continue to argue and speculate on the advantages of simultaneous orgasm over sequential orgasm (as though we have a lot of choice). Some sexual partners reach orgasm at the same time out of coincidental timing of their sexual response. Yet, some couples are gratified by adjusting the height of their arousal by one partner holding back and pacing response until both partners can come together.

To strive for simultaneous orgasm may involve so much pressure that it may detract from the sexual gratification of one or both partners. Both partners bring to the sexual event their preferred sexual activity, depending on how they are feeling. She may prefer deep thrusts, while he may find rapid thrusting more pleasurable.

Couples should not be trapped into believing that simultaneous orgasm is synonymous with

sexual compatibility. In fact, placing too much emphasis on simultaneous orgasm may lead to frustration and disappointment if it doesn't occur.

Actually, the degree of mutual enjoyment of sexual intercourse is a stronger indicator of sexual compatibility than whether both partners arrive at orgasm at the same moment or whether, in fact, each partner has orgasm every time. Flexibility in sexual behavior encourages creative experimentation that allows for varied ways of achieving sexual arousal and protects against the sexual sameness that erodes relationships. The elements of surprise and excitement in coital sex bring newness to the relationship and help to avoid the monotony that snuffs out sexual desire.

Finally, whether or not a woman experiences orgasms through intercourse depends more upon her ability to respond psychologically than it does in the male. As we discussed earlier, intercourse only indirectly stimulates the clitoris and may or may not lead to orgasm. If it does lead to orgasm, it may be that the orgasm can be partially attributed to the woman's psychological view of her sexuality. That is, through the fusion of the penis and vagina, a woman is reassured about her need to feel loved and her ability to create an intimate and mutual love (Bardwick 1971). These feelings may be the psychological trigger that, along with indirect stimulation of the clitoris, produces orgasm.

Multiple Orgasm

A myth that has been dispelled by years of research is that males have a greater natural capacity for orgasm than females. Both Kinsey (1953) and Masters and Johnson (1966) found that, when fully aroused, women were capable of many orgasms. Of course, most women knew that all along.

There is no definition for **multiple orgasm** that is accepted by all. Generally, it refers to having one orgasm after another within a short period of time. Kinsey (1948) defined multiple orgasm as "the capacity to achieve repeated orgasm in limited periods of time." Masters and Johnson (1966) made a distinction between males and females. For males they described multiple orgasm as "a second ejaculation developing in a short interval after a first emission." They said that women

> have a response potential of returning to another orgasmic experience from any point in the resolution phase. . . . This facility for multiple orgasm is evident particularly if reversal is instituted at plateau tension level.

While multiple orgasms can be achieved by both women and men, a multi-orgasmic sexual experience should not be a predetermined goal. A goal orientation doesn't enhance sexual response. In fact, it only tends to interfere with it. Thus, the harder we strive to produce multiple orgasms, the less likely that we will be successful.

Physiologically, both females and males enter the resolution phase following orgasm. For the male, this means the refractory period, during which he cannot be immediately aroused again. The female, however, is likely to experience a series of orgasms if effective stimulation continues.

Females

Kinsey estimated that about 13 percent of all women have multiple orgasms. Masters and Johnson believe that many more women are *capable* of having multiple orgasms, given the proper stimulation. They found that multiple orgasms can easily occur, particularly if resumption of arousal is started when sexual tension is still at the plateau phase. Two other factors are also important in females experiencing multiple orgasms.

First, Masters and Johnson report that clitoral stimulation is more likely to induce multiple orgasms than is vaginal stimulation. Clitorally induced orgasms result in a higher frequency of uterine and rectal contractions, indicating a higher level of pelvic congestion.

Second, the clitoral stimulation must be maintained. If effective stimulation is continued, each orgasm increases the orgasmic potential, and second or third orgasms may require less effort than the first.

> Since each orgasm tends to increase pelvic vasocongestion, the more orgasms achieved, the more can be achieved until physical exhaustion occurs. (Bardwick 1971, p. 61)

The extent of female orgasmic potential thus appears to depend upon the woman or her partner centering the stimulation in the highly erotic clitoris. If the woman can either direct the location or pressure of stimulation of the clitoris (such as during masturbation or in directing the hand or mouth of her partner), she is more able to achieve repeated orgasms. During vaginal coitus, without accompanying direct clitoral stimulation, the female may experience only one, or perhaps no, orgasm during intercourse (Federation of Feminist Women's Health Centers 1981).

Some women who understand and have experienced multiple orgasms are quite satisfied during sexual intercourse with only a single orgasm. The quality of the orgasm is of more significance than the quantity. In a real sense, if a woman has developed the capacity for multiple orgasm, she has the option of choosing the degree of sexual arousal she prefers in terms of the strength of her sexual drive at that time. In the absence of a strong need or a powerful sex drive, some women may be quite satisfied with the psychological intimacy experienced during vaginal intercourse even if orgasm does not occur.

Males

Multiple orgasms are much less frequent among males. Kinsey reported an incidence of multiple orgasm of only 12 percent for males at age 20. Some males, however, may routinely experience more than one orgasm during a single lovemaking session. As Alex Comfort (1972) states:

> . . . most men can get a second by slow handwork and a third from self-stimulation within an hour of full intercourse. (p. 63)

For the male, a second ejaculation produces a smaller quantity of semen than the first one. Some men perceive a second orgasm as less intense and pleasurable than the first, although other males do not. Yet, for the male, the number of orgasms may not be the thing that matters most:

> . . . it is rather the ability to hold off your own orgasm as long as you want, or to go on after, or soon after it, even if you don't come a second time. (Comfort 1972, p. 63)

With or without a second orgasm, the male may find pleasure in continuing sexual activity after a first orgasm. Perhaps to his surprise, as a "reward for his patience," he may be able to regain erection. This may or may not result in climax, but the continued sex play may be very gratifying to both partners. By slowing down the pace, the male may in fact discover that he is able to ejaculate a second time.

---

1. What is meant by the refractory period? Why does it occur only in males?
2. Explain the significance of the coital relationship of the penis to the vagina versus the anatomical relationship of the penis to the clitoris.
3. How might a higher incidence of masturbation benefit young females?
4. If you are a woman and sexually active, do you ever have trouble achieving orgasm? If you are a male and sexually active, does your partner ever have trouble achieving orgasm? If so, what do you think might be the causes of this problem?
5. Why might a woman *perceive* a clitoral orgasm as different from a vaginal one?
6. Why might multiple orgasms occur more frequently in females than in males? If you or your partner have experienced multiple orgasms, how would you describe the second or third orgasm in comparison to the first orgasm?

"Thanks."

"For what?"

"For caring. Last night was the first time in a long, long time that I have really let myself go. Sex was incredible for the first time in ages."

"I didn't know it was that bad for that long, but I knew I had to do something. You are far too important to me. I couldn't go on making love, all the while knowing that I wasn't doing it right for you."

"Well, you did it right!"

"It sounds boring, but I went to the library and checked out a "How to" book. It was a little much to take, but I did learn a lot about how to please a woman."

"Boring or not, it worked. I think I'd like to take a look at your book. . . . Maybe I can learn a little more about myself so that I can help you to know what to do."

Summary

1.   Sexual response is initiated by feelings of sexual desire, or libido. Sexual desire is an appetite or drive and results in both males and females from the activation of a part of the brain under the influence of the hormone testosterone.

2.   The research of Masters and Johnson provided the first detailed portrait of the human sexual response cycle. Masters and Johnson divided the cycle into four phases—excitement, plateau, orgasm, and resolution—yet noted that there was no break between the phases. The phases form a continuum.

3.   The excitement phase marks the beginning of erotic response. Pelvic vasocongestion and generalized myotonia occur. Response includes erection of the penis and lubrication of the vagina.

4.   The plateau phase is a continuation and intensification of the events that occurred during the excitement phase. Females show a reddening of the labia minora, formation of the orgasmic platform, and sex flush of the skin. Erection becomes firmer in the male.

5.   Orgasm is the peak, or climax. It consists of an explosive discharge of neuromuscular tensions brought on by intense pelvic vasocongestion and skeletal myotonia. In the male, orgasm occurs in two stages: a feeling of inevitability and ejaculation. In the female, orgasm may produce feelings of suspension, followed by intense clitoral and pelvic sensations of warmth. Freud theorized that there were two types of female orgasm: vaginal and clitoral. Masters and Johnson concluded that there is only one type of orgasm and that clitoral stimulation is always involved in producing orgasm.

6.   Resolution is the return of the body, following orgasm, to the unaroused state. Vasocongestion, myotonia, and other signs of arousal rapidly subside, leading to a state of deep body relaxation.

7.   Sexual response cycle "traps" we can fall into include (1) believing that everyone's sexual responses are exactly alike; (2) not understanding or taking into account our (and other persons') day-to-day fluctuations in sexual response; (3) viewing
the individual phases of the sexual response cycle as separate events; and
(4) expecting too much too often of our sexual experiences. Also, it is important to
remember that the measure of a good sexual relationship is the ability of the partners to discover their sexual potentials, to communicate their feelings, and to let
each other express as full a range of sexual responses as possible.

8.   Along with the fundamental similarities between male and female sexual response patterns, there are some significant differences.

9.   The male experiences a refractory period following orgasm, during which he
is temporarily unresponsive to continued stimulation.

10.   The female sexual response pattern may be more variable than the male sexual
response pattern, depending on the site of arousal, arousability, and the psychological factors involved.

11.   Multiple orgasms (two or more orgasms for one arousal) are more likely in
women than in men when women are able to center stimulation on the highly erotic
clitoris. While multiple orgasms are desirable, they are not essential to effective
lovemaking and should not and need not be a goal.

9

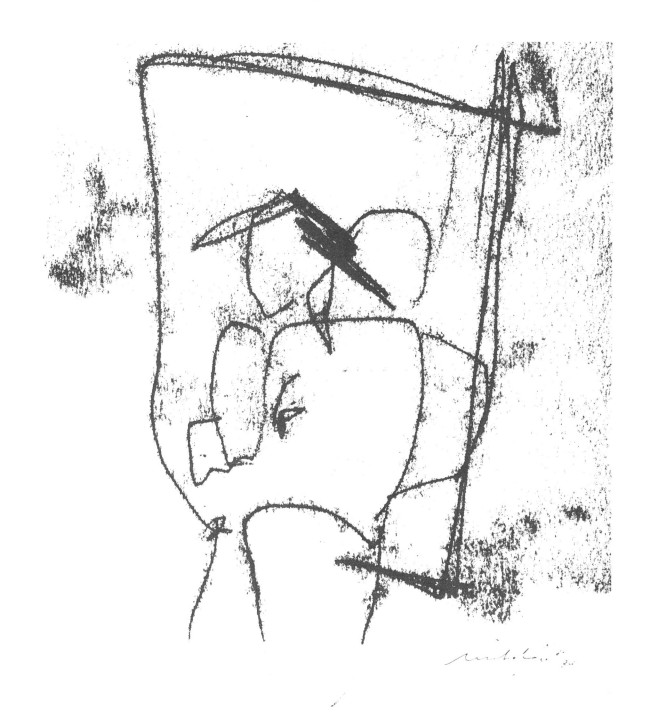

Sexual Stimuli
Emotional Stimuli/Physical Stimuli

Autoarousal
Masturbation/Fantasy

Nocturnal Orgasms

Partner Arousal
*Kissing/Use of the Hands/Genital Play/Oral-Genital Sex/
Anal Sex/Other Aspects of Arousal*

Coitus
Coital Positions/Reasons for Coitus/Frequency of Coitus

Sex and Drugs
*Aphrodisiacs and Anaphrodisiacs/Nonprescription Drugs/
Prescription Drugs*

What really turns me on in a man? Eyes. Big, brown eyes that are dark and sexy do it to me every time. Also, I get horny every time I see a really great body. I love a guy with broad shoulders and a tight ass. Most important, though, is his personality. A guy can be incredibly good-looking, but if his personality is lousy— forget it! There are some men I know that don't *look* very sexy, but get them alone, one on one, and look out! They know how to really turn a woman on—a tongue down the neck to the breasts . . . a nibble around the navel . . .

One of the first things I notice on a woman is her legs. Long, slender legs with tight thighs and round calves are a real turn-on for me. Then I check out the breasts. Nice and firm with round, hard nipples are sexy but not necessary. Long hair and a pretty face are nice. What I find really sexy in a woman, though, is how she feels about herself sexually. I can really get turned on by a woman who knows how to seduce a man. I don't mean tight sweaters and wiggles. I mean the way a woman can look right into your eyes, and you know she wants to make it with you right then and there. Now that's *sexy!*

In this chapter, we discuss self and partner arousal and the intense physical intimacy of intercourse. We explore the richness of sensory awareness, of fantasy, and of genital play. While we absorb all of the information and techniques this chapter provides on sexual pleasuring, however, it is important that we keep several things in mind.

First, we live in a society that tends to curtail emotional expression and to channel physical intimacy into a narrow, mechanical definition of sex. Sexual activity, however, should not be stereotyped. The freedom should be ours to have sex to orgasm or not to orgasm, to give and receive genital or oral stimulation, to engage in coitus in any pleasurable position. Nor need the goal always be intercourse.

Second, emotional closeness and intimacy should be one of the most pleasurable aspects of sexual activity. Therefore, the information presented in this chapter on the "techniques" of sexual pleasuring is only part of what will provide a satisfying sexual relationship.

Finally, no standard for sexual performance exists against which we need to measure ourselves. We are each individuals, with our own preferences and limitations.

This chapter, limited though it is, is meant to help each of us to explore and discover our sexuality and thereby help to make our relations with others everything we want them to be.

Sexual Stimuli

All healthy persons have the ability to respond to sexual stimuli, and a wide range of stimuli can be perceived as sexual. For any one of us, it may be the smell of perfume or after-shave on a person passing us, a touch on the shoulder, a sexy voice, or a beautiful or handsome face. Any of these may ignite arousal and set off a series of sexual thoughts (fantasies). During a busy day, any such sexual thoughts may soon be crowded out by more demanding nonsexual activities. But if there is time, we may enjoy a reverie of reflective meditation. We may construct a series of sexual images that may even result in the beginnings of sexual response in the vagina or penis.

People vary in the degree to which they view their world sexually. One person, exposed to certain events, will not respond sexually. Another person, exposed to the same events, may actively perceive erotic images. The difference in response will depend on the sexual meanings we give to certain events, and whether or not we view the stimulus as appropriate for a sexual response.

Even though there is a wide range of sexual stimuli, the underlying physical response of the body is the same. The intensity of response is as varied as the assortment of stimuli: The response may amount to nothing more than a passing thought or it may lead to full arousal to orgasm.

Some sexual stimuli are emotional; others are physical. Although we separate these two forms of stimuli in the following discussions, emotional and physical stimuli are often interwoven. Our minds and bodies tend to respond together when stimulated sexually.

Emotional Stimuli

Before being able to respond sexually, many people require a certain emotional readiness. We expect some emotions, such as feelings of love, to lead to erotic responses. What we may find surprising, however, is that other emotions that seem to have little to do with sex may also lead to unexpected arousal.

For example, forms of excitement can cause arousal. The Kinsey researchers (1948) found that young boys reported erections from such things as being chased by the police or hearing the national anthem. Negative emotions, such as anger or anxiety, can also lead to arousal (Dutton and Aron 1974). This may be particularly true if these emotions are experienced in the presence of an acceptable sexual partner.

Not all emotions produce arousal. In fact, some emotions are sexual turn-offs. Fears of various sorts—of intimacy or of romantic success—may inhibit sexual arousal. Some people follow patterns of avoiding intimacy to prevent being hurt, feeling guilty, or having fun. Their fears eliminate the possibility of pleasurable responses.

Most commonly, however, people need to feel affection or love to be aroused sexually. Such positive emotions are enhanced by feelings of mutual security and acceptance, and are nurtured within an atmosphere of mutual trust.

Affectionate talk reinforces sexual feelings. Words can affect sexual arousal, especially when they are sincere and voluntary. Words are, in fact, such a common tool of arousing sexual feelings that partners often play romantic games with "sweet" words, even though both partners recognize the words' exaggerated use. Such excess may be excused if there is no loss of contact with the real world, and there is no undue fear of creating deceit. Such "sweet talk" can serve to fuel our sexual fantasies, a common form of sexual arousal.

While physical stimuli are more intense in stirring up sexual arousal, they are initially fueled by the sexual feelings created by our emotions.

Physical Stimuli

We constantly interpret the meaning of events, making connections between stimuli and responses. We learn what different things mean in our culture. A given touch, for example, becomes a sexual stimulus only when we *decide* that the touch is sexual. Then we must decide to give, or not to give, a sexual response.

| aural | olfactory | fustatory |
| (aw'ral) | (ol-fak'to-re) | (gus'tah-to''re) |

Nonsexual Sources of Erotic Response among Preadolescent and Younger Adolescent Boys

Chiefly Emotional

Being scared	Band music
Fear of a house intruder	Adventure stories
Being late to school	National anthem
Reciting before a class	Finding money
Tests at school	Seeing name in print
Seeing a police officer	Detective stories
Cops chasing him	Entering an empty house
Getting home late	
Receiving grade card	
Harsh words	
Fear of punishment	
Being yelled at	
Being alone at night	
Playing musical solo	
Long flight of stairs	
Big fires	
Hearing revolver shot	
Anger	
Watching exciting games	
Playing in exciting games	
Marching soldiers	
War motion pictures	

Chiefly Physical

Sitting in class
Friction with clothing
Taking a shower
Punishment
Accidents
Fast elevator rides
Carnival rides, Ferris wheel
Fast sled riding
Fast bicycle riding
Fast car driving
Skiing
Airplane rides
A sudden change in environment
Sitting in church
Motion of car or bus
A skidding car
Sitting in warm sand
Urinating
Boxing and wrestling
High dives
Riding horseback
Swimming

Source: Kinsey, A. C., W. B. Pomeroy, and C. E. Martin. *Sexual Behavior in the Human Male*. Philadelphia: Saunders, 1948, pp. 164–65. Courtesy Institute for Research in Sex, Gender & Reproduction, Inc.

Sexual stimuli can be communicated through all modes of sensory perception. But for many persons, **tactile (touch) perception** is the predominate means of evoking erotic arousal. It is also the only type of stimulation to which the body can respond reflexively, independent of the brain. For example, a male with spinal cord injuries that keep impulses from reaching the brain or a male who is unconscious may still experience an erection if his genitals are caressed.

Other modes of sensory perception that may be involved in sexual arousal to varying degrees include visual, **aural** (hearing), **olfactory** (smell), and **gustatory** (taste) sensations. None of these, in contrast to touch, operates reflexively. We *learn* to experience the stimuli conveyed by each of these other sensory perceptions as either erotic, offensive, or neutral. Our responses to each of these stimuli is likewise learned.

erogenous
(e-roj′ē-nus)

We need to clarify several terms before proceeding. A **sensation** or sensory perception is an awareness of stimulation of a sensory receptor. Sensations come via the skin, eyes, ears, nose, and taste buds. The sensation produced by pricking skin with a needle may be painful; the sensation produced by genital caresses may be pleasurable. Sensations that are gratifying or pleasurable are called **sensual.** Some sensual pleasures are sexual, such as those involving the genitals; others may be nonsexual, such as those involving the satiation of appetite. Sensory perceptions that are both sensual and sexual are called **erotic.** Areas of the body that are particularly sensitive to erotic tactile stimulation are known as **erogenous zones.**

Touch

Touch, or tactile stimulation, is prominent in most instances of sexual arousal leading to orgasm. The beginning point of all lovemaking is close body contact; the entire body surface can serve as a source of sensual and erotic pleasuring.

Perception of Touch   Touch is perceived through sense receptors in the skin and underlying tissues. Stimulation of these tactile receptors creates nerve impulses that are then carried to the spinal cord and brain.

Tactile receptors are not evenly distributed throughout the skin but occur in groups called **touch spots** (E. Gardner 1975). Only by stimulation of one of these touch spots can the sensation of touch be aroused. Between these spots, sensation is decreased or absent. Some body parts have far more touch spots per given area than do other parts. Touch spots are numerous in the fingertips, lips, and genitals. They are scarce in areas such as the skin of the back. Those areas that are more richly innervated with touch spots are more sensitive and have a greater potential for stimulation.

Erogenous Zones   Some of the areas of greatest sensitivity are particularly susceptible to sexual arousal and are called erogenous zones. Erogenous zones include the clitoris (particularly the glans), the penis (particularly the glans and the corona of the glans), the shaft of the penis, the labia and the vestibule the labia enclose, and the vaginal opening. The area around the genitals, the perineum (the area between the genitals and the anus), the anus, the breasts (particularly the nipples), the buttocks, the inner surfaces of the thighs, the mouth (lips, tongue, and interior), and the ears (especially the lobes) are also considered erogenous zones.

What makes these zones erotic is the setting in which they are touched and the meanings given to that touching. Not all touchings of sensitive areas are sexual. A woman's breasts, for example, may be touched in the context of a medical examination or washed in bathing without the woman becoming sexually aroused. Extended touching of her breasts in a sexual setting, however, will probably produce a sexual response. In this way, we learn to associate some sensitive body parts with sexual desires.

The stimulation of body parts not normally considered erogenous can also lead to arousal. The caressing of an elbow, the sucking of a finger, or the licking of a palm have produced orgasm, especially in women. Unconditioned areas may become erogenous through extended caressings within a sexual context.

Erogenous zones differ somewhat from person to person due to the distribution of touch spots and the sexual conditioning that has occurred. No two people are exactly alike. Communicating lovers will learn the erogenous zones of their partners and may even attempt to extend their partners' erogenous areas, particularly if these zones appear to be limited.

Vision

For many people, visual stimuli are second only to touch as effective forms of sexual arousal. It is common knowledge that men become sexually excited by the sight of the female genitals, whether in films, magazines, or striptease shows (Kinsey 1948, 1953). That women are similarly aroused by seeing male genitals is of more recent observation (Fisher and Byrne 1978). Men are more aroused by seeing pictures of naked women than women are by seeing pictures of naked men (Stauffer and Frost 1976). Yet the extent of sexual arousal is quite similar when men and women are shown pictures of sexual activity (Schmidt and Sigusch 1970).

It appears that women today are seeing much more erotic material than they did in the past, in contrast to men, who have consistently been exposed to a large assortment of visual erotic material. Whatever changes are taking place in our culture, however, there is little disagreement as to the effect of visual stimuli on our obsession with bodily features and attire. All of this helps to make visual stimuli a primary source of information for fantasy.

Hearing

Although sounds, or aural stimuli, tend to be less sexually exciting than tactile or visual stimuli, they can play a part in sexual arousal.

Certain kinds of music, for example, may create given moods. Loud, pulsating music may be used to stimulate physical activity and a desire to dance, clap hands, and move around. Softer music may be used to create a setting of quiet conversation and other forms of social interaction. Which type of music enhances a mood of sexual arousal will depend, in addition to the specific sexual atmosphere, on our personal taste and how we have been scripted. Music that turns one of us on may inhibit another.

In addition to carrying messages in music, sound conveys meanings in conversation. Words communicate sexual intent and willingness. Sex talk is often indirect, especially when determining a person's sexual availability.

pheromones
(fer'o-mōnz)

Words also convey important meanings in sexual interaction. Males may use words like "fuck," "ball," and "screw" more commonly during intercourse, while women more often use romantic phrases, such as "making love." Women often use words more indicative of sexual activity *with* a partner, while men may more often use words implying sexual activity *to* a person (Walsh and Leonard 1974).

Talking about sex, as a form of communication, relates directly to good sex. The ability to share thoughts and feelings about sex with a partner is the single factor most highly correlated with a good sexual relationship, according to a *Redbook* survey (October 1980). The *Redbook* survey found that good communicators had intercourse oftener, found sex more satisfying, and had fewer sexual problems. More than any other factor, effectiveness in communicating one's preferences and feelings about sex is the secret to a good sex life.

Smell and Taste

We *learn* to view certain scents or tastes as erotic or obnoxious. By acquiring preferences, we become conditioned to smells or tastes that either turn us on or inhibit our sexual arousal. Various genital odors and excretions may be exciting to some of us and repulsive to others. No one taste or odor appears to have universal sexual attraction to either human males or females.

Scent arousal, in particular, is highly erotic for some people. Women dab themselves with Charlie, Jontue, or Tabu, while men douse on Brut, Old Spice, or Musk—all in an effort to give themselves a "gorgeous, sexy-young fragrance." Some women are very turned on by the male's genital scents, especially those that are musklike (a hormone-related secretion from the male musk deer).

One interesting note: Smells are often as or more important than visual stimuli in causing sexual arousal in animals other than humans. Chemical signals, or **pheromones,** given off by certain female animals during their fertile periods invariably attract the male animals. Although the evidence is still inconclusive, some researchers propose that humans may produce similar secretions (Michael, Bonsall, and Warner 1974).

---

1. How might negative emotions cause sexual arousal?
2. If affectionate words can provoke sexual arousal, what effect do you think obscenities might have on arousal when used during lovemaking?
3. How might you go about conditioning your partner in developing new erogenous zones? Compare your nonerogenous zones with those of someone else in your class.
4. Do you think that males or females are more aroused by nude photos of the opposite sex? Why?
5. What effect does music with sexually explicit words have on your sexual arousal?

Vibrators—Devices That Help or Detract?

A vibrator is a pulsating device that is used for a variety of purposes—relaxing massages, pleasurable body sensations, and gratifying genital arousal. In sex play, vibrators add erotic pleasure and variation.

The most popular type of vibrators are the plastic, battery-operated, penis-shaped ones. More effective are the larger, electric-motor-driven vibrators that are either hand-held or strapped to the back of the hand. These come with a variety of attachments and have variable speeds.

While both men and women use vibrators for sexual pleasure, women tend to use them more frequently. One reason for this might be that vibrators provide the strongest, most intense clitoral stimulation known (Kaplan 1974). Some women prefer vibrators because vibrators provide continuous pressure and because the woman can remain "in control" (Steinhart 1980). Some women, in fact, become dependent on the vibrator as a mechanical means of reaching orgasm. On the other hand, some women feel let down after using a vibrator because the vibrator-induced orgasm may come too fast and too easily when compared with coital orgasm, which usually takes longer and requires more effort.

Since vibrators can induce sexual arousal in almost any woman, they are useful in teaching sexually inexperienced women to stimulate their own sexual responses and may also be used in the treatment of orgasmic dysfunction. The goal of therapeutical use of vibrators is to enable the woman to transfer the vibrator-induced orgasmic ability to sexual intercourse. To make this transfer easier, many therapists urge their patients not to make sole use of vibrators to produce orgasm and to find other ways of creating arousal to avoid becoming "hooked" on the easily induced vibrator orgasm.

Autoarousal

Some sexual activities, such as masturbation and sexual fantasies, are self-induced, or **autoerotic,** a word coined by Havelock Ellis. Individuals may engage in autoerotic activities either alone or in the company of others, but the activities themselves still represent self-created sexual pleasuring.

Masturbation

Derived from the Latin words *manus* (hand) and *tubare* (to disturb), **masturbation** usually means manipulation by individuals of their own genitals for erotic gratification. We use the term as meaning voluntary self-stimulation (frequently to orgasm) of the genitals, either by the hands or by various devices. While most masturbation involves genital stimulation, some people (most often women) can reach orgasm by caressing their breasts or other body parts they find erogenous.

During masturbation, the primary targets of stimulation are the external genitals. Through their manipulation, the external genitals undergo vasocongestion, and the body shows increased muscular tension.

Figure 9.1 Female
masturbation.

Female Masturbation Techniques

Among females, the most common technique of masturbation involves stimulation
of the clitoral shaft, the clitoral area, or the area surrounding the vestibule. (See
figure 9.1.) A female may caress up and down along either side of the clitoral shaft
or use a circular movement around it. She may tug on the labia minora and thus
indirectly stimulate the clitoris. Shallow insertion of one or more fingers or objects
into the vaginal canal is another variation. A female may rub pillows against her
genitals or direct a stream of water from a shower or bathtub onto her genitals.
Vibrators of various types may be employed. A woman can also masturbate by
crossing her legs and exerting rhythmic thigh pressure against the genital area. The
breasts, nipples, or mons veneris may be caressed during the masturbation experience.

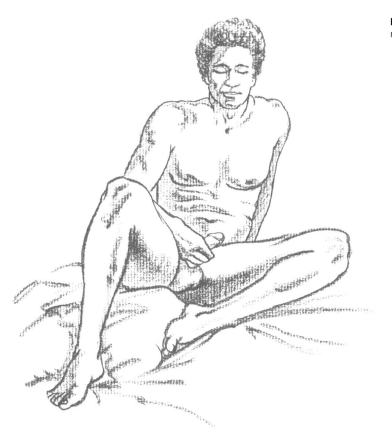

Figure 9.2 Male masturbation.

Male Masturbation Techniques

Males usually show less variety than females in masturbatory techniques. Most males grip the penis with one or both hands and use an up-and-down movement to stimulate the shaft and the glans. (See figure 9.2.) The degree of pressure, the speed of movement, and the extent of contact may be varied. The rapidity of movement is increased as orgasm nears. Males may also touch the penis, tug the skin around the frenulum, or tap the head or neck of the penis with the fingers. Vibrators or artificial vaginas may be used. While direct penile stimulation is common, fondling of the testicles, the perineum, or the anus may heighten the arousal. As with women, men may use warm water jets on the genitals or may massage their nipples.

Incidence and Frequency of Masturbation

Masturbation is very common among both males and females. In 1948, Kinsey reported that 92 percent of the males he had studied had masturbated to orgasm. Of the females in his study (1953), 62 percent had masturbated, although only 58 percent had masturbated to orgasm. In a more recent national study, Hunt (1974) found that 94 percent of males and 63 percent of females said that they had masturbated at some time.

Among adolescents, Kinsey's study found that the number of boys who masturbated during their teen years increased much faster with age than it did with girls. Among twelve-year-olds, 21 percent of the boys masturbated, compared to 12 percent of the girls. Among fifteen-year-olds, however, the percentage of boys who masturbated had risen to 82 percent, while the percentage of girls who masturbated was only 20 percent. Subsequent surveys of same-age adolescents show higher percentages of both males and females who masturbate.

The incidence of masturbation among college students is higher than that of adolescents. In 1974, Arafat and Cotton found that, among students sampled in three New York universities, 89 percent of the males had masturbated, compared with 61 percent of the females.

Both the Hunt and Kinsey studies showed not only a higher *incidence* of masturbation among young males than females, but also a higher *frequency* of young male masturbation. This difference may be due to various factors. The male sex drive peaks earlier and with more intensity than the female sex drive (Kaplan 1979). Also, sexual experimentation usually occurs earlier with males than it does with females. Women are more apt to learn how to masturbate *after* they have had orgasm from intercourse, while men are much more apt to have masturbated *before* first intercourse (Gagnon 1977). Finally, as discussed in chapter 8, some females have been scripted to serve others more than themselves and to give less value to making themselves feel good than males do. Until these women associate genital feelings with two-person lovemaking, they may not even define themselves as sexual (Gagnon and Simon 1973).

With increasing age, the masturbation patterns of males and females appear to reverse. With males, the incidence of masturbation drops off by age thirty. Females, on the other hand, show a pattern of increasing masturbation through their twenties and into their thirties (Hunt 1974; Kinsey 1953). Kinsey gave several explanations for this reversal: (1) women's capacity for erotic arousal may increase with age; (2) other sexual outlets may become more scarce with age; (3) women may rid themselves of learned sexual inhibitions with age; and (4) from sexual experiences, women may gain greater confidence in self-arousal and in their ability to provide it for themselves.

clitoridectomy
(kli''to-rǐ-dek'to-me)

Functions of Masturbation

Masturbation has various functions. First, during adolescence, masturbation is an important part of our psychosexual development since we learn about our personal sexual responses. Among adults, masturbation can bring relief from sexual tension when, for example, the male fails to bring his female partner to orgasm or when a sexual partner is unavailable due to absence, illness, pregnancy, or lack of inclination. Of all the alternatives to sexual coitus, masturbation is the least threatening. Through its use, we can more freely revel in sexual fantasies, avert relations with a demanding partner, or avoid humiliation due to some sexual dysfunction. Some people masturbate to combat loneliness, to release occupational or personal tensions, or simply as an aid in falling asleep.

Most importantly, however, masturbation helps us to discover our personal patterns of arousal and those caressings that bring us to the levels of sexual response desired. This information can then be communicated to our sexual partner, who can then provide those caressings that bring the most satisfying responses. We cannot communicate our sexual preferences to our partner unless we ourselves know what we desire or what our bodies are capable of responding to, and masturbation is a convenient way to make these discoveries.

Viewpoints on Masturbation

Many people are uneasy about masturbation. Both cultural folklore and religious teachings have contributed to these feelings.

Cultural   Some attitudes toward masturbation come from the writings of Tissot (1723–1787), a Swiss physician. Tissot theorized that various body fluids, such as semen, were important to our survival. He believed that semen was important in maintaining bodily integrity and that any loss of it (through masturbation, nocturnal emissions, or coitus) could weaken the body and create illness. Tissot suggested that various illnesses, including mental illnesses, could result from losing semen through ejaculatory excesses. He contended that, thus weakened, a man would not have the energy for productive work in society. Other writers argued that masturbation could lead to blindness, epilepsy, amnesia, and tuberculosis.

Writings such as these caused people to become so obsessed with fears of masturbation that some physicians performed **clitoridectomies** (surgery removing the clitoris) to prevent masturbation among young women. Penile rings (with sharp points turned inward toward the penis) and other appliances were still available as late as the 1920s to discourage masturbation among adolescent males.

The influence of cultural folklore such as this is still prevalent today. Such cultural views are often transmitted, without examination, by parents to children. As a result, adolescents, fearing parental disapproval, masturbate in secret. In this way, masturbation easily becomes a source of guilt and anxiety.

Religious Some religions, such as Orthodox Judaism, the Eastern Orthodox churches, certain Protestant churches, and the Roman Catholic Church, condemn masturbation, basing their condemnation on the Old Testament story of Onan, who committed a sin by spilling seed (semen) on barren ground (Gen. 38:8–10). Since during Biblical times any sexual activity that did *not* increase the population was condemned, any "waste of seed" was abhorred. It is now generally accepted that Onan was, in fact, practicing coitus interruptus by withdrawing his penis before ejaculation and thereby failing to fulfill his social duty to impregnate the widow of his brother. It was this, rather than the mere loss of semen, that was condemned (Cole 1959).

The medieval church, however, viewed masturbation as a more flagrant sin than adultery or rape; this was part of the "superstitious reverence for semen" during the Middle Ages (Bailey 1957).

Even today, Orthodox Jewish codes cite the discharge of semen in vain as the gravest sin mentioned in the Torah (Ganzfield 1961). And in its "Declaration on Certain Questions Concerning Sexual Ethics" (1975), the Catholic Church officially restated its position that masturbation is a "grave moral disorder."

Hunt (1974) reports that religious people are less likely to masturbate, start masturbating at a later age, and are less likely to continue masturbation into adult life and marriage. Hunt also states that the effect of religion is more marked among women than men.

Contemporary Regardless of any contrary teachings, masturbation can be part of a healthy sexual experience. Medical authorities today view masturbation as harmless, noting that there is no evidence to support any claims of physical damage resulting from masturbation.

From a psychological point of view, masturbation is a normal, universally practiced activity of childhood and adolescence. Many view masturbation as an acceptable part of adulthood when coitus is not available.

Masturbation could be considered harmful if it produces guilt or anxiety. In place of a relationship with another person, masturbation might be a symptom of sexual immaturity or insecurity. As such, masturbation can be viewed as a liability when compulsively chosen at the expense of what *should* be far more rewarding interpersonal encounters.

---

1. Why do you think that the incidence of masturbation is higher among both teenage and college males than among females of the same ages? Do you expect this incidence to change during the next decade? If so, how and why?
2. Why might males tend to begin masturbation *before* first intercourse and females *after* first intercourse?
3. How were you taught to view masturbation? Were you ever told not to masturbate? If so, what reasons were given to keep you from masturbating?

Fantasy

In addition to masturbation, autoerotic activities include sexual fantasies. A sexual **fantasy** is any daydream with an elaborate script that is sexually exciting. Sexual fantasies usually are confined to the mind, never to be acted out. All of us have reservoirs of repressed wishes that surface occasionally but do not define us as persons. Fantasizing about an experience does not mean we want to go through with it even if we could.

Virtually everyone experiences sexual fantasies, consciously or unconsciously, much of the time. Frequently, the fantasies relate to sexual activities, such as masturbation and coitus, either as a prelude to or along with the activity.

The material for erotic fantasies develops early and unfolds over a lifetime of psychosexual development. Erotic fantasies do not indicate maladjustment but relate to sexual satisfaction and increase the incidence of orgasm. Except when fantasies are out of control, there is little need to repress or deny them.

Fantasies are particularly common among teenagers coming to terms with their sexual feelings. Adolescents lay elaborate plans for the sexual activities they hope to share in. This is especially true when they are in love.

Content of Fantasies

People have sexual fantasies throughout their adult lives. Even sexually satisfied adults relive past experiences or reflect on missed or potential opportunities. We may fantasize about known, identifiable figures who may be friends, or about characters known only remotely or through reputation, such as idols in the performing arts. Fantasies may center on fictitious figures to whom we are unable to give a name.

Fantasies vary in intensity. Many are fleeting and momentary and rarely intrude into our primary nonsexual activity. At other times, fantasies are so strong that they crowd out all other thoughts and call for sexual release. Their frequency and intensity are influenced by our creativity, by our unconscious wishes, or by our success in keeping the fantasies out of our consciousness by directing our thoughts to other things.

Some people feel that they must limit the content of certain of their fantasies. They perhaps agree with the scriptural teaching of Christ, that a man who looks on a woman lustfully has already committed adultery with her in his heart (Matt. 5:28). In other words, these people believe that fantasizing about a wrong act also makes the fantasy wrong.

Functions of Fantasies

Fantasies have various functions. They are a source of pleasure, offering many mental delights. They may be a means of escape from the monotony, disappointment, or boredom of everyday routines. They may substitute for real-life sexual activities. This replacement may be a temporary satisfaction while waiting for upcoming events to materialize. Fantasies can also be replacements for goals that will never come true, for some we wish could develop (for example, marriage), and others we would not want to see happen (for example, rape). Fantasies may take the form of sexual rehearsal, in which we try out activities in our minds and work out a plan of action in the event that the real activity occurs sometime in the future. We may also use fantasies to assist us in sexual arousal, when arousal may not develop as easily as usual.

Male and Female Fantasies

Male sexual fantasies tend to place the male in a setting where he is powerful and aggressive in obtaining sex in a relatively impersonal encounter (Hunt 1974). A man's fantasies may center on coercing others to have sex with him or on other persons complying after initially resisting. Men have a greater tendency than women to fantasize about some imaginary lover (Sue 1979).

Female fantasies are often either highly romantic, pertain to the woman being forced to submit in a sexual situation, or involve sex with more than one partner. Women's fantasies tend to involve more sensory imagery—touch, sight, sound, taste, and smell. Female fantasies more often focus on the social and psychological aspects, rather than the physical aspects, of the fantasied relationships (Shope 1975; Barclay 1973).

Both males and females fantasize about more activities than they would care to engage in in real life. Few really want *all* of their fantasies to become actual experiences. To some degree, the arousal of fantasy lies in imagining what is forbidden.

Abnormal Fantasizing

Although sexual fantasies are virtually universal, beyond a certain point, fantasizing becomes wasteful and maladaptive. Fantasies may be viewed as emotionally abnormal if they interfere with work or study, or if they replace satisfactory interaction with others (Katchadourian and Lunde 1980). For example, when the sexual fantasies associated with masturbation become necessary conditioned stimuli for arousal for sex with a real partner, the fantasies are no longer considered a healthy outlet (Zimbardo 1980).

There are no reliable criteria for judging the "normality" of fantasies. Some people are disturbed by fantasies of very common activities, while other people go undisturbed by very bizarre thoughts. Many people fantasize about socially unacceptable behavior.

Whether our fantasies are merely silly or deal with highly disturbing behavior is usually irrelevant since most fantasies are never acted out. Just because we fantasize about sadomasochism does not mean that we would engage in sadomasochism even if we had the opportunity.

We should view disturbing fantasies as isolated, innocuous thoughts. Since we have some control over our thoughts, we can also exert some control over how much time we allow such fantasies.

If, however, a person sees a fantasy as any indication of potential action and feels that he or she is losing control and may commit some serious antisocial act, that person should seek professional help.

Nocturnal Orgasms

According to Kinsey (1953), most males (83 percent) and more than a third of all females (37 percent) have reported erotically stimulating dreams that led to orgasms, called **nocturnal orgasms.** For men, these orgasms are known as **nocturnal emissions** or "wet dreams."

Dreams almost always accompany the nocturnal orgasm. While the dream may or may not be erotic, there is usually some sense of sexual arousal. The male may awaken as a result of the ejaculatory experience or of the resulting wetness of the ejaculate. In a few cases, some individuals have reported nocturnal orgasms without dreams.

Because there is pleasure with the sense of sexual arousal that usually occurs with nocturnal orgasms, some persons feel unnecessarily uncertain or even guilty about nocturnal orgasms. They feel that they have taken part in a condemnable action. Yet, we have no control over our dreams, and nocturnal orgasms are a common and natural phenomenon.

In males, as a matter of fact, nocturnal orgasms are commonly viewed as the body's way of releasing built-up sexual tension. The adolescent male's body produces increasing amounts of semen. If the semen are not released in coitus or masturbation, the body will naturally (and harmlessly) release the surplus semen.

---

1.   Should sexual fantasies be shared with sexual partners? Why or why not?
2.   What is lust? How might some fantasies create problems for some people of strict religious principles?
3.   How does a nocturnal orgasm differ from a sexual fantasy?

Partner Arousal

Close body contact is the starting point for all lovemaking. This virtually always includes sex play of some kind, such as embracing, kissing (on the mouth and elsewhere), touching, and stroking erogenous areas of the body. Because such arousal play usually precedes coitus, it is commonly referred to as **foreplay.** Regardless of this association, such an array of sex play is in and of itself pleasurable, whether or not it culminates in sexual intercourse.

A discussion of the many techniques for erotically stimulating a partner, such as the one that follows, may seem too elementary or commonsensical to some people, but it may be appropriate for several reasons.

First, we can easily fall into ruts, or monotonous patterns, of stimulating our partners. A refresher course in erotic techniques can be "stimulating."

Second, we undoubtedly know ourselves well as males and females, but it may never occur to us that there may be significant differences in the body parts that males and females want caressed and the way in which males and females enjoy having these body parts caressed. In the pages that follow, we discuss arousal techniques that work well for both sexes and, more importantly, specific arousal techniques that each sex tends to favor.

Third, some people know so little about their own bodies that they do not know what to ask for from their partners. A discussion of arousal techniques gives them the basics to begin—perhaps through masturbation at first—to understand the arousal potentials of their bodies as well as the bodies of their partners.

It is important to remember during this discussion of arousal techniques that no one can presume, without communication, to understand the arousal preferences of anyone else. To understand our partner's sensitivities, we need to freely communicate our sexual feelings and preferences. Such communication and willingness to learn is the keystone to any successful sexual relationship.

Kissing

A very common part of erotic play is use of the tongue and lips in kissing. Kissing expresses sexual feelings as well as serving as a stimulant and may take a number of forms. In the simplest form, we use our lips to gently touch the lips of the other person. The lips may be used to stroke or nibble.

During tongue kisses, we use our tongue to caress and probe the other person's mouth. The tongue can also be used for deep thrusting in and out of the other person's mouth. Some refer to tongue kisses in sex play as "French kissing."

Kissing should not be confined simply to the other person's mouth or face:

> If you haven't at least kissed her mouth, shoulders, neck, breasts, armpits, fingers, palms, toes, soles, navel, genitals, and earlobes, you haven't really kissed her: it is no trouble to fill in the gaps for completeness and make a touching compliment. (Comfort 1972)

While kissing is an exciting prelude to lovemaking, it can also be arousing to continue a prolonged kiss through the entire cycle of coitus.

Kissing opens up a whole world of feelings. Kisses can be put anywhere on the body.

Use of the Hands

The use of the hands is basic in discovering our own bodies, as well as in discovering the bodies of our lovers. The hands are sensitive and versatile instruments of sex play. They express affection, help produce sensual gratification, and actively stimulate erotic responses.

Caressing

All parts of the body deserve to be caressed. Contrary to some of the antiquated sex manuals, there is no one best place to begin caressing a partner's body or any best sequence of parts to caress. The hands should be played generously over the whole body during the entire period of sex play.

Hand sex play is most readily heightened by maneuvers of advance and retreat. Once stimulation is begun, there can be small buildups, then teasing withdrawals. Stimulation can be resumed, carried to a further buildup, then again tantalizingly withdrawn. Timing these advances and retreats until the desired level of sexual arousal is achieved is one of the keys to lovemaking. To continue beyond this optimal point may actually create discomfort for the partner being caressed.

The fingertips are ideal for the light stroking used for exploration and advance and retreat. The palms of the hands are useful for more intense fondling beyond the early buildups.

A light touch is often preferred for early excitement than is pressure. The early, general caressing should be gentle and slow. As arousal mounts, the caresses can become more specific, pressured, and excited.

Breast Stimulation

Fondling of the breasts is for many women a reliably arousing type of erotic play. (See figure 9.3.) Next to the genitals, the breasts are probably the most prized parts of the body for stimulation.

The size of the breasts is unimportant, as is the age at which the breasts began developing or how they respond to fondling. Breast sensitivity varies from woman to woman as well as with the same woman at different times. Some women do not enjoy breast stimulation, and others do not at certain times, such as during their menstrual period.

As with other parts of the body, breast stimulation is enhanced when both the hands and the mouth are used. While the nipples are the most responsive, fondling of other parts of the breasts is also pleasurable. The breasts may be fondled, sucked, kneaded with the lips, or tongued. The pressure of the touching and the type of play will depend upon the woman's preferences, which she should freely relay to her partner. She may enjoy fondling of the entire breasts or of the nipples only.

As with other forms of caressing, it is essential that adequate time be taken to caress the breasts. There is no advantage in hurrying to get on to the genitals. In

Figure 9.3 Fondling of the female breasts is an erotic and reliable way of arousing a partner. Such caressing often results in clitoral response.

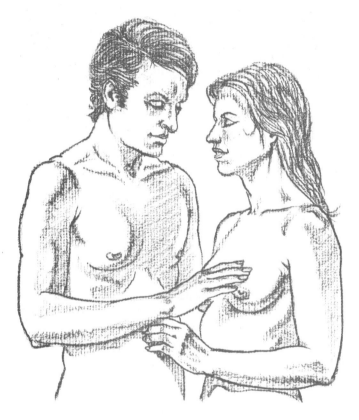

some women in particular, there is a strong connection between the breasts and genital arousal, and fondling of the breasts serves well as a preliminary stimulant for the genitals. Some women, in fact, are able to orgasm from breast stimulation alone.

Although breast stimulation usually is followed by genital stimulation, there is no reason why breast stimulation must *end* when genital stimulation begins. Continued breast caressing, combined with intercourse, can accentuate the pleasure a woman receives.

The male breasts may also be sensitive to stimulation. The sensitivity is mainly centered in the nipple. Some men may enjoy nipple stimulation; others may be annoyed by it. Again, it is important for the partners to freely explore each other's bodies to discover as many areas of erogenous delight in the other as possible.

Figure 9.4 Hand caressing of the female genitals (especially the clitoris) by the male and of the male genitals by the female is an exciting form of stimulation.

Genital Play

Both male and female genitals are highly sensory, and most people are easily aroused when their genitals are caressed. (See figure 9.4.) Most commonly, the genitals are stimulated before coitus.

Stroking or kissing the abdomen, buttocks, and inner thighs, with a general movement in the direction of the genitals, is an exciting preparation for more direct genital stimulation. As the genitals are first approached, they should be caressed lightly since genital tissue is sensitive and easily irritated. The pressure and speed of the caresses can be slowly increased as arousal builds.

Both partners may add to their pleasure by caressing each other's body and genitals simultaneously. Or they may wish to concentrate on the pleasure their partner is giving them.

Care should be given to the hands before using them in lovemaking, especially genital play. They should be washed and the nails smoothed.

Stimulation of the Female Genitals

How a woman's genitals are caressed should depend on what she prefers, and what she prefers one time may be different from what she prefers another time. Thus, each time they make love, the female should direct her partner in the type and speed of touchings she finds most pleasurable. The male can also learn more about the caresses the female finds arousing by observing the female while she masturbates.

Before a woman is sufficiently aroused, she may not prefer too much pressure on the clitoris or vaginal opening. Some women are sensitive to direct caressing of the glans of the clitoris and prefer touching to the side of the clitoral shaft, around the clitoral area, of the mons veneris, or of the general genital area.

During stimulation of the female genitals, it is important not to neglect the labia in favor of the clitoris or vagina. The pleasure the female receives from having the labia caressed may be roughly comparable to the enjoyment the male receives from having his scrotum caressed. A gentle opening of the labia with the middle finger can introduce caressings of the vaginal vestibule. Comfort (1972) suggests using

> the flat of the hand on the vulva with the middle finger between the lips, with its tip moving in and out of the vagina, while the ball of the palm presses hard just above the pubis. . . .

Stimulation of the Male Genitals

A female can learn much about the types of genital caresses a male prefers by watching him masturbate. It may be a tender tugging on the penis or a stroking of it. He may prefer the female gripping the penis gently between her fingertips and thumb tip. Gripping the penis just behind the corona, stroking it up and down, and causing the foreskin to move back and forth can cause a buildup of arousal. At the same time, the woman's other hand can be fondling the scrotum, caressing the perineum and anus, or stimulating the nipples. A man's pleasure can be intensified if the pressure and speed of the caressings is varied.

As with a woman, a man may feel different from one time to another and prefer different modes of touching. A partner can learn this only if the male tells her the types of caressing he prefers and how they make him feel.

---

1. Explain why communication is so essential in partner arousal.
2. How might the lips, tongue, and hands best be used for sexual arousal?
3. What are some reasons for gradually working toward the genitals when caressing your partner?
4. If you are a male, describe how you would caress your female partner's genitals. If you are a female, describe how you would caress your male partner's genitals.

---

cunnilingus
(kun''i-ling'gus)

fellatio
(fē-la'she-o)

Oral-Genital Sex

A very erotic form of kissing is genital kissing, or **oral-genital sex.** During oral-genital sex, the mouth and the genitals (both very erogenous zones) are stimulated simultaneously. **Cunnilingus** is oral-genital stimulation of the female, while **fellatio** is oral-genital stimulation of the male.

People's feelings toward oral-genital sex have been changing in recent decades. Kinsey (1953) found that oral-genital sex was practiced to some extent by 60 percent of the married couples who had gone to college. In Hunt's 1974 survey, more than 90 percent of married people under the age of twenty-five had practiced oral sex within the year. In the 1975 *Redbook* survey (Levin and Levin 1975), it was reported that the number of women between the ages of twenty and thirty-nine who practiced oral-genital sex was 91 percent. Of these, 40 percent engaged in oral-genital sex often and 45 percent occasionally. Today, both fellatio and cunnilingus are practiced by a majority of high school educated persons and by a large majority of those with some college education.

Interestingly, both fellatio and cunnilingus are illegal in many states. In fact, in most of these states, anyone engaging in fellatio or cunnilingus could, if prosecuted, be convicted of a felony. Such laws, however, are seldom, if ever, enforced, and most people simply ignore them.

Cunnilingus

From the Latin for "licking the vulva," **cunnilingus** is the use of the tongue and lips to stimulate the female genitals (vulva)—the clitoris, labia, vestibule, and vaginal opening. (See figure 9.5.) While any part of the vulval area may be stimulated in oral-genital sex, the primary focus is most often on the clitoral area.

The type of contact women prefer is quite variable. Some enjoy pressure on either side of the clitoral shaft, around the hood, or on the clitoral glans itself. Others prefer having the labia minora licked or the tongue inserted into the vaginal opening. The preferred type of movement also varies and must be communicated by the woman to her partner.

Many women enjoy cunnilingus because the tongue is moist and gentle, and there is less chance for pain than with manual clitoral stimulation. As one woman put it:

> A tongue offers gentleness and precision and wetness and is the perfect organ for contact. And, besides, it produces sensational orgasms! (Hite 1976, p. 361)

As pointed out in the *Redbook* survey (Levin and Levin 1975), a significant percentage of women reach orgasm only through cunnilingus. Some couples perform cunnilingus to heighten sexual tensions and then conclude their sex play with coitus.

Figure 9.5 Cunnilingus.

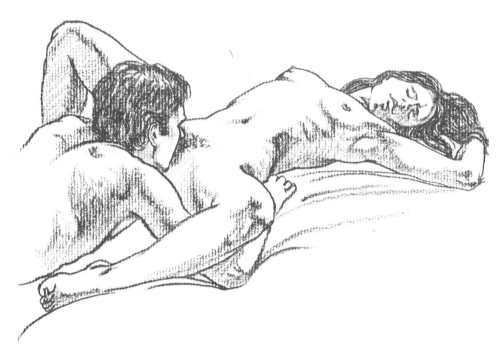

Some women must conquer the notion that a man may not willingly perform oral-genital sex on them. Actually, the partner performing cunnilingus can become very aroused at the same time as the woman. To fully enjoy oral sex, a woman must learn to appreciate the beauty and acceptability of her genitals. Some women need help in this, particularly if they have been taught that their genitals are "dirty." Some resort to the unnecessary, and sometimes dangerous, use of vaginal cosmetics to "make" themselves smell acceptable. Freshly bathed and disease-free, the female genitals are as clean as any other part of the body.

Cunnilingus should only be engaged in if it is mutually agreeable to both parties. If it is new to the couple, they may wish to experiment. If, after an attempt to enjoy cunnilingus, one or both of them are adverse to it, they shouldn't force the issue. There are many other pleasurable sexual arousal techniques from which to choose.

Fellatio

From the Latin meaning "to suck," **fellatio** is the oral-genital stimulation of the man's genitals. (See figure 9.6.) While fellatio techniques vary, the most common method is the sucking or licking of the glans and neck of the penis. Variations to this include nibbling of the glans, licking the scrotum, or placing part or all of the shaft of the penis into the mouth. This latter technique may be impossible unless

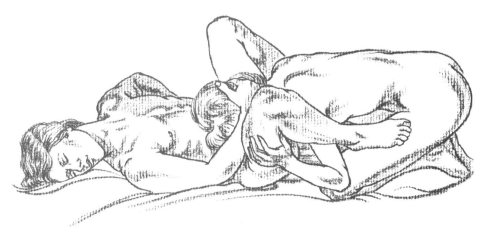

Figure 9.6 Fellatio.

the partner is able to relax the throat muscles. Any type of sucking or tonguing action may be used.

Whether during fellatio the male is stimulated to the point of ejaculation or not is a matter for agreement between partners. While some people enjoy having a partner ejaculate into their mouths, others do not, and fellatio in no sense must include this.

Fellatio is highly stimulating for most men. While fellatio is a common practice of homosexuals, a heterosexual male's enjoyment of it in no way compromises his masculinity or heterosexuality. The performance of fellatio on the male can also be very stimulating to the partner.

As with cunnilingus, it is important that fellatio be practiced only with the mutual acceptance of both partners, and the penis and other genitals should be clean and free of disease.

Mutual Oral-Genital Stimulation

Both fellatio and cunnilingus may be performed by each partner on the other at the same time if the partners face each other, but in opposite directions. Some refer to this as the "69 position" because of the resemblance of these figures to the posturing of the two bodies. (See figure 9.7.)

While simultaneous oral-genital stimulation may be very exciting to both partners, some couples find the necessary positioning too acrobatic. In addition, some find that trying to satisfy the other partner while receiving pleasuring at the same time calls for too much concentration and interferes with their enjoyment.

Some couples begin their sex play with mutual oral-genital stimulation and then, after the arousal becomes very intense, shift to coitus.

anilingus
(a''ni-lin'gus)

Figure 9.7 Simultaneous oral-genital stimulation.

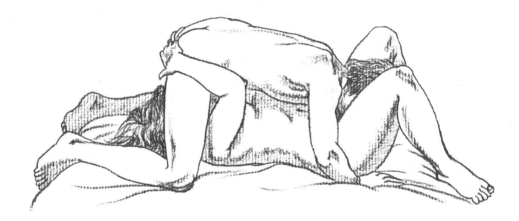

Anal Sex

Many heterosexual couples occasionally practice some form of anal stimulation—either manually, orally (**anilingus**), or as **anal intercourse** (inserting the penis into the anus)—as a part of their sex play. Anal sex in any form can be highly arousing and lead to orgasm.

Some people consider anal sex taboo because of its association with excretion. Others view anal sex as perverted, unnatural, unclean, or a sexual turn-off. Some "relearning" may be necessary before anal contacts can be enjoyed by some people.

While anal intercourse can induce pleasure, it can also be uncomfortable for the woman. The anal sphincter muscle normally keeps the anus shut tightly and usually tightens more when stimulated. In addition, the anus lacks natural lubrication, in contrast to the aroused vagina. Thus, the man should always lubricate the anal area and penis head well and manually dilate the anus before gently attempting to insert the penis. Some suggest inserting the penis no further than the penile glans. Under no conditions should the penis be forced into the anus.

Although the skin around the anus can be as clean as any other body area, bacteria and other organisms are normally present within the anus and can cause vaginal, as well as urethral (in both male and female), infections. Anything that has been inserted into the anus can cause infection unless thoroughly washed before insertion into the vagina. To minimize such risks of infection in anal intercourse, it is recommended that a lubricated condom be used and removed before vaginal intercourse is begun.

Other Aspects of Arousal

Anticipation, cleanliness, and the setting in which lovemaking takes place can greatly affect the quality and meaning of the experience.

Anticipation

Most of us have considerable control over the creating of sexual desire in our minds long before we actually see our lovemaking partners. In spite of the important business and routines that sometimes clog our days, we can direct our minds to pleasant fantasies about arriving home or meeting a special person. This type of anticipation can greatly enhance the actual lovemaking that may follow later.

Anticipation can also result from partners using various signals to convey the message that they want sex. The signals not only help provide subtle negotiating, they also give either partner the opportunity to say yes or no without making an issue out of the invitation. The mood can be signaled by certain clothes we choose to wear, by a candlelight dinner, by taking a shower before going to bed, by coming to bed nude, or by particular displays of affection. Such subtleties create the anticipation of sexual arousal and can add interest and freshness to a relationship.

Cleanliness

Attention to matters of personal grooming enhances sexual desire long before lovemaking begins. We should make an effort to wear clean and attractive clothing and to keep our bodies smelling pleasant so that sexual interest in our sexual partners is sustained.

Body cleanliness is particularly important during sex play. Both partners should be freshly showered or bathed, have clean-smelling breath and hair, and be wearing clean lingerie (if any is worn).

The sense of smell is an important stimulus to sexual arousal, and many people are highly aroused by the natural smells of a clean body. Hair, mouth, underarm, and genital odors that are offensive, on the other hand, interfere with sexual activity.

Uncleanliness may be used intentionally as a signal of displeasure or of sexual unavailability. The reverse, however, is also true. A partner who usually showers in the morning may indicate intended interest in lovemaking by an obvious nighttime shower.

Setting

Sex can easily become unimaginative and ritualized. Too often it is performed only after the late news or merely as relief from personal sexual and emotional tensions. Variation in the where and when of lovemaking can provide a sure stimulus. A couple may try moving away from the bedroom to a carpeted living room floor in front of a warm fire. They may try making love while showering together, while lying in a patch of fragrant grass on a warm summer night, while relaxing in a Jacuzzi or on a waterbed during an occasional weekend away from home in a motel.

Surprising a partner by being partially or completely disrobed at a time when he or she would not usually expect sex also can be arousing. When the children are out of the house for several hours, stopping everything, closing the bedroom door, and taking the telephone off the receiver can be the setting for an erotic interlude. Going for an early evening walk and then taking a long, warm shower together can create a setting for exciting sex. Just breaking the routine and then giving our best, most relaxed moments to lovemaking can be a sure formula for profound sexual happiness.

Such books as *The Joy of Sex* by Alex Comfort (1972) can provide additional ideas and be an exciting adventure in fantasy and experimentation.

1. Do you have adverse feelings about performing or receiving cunnilingus? What do you think is the basis for your feelings?
2. Some women are reluctant to engage in fellatio. What might be the basis for such reluctance?
3. Explain what is meant by the "69" position. Give some of its advantages and disadvantages.
4. Why do you think that people's feelings about oral-genital sex are changing?
5. What precautions should a couple exercise when engaging in anal intercourse?
6. List some ways, besides those mentioned in the text, in which couples can enhance their anticipation of lovemaking. What might be some imaginative settings (other than those mentioned in the text) for lovemaking?

Coitus

Coitus ("coming together") or **sexual intercourse** ("sexual exchange") usually means inserting the penis into the vagina. (See figure 9.8.) Sometimes, these words are used to signify other forms of sexual activity, such as femoral intercourse (placing the erect penis between the female's tightly squeezed thighs), intermammary intercourse (placing the erect penis in the cleavage between the breasts), or anal intercourse.

How coitus is performed depends on a person's expectations. Some believe it should be done *only* in one position. Others allow for much variation. Some coital positions are very restful, while others demand acrobatic prowess. In any given session of coitus, the imaginative couple may use several positions—ones that allow for rapid arousal, prolonged caressings, and climax, perhaps followed by relaxation and sleep in the final position.

There is no one "normal" or "natural" position. Nor is there any "abnormal" or "perverted" position. The sex act involves two persons, both of whom deserve pleasure from every act of coitus. To achieve pleasure, each partner's expectations need to be communicated and fulfilled. Any coital practices that both partners enjoy are normal for that couple and fully acceptable, and there need be no guilt, shame, or accountability to others about those practices a couple prefers.

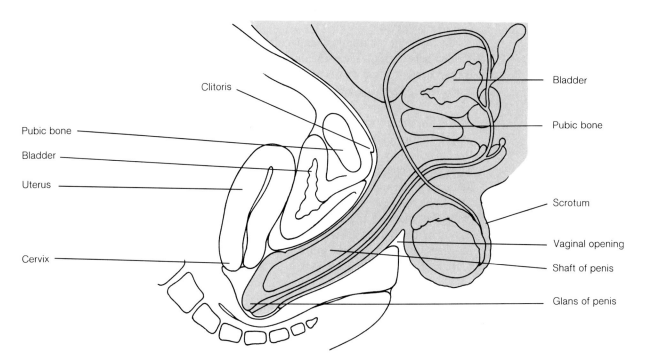

Clitoris

Pubic bone

Bladder

Uterus

Cervix

Bladder

Pubic bone

Scrotum

Vaginal opening

Shaft of penis

Glans of penis

For humans, there are many coital positions. This is in contrast to nonhuman primates, where only a single position, the rear-entry approach, is most often used (Goldstein 1976). The vaginal canal of most nonhuman primates, such as chimpanzees, is located more posteriorly than in humans. This makes a rear entry the easiest approach. Humans have a vaginal canal with a more frontal position. Thus, many persons prefer coitus in one of the face-to-face positions because it provides for more stimulation of the mons veneris and clitoris than do any of the rear-entry positions.

Preferences in coital practice may be influenced by pregnancy, change in body stature, illness, or physical agility. Culture also has a bearing on which coital positions are most commonly practiced. The social status of the sexes in the society influences whether the usual coital position is woman on top, man on top, or man and woman side by side (Goldstein 1976). If women have a privileged cultural status, they usually have the option of volunteering their participation in coitus. In such cultures as the Hopi and Crow Indian tribes and South Sea Trobriand Islanders, in which the female's sexual satisfaction is viewed as being as important as the man's, woman-on-top positions seem to predominate. In Western societies such as ours, which are male-dominated and in which the woman's social status is less privileged than that of the man's, man-on-top positions are more common (Langmyhr 1976).

Figure 9.8 Male and female genitals during coitus. Varying body positions can create greater satisfaction because pressure is exerted on different genital organs.

Coital Positions

Aside from the anatomical and cultural interpretations, the coital positions described here are in no way meant to suggest that there is one "best" position. Each couple needs to find those combinations of positions that give them the greatest amount of pleasuring and excitement.

Male-Superior (Face-to-Face) Positions

Male-superior face-to-face positions are so common in our society that some view them as the only "normal" ones. In these positions, also known as "missionary positions," the couple has the advantage of being able to look into each other's eyes, and engage in mouth kissing and breast caressing. (See figure 9.9.) The female is able to lie relaxed, while the male takes the initiative and is allowed to psychologically feel like the aggressor. Entry is simple, and pelvic thrusting by the male is easy. For many men, these are the most satisfying and exciting positions. These positions also tend to place more pressure on the woman's pubis, causing more stimulation of the clitoral area.

Figure 9.9 Variations of the male-superior face-to-face coital position.

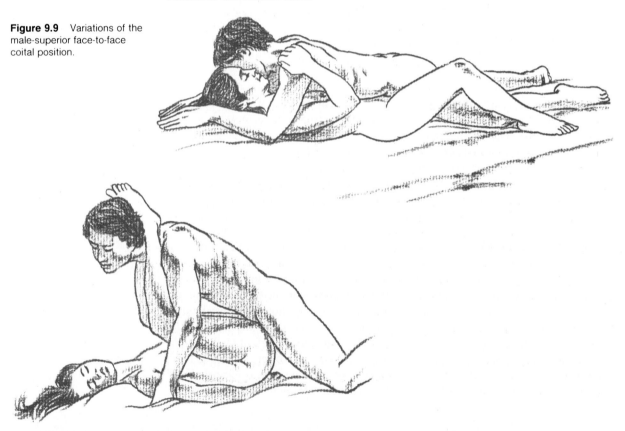

Male-superior positions may be disadvantageous if the man finds them too arousing. He may penetrate early, thrust rapidly, and ejaculate so quickly that his partner may not reach orgasm. They may not be good positions if the male is bothered by persistent **premature ejaculation** (unintentional and early ejaculation). Also, the man's weight may be too great for the comfort of the woman. She may feel "pinned down" and be unable to move freely, particularly if he rests too much weight on her. Some men support their weight with their arms and legs, but this can quickly become very tiring.

Male-superior positions increase the possibility of pregnancy. Since the female is on her back in male-superior positions, the vaginal barrel slopes downward into the blind end, or cul-de-sac, of the vagina, and as sexual arousal mounts, this cul-de-sac enlarges. This allows the semen to collect in the cul-de-sac of the vagina after ejaculation. Following the female's orgasm, the uterus returns to its beginning position and the cervix dips into the seminal pool in the vaginal cul-de-sac, allowing for the easier movement of the sperm into the uterus.

There are many variations of male-superior coital positions. Both partners may lie flat with legs extended. The woman may bend her knees and draw them toward her chest with the man between them. Or she may rest her feet on his shoulders. The man can rest all of his weight on the woman's body or support his weight with his arms and legs to give the woman more freedom of movement.

Female-Superior (Face-to-Face) Positions

Female-superior positions are the most frequently used coital positions around the world (Langmyhr 1976). These positions may provide greater pleasure for the woman because they allow her to have greater control over the rhythm and angle of penile-vaginal friction and thus have more clitoral stimulation. (See figure 9.10.) The woman can also exercise more control over the depth of penis penetration. She can, merely by flexing the hips, shorten the length of the vaginal barrel, placing the tip of the penis deeper into the vagina. Depending on the length of her vagina, she may prefer the penetration to be deeper or more shallow. Some women find that female-superior positions make them feel more involved and less passive, instead of feeling that intercourse is something that is "done" to them.

Female-superior positions are helpful for a woman who has trouble reaching orgasm because she can allow penetration to occur in a way she finds more exciting and can experiment with the kinds of movements she finds erotic. These positions are also helpful in treating a male who has trouble with premature ejaculation. Since in female-superior positions, the female can more easily control the tempo of penile penetrations of the vagina, she is able to slow the rhythm down to help the male from becoming aroused too quickly. If the male is bothered by erectile problems, female-superior positions may allow the female to work the semierect penis into the vagina to help enhance full erection.

Figure 9.10 Variation of the female-superior face-to-face coital position.

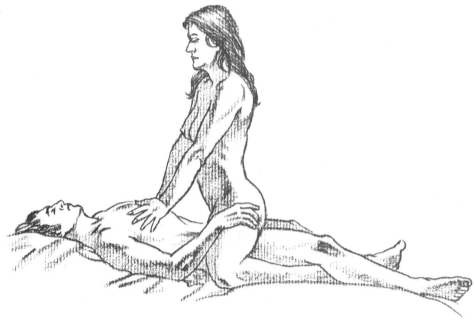

The female-superior positions make some men feel that they are being forced to "surrender" what they feel should be their dominant role. As with all coital positions, both partners must be sensitive to each other's feelings and be willing to discuss them.

Variations of female-superior positions include the woman sitting upright astride the man's body and facing him, which allows for talking, kissing, and his caressing of her clitoris or fondling of her breasts, or she may rest her full body on his body or between his spread legs. In any of these variations, female-superior positions demand more exertion from the woman and may be more restful for the man.

Side-to-Side and Lateral Positions

In side-to-side coital positions, both partners lie on their sides facing each other and fully bear their own weight. Often, their legs are intertwined. (See figure 9.11.)

The side-to-side positions are very restful for both partners and allow for kissing, breast fondling, and freedom of movement. The depth of penetration is easy to control by the positioning of the legs of each partner. Since these positions are less active, they allow for greater ejaculatory control by the man, and, thus, can be useful in countering premature ejaculation.

Figure 9.11 Side-to-side coital position.

The lateral coital position is a variation of the side-to-side position and was devised by Masters and Johnson for certain therapies. It is recommended to help give the man more control over his ejaculation and to give the woman more freedom to regulate her hip movement. In this variation, the couple shifts from a female-superior position to a lateral position, with the man partly supporting the woman's body. This position frees one arm of each partner for caressing, yet provides comfort and support for the woman's free pelvic thrusting.

Rear-Entry Positions

In rear-entry positions, the man faces the woman's back and enters her vagina from the rear. (See figure 9.12.) Most commonly, this position is used with both partners lying on their sides. Or the woman may be standing and leaning over, or kneeling and resting on her hands or elbows. In another variation, the man sits on a low stool while the woman sits astride him facing away.

As with other positions, rear-entry positions have both advantages and disadvantages. In rear entry, the woman's hips are likely to be flexed, bringing the thighs forward. Such flexing action shortens the vaginal barrel, placing the penis deeper into the vagina. For some women, this deeper penile penetration is pleasurable; for others, it may be uncomfortable. Rear-entry positions also provide less clitoral stimulation for the woman, but manual caressing of the clitoral area by either partner can compensate for this. Some men find rear-entry positions advantageous because these positions allow for full exposure to and contact with the woman's buttocks, which some men find especially arousing.

Because some rear-entry positions allow both partners to bear their own weight on their sides, these coital positions require less exertion and are very restful when the partners are tired, old, debilitated, or recovering from illness or surgery. They are also comfortable positions for late pregnancy or for obese persons.

Figure 9.12   Rear-entry coital
position.

Some persons object to rear-entry positions because they are reminded too strongly of anal intercourse (which they find repugnant), because this is the posture that most animals other than humans assume in intercourse, or because rear-entry positions lack the face-to-face intimacy of other positions.

Sitting Positions

In sitting coital positions, the man is usually sitting in a chair or on a bed, while the woman sits astride him and either faces toward or away from him. (See figure 9.13.) Unless the woman's weight is excessive, these positions can be very restful for both partners. These positions also allow the man to embrace the woman and to fondle both her breasts at the same time or to caress her clitoral area.

In cases of male paraplegia (paralysis of the lower half of the body), sitting positions may be helpful in performing coitus. Also, some women prefer these positions during late pregnancy.

Figure 9.13 Sitting coital positions.

Other Positions

Numerous other coital positions are possible. (See figure 9.14.) Some require extensive agility and athletic ability, but they also allow for much imagination. While experimenting may be exciting for one or both partners, both need to agree on what is acceptable and pleasing for each of them separately as well as together. For many couples, the fun of experimenting with changes in coital techniques has been the formula for a happy sex life.

Figure 9.14   Other coital
positions.

1. What bearing might culture have on whether the male or female predominantly assumes a superior position in coitus?
2. Give some pros and cons of the male-superior coital position. Why might some consider it the "normal" position for intercourse?
3. The female-superior position is recommended for use by some couples undergoing various sex therapies. What advantages might this position have in such therapies?
4. Explain why the lateral coital position has value in treating males with ejaculatory problems.
5. Some people are repelled by a rear-entry coital position. What might be the basis for such objections?

Reasons for Coitus

In a biological sense, coitus is the manner in which humans reproduce. Through it, we express human potential. Yet, the human female is able to be impregnated during only one or two days out of each monthly menstrual cycle. By far, most coitus occurs during times when it could not result in reproduction.

In a sense other than biological, coitus has broad nonreproductive significance. It may express passion, love, intimacy, lust, or simply physical gratification. It may involve the need for variety, pleasure, or relaxation. It may be a call for closeness or be a way to prove a point. Coitus can also be one of the most delightful ways in which we can play. Coital play can not only be a way of dealing acceptably with our anxieties and aggressions, it can also be a way of unabashedly expressing pleasure or having fun. This need not be exclusive of the more serious reasons for having coitus. Many of us, however, have trouble accepting the necessity for sex play. Comfort (1972) says: "One of the things still missing from the 'new sexual freedom' is the unashamed ability to use sex as play."

At its best, coitus can be a highly intimate way in which we express tender feelings and wishes to another. It can be a way of sharing commitment, a way of pledging ourselves to another. Coitus also strengthens the bond between two people and reinforces a partnership based on care and affection (Goldstein 1976). Some believe that the emotional ties that are reinforced through coital pleasure may be the biological foundation upon which patterns of family life are built.

When coitus is positive, there is both physical and psychological pleasure. We express love to obtain social and psychological reinforcement, a kind of validation of our self-worth. Once such an emotional climate is established, our love can positively feed back and add to the original physical pleasure we find in coitus.

Just as, at its best, coitus is pleasurable and positive, at its worst, coitus can be exploitative and manipulative. Coitus can be used to coerce others, to obtain a favor or to repay one, to capture and retain another's interest, or to prove a person's wish for power and sophistication. Coitus may result from **seduction,** when one partner agrees to the act upon the promise of a reward. On an occasional basis, such misuses may be harmless. But over a span of time, after becoming entrenched and routinized, such misuses begin to rob a relationship of its joy and spontaneity. Rather than reinforcing closeness, such coitus creates distance between two people and may leave one or the other with pain, shame, guilt, or resentment.

Coitus is healthy when it is desired and performed freely within the context of a sound relationship between two adults as equal partners. Compromise in any of these elements eventually exacts a price in terms of disappointment and disillusionment (Racy 1971).

1. Aside from reproduction, what might be some reasons for engaging in sexual intercourse?
2. Have you ever "misused" coitus or been on the receiving end when a partner misused coitus? What were the circumstances? How did you feel?

Frequency of Coitus

Some couples feel that they must quantify their sex. They may practice coitus once every day, limit it to once every other day, allow it no more than once a week, or whatever. In actual fact, studies show that, in the United States, the frequency of intercourse is highly variable and reflects such factors as personal preferences, availability of a willing and acceptable partner, education, and age (Wilson 1975).

What the *preferred* frequency of sexual coitus is may or may not be the *actual* frequency. The actual frequency of marital coitus is partly determined by our desires and partly by our subjective interpretation of our partner's preferences. Men, especially early in marriage, tend to desire more coitus than they are actually experiencing (Levinger 1970). The actual frequency reported by women, however, more closely matches women's preferred frequency. Furthermore, wives tend to overestimate their husband's preferences for coital frequency, while men tend to underestimate their wives' preferences. And the higher a wife's intercourse frequency, the more likely she is to believe that her husband's preferred frequency exceeds her own. The wives and husbands who are most accurate in estimating the preferences of their partners are those who are noticeably more satisfied with their marriages and sexual relationships.

A recent study (Petersen et al. 1983b) of cohabitants found that the frequency of sexual intercourse drops the longer the couple lives together. For those living together four or fewer years, over half of cohabitants reported intercourse four or more times per week. But for those together after four years, only 28 percent of males and 14 percent of females surveyed reported the same frequency. A similar drop was reported for singles and for married people.

Hite (1981) found that the male sex drive usually is somewhat greater than for the female during early years of marriage among younger persons. This did not hold true for persons who marry or remarry later in life. The report showed that regardless of marital status, men tend to want more sexual intercourse than they actually experience.

The 1980 *Redbook* survey (Levin and Levin 1975) found that men and women who had sexual intercourse very frequently (four or more times per week) had the most satisfactory sex lives. In fact, five times as many of these women and men were likely to say that their sex relationship was "good" or "excellent" as were those who made love less often. This may be a cause and effect situation—those who enjoy sex more may want to have it more often. According to *Redbook* (1980), 57 percent of the couples surveyed had sexual intercourse one to three times per week, 28 percent had it three to four times per week, and 15 percent had it one to two times per month or less.

Most married men engage in marital sexual intercourse. But partner coitus is not their only sexual outlet. Among married men, Kinsey (1948) found that marital coitus accounted for about 85 percent of their total sexual outlet, with the balance of their sexual activity occurring in masturbation, petting, nocturnal emissions, extramarital sex, and homosexual activities.

These results appear somewhat education-related. Kinsey found that among college-educated males, marital coitus accounted for more of the total sexual outlet during the early years of marriage than it did with the less-educated males. This reversed with more years of marriage. After being married for more years, coitus accounted for a *higher* percentage of the total sexual outlet among the less-educated males than it did among the college-educated males. Perhaps this suggests a greater sense of freedom on the part of the older, college-educated male to "do his thing."

Virtually all married women share in marital coitus (Kinsey 1953). While the incidence of marital coitus declines after the early years of marriage, the incidence of female masturbation and nocturnal dreams increases after marriage and remains fairly steady up to and beyond the age of sixty (Kinsey 1953).

While male sexual desire reaches its peak during the late teens and early twenties, women reach their peak of sexual drive during their thirties (Kinsey 1953; Kaplan 1979). How is the decline in the frequency of female coitus then explained? It may be that the male's earlier decline in sexual desire reduces the female's opportunity for marital coitus. As stated earlier, a decline in frequency of coitus with a partner does not mean a drop in the combined total of forms of sexual activity, since studies show an increased incidence in female masturbation and nocturnal orgasms.

---

1. Why might people overestimate or underestimate their partner's desire for coitus?
2. Give reasons why the sexual practices of a college-educated person might differ from those of a person who does not have such education.
3. Why might frequency of coitus decline after the early years of marriage?

aphrodisiac
(af''ro-diz'e-ak)

cantharidin
(kan-thar'ĭ-din)

priapism
(pri'ah-pizm)

placebo
(plah-se'bo)

anaphrodisiac
(an''af-ro-diz'e-ak)

Sex and Drugs

All of us feel more erotic at some times than others, but to become aroused, we need to perceive the situation as erotic. Negative thinking, normal distractions, embarrassment, disgust, a noncompliant partner, and numerous other problems may get in the way of our erotic perception. For centuries, some people have turned to artificial mood modifiers, such as substances a person ingests, drinks, or smokes, when they feel a need to increase their erotic perception and thus aid in their sexual arousal. Some of these modifiers arouse only because they are perceived as relating to pleasure, while others actually act in the body physiologically. And some—especially if used to excess—may increase sexual desire but detract from actual sexual performance.

Aphrodisiacs and Anaphrodisiacs

Throughout recorded time, there has been a search for substances that could improve our love life. Such substances, called **aphrodisiacs,** are reputed to increase sexual desire, performance, and frequency. Especially sought after are substances that aid in the seductive process, increase penile erection, heighten sexual sensation, and produce more intense and frequent orgasms. Thousands of natural and synthetic drugs have been tried, such as deer penises, bananas, oysters, raw bull testicles ("mountain oysters"), clams, powdered rhinoceros horn, and various brews.

One of the most reputed aphrodisiacs has been **cantharidin** ("Spanish fly"), derived from *Cantharis vesicatoria,* an iridescent beetle of southern Europe. A powerful irritant when ingested, cantharidin burns the lining of the bladder and urethra, causing a reflex stimulation of the sex organs, but without creating sexual desire. In females, cantharidin causes erection of the clitoris, engorgement of the labia, and vaginal sensations. In males, it causes erection of the penis, often with **priapism** (a persistent and painful erection without desire). Cantharidin may also cause digestive ulcers, diarrhea, and in some cases, death.

Some reputed aphrodisiacs may have a placebo effect on the user, who may respond psychologically because he or she *believes* the substance to have certain properties. (If, as a few insist, an aphrodisiac, by definition, produces any *perceived* enhancement of sexual pleasure, then some drugs qualify.) So far, however, no substances have been found that physiologically, on their own, increase sexual desire.

Various substances, called **anaphrodisiacs,** have also been used in attempts to *decrease* sexual desire—invariably other people's. Despite its wide reputation, saltpeter (potassium nitrate), while increasing urine flow, has no such success. But other substances have inadvertently created an anaphrodisiac effect. The side effects of certain prescription drugs, such as tranquilizers, may decrease sex drive. Tobacco smoking, by its lowering of the testosterone level and constricting of blood vessels, may do likewise (Winter 1980). And as we will see, large doses of alcohol may significantly depress sexual desire and response.

Nonprescription Drugs

Alcohol

In *Macbeth,* Shakespeare writes that alcohol "provokes the desire but takes away the performance" (act 2, scene 3). Alcohol's reputation as an aphrodisiac is fully explained in this statement. In small amounts, it lessens sexual inhibitions, but in larger amounts, it leads to erectile and orgasmic problems in both men and women.

As alcohol affects the brain, it dilates blood vessels in the body surface, thereby producing a feeling of warmth and well-being. As alcohol sedates brain centers, it initially diminishes sexual inhibitions and improves sexual performance. With increasing intoxication, however, alcohol progressively diminishes the performance.

Since wine is relatively low in alcoholic content, a person may feel its warming and inhibition-releasing effects before becoming drunk; thus, wine's reputation as an aid to love and romance. Beer does not have the sexual reputation of wine. While having a lower alcohol content than wine, beer fills the bladder sooner, requiring more frequent urination (readily interrupting the mood of lovemaking). Hard liquor contains three to four times the amount of alcohol (per volume) of wine. Thus, before a person begins to feel its warming effects, he or she is more apt to have drunk it in excess amounts that adversely affect his or her performance abilities (Bush 1980).

In a study in which males were given different dosage levels of alcohol while viewing erotic movies, the erectile responses at very low levels of intoxication were enhanced somewhat: there was increased desire, and the males had better control of premature ejaculation. As the dose level increased, however, doses even below the legal levels of intoxication suppressed erection (Farkas and Rosen 1976). In another study (Bush 1980), moderate levels of alcohol intake in men made erection more difficult and reduced the frequency of orgasm. In women, low levels of alcohol consumption tended to release inhibitions, increase desire and arousal, and improve orgasm, while moderate alcohol intake led to less vaginal lubrication and a decrease in the frequency and quality of orgasm. In large-dose levels of alcohol, in both men and women, there was noted deterioration in responsiveness. Throughout the range of consumption, the desire for sex remained high, while the sexual performance deteriorated.

Part of the social mythology is that, at best, alcohol either increases sexual arousal, or, at worst, leaves it unaffected (Wilson, Lawson, and Abrams 1978). Yet, chronic heavy drinking destroys the ability to respond at all to sexual arousal due to damage to the nerve centers involved in erection and orgasm in both genders (Lemere and Smith 1973).

Alcohol use may also have a psychological effect in that some people hold the *expectation* that alcohol will increase their sexual functioning. Briddell et al. (1978) found that drinking males holding such an expectation experienced greater sexual arousal than those *not* holding such an expectation. Other studies have shown that,

amphetamines
(am-fet'ah-minz)

with females, the arousal response is due only to the alcohol content of the drink rather than to any expectation of its effects (Wilson and Lawson 1978). Thus, with men, drinking seems to have a heavier psychological impact.

Alcohol may also stimulate sexual performance by providing an excuse for behavior that might otherwise conflict with a person's moral training or value system. Thus, as an ego defense, the guilt-producing behavior can always be blamed on the alcohol.

Marijuana

Many marijuana users claim that the drug enhances their sexual feelings and enjoyment of lovemaking. Both males and females report more intense subjective perception of touch all over their bodies, longer lovemaking sessions, more relaxed feelings, and greater feelings of harmony between the partners. Research by Koff (1974) has shown that females, more often than men, report a desire-enhancing effect from marijuana, perhaps because it helps loosen learned inhibitions against experiencing and expressing sexual desire.

Increased use of marijuana, however, may have various reduced sexual effects. The more marijuana a person uses in a situation, the greater the chance of intoxication and the greater the tendency to withdraw into the self or to become sleepy (Koff 1974). In addition and more importantly, however, heavy use of marijuana may depress the production of sex hormones by the ovaries and testicles. In females, marijuana use during pregnancy can affect fetal hormone supply during important periods of fetal development, contributing to low birthweight newborns (Jones and Jones 1977). In males, the depressed hormone production causes reduced sperm production. Also, erectile problems affect about 20 percent of the men who use marijuana daily (Masters, Johnson, and Kolodny 1982).

Cocaine and Amphetamines

Users of cocaine and amphetamines report that any kind of sexual stimulation is more intensely pleasurable when these drugs are used in low doses. This may be due to these drugs acting directly on the brain to produce feelings of euphoria. It may also be because cocaine and amphetamines increase blood pressure and muscle tension in the genital area, allowing the genitals to abnormally engorge with blood for long periods of time.

Prolonged lovemaking sessions while using these drugs may be painful because orgasm may not relieve the artificially created blood congestion and muscle tension as it would in normal resolution (Jones and Jones 1977). Further, there are reports that cocaine has led to sexual dysfunction (Gay et al. 1975; Bush 1980) and that in some it becomes psychologically addictive, leading to a decrease in sexual feelings (Kaplan 1974).

opiate
(o'pe-at)

lysergic acid diethylamīde
(li-ser'jik as'id
di''eth-il-am'īd)

amyl nitrite
(am'il ni'trīt)

Narcotics

Opiates, such as heroin and morphine, cause the suspension of sexual function. They affect sexual activity adversely through their cerebral depressant effect. Dose-related, erectile problems from narcotics use may be reversible in lower doses, but in higher doses may become permanent due to neurological damage. Even after stopping the prolonged use of these drugs, sexual function may not be restored (Renshaw 1978).

Hallucinogens

While people's experiences with LSD (lysergic acid diethylamide), mescaline, and other psychedelic drugs vary widely, users commonly report that these drugs do little for lovemaking. Their use is primarily for the creation of mental imagery during the "trip," not for sexual effects. Subjective perceptions may change, making sex better or worse, depending on individual judgment. Various other possible body hazards also are reported (Jones and Jones 1977).

Amyl Nitrite

Amyl nitrite ("snappers," "poppers") is taken to intensify and prolong the sensation of orgasm by aiding the genital blood vessels in dilating. But it may also cause severe headaches, dizziness, and fainting. While studies are incomplete, there have been reports of users dying from cardiac arrest (Kaplan 1974) and of suppression of the immune response, leading to severe infections.

Prescription Drugs

Barbiturates and Tranquilizers

In lower doses, both barbiturates and tranquilizers, which are sedating drugs, reduce sexual anxiety, thus producing a relaxing sense of euphoria and a reduction in inhibitions. Because some persons temporarily lose their feelings of sexual inhibition, which they may interpret as a sexual "stimulant" effect, some of these drugs are reputed aphrodisiacs. But as dosages become higher, libido and erection are depressed, and sexual interest is lost. At continued high doses, these drugs are very addictive, with overdosing a real possibility as the user increases intake to get the desired effects. Overdosing may cause severe body reactions and death, and withdrawal from the addictive use of these drugs is also very hazardous (Jones and Jones 1977).

Antihistamines

Antihistamines are used primarily as allergy pills and nasal decongestants. One of the side effects of antihistamines is drowsiness, not a quality related to improved lovemaking.

1. On what basis might any reputed aphrodisiac mislead a person into believing that the substance increases sexual arousal?
2. What experience, if any, have you had with reputed aphrodisiacs, including alcohol, marijuana, and the other substances mentioned in the text? Did you feel that these substances increased your sexual desire or improved your performance? How do you explain your reaction to these substances?

When a guy thinks he's God's gift to women, that's what really turns me off. I hate men who strut in front of women like they have more in their pants than anybody else. They act like they're doing you a favor just to talk to you. Well, you can keep them! Another thing is I don't know which is worse—studs who wear a ton of cologne or creeps who smell like they shower maybe once a year. They both turn me off!

I know this sounds really stuck up and sexist, but ugly or fat women really turn me off. Oh, I know I should try to get to know them, and I know that plain women can be just as nice as pretty, if they're given the chance. But plain women could look pretty if they just tried a little harder. I get turned off by women who don't take care of themselves at all. I don't think they need to spend hours looking nice for others, but they should do something for *themselves*. Of course, the same holds true for guys, too.

Summary

1. We have the ability to respond sexually to a wide range of stimuli, although each of us is not necessarily aroused by the same stimuli. Some stimuli are emotional; others are physical. Regardless, the underlying physical response of the body is the same.

2. Among emotional stimuli, excitement and some negative emotions, such as anger or anxiety, have little to do with sex but may cause arousal. Other emotions, such as fear, may inhibit arousal. Most commonly, arousal relates to feelings of acceptance, love, and affection.

3. Physical sensations that are gratifying are called sensual, and those that are both gratifying and sexual are called erotic. The predominant sensory stimulus is touch, and the body areas most sexually susceptible to touch are called the erogenous zones. Some body parts, such as the genitals, are inherently erogenous; other body parts may be conditioned to become erogenous. Sexual arousal may also come through the senses of vision, hearing, smell, and taste.

4. Sexual arousal may be self-induced. Masturbation is self-stimulation of the genitals to induce erotic gratification. Females commonly masturbate by stimulating the clitoral or labial areas. Males commonly masturbate by stroking the shaft or head of the penis.

5.   The incidence and frequency of masturbation is higher among males than among females during the early adult years, but the reverse is true during later adult years. Most men first masturbate *before* first intercourse, while most women first masturbate *after* first intercourse.

6.   Masturbation helps us to learn about our personal sexual response patterns, provides relief from sexual tension when our partner fails to induce orgasm, and provides compensation when our sex partner is unavailable.

7.   Viewpoints vary widely on masturbation. Some religions still condemn it, and many people still find it a source of guilt and anxiety. Yet, masturbation is a normal, almost universal practice that produces no adverse effects unless it becomes compulsive or is chosen over interpersonal encounters.

8.   A sexual fantasy is any daydream that is sexually exciting. Fantasies provide pleasure, relief from frustration or boredom, and replacement for real-life sexual activities. Fantasies do not threaten a person's sanity or integrity, and relate positively to sexual satisfaction and increased incidence of orgasm. Fantasies may be considered emotionally abnormal if they interfere with work or study, or if they replace satisfactory interaction with others.

9.   Nocturnal orgasms are common to both sexes. With males they are accompanied by ejaculation and thus are known as nocturnal emissions or "wet dreams."

10.   There are many techniques for erotically stimulating a partner. Partners who wish to please each other must communicate their arousal preferences. Such communication between partners is the keystone to any successful sexual relationship.

11.   Erotic stimulation of a partner may include kissing and caressing of all body parts, particularly erogenous zones.

12.   Genital caressing is very arousing since the genitals are highly sensory. Observing our partner masturbate can be very helpful in learning the techniques of effective genital stimulation.

13.   Oral-genital sex is very erotic and is widely practiced. Cunnilingus is the oral stimulation of the female genitals, primarily the clitoral area. Fellatio is the oral stimulation of the male genitals, primarily the glans and neck of the penis. Mutual oral-genital sex is partners' stimulation of each other's genitals simultaneously, usually while in the "69 position."

14.   Anal sex (manual, oral, or anal intercourse) is practiced by many heterosexual couples at least occasionally. Even though it is tabooed by some people, anal sex can be highly arousing. Anal intercourse should be practiced with care to avoid pain and discomfort and the transfer of infectious bacteria to the vagina.

15.   Sexual arousal also relates to the anticipation of being with a sexual partner, cleanliness of the body, and a setting that is imaginative and unexpected.

16.   Coitus, or sexual intercourse, is the inserting of the penis into the vagina. A couple's desires and expectations determine when and where coitus is performed.

17.   Although there are many coital positions, none is more normal than any other. Desired positions relate to age, physical condition, size, agility, and culture. Each of the basic coital positions has many variations. Each couple needs to find those combinations of positions that give them the greatest amount of pleasure and excitement.

18.   Positive reasons for coitus include reproduction; to express passion, love, intimacy, or lust; to provide variety, pleasure, and relaxation; and to create partner bonding. Coitus, however, may be misused if engaged in to exploit, manipulate, seduce, alienate, coerce, or obligate a partner.

19.   The frequency of intercourse and other sexual activity among people is highly variable and reflects our personal preferences and our subjective interpretation of our partner's preferences. Frequency tends to decline after the early years of marriage.

20.   Drugs have long been used as modifiers to artificially create a sexual mood. Aphrodisiacs are substances that increase sexual desire, performance, and frequency. Contrary to reports, there are no true aphrodisiacs. Drugs used for perceived sexual arousal include alcohol, marijuana, cocaine and amphetamines, narcotics, hallucinogens, amyl nitrite, barbiturates and tranquilizers, and antihistamines.

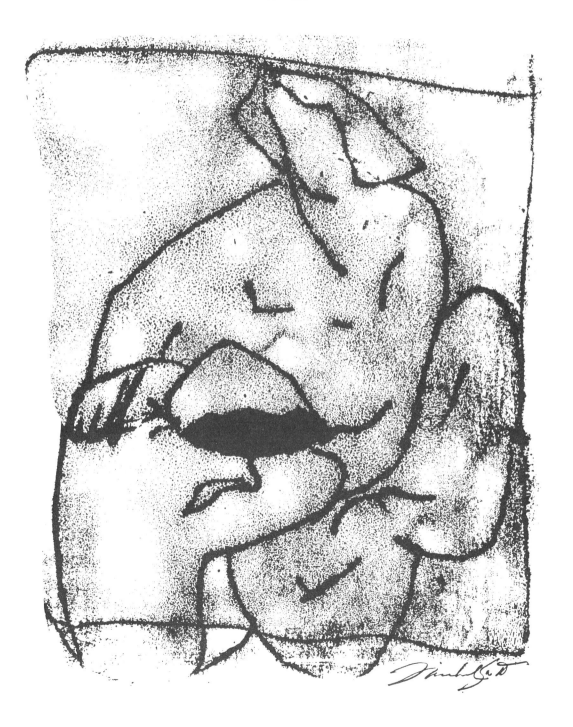

Bob and Phyllis have been married for eleven years. He is thirty-three, a successful, competitive executive, sensitive to failure and anxious to please his attractive wife. Phyllis is thirty and a college graduate.

Very attractive as a teenager, Phyllis dated quite frequently and began having intercourse at age thirteen. She was usually orgasmic, and her arousal increased the pleasure of her partners.

Following a six-month courtship, Bob and Phyllis became engaged and began having intercourse. Bob found that he would ejaculate rather quickly after entry, although he would always caress Phyllis to orgasm. After marriage, Bob improved somewhat in ejaculatory control, although not enough to bring Phyllis to orgasm during intercourse. He sensed that Phyllis was disappointed and was comparing his technical performance with that of the other men she had known, who could maintain erection longer than Bob. These men had given Phyllis immediate gratification, although she had often felt sexually exploited.

Now Bob's awareness of his repeated failure to measure up to Phyllis's previous lovers has increased his sense of anxiety. He has become emotionally withdrawn and defensive, and has compensated by immersing himself in his work. Sexual rejection by Phyllis is equated with personal rejection, particularly since Phyllis has sought out two extramarital partners. Bob, who is otherwise successful, feels humiliated by his experience with Phyllis.

Increasingly impatient with Bob's manual stimulation, Phyllis has become increasingly unresponsive. Having tried "faking" orgasm, Phyllis feels herself becoming alienated and withdrawn . . .

paraphilias   dysfunctions
(par''ah-fil'e-ahz)   (dis-funk'shunz)

Much of what we know as sexual learning takes place behind the scenes in an "un-official" way. Impressions are picked up from family, friends, movies and television, magazines and newspapers. Some of this "information" is rich in unreal expectations, mythology, and excessive restrictions. As a result, what should be one of the most pleasurable of activities—sexual expression—often ends up colored with unnecessary feelings of guilt and fear.

Many males in our culture, for example, are taught to feel shame about acts of masturbation. As adolescents, they learn to "come" quickly in an atmosphere of secretiveness and guilt. Later, with sexual partners, they may develop fears of incompetence unless they can ejaculate quickly and without fail.

Similarly, many females in our culture are taught to be fearful of obtaining a bad reputation if they take too much pleasure in their genitals. When they begin to menstruate, they are made to feel that their genitals are dirty, a body part that no one would ever want to caress or take pleasure in.

It is easy to see from these examples how cultural learnings can alienate us from our genitals and our sexual needs. A part of ourselves we should freely accept and receive gratification from, we learn to deny and to be ashamed of. The physical-emotional drives that should be fulfilling frequently become disordered. Such faulty beginnings can influence sexual conduct years later. The frequent results are wide-spread sexual disappointments and failures.

This chapter focusses on the sexual dysfunctions that are common to each sex. We identify the various factors that may be responsible for these dysfunctions and also the therapies and treatments available to relieve the dysfunctions. The chapter concludes with an examination of the sexual problems (and prejudices) faced by the physically and mentally disabled.

Sexual Disorders

Sexual disorders can be divided into paraphilias (variations) and dysfunctions. Sexual **paraphilias** are those actions that are pleasurable and gratifying, yet whose object (with whom or what one has intercourse) and/or aim (a goal other than seeking intercourse) deviate from the norm (see chapter 19). A paraphiliac, for example, may be aroused by sexually abusing children or by exposing his or her genitals to surprised adults or children (Kaplan 1974).

Sexual **dysfunctions,** on the other hand, are disorders that make it impossible for a person to have or to enjoy sexual intercourse. The term *sexual dysfunction* means difficult or painful sexual functioning and is used to help avoid the impression, intended or not, of implying motive on the part of the person reporting the problem. Sexual dysfunctions range from lack of sexual desire to prematurely completing the sexual response cycle. Many sexual dysfunctions are the result of *psychosomatic* disorders, meaning that a person's emotional state can strongly affect physiological processes (Kaplan 1974). Chronic stress, depression, acute fear, or anger, for example, can interfere with the body's control of blood vessel reflexes, which produce male erection and female lubrication.

Sexual paraphilias are examined in detail in chapter 19. In this chapter, we concentrate on the causes of, types of, and therapies for sexual dysfunctions.

Identifying Sexual Dysfunctions

What qualifies as a sexual dysfunction? Since people typically vary in their sexual desire and response, sexual dysfunctions are sometimes difficult to identify. Even satisfactory sexual functioning involves considerable fluctuation. At times, everyone experiences fluctuations in sexual desire, sexual performance, and sexual gratification. Some variation in these three aspects of our sexual lives is to be expected. Yet, beyond certain limits, the extent of our dissatisfaction with our or our partner's performance may be considered out of the ordinary, inadequate, and a problem.

One aspect of identifying sexual dysfunctions is deciding to *whom* the behavior is a problem. The source of the disappointment may be either *within* one person or *between* partners. One partner may take most of the weight of the disappointment, as with a woman who shares in intercourse but is unable to attain orgasm. In other cases, the problem may be of equal disappointment to both partners, as when intercourse is impossible because the man is unable to obtain erection. When both partners are perceived as being a part of the problem, both may take responsibility for it and be involved in **sex therapy,** which is the treatment of sexual dysfunctions. In this respect, sex therapy differs from other forms of medical treatment, in which only the person with the primary symptoms may be given therapy.

Another aspect of identifying sexual dysfunctions is that there may be little uniformity of cause and effect. Each person reacts somewhat differently to the stresses he or she faces. Similar causes may result in very different symptoms, and similar symptoms may be the result of very different causes. For example, a similar set of psychological problems may lead to an inability to climax in one woman and to vaginal muscle spasms in another. Diabetes may be the physical cause of one man being unable to gain an erection, while another man may have the same symptom from causes that are entirely psychological. Some persons are severely affected by certain pressures, while other persons show no symptoms whatsoever in reaction to the same sorts of stresses. Thus, the symptoms of sexual dysfunction may be only a relative indication of the background causes.

The difficulties in identifying sexual dysfunctions make determining their prevalence difficult to assess. William Masters (1978) observes that there are mil-

psychogenic   Peyronie's
(si''ko-jen'ik)   (pa-ron-ēz')

lions of sexually dysfunctional men in this country. Helen Singer Kaplan (1977) states that "sexual problems are the most prevalent medical complaint in the whole world."

---

1. Describe how sexual paraphilias differ from sexual dysfunctions. Would you expect sexual paraphilias or sexual dysfunctions to be more common?
2. Suppose a woman is unable to attain orgasm during intercourse. Would you say that this is a sexual dysfunction of the woman, her sexual partner, or both? Why?
3. If you were a sexual therapist and a man came to you for help because he was unable to attain an erection, what absolutes could you surmise about the cause of his dysfunction before actually talking to him?

Sources of Sexual Dysfunctions

Sexual dysfunctions arise from a wide variety of experiences and influences that can be categorized as organic, psychogenic (psychological), or cultural. *Organic* factors are biological causes, such as illnesses, drugs, and structural abnormalities. *Psychogenic* factors are behavioral causes that may grow out of our views of ourselves, of others, and of how we relate to others. *Cultural* factors are those causes that arise from growing up in a society that alienates people from their sexuality.

Organic Factors
About 10 percent of all sexual dysfunctions show some organic cause (Kaplan 1974). A variety of physical illnesses and drugs can inhibit sexual interest and performance.

Factors Affecting Males
Erectile response in males is highly sensitive to various diseases and drugs and to changes in hormone levels. In fact, erectile problems may be the first clue to illness in a man. He may be exhibiting the first symptoms of diabetes, multiple sclerosis, or alcohol or drug abuse.

Loss of **libido** (sexual desire) may be due to various diseases, changing hormone levels, or depression and fatigue.

A very tight foreskin in the uncircumcised male, **Peyronie's disease** (incurving of the penis due to the buildup of calcium and fibrous deposits in the cavernous bodies of the penis) or congenital absence of testes also can impair sexual performance in the male.

episiotomy
(ē-piz″e-ot′o-me)

Factors Affecting Females

Female sexual responses are somewhat less sensitive to increasing age, illness, and drugs than are the male's. However, debilitating illness, depression, fatigue, or the use or misuse of specific drugs may affect a woman's interest in or responsiveness to sexual arousal. Changing hormone levels, as during the menstrual cycle, or the use of oral contraceptives also may inhibit sexual functioning.

An **imperforate** (obstructed) or thick **hymen,** vaginal infections, and ovarian and uterine tumors and cysts can all lead to sexual disorders in women, as can obstetrical or surgical damage, as with a poorly done **episiotomy** (cutting into the perineum behind the vagina during childbirth).

Psychogenic Factors

Most sexual dysfunctions have psychogenic roots. More difficult to identify than organic causes, they arise out of our experiences, both past and present. Some of these factors operate in the here and now, growing out of the *immediate* stresses of an antisexual environment. These are reflected in surface personality problems in the individual. Sometimes, the factors are out of the past and stem from deep personality, or *intrapsychic,* causes. Other conditions depend on the relationship between sexual partners. If the partners do not respond positively to each other, these *interpersonal* conflicts can provoke the dysfunction.

Immediate Causes

To be at their best sexually, people must be able to give up their self-control to the erotic experience. Any events that inhibit that feeling of openness and trust may impair the sense of abandonment and result in a sexual dysfunction. Various immediate obstacles and surface personality problems interfere with this letting go.

First, out of sexual ignorance, the partners may not understand each other's basic anatomy and functioning. They may not see the importance of mutually caressing and loving each other to the point of satisfying arousal and climax. Neither partner may be prepared for the effects that life pressures and advancing age have on a person's sexual responsiveness.

Second, some people, for a variety of reasons, feel guilty about enjoying sex. As a result, they may feel uncomfortable in accepting effective sexual stimulation, and they may also tend to withhold the kind of sex play their partner finds arousing.

A third immediate cause of sexual dysfunction is the competition and achievement that play a dominant role in our culture, even in our sexual lives. Since many of us perceive the performance of the sexual act as important, any fear or experience of failure becomes a source of sexual anxiety. This is especially true for the male who fails to erect or loses erection before the sex act is completed. However, the female may also have arousal problems, although she may comply with her partner by allowing him to "use" her body for intercourse. While his failure is more conspicuous, hers is no less destructive to her sense of sexual adequacy. In both males and females, the anticipation of failure in arousal and response may become a self-fulfilling prophecy.

Sexual dysfunctions can also result when we construct defenses against any display of erotic feelings. Some people carefully control their emotions and monitor their sexual reactions and become "spectators" to their own sexual performance (Masters and Johnson 1970). Such "**spectatoring**" is more common in persons who are afraid to trust others, who often feel insecure, or who are perfectionists.

Some feel that they may lose their sense of identity if they allow themselves to be overwhelmed by another person, particularly if this "overwhelming" is accompanied by the "invasion" of an erect penis into the most protected part of their bodies. There may be apprehension over a feared loss of respect from their partner if they "let themselves go" and freely express their passions and impulses. The consequence may be that a man, without understanding why, fails to erect or a woman fails to become aroused or to climax.

Adding to these anxieties may be failure of the couple to freely verbalize their sexual feelings. While not often the direct cause of sexual dysfunction, communication failures often allow other troubles to ferment. Open and honest communication allows true feelings and expressions of wants to flow freely between loving partners. Good communication is free of recrimination and not only builds bridges between partners; it also creates assurance of support if and when more severe physical or emotional emergencies arise.

Intrapsychic Causes

Many of the deeper causes of sexual dysfunctions result from internal conflicts basically related to past experiences. Lodged in the unconscious, such conflicts are considered primarily *intrapsychic* (within the person).

Psychoanalysts see the source of some sexual conflict as arising out of the early incestuous wishes of the child toward his or her parents. They believe that, during early childhood, the child chooses the parent of the opposite sex as the focus of erotic aims and that this causes guilt and anxiety in the relationship with the parent of the same sex.

According to this theory, the son, for instance, fears and hates his father, who is his rival, yet whom he loves. The son experiences "castration anxiety," in which he fears that his penis will be removed by the jealous father as punishment for the son's wish for his mother. The son represses all of this. But, as an adult, when he is ready to have sexual intercourse with a woman, these old fears may emerge and inhibit his erection. The daughter focuses on the father in the same way. Later in life, she may avoid or feel uncomfortable in having intercourse with any man whom she identifies with her father because of any similarities between the two (Kaplan 1974).

dyadic
(di-ad'ik)

Past experiences can also be a source of sexual dysfunction since they can *condition* a person and thereby set the stage for similar reactions to similar situations later on. The conditioning may have come from a disappointed or frustrated parent transmitting negative sexual values to the individual as a child. A woman, for example, may fear any penis because of some trauma suffered long ago by her mother at the hands of an inconsiderate sexual partner or rapist.

Interpersonal Causes

Sexual dysfunctions can also be *dyadic* in that the problems arise between the two partners. The particular relationship may be generating feelings of fear, rejection, anger, humiliation, or misunderstanding, and these feelings are often reflected in sexual dysfunction.

Some couples become locked in power struggles, out of which may grow anger and rage. One or both partners may pick quarrels, make demands, criticize or insult the other, and use subtle and covert methods to sabotage sexual expression. One partner, for example, may delay sex when the other partner is aroused and prepared for lovemaking, and then demand sex when the other partner is out of the mood. The sabotaging partner is very alert to what the other partner desires and withholds that very thing for what may *sound* like a good reason. In this type of situation, it doesn't take long before one or both partners experiences sexual arousal and response problems.

Only a loving, trusting relationship and open and honest communication can help to ensure good sexual functioning. For the woman in particular, it is one of the most important factors affecting orgasmic capacity.

Cultural Factors

The pleasures of sexuality can easily be distorted or impaired by cultural prohibitions. Such restrictions come about because all cultures regulate sexuality in various ways to maintain social order. Also, some religions and sects seriously restrict certain sexual activities because they believe the activities to be sins against God.

A child growing up in any culture faces some conflict between his or her developing sexual urges and sexually alienating cultural prohibitions. Some individuals end up feeling that sexual urges should be treated as shameful and that they should be denied and curtailed. Rather than being something beautiful, sex becomes something to be conquered or submitted to. The personal conflicts created from these cultural restrictions can show up in sexual dysfunctions.

Fortunately, most of us are able to think for ourselves and avoid such behavioral recriminations by placing restrictive cultural and religious teachings into proper perspective.

Sexual problems are often the result of nonsexual conflicts in a relationship.

1. What are some organic factors that can lead to sexual dysfunctions?
2. Can you explain how self-fulfilling prophecy may play a role in sexual dysfunction? Have you ever self-fulfilled a personal prophecy, sexual or otherwise? What were the circumstances?
3. Have you ever been involved in a relationship in which negative personal feelings between you and your partner were transferred to and expressed in your sexual relationship? How did you handle the situation? What was the outcome?

Types of Sexual Dysfunctions

Sexual dysfunctions can be organized into those disturbances that relate to arousal, orgasm, and penetration. Any of them may be lifelong or acquired (developed after a period of normal functioning), generalized (usually occur) or situational (limited to certain situations or with certain partners), and total or partial (in degree or frequency of disturbance). While many dysfunctions occur in both males and females, some are unique to one sex.

Male Sexual Dysfunctions
The male sexual dysfunctions can be divided into three major types: erectile dysfunction, premature ejaculation, and retarded ejaculation. Since the three conditions respond to different therapies, the methods of dealing with each dysfunction are discussed briefly with each condition. We also discuss painful intercourse in this section, even though some therapists do not consider painful intercourse a sexual dysfunction.

Erectile Dysfunction
Inhibitions in the arousal, or vasocongestive, phase of sexual response can result in **erectile dysfunction**—the male is unable to attain or maintain an erection of sufficient firmness to permit intercourse to be completed. Also known as *inhibited sexual excitement* (American Psychiatric Association 1980), this condition may occur in males of all ages, although it becomes more common as males grow older. For about ten million American males, erectile dysfunction is a devastating chronic disorder.

In *primary* erectile dysfunction, the man has never been able to reach or maintain erection for coitus, although he may attain good erections during masturbation or dreams. In *secondary* erectile dysfunction, the man has had successful coitus at some time prior to the erectile difficulty. *Transient* (occasional) erectile dysfunction is very common. Estimates are that about half of all males experience transient erectile dysfunction. Such minor episodes are considered within the range of normal sexual response (Kaplan 1974).

Penile Implants

For severe erectile dysfunction arising from physical problems, one of the remedies is a **penile prosthesis** (a prosthesis is a synthetic substitute for a missing part of the body). This is a mechanical implant that can mimic a natural erection.

The most popular type of penile implant consists of semirigid silicone rods inserted into the two cavernous bodies of the penis (box figure 10.1a).

The disadvantage of this implant is that the man is left with a permanently semierect penis, although a jock strap or tight shorts make it undetectable under street clothes. Some physicians now insert bendable rods that can be turned downward.

(a)

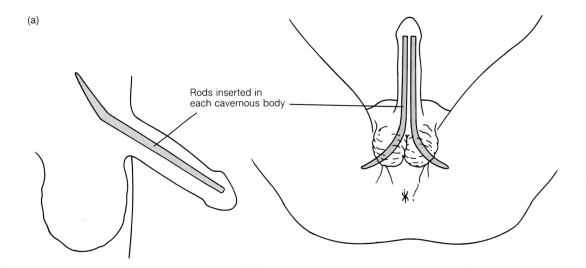

Rods inserted in each cavernous body

Box Figure 10.1 Penile prostheses. (a) Semirigid implant. (b) Inflatable implant: (1) front view, (2) erection, (3) side view.

The other, less widely used and more sophisticated implant is an inflatable prosthesis (box figure 10.1b). Two expandable, balloonlike cylinders are slipped into the cavernous bodies of the penis. The cylinders are connected by tubing to a small spherical reservoir filled with fluid (placed near the bladder under the muscles of the abdominal wall). This reservoir is connected to a pump that has been inserted into the scrotum. To create erection, the man squeezes the pump, forcing fluid into the cylinders and distending the penis. The process is reversed by pressing a release valve on the pump. The disadvantages of the inflatable prosthesis are the greater medical difficulties involved in its installation and a cost about twice that of having a fixed rod implanted.

Such implants are less-than-perfect substitutes for normal erections. But they do, however, provide the enjoyment of intercourse to many men who would otherwise find it impossible.

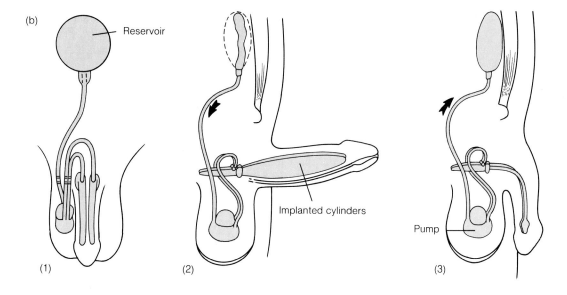

(b)

Reservoir

Implanted cylinders

Pump

(1)   (2)   (3)

Factors   For the penis to become erect, the vascular reflex mechanism must pump sufficient blood into the penile erectile tissues, and this biological mechanism can be influenced by both physical and psychological factors.

Physical causes for erectile dysfunction include stress and fatigue, diabetes, low testosterone levels, general illness, and the use and abuse of narcotics, alcohol, and various types of medication. Diseases affecting the spinal cord (such as multiple sclerosis), Peyronie's disease of the penis, prostatic surgery, and hormone problems can be other physical causes of erectile dysfunction. Also, at least half of all diabetics may have trouble getting or maintaining erections (Gross and Hershberger 1981).

Other cases of erectile dysfunction may have a psychological basis. For example, many males today understand women's orgasmic needs and are assuming greater responsibility for their female partner's sexual satisfaction. Some men, however, fear women and women's increasing expectations for male sexual performance. They experience performance anxiety and fear sexual inadequacy. Fear of failure in coitus is one of the common psychological causes of erectile dysfunction.

Treatment   Counseling and sex therapy are helpful when the cause of erectile dysfunction is psychological (about half of all cases). The aim of therapy is to reduce anxiety so that physical responses can take their course. Therapists impress upon the client that no man can "will" an erection. Erections develop as involuntarily as breathing, and conscious efforts have an inhibiting effect and hamper the input of sensual pleasures. Therapists make no demands for any immediate successful coital performance, which relieves the man of any performance fears.

Therapy includes **sensate focus** exercises without any demand for sexual performance. The chief goal of these exercises is for the couple to establish communication and to focus attention on each other rather than on being spectators to their own performance. Sensate focus exercises are discussed in more detail later in the chapter.

With such a nondemanding approach, erection often appears without the man forcing it or the woman demanding it. Repetition of the exercises assures the man that he can repeatedly reach erection, even when it is temporarily lost.

Premature Ejaculation

Premature ejaculation affects many men and is a condition variously defined. In simplest terms, the premature ejaculator wants his erection to last longer during sexual activity but cannot achieve this due to an absence of reasonable control of ejaculation. Opinions differ as to what constitutes "reasonable control," but age, newness of the sexual partner, and frequency and duration of coitus all enter in as factors.

For the purposes of this text, we choose to use the Masters and Johnson (1970) definition of the premature ejaculator as one who cannot control ejaculation during penile-vaginal containment for a sufficient length of time to satisfy his partner during at least 50 percent of the couple's coital acts.

Typically, failure to control ejaculation results in feelings of inadequacy, shame, and guilt in males who are aware of the sexual needs of the female and who know that premature ejaculation severely curtails the woman's pleasure. Some males respond to these negative feelings by avoiding intercourse or even by experiencing erectile failure.

Factors Premature ejaculation in a person who has had a history of good ejaculatory control may be due to physical factors, such as urinary or neurological diseases, but this is rare.

Most cases of premature ejaculation can be attributed to various psychological causes. Some therapists see premature ejaculation as an unconscious defying of the woman and an attempt to deprive her of pleasure or to cause her pain and disappointment. Others see it as the result of a power struggle in which a woman unconsciously delays orgasm in an attempt to control her partner. A few see premature ejaculation as a high sensitivity to erotic sensation. Masters and Johnson (1970) view premature ejaculation as the result of stressful conditions during some young males' first experiences with intercourse. Those experiences in semiprivate conditions (such as the backseat of a car at a drive-in theater) or those that encouraged rapid orgasm (such as with a prostitute) may have conditioned the male to ejaculate as soon as possible. Frequent repetition of such experiences sustains the conditioning process.

Treatment The goal of therapy for premature ejaculation is to train the man to focus his sensations so that he can learn to anticipate orgasm and to control his level of arousal accordingly.

The first step is instructing the man and his sexual partner in the **squeeze technique** of controlling premature ejaculation, a technique that the couple then practices at home (figure 10.1). To apply the squeeze technique, the woman sits comfortably while the man lies on his back facing her. Provided with full and easy access to the man's genitals, the woman manually stimulates his penis. When the man reaches full erection and is about to ejaculate, the woman holds the neck of the penis between her thumb and first and second fingers and squeezes the penis firmly for three to four seconds. Then after another fifteen to thirty seconds, the woman resumes penile stimulation. When ejaculation is again imminent, the procedure is repeated. A variant of the squeeze technique is the *basilar* squeeze technique, in which the woman applies firm pressure at the base of the penile shaft.

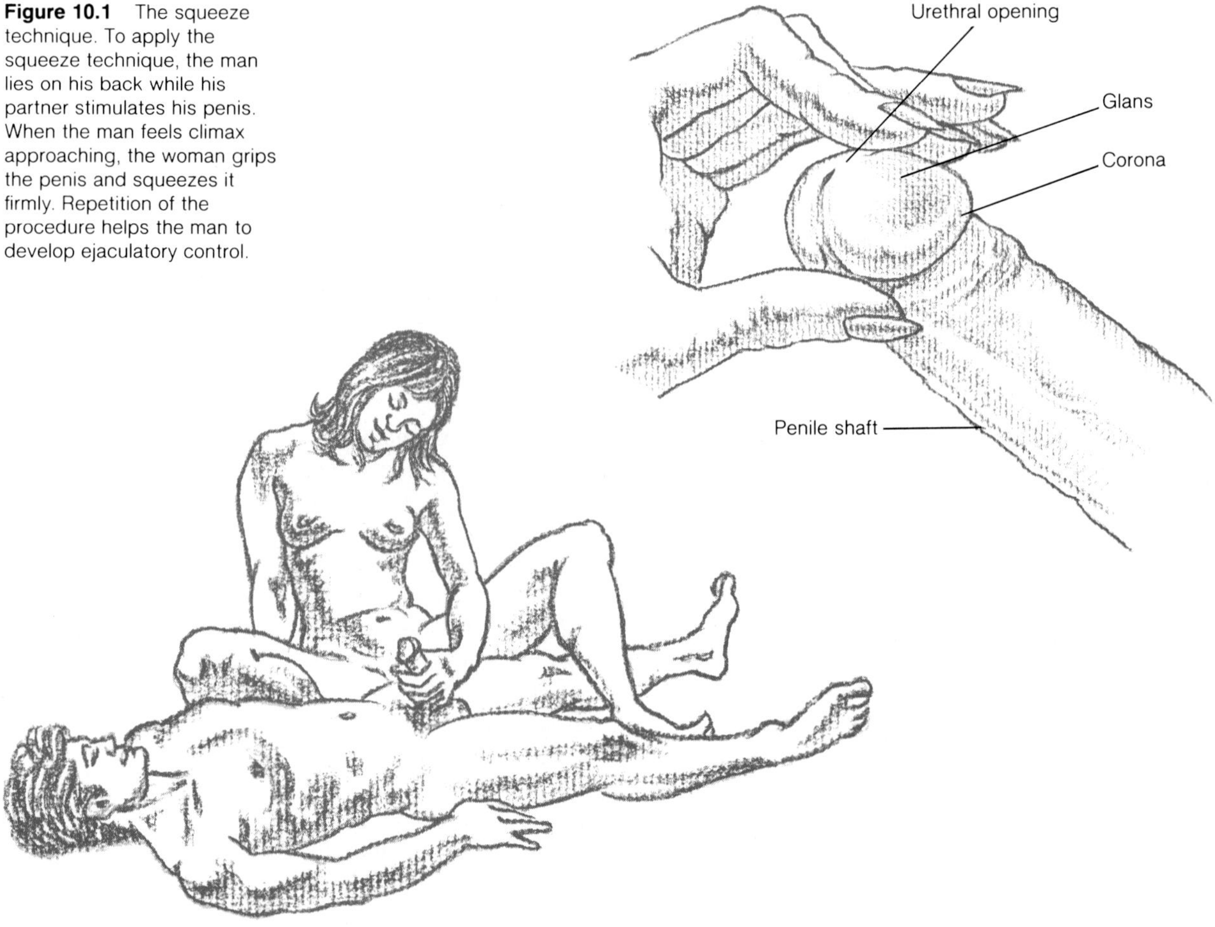

Figure 10.1 The squeeze technique. To apply the squeeze technique, the man lies on his back while his partner stimulates his penis. When the man feels climax approaching, the woman grips the penis and squeezes it firmly. Repetition of the procedure helps the man to develop ejaculatory control.

Urethral opening

Glans

Corona

Penile shaft

In the second step, the man is gradually able to develop sufficient control to allow for nondemanding intercourse in a female-above coital position. Whenever he feels the urge to ejaculate, the woman withdraws the penis and repeats the squeeze technique. She then reinserts the penis. The object is to get the man to focus on the sensations of impending orgasm while he is making love to his partner and to avoid being distracted by the process of penile containment in the vagina. The couple is instructed to employ the squeeze technique whenever needed.

Therapies that *reduce* penile sensations (such as use of condoms, applying anesthetic ointments to the penis, focusing on unpleasant fantasies, cold showers, strenuous exercise, use of alcohol, repeated intercourse, or masturbation to orgasm prior to intercourse) have also been suggested for treating premature ejaculation.

But their effectiveness is questionable in light of Kaplan's finding (1974) that some men with premature ejaculation report a loss of erotic sensation once they have become intensely aroused (a kind of genital anesthesia) and that after attaining control over ejaculation, these men usually report more enjoyable penile sensations.

Retarded Ejaculation

The delay or absence of ejaculation following an adequate period of sexual excitement is known as **retarded ejaculation** (also known as *ejaculatory incompetence* and *inhibited male orgasm*). The retarded ejaculator can respond to sexual stimuli with erotic feelings and a firm erection but experiences an inhibition of the orgasmic, or myotonic, phase of the sexual response cycle. He is unable to ejaculate even though he wants orgasm and receives stimulation that should be more than sufficient to produce it. The severity of inhibited orgasm varies considerably, ranging from occasional inability to ejaculate to never being able to ejaculate.

In the condition's primary form, the man has had difficulty ejaculating from his first attempt at sexual intercourse. Yet, he may be able to ejaculate with solitary masturbation. Men experiencing secondary inhibition date the onset of their problem in terms of having experienced a specific trauma, such as being discovered engaging in forbidden sexual activity.

Factors   Retarded ejaculation from organic causes is quite rare. Much more often, its onset is preceded by a traumatic event, such as discovery of a wife's infidelity or the infliction of harsh punishment by some authority figure for some sexual misbehavior. The mechanism by which these factors impair the ejaculatory reflex involves an involuntary, unconsciously conditioned inhibition. It is believed that the ejaculatory response is involuntarily associated with the painful experience or the anticipated fear of punishment.

Treatment   The goal of therapy for retarded ejaculation is the elimination of the inhibition that prevents orgasm. The first step of the therapy involves private sexual practice between the man and his sexual partner. The man's sexual partner is instructed to manipulate her partner's penis, asking for verbal and physical direction to increase stimulation that the man finds most satisfying. After several sessions, the woman should be able to bring the man to orgasm manually, although the couple needs to feel assured that there is no hurry. Once the man has ejaculated in response to the woman's manual caressing, he can begin identifying his partner in his mind as a symbol of pleasurable ejaculatory release. He is then encouraged to provide her with orgasmic satisfaction. In this way, he not only experiences the pleasure of being satisfied but feels stimulated by her responses to his sexual stimulation of her.

The next step in treating retarded ejaculation is to establish competence in reaching orgasm with the penis inside the vagina. The woman is instructed to stim-

dyspareunia   chordee
(dis″pah-roo′ne-ah)   (kor′de)

ulate the man manually to a high level of excitement and to then, atop him, rapidly insert his penis into her vagina when ejaculation becomes imminent. If not successful, she removes the penis and repeats the manual stimulation. Eventually, the man's mental block against ejaculating within her vagina may be broken, and his confidence in his ejaculatory competence begins to become established.

Painful Intercourse

Painful intercourse, or **dyspareunia,** occasionally affects males as a severe, jabbing pain during intercourse. Such pain may be the result of one of a number of physical conditions. Infections, irritations from contraceptive chemicals used in the vagina, **penile chordee** (painful downward curvature of the penis on erection, caused by infections such as gonorrhea), or Peyronie's disease may cause dyspareunia. Congestion of the prostate gland, seminal vesicles, or ejaculatory ducts also may produce such pain. Men who experience pain during intercourse should consult a physician.

1. If you are a male, have you ever experienced erectile dysfunction? What do you think caused it? How did your sex partner react?
2. What is the Masters and Johnson definition of premature ejaculation? According to this definition, would a man be considered a premature ejaculator if he was able to control his ejaculation enough to satisfy one sexual partner 75 percent of the time but another sexual partner only 25 percent of the time? Why might there be such a variance in his sexual performance between partners?
3. Explain why the onset of retarded ejaculation is often preceded by a traumatic event.

Female Sexual Dysfunctions

Female sexual dysfunctions are less clearly understood than those of men but can be divided into three distinct types: general sexual dysfunction, orgasmic dysfunction, and vaginismus. Sexual anesthesia and painful intercourse in the female also are discussed in this section, even though some therapists do not consider them dysfunctions.

General Sexual Dysfunction

An inhibition of the excitement, or vasocongestive, phase of the sexual response cycle characterizes **general sexual dysfunction** (inhibited sexual arousal). General sexual dysfunction in the female is comparable to erectile dysfunction in the male. Psychologically, there is a lack of erotic feelings. Physically there is an impairment of the vasocongestive mechanism of sexual response. As a result, the female either does not lubricate or does so very slightly, her vagina does not expand ("balloon out"), and no orgasmic platform forms.

anorgasmia
(an-or-gaz′me-ah)

Some see inhibited sexual desire and inhibited sexual excitement as two separate female dysfunctional categories (American Psychiatric Association 1980). We have chosen to place these two conditions together in the same category for purposes of discussion.

General sexual dysfunction is the most severe of the female inhibitions. The condition varies from women who respond sexually only in certain situations to women who have never responded in any situation. Some women react to this dysfunction with feelings of great distress, while others accept it casually or see their primary role as providing men with sexual pleasure and bearing children. Other women develop strong aversions toward sex and intense hostilities toward their partners, or turn inward in self-hatred and depression. These negative attitudes do women the greatest psychological damage. Yet others are able to suppress their sexual cravings without visible damage.

Factors Physiologically, female sexual arousal is a genital vasocongestion under the control of the autonomic nervous system. If a woman is upset, the autonomic nervous system is disrupted and serves her negative emotions by inhibiting the excitement and plateau stages of sexual arousal. The causes of negative emotions may be sexual as well as nonsexual. A woman may fear not being able to reach orgasm, may not communicate her erotic wishes to her lover, or may judge her performance adversely. While deep psychological problems may be responsible for general sexual dysfunction by causing anxiety at the time of lovemaking, the first step in treatment is to modify immediate sources of sexual anxiety.

Since many therapists use similar treatment procedures for both general sexual and orgasmic dysfunctions in females, both therapies are discussed together in the following section.

Orgasmic Dysfunction

By far the most common sexual complaint of women, **orgasmic dysfunction** is the impairment of the orgasmic phase of the sexual response cycle. Some therapists have labeled this condition *anorgasmia* or *inhibited female orgasm* (American Psychiatric Association 1980). Usually sexually responsive, women with orgasmic dysfunction may experience erotic feelings, lubricate adequately, and show genital vasocongestion. Yet they are unable to be aroused beyond the plateau phase. They simply do not reach orgasm. This condition in the female is comparable to the more rare retarded ejaculation problem in the male.

Some women have never been able to reach orgasm (primary dysfunction); others were once able to but no longer can (secondary dysfunction). Some are unable to achieve either a clitorally or coitally induced orgasm under any circumstances with a particular man but do reach orgasm with other partners (situational dysfunction).

Some women are not adversely affected by their inability to orgasm. They may tend to deny its importance, enjoying the nonorgasmic aspects of sex play. Other women become distressed and enraged by repeated failure to orgasm.

Factors   Psychological factors usually underlie a woman's inability to reach orgasm. She may be uncertain about her commitment to the relationship, fear being abandoned, feel guilt about her sexuality, or feel hostility toward her partner. Any of these feelings may cause her to involuntarily exercise "overcontrol" of the orgasmic reflex. Such involuntary inhibition of the orgasmic reflex may have started with a conscious "holding back" when relational feelings became intense. But after a while, the woman becomes unable to climax even when properly stimulated when in love and otherwise responsive. Some women whose partners are premature ejaculators are anorgasmic. While most of the causes of orgasmic dysfunction are psychological, there are a few rare cases in which it is caused by physical factors.

Treatment   Some therapists, such as Masters and Johnson, use a similar procedure for both general sexual (arousal) and orgasmic dysfunctions in the female. Others, such as Helen Singer Kaplan, separate the two. We discuss both approaches in turn.

Masters and Johnson's Approach   With the Masters and Johnson approach, the therapist's aim with arousal inhibition is to help the woman learn how to "let go"; with orgasmic difficulties, the inhibition that prevents orgasm needs to be eliminated.

The therapeutic procedures are similar to those for the male disorders, except that the man takes the lead in stimulating his partner. The couple is first encouraged to identify those things the man does or fails to do that displease the woman sexually. The woman also is encouraged to discover and share sexually stimulating experiences and is thereby given "permission" to express her sexual feelings. The therapists emphasize that sexual arousal and orgasmic release by the woman cannot be willed or forced. She must *accept* erotic stimulation. The therapists also request that the couple avoid tension-provoking behavior if at all possible.

Initially, the couple engages in **sensate focus** exercises, or nondemand pleasuring (figure 10.2). These are performed with the man in a seated or slightly reclining position and the woman between his legs with her back against his chest. This creates a kind of back protection and reduces the woman's self-consciousness or feelings of being a spectator. The woman guides the man's caresses. There is no demand on the woman for performance. The man does not try to force responsiveness but rather accommodates the woman's desires with warmth and cooperation. Initially, there is much caressing of the nongenital areas. This is later followed by genital play.

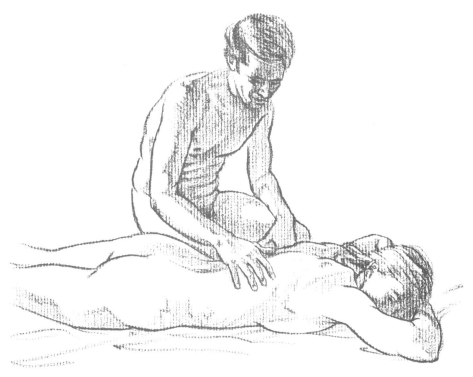

Figure 10.2 Sensate focus. These exercises, designed to teach people to focus on the sensations involved in giving and receiving sensual pleasure through touching, are used in the treatment of both female and male sexual dysfunction.

The woman, freed from pressure to produce an orgasm and to "serve" her partner, may experience erotic sensations for the first time. She also may learn to begin taking responsibility for her sensual pleasure and understand that her mate will not reject her for her assertiveness. This requires that the man defer his orgasmic gratification. His willingness to do so shows the woman that he cares for her pleasuring.

Following arousal and orgasmic success in manual genital excitation, the woman and man engage in nondemand intercourse, using the female-superior position. The woman slowly controls the pelvic thrusting to become aware of penile containment, thinking of the man's penis as hers to play with and enjoy. Periodically, the couple may disengage and simply lie together in each other's arms, only to return to lovemaking and intercourse. Many women find this teasing, leisurely lovemaking extremely arousing. Once the woman's confidence has been built up and she finds pleasure in having the man's penis in her vagina, the couple is instructed to use the lateral coital position (see chapter 9), which permits mutual freedom of pelvic movement.

Sensate Focus

Meaning "to feel or think sensually," **sensate focus** is a technique of graduated touching exercises assigned to couples in sexual therapy to reduce anxiety and to teach nonverbal communication skills. The couple learns that touching and being touched reduces performance pressures and failure-fear cycles.

In the first phase of sensate focus, the partners take turns silently touching each other's body to become aware of touch sensations (both in touching and being touched). Sexual body parts (breasts and genitals) are off-limits. The touching partner chooses body areas that interest him or her, with no goal of sexually arousing the partner.

In the next stage, the touching is expanded to include the breasts and genitals, yet with emphasis on awareness of physical sensations rather than on any sexual response. The couple also uses a "hand-riding" technique in which they take turns placing one hand on top of their partner's hand while the partner is touching. A woman "riding" her husband's hand while he touches her, for example, can nonverbally indicate when she desires more or less pressure, a faster or slower stroking, or a moving to a new area.

The next stage of sensate focus consists of both partners touching each other at the same time. This mutual touching helps each partner to shift attention away from watching his or her own personal response to the other partner's stroking and to concentrate instead on touching any part of the partner's body. Intercourse is still not permitted at this stage.

In the final stage of sensate focus, the couple uses a female-superior coital position without penile insertion. The woman plays with the man's penis, possibly rubbing it against her genitals while focusing on the physical sensations. When the couple is comfortable in this stage, they can move on to intercourse.

Sensate focus exercises remove the demand for performance. Even if the man, for example, experiences an erection early in the exercises, the erection is not necessarily expected, nor is it to be used in intercourse. This freedom from performance is a big help to either partner in reducing anxiety. By engaging in mutual touching, the couple learns nonverbal communication skills, and in so doing, the couple may each rediscover sensory reactions. Testimony to the effectiveness of sensate focus exercises in restoring sensory perception is the dramatic help these exercises have been in cases where sexual dysfunctions have been observed for many years (Masters, Johnson, and Kolodny 1982).

Kaplan's Approach Kaplan treats general sexual dysfunction and orgasmic dysfunction in women as two separate disorders, which is her most significant divergence from the therapy techniques of Masters and Johnson. Her therapy routine for female general sexual dysfunction is basically similar to that of Masters and Johnson, so we need not reexamine the procedure. Her main contribution has been success in treating female orgasmic dysfunction, especially in women who have *never* been able to reach orgasm.

First, Kaplan suggests identifying and removing any intrapsychic and dyadic (interpartner) hindrances to intercourse that may exist. Second, she suggests erotic

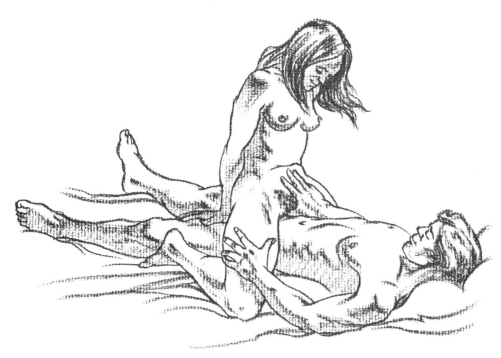

Figure 10.3 This position allows for simultaneous stimulation of the clitoris during coitus in the nonorgasmic woman. She may stimulate herself, or the man may stimulate her. When she reaches the point of climax, the couple can thrust vigorously and bring on orgasm.

tasks that are designed to heighten sexual arousal. The woman is instructed, for example, to masturbate in private to enhance her awareness of and pleasure in her vaginal sensations and clitoral stimulation. Then, with her partner, the woman attempts further sexual arousal by pleasuring and sensate focus methods and by nondemanding lovemaking techniques. The man is instructed to use a vibrator or manual stimulation to bring the woman to orgasm, following the woman's instructions for the techniques she finds most stimulating.

When the woman finally participates in intercourse, she is encouraged to engage in nondemanding, female-controlled coital thrusting in a female-superior position. In this position, either of the partners can easily stimulate the clitoris during coital thrusting (figure 10.3). This stimulation is continued until the woman is near orgasm, at which point it is stopped, allowing the woman to climax with penile thrusting. The couple may use either manual stimulation or a vibrator.

The reason for much of the success of Kaplan's therapy is that the woman learns how to allow herself to reach climax. She may, through therapy, overcome her fear of losing her partner or his approval and gain a love for sex and for the pleasure she derives from it. She must learn to feel secure enough to express her own sexual needs without fear of being rejected.

vaginismus
(vaj''ĭ-niz'mus)

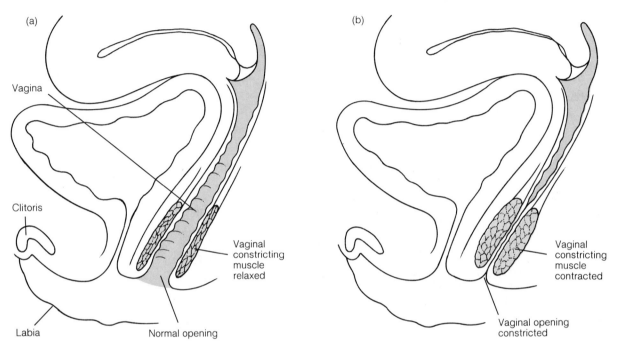

(a)

Vagina

Clitoris

Vaginal
constricting
muscle
relaxed

Labia   Normal opening

(b)

Vaginal
constricting
muscle
contracted

Vaginal opening
constricted

Figure 10.4   Vaginismus, the spastic (involuntary) contractions of the muscles surrounding the vaginal opening. (a) Relaxed vaginal muscles. (b) Contracted vaginal muscles.

Vaginismus

Involuntary spasms of the muscles surrounding the lower vagina are known as **vaginismus.** In vaginismus, whenever penetration by the penis is attempted, the vaginal opening closes so tightly that intercourse is impossible, and intercourse attempts are frustrating and painful (figure 10.4).

Women with vaginismus are usually very fearful of intercourse and vaginal penetration. Yet, many of them are sexually responsive, seek sexual contact, and enjoy sexual play. They are often orgasmic with clitoral stimulation, as long as the sex play does not lead to intercourse.

While the disorder is relatively rare, vaginismus can have a devastating effect both on the woman and her partner. The woman may want to be helped but be frightened of the cure. She may at the same time feel frustrated and humiliated. Her partner may feel frustration or rejection. Some men retain their ability to function sexually, but others develop secondary erectile dysfunction in response to the woman's vaginismus.

Factors   Pain connected with various physical conditions may unconsciously condition a response with the vagina and result in the vaginal muscle spasms of vaginismus. The pain may be caused by a firm hymen, endometriosis, pelvic inflammatory disease, childbirth disorders, hemorrhoids, or a dislocated uterus.

Psychological conditions may also be responsible for vaginismus. The woman may still be suffering emotional damage from a rape or other brutal sex experience. The home a woman came from may have helped to create feelings of guilt and anxiety about sex and a fear of men. The woman may feel hostility toward or fear of her partner. In addition, some women's fear of pregnancy and childbirth takes the physical form of vaginismus.

Women suffering from vaginismus are difficult to stereotype. Some are extremely disturbed psychologically; others are well adjusted. If they are married, their marital relationships may range from being excellent to being deeply troubled.

Treatment   Treatment of vaginismus is directed toward eliminating the involuntary muscle spasms, and usually the muscle spasm symptom is relieved when the client's intense fear of vaginal entry is eased.

The most common method of neutralizing a woman's fear of vaginal entry involves desensitizing the vaginal opening by gently inserting into the vagina a series of plastic dilators. The woman uses these dilators at home and inserts them with lubricating jelly. Initially, the woman inserts a very thin dilator. Eventually, she progresses to a dilator the size of an erect penis. The dilators are left in place for ten to fifteen minutes at a time, and usually within five or six days the woman is able to accept the largest dilator (figure 10.5).

The transition from the dilators to sexual intercourse is usually easy at this point. In initial coitus, however, it is important that the woman guides her partner's penis into her vaginal opening with her hand so that she feels she is in control.

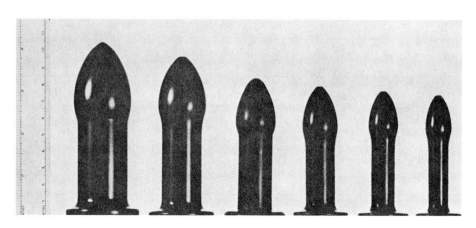

Figure 10.5   Plastic dilators used to treat vaginismus allow a woman to learn how to recondition the reflex response of the muscles surrounding her vagina. Treatment begins with the smallest dilator and progresses gradually to the larger sizes.

Sexual Anesthesia

Some women report they "feel nothing" from sexual stimulation, a condition known as **sexual anesthesia.** While these women may enjoy the warmth and closeness of physical contact, even clitoral stimulation does not arouse erotic feelings. They feel general tactile sensations only, and there are no special sexual feelings upon entry of the penis into the vagina.

Kaplan (1974) views sexual anesthesia as a form of neurosis (mild emotional disorder), in which internal psychic conflicts are expressed physically to avoid anxiety. For this reason, sexual anesthesia is not viewed as a true sexual dysfunction, and no suggested causes or treatments of sexual anesthesia are presented here.

Painful Intercourse

While painful intercourse, or **dyspareunia,** may affect both males and females, women appear to be affected far more often than males.

Factors   There are many varieties of dyspareunia. While many of them have a physiological basis, the true cause may be difficult to identify. With the woman who says that "it hurts when I have intercourse," it may not be easy to determine whether the "hurt" is due to pelvic disorders or due to a means the woman has found of avoiding or reducing vaginal entry in sexual intercourse. While other excuses for not having intercourse may be overruled by a persuasive sex partner, the complaint of painful intercourse is one that few concerned partners can ignore.

The major sources of painful response in the female are pelvic disorders. Irritating remnants of the hymenal ring, irritation around the clitoral foreskin, infections in the vaginal barrel, perineal damage from episiotomies, tissue damage from rape, poorly performed abortions, sensitivity reactions to contraceptive materials, insufficient vaginal lubrication, pelvic infections, and endometriosis are just a few of the physical causes. Psychological causes of painful intercourse may include fear of sexual performance, pregnancy, or social compromising.

Due to the wide variety of causes of painful intercourse, there are no typical therapies to use in dealing with them.

---

1. If you are a female, have you ever experienced general sexual dysfunction? What do you think caused the problem? How did your sex partner react?
2. What are some of the psychological factors that underlie a woman's inability to reach orgasm?
3. Compare and contrast Masters and Johnson's approach to orgasmic dysfunction with Kaplan's approach.
4. What is vaginismus, and how is it usually treated?

Sex Therapy

Sex therapy is the treatment of sexual dysfunctions. The whole idea is relatively new and is aimed at improving sexual functioning by reducing difficulties in sexual interaction.

Sexual dysfunctioning may be temporary and mild, or it may be severe and long-lasting. The therapies for sexual disorders vary from short-term programs to intensive, highly specialized programs that may last for months. Because sexual unhappiness reduces the full enjoyment of life, many people have sought help from sex therapists, and various treatment methods are now available.

Approaches to Therapy
Sex therapy arises from two traditions—the psychoanalytic and the behavioral.

Psychoanalysts generally hold that most sexual difficulties are symptoms of emotional conflicts arising in childhood. They feel that such problems are likely to persist unless the underlying, unconscious conflict can be resolved and the personality restructured. The drawback to psychoanalysis is that it is expensive, time-consuming, and does not always work (Adams 1980).

Behavioral psychologists hold that a person may be emotionally healthy and still have sexual difficulties. They insist that the way to treat sexual dysfunctions is to use conditioning techniques designed to eliminate anxiety.

Sex therapy today is largely behavioral in method and has gained a reputation for brevity and effectiveness. Masters and Johnson have popularized the behavioral approach, and many therapists today use the Masters and Johnson approach or some form of it. A newer form of sex therapy, advocated by Helen Singer Kaplan, combines behavioral methods with some of the techniques of psychoanalysis.

Masters and Johnson's Methods
The development of current sex therapies has largely followed the pioneering work of William Masters and Virginia Johnson at their Reproductive Biology Research Foundation in St. Louis, Missouri. Through formulating new therapy approaches and training numerous other therapists, Masters and Johnson have influenced most sex therapy programs being used today.

Masters and Johnson's approach is one of behavior modification. It is based on the premise that there is no such thing as an uninvolved partner in a relationship in which a sexual problem exists. The focus of therapy is to eliminate the dysfunctional symptoms without trying to change the personality structures of the persons involved.

By treating both partners, Masters and Johnson affirm their belief that sexual functioning is a form of interaction between two persons. The problem is treated as a marital-unit problem; the relationship is treated as the client.

The Masters and Johnson approach involves a therapy team composed of both a male and a female therapist. This provides a therapist of the same sex with whom each partner (theoretically) can best communicate. This practice also is based on the assumption that a combination of therapists encourages communication between partners about what is going on and how they feel.

The couple receives intensive therapy for a two-week period, during which time they reside at a motel. Isolated from their usual vocational-home world, the couple has time and energy to focus on their sexual relationship.

The Masters and Johnson therapy combines daily therapeutic sessions in the clinic with specific tasks the couple is instructed to carry out on their own. Initially, extensive medical history-taking, physical examinations, and individual interviews help the therapists to gain an understanding of the couple and to create a comfortable atmosphere. The daily sessions consist of roundtable discussions, involving the couple and therapists, that include sex information designed to combat misconceptions. Also, each day the therapists give the couple specific exercises to practice in the privacy of their motel room. These exercises are designed to help the couple to feel and respond to simple touching and stroking and to communicate which sensory experiences are pleasurable. The goal is to shift the couple's attention away from the achievement of response to the giving and receiving of pleasure. The couple's attention is diverted from erection and orgasm and focused rather on experiencing erotic feelings. These exercises also help to alter the couple's tendency to perceive themselves as spectators and to judge the sexual experience on the basis of their abilities to produce and perform. The couple discusses the exercises and their responses the following day with the therapists and then the next sequence of sexual behavior to be conducted in private by the couple is prescribed.

Kaplan's Methods

Helen Singer Kaplan of the New York Hospital-Cornell Medical Center has developed a significant new approach in sex therapy. She combines Masters and Johnson's model of behavior modification with in-depth psychoanalysis.

Kaplan believes that many sexual difficulties arise from superficial causes and that brief therapy works best for a couple whose relationship is basically sound and whose personalities are fundamentally healthy. Even when underlying conflict is at the base of the problem, Kaplan asserts that it may still be possible to relieve the symptoms fairly quickly without reshaping the personality. For example, if a couple's problem involves a power struggle, then perhaps marital therapy can resolve the conflict; if the couple has a learning problem, then information and instruction may be all that is needed.

In any case, according to Kaplan, the *first* approach is always behavioral. Only in a severely troubled relationship, when a partner may unwittingly be sabotaging treatment or when sexual symptoms are so strong that they keep fears from being

PLISSIT

Jack Annon (1974) developed what he called the PLISSIT model for sex therapy. PLISSIT consists of four sequential therapeutical steps—the "P" step, the "LI" step, the "SS" step and the "IT" step. Some people's sexual problems are resolved at each step, and fewer people need to proceed to the next step (see box figure 10.2). Only a few people need to progress all the way to the fourth step of PLISSIT.

The "P" of PLISSIT stands for *permission:* giving a person permission to talk about his or her sexual concerns. In our sexually ambivalent society, people often feel reluctant to talk about sexual matters, especially their personal sexual concerns. Giving permission amounts to making people feel that we won't be shocked or judgmental over what they say. Once people feel free to talk about their sexual concerns, the mere process of vocalizing them can often help to resolve the problem. And, of course, open communication helps to prevent most sexual problems from arising in the first place.

The "LI" of PLISSIT stands for *limited information:* gaining some knowledge of the subject. At this step of therapy, we may learn that what we have perceived as a problem is actually a feeling or behavior pattern that is typical of most other people as well. Put in this new perspective, what was once viewed as a problem may now be perceived as no problem at all.

The "SS" of PLISSIT stands for *specific suggestion:* the suggestion of a specific behavioral or attitudinal change that may solve the problem. For example, the specific suggestion might involve how we relate to our partner in some specific situation that has been a source of conflict.

Finally, the "IT" of PLISSIT stands for *intensive therapy.* Only a few people need to progress to this stage, in which one works with a trained and certified counselor or sex therapist. Most problems can be resolved through one of the earlier three steps in PLISSIT.

The first three steps of PLISSIT may only involve brief, simple therapy consisting of just a few visits. Or, a human sexuality course can serve the same purpose as the first two steps of PLISSIT, since the course can help a student to resolve a perceived problem or, through expanded knowledge and improved communication skills, to prevent future problems from arising.

Permission   Limited Information   Specific Suggestion   Intensive Therapy

Progressively fewer people at each step

Box Figure 10.2 PLISSIT model of sex therapy. Fewer people need to progress to each step.

easily worked out is more prolonged treatment required. Then the therapist may use psychoanalysis to probe deeper into the client's personality and explore and/or reshape it (Adams 1980).

Seeking a Therapist

With the increased demand for sex therapy since the early 1970s has come increased interest in the proper training and credentialing of sex therapists. Many states do not have licensing requirements for sex therapists (as they do, for instance, for psychologists).

The major training and credentialing agency for sex therapists in North America is the American Association of Sex Educators, Counselors, and Therapists (AASECT), which is headquartered in Washington, D.C. AASECT has created a code of ethics, criteria, and procedures for officially certifying educators, counselors, and therapists. Also involved in credential-granting programs involving sex therapy are the American Psychological Association, the American Psychiatric Association, and the American Association of Marriage and Family Therapists.

The individual seeking a personal sex therapist may need to do some research and obtain some references. A psychology or human sexuality instructor or the family physician may be able to direct him or her to a reputable and licensed therapist in the area. AASECT can also provide names of local therapists.

An interview with a potential therapist to discuss the individual's expectations for the therapy and the therapist's approaches and procedures is recommended. Such an interview is also helpful in that both the potential client and the potential therapist have a chance to see whether they can establish a positive rapport. For therapy to be successful, there must be a feeling of comfort and understanding between the therapist and the client.

Sex therapy may be expensive, and fees vary. The higher fees (which may exceed one hundred dollars per session) are usually found with psychiatrists and the lower fees with psychologists and counselors. Also, individual therapy requires higher fees than group therapies. The individual seeking therapy would be wise to investigate whether his or her health insurance plan covers such therapy, and if so, with what type of therapist.

Additional guidelines that the individual seeking the services of a sex therapist should follow include being cautious about paid advertising. Many qualified professionals will not use this means of promoting their services. Also, only licensed and/or credentialed therapists (psychiatrists, psychologists, social workers, or counselors) should be considered. The licensing and/or credentialing gives the client some legal protection.

1. Explain the approach to sex therapy used by Masters and Johnson.
2. In what way does Kaplan's approach to sex therapy differ from that of Masters and Johnson?
3. What guidelines would you want to follow in selecting a sex therapist?

Sexuality and the Disabled

To understand the subject of sex and the physically and mentally handicapped is to appreciate that all people are sexual beings. Just because some people have handicaps that limit their physical motion and feeling or their intellect does not mean that they cannot, and do not, enjoy sex and contribute to their partners' sexual pleasure (Sha'ked 1978).

As in any sexual partnership, the most important factor determining the sexual success of a handicapped person is the quality of the total relationship with his or her partner. Within the context of a mutually caring partnership, even severely handicapped individuals and their partners can enjoy fulfilling sexual relationships.

Physical Handicaps

In this section, we are mainly concerned with the sexual difficulties of people who have suffered amputations and spinal cord injuries with subsequent paralysis and loss of feeling. However, other physical problems, such as diabetes, kidney failure, cancer surgery, extreme obesity, arthritis, and the results of alcoholism and other substance abuse, can also affect sexual function.

Not all physically handicapped people have come to terms with their loss and adapted to a different body image. Those who have not yet made this adjustment are generally not interested in initiating sexual relationships. However, many others have made the necessary adjustments to their condition and have accepted themselves as they are. These people feel good about themselves and want a full range of life experiences, including sexual interaction.

Many physically handicapped people have extremely fulfilling sex lives. The limitations placed upon them by their physical problems motivate them to learn adaptive ways of enjoying their own sexuality and of pleasuring their sex partners. They are often more willing to experiment with alternate methods of sexual satisfaction than are other people. They understand, as we all should, that no enjoyable sexual position, technique, or response is abnormal. Further, physically handicapped people derive considerable satisfaction from giving their sex partners pleasure. This increases their own sexual pleasure and contributes to feelings of personal worth and usefulness.

Many physically handicapped
people have extremely fulfilling
sex lives.

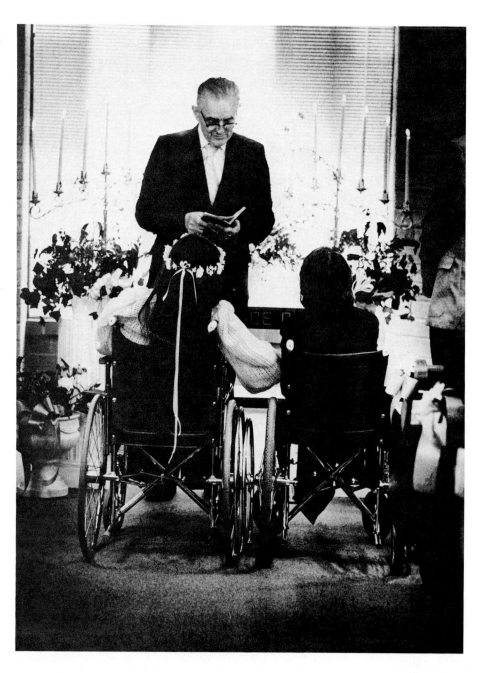

Amputees

The loss of a visibly obvious and highly functional organ such as an arm or leg may have a significant psychosexual impact on a person of either sex. Even though an arm or leg is not directly essential for normal sexual function, amputation of a limb creates a psychological impact surprisingly similar to the loss of the penis or testes (Mourad and Chiu 1974).

Amputees may have difficulty adjusting to their new body image and often experience anxiety about their future sexual desirability and function. A disproportionate number of amputees are young males who have lost limbs through vocational or vehicle accidents. Sexual readjustment is extremely important to this group. Another youthful group that includes both sexes contains victims of bone cancer. Sixty percent of these amputations occur before age forty and almost 30 percent in the teen years. Those who lose limbs due to diseases such as diabetes and atherosclerosis tend to be older (60 percent over age sixty) and are often already in a relatively poor state of health and sexual function (Mourad and Chiu 1974).

When an amputee already has a regular sex partner at the time of the loss, his or her sexual adjustment tends to depend on the quality of the relationship with that partner. If the relationship is sound, the period of sexual difficulties is usually brief, perhaps only a few weeks (Mourad and Chiu 1974). The acceptance of the partner reassures the victim of his or her continued sexual adequacy, and adjustment is quickly made. (Often, new sexual positions are adopted for comfort and convenience.)

But if the sex-partner relationship was troubled prior to the amputation, adjustment within the relationship may be more difficult or even impossible. The added stress of the limb loss may be beyond the adaptive abilities of the relationship, and separation may occur.

Paralyzed Women

Many paralyzed women have no sensation in the genital area of the body. Also, their responses during intercourse may have to be physically passive as far as the lower part of the body is concerned. For example, it may be impossible for them to thrust their hips or to lift their legs. Yet, these women are often extremely sensitive to stimulation of the face, neck, and breasts. They demonstrate verbal and nonverbal responses to this stimulation, which reinforce the efforts of their partner. In addition, they are usually extremely aware of the presence of their sexual partner—his breathing, heartbeat, and sexual arousal—and derive pleasure from this closeness. They generally do not experience a true physical orgasm, but they do often feel an emotional release that rivals the intensity of orgasm.

In addition to being able to enjoy a sexual relationship, many paralyzed women have regular menstrual cycles and are capable of becoming pregnant and bearing healthy babies.

paraplegic
(par''ah-plej'ik)

Paralyzed Men

Depending on the location and severity of spinal cord injuries, a paralyzed male may experience various degrees of sexual response (Comarr 1973; Cottrell 1975). Cottrell (1975) reported that about 60 to 80 percent of paraplegic males (males whose lower half of the body, including both legs, is paralyzed) are capable of erection but that only about 15 percent are successful in copulation, that only 5 percent experience intravaginal ejaculation, and that the conception rate, where pregnancy is desired, is only about 1 to 4 percent.

However, even those who cannot achieve erection still can and do engage in pleasurable sexual activity. For example, the male's sexual partner may massage her clitoris against the flaccid penis to achieve orgasm. If vaginal penetration is desired, a prosthetic device of some type can be worn externally or implanted within the penis.

Paralyzed males who do achieve erections do this in one of several ways. Some experience reflex erection in response to physical stimulation of the penis or some other body part. Their sexual partner must learn by experimentation what form of stimulus will create the erection and also release it. Reflex erections may last for very extended periods, allowing extremely prolonged intercourse. This delights some partners but causes anxiety in others when the erection they have created persists after their own satisfaction is complete. Reflex erection cannot be perceived by the paralyzed male unless he can see it or feel it with a nonparalyzed body part, such as a hand.

Other paralyzed males can produce erections through psychogenic means; that is, the erection can be indirectly brought on by the thought processes or emotions, just as in an unimpaired male. As is also true of an unimpaired male, this type of erection in a paralyzed male cannot be directly willed. Erection is controlled through the autonomic nervous system, which is largely involuntary. Since the penis of a paralyzed male is often unable to feel the vagina and the thrusting of the sexual partner, this type of erection may also be maintained much longer than the erection of an unimpaired male (Comarr 1973).

Paralyzed males usually participate in intercourse in one of the female-superior positions. The woman must be the more active one, since a paralyzed male cannot lift his legs or buttocks or thrust his pelvis. As with the paralyzed female, the male does not feel the friction of intercourse or his ejaculation, should that occur. However, he is intensely aware of the sexual act through his partner's verbal and nonverbal behavior. The sight of the aroused partner and the sounds and odors that accompany her sexual excitement all provide satisfaction to the paralyzed male.

As mentioned earlier, physically handicapped people tend to be very successful in breaking away from the narrow concept of penis-in-vagina as the only legitimate sexual activity, an attitude that unnecessarily limits the sexual fulfillment of many unimpaired persons. A paralyzed male, for example, usually develops caressing techniques that meet the needs of his partner. Also, among physically hand-icapped people, oral sex is far more accepted than among other people (Pepmiller 1980). A paralyzed male may develop techniques of cunnilingus that provide his partner with satisfying orgasms and himself with an extremely pleasant and satis-fying sexual experience. The partner of a paralyzed male often practices fellatio on him even though he cannot directly feel her oral stimulation. Regardless, he gets considerable satisfaction from seeing and hearing his partner enjoy the oral ca-ressing of his penis.

Sexuality and the Mentally Retarded

Millions of Americans suffer from some degree of *mental retardation* (basic lack of intellect). Depending on where the line is drawn, 1½ to 3 percent of the popu-lation may be retarded (Kempton 1974; Valente 1975). People who might be con-sidered retarded fall among a continuum ranging from cases so severe that they require twenty-four-hour nursing care to many whose intelligence allows an essen-tially normal life-style. Some are destined to a lifetime of dependency; others, with proper education and training, are capable of productive, rewarding, self-sufficient lives.

There are many causes of retardation. Some cases are hereditary; others are the result of noninheritable factors, such as infectious diseases, toxic agents, phys-ical injuries, lack of oxygen, and many unknown factors. The brain is especially sensitive to lack of oxygen, with permanent damage occurring in just a short time.

Mental retardation is rather arbitrarily defined as having an intelligence quo-tient (I.Q.) of less than seventy (Valente 1975). However, it is not merely a low I.Q. that causes retarded persons to have sexual problems, but also a deficiency in social skills. According to Kempton (1974):

1. Retarded persons often overly respond to attention and give affection indis-criminately in return.
2. They often have poor judgment and deficient reasoning in developing and car-rying on relationships.
3. They often cannot explain or verbalize feelings, thoughts, or experiences.
4. Because so many do not reach emotional maturity, they are generally inept in delaying gratification, be it from an ice-cream cone or sexual intercourse.
5. They often do whatever is asked of them without questioning and conse-quently are more likely to be exploited.
6. They often are not capable of distinguishing reality from nonreality and readily believe myths and half-truths.

Historically, retarded people have been segregated from society and subjected to prejudices that deny their sexuality. In recent years, however, increasing numbers

Society is becoming increasingly aware of the sexual needs, feelings, and rights of retarded people.

of retarded people have begun to reside outside of institutions. Further, the concept that retarded people have sexual needs and feelings and should have the right to express them is becoming more widely accepted. This is part of a broader awareness of the needs and rights of handicapped people in general. The right to express sexuality to the highest degree possible is part of the right to human fulfillment at the highest degree possible for all handicapped people.

Sweden has been a leader in developing programs to assist handicapped people to attain fulfilling lives (Curry and Peppe 1978), and the United States is adopting some of Sweden's methods and attitudes. For example, masturbation is now beginning to be seen as acceptable behavior for retarded people just as it is for everyone. Like all children, retarded children are taught that masturbation is something to be done privately, rather than in public.

Also, loving relationships are beginning to be recognized as both possible and fulfilling for many retarded people. Training programs emphasize selection of appropriate partners, awareness of the potential for retarded persons being exploited by nonretarded persons, and the importance and methods of effective fertility control.

Marriage is increasingly seen as a rewarding life-style for retarded people. It offers companionship, independence, sexual fulfillment, and increased feelings of accomplishment, security, self-confidence, and personal worth (Kempton 1974). In one study, about 60 percent of marriages of two retarded persons resulted in mutually affectionate and supportive relationships (Mattinson 1970). (About half of all marriages of nonretarded people end in divorce.) Retarded people are often sensitive to their own and each other's needs. One partner compensates for the other when necessary.

Retarded couples are generally discouraged from parenthood, even though their conditions might have no hereditary basis (Kempton 1974). The reasoning behind this position has been that even in cases where a marriage relationship between two retarded individuals was fairly strong, the added emotional and financial strain of parenthood tended to destroy it. Characteristics that retarded people often lack but that are essential for adequate parenthood include the ability to plan for the future, sound judgment and emotional maturity, the ability to provide intellectual stimulation, and the ability to handle frustrations.

Assisting the Handicapped

Most physically and mentally disabled persons have an overwhelming interest in receiving counseling and instruction about their sexual function and activity. In fact, handicapped people who have received sexual counseling often report that it was the most valuable of the human services they received (Sha'ked 1978).

Yet the sexual concerns and difficulties of the physically and mentally disabled are often inadequately attended to by health-care professionals. Schools similarly tend to ignore the special sexual needs of their handicapped students. Home sex education is equally ignored, sometimes because parents deny the sexuality of their handicapped children and sometimes because parents wish to prolong the dependency status of their children (Delp 1971).

Sexual concerns and anxieties of handicapped persons are compounded by the lack of training, experience, and confidence of many of those people who might be in a position to deal with these needs. Some underestimate the importance to handicapped people of maintaining a sense of sexual adequacy. Others are too insecure or uncomfortable with their own sexuality to effectively counsel anyone else on sexual matters, and especially those with special sexual needs.

Health professionals, educators, and parents must begin to accept the physically and mentally disabled as sexual human beings and to provide them with attitudes and information that assist them in the acceptance and expression of their sexuality.

---

1. Tomorrow afternoon, while driving to work, you forget to use the seat belt in your car. Someone runs a stop sign, and you know there is going to be a crash. Your next memory is of regaining consciousness in a hospital room. The funny thing is that you don't hurt. In fact, in your legs and lower torso, you don't feel anything. In a few days, a physician confirms what you have come to suspect—you are now paralyzed in the lower body and are going to stay that way.
   a. What changes will this bring about in your life, and how would you rank the importance of each of these changes, relative to each other?
   b. Several months of treatment have gone by, and no one has said anything about your sexual future. What things would you want to know?
   c. The person who was your sex partner prior to the accident has stayed close to you during your period of treatment, but the two of you have not discussed the future of your relationship—sexual or otherwise. What would you want the two of you to discuss, now that it is time for release from the hospital?
2. A young retarded man and woman have begun to date. They have both been recently discharged from institutions where they had no regular contact with the opposite sex. They know no basic facts about sexuality, even that sexual intercourse exists. Should the persons responsible for them explain intercourse and contraception? How?
3. You are the parent of a twenty-year-old son who is mildly retarded. He has a lot of time on his hands since he has completed school, but he has been unable to find a job. The police have reported to you that he has been seen at the local grammar school watching little girls on swings and has been looking in neighbor's windows. On one occasion, police picked him up while walking down the street with a little girl and offering her some candy. How would you handle the situation?

Phyllis and Bob finally agreed to seek therapy. Because they had a variety of problems, their therapist suggested both marital and sexual counseling.

Bob's sexual dysfunction—premature ejaculation—caused Phyllis to be secondarily anorgasmic. Her dysfunction may have been produced by Bob's basic inability to control his ejaculatory reflex, as much as by his growing insensitivity to her emotional needs.

Through marital therapy, Phyllis was able to see that, although her former boyfriends were *technically* good lovers, they completely separated sex and love. Bob was a caring young man who, although he had a problem with prematurity, was trying to communicate a true love for Phyllis.

Bob perceived that while Phyllis was disappointed with his sexual performance, she still loved him. Through co-marital sex therapy, Bob was learning how, with Phyllis's use of the squeeze technique, to delay ejaculation.

Both Bob and Phyllis are seeing that when the goal of intercourse is the expression of mutual love, sexual adequacy can be learned and can, in fact, become the product of such a relationship.

Summary

1. Much of our sexual learning takes place "unofficially." These cultural lessons may alienate us from our genitals and our sexual needs, resulting in widespread sexual failures.

2. Sexual disorders are of two types: those in which the sexual activity is gratifying but which require some unusual stimulus for arousal (sexual paraphilias) and those in which the sexual activity provides little, if any, gratification (sexual dysfunctions).

3. Sexual dysfunctions may be problems within one partner or between the two partners. There may be little uniformity of cause and effect. Similar causes in different persons may lead to different sexual problems, while in others, the same types of sexual problems may arise from quite different causes.

4. The factors behind sexual dysfunctions may be organic (or biological) causes, such as illnesses, drugs, and structural abnormalities; psychogenic (or psychological) causes that grow out of our views of ourselves and others; or cultural (or social) causes that alienate us from our sexuality.

5. Organic factors include alcohol or other drugs, physical illnesses, hormone levels, and structural abnormalities. Psychogenic factors may be due to stresses that are immediate (surface problems within the person), intrapsychic (deep problems within the person), or interpersonal (problems between partners). Cultural factors may be due to cultural or religious learnings that distort and unduly restrict sexual expression.

6. Sexual dysfunctions may be organized into disturbances that relate to arousal, orgasm, or penetration. These disturbances may be lifelong or acquired, generalized

or situational, and total or partial (in degree or frequency of disturbance). Some problems occur in both sexes; others are unique to one sex only.

7. Male sexual dysfunctions include:
    a. Erectile dysfunction (inhibited sexual excitement), which is inability to attain or maintain an erection of sufficient firmness to permit intercourse to be completed
    b. Premature ejaculation, in which a man cannot control ejaculation during intercourse for a sufficient time to satisfy his partner in at least 50 percent of their coital acts
    c. Retarded ejaculation (ejaculatory incompetence, inhibited male orgasm), in which there is delay or absence of ejaculation following an adequate period of sexual excitement
    d. Painful intercourse (dyspareunia), usually resulting from physical conditions

8. Female sexual dysfunctions include:
    a. General sexual dysfunction (inhibited sexual arousal), in which there is lack of erotic feelings and vaginal lubrication
    b. Orgasmic dysfunction (inhibited female orgasm, anorgasmia), in which there is an inability to reach orgasm
    c. Vaginismus, in which there are involuntary spasms of the muscles of the lower vagina, preventing entry of the penis
    d. Sexual anesthesia, in which the woman feels nothing from genital stimulation
    e. Painful intercourse (dyspareunia), which can result from either physical or psychological causes

9. Sex therapy is the treatment of sexual dysfunctions. Therapy follows one of two basic approaches: the behavioral, in which the person is viewed as basically emotionally healthy but with some immediate problems, and the psychoanalytical, in which the person is viewed as having deep emotional problems that affect the personality.

10. The Masters and Johnson approach to sex therapy is based on behavior modification and the premise that there is no such thing as an uninvolved partner in a relationship in which a sexual problem exists.

11. The Kaplan approach to sex therapy combines Masters and Johnson's model of behavior modification with in-depth psychoanalysis when needed. The first approach is behavioral. Psychoanalysis is only used in severely troubled relationships.

12. The major training and credentialing agency for sex therapists in North America is the American Association of Sex Educators, Counselors, and Therapists. Guidelines for choosing a therapist include seeking referrals, checking qualifications, seeking a licensed and/or credentialed person, and being cognizant of paid advertising.

13.   Disabled persons are sexual beings, with sexual needs, interests, and abilities that are often underestimated by others. Within the context of a mutually caring partnership, even severely handicapped individuals and their partners can enjoy fulfilling sexual relationships.

14.   Physically handicapped people need to adjust to their new body image and may need to develop new methods of sexually satisfying themselves and their partners.

15.   The mentally retarded have special sexual problems: They may have trouble identifying appropriate times, places, and partners for sexual relationships, and they are easy targets for sexual exploitation. Yet, marriage is increasingly seen as a rewarding life-style for some retarded people. They are generally discouraged from parenthood, however, since they often lack some of the characteristics that are essential for adequate parenting.

16.   People who deal with the physically or mentally handicapped must accept them as sexual beings and provide them with attitudes and information that assist them in the acceptance and expression of their sexuality.

3

PSYCHOSEXUAL LIFE-STYLES

11

"Tommy! What are you doing? Get dressed this instant! Susie, would you go and wait in the living room? I want to talk to Tommy alone. Oh, and Susie, stay there. I'll take you home in a little while."

"What's wrong, Mommy?"

"What do you think you two were doing in here? You *never* take all of your clothes off in front of a girl, do you hear me? I don't want to hear any excuses. I won't have a son of mine exposing himself to neighbor girls. What am I going to do with you?"

"Mommy, I'm sorry . . . I . . . I . . . didn't do nothin'. We were just playin'."

"I know what you were playing, and I won't permit it. You've been a very bad boy. I don't know how I'm going to explain this to Susie's parents."

"But, Mommy . . . I'm sorry! What did we do wrong?"

From birth to death, our sexuality is a basic part of each one of us. This is the first of a series of four chapters that explore our sexuality progressively, as it develops through the course of our lives.

In this chapter, we examine the emerging sexuality of infants and children. One goal is to provide information of value to us as potential parents, parents, or other concerned adults about the sexuality of children and how best to nurture it. Another goal is to help us interpret some of our personal childhood sexual experiences and how they may be influencing our adult sexuality. We also examine the issue of sex education—how important is it and where should it come from?

Children *Are* Sexual

Some people doubt the sexual nature of infants and children, preferring to believe that the very young are asexual. Even the thought that children *might* be sexual elicits feelings of anxiety in many people who have not come to terms with their own sexuality and find that any display of sexuality causes them to feel uncomfortable.

Parents who are comfortable with their own sexual selves are more likely to perceive their children's sexuality in its widest and most positive dimension (Curry and Peppe 1978). Less secure parents may have a very restricted and negative view of the implications of sexual development in their children. Their problems in handling the sexual development of their children may arise from a number of sources. Parents may want to avoid being confronted with a reawakening of those uncomfortable feelings that occurred during their own entry into puberty. Religious or societal prohibitions may be in conflict with scientific views regarding sexual expression. Parents may fear loss of control over their children or wish to keep them in a dependent state for the satisfaction of the parents' own emotional needs (Curry and Peppe 1978).

The world's cultures vary in their acceptance of infant and childhood displays of sexuality. Many people in the United States tend to be disturbed by evidence of infant or childhood sexuality. Parents commonly discourage childhood masturbation, and children's sex play with peers is likely to evoke a strong parental reaction, often a mixture of fear, anger, anxiety, and/or disgust.

Some of our adult sexual inhibitions, anxieties, and dysfunctions can be traced back to negative parental reactions to childhood sexual behavior (Chamberlin 1974). For example, someone who was on numerous occasions punished for childhood sex play may years later experience an inability to respond freely in adult sexual activities (Carrera 1981). There may be a lingering fear of punishment for engaging in sexual interaction. Some people report that just when they start to respond sexually, the image or voice of a parent appears before them, and they just "turn off."

The emotional damage of unhappy childhood sexual experiences can extend beyond the sexual arena to impair our entire self-concept (Chamberlin 1974). Children, for example, are often spanked, shamed, or scolded for sexual behavior. They are likely to interpret this punishment as meaning that they should not even have sexual feelings. But sexual feelings exist in people of all ages. They are part of us. And if we perceive that a part of us is bad, evil, or shameful, this can lower our entire opinions of ourselves—it damages our self-esteem: "I have these evil feelings, so I must be a bad person." As adults, we may understand intellectually that our sexual feelings are perfectly normal and healthy. Yet, at an emotional level, we may still carry residual guilt, shame, or anxiety about our sexuality.

This situation is perpetuated from generation to generation because many parents deal with their children's sexuality in much the same way as their parents dealt with *their* sexuality. After all, the main role models we have for parenthood are our own parents (Hetherington and Parke 1979; Papalia and Olds 1979). Even when we try to deal with childhood sexuality in positive ways, any sexual anxieties, doubts, and inhibitions we may feel are revealed to our children in countless verbal and nonverbal ways. A powerful message can be conveyed by something as simple as the tone or inflection given to a word. For example, if the voice of a parent conveys anxiety or disgust when a child is discovered masturbating, regardless of the words spoken by the parent, the message is clear. The child internalizes the concept of sex as shameful. In later life, even though it is intellectually understood that it is "OK" to feel sexual and act sexually, the feelings of shame persist at an emotional level (Carrera 1981). Among the many results are difficulties in adult sexual adjustment and interaction and reluctance to focus attention on the sexual body parts, as in breast self-examination or arranging for routine medical examinations such as pap smears or rectal prostate examinations.

Even what we leave unsaid can effectively communicate our attitudes. The mere fact that sex is never discussed in some families conveys the idea that it must be a disgusting subject. Cross-cultural studies have shown that children are not born with sexual guilts or anxieties; they acquire them (Mead 1963; Beach 1977; Tannahill 1980).

---

1. How can unhappy childhood sexual experiences cause problems for people years later?
2. How did your parents deal with your own childhood sexuality? Would you do anything different with children of your own?

Expressions of Childhood Sexuality

For the purposes of this discussion, childhood will be considered to extend from about ages two to twelve years (or to the approximate onset of puberty). During this period, profound physical and mental changes occur in the child. The older the child, the more specific is the form of sexual expression (Renshaw 1975). While infants may experience a diffused sort of pleasure from genital stimulation, older children may fantasize about or engage in more specific sexual interaction with other people.

Childhood Masturbation

At an early age, often during infancy, children discover that the sex organs can be a source of pleasure. Starting early in infancy, many develop methods of masturbating (Bakwin 1974). Infants probably do not perceive the pleasures of masturbation in a sexual sense as do older children and adults. Yet, it must be a pleasant experience, as many infants do stimulate their genitals. With increasing age, masturbation becomes both more prevalent among children and more frequent in individual children. Also, unlike infants, older children are likely to accompany their masturbation with elaborate fantasies that are specifically sexual in content (Bakwin 1974).

Childhood masturbation is a normal and harmless behavior that need be no cause of parental concern. A child may need to be cautioned against inserting objects into body orifices or told that masturbation is done in private, but a general prohibition is neither necessary nor desirable.

Childhood Sex Play

Parents are sometimes shocked to find their young children deeply engrossed in sexual forms of play behavior. Perhaps two or more children of the same sex or both sexes are engaged in examining each other's genitals (playing "doctor" or "show") or in watching each other urinate. They may even be simulating coitus.

A frequent parental reaction is visible horror, anger, and/or disgust. The children may be scolded, perhaps physically punished, and left feeling confused, guilty, and less good about themselves. What had seemed like pleasurable body parts and activities are now sources of shame. Such childhood experiences are believed to contribute to the problems of sexual adjustment and function that plague so many adults in our society (Chamberlin 1974; Carrera 1981; Orr 1981).

Sexual curiosity is natural and healthy in children, and parental overreaction is harmful (Carrera 1981). Childhood sex play does not lead to precocious intercourse. Nor does sex play among children of the same sex lead to or indicate a future homosexual orientation (Carrera 1981).

Childhood sex-play is important in the normal psychosexual development of any child and should be no cause for alarm.

Childhood sex play can be viewed in the same context as any childhood play. Authorities on child development view play as highly important to the normal development of any child (Hetherington and Parke 1979; Papalia and Olds 1979). In play, children prepare for adult roles, get the physical contact they need, are able to act aggressively in socially acceptable ways, and develop ways of getting along with other people. They enjoy a temporary refuge from life's frustrations. They are able to develop their imaginations and cultivate needed social skills.

Perhaps part of the shock parents experience when confronted with the sexual play of children is due to misinterpretation of the *meaning* of the play. Parents may interpret their children's sex play from an adult point of view, rather than from that of a child. To children, sex play is just that—it's play. It provides immediate pleasure and fulfillment of curiosity and helps fulfill important developmental needs.

Parents who observe their children in genital exploitation are usually advised to keep their responses nonpunitive (Carrera 1981). They might do well to ask the child what he or she has learned in the play. Childhood misconceptions may be revealed and clarified at this time. Similarities and differences between the sexes can be productively discussed in this context, as can be the proper time and place for particular behaviors. Nonpunitive limits on public sexual activity can be set. A positive attitude toward the body can be conveyed in these discussions. Parents can encourage a child's questions rather than activities (Chamberlin 1974; Orr 1981).

Obviously, some limitations are necessary. Children need to be cautioned in a nonthreatening and nonjudgmental manner not to insert objects into their various orifices. The sexual orifices are no different than the nostrils and ear canals in this respect. Children also need to know that individual or shared sex play, just like matters of personal grooming and hygiene, ought to be done in private to avoid offending the sensitivities of other people. Always, though, sex and sexuality can be approached positively and in perspective as important parts of our total beings.

Children and Pornography

Another potentially mishandled family situation is the discovery by parents of pornographic material in their child's possession. (**Pornography** is usually defined as material, such as books, photographs, or films, that is intended to cause sexual excitement. See chapter 20 for a more detailed discussion of pornography.)

Children are extremely curious about sexual subjects, and if sex is not a subject of open discussion at home, pornography may be sought out as an alternate source of information. Few parents seem to realize how prevalent pornography is among young people.

Most pornography represents a poor basis for the formation of sexual attitudes and is a source of much factual misinformation. It presents a hostile, exploitative, distorted, dehumanized, and degrading approach to sexuality. Physical and emotional abuse of females is a common theme. People of both sexes are portrayed merely as sexual objects. Physical aspects of sexual interaction are exaggerated, while interpersonal relationships are ignored. Other common pornographic themes include exaggeration of the significance of physical characteristics, such as breast or penis size. Sadomasochism is quite prevalent. Less commonly, children are portrayed in sexual acts with adults.

While pornography that portrays a distorted sexuality may damage the **psychosexual** (pertaining to the emotional or mental aspects of sexuality) development of children, it is not helpful for parents to overreact to it with fear, anger, visible anxiety, and harsh discipline. This turns a potentially good opportunity for constructive sex education into a damaging, negative childhood experience (Paddack 1981).

If parents calmly mention the discovery of pornographic material, the situation can provide an excellent opportunity for a productive discussion of sexuality. Depending on the type of pornography and the age and understanding of the child, the discussion might include sexual function, sexual orientation, and the nature and quality of relationships.

This might also be an appropriate time to provide a child with sex-education books specifically intended for his or her age group. Most large bookstores carry such books. An example of the many available is *Where Did I Come From?* by Mayle (1973). *Changing Bodies, Changing Lives* by Ruth Bell (1981) is recommended for older children and adolescents.

1. What is the earliest age at which you can remember experiencing your sex organs as a source of pleasure? At that time, did you interpret this pleasure in the same way as you now interpret genital pleasure?
2. If you discovered your child (or little brother or little sister) engrossed in sex play with a neighbor child, how would you handle the situation? What would you say to the child?
3. How can parents turn the discovery of pornography in the possession of their children into a constructive educational experience?

Parental Affection and Childhood Sexuality

Child development authorities believe that the most significant role models in children's lives are their parents or those adults who serve in that capacity. Very early in life, children develop concepts regarding sexuality, love, affection, and caring that are based largely on what they have observed in their parents. Children come to perceive sexuality as either a positive or negative force. Ideas are developed as to appropriate expressions of love and affection. At the same time, the child's own sexuality influences how he or she perceives the behavior of adults. Parents may be unaware of their influence on their children or, conversely, knowing that they are role models, may feel uncertain about appropriate expressions of their love, affection, and sexuality.

In the following paragraphs, we briefly examine the effects of parental displays of affection for their children and for each other on childhood sexuality. Special attention is given to how children react to the new love relationships of a divorced or widowed parent.

Parent-Child Affection

Most parents feel a great amount of affection for their children, but this parental love is not always demonstrated. A variety of hypotheses may explain why so many parents fail to be more affectionate with their children. One obvious answer lies in the great demands placed upon the time of many parents. With career pressures, social obligations, keeping a home functioning, and all the other adult responsibilities, children sometimes seen to get lost in the shuffle.

However, authorities on child development place great emphasis on the importance of parental demonstrations of affection for their children (Thornburg 1975; Hetherington and Parke 1979; Papalia and Olds 1979). Having affectionate parents contributes to a sense of self-esteem that serves us well in all phases of our lives. It helps us to weather the hard knocks of childhood. It contributes to our academic and social success in school and to later career success as an adult. And having had affectionate parents helps us in our relationships with others throughout our lives since people who are shown plenty of affection as children are better able to display affection to others as adults. In addition, it is well known that people relate to their children much as their own parents related to them (Pomeroy 1976). Problems such as child neglect or other abuse tend to perpetuate themselves from generation to generation.

Affection between Parents

Many young people would find it almost impossible to believe that their parents still carry on a sexual relationship with each other. They never see their parents kissing each other, nor do they hear affectionate verbal exchanges between them. Many parents are so uncomfortable with their sexuality or carry such negative feelings about sexuality in general that they feel that children must be "protected" from any display of sexual feelings. But what better role models for adult mate interaction could children have than a pair of loving, caring parents?

If children observe little open display of affection between their parents, they will probably be inhibited in their own ability to demonstrate affection as adults.

primal
(pri'mal)

While children sometimes verbally reject everything their parents stand for, in reality, as we've stated before, parents are the most significant role models in their children's lives. Children tend to rather closely pattern their attitudes and behaviors on what they have observed in their parents. If children observe little open display of affection between their parents, they may be inhibited in their own ability to demonstrate affection when they reach adulthood (Pomeroy 1976).

To what extent should parents express love or sexuality in the presence of their children? The answer to this question is unclear. It is unquestionably beneficial for children to know that their parents love each other. In many of the world's societies, adults and children all share one sleeping room (Mead 1963; Beach 1977). Gardner (1975) reports that three-quarters of the world's children sleep in the same room as their parents. In such situations, children openly observe their parents' sexual activities from birth and seem to suffer no damage to personality or sexual adjustment (Myers 1974; Harrison 1976). However, it is uncertain how this relates to the very different cultures of most industrialized nations, such as the United States. Here, children experience sexual and romantic preoccupations and hold extreme interest in their parents' more mysterious sexuality.

When a child has never observed sexual intercourse before, the sight of parents actively engaged in coitus can be confusing and even frightening. Not understanding what is happening, but hearing moans and screams, a young child may conclude that one of the parents (probably the mother) is being hurt by the other (Harrison 1976). Older children experience less confusion and misunderstanding in this situation.

Psychoanalysts of the Freudian school of thought sometimes place a great significance on the psychological damage a child may suffer from observing parental intercourse, calling this the *primal scene* (Myers 1974). However, if good communication exists in a family so that the child feels free to ask questions about what has been seen, there should be little or no harm done by a child's accidentally observing parental coitus (Harrison 1976; Hoyt 1982). The parents' response to the episode is significant. A child may be particularly upset if parents display anger, anxiety, or guilt, or if the child is punished for the accidental intrusion (Myers 1974). Children should be told that the activity they observed was loving and enjoyable (Hoyt 1982).

Divorced or Widowed Parents and New Love Relationships

Separated, divorced, or widowed parents often feel quite uncertain as to how much should be revealed to their children regarding any new love relationships. These situations can present some special problems not present in a marital partnership. Children may feel very threatened by a parent's relationship with someone other than the original spouse. There may be a sense of loyalty to the original spouse.

There may be the fear that another parent is about to be taken away from them. There may be lingering hopes that the two original parents may someday get back together. There may be a reluctance to share the attention of the parent with whom the child lives with an "outsider." There may be fear that the new relationship won't last and that the child's sense of loss will have to be repeated. Children seem to be especially possessive of a parent of the opposite sex. (Freudians would say that this reflects the child's sexual desire for the parent.)

Many single parents find themselves in a quandry. On the one hand, they desperately need to establish and maintain new relationships. But they care about their children and do not want to upset or damage them. While there may not always be an ideal solution to this situation, a good, workable plan can usually be devised. In most cases, it is preferable to be open and honest with children, explaining why the parent needs adult companionship and trying to deal with specific anxieties as they appear (Adams 1978). Having the child and the new friend become well acquainted may help with the child's acceptance of the friend.

Looking ahead, there are many potential positive effects for children in having a caring stepfather or stepmother in the home. This situation provides adult role models of both sexes, both as individual role models and as models of couple interaction. It shows a child that he or she can be accepted and loved by adults of both sexes. Even though someone is not a child's natural parent, his or her presence can create many positive feelings and experiences for the child.

---

1. Would you describe your parents as affectionate or nonaffectionate? How do you think their affection or nonaffection has affected you?
2. How do you feel about your parents having a sexual relationship? Does it seem perfectly natural or very unnatural?
3. Imagine that you are recently divorced and that you have custody of your four-year-old son. He is openly hostile toward any person of the opposite sex that you date. How can you best deal with this situation?

Home Nudity

The world's cultures vary immensely in their approaches to covering the human body (Mead 1963; Beach 1977). In some cultures, little or no clothing is worn under any circumstances. In other cultures, nudity within the home or on the beach prevails. Other cultures require keeping almost the entire body covered at all times. Within each culture, people apparently feel comfortable about their particular state of dress or undress (Gardner 1975).

Within many families in the United States, there exists considerable anxiety about exposure of the breasts or genitals, even within the privacy of the home. Children are told from an early age that these parts must be kept covered. What does this really tell a child? The implicit message is that part of the body is basically unacceptable or "shameful" (Gardner 1975).

Childhood training that the sexual parts must be kept covered can influence adult sexual relationships years later. There may be discomfort about nudity even during sexual interaction. There may also be anxiety about touching or having touched the sexual parts of the body. This anxiety may translate into sexual dysfunction (Gardner 1975).

A more relaxed attitude toward home nudity can help children to develop more positive feelings about their sexual anatomy and their sexuality (Finch 1982). Some people might say that home nudity tends to provide more sexual stimulus than is beneficial to children. But the truth is that by selectively covering a particular part, we actually emphasize that part. The bikini is a case in point. Most people who spend any time at nude beaches or resorts are surprised at how being nude deemphasizes the sexual body parts.

As adults, our attitudes toward nudity are rather deeply ingrained. Many adults would find it quite uncomfortable to be nude in the presence of their children, even if they intellectually understood that nudity was acceptable behavior. In such cases, the discomfort of the parents would be nonverbally conveyed to their children—the message would be just the opposite of what the parents intended to convey. However, such parents may be able to allow their children the freedom of home nudity without undue anxiety.

Finally, adults who are comfortable with nudity should not flaunt their nudity before their children in a seductive way (Gardner 1975). Nor should they insist on their children's nudity. If a child feels uncomfortable without clothing, it is counterproductive to force nudity upon the child. This is especially true of adolescents, who may be highly self-conscious about their changing bodies.

1. How much emphasis was placed on modesty in your childhood home?
2. In raising children of your own, would you place more or less (or about the same) emphasis on modesty?

Sexual Differentiation in Children

Of extreme importance to a discussion of childhood sexuality is the question of inherent differences between the sexes. How are boys and girls different, and just how different are they?

Certain anatomical differences between males and females are indisputable. Obviously, the reproductive organs are different. Obviously, mature males are, on the average, taller and more muscular than females (Gersh and Gersh 1981). Physiologically, it is proven that the male metabolic rate averages about 25 percent higher than the female rate, even if all other variables, such as weight, are the same. But it is in the area of behavioral differences between males and females that controversies occur.

Valid research in this area is difficult to perform, as differences may be quite subtle. It is virtually impossible to eliminate cultural influences from research on basic male and female differences. Not only are the subjects of the research influenced by cultural factors from birth, but the researchers themselves also carry numerous, inescapable cultural biases. As a result, much conflicting data is obtained, and almost every research finding in this area is challenged by other authorities (Hooper 1981).

Biological Brain Differentiation

Many authorities now feel that the hormones of human males and females condition their brains in subtly different ways, even before birth. These differences are indisputable in other animal species but are much less pronounced in humans (Gelman 1981).

If such brain differences exist, they may account for ways in which males and females seem to experience the world differently. Perhaps females and males perceive events differently not just because of their different cultural conditioning, but because they feel with a different sensitivity of touch and puzzle out problems with subtly different brains.

What must be emphasized, however, are the great mental *similarities* between the sexes, rather than the differences. Any real difference in the mean (average) mental abilities of the two sexes is quite small compared to the range of abilities within each sex. Also, the influence of these minor, hormone-related differences, if they exist at all, would be trivial in contrast to the impact of our different cultural expectations and conditioning for males and females. And finally, even if these biological differences were absolutely proven valid, they would provide no justification for imposing any selective limitations on either sex. The inherent mental abilities of the two sexes are extremely similar, if not identical.

Social, Cultural, and Learning Experiences

A society is a group of interacting people who share the same territory and participate in a common culture. A culture consists of all the shared material and nonmaterial products of a society. Material culture consists of homes, schools, clothing, cars, and all of the other objects we create. Nonmaterial culture consists of our abstract creations—our languages, ideas, beliefs, rules, customs, family patterns, and political systems (Robertson 1977). Our sexuality is greatly shaped and influenced by such nonmaterial cultural factors.

It is well documented (Papalia and Olds 1979; Woods 1979) that right from birth, parents, or any others who have any form of contact with an infant or child, treat males and females differently. People tend to hold female infants more than males. They play more roughly with males than with females. A different tone of voice is used in speaking to each sex. Females are spoken to and sung to more than males. Different types of toys are offered to each sex. Discipline may be handled differently. Parents encourage their daughters to remain closer to them, while they encourage independence in their sons. Rooms are decorated differently for each sex. And in countless other ways, the two sexes undergo different kinds of behavior-conditioning experiences. All of these differences are certain to influence the development of a child's personality.

Most people who recognize these differences in relating to male and female children presume that there are innate differences between the sexes. But is this true? Interesting experiments have been done (for example, Gelman 1981) in which the same infants have been dressed in different colors and their behavior evaluated by observers who were not told the sex of the infants. When dressed in blue, the children were described by the observers as "very active." The same babies dressed in pink were perceived as "very gentle." When the infants were dressed in yellow, the observers became very frustrated. They were not sure how to react and were eager to know the sex of each baby so that they could respond "appropriately."

Again, we must conclude that the two sexes are inherently very similar in terms of behavioral responses and that most of the differences that are commonly perceived between the sexes are culturally induced if, indeed, they exist at all. Table 11.1 points out some probable, possible, and mythical sex differences.

Different types of toys are offered to each sex and are thought to influence the development of children.

Table 11.1 Probable, Possible, and Mythical Sex Differences.

Probable Sex Differences (Either Definitely Proven or Supported by Most Published Studies)

Size	Males are longer and heavier at birth, and remain taller and heavier throughout life.
Musculature	A greater percentage of body weight is muscle in males than in females.
Physical, motor, and sensory	Females are physically and neurologically more advanced at birth, are earlier in walking and attaining puberty. Female infants have greater sensitivity to pain. More males are conceived, but the male miscarriage rate is much higher. The male infant mortality rate is higher. Males are more vulnerable to disease, malnutrition, and hereditary disorders at all ages. Females could be said to be biologically superior to males.
Social and emotional development	Males are more aggressive, even in early social play. Females are more compliant to parental wishes as early as age two.
Developmental problems	Males are more likely to have school problems, reading disabilities, speech defects such as stuttering, and emotional problems.

Possible Sex Differences (Reported by Some Authorities but Doubted by Others)

Activity level	When differences in infant activity level are found, males are usually reported as being more active than females. Many studies find no differences.
Dependency	There is no difference in dependency between younger males and females. As older children and adults, females tend to rate themselves as more dependent.
Recognition of faces	Some studies have shown that female infants recognize different faces at an earlier age than male infants.
Confidence	No consistent differences in levels of timidity in young males and females have been proven. Older females report themselves as being more fearful than do males. Males are more likely to engage in dangerous occupations and activities (to prove "masculinity"?).
Curiosity	Some studies have shown males to be more curious and exploratory. Other studies dispute this finding.
Stress management	Some studies suggest that males are more vulnerable to problems resulting from family disharmony and interpersonal conflicts. The findings are uncertain at this time.
Cognitive abilities	Females are possibly superior in verbal abilities—talk earlier, excel at vocabulary, reading comprehension, and verbal creativity. Males possibly excel in visual-spatial ability, such as manipulating objects in three-dimensional space or reading maps. Male superiority at mathematics is supported by some authorities and challenged by others.

Table 11.1   *continued*

Mythical Sex Differences (Believed by Many People but Definitely Disproven)

Myth	*Reality*
Males are more responsive to visual stimuli and females to auditory stimuli.	Not true—there are no documented differences in this respect.
Females are better at simple, repetitive tasks; males are better at complex tasks.	Not true.
Females have lower self-esteem than males.	Self-esteem, in general, is about equal in both sexes. Females rate themselves more highly in social skills, while males tend to view themselves as having more power (a realistic view in our culture).
Males are biologically superior to females.	Males are (on the average) larger and more muscular than females. Males, however, are more likely to die than are females, at any age beginning at conception.
Males are less social than females.	Males and females spend equal time with others and are equally responsive to others.
Females are more likely to respond to suggestion.	Females are not more suggestible. Females are not more likely to conform to standards of a peer group or to imitate others.

Sources: Paraphrased from Maccoby, E. E., and C. N. Jacklin. *The Psychology of Sex Differences.* Palo Alto, Calif.: Stanford University Press, 1974 and Hetherington, E. M., and R. D. Parke. *Child Psychology: A Contemporary Viewpoint.* New York: McGraw-Hill, 1979.

Note: All statements are generalizations and refer to the average of all members of each sex. Where sex differences do exist, the range of characteristics of individuals within each sex is usually much greater than the difference between the two sexes.

1. In your opinion, are "masculinity" and "femininity" influenced more by inherent biological factors or by culture?
2. Why is valid research on question 1 difficult to carry out?

Gender Identity

In the preceding section, we discussed the biological and cultural differences that promote sexual differentiation in children. But when and how do children develop a sense of their gender identity, their concept of themselves as being either male or female?

Actually, little is known with certainty about how children develop a sense of gender identity. While almost all authorities agree that gender identity is firmly

dysphoria
(dis-fo're-ah)

ingrained quite early in life, and probably is irrevocable by age four (Pattison 1982), they do not agree on how this happens.

Both biological and psychological theories have been proposed. Most research to date (as surveyed by Ehrhardt and Meyer-Bahlburg 1981) seems to indicate that prenatal or postnatal hormones or other biological forces are not as important in gender identity development as the way in which we are reared (see also chapter 7). If a child is reared as a male, the child feels male. If a child is reared as a female, the child feels female. And, if the child is reared ambiguously, an uncertain gender identity may result.

Once gender identity has been established, it cannot be easily changed. For example, if a person has been consistently raised as a female but suddenly (perhaps due to an adrenal hormone disorder) develops a low voice and grows a beard and the clitoris enlarges to resemble a penis, her gender identity remains female (Ehrhardt 1979). (Obviously, such physical changes would be very disturbing, and their cause would need to be corrected without delay.)

When a child is born with ambiguous-appearing sex organs, it is essential that a definite sex assignment be made immediately because the concept of being male or female is so important in any society. Sex assignment is often, though not always, made on the basis of the sex chromosomes carried in the baby's cells (see chapter 7).

If surgical and hormonal corrections result in a physical appearance that is clearly female or male, and if parental doubts about the child's sex are resolved early, the gender identity of the child will almost always develop in agreement with the sex of assignment. This is true even if the child is assigned the opposite sex from that indicated by the sex chromosomes. For example, some physicians feel that it is preferable to automatically assign the sex of female because a normal appearing and sexually functioning female can be surgically created more successfully than a male. The fact that a child's sex can be rather arbitrarily assigned at birth and that the child usually grows up with the gender identity appropriate to the assigned sex tends to point toward a more psychological theory on development of gender identity.

Most individuals' gender identity conforms well to their biological sexual development. If they appear to be female, they think of themselves as being female. If they look like males, they feel like males. But not everyone's gender identity conforms so well to their biological sex. Some people go through much or all of their lives feeling uncertain as to just which sex they belong. A general term given to any degree of difficulty in gender identity is gender **dysphoria,** a term referring to an unwell or uneasy feeling.

A few people feel quite certain that their true gender is actually the opposite of what their physical appearance seems to indicate. These people are called *transsexuals.*

transvestism
(trans-ves'tizm)

Transsexualism

Transsexualism is the most extreme form of gender misidentification. A transsexual
is a biologically normal-appearing male or female who believes that he or she should
have been born a member of the opposite sex. Transsexuals believe that a biological
mistake has been made and that they were born with the wrong body for their feelings. This is sometimes described as the feeling of being "trapped" in the body of
the wrong sex. Many transsexuals seek medical help with the goal of changing their
body to fit their feelings. The term *transsexual* is used for these people whether
they undergo sex-change surgery or not.

Transsexualism is not to be confused with **homosexuality** (being sexually attracted to people of one's own sex) or **bisexuality** (being sexually attracted to people
of both sexes) (see chapter 18) or **transvestism** (deriving sexual gratification from
dressing in the clothing of the opposite sex) (see chapter 19). Since a transsexual
male believes that he is really a woman, he desires a relationship with a male. He
has romantic and emotional responses to men and sexual fantasies about them. Similarly, a female transsexual believes that she is really a man and therefore desires
a relationship with a heterosexual female. She has romantic and emotional responses to women and sexual fantasies about them. For both males and females,
these may seem like homosexual attractions, but they are not because transsexuals
perceive themselves to be of the opposite sex of the people to whom they are attracted.

Another distinguishing feature between transsexuals and homosexuals is in
how they view their own genitals. Homosexuals may take pride in their sex organs
and receive great pleasure from their sexual activities. In contrast, transsexuals despise their genitals and do not even want to use them (Silber 1981). They do not
enjoy masturbating and do not want any partner to touch their sex organs. A transsexual male despises his erections. While transsexuals may have elaborate sexual
fantasies, actual sexual interaction tends to be infrequent. A male homosexual views
himself as a man, has a sexual preference for other men, and enjoys using his genitals in activities with other men. The male transsexual views himself as a woman,
and his male sex organs are an incredible impediment to him.

Transsexuals differ from transvestites in that the gender identities of transvestites coincide with their biological sex. Transvestites are usually married heterosexual males who prefer sexual relationships with women but find dressing in the
clothing of the opposite sex sexually arousing.

There are no accurate figures on the number of transsexuals in the United
States. It is estimated that several thousand people have undergone sex-change surgery and that an additional eight to ten thousand identify themselves as transsexual
but have not had the surgery (Carrera 1981). Since most United States gender clinics
set rigid qualifying standards for their sex-change procedures, it is believed that
many transsexuals go to Europe or Mexico for their operations.

Sex-Change Surgery

In ethical gender clinics, sex-change surgery is the final step in a long and difficult process and is only performed eighteen to twenty-four months after the patient has entered a gender identity program. All of the following must be accomplished before surgery takes place (Carrera 1981):

1. Psychological tests must confirm that the patient is a true transsexual and not suffering from some emotional health problem in which apparent transsexualism is a symptom.

2. Medical tests must confirm that the patient is physically able to withstand the surgical and hormonal stresses involved in sex change.

3. Family and friends are interviewed to determine the patient's family, social, and employment situation.

4. The patient must fully live the life of the intended sex for at least one year before surgery. This trial period should include dressing in the desired sex, assuming a name suitable for that sex, and learning the behavior that is socially sanctioned for the intended sex.

5. Extensive counseling is necessary to help the patient to prepare for surgery and its consequences. Issues of employment and family and personal relationships must be resolved.

6. Legal issues must be dealt with. These can be among the most difficult problems facing the patient. Legally changing one's name and getting it on a new birth certificate is difficult, time consuming, and costly in some states. Obtaining a new driver's license, social security card, credit cards, and medical and life insurance can be very difficult as well. Also, many transsexuals have found little legal protection from job loss as a direct result of their sex changes.

7. Long before surgery, both sexes begin the hormone therapy that they must continue throughout their lives. Males receive estrogen, which develops breast tissue; reduces testicle size and testosterone production; promotes subcutaneous fat deposits, producing softer skin and more feminine contours; causes erectile loss; and reduces muscular strength. Females receive testosterone, which stops or reduces menstruation, increases facial and body hair, deepens the voice, and enlarges the clitoris. It also often increases sex drive and may lead to the development of acne. Surgical breast removal may take place during this period.

The actual sex-change surgery completes the sexual conversion. In male-to-female surgery, the more successful of the two procedures, the testes are removed, though the scrotum and some of the penile tissue is retained for construction of a vagina and labia. The vagina is usually functional for intercourse, although a lubricant is necessary as it does not lubricate upon sexual arousal. Enough sensory tissue is retained to allow the attainment of orgasm. If breast development, under stimulus of hormones, is viewed as inadequate, silicone implants can be used to augment breast contours.

In female-to-male conversions, ovaries, uterus, vagina, and breasts are removed. While a realistic-looking penis can be constructed of existing tissues, it has not yet been possible to construct a penis that becomes erect upon sexual arousal and is flaccid at other times. This difficulty can be overcome either by placing a semirigid implant into the penis or by inserting a device that can be pumped up with fluid from a reservoir implanted in the groin region (see chapter 10). In any case, no ejaculation occurs, although orgasm does take place. Following either sex-change surgery, natural parenthood is impossible.

Authorities do not agree on the success of sex-change surgery, as measured by the happiness of the individual who has gone through a gender reversal. Johns Hopkins Hospital and Stanford University Hospital, which pioneered sex changes, eventually discontinued sex-change surgery when follow-up studies showed that their patients' lives had not been improved sufficiently to warrant such drastic and expensive treatment. Many other clinics, however, and certainly many people who have undergone gender reversal, feel that the operation is well worthwhile.

A first-person account of a successful sex change is *Conundrum* by Jan Morris (1974). In this book, Morris chronicles her earlier life as a male, her sex transformation, and the later, more rewarding, life as a woman.

For reasons that are unclear, the number of male transsexuals exceeds the number of females, at least in terms of those seeking treatment. The ratio of males to females at different clinics ranges from 2:1 to 8:1 (American Psychiatric Association 1980).

---

1. Do you have any memory of developing your own sense of gender identity? What does this tell you about when the process occurred?
2. Describe how transsexuals differ from homosexuals and transvestites.

Freedom from Gender-Role Stereotyping

Traditionally, most parents have raised their children to conform to rather stereotyped concepts of masculinity or femininity. A son has been strongly encouraged to grow up to be a "real man," a girl to be "ladylike." But increasing numbers of people feel that encouraging gender-role distinctions artificially limits children's potential for finding personal fulfillment or self-actualization (Olds 1981). In order to be a "real man" or to be "ladylike," there are, in addition to those things we *must* do, many things we *may not* do. And those latter things might be just those that would provide us with personal fulfillment. Also, our sexual and other relationships with people suffer because many of the prohibited behavioral traits for each sex are traits that help build rewarding relationships when they are present in either sex (Bem 1975a). For example, free expression of emotions, more associated with females in our society, is helpful in either sex.

Even if parents are careful to avoid creating stereotyped gender-role concepts in their children, however, there is no way a child can grow up in our culture without considerable exposure to these concepts. A child's peers are almost certain to hold many ideas of what is appropriate masculine or feminine behavior and may be cruel and relentless in seeing that all members of the peer group conform to these notions. Despite some efforts to eliminate stereotyping, television is still full of rigid gender-role concepts, both in program content and in commercials. Males are portrayed as assertive and independent, females as passive, indecisive, and dependent. Even some schools still promote gender-role stereotyping through their academic, sports, and extracurricular activities (Powell 1979). But parents can help to counteract these limiting influences on their children.

One thing parents can do is to set an example of a smoothly working relationship that is relatively free of role stereotyping. It is very beneficial for children to see that either parent can cook dinner, wash dishes, do the laundry, fix the car, balance the checkbook, have a career, or nurture children.

It is very beneficial for children to see that either parent can cook dinner, fix the car, or have a career.

Another thing parents can do is to be very careful not to instill stereotyped thinking by what they tell their children, especially relative to adult life-styles and careers. If all a daughter ever hears is, "When you grow up and have children. . . ," she will have difficulty thinking of her future in other terms. If parents speak to their daughters only in terms of traditionally female jobs (secretary, nurse, etc.) and to their sons only in terms of traditionally male jobs (mechanic, construction worker, etc.), this again will have the effect of limiting the options the children consider for themselves (Powell 1979).

Children's play behavior also has been shown to influence their gender-role concepts (Pogrebin 1981). Play situations tend to be adult power relationships in miniature, and patterns of interaction established in sports and games carry into adult life. Boys must be the competitors and girls the cheerleaders. Boys must be strong; girls must be graceful.

Parents are partially responsible for this gender-role stereotyping of children's play behavior. Parents play differently with boys and girls and encourage them to be involved in different kinds of play activities (Brooks-Gunn and Matthews 1979). Boys are encouraged to play outdoors, allowed to explore farther from home, and are rewarded for problem solving. Girls are restrained, sheltered, chaperoned, and encouraged to seek adult help in solving their problems. Mothers often stay indoors and play with their girls; fathers take their boys outside and play sports with them.

androgyny
(an-droj'ĭ-ne)

Boys' play teaches them to be active, constructive, and inventive. Girls' play teaches them to be dependent, domestic, and decorative. Overall, boys' play teaches strategy, group dynamics, problem solving, mediation, and reaching beyond their grasp; girls' play does not. Conversely, girls' play teaches nurturance and empathy, also valuable traits; boys' play does not (Bem 1975b; Pogrebin 1981). The message here is clear: Parents who want their children to be free of gender-role stereotyping must encourage their children to engage in a variety of play activities that is balanced across the spectrum of play activities common to each sex.

Another influence on children's gender-role concepts is their *separate* play behavior: boys play with boys, and girls play with girls. It is not clear whether this tendency is innate or whether it is the result of social and parental pressures. As it now stands, a boy who plays with girls is called a "sissy," which is not a compliment. His parents and other people worry or wonder about his ultimate sexual orientation (Deisher 1981; Pattison 1982). On the other hand, a girl who prefers to play with boys is a "tomboy." While her parents and teachers may worry about her future sexuality and gender role, she probably is developing skills and attitudes that will serve her well in adult life, in contrast to the passivity characteristic of more "feminine" girls (Powell 1979; Brooks-Gunn and Matthews 1979; Pogrebin 1980).

While boys and girls playing separately tends to solidify gender-role stereotypes, boys and girls playing together breaks down gender-role stereotypes. Playing together from early childhood gives boys and girls a shared history. It gives them an interest in one another beyond the relatively narrow objective of sexual gratification. It prepares them to be much better partners as adults and probably decreases the sexual segregation that is so typical of adult leisure activities. Adult men and women would be more likely to enjoy the same sports, games, and leisure activities if they had played together as children.

Some people now use the term **androgyny** in reference to child development. Derived from the Greek *andros* (man) and *gyne* (woman), androgyny means being able to choose from the whole range of human behaviors those that best suit our own personalities or seem most appropriate in a given situation, rather than being limited to those behaviors traditionally associated with our particular gender (Olds 1981).

Some people fear that androgynous child-raising might lead to an asexual adulthood—that if men and women became too much "the same," they would just lose interest in each other as sexual partners. Research has shown that this is not the case. Walfish and Myerson (1980) found that relatively androgynous females were more comfortable with heterosexual intercourse than were more traditionally "feminine" females. Similarly, relatively androgynous males felt more comfortable about heterosexual intercourse than did more conventionally "masculine" males. Apparently, when people of the opposite sex are perceived as being more similar to one's own self, some of the anxiety associated with heterosexual interaction is relieved.

1. Do you feel that you grew up in a gender-role stereotypical household? How has your upbringing affected how you feel about "masculine" and "feminine" stereotypes?
2. How would you feel if your little boy enjoyed playing with dolls more than trucks or your little girl enjoyed playing with trucks more than dolls? Would you feel more strongly about one than the other?

Sex Education of Children

There is no question of *whether* children receive sex education, only one of *how*. Children are constantly bombarded with sexual information from peers, the media, and every area of the cultural environment. In one way or another, an informal sex education is obtained, but often with much confusion and without constructive purpose. With effective school and home sex education, children are guaranteed the factual information they need so that their sexual decisions can be made wisely and knowledgeably.

Goals of Sex Education

The adequate sex education of children holds many lifelong benefits (Kirkendall 1965). First, quality sex education helps a child to develop a positive attitude about his or her sexual nature, which, in turn, contributes to the child's total self-esteem and certainly leads to more rewarding sexual relationships.

Second, a sound, factual background of sexual information enables a child to recognize and ignore the sexual misinformation he or she so often receives from peers and other sources. Many sexual problems, such as sexual diseases and unwanted pregnancies, can be prevented through the knowledge and positive attitudes that result from sex education. *Attitudes* are emphasized here, as research has shown that factual knowledge in itself does not result in healthful behavior unless accompanied by healthful attitudes (Kirkendall 1965; Spanier 1977).

Sex education also helps to develop the skills needed for effective communication of sexual ideas and feelings. The ability to freely communicate sexual needs and feelings is important at all ages, but it is a difficult ability to develop without a lifelong history of open sexual communication. When sexual education has been an ongoing process from an early age, the communication of sexual information seems no different than any other form of communication.

There is yet another reason why sex education is essential. In years gone by, there were very few "respectable" options for sexual behavior or sexual life-styles. Now, children are free to choose from many sexual alternatives with less concern about social condemnation. Unless at an early age children learn tolerance for others and develop adaptability in their own lives, they are likely to encounter many problems in their relationships with other people.

Effective sex education also includes training in decision-making skills. Knowledge and attitudes are not quite enough. Underlying values need to be explored and ways of clarifying personal values explained. Children need to learn how to translate their knowledge and attitudes into well-grounded decisions, based on a clear understanding of their personal values. Indecisiveness or impulsiveness are common symptoms of poorly developed decision-making abilities. Many people have simply never been taught how to make valid decisions—sexual or otherwise.

Finally, when we speak of sex education, it must be understood that sexuality includes much more than various coital techniques, pregnancy, and other physical concerns. The sex education of children too often consists of little more than reproductive physiology and sexually transmitted diseases. While it is important that children have a knowledge of these things, it is even more important that they understand the relationships between people and that they value themselves and respect others as well.

In other words, sexuality is an integral part of the whole being, and this is the essence of what sex education should be.

Home Sex Education

Giving children a sound factual and attitudinal basis for their sexual decisions is among the most important aspects of parenting. And, sadly, it is among the most mishandled or just simply ignored of all parental tasks. Little in our educational experience prepares us to be parents, and we are especially unprepared for conveying sexual information to our children.

There are many reasons for parents' difficulties as sex educators. One is that parents themselves are often uninformed. Another is uncertainty about what information a child needs at any particular age. Still another reason is doubt about which terms are best to use with children. Most of the sexual words we know seem either too technical or too vulgar to use with children. Finally, many people are just too uncomfortable with their own sexuality to feel at ease discussing sexual matters with their children.

All too often, a parent's efforts at sex education consist of one day sitting the child down and awkwardly attempting to explain the "facts of life." This is a classic symptom of inadequate home sex education. Effective sex education is an ongoing process, throughout childhood, and is well integrated with other life education. It cannot be accomplished in one lesson. It is planned and anticipates, as well as responds to, the needs of the child.

A child's sexual questions demand answers—immediately, honestly, and as fully as his or her level of understanding will allow. In their embarrassment or sexual discomfort, parents often make mistakes. One is to put off answering a question—"I'm busy right now, I'll tell you later" or "I'll tell you when you get older." Another mistake is to be dishonest—"The stork brought you" or "Babies come from hospitals." Perhaps the worst mistake of all is to chide or scold the child for having asked a question—"Nice little girls don't ask such questions." The child feels guilty for having asked, learns that sex is shameful, and suffers a loss of self-esteem for possessing shameful interests and feelings.

Parents who are committed to home sex education believe that few duties rate a higher priority than answering the sexual questions of their children. Other tasks can usually be set aside until all of the child's concerns are satisfactorily answered. "Later" never seems to arrive when sexual questions are put on hold.

Parents who honestly answer their child's original question often find that the answer usually stimulates further questions. The child's questions are usually a good indicator of his or her capacity to understand the answers and thus should guide parents in how detailed they should make their explanations.

Parents need not always wait for a child's questions. Many other good opportunities for sex education present themselves. Perhaps a pregnancy or birth may occur within the family or among family friends. This is an excellent discussion opener. Perhaps dogs or other animals are observed in mating or other sexual behavior. What the child sees can be explained and related to human behavior.

As for a specific schedule for sex education, in addition to answering questions, parents must make sure that potential anxiety-causing events in the life of the child are understood well in advance of their taking place. Parents can anticipate the kinds of information their child will need and can develop a pool of knowledge and plan for the presentation of this information. Appropriate books can also be made available to children. With males, ejaculation and nocturnal emission should be anticipated and explained before they occur. With females, breast development and the first menstrual period need to be discussed in advance. In particular, the wide range of ages at which these events may normally occur should be discussed since many young people feel quite concerned if their sexual development seems to be happening earlier or later than that of their friends. Another troublesome source of anxiety is concern over various physical proportions or anatomical details. Girls worry about their breast size, while boys often have misgivings about the size of their penises. Young people need to know that sexual adequacy is not determined by details of body size or shape. It is also very helpful for a child to understand the physical changes that will be occurring in children of the opposite sex.

Studies have shown (Papalia and Olds 1979) that particularly ignored areas of home sex education are the important subjects of fertility control and sexually transmitted diseases. Very few parents adequately inform their children on these subjects, often because very few parents are themselves well informed. Parents should first make sure that they themselves are fully informed on these subjects and only then should they approach their children with the information.

Sex education is an ongoing process throughout childhood. It cannot be accomplished in one "facts of life" lesson.

Parents also need to discuss with their children the possibility of sexual molestation. Children need to be aware of the general dangers involved in sexual advances from adults. They also need to know of the possibility of sexual exploitation by adults or older children. Parents should encourage children to report any unusual occurrences (Westman 1975).

Above all else, home sex education should convey a strongly positive view of sexuality. Children need to perceive their parents as being happy and comfortable with their own sexuality. Here, nonverbal communication is often more meaningful than what is expressed in words. Children will perceive that their parents are at ease with their sexuality, just as they will be aware if this is not the case.

School Sex Education

Ideally, there might be no need for any extensive sex education in schools if parents were doing a good job at home. Unfortunately, we do not live in an ideal world, and many parents either cannot or do not give their children adequate home sex education. Thus, there is a clear need for well-developed and carefully administered sex education programs in our schools.

Not everyone in our society is in agreement as to what the content of school sex education programs should be or even whether or not these programs should exist. But virtually all authorities in the fields of human sexuality, psychology, and sociology feel that effective school sex education benefits both the individual and society. They further agree that an adequate program goes beyond sexual biology to encompass the emotional, cultural, and ethical aspects of sexuality. The goal of sex education is not to make children's decisions for them, but to provide them with a sound basis for making their own decisions.

People teaching human sexuality at any level should be carefully chosen and adequately trained for this important job. They need, first of all, to be comfortable with their own sexuality. They should also be objective about controversial issues and able to understand and appreciate the views of other people. A good sense of humor is also helpful. Sex educators need the broadest possible kind of knowledge, including familiarity with the biological, psychological, and cultural bases of sexuality.

Concerns Regarding Sex Education

Several widely held fears may inhibit parents in their role as sex educators and bring pressures to bear on school sex education programs. Most of these fears, however, are unfounded and can be easily dispelled.

Some people fear that sex education may stimulate or motivate children into premature sexual activity. The facts, however, do not support this fear (Kirkendall 1965; Taylor 1970; Spanier 1977). Often, a clear understanding of sexual feelings and motivations means a better ability to control these feelings and motivations. Much of the sexual activity of young people is motivated not by sexual need alone, but by a variety of peer and cultural pressures and nonsexual emotional needs. Sex education helps young people to recognize these forces and to deal with them more effectively.

From the opposite perspective, *withholding* knowledge of sexuality from young people does not deter them from participating in sex any more than the availability of sexual information encourages sexual activity. There are plenty of sources of awareness of the possibility of sexual activity and a similar abundance of sexual misinformation.

Another fear of parents is that sex education may begin at too early an age. Sex education, however, cannot be premature. It will only bore the child if it is too complicated or advanced for his or her understanding. It can, however, be too late, and the lack of understanding of a sexual phenomenon can be harmful. Menstruation, for example, in an unprepared girl can be frightening and embarrassing. Similarly, the sexually naive child is at increased risk of sexual molestation or exploitation by older children or adults.

1. How have you acquired sexual information up to this point? Was most of the information you acquired accurate?
2. Can you and your parents discuss sexual matters without embarrassment? Why or why not? What effect has this had on you?
3. Where do you think sex education belongs—in the home, in the schools, in both the home and the schools, or not at all?

"I'm sorry, Mrs. Johnson, but I don't think Susie and Tommy should play together anymore."

"Why? Has something happened? Did they get into a fight?"

"No, I . . . well, actually, it's because *I* don't want them to play together anymore. You see, today I found Susie and Tommy . . . playing in the bedroom without their clothes on!"

"I see, and what were they doing?"

"*Doing?* They were playing with each other! Touching each other and . . . well, you know! It was disgusting, and I put a stop to it."

"You think what they were doing was disgusting?"

"Well, of course, don't *you*?"

"No, I'm afraid I don't. More importantly, I don't want Susie to think so either. I think it's healthy for children to discover themselves and each other. I don't think that playing 'discovery' at the age of four will turn Susie or Tommy into sex perverts when they grow up."

"But what they were doing is wrong."

"Maybe in your mind, but not in mine. I don't want Susie to grow up thinking that her body is disgusting and that sex is bad."

"Well, suit yourself, but keep your Susie away from my Tommy."

Summary

1.   Sexuality becomes apparent early in the life cycle. The world's cultures vary in their acceptance of infant and childhood sexuality, and many people in the United States are uncomfortable with it. Some adult sexual problems can be traced back to negative parental reactions to childhood sexual behavior.

2.   Childhood masturbation is normal and harmless behavior. Infant masturbation is thought to be physically pleasant, though not perceived as sexual. Older children accompany their masturbation with elaborate sexual fantasies. Sex play is useful in the psychosexual development of a child, and parental overreaction is not beneficial. Exposure to pornography that portrays a distorted sexuality may be harmful to a child, but so may parental overreaction to its discovery in the child's possession.

3.   Parental demonstrations of affection for their child contribute to the child's self-esteem and academic and social success. Parents are the primary role models for their child's own parenting behavior.

4.   Displays of affection between parents give a child a sense of security and provide a role model for the child's ability to demonstrate affection when he or she reaches adulthood. A child's observation of parental coitus may be confusing or frightening, and the child may need to be reassured that the activity observed was loving and enjoyable.

5.   Divorced or widowed parents may find that their children are threatened by the parent's new relationship with someone other than the original spouse. Having the child and the parent's new friend become well acquainted may help with the child's acceptance.

6.   The world's cultures vary immensely in their approaches to covering the human body. The message in extreme modesty is that sexual parts of the body are shameful, which conveys a negative view of sexuality. A more relaxed attitude toward home nudity can help children to develop more positive feelings about their sexual anatomy and their sexuality. Parents, however, should not flaunt nudity before children in a seductive or erotic way, nor should they insist on their children's nudity.

7.   Basic behavioral differences between the sexes may be subtle and are difficult to prove or disprove since it is virtually impossible to eliminate cultural bias from research in this area.

8.   Many authorities believe that the human brain is sexually differentiated even before birth because of the influence of sex hormones. Regardless, the brains of the two sexes are much more similar than different.

9.   Social conditioning of males and females is quite different and is believed to have more of an influence on the behavioral differences between the sexes than any biological differences.

10.   Gender identity is our concept of ourselves as being either male or female. Little is known with certainty about how gender identity develops, except that it is firmly ingrained early in life. Both biological and psychological theories are pro-

posed, but evidence favors psychological development of gender identity. When a child is born with ambiguous genitals, sex assignment should be made immediately for successful development of gender identity.

11. Some people have ambiguous gender identity. The general term for difficulty in gender identity is gender dysphoria. Transsexuals believe that their true gender is actually the opposite of what their bodies appear to be, and some of them undergo sex-change surgery.

12. Some people feel that raising children to conform to rigidly stereotyped gender roles artificially limits the children's potential for personal fulfillment. Children acquire gender-role stereotypes from parents, other relatives, friends, schools, the media, and society in general.

13. Androgyny means being able to choose from the whole range of human behaviors those that seem most appropriate in a given situation, rather than those that always conform to stereotyped gender roles. Androgynous people feel more comfortable in heterosexual relationships than more traditionally "feminine" or "masculine" people do because the opposite sex is perceived as less different and thus less threatening.

14. Parents are often poorly prepared for the sex education of their children. Effective home sex education is an ongoing, planned process that anticipates, as well as responds to, the needs of the child.

15. School sex education is needed because many parents cannot or do not give their children adequate information.

16. Sex education does not stimulate premature sexual activity, nor can it come at too early an age. It can, however, come too late.

12

Biological Aspects of Adolescence
Puberty in Males/Puberty in Females

Psychological Aspects of Adolescence

Adolescents and Society

Adolescent Sexual Outlets
Masturbation/Petting/Nonmarital Sexual Intercourse

Adolescent Marriage

Adolescent Pregnancy
Reasons for Adolescent Pregnancy/Dealing with Adolescent Pregnancy/Adolescent Fathers

Sexual Orientation

Parent-Adolescent Communication

Common Adolescent Sexual Myths

"Kathy, can I come in?"

"Yeah."

"Kathy, Mom's worried about you. Is there something wrong?"

"I don't want to talk about it."

"Listen, Kath, Mom thought you might talk to me because I'm closer to your age. I think she really believes that maybe you could use some help. Is that what you need?"

"Mary, I know you want to help, but there is nothing anyone can do!"

"Kathy, look at me. Are you pregnant?"

"Mary, I'm sorry! I was trying hard to keep things from going too far. Brian and I would always stop before anything happened. Mom's going to be so angry . . . she'll hate me! I can't tell her. I haven't told Brian yet. What's he going to think? I've got a whole year of high school left. I'd rather die than go to school pregnant. What am I going to do??"

"Calm down and try to stop crying. That's not going to help you or the baby."

"I keep telling myself I *can't* be pregnant. We only did it once. You can't get pregnant from screwing just one time!"

"Kathy, be quiet! Are you sure you are pregnant? Who did you go to?"

"I went to the clinic downtown. They did the test and said that I should come in to talk with the counselors as to what I want to do."

"What *do* you want to do?"

"I don't know."

"Listen, Kath, I won't say anything, but I wish you would talk to Mom. Keeping her in the dark only makes matters worse."

"But she'll kill me!"

"No she won't. Come on, she loves you. You've always been able to work things out together in the past."

"Yeah, but this is different."

"Of course it's different. You're pregnant. You are carrying a life inside of you, and the sooner you share that burden with someone else, the easier it will be to carry."

"All right, but I want you there to protect me when I tell her."

"I will be, don't worry."

pubescent
(pu-bes'ent)

There is probably no period in the life cycle during which physical and emotional changes are as rapid and as profound as they are during adolescence. **Adolescence** can be roughly defined as the period from the onset of puberty until the attainment of adulthood, about ages twelve to twenty. During this brief span, a young person is challenged with adjusting to an entirely new body image and a transformed identity as he or she relates to other people.

In this chapter, we explore some of the biological, emotional, and social aspects of adolescence. Some readers of this text are barely beyond adolescence themselves and may still be dealing with some of the adjustments this entails. Others are looking ahead to how they, as adults, may most effectively relate to young people, at home or in careers. This chapter provides information that should be useful to all readers.

Biological Aspects of Adolescence

Throughout childhood, the sex organs remain in a basically infantile (infantlike) condition; they grow very little. But in a relatively short time, prior to and during puberty, the genital organs develop rapidly, finally reaching maturity.

The term **puberty** is used for the earlier portion of adolescence, during which a person becomes functionally capable of reproduction. Puberty typically occurs between the ages of twelve and sixteen in boys and from nine to sixteen in girls.

The age of puberty in the United States and Western Europe has dropped significantly in the past one hundred years or so. In the mid-1800s, the average age for female puberty was over sixteen; now the average age is less than thirteen (Lein 1979). Sullivan (1971) reports a corresponding drop in age for male puberty, although males continue to mature later than females. The prevailing opinion among authorities is that the decline in age of puberty relates to improved nutrition.

Puberty usually takes from two to four years and is marked by great physical and psychological changes. The body becomes sexually functional, and attitudes and behavior become somewhat more mature.

Puberty is an ongoing process and can be divided into three stages. In the **prepubescent stage,** the secondary sex characteristics (nongenital features that distinguish the sexes) begin to appear (see chapters 5 and 6). In the **pubescent stage,** the secondary sex characteristics continue to develop, and the reproductive organs become capable of producing mature eggs and sperm. In the **postpubescent stage,** the secondary sex characteristics are well developed, and the sex organs are capable of adult functioning.

Puberty in Males

In males, the testes are only about 10 percent of their mature size at the time of birth, and little growth occurs until puberty. During the first year or two of puberty,

Adolescents of both sexes frequently are concerned about their physical development and appearance. Those who develop either faster or slower than their peers are most likely to experience anxiety about physical proportions.

the testes grow rapidly. Then growth slows, and the testes do not reach their maximum size until the age of twenty or twenty-one.

Shortly after the testes begin to develop, the penis starts to grow in length and diameter, and the glands that produce seminal fluid enlarge. Though the penis is capable of erection by contact stimulation from birth, only during puberty does it begin to erect without contact, in response to sexual sights, sounds, or thoughts. Some erections are spontaneous, independent of any sexual stimulus.

During male puberty, there is often a relatively rapid increase in height and weight, along with a broadening of the shoulders. Pubic hair and the beard begin to grow. Hormone levels increase, and the desire for ejaculation becomes urgent. Frequency of masturbation may increase to several times daily. Nocturnal emissions may begin (see chapter 9). Production of sperm begins early in puberty, and even the first ejaculations should be considered to contain sperm for purposes of contraception (Abrahams 1982).

Details of physical development may seem extremely important to boys going through puberty. The common belief that masculinity can be equated to the size of the penis and testes contributes to this concern. Many males worry that their penises are too small. A few are concerned that they may be too large. Young men need to know that the size of the penis does not reflect their masculinity and is not an important factor in either experiencing or providing sexual gratification. Similarly, muscle size may also seem disproportionately important, since size of muscles is so closely related to masculinity in our culture.

gynecomastia
(jin''ē-ko-mas'te-ah)

Another source of concern in males during puberty is **gynecomastia**—swollen breasts. This condition is so common that it should be viewed as a normal developmental event (Woods 1979). Usually disappearing without treatment, gynecomastia is caused by a small amount of glandular growth under stimulation of the high hormone levels of puberty. It does not represent any lack of masculinity and need be no cause for concern.

In both sexes, aspects of growth, such as height, weight, and skin problems, especially acne, create anxiety. Insecurities are amplified during this difficult period, and minor physical characteristics may be assigned significance far beyond their true importance. The impact of such anxieties is minimized by a well-developed sense of self-esteem. Parents can perform no more vital service for their child, especially during puberty, than to contribute to their child's developing a strongly positive self-image.

Puberty in Females

Female puberty often begins at a somewhat younger age than male puberty does. Researchers believe that the onset of female puberty relates closely to body weight and fat deposition. Puberty generally takes place when a girl's body weight reaches about 100 pounds (Lein 1979). Puberty occurring at a body weight of 85 or 90 pounds, however, is not necessarily premature, nor is puberty necessarily delayed if it has not occurred at a body weight of 115 pounds or more. The relationship between weight and puberty is not necessarily one of direct cause and effect. Many other factors are involved in puberty.

Athletic girls, particularly those who engage in endurance sports (such as running) and in sports in which there is emphasis on a "thin" body image (such as gymnastics), may undergo puberty later than other girls. All evidence indicates that it is not just total body weight, but fat deposition as well that affects the hypothalamic-pituitary-ovarian-hormone processes that initiate puberty. Michelle Warren (1982) found that girls who exhibit delayed puberty because of low fat deposition undergo puberty when a weight gain and/or cessation of strenuous exercise occurs.

For most girls, however, puberty begins sometime between the ages of nine and sixteen. Its onset is characterized by a marked increase in growth rate, accompanied by broadening of the hips, enlargement of the breasts, and the appearance of pubic hair. The uterus, fallopian tubes, vagina, and labia grow rapidly during puberty. The ovaries also grow during puberty, and, while they become functional by midpuberty, they do not reach their full size until age twenty or twenty-one (Woods 1979).

Within one to two years after hip broadening and breast enlargement, underarm hair grows and the normal, whitish vaginal secretion characteristic of adult females appears. After several additional months, the first menstrual period (**men-**

anovulatory
(an-ov′u-lah-to″re)

arche) occurs. Early menstrual cycles are sometimes **anovulatory** (no ovulation occurs) and irregular. Young women may experience several years of irregular cycles before their menstrual periods become regular and predictable (Chiazze 1968), making "natural" methods of fertility control unreliable for many in this group.

Physical concerns of girls during puberty often center on breast development and menarche. Breast development either somewhat before or somewhat after that of friends can be a major source of anxiety. Breast size is also assigned a great importance. Breasts perceived as being larger or smaller than those of peers can cause both anxiety and embarrassment.

In reality, breast size is unrelated to sexual adequacy. A woman with very small breasts can give and receive just as much sexual pleasure as a woman with large breasts. Further, there is no relationship between breast size and breast-feeding ability. The difference between larger and smaller breasts is primarily in the amount of fat tissue, rather than in glandular, milk-secreting cells (see chapter 6).

Several types of menstrual anxieties also are common in adolescent girls. A girl's anxiety level may become quite high if all of her friends have begun menstruating and she has not. Conversely, menarche in a younger girl who has not been properly prepared for the event can be extremely frightening. Well before the possible onset of menstruation, a girl should know about the process and function of menstruation and the techniques of menstrual protection through the use of pads and/or tampons. She should also understand that irregular periods for a year or so are not abnormal.

Many of the anxieties of adolescents (and adults!) can be traced directly to the advertising industry. We are frequently the targets of advertising campaigns intended to create anxieties where none might previously have existed. Then, of course, products are offered whose purchase promises to relieve those anxieties. The advertising industry needs and promotes the feeling in people that they are sexually inadequate unless they purchase the right products. Bra ads, for example, emphasize that a woman's breasts are probably either too small or too large. (How often do we see a bra ad telling a woman that her breasts are just right?) The ads imply that anyone who buys the wrong brand of shampoo, toothpaste, or even floor wax or coffee will not be sexually attractive. The tragic part is that many people believe such advertising and have diminished self-esteem as a result.

---

1. Recalling your own early adolescence, what were your main sexual anxieties or worries? Do you still feel concerned about these same things? If not, how did you overcome your concerns?
2. How would you help an adolescent in dealing with the common anxieties of adolescence?

Psychological Aspects of Adolescence

The psychological developmental challenges for adolescents include accepting a new body image, establishing a new identity, adjusting to physiological changes, and developing new forms of relationships with other people, including parents (Thornburg 1975; Papalia and Olds 1979). Each of these areas can involve some difficult adjustments.

The majority of adolescents are more concerned about their physical appearance than about any other aspect of themselves (Papalia and Olds 1979). What worries adolescents the most? Everything—height, weight, physical proportions, complexion, hair, and above all else, the timing of their sexual maturity. Boys want to look masculine, and girls want to look feminine.

Our mass media, and especially advertising, set impossibly high standards for adolescent appearance. Peers also can create anxiety, teasing or avoiding anyone whose appearance or development is a little different from the majority. Papalia and Olds (1979) report that boys are more affected by differences in growth and maturity than are girls and are more likely to tease each other than are girls.

Along with accepting a new body image, an adolescent must work at establishing his or her identity. Erik Erikson, in his classic *Childhood and Society* (1950), saw this, in fact, as the most important task in adolescent development. Adolescents who successfully develop their sense of identity are characterized by feelings of self-assurance. They have a definite sense of who they are, where they are, and in what direction they are moving. They are certain of their gender identity and their sexual orientation. They have been able to integrate their varied identities, such as their relationships with significant adults, their sexual identity, their emotional characteristics, and their social roles, into a single identity. Because of this successful integration of identities, these adolescents have a sense of rightness about who they are and what they are doing—a well-developed self-esteem.

Puberty also brings on many physiological changes. Young women need to adjust to the many effects of cycling hormone levels. Both sexes experience increased sex drive. Young men find that sexual maturity brings erections at embarrassing times. Hormonal changes influence the emotions in both sexes. All of these changes require adjustments.

Finally, sexual maturity brings changes in adolescents' relationships with others. Relationships with parents may be strained by conflicts over levels of independence. At the same time, parent-adolescent relationships may be more fulfilling as young people gain maturity. Even though physical/sexual relationships may still be in the future, sexual tensions now influence much of an adolescent's interpersonal interaction. In relating to the opposite sex, the *possibility* of a sexual relationship always exists. Members of the same sex may be viewed as competitors for sexual partners, even before actual sexual activity begins. The possibility of homosexual interaction also may influence relationships between members of the same sex, either drawing people together or causing them to keep a cautious distance apart. In many of their relationships with others, adolescents are in the confusing position of being neither child nor adult. The following section examines this ambiguity.

Adolescents and Society

Most societies throughout history have perceived adolescence as a particularly significant time in a young person's life but have dealt with adolescence in differing ways. Some, primarily the less industrialized societies, have a "rite of passage" into adulthood, at which time the adolescent formally assumes the adult role. In this way, the individual's identity in the society is never ambiguous—either to the individual or to other society members.

In our society, however, adolescence often blends gradually into adulthood because there are no clear rites of passage from girl to woman or boy to man. This results in the relationship of adolescents to society being ambiguous in many ways. There being no clear demarcation of adulthood, adolescents are viewed neither as children nor as adults. They are given many adult responsibilities, yet denied many adult privileges. They are often misunderstood, occasionally mistrusted, sometimes even feared by adults. Yet their youthfulness is admired, envied, and often emulated by adults as well. Although they are physiologically mature and experience intense sexual drives, society places both legal and moral limitations upon their sexual activities.

These ambiguities are magnified by the fact that in our industrialized and technological society, the period of adolescent status has been extended considerably. There are several reasons for this. First, as we mentioned earlier, adolescence tends to begin at an earlier age now than in the past, probably because of the improved nutrition available in this country. In addition, however, adolescence also tends to end at a later age than in the past. This is due primarily to the fact that careers in an industrialized and technological society often require years of education and preparation. Full adult status, as signified by a career and economic independence, then, takes much longer to attain.

---

1. What are some of the special adjustment challenges for adolescents?
2. Can you think of other ways (other than those mentioned in the text) in which adolescents in the United States play ambiguous roles in society?

Adolescent Sexual Outlets

During the years of adolescence, the relationships of young people typically become gradually more intimate, in both sexual and emotional senses of the word. Each young person progresses at his or her own particular pace, as influenced by individual rates of physical, psychological, and social development, as well as by religious, ethnic, and socioeconomic affiliations.

Masturbation

The least intimate sexual outlet of adolescents is masturbation, which may or may not lead to orgasm. Masturbation begins at widely varying ages. As noted in chapter 11, some children discover long before puberty that stimulation of their genitals can be a pleasurable experience. In younger children, this pleasure is not perceived as sexual. With the physical and emotional changes of puberty, however, masturbation becomes more sharply identified as a sexual act (Bakwin 1974), and increases in both incidence and frequency.

Statistics on masturbation were presented in chapter 9. For our present purposes, it is sufficient to restate that the great majority of males and females do masturbate at some time during their lives and that for many adolescents, masturbation provides the principal sexual outlet.

Medical authorities have been in agreement for many years that masturbation causes no physical or mental harm, and sex therapists often recommend masturbation as part of sex therapy. Yet for some young people, masturbation is still laden with guilt and anxiety (Carrera 1981). This is partly due to ignorance of the fact that masturbation cannot be harmful and partly due to centuries of religious teaching that masturbation is sinful. Some religions, incuding Orthodox Judaism, Roman Catholicism, some Protestant sects, and the Latter Day Saints (Mormons), still maintain that position today.

Petting

Another sexual outlet of adolescents, one that requires two participants, is **petting.** Petting is defined as including all activities more physically sexual than kissing but short of vaginal intercourse. It typically includes manual or oral stimulation, or both, of the breasts and genitals. It may or may not lead to orgasm in either partner.

Petting is usually seen as a normal step in the development of the psychosexual maturity of adolescents. It enables young people to learn their own sexual responses as well as those of the opposite sex. The great majority of adolescents engage in petting by the age of eighteen and report their petting experiences as primarily enjoyable (Hass 1979).

Petting is a normal step in the development of psychosexual maturity. It enables young people to learn their own sexual responses as well as those of the opposite sex.

Many couples develop techniques of petting to mutual orgasm as an alternative to vaginal intercourse. This can effectively satisfy the immediate needs for sexual relief and shared intimacy, while also satisfying the desire to reserve vaginal intercourse for some future partner or situation, such as marriage. Couples petting to orgasm, however, must be careful that the male's semen is kept away from the vaginal opening since pregnancy can occur even without vaginal penetration by the penis.

Any value judgment regarding petting must be based on such considerations as the age and emotional maturity of each individual. The role of petting in the total relationship must also be considered. Is petting just one of many varied activities of the couple, or is it their only shared activity? Is it contributing to the growth of each individual, or is so much time spent petting that it is inhibiting growth?

Nonmarital Sexual Intercourse

Published incidence figures for nonmarital sexual intercourse (intercourse that occurs outside of marriage) are highly variable, depending on survey methods and the group surveyed. Zelnik and Kantner (1980), for example, found that 69 percent of unmarried urban females had experienced vaginal coitus by age nineteen (49 percent by age seventeen, and 38 percent by age sixteen). Male percentages reported typically run somewhat higher than female figures (Hass 1979).

Commonly Asked Questions about Masturbation

"Are You Sure It's Normal to Masturbate?"
By any definition of "normality," masturbation must qualify. If you think of normality in terms of what most people do, masturbation must be among the most "normal" of all behaviors since the great majority of both males and females masturbate at some time in their lives. If you think of the normality of behavior in terms of its consequences, again, masturbation must be normal since it has no harmful effects.

"Could I Masturbate Too Much?"
No. The idea that a person might have only a certain number of orgasms to last a lifetime was disproven long ago. You won't use up your supply of anything by masturbating. No physical or mental harm will come to you regardless of your frequency of masturbation.

"Could I Like Masturbation So Much I Wouldn't Want to Have Sex with a Partner?"
Masturbation does seem to have certain advantages over intercourse. It is simple, can be done quickly, and you don't have to be concerned with the desires and needs of a partner. Also, some people find the intensity of orgasm from masturbation to be greater than that of orgasms they attain through intercourse. Regardless of all of

this, most people still prefer partner sex over masturbation because of the many rewards partner sex provides in addition to orgasm. If a person at all times (not just occasionally) preferred masturbation over partner sex, it would likely be a *symptom* of that person having difficulty in interpersonal relationships. The masturbation would not be the cause of the problem (Carrera 1981).

"I've Heard That Women Use Coke Bottles and Cucumbers and Things Like That for Masturbation. Is That True?"
Usually not. Most women masturbate by stimulating the clitoris, labia, and outer portion of the vagina because these areas contain most of the sensory nerves (Hite 1976). Hite found that less than 2 percent of all women masturbate by inserting objects into their vaginas.

"Is There Something Wrong with a Person Who Sometimes Masturbates Even Though He or She Is Married or Has a Willing Sex Partner?"
Not at all. Even happily married people who have excellent sexual relationships with their spouses sometimes masturbate. Perhaps their partner is unavailable for sex at times, or sometimes they might just feel the need for solitary pleasure or relaxation (Carrera 1981).

Making the Decision

Some adolescents pass through a period of uncertainty over whether or not to engage in full vaginal intercourse. For those holding conflicting or ambivalent values, this decision may involve emotional turmoil and may never be satisfactorily resolved.

Many conflicting external forces will probably influence the decision. First of all, peers may exert pressure for or against sexual activity, and adolescents value the opinions of their peers highly.

Parents also may try to influence their offspring in either direction. Sons are often pushed, especially by their fathers, to become sexually active. A father or older brother may teach a young man to use trickery, deception, or even begging to gain sexual privileges. Daughters, on the other hand, are more likely to be discouraged from sexual activity. Parents may worry about their daughter becoming pregnant or may perceive their daughter's virginity as an important asset to preserve.

Parents also may project their own sexual fears and inhibitions onto their children. If sex has been a source of anxiety for a parent, efforts may be made to "protect" children from sexual involvement. Sometimes, parents just try to prevent their children from growing up in any way. This may reflect the parents' unhappiness in their own adult roles. It may also be characteristic of parents who have little identity of their own beyond their role as parents. The maturing of their children threatens that identity.

The ambivalent sexual attitudes of our society also will influence the adolescent's decision about becoming sexually active. Our society presents sexuality as simultaneously good and bad. For example, sexual attractiveness is highly valued, and the media tell us that we simply *must* be perceived as sexually attractive and available. But actual sexual interaction by unmarried individuals still is not accepted by many. Also, the "double standard," or permissiveness for males but restrictiveness for females, is still held by many people. There is little wonder that a young person in such a culture might have difficulty in making sexual decisions.

Ultimately, the decision of when to engage in coitus can be made only by the individual. Ideally, the decision will reflect the emotional and social maturity of the individual as well as his or her personal values. Of all the conflicting values of society, religions, peers, parents, and others, those that are meaningful to us as individuals are internalized—taken as our own. Once a person really understands his or her values, they may form a basis for decisions on appropriate behavior.

First Intercourse

Few human experiences can be as simultaneously thrilling and anxiety provoking as our first sexual experience. An individual's perception of first intercourse is influenced by the person's age at the time, as well as by his or her emotional and social maturity. The total circumstances surrounding the event also influence how first intercourse is perceived. And the partner with whom the experience is shared is significant. First intercourse in the context of a valued personal relationship is likely to be more emotionally rewarding than a sexual initiation with someone with whom no intimacy exists.

Sometimes, first intercourse is a carefully planned event; sometimes it is highly spontaneous. In the latter case, alcohol or other drugs are often a factor in lessening inhibitions. Sometimes, a young couple just makes a gradual transition from petting to vaginal intercourse as a natural sequence of events.

The outcome of first intercourse is highly variable. It may be perceived as anywhere from one of life's real peak experiences to one of life's major disappoint-

It's Up to You: Decisions about Sex

(The following is based on an excellent brochure prepared by the Los Angeles Planned Parenthood—World Population organization. While the brochure is intended for teenagers, much of it applies to adults as well.)

How do you know when you're ready for sex? Many people will tell you what to do, and this can be very confusing. As a teenager, you are physically capable of having and enjoying sex. But there's more involved than physical needs, including your feelings, your relationship, and your view of yourself. Sex is used by people for many purposes. Although most people desire the pleasure of sex, it is often used for other reasons, many of which lead to pain. Sex can be one of life's most pleasurable experiences, or it can be equally as devastating. Because sex can be such a strong force, deciding when you are ready for sex is not a decision to be made in a moment of passion. It is a decision that you alone can make. Because remember—in the end, it's up to *you*.

Answering the following questions should help you in making decisions about your sexual activity.

You

1. Have you thought about your sexuality?
2. Are you prepared to make sure an effective form of contraception is used?
3. If you don't use contraception, are you prepared to cope with a pregnancy?
4. There are many types of sexuality; which will you choose?
5. How will you handle it if your sexual experience is unpleasant?
6. Sexually transmitted diseases are a definite risk. Can you deal with that?
7. If the sexual life-style you choose is not legal (for example, prostitution), are you willing to deal with the consequences?
8. Do you use sex to shock people?
9. How will you feel the next day?

Your Relationship

1. Is there mutual consent to have sex?
2. Is sex being used as a weapon or bribe?

3. Do you or your partner feel like a sex *object* or feel exploited?
4. Is sex a last resort to hold the relationship together?
5. What kind of commitment are you willing to make to one another?
6. Can you have a good relationship without sex?
7. Do you feel comfortable talking about sex with one another?
8. Will sex enhance your relationship?

Your Parents

1. How will your parents react?
2. Have you ever discussed sex with your parents? Or their values about sex?
3. Will you have to lie to your parents? Can you cope with that?
4. Are you using sex as a way to hurt your parents?
5. How have your parents' attitudes toward sex influenced you?

Your Friends

1. Do you feel pressured to have sex?
2. Would you be considered "out of it" if you didn't have sex?
3. Do you need to be sexually active to be popular?
4. Are you tempted to have sex when and if you get high or drunk?
5. Does it really matter what your friends think?

Back to You

Many of these questions can be answered only by you. To answer them, it is helpful to understand your personal values, needs, and desires, as well as the consequences of your actions. If any of these questions are difficult to answer, perhaps you need more time to think before you make a decision or take an action. These questions should help you in making the best decision for yourself, because, basically, *it's up to you.*

Source: Courtesy of Planned Parenthood, Los Angeles, California.

ments. If first intercourse is with a valued partner, with whom both sexual and emotional intimacy has gradually developed, there is a good chance that the experience will be rewarding. On the other hand, if there is little or no affection for the first partner and little time has been spent in preliminary sex play, the experience is likely to prove disappointing.

Events that might be considered sexual dysfunctions in an established sexual relationship are no cause for concern in light of the high anxiety levels associated with early efforts at intercourse. Males, for example, may have difficulty gaining an erection. In his first vaginal intercourse, a young male is very likely to experience what might seem to be premature ejaculation. He may ejaculate immediately upon entry, or maybe even before. In their first efforts at vaginal intercourse, young females may fail to lubricate, may experience vaginismus (spasm of the vaginal muscles), and very possibly will not experience orgasm. Again, none of these male or female experiences should be perceived as problems that are likely to interfere with future sexual interaction. They are entirely predictable in view of the inexperience and high anxiety levels typical of first intercourse.

Adolescent Marriage

Adolescent marriages are statistically the least successful of all marriages, as measured by divorce rates (see table 12.1). Why, then, do adolescents marry? Even in an era of readily available contraception and abortion, pregnancy remains the chief motivating factor in adolescent marriages. And, unfortunately, adolescent marriages in which the bride is pregnant have the poorest chances of success.

Various unfulfilled emotional needs are also associated with early marriage. Low self-esteem is foremost among these characteristics. Not appreciating their own potential for personal growth and development, many young people are unable to set significant educational and career goals for themselves. They are more interested in anything that promises to provide more immediate identity and fulfillment. Marriage often seems to hold that promise (Thornburg 1975; Ambron and Brodzinsky 1979).

Table 12.1 Divorce Rates for Early Marriages.

	Persons Under Twenty Years of Age	
	Percent of All Marriages	Percent of All Divorces
Women	21	38
Men	8	17

Sources: National Center for Health Statistics, *Monthly Vital Statistics Report,* vol. 32, no. 5, 18 August 1983 (marriages); National Center for Health Statistics, *Monthly Vital Statistics Report,* vol. 32, no. 9, supplement 2, 17 January 1984 (divorces).

Limited awareness of the many options life holds is another shared characteristic of individuals who marry during adolescence. In particular, limited dating experience is quite common. Adolescents who marry have, on the average, dated fewer people than those adolescents who do not marry. Having had few, if any, prior relationships, and finally enjoying the attention of someone who seems to feel that they are special, these individuals feel a strong tendency to want to make that relationship "permanent." There is often the feeling that maybe this is the "last chance." In these situations, not only do people marry prematurely, but they often make poor choices of partners, since they lack a broad range of prior relationships to use as a basis for comparison.

Regardless of the reasons why adolescents choose to marry, few people who are seventeen years of age or younger are emotionally, socially, and economically prepared for marriage. Their degree of emotional and social development, for example, may prepare them neither for appropriate partner selection nor for the difficult interpersonal, social, and financial tasks of maintaining a marriage. In addition, many adolescents have yet to completely resolve their sense of identity. Because they are still trying to resolve personal identity conflicts, married adolescents often try to use each other for ego support, commonly through physical attractiveness and intense sexual interaction. However, pregnancy, childbirth, and parental responsibilities may disrupt this pattern of interaction rather quickly.

Another problem is that early marriage commonly acts to inhibit the personal growth and development of young people. Each is denied some of the social experiences that contribute to personal development. Some of the options open to a single person of the same age are closed or rendered more difficult.

Most married adolescents find that their educational and economic achievement is also limited. Many, for example, fail to complete even high school. Immediate financial need takes them out of school and into low-paying, menial, dead-end jobs. Some are able to complete school or vocational training later on, but many remain in low-paying jobs for long periods of time. Financial difficulties contribute to the high failure rate of such early marriages.

While there are exceptions, very young women do not always make ideal mothers. They often resent their children, perceiving the children as being the cause of their own unhappiness.

Children born to very young parents (really children themselves) may be in for a rough time of it. Various studies (for example, Thornburg 1975) have shown that very young people do not always make ideal parents. Many tend to be impatient and intolerant with their children. They may resent their children, perceiving the children as being the cause of their own unhappiness. Younger parents are often irritable with their children and quick to punish them. Early parenthood is a recognized factor in child abuse and neglect (Smith, Hanson, and Noble 1973).

In 1980, about 117,000 females and 19,000 males aged seventeen or younger got married in the United States.* Although these figures may seem large, they

*Some of the statistics in this chapter are for the age groups fourteen to seventeen or fifteen to seventeen while others are for the age group fifteen to nineteen because different federal agencies use different age groupings in gathering their statistics.

represent a sharp decline in the incidence of adolescent marriage. Between 1970 and 1981, the United States marriage rate for previously single women fifteen to seventeen years of age dropped 25 percent, from 25.6 to 19.1 marriages per 1,000 women per year (National Center for Health Statistics, 29 February 1984.)

Many social and technological changes seem to have contributed to the decrease in the incidence of adolescent marriage. Some possible factors include:

1. Rising career expectations of young women, requiring longer periods of preparation
2. Relaxation of traditional restrictions on premarital sexual activities, which, in the past, motivated people to marry early in order to experience sexual fulfillment
3. Improved contraceptive methods and availability to young people
4. Greater accessibility of safe abortions
5. Greater willingness of women to raise children without marrying
6. Success of programs trying to discourage premature pregnancy or marriage

Schools and organizations such as Planned Parenthood sponsor many effective sexuality programs for adolescents. These programs typically stress communication and decision-making skills as well as factual information about sexuality and contraceptive methods and their availability (Oettinger 1979). Some programs, established by the National Center of Child Advocacy, arrange for adolescents to spend time caring for children in day-care centers and kindergartens. Changing diapers seems to change attitudes. Oettinger quotes one adolescent male following such training: "Before I went in, I thought I'd get married right away and have children. Now, I want to wait until I'm mature enough to be a good parent."

---

1. Sometimes, adolescents receive inconsistent and inaccurate information about sexual matters. When you were younger, how much agreement did you find among your particular sources of information (your friends, parents, school, religion, etc.) on masturbation? Did your sources seem to agree on petting? How about nonmarital intercourse?
2. How would you counsel a couple, both age seventeen, thinking about getting married? What questions would you ask?

Adolescent Pregnancy

A fair estimate of the incidence of adolescent pregnancy may be reached by totaling the rates of live births, induced abortions, and spontaneous abortions (miscarriages) of adolescent females.

The live birthrate among adolescent females has been declining rather steadily since 1957. In that year, 96 out of every 1,000 (almost one in ten) women of ages fifteen to nineteen gave birth. By 1980, the annual rate had dropped to about 52 live births per 1,000 women in the same age group (National Center for Health Statistics, 28 September 1981).

The drop in the live birthrate, rather than indicating a decrease in adolescent pregnancy, represents a significant rise in the induced abortion rate during this period. In 1957, most abortions performed were illegal, so there are no accurate figures for that era. Even today's figures are just estimates. Currently, among women of ages fifteen to nineteen, there are an estimated 750 induced abortions per 1,000 live births. In this group, the abortion rate is highest among fifteen-year-olds, who experience more abortions than live births by an estimated ratio of 1,180 to 1,000. This ratio declines to 580 induced abortions per 1,000 live births among nineteen-year-old women (National Center for Health Statistics, 28 September 1981). Of course, all of these figures change annually.

The spontaneous abortion rate for this age group is even less precisely known, as many young women have miscarriages without benefit of a physician's attention. However, a conservative estimate is that at least 10 to 15 percent of adolescent pregnancies spontaneously abort (Pritchard and McDonald 1980).

Putting all of these figures together, we can estimate that the total pregnancy rate for fifteen- to nineteen-year-old women is about 100 per 1,000 women (one in ten) each year.

How many of these pregnancies are intentional, and how many are unwanted? Such an either/or classification is actually an oversimplification of the situation. Women often hold ambivalent feelings about pregnancy, at the same time wanting and not wanting to be pregnant.

While another oversimplification, one way people try to quantify unwanted pregnancies is through the induced abortion rate. The obvious inadequacies of this approach are that some unwanted pregnancies are not terminated, while some initially desired pregnancies are aborted. In any case, as we have mentioned, among fifteen- to nineteen-year-old women, there are about three-fourths as many abortions as live births, indicating that many of the pregnancies among this age group are definitely not wanted. It is officially estimated that about one million unmarried American women under age twenty experience unwanted pregnancies each year (National Center for Health Statistics 1980).

Reasons for Adolescent Pregnancy

A number of factors have been identified as reasons for adolescent pregnancy, and the reasons seem to depend somewhat on whether the pregnancy is intentional or unintentional. Among adolescent females who intentionally become pregnant, unstable or unhappy home environments are common, although certainly not universal. Pregnancy may be an effort to bring stability to a chaotic existence. It may be an attempt to achieve adult status. Parenthood may seem to offer a more defined identity than has otherwise been attained. It may be an effort to feel loved. People often hope that a baby will give them love, a need that is strong and often unfulfilled. Pregnancy may be an attempt to gain love and recognition from parents. Many emotionally neglected young people are willing to try almost anything to gain the attention of their parents.

Among adolescent females who unintentionally become pregnant, a lack of accurate information about conception and contraception—both on their and their sexual partner's part—are common. But knowledge alone does not always result in effective contraceptive practice (Woods 1979). Several other factors that influence whether or not a young person will use a contraceptive include the influence of other people, especially parents, peers, and sexual partners. Values and attitudes about sexuality, children, contraceptives, and gender roles also are important. So are self-esteem, degree of assertiveness, and ability to communicate with one's sexual partner. Of greatest impact is the adolescent's acceptance or nonacceptance of his or her sexuality and sexual behavior. Young people who accept their sexual behavior as positive are more likely to use contraceptives than are those who believe their sexual behavior to be wrong or shameful. For this reason, parents and professionals working with adolescents are much more effective in preventing unwanted pregnancy if they take a positive approach to sexuality (Oettinger 1979).

Dealing with Adolescent Pregnancy

Life presents few situations more difficult than being young, unmarried, and pregnant (Cheetham 1977). A young woman in this situation may delay seeking help and may find few sources of support if she does. She may find herself abandoned by the father and maybe even by her parents. Social services available to her depend upon where she lives (Child Welfare League 1976).

Supportive parents are without doubt the most valuable asset a pregnant adolescent can have. A good parental relationship encourages the young woman to face the reality of pregnancy more promptly. And the sooner she accepts the fact that she is pregnant, the more options she has in dealing with her situation.

Many pregnant adolescents choose to abort their pregnancies, with or without the knowledge of their parents (Oettinger 1979). If abortion is being considered, a decision one way or the other must be made very early in the pregnancy. With delay, abortion becomes more dangerous, more expensive, and psychologically more traumatic. Early abortion by a licensed physician is relatively safe—actually, it is less dangerous than carrying the pregnancy to term (Cheetham 1977). But the decision to abort must be compatible with the young woman's personal philosophy and values or guilt may result.

In many cases, giving the child up for adoption is the best course of action. Adoption should assure the child of a loving home with adequate human and eco-

Supportive parents are the most valuable asset a pregnant adolescent can have. A good parental relationship in which the young woman feels confident she will receive parental support encourages facing the reality of pregnancy more promptly.

Some Facts about Adolescent Pregnancy

About one million unmarried women under age twenty become unintentionally pregnant each year in the United States.

Nearly two-thirds of all teenage pregnancies are unintentional.

One-third of all abortions in this country are for teenage women.

Nine out of ten teenage mothers who give birth keep their babies.

Sixty percent of women who bear a child before age sixteen have another baby before age eighteen.

Pregnancy is the most common reason for young women failing to complete high school.

Only 20 percent of sexually active teenage women use contraceptives on a regular basis.

Death rates for babies born to mothers under age eighteen are nearly twice that for babies born to mothers aged twenty to twenty-nine.

The rate of physical and mental birth defects is much higher among babies born to mothers under age eighteen than among babies of women aged twenty to twenty-nine.

The maternal death rate from complications of pregnancy is much higher among women under age fifteen than among older mothers.

Despite the inherent risks in teenage pregnancy, nearly half of all pregnant teenagers receive no prenatal care in the first trimester (three months) of pregnancy.

Sixty percent of pregnant teenage brides separate or divorce within six years after their marriage.

Sources: *Leaders Alert Bulletin* 30, March of Dimes Birth Defects Foundation, White Plains, New York, 1980; U.S. Public Health Service, Health Services Administration, Publication 78–5624, 1978.

nomic resources. There is currently a strong demand for newborn infants for adoption.

Marriage is another possibility, if the father of the child is willing and able to do so. However, the success rate of such marriages is very poor. A high percentage of marriages motivated by pregnancy lead to divorce or, even worse, to bitter, meaningless coexistence that hurts everyone, including the child for whose supposed benefit the marriage took place. Unless both parties truly want to marry each other, it is usually better to take one of the other options.

Single parenthood is another option and has become increasingly prevalent in recent years. Raising a child as a single mother is often more rewarding in fantasy than in reality, however. Parenthood is challenging under the most favorable of conditions, and being a young, single mother is among the least favorable of conditions. Few adolescent girls possess either the emotional or the financial resources for successful parenthood (Child Welfare League 1976).

In all fairness, some young, single mothers cope very well with the financial and emotional realities of their situation and do an excellent job of raising their children. But, often, the experience is damaging to both the mother and her child.

In an age in which a career is highly valued by many women, an adolescent mother finds her options in terms of career preparation severely limited. While perhaps any goal is still theoretically possible to achieve, the probability of actually doing so is greatly reduced (Cheetham 1977).

Perhaps the greatest emotional difficulties of young single mothers relate to their loss of personal freedom (Oettinger 1979). Until someone (single or married) has had the experience of raising a child, there is just no way he or she can appreciate how a child limits personal freedom. When a single mother is young and wants to be out doing the things her peers are doing, it is easy for her to start resenting her baby, blaming it for her loss of freedom. The incidence of emotional or physical abuse or neglect among children of very young mothers is quite high (Smith, Hanson and Noble 1973).

Society can do much to assist pregnant adolescents and the babies they produce. Schools do a great service when they provide well-funded, caring programs to help young mothers finish their educations. The ability to earn a living is of utmost importance to the mother and her child. Many other social services are needed (Child Welfare League 1976). Many pregnant adolescents need counseling services. Some need housing. Without adequate social services, many young women slip into a cycle of desperation and repeated pregnancies.

Adolescent Fathers

There is every reason to believe that the social, educational, occupational, and emotional consequences of adolescent fatherhood are just as difficult and handicapping as those of adolescent motherhood (Earls 1981). The view that the female is primarily responsible for the care and rearing of children has been replaced by a concept of mutual responsibility for children between men and women. Some cities have responded by instituting counseling services for young fathers as well as mothers.

Many young fathers need the opportunity to bring their feelings about the situation into the open in order to understand more clearly their own involvement and responsibility. The father may require some assistance with his feelings about the past, present, and future relationship with the mother and his moral or legal responsibility to the child.

The unmarried father is increasingly available and anxious to help in planning for his baby (Child Welfare League 1976). In fact, more and more often, the father is being viewed as a resource for the physical custody of the child if he displays such interest and has a plan that is in the best interests of the child (Child Welfare League 1976). His sense of responsibility for the child, as well as the legally defined responsibility of an acknowledged father, leads him in many cases to willingly contribute to the care of the child and to offer support to the mother.

It is important that adolescent fathers be treated not just as prospective or actual parents, but as individuals with their own needs and problems. Relationships

The view that the female is primarily responsible for the care and rearing of children has been replaced by a concept of mutual responsibility of both parents.

between young, unmarried parents are often very meaningful, and the father should be regarded as more than just a source of financial support.

1. Did your junior high school and/or high school seem to have effective programs to help prevent student pregnancies?
2. How well did the students in your high school deal with the pregnancies that did occur?
3. If you were given free rein to set up a program in the high school you attended to help prevent and deal with unwanted pregnancies, what would you include in your program? What services would you offer to couples faced with an unwanted pregnancy?

Sexual Orientation

Sexual orientation reflects one's preference for partners of the same sex (**homosexuality**), opposite sex (**heterosexuality**), or both sexes (**bisexuality**). A more detailed discussion of homosexuality and bisexuality appears in chapter 18. Here we briefly discuss the development of sexual orientation as it relates to adolescents.

As part of the healthy development of psychosexual maturity, many young people may at some time wonder if they are homosexual, heterosexual, or bisexual in orientation. It is common for adolescents to have crushes or close friendships with peers or older persons of their own sex, and contact with these individuals sometimes results in sexual arousal. Hass (1979) found that 11 percent of girls and 14 percent of boys ages fifteen to eighteen reported at least some homosexual experience. It can be assumed that many more felt homosexual attraction but didn't act on it. Young people are aware of our society's primarily negative attitude toward homosexuality, and this contributes to anxiety about homosexual acts, impulses, and feelings (Jensen 1981).

Adolescents tend to relate their physical development to sexual orientation. For example, a young male who is smaller or slighter than his peers or who seems to conform less to stereotypical ideals of masculinity may wonder whether this means he is homosexual. A young woman who develops later than her peers or who has smaller breast development may feel that there is something sexually different or homosexual about herself (Jensen 1981).

Adolescents also sometimes confuse gender-role behavior with sexual orientation. A nonstereotypical style of masculinity or femininity does not in any way indicate a homosexual orientation. A male can be sensitive, emotionally expressive, and noncompetitive, all of which contradict the standard male-role stereotype, and still be strongly attracted to females as sexual partners. Similarly, a female can be

Many adolescents of both sexes have transient or longer-term experiences with homosexual activity. Such experiences do not mean that one's adult sexual orientation will be homosexual.

Some Facts about Sexual Orientation

Adolescents may benefit from an awareness of the following facts about sexual orientation (Gordon 1981; Jensen 1981):

1. Many young people worry about their sexual orientation.
2. About a fourth of all young people have some homosexual experience during their teenage years.
3. Homosexual experiences or thoughts do not mean that a person is homosexual.
4. Attraction to a person of the same sex is normal and healthy and does not mean homosexuality.

5. Homosexuality is eventually indicated by a person's *predominant and consistent* attraction and sexual arousal to people of the same sex.
6. Sexual orientation is probably determined very early in life, possibly in the first seven years.
7. Experiences that come later do not cause homosexuality; they merely affirm it.
8. Unwanted sexual advances can be dealt with by saying, "That's your preference, which is fine, but it's not mine."

willful, ambitious, independent, and assertive, and still prefer male lovers. Gender-role behavior and sexual orientation are separate personality elements in each of us (Ambron and Brodzinsky 1979).

Most young people who worry about their sexual orientation are heterosexual or predominately so. Some are homosexual, but their sexual preference may be unclear to them for some years because clearcut homosexual identity manifests itself slowly. In retrospect, most homosexual adults can recall that during their teenage years they felt some sexual attraction for same-sexed persons (Jensen 1981). Yet many heterosexual adults have similar memories. It is sometimes difficult for adolescents to be sure about their ultimate sexual preferences until after several years of sexual activity.

1. At what age did you first become aware that there are various sexual orientations?
2. Can you recall a period when you were uncertain about your sexual orientation?

Parent-Adolescent Communication

A near-universal complaint among both adolescents and their parents is lack of communication between the two generations. Neither "side" feels that the other listens to what is said. In many families, there is virtually no effective communication between parents and adolescents. The great majority of adolescent sexual problems can be resolved, if not prevented entirely, through effective communication with understanding and caring parents.

Patterns of effective communication cannot be developed overnight. Ideally, the process begins while children are still infants. Children need to learn, through years of experience, that they can depend on their parents to take the time to listen to them, to really hear what they are saying, and to give honest, nonjudgmental responses. Having this expectation, adolescents feel no reluctance to bring sexual or other concerns to their parents' attention. Another benefit is that children who grow up in such an environment are likely to carry habits of effective communication into their adult relationships.

As we discussed in chapter 4, successful communication requires two *active* participants: one who honestly expresses a feeling or idea and one who truly wants and tries to understand the message, not just hear the words. Many of us tend to view the speaker as taking an active role while the listener is passive. But the listener is also an active participant, of whom much is required for communication to be successful. Many people fail as listeners because they are so wrapped up in their own problems that they are unable to direct their attention and concern to the needs of others.

Sometimes, people try to listen but fail to understand or misunderstand what is said to them. Often, people take messages as being critical when they were not intended as such. Minor misunderstandings can easily grow into major hostilities. When someone makes a statement that causes us to feel defensive or angry, these feelings should not be concealed in the hope that they will disappear. We should immediately ask for clarification of any ill-taken or vague statement. We might say, for example, "Could you rephrase that? I'm not sure what you mean" or "What I understand you to say is. . . . Is that what you mean to say?" Many family problems can be avoided by this simple step.

In some families, unsuccessful sexual communication results from inadequate vocabulary or feelings of discomfort with sexual terms. Actually, the English language as spoken in the United States lacks a good, everyday sexual vocabulary. Most sexual words are either too technical for everyday use or have been debased by vulgar or hostile use. The options available to describe sexual intercourse are good examples. The terms *intercourse* or *coitus* seem too stilted or clinical for informal use. *Making love* is not entirely accurate because intercourse may or may not reflect love, and we also express love in many ways other than intercourse. *Fuck* and *screw* are too often used to express hostility or anger to be acceptable to everyone for nonhostile use. It seems that we need some new words in our sexual vocabulary.

Communication is not limited to spoken language. Our nonverbal behavior, commonly called body language, conveys much of our message, particularly its emotional content. Our true feelings are often more accurately perceived by others through our facial expressions, posture, and body gestures than through our words. Feelings that we may *not* desire to express are communicated nevertheless. If par-

Discussing Sex with Young People

George Orvin (1981) has some helpful suggestions for adults discussing sex with young people:

1. People talk more freely when they are not compelled to talk. We should not make people feel that they have to talk.

2. Let people finish what they want to say without interrupting.

3. Listen purposefully and with genuine interest.

4. Avoid showing excessively emotional responses, including shock, horror, or vicarious sexual interest.

5. Your only motive should be having the young person share a sensitive part of his or her life with you. Try not to cross-examine or see if you can trap the person in an inaccuracy.

6. Treat the information shared with you with sensitivity and respect.

7. Let the young person know your ideas and feelings as well as any advice you may wish to give. Disagree if you choose, but do so without making him or her feel like a bad person.

8. Respect his or her confidence (don't tell others what you learn).

9. Do not use the information against him or her in future interactions.

10. Ask how you might help.

ents feel uncomfortable about sex or sexuality, their children will perceive this regardless of the words said.

Again, the basic reason children of any age do not approach their parents with sexual questions or concerns is not a lack of interest, but a fear that their questions will not be well received. This sense of uncertainty may not even be a product of the home environment. It may come from outside experiences, perhaps at school or in the neighborhood. This makes it extremely important that parents be approachable. Children must be able to feel that they can raise any question without fear of an unpleasant response.

Perhaps the most basic factor in parent-child sexual communication is that the parent must be comfortable with his or her own sexuality. Being comfortable with our sexuality means freedom from guilt about being sexual, about having sexual feelings, and about enjoying sexual expression. It includes liking our body, including all of its sexual attributes. It means feeling good about our maleness or femaleness and being free from embarrassment or shame in the expression of our sexuality. Our sexuality should be integrated comfortably into our total being and not set aside as an alien function.

Beyond the realm of sexuality, the approachable parent must have the child's trust. The more the channels of communication are kept open and the free exchange of ideas takes place, the easier it is to communicate in the critical sexual area.

Common Adolescent Sexual Myths

Adolescence is often a time of ambivalent sexual feelings, unrewarding sexual relationships, and unwanted pregnancy. Certain widely held myths among young people serve to perpetuate these problems. We now examine a few such myths.

Myth: *Sex produces instant adulthood.*

Facts: Young people often fantasize major personality changes as an immediate result of their initiation into sexual intercourse. They expect these changes to occur in themselves and sometimes believe that they *have* occurred. Commencement of sexual intercourse is seen as a sudden step into adulthood. This myth can have at least two adverse effects. First, it can help push young people into relationships that are inappropriate in terms of personal maturity or choice of partner. Also, when sudden adulthood fails to materialize, there may be disappointment and loss of self-esteem. On the other hand, when individuals believe that their sexual initiation has actually caused them to be fully mature, this can have the effect of inhibiting further personal growth and development.

Myth: *Sex means love.*

Facts: This myth affects young women especially. Even today, young women are more likely than young men to believe that sex and love go together (Scales 1981). Adolescents may interpret someone's sexual advances as indicating love or commitment and feel very disappointed when that proves to be untrue. Or they may feel that love, if not a necessary condition for having sex, will be an inevitable outcome of it. Young people often believe that, if they have sex with someone, he or she will be more likely to love them. While this may happen at times, it is certainly not inevitable.

Myth: *No means yes.*

Facts: This primarily male myth creates problems for women of all ages and is especially troublesome in adolescent relationships. Many males believe that the proof of their masculinity requires taking advantage of every possible opportunity for sexual activity. They also believe that most women who say "no" to sexual advances really mean "yes." As a result, the phenomenon of "date rape" (see chapter 21) is quite prevalent, though most cases go unreported. To the woman who finds herself in the position of having a date who does not believe that her "no" really means "no," Scales (1981) suggests telling him, "You just don't turn me on sexually." Very few people misunderstand this statement.

We should point out that it is not always the female who is pressured into undesired sexual activity. Many males report similar experiences. And saying "no" can be particularly difficult for a male, who may fear that his masculinity will be subject to ridicule as a result. A rejected female, for example, may find it necessary to perceive her rejection as reflecting the male's inadequacy, not her own lack of attractiveness, in order to protect her self-esteem. In reality, of course, a sexual refusal may have a totally different basis. For example, it might be based on ethical grounds or a sense of commitment to someone else.

Myth: *I can't get pregnant.*

Facts: Many sexually active young people make no attempt to use effective contraceptive methods. The myth of "I can't get pregnant" is based on a lack of factual information plus the use of denial (unconsciously refusing to perceive a stressful situation) as a defense against anxiety.

One possible reason for failure to use effective contraception is the unconscious wish for pregnancy to occur. Among the many motives for this wish are the proving of femininity or masculinity, desire for a more adult status, the need to feel loved and the fantasy that a baby will fulfill this need, and even revenge toward a parent or former lover.

In the more likely event that pregnancy is not really wanted at any level of consciousness, there may still be psychological barriers to contraceptive use. Effective contraception requires some advance planning. Most effective methods require a prescription or fitting by a physician, or, at the very least, a visit to a pharmacy or other business offering contraceptives. To take this step requires the conscious acceptance of the probability that sexual intercourse is going to take place, and that it will not just "happen" but is going to be planned. Such a conscious decision causes an intolerable level of anxiety and/or guilt for many young persons. Some have not yet fully accepted their status as sexual beings. Others have ambivalent feelings about being sexually involved at their particular stage in life. Obtaining contraceptives requires acknowledging their sexuality as well as the conscious decision that they are going to be sexually active. Thus, uncomfortable feelings are avoided by letting sex just "happen" without any advance preparations.

There also are some factual inaccuracies that lead to unwanted pregnancies. Many young people (Scales [1981] says over half of teenagers) do not know when, during her menstrual cycle, a woman is most likely to become pregnant. Many believe that they are too young or have sex too infrequently to get pregnant. Some people believe that women won't get pregnant if they do not have an orgasm. Finally, after having unprotected intercourse a few times without becoming pregnant, some young women feel confirmed in their belief that, "It can't happen to me."

Myth: *Condoms allow no feelings.*

Facts: Many young people are extremely resistant to the idea of using condoms (rubbers) for fertility control. This is primarily true of those who have never tried condoms. The younger boys listen to the older boys, mimic their words, and come to believe that "real men" are not supposed to like condoms because they allow no pleasure. The reality, of course, is that condoms detract very little from the pleasure of either partner. And, as a bonus, condoms help prevent disease transmission.

Myth: *And one adult sexual myth: Knowledge leads to experimentation.*

Facts: Parents and other responsible adults are sometimes reluctant to give young people accurate sexual information. Some fear that knowledge about sexuality leads to premature sexual activity or that talking openly about sex stimulates casual sexual partnerships. Adults who try to protect young people from the information they need to make responsible sexual decisions simply push these adolescents toward irresponsible sex. The fact is that talking about sexual issues encourages responsibility. Research shows that, in families where sex is openly discussed, children wait longer to have sexual intercourse, and when they do, are more likely to use effective contraception (Scales 1981). Often, adults' real reason for avoiding sexual discussions is their own anxiety about the subject.

---

1. How do you and your parents communicate about sexuality? Could your communication be better? How could you improve it?
2. Did any of the myths listed influence your adolescent sexual attitudes? What other myths would you add to the list?
3. Under what circumstances do you feel a woman should report a "date rape" to the police? Have any of your acquaintances ever reported a "date rape" to the police? If so, what was the outcome of the report?

"Mom, do you think I made the right decision?"

"About what, Kathy?"

"About the baby?"

"Honey, that was five years ago. Do you still think about her?"

"Of course I do. I don't regret my decision to put her up for adoption, but every once in a while I wonder how she is doing, what she looks like, and I wonder how she'll feel about me when she discovers that she's adopted."

"Kathy, you had just turned seventeen when you got pregnant. You needed to complete high school, and you wanted college and a career. Of course you made the right decision. You couldn't have married Brian then. You're not even sure of yourself now—how could you have been back then?"

"Oh, I know I did what was right for me, but what about the baby?"

"The agency is very careful in screening prospective parents. That couple desperately wanted that baby. You know they must be giving her all the love and guidance you would want for her, don't you?"

"I know that. I am glad she's with a good family, only maybe someday . . . no, I'll stay out of her life. It would be for the best I guess."

Summary

1. Puberty is the early portion of adolescence, during which a person becomes functionally capable of reproduction. In addition to the maturation of the sexual organs, bodywide physical changes occur and many emotional adjustments are required.

2. Various anxieties may accompany puberty. Anxieties about details of physical development and one's new self-image are not unusual.

3. The psychological development demanded of adolescents includes accepting a new body image, establishing a new identity, adjusting to physiological changes, and developing new forms of relationships with other people, including parents.

4. The period of adolescence is prolonged in our technological society. Adult status comes gradually, there being no clear demarcation of adulthood.

5. Adolescent relationships tend to gradually become more intimate, both emotionally and sexually. Each young person progresses at his or her own particular pace.

6. Masturbation, the least intimate sexual outlet, increases in both incidence and frequency during adolescence. Masturbation is normal and harmless behavior.

7. Petting is another important adolescent sexual activity, enabling young people to learn their own sexual responses as well as those of the opposite sex.

8. Most adolescents progress from petting to nonmarital sexual intercourse, although our culture holds ambivalent attitudes on intercourse between unmarried partners.

9. First intercourse is a highly varied experience. An individual's perception of the event is influenced by his or her age, emotional and social maturity, choice of partners, and the surrounding circumstances.

10. Reasons adolescents marry include pregnancy, various unfulfilled emotional needs, and limited awareness of the many options life holds. Few adolescents, however, are emotionally, socially, and economically prepared for marriage, and the failure rate of adolescent marriages is high.

11. In any given year, about one in ten females between the ages of fifteen and nineteen become pregnant, either by choice or by accident.

12. Reasons for adolescent pregnancy include unstable or unhappy home environments, a desire to achieve adult status, a need to feel loved, or a lack of accurate information about conception and contraception.

13. Pregnant adolescents must decide whether abortion, adoption, marriage, or single parenthood is the most viable option. Supportive parents and social services can aid in this decision.

14. The social, educational, occupational, and emotional consequences of adolescent fatherhood are just as difficult and handicapping as those of adolescent motherhood. Counseling is now often available to the adolescent father as well as to the adolescent mother.

15.   Many young people wonder if they are homosexual, heterosexual, or bisexual and tend to relate physical development and gender-role behavior with sexual orientation. Many anxieties can be relieved with adequate information.

16.   The great majority of adolescent sexual problems can be resolved, if not prevented entirely, through effective communication with understanding and caring parents.

17.   Certain myths that tend to perpetuate adolescent sexual problems include: sex produces instant adulthood; sex means love; no means yes; I can't get pregnant; condoms allow no feelings; and sexual knowledge leads to experimentation.

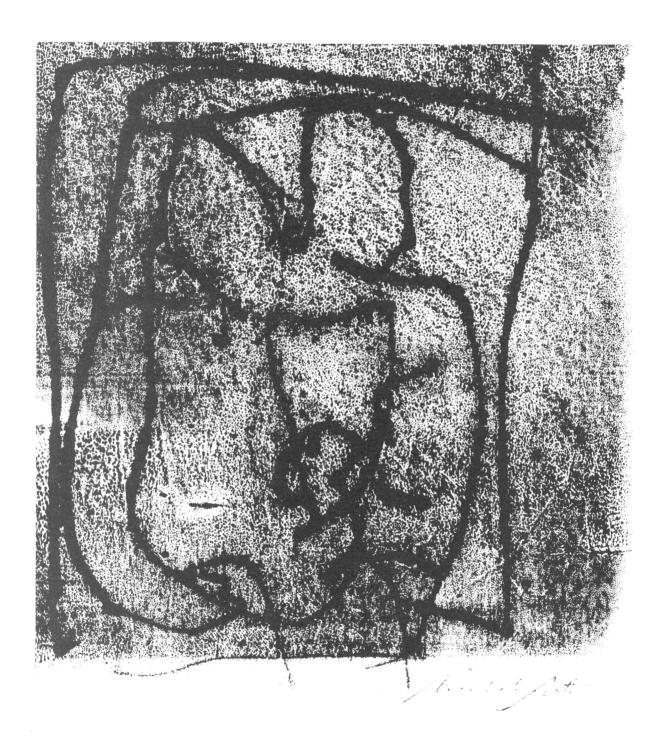

"Kiss today good-bye and point me toward tomorrow. We did what we had to do, won't forget, can't regret, what I did for love . . ." The melody lingered in her ear long after she left the theater. She loved that play. It always made her cry. She had bought one ticket. The box office always had a single left somewhere down front. The seating always allowed for the odd person out. She was always it.

She usually didn't mind being alone. Cooking was sometimes a problem. She loved to cook, but it was tough to cook for one. She did love her privacy, though; no one to pick up after, no one to complain if she didn't. She could go when and where she wanted. She could play loud music or wear loud clothes and no one would object.

Yet, it might be nice to have someone to hold hands with when an old Cary Grant movie came on the late, late show, someone to share the bowl of popcorn with and fight over the seeds with. . . . Maybe it would be nice to be married . . . maybe. . .

Her brother Tom told her not to worry about it, that marriage wasn't all that it was cracked up to be. She envied Tom and his wife Carol. They seemed to be really happy. He had a great job, she was busy with her clubs, their kids always seemed so well mannered. If she did find someone, could they have a marriage as perfect as Tom and Carol's? She wondered.

At some point, each of us expects to be "grown-up." But just what does that mean? Part of it has to do with physical growth—the attainment of our mature height and body proportions. Yet, adulthood also refers to social identity. Being an adult means not being a child or adolescent. It generally means being financially independent of our parents. It means establishing mature types of relationships with others.

In our society, the assumption of adult roles often occurs gradually and at different rates in different individuals, there being no specific rite of passage into adulthood in our culture. In very arbitrary terms, the period of young adulthood may be considered to extend from about ages eighteen to thirty or perhaps even forty.

Early adulthood is characterized by much more diversity than the earlier stages in the life cycle. Some twenty-year-olds, for example, are still students, studying for exams, accepting financial assistance from their parents, and experimenting with various types of relationships. Other twenty-year-olds are parents, involved in child care, careers, and financial planning. Some people enter the job market immediately after high school. Others, such as physicians, may not undertake full-time employment until around the age of twenty-eight.

Early adulthood is the period during which we often form serious personal commitments, marry, begin families, and take our place in the world of work. It is in early adulthood that we define our relationship to society through work, love, and play. The number of years we take to accomplish this varies, and the break between adolescence and adulthood is often gradual and unclear, even in a specific individual.

In this chapter, we explore young adult sexuality. Since physical sexual development is largely complete in the young adult, we primarily concern ourselves with the types of relationships characteristic of young adults.

Intimacy in Young Adults

If the major task during adolescence is the resolution of our personal identity, the challenge during early adulthood is to develop intimate relationships with others. These two tasks are accomplished most effectively in that sequence; that is, intimacy can develop only after identity is established. This means that many people who are well beyond adolescence are unable to establish intimate relationships because they have yet to resolve their identity. It is only after we achieve an identity that we feel comfortable enough to risk revealing this identity to another and to develop a new, adult kind of intimacy. This is the kind of intimacy freely chosen by two equal persons who have both worked through their adolescent identity crises and know basically who they are.

In chapter 4, we distinguished between emotional intimacy and sexual intimacy, and the distinction is worth repeating. Many of us use the word *intimacy* as a synonym for sexual intercourse. When we ask, "Were you ever intimate with him?" we mean, "Did you ever have sexual intercourse with him?" Yet, it is quite possible to have emotional intimacy without sexual interaction or to have sexual relationships without emotional intimacy.

Before we resolve our identity, most of our sexual relationships are of the searching, self-serving kind. We share our inner self very little. Communication is superficial at best. When we are at this stage of development, we are afraid of losing ourselves in an intimate relationship because we do not really have ourselves to begin with.

In contrast, intimacy is characterized by mutuality. Ideally, we care for our partner as much as we care for ourself. Mutuality includes the willingness to make sacrifices and compromises. It also involves mature sexual functioning in that there is a mutual sharing of sexual pleasures. It is emotional intimacy that most distinguishes the sexual relationships of young adults from those of adolescents.

In studies of college students, who as a group tend to span the indefinite gap between adolescence and young adulthood, those having well-developed identities tend to score high on intimacy as well (Ambron and Brodzinsky 1979). They are able to share worries and express anger as well as affectionate feelings toward their partners. Those scoring low on measurements of identity tend to develop alternatives to intimacy, such as superficial, stereotyped relationships or a "pseudointimacy."

Of course, intimacy is not an either/or situation. There are all degrees of intimacy in our relationships. Even in a continuing relationship between the same two individuals, the level of intimacy fluctuates from day to day and year to year. As each individual has his or her own emotional ups and downs, the nature and quality of the interaction between the two naturally varies in response. It would be unrealistic to expect any relationship to exhibit a high level of intimacy at all times. It is just such unrealistic expectations that cause some people to become disenchanted with what are actually very good relationships, perhaps feeling an unwarranted sense of failure.

The opposite of intimacy is emotional isolation. Some young adults intentionally isolate themselves from intimate relationships. Their bodies may be rather freely available to others, but their true selves remain closely guarded. Perhaps a young man has been so hurt by a parent or former lover that he is simply unable to take the emotional risk involved in satisfactory interpersonal relationships. Or perhaps a young woman is in the midst of an intentional, temporary "moratorium" on intimacy. She may be at a point where problems involved in breaking free of parents or choosing and preparing for a career make it easier for her not to "get involved." For these and other reasons, many young adults engage in superficial sexual relationships, turning away from the challenge of intimacy to become self-absorbed and emotionally excluding others.

Most of us place considerable importance upon our personal fulfillment (self-actualization) through our careers or other personal achievements. But some of us mistakenly seek self-actualization through totally self-centered approaches. Actually, self-actualization is the process of fulfillment of self through both personal growth and growth in our relationships with others.

Those who misunderstand the process of self-actualization may place a decreased emphasis on interpersonal relationships as bases of self-fulfillment. Becoming deeply involved in their own personal growth, they may devote little time and energy to the development and maintenance of their marital or other partnerships. Some couples become almost strangers to each other. Each comes and goes on his or her own busy schedule. There is little relaxed conversation, and meals are seldom eaten together. Soon, beyond sexual, social, or economic convenience, there is little basis for maintaining the relationship. In our search for self-actualization, we need to remember that our relationships with others are a very necessary part of our ultimate fulfillment as individuals.

While avoiding intimacy may seem to be the easiest and most efficient way to live one's life, in the long run, it is not the most fulfilling. People who take this route often complain that their lives seem empty and lack meaning. What is missing is the satisfaction that can come only from shared intimacy.

---

1. Some of your friends have been saying that they have been "burned" so often in relationships that they are going to intentionally keep their future relationships at a superficial level—sexual activity, but no emotional involvement. What are some possible outcomes of this effort?
2. How can someone who has not been successful in developing intimate relationships achieve the ability to form such relationships?

Adult Gender-Role Concepts

Perhaps no aspect of sexuality arouses more interest and concern today than the appropriateness of various male and female roles. Controversies rage. On the one hand stand those who feel that male and female roles should be clearly defined, preferably along traditional lines. On the other hand are those who feel that people of either sex should be free to assume any kinds of roles they find fulfilling.

Gender-role concepts influence almost every aspect of our lives. Our choice of career may reflect what we feel is appropriate for a person of our sex. What tasks we feel comfortable doing at home is another reflection of what we feel is appropriate for our sex. Even how we interact with each other sexually reflects our gender-role concepts.

Recent years have seen considerable blurring of distinctions between "a man's job" and "woman's work," a trend that is ultimately highly beneficial to people of both sexes.

Young adults of today often feel that they are caught in the middle between those who encourage them to try nonstereotypical behavior and those who would make life difficult for them if they did so. There is often an additional element of internal conflict—many people are just not sure how they define their personal sex roles.

Career Gender-Role Conflicts

While many types of employment are still dominated by one sex or the other, there are many more options for a person of either sex than there were in the past (table 13.1). Women who in the past might have become nurses, secretaries, or teachers now become engineers, physicians, attorneys, ministers, coal miners, or truck drivers. Men who might once have been firefighters or construction workers become airline flight attendants, telephone operators, or nurses.

For some people, these changes have meant taking the risk of expressing interests, abilities, and life-styles believed by prior generations to belong to the opposite sex. Parents and older coworkers may be nonsupportive or even hostile. A mother may caution her executive daughter that her success may stand in the way of her personal fulfillment in marriage. A middle-aged male steelworker may make on-the-job socializing difficult for his young female coworker. A male nurse may find that, because of his career choice, many people assume that he is gay, regardless of his actual sexual orientation.

Table 13.1   Jobs Where Women Are Gaining.

Occupation	Women As Percentage of All Workers	
	1960	1980
Accountants	16.4	36.2
Bakers	15.9	42.9
Bank financial officers	12.4	33.6
Bus drivers	9.8	44.9
Buyers, purchasing agents	17.7	33.6
College professors	21.3	33.9
Food-service managers	24.0	39.4
Lawyers and judges	3.3	12.8
Physicians	6.8	13.4
Police and firefighters	4.1	9.5
Retail sales managers	28.2	40.5

Source: U.S. Bureau of the Census, 1981.

Female Gender-Role Conflicts

In our current redefinition of gender rules, it appears that women are in the greatest state of internal emotional conflict (Ambron and Brodzinsky 1979). Many women demonstrate this conflict in the way they plan and implement career goals. They may find themselves caught between a need for achievement and a fear that too much success may compromise their femininity.

The "Cinderella Complex"

Colette Dowling (1981) has identified and named a psychological phenomenon that, she believes, thwarts many women in their efforts to achieve personal and career fulfillment. Called the "Cinderella Complex," it is the culturally derived desire to be taken care of by others. Whether felt consciously or experienced unconsciously, this is the chief force holding women down today, according to Dowling. Like Cinderella, many women are still waiting for someone or something external to transform their lives. Until these women become aware of their deep wish to be taken care of and assume the responsibility for their own well-being, Dowling believes that they will remain emotionally dependent on others and never know the joy of their own autonomy.

The Housewife Conflict

With the majority of adult women now in the full-time work force, it has become more common for women to define or identify themselves in terms of the work they do outside the home. This has created major conflicts for those women who are not employed. Perhaps they have felt fulfilled and satisfied with their roles for some years (although, according to Oakley [1974a], this is unlikely). Suddenly, the role that once brought needed social approval and reinforcement is no longer adequate for this purpose. People want to know what women *do*—meaning how they are employed. And quite apart from what other people think, more and more women feel unfulfilled without a career of their own.

Ann Oakley (1974a, 1974b) and Susan Strasser (1982) give a feminist's outlook on housework and the housewife's role. Their conclusions, based on considerable research and interviews with many women, are that the life of the housewife is boring, socially isolated, physically demanding, mentally demeaning, and often very low in social status. For many women, housework offers few intrinsic rewards (pleasures in doing the work) and gains little recognition from others for a job well done. This is true for most women employed outside the home, as well as for most who are not.

In response to the low social status some currently give the role of "housewife" and perhaps also as a part of the current trend back to more traditional values, a phenomenon of "housewife backlash" has appeared in some parts of the country.

Women are pushing for acceptability and respect for their roles as wives and mothers, pointing out that their services in this capacity are of great value to society and to their husbands and children. They also point out what it would cost to hire someone to do all the many tasks that comprise the housewife role.

Male Gender-Role Conflicts

For men, the gender-role situation has not changed so drastically. Men have always been expected to be employed, and they still are. Newspapers and magazines publish stories on "househusbands," but few people view this as a major trend, and few men are taking this option. However, as we mentioned earlier, more men now feel free to pursue what were once considered to be women's jobs.

One gender-role change that many men may now be faced with is that they are not the principle source of income in their marriages. While women are still seriously underpaid (the average working woman earns only about 59 percent of the average man's wages), increasing numbers of women are making their way into the higher income levels. Some men have difficulty adjusting to their wives' incomes being higher than their own since part of the traditional male's ego support has come from being the "breadwinner."

Another area in which the traditionally oriented male is likely to have difficulty in adjusting to today's realities is the working out of an equitable division of labor at home. If each member of a partnership is working full time outside the home, it seems only logical that the home duties would be shared about equally. But some males (usually middle-aged, but a surprising number of young males as well) are quite reluctant to do what they perceive as "women's work," such as cooking, housekeeping, and laundry. These men perceive such work as a threat to their masculine image (not to mention that the work is often tedious and unpleasant). The same type of men may also have trouble in their sexual and other relationships with contemporary women, feeling threatened by the women's self-confidence and assertiveness (Gould 1977).

The Breaking Down of the Sexual Double Standard

To a surprising degree, the sexual double standard still exists—the male is to be dominant and aggressive, the female is to be sexually passive. Further, according to the double standard, males are allowed to pursue a variety of sexual partners, while females are expected to be monogamous (faithful to one partner). Obviously, such an arrangement is most favorable to males, and, not surprisingly, it is males who most often support the double standard.

Fortunately, many women are forcing the slow breakdown of the sexual double standard by feeling just as free as males to initiate sexual activity, either with an existing sexual partner or someone new. Those men who can accept female sexual assertiveness are finding their sex lives more fulfilling than ever before. Those who feel threatened by female sexual assertiveness are sometimes experiencing impotence or premature ejaculation or are withdrawing from the sexual arena altogether. These, of course, are men who carry lingering doubts about their masculinity, primarily as a result of their early conditioning to conform to rigid and demanding masculine gender-role stereotypes (Gould 1977).

All in all, some people of each sex may have difficulty adjusting to less rigid concepts of what is appropriate male and female behavior. But the great majority of people of both sexes are able to live much more rewarding and fulfilling lives once they free themselves of the old, arbitrarily imposed restraints on male and female behavior.

1. What is wrong with such statements as: "She's a good driver for a woman," or "He's a good cook for a man"?
2. Will we ever achieve gender equity in this country? If you answer yes, how do you think this will come about? If you answer no, what do you see as the barriers to gender equity?

Nonmarital Life-Styles

Most Americans are married at least once during their lives. Yet nonmarital life-styles, such as cohabitation and living alone, are also important to most of us at various times—before marriage, between marriages, and as a permanent choice.

Cohabitation

Cohabitation (living together), now prevalent in all socioeconomic strata and all age groups in the United States, provides life satisfactions, developmental possibilities, and potential problems that are only now beginning to be appreciated.

Some couples live together for seemingly unromantic reasons. For example, a woman chooses a male roommate (and incidentally, a sexual partner) because she cannot afford to live alone, dislikes living with women, or feels more secure living with a male.

Other living-together relationships constitute "trial marriages," during which each partner works at developing emotional commitment (or tests emotional commitment) with the security of knowing that he or she can pack up and leave on short notice.

In still other cases, two people live together without marriage because they cannot legally marry. Perhaps one or both are still legally married to other persons. Perhaps both are of the same sex.

Many people find living alone to be a most rewarding life-style.

No one knows exactly how many unmarried couples live together. Some represent themselves as being married, simplifying relationships with landlords and others. Some technically retain two addresses to appease parents or others but seldom sleep apart. In any case, many millions of Americans now cohabit.

Legal considerations regarding cohabitation vary from state to state (Douthwaite 1979). A few states prohibit cohabitation, but enforcement of such laws is rare. Common-law marriage statutes in Alabama, Colorado, Georgia, Idaho, Iowa, Kansas, Montana, Ohio, Oklahoma, Pennsylvania, Rhode Island, South Carolina, Texas, and the District of Columbia recognize a couple as legally married after they cohabit for a specified period (Zepke 1983). A couple considering cohabitation would be wise to check the laws of their state before moving in.

The economic considerations of cohabitation are more complex and also vary from state to state (Douthwaite 1979). A couple living together is not usually recognized as an economic unit in the same manner as a married couple. However, they can own property of any kind jointly, and they can incur debts and obligations jointly. They file their income tax separately.

Most of the really difficult economic questions arise if the living-together relationship is terminated. Depending on how title to items purchased jointly has been registered or recorded, a fair and equitable division of property may or may not occur. Further, there have been well-publicized cases of "palimony" being granted to one partner when he or she has been financially supported by the other. It is strongly recommended that individuals considering cohabitation engage an attorney to draw up a binding financial agreement to protect the rights of both parties.

Living Alone

One of the significant changes in American living habits in recent years has been a sharp increase in the number of people living by themselves. The 1980 census revealed that 22 percent of all United States living units consist of only one person. Among these fifteen million people are those who have never married, those who are now separated or divorced, and those who are widowed. Some live alone by choice; some by necessity. Some find it a highly rewarding life-style; many do not. Like other life-styles, living alone has its advantages and disadvantages.

One advantage of living alone is that it offers more freedom than any other life-style. There is usually plenty of time to travel, to develop talents and skills, to enjoy hobbies, to relax, to entertain and be entertained, and to discover one's own individuality. For some self-sufficient people, living alone offers the greatest potential for personal fulfillment of all life-styles (Simenauer and Carroll 1982).

Other people, however, find coming home to an empty house or apartment, eating alone, or sleeping alone difficult and depressing. Except for those who choose it as a life-style, few people consider living alone a positive experience. Some even remain in relationships that are unproductive and unfulfilling only because they

Making the Single Life-Style Rewarding

For those having difficulty establishing a rewarding single life-style or those who might like to try it but have been reluctant to do so, Lynn Shahan (1981) offers almost two hundred pages of advice. The following are a few of her ideas.

First, Shahan suggests that we appreciate the advantages of living alone. It provides more freedom to cater to our personal tastes and interests than does any other life-style. We can design our life-style on the basis of who we are. We can choose what our opportunities and relationships will be rather than having them forced upon us.

Living alone, according to Shahan, also gives us a tremendous opportunity to establish true personal independence. Because we must learn to take care of our own needs, we are in a position to acquire the kind of inner strength and self-esteem that results from being our own primary source of support. Being self-reliant is highly rewarding. There is no feeling quite like knowing that we can take care of ourselves. In the process, we discover that no other person can ever give us the security we can't provide ourselves.

Finally, in living alone, according to Shahan, we are guaranteed the luxury of privacy—to come home to peace and quiet, to sleep undisturbed, to collect our thoughts, to drop all guards and shed all facades—to be completely ourselves. Many people live entire lifetimes without knowing this pleasure.

To overcome the primary disadvantage of the single life-style—loneliness—Shahan suggests a two-phase process. First, we must face our loneliness. Loneliness is something to which we seldom like to admit, either to ourselves or others. We feel it implies that we are somehow lacking. To maintain self-esteem, we try to construct a protective, confident, false front. But to deal with loneliness, we must acknowledge that there are times and situations in our lives that produce feelings of loneliness.

The second phase, according to Shahan, is to actively combat loneliness. We must identify what causes the problem and then attempt to modify the conditions that produce our lonely feelings. We can do this by aggressively working toward establishing worthwhile social contacts and maintaining our present valuable friendships. Calling someone we have not spoken to in a while or inviting a friend over for dinner or out for an evening are positive approaches to the problem. Supportive personal relationships can go a long way in combating loneliness. The establishment and maintenance of such relationships is, according to Shahan, one of the most important responsibilities we have to ourselves if we live alone.

cannot conceive that living alone can be anything but a lonely, negative experience. It does not have to be that way. Regardless of whether an individual lives alone by choice or necessity, viewing it as a positive life-style is the first step toward making it such.

1. An unmarried couple is planning to live together. What are some potential sources of conflict that they might profitably discuss and reach written agreements on before they begin cohabitation?
2. Do you see living alone for a period as a potentially rewarding life-style for yourself? What would be some of the more difficult problems you would face by living alone?

Marriage

Despite all of the predictions during the 1960s and 1970s that the institution of marriage was about to meet an untimely demise, marriage is still thriving and has every likelihood of outliving all of us. This is not too surprising, considering that every past or current culture has had marriage in some form. Marriage, or something that approximates it, can be an ideal way for many people to live highly fulfilling lives. And, even today, most people do marry at some time during their lives.

Although marriage has not died, there have been changes. The "traditional" American family, as still portrayed by advertising and the popular media, now is in a minority. According to 1980 census figures, only 13 percent of the nation's families include a working father, nonworking mother, and one or more children. People marry later, delay or avoid having children, and divorce more freely. With or without children in the home, a married woman today is likely to have a job or career that she views as important for both financial security and personal fulfillment.

Readiness for Marriage

About half of all marriages now end in divorce, and quite a few of the rest are maintained more for convenience than for desire. Obviously, we need to be pretty careful about who, when, and even whether we marry.

Marriage is definitely not for everyone. Some people are unready for marriage in terms of their social and/or emotional maturity. Others have particular personality types or life-styles that would make it very difficult for their marriage to succeed. Those who hold little expectation of success in marriage are probably not ready to marry, nor are those who would demand perfection in their marriage. There is no totally reliable way to know who is ready for marriage, but the following criteria may be helpful.

Age

Certainly not everyone at a particular chronological age represents the same degree of maturity. Yet chronological age at the time of marriage is one of the most reliable predictors of the success of a marriage. Many studies have shown that the level of satisfaction and success in marriage increases with the age of the partners at the time of marriage. Marriages where both partners are quite young, perhaps under age twenty, are particularly likely to be unhappy. U.S. Census Bureau figures reveal that three out of four teenage marriages fail.

A source of the problems with young marriages is that many people experience considerable growth in their value systems somewhere between the ages of sixteen and twenty-four. During this period, our interests, tastes, ideals, standards, and goals often undergo a complete change. If people marry before this change, they may relieve parental or social (peer) pressures to marry, but there is a strong possibility that they will not meet each other's needs in the future (McCarthy 1981).

Emotional Maturity

In a successful marriage, each partner contributes to the need fulfillment of the other. One measure of emotional maturity is how well a person has developed the means of satisfying his or her own emotional needs without exploiting others in the process. Anyone with a number of unfulfilled needs is going to have trouble contributing to a partner's need fulfillment.

Even the most enthusiastic supporters of marriage agree that maintaining a smoothly working marital relationship is not often easy. Marriage requires ongoing patience, tolerance, and compromise. All of these require a good measure of emotional maturity.

The presence of outright emotional maladjustments in a marriage can be destructive to both partners as well as to the relationship. Generally, someone experiencing extremes of moodiness, rage, jealousy, anxiety, depression, or insecurity will have a difficult marital relationship and should consider postponing marriage until such problems are successfully resolved.

Social Maturity

Social maturity develops through social interaction, such as dating many different individuals. Dating provides a basis for the selection of a marriage mate and helps to satisfy social and sexual curiosity.

Another way of developing social maturity is experiencing a period of single, independent life before marriage, a time of freedom between the former dependence on parents and the future responsibilities of marriage. Living away from parents for a time is a good way to get to know oneself, to develop social competency, and to learn to manage one's own affairs. On the other hand, given today's high rents and other living expenses, it is often necessary for young people to remain in their parents' homes even though they might prefer to be out on their own. Even in this situation, considerable growth is possible as the young person learns to manage his or her financial and social affairs with increasing independence.

Flexibility

Successful marriage always requires a degree of compromise. Two people cannot always have exactly the same interests, tastes, needs, and desires at the same time. Ideally, two partners are fairly similar in their preferences. And, also ideally, each partner is willing to meet the other halfway when compromise is necessary. A good marriage does not result when one partner does all of the compromising and the other does little or none. In this situation, hostilities build quickly and will certainly be expressed, if not openly, then in numerous ways, such as sexual problems, financial mismanagement, and extramarital affairs. People who find compromise difficult might seriously consider remaining single.

Choosing a Marital Partner

For any one of us there are literally thousands of people who would be good choices for marital partners. (There is no such thing as a "one and only" love.) At the same time, of course, there are thousands of other people who would be very poor marital choices. The desirability of any potential partner depends on his or her personal traits and how those traits interact with our own.

Personality Traits

By far the most important characteristic in a potential marriage partner is his or her personality. Some people have highly positive personality traits that enable them to enjoy life to its fullest and to bring joy to anyone with whom they have contact. Others have so many unresolved emotional conflicts that their own happiness is impossible, as is that of anyone who must live with them.

Traits that produce happy marriages include optimism, a sense of humor, an honest concern for the needs of others, a sense of ethics, the ability to adjust easily to changes in conditions, and freedom from severe emotional problems such as extreme anxiety, depression, and jealousy. The single most important emotional characteristic and the basis for most other desirable characteristics, however, is a well-developed sense of self-esteem.

Mutual Need Satisfaction

The happy and lasting marriage is one in which the needs of each individual are adequately fulfilled. While the idea may not appeal to romantics, the basic reason why people marry is to satisfy various needs. A successful marriage satisfies many needs—love, companionship, sex, self-esteem, security, and other psychological needs. Usually without conscious awareness of what we are doing, we tend to be attracted to people who we perceive as being best able to satisfy our needs. Our perception may or may not be accurate. Only through a long period of interaction in a variety of situations (both pleasant and unpleasant) can two people learn whether they are really able to fulfill each other's needs.

At the same time, many marriages fail because people hold unreasonable expectations of need fulfillment by their partners. Many needs just cannot be fulfilled by someone else. For example, it is unrealistic to expect another person to ensure our happiness. Certainly, someone else can contribute to our happiness, but true happiness must come from within. Similarly, while a caring partner can contribute to our self-esteem, true feelings of personal adequacy can only arise within ourselves.

Communication

Some of us are fortunate to have grown up in families in which parents set an example of open, effective communication. Others of us know that our communication skills need further development. Fortunately, a person who decides to work toward improving his or her communication skills has an excellent chance of success. Many colleges, community groups, and organizations now offer excellent courses and seminars in interpersonal communication.

Effective communication is essential to a smoothly working marital partnership. If either partner is unable to freely communicate needs, desires, preferences, thoughts, and feelings to the other, serious difficulties are likely to develop.

For example, before marriage a couple needs to discuss money management—where it is to come from and how it is to be spent. They need to discuss parenthood—whether each prefers to have children, when, and how many. If there are to be children, it is desirable for a couple to hold similar feelings on how the children are to be raised, a major source of conflict in many marriages. Also, free and open communication on sexual matters can help prevent conflict in this critical area.

A lack of open communication is usually indicative of a relationship that lacks emotional intimacy. Such a relationship is a weak basis upon which to build a marriage.

Marital Adjustments

Adjustment to marriage has always been challenging. Today, however, it may be even more so because the expectations by and for each partner may be less clearcut than in the past. Even when a couple has already lived together for several years, marriage can require new adjustments. When two people marry, each assumes a new role, that of "wife" or "husband." This new role requires more personal, social, economic, and sexual adjustments than most unmarried people anticipate.

Being married carries many psychological, social, and economic implications. A married couple is a social and economic unit, beyond the particular social and economic role of each partner as an individual.

Adjustments to Each Other

Even after several years of cohabitation, the new relationship of marriage usually demands some reevaluation of old patterns of interaction. Marriage usually implies a new level of commitment. Where before, each partner may have felt as if he or she could easily walk out the door if so desired, now there may be an uncomfortable feeling of being tied down. Difficult adjustments in many marriages include patterns of dominance, dependence versus independence, self-assertion versus compromise, and prioritizing one's own needs versus the possibly conflicting needs of one's partner (Ambron and Brodzinsky 1979).

Social Adjustments

People, even relatives and old friends, suddenly relate to a newly married person in a different manner. Social activity now more often involves the couple as a unit, rather than as individuals. At the same time as marriage creates new social opportunities, it may also seem to limit one's social activities. Newly married people often find that they, as individuals, are no longer included in activities and primarily single social groups in which they might still wish to be involved.

In-law relationships also may call for some adjustments. Parents may have difficulty in accepting a new son- or daughter-in-law or in releasing their hold on their own son or daughter.

Economic Adjustments

Though state laws vary, a married couple is usually viewed as being an economic unit beyond the economic roles of each individual. For example, in "community property" states, the earnings of either partner are considered to belong equally to both while financial obligations made by either partner are binding upon both. Conflicts arise when partners are reluctant to pool their earnings or when the spending habits of one partner meet with the disapproval of the other partner. Serious disagreements over money often reflect more basic conflicts in the partnership, such as questions of dominance and dependency.

Sexual Adjustments

The sexual success of a marriage depends both on the individual characteristics of the partners and how the partners interact with each other. Significant individual characteristics include self-esteem, assertiveness, concern for the partner, and freedom from sexual anxieties or inhibitions. Significant characteristics of the partnership include open and honest communication, shared emotional intimacy, and freedom from hostilities and conflicts, such as struggles for dominance. A good sexual relationship is generally assured if two partners are relatively free of individual emotional conflicts and enjoy a mutually rewarding total relationship.

However, many couples do experience difficulties in sexual adjustment. Sexual dysfunctions are discussed in chapter 10. Here we are concerned more with sexual disagreements. Common areas of disagreement include frequency of sexual activity, time of sexual activity, choice of sexual activities, and amount of nonsexual attention.

Frequency of Sexual Activity   The need for sexual release varies considerably among different people. Some strongly feel the need for sexual pleasure daily or more often. Others are satisfied with much less frequent activity. Further, the sexual interest of any individual tends to vary with that person's emotional and hormonal state. Emotionally, the majority of people are more sexually interested and responsive during periods of emotional well-being. Some, however, respond to stress and anxiety by increased desire for sexual release. Hormonally, the female menstrual cycle is the best understood example of the relationship of cycling hormone levels to sexual interest (see chapter 6, or, for more detail, Bermant and Davidson [1974] or Schrotenboer and Subak-Sharpe [1981]). All of these variables ensure that, in almost any relationship, there will be times when one partner desires sexual activity, but the other is uninterested.

Sexual frequency can become a major source of conflict in a relationship. Ideally, each partner can compromise to some extent, and a mutually satisfactory frequency of sexual activity can be achieved. But this does not always happen. Sometimes, the giving or withholding of sexual favors is used as a bargaining device—a barter. Some relationships deteriorate into a struggle for dominance. Each partner wants to be the one to initiate sexual activity and may refuse to take part if the other takes the initiative. Obviously, in situations such as these, sexual frequency is not the real issue at all. It is merely the battleground on which basic marital conflicts are fought. If those conflicts can be resolved, issues of sexual frequency usually resolve themselves.

Time of Sexual Activity   Many of us are basically morning people or night people. That is, some of us function best early in the morning, others late at night. These functional discrepancies may cause some people to hold a definite preference for sexual activity at a particular time—early morning, afternoon, or late at night.

Generally, if the overall relationship is sound, a couple can agree on a mutually acceptable time for sexual pleasuring. As with sexual frequency, however, basic power conflicts between a couple may emerge as disagreements on when sexual activity should occur.

Choice of Sexual Activities   Not all couples can agree on just what specific sexual activities and techniques they want to enjoy. Some people are eager to try almost any form of sexual activity. Others, perhaps coming from more sexually restrictive backgrounds, feel comfortable with a more limited sexual repertoire.

Oral sex, for example, is sometimes an area of contention in a relationship. Most younger people today quite enthusiastically give and receive oral stimulation of the genitals. But many older people and some younger ones just do not enjoy oral sex. Their reasons are probably more emotional than rational—personal modesty, religious inhibition, etc.—but their feelings are very real, often strong, and should be respected.

As with the previously discussed conflicts, those concerning specific sexual practices are usually not too disruptive to a strong total relationship. But in a relationship with such basic conflicts as struggles for dominance, issues such as oral or anal sex, choice of positions, and countless other technical matters may emerge as severe impediments to pleasant lovemaking.

Amount of Nonsexual Attention   In some marriages, one partner, in a hurry to obtain sexual release, ignores the other partner's needs for nonsexual attention and affection prior to lovemaking. This often results in a feeling of being used on the part of the ignored partner and general hostility in the marital relationship.

Most people are more easily aroused in the context of an emotionally intimate relationship. For that reason, married couples need to spend time together in nonsexual activities, such as relaxed dining, conversation, and enjoying shared interests, as an important preliminary to sexual activity. It assures both partners of acceptance as total persons, rather than mere sexual objects, and improves and strengthens not only the sexual relationship but the marital relationship as well.

---

1.   Numerically rank (1–10) the following characteristics of a potential marriage partner for yourself as to how important these characteristics would be in influencing your happiness if you would marry that person (1 = most important; 10 = least important):
    a. _____ Sexually attractive to you
    b. _____ Wealthy
    c. _____ Viewed as attractive by others
    d. _____ Cheerful
    e. _____ Intelligent
    f. _____ Well-educated
    g. _____ Optimistic
    h. _____ Practical
    i. _____ Stable personality
    j. _____ Sexually "faithful" to you
2.   Which (if any) of the characteristics in question 1 is so important that you would not consider marrying someone who lacked it, even if that person possessed the other nine characteristics listed?

Sexual Fidelity

Much of this discussion of sexual fidelity applies equally to married couples as well as to emotionally committed unmarried couples, whether or not the unmarried couple is living together. The expectation of sexual exclusivity is generally the same in either case, unless other agreements have been made. While the outside affairs of unmarried people have been much less studied than the affairs of married people, the motivations for these outside relationships are probably similar. Also, the emotional responses of the other party, upon discovery of an affair, are also probably similar to those of a married person. In this discussion, substitution of the term *relationship* for the term *marriage* and substitution of the word *partner* for *spouse* will generally make the discussion applicable to unmarried couples.

Most people still marry with the expectation that both they and their spouses will be sexually exclusive to each other. Regardless of this ideal, the fact is that, within a few years after marriage, one or both spouses in many marriages will have had outside sexual partnerships. Statistics on infidelity are notoriously unreliable. Some people lie to cover up affairs they have had, while others fabricate affairs that never took place. However, it seems almost certain that outside affairs are a part of over half of all marriages at one time or another (Appleton 1981).

Hunt (1974) did extensive research on the incidence of extramarital affairs. He found that, compared with Kinsey's survey (1948), the incidence of affairs among married males had remained about the same over the years. In the 1970s, as in the 1940s, about half the men reported having had one or more affairs. In young (eighteen- to twenty-four-year-olds) married women, however, the incidence had changed during those decades. For this group, the incidence of extramarital affairs had tripled, from about 8 percent in 1948 to about 24 percent in 1974. Hunt felt that as these women grew older, their cumulative incidence of having ever had an affair would rival that of the men in their age group.

Certainly, the opportunities for having affairs have never been greater. Many people's lives place them in contact with an abundance of interesting, attractive, and eager potential lovers. More people than ever have the time, money, and mobility to carry on affairs. Effective contraception makes the fear of pregnancy a minor concern. While society "officially" disapproves of extramarital affairs, many people find that they receive plenty of emotional reinforcement from friends who are either involved in affairs or would like to be. The level of temptation has reached the point where books have actually been written on how to *avoid* having an affair (Kreitler 1981).

Outside affairs are a part of over half of all marriages at one time or another. Affairs are motivated by a great variety of sexual and nonsexual needs.

Motivations for Affairs

Affairs are motivated by all of the factors that move us toward any sexual relationship, plus some additional factors. The motivating forces for any *particular* affair, however, are often difficult to identify. The participants may not recognize their true motives or may be reluctant to reveal their motives. In most cases, a number of forces are likely to be involved.

Sexual Need

Sexual need is the most obvious motivator of affairs, though not necessarily the most important one. In many marriages, the sexual needs of one partner may greatly exceed the needs, interest, or ability of the other. Perhaps too much of the other partner's time, energy, and attention is directed toward career goals. Perhaps the relationship has deteriorated to the point where one partner has simply lost interest in the other. Mental depression is another common cause of loss of sexual interest. Physical disability or illness of one partner might also preclude active sexual exchange.

But pure sexual need, however, is not the main motivation behind most affairs. That need could be fulfilled very simply through masturbation. Obviously, most affairs must be motivated by more than just the need for orgasm.

Sexual Novelty

Novelty is another motivator of extramarital affairs. Novelty is prized and enjoyed by most people. Anything new and different is in demand—new clothing, a new hairstyle, a new model of car, a new food or beverage, or a new song, just to name a few. Sexual novelty is no exception. The thought (or reality) of making love with someone new is highly exciting to many people. Sad but true, the most exciting sexual activity in many relationships occurs during the first few months. Once each partner's personality and sexual responses become known and predictable to the other, one source of excitement is gone. Couples can do much to keep both their emotional and sexual relationship interesting and exciting, but for those who are *addicted* to the novelty aspect of sexual relationships (see chapter 4), the motivation to start a new affair is often overwhelming.

Need to Feel Loved

The need to feel loved, one of the most basic of human needs, also motivates many affairs. Most people require frequent reassurance that they are loved, but many spouses fail to express love to their partners on a regular basis, especially in a variety of nonsexual situations. In this circumstance, especially if love is only expressed sexually, it is easy for a partner to feel unloved. And the feeling of being unloved is intolerable for many people. The quickest remedy for this unpleasant feeling is often an extramarital affair.

Need to Prove Sexual Attractiveness

Doubts about one's sexual attractiveness can also lead to repeated extramarital involvements. Many people require frequent reassurance that they can attract and arouse sexual partners. Affairs motivated by this factor tend to be short-lived, since each relationship has served its emotional purpose as soon as the affair is "consummated."

Desire to Hurt

Some affairs are begun as conscious or unconscious attempts to hurt one's marital partner. These efforts to seek revenge or retaliation may be in response to extramarital affairs the other partner has had or other real or perceived hurts that have been suffered. When revenge is the motive, the spouse having the affair often makes sure that the affair is discovered, perhaps leaving little clues such as motel matchbooks or other physical evidence.

Midlife Crisis

Midlife crisis is a major factor in the affairs of many people in their thirties through fifties. This problem is discussed in depth in chapter 14, so we will be brief at this point.

Basically, midlife crisis occurs at a time in life when people begin to doubt the validity of the way they have lived their lives. They may feel disappointment at unfulfilled career ambitions. If career goals have been achieved, they may doubt the validity of those goals or whether the achievement was worth the effort and sacrifice it required. The validity of a long-term marital partnership may be questioned. Individuals going through a midlife crisis may wonder what life would have been like with someone different. As physical signs of aging begin to appear, they may doubt their sexual attractiveness.

For several reasons, partners in the affairs motivated by midlife crisis are often much younger than the midlife individual. There may be the hope of regaining lost youth through association with a younger person. There may be extra reassurance of continued sexual attractiveness by winning a younger partner. There may be ego gratification by being seen with a younger person. Males may hope to regain a more youthful potency through the stimulus of a younger woman.

All in all, midlife crisis is a time of great emotional turmoil in the lives of many people.

Dealing with Infidelity

With infidelity, as with so many aspects of sexual behavior, the double standard still commonly exists. Thus, infidelity by a husband is often seen by other men as no big deal (Goldberg 1981). It is almost expected that husbands will have affairs and that wives will be tolerant of this behavior. But infidelity by a wife is a different matter. Here, the outraged husband is likely to regard the adultery as a good reason for divorce. Husbands are much more likely to view infidelity as an unforgivable outrage, to brood incessantly over it, and to end the marriage because of it. This difference probably relates to the lingering concept of a wife as "property" of her husband, as well as to the reluctance of many men to have their sexual performance compared with other men.

On the surface, infidelity seems to be a major factor in many divorces. Most authorities, however, view infidelity as one of the *results* of marital deterioration, rather than one of the causes. Severe marital incompatibilities, interpersonal conflicts, personality disorders, and chronic hostility all serve to produce the kinds of situations in which infidelity is likely to occur. Such troubled marriages often lack the resources to deal constructively with infidelity and, thus, break up when the extramarital affair of one spouse is discovered.

Rather than automatically assuming that the discovery of infidelity must lead to divorce, couples in this situation might try marital therapy (counseling). There is little chance that such therapy will be successful unless both marital partners are involved because there is no such thing as an uninvolved spouse in a case of marital infidelity. The couple must understand that each has contributed to the problem and that each must be involved in solving it. Interestingly, the partner who is most resistant to trying marital therapy is often the one whose behavior contributed most to the development of the problem (regardless of who appears to be the "guilty" individual).

Incidentally, in cases where there has been no discovery of or confrontation about one's infidelity, it is rarely advisable to confess to one's spouse. Goldberg (1981) felt that, at an unconscious level, every man or woman whose spouse is having extramarital sexual encounters knows about it. Infidelity can be detected or perceived through hundreds of nonverbal and behavioral clues. But many people do not want to know about a spouse's infidelity. For these people, this knowledge is just too threatening and anxiety provoking to allow into their consciousness. There is rarely anything to be gained through a confession of infidelity unless one's real intent is to hurt the partner or to precipitate a divorce (Appleton 1981; Goldberg 1981).

1. Assume that you have been married for three years and that you have been personally quite satisfied with your marriage and thought your spouse felt the same way. However, you have accidentally discovered that for the past six months your spouse has been sexually involved with someone in addition to yourself. How will you deal with this situation?
2. How many of your married friends seem to be involved in extramarital affairs? How well do they seem to be able to handle their marital and extramarital relationships?

Divorce

Divorce rates in the United States have more than doubled since the 1950s, and the current rate is over half the marriage rate. Thus, a marriage taking place today stands better than a 50–percent chance of ending in divorce. Focusing on statistics for a moment, the divorce rate is highest in the twenty- to twenty-four-year-old age group and declines progressively with increasing age. Also, divorce rates peak during the second and third years of marriage, and decline steadily thereafter. The divorce rate for second and subsequent marriages is at least twice as high as that for first marriages. And finally, the rate for couples with children under eighteen is lower than for comparable couples with no minor children (all statistics from U.S. Vital and Health Statistics, March 1978).

Factors Responsible for Increased Divorce Rate
A number of factors are believed to contribute to today's sharply increased divorce rates, although it is virtually impossible to determine the relative importance of each factor.

One factor is the liberalization of divorce laws that occurred during the 1970s. Many states abandoned the traditional approach of granting a divorce to the "innocent" party because of the objectional behavior (usually adultery) of the "guilty" party. Now, in these states, neither party is recognized as guilty and "no-fault" divorces are granted for what the laws describe as "irreconcilable differences."

Increased expectations for marital and sexual fulfillment have probably had an even greater impact on divorce rates than liberalization of divorce laws. People today are less willing to stay with an unfulfilling marriage simply because of religious or social pressures or as a matter of economic convenience than they were in the past. The media have created an idealized concept of marital bliss against which many people measure the success of their own marriages.

Changes in childbearing patterns also have contributed to the rising divorce rates. According to U.S. Census Bureau data, people now tend to start families later, to have fewer children, and more often to remain voluntarily childless. All of these factors increase the ease with which marriage can be terminated. By delaying children for a few years, the still-childless couple can more easily part company if their marriage does not succeed. And when children are present, the fewer their number, the more easily divorce can be accomplished.

Divorce Alternatives
Regardless of relaxed legal and social attitudes toward divorce, it is almost always very painful for all concerned. Divorce often involves persistent psychological problems for one or both spouses and any children they may have.

United States divorce rates have more than doubled since the 1950s. The current divorce rate is over half the marriage rate.

For these reasons, divorce alternatives should be explored before any irrevocable decision to terminate marriage is made. This suggestion is based not on any traditional moralistic or religious grounds, but on the pragmatic reasoning that staying married is often the happiest solution for everyone concerned. While there are situations in which the damage done by staying together is greater than that of breaking up, this is definitely not always the case.

Professional marital therapy (counseling) is one alternative that should be considered before any decision to divorce is finalized. While often expensive, the cost of therapy is small when compared with the financial costs of divorce and trivial when compared with the emotional costs of most divorces.

With surprising frequency, what seem to be insolvable problems are successfully resolved through counseling. Many marital conflicts reflect one or both spouses' individual psychological problems. Instead of representing an inability to live with a specific spouse, the problem may be difficulty in living with oneself. If an individual in this situation were to divorce and remarry without counseling, the same problems would be likely to develop in the new marriage.

Another divorce alternative to consider is a period of temporary separation rather than immediate divorce. Partners may wish to agree upon a set period of separate living—one, two, or six months, for example. After this time, they may decide to try living together again, to file for divorce, or to continue living separately for another period of time. The partners need also to agree on the "rules" for the trial separation. Freedom to interact with new partners, financial arrangements, and care and custody of children, if any, all need to be discussed.

The results of a trial separation are usually positive. Maybe the partners proceed with divorce, more confident that they are doing the proper thing. Or maybe they reconcile their differences, seeing that they really do want to continue with their marriage.

Dealing with Divorce

If, after exploring divorce alternatives, a couple decides that divorce really is the best course of action, the partners should try to carefully plan together the details of the divorce, including the timing of the divorce, money matters, and child custody.

The timing of the divorce can be important. A delay may allow improvement in a couple's financial situation, a move to an area where the couple has supportive relatives, or the children to grow older so that they are better able to understand what is happening and are less disturbed by the divorce.

If possible, the divorcing couple should also try to reach some basic agreements on finances and child custody before engaging any lawyers. These matters can often be more successfully resolved—and with less conflict—between the two spouses if third parties are not involved. It is also true, however, that by the time

Marriage and Increasing Life Expectancies

The addition of twenty to twenty-five years of life expectancy during this century has had an impact on our ideas regarding marriage and divorce. As box figure 13.1 shows, a young couple entering into marriage is making a significantly longer commitment than in the past. Not only do couples live longer now, they also have more leisure time to spend together and have higher expectations for happiness in marriage than was once the case.

Most people today expect to live seventy-five or eighty years or more, compared with fifty or fifty-five years in the past. If one is thirty years old and unhappy in one's marriage, the thought of another *fifty* years with the same partner may be too much to face. It appears that many people who in the past might have stayed with an unhappy marital situation are today feeling strongly motivated toward divorce and remarriage.

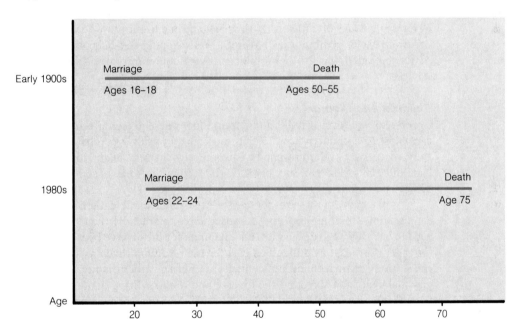

Box Figure 13.1 Graph of age at marriage and death, 1900 versus now.

divorce takes place, many relationships have deteriorated to a point where cooperation between spouses is unlikely.

Along with working out all the *material* details of the divorce, each spouse may want to consider personal counseling to help him or her sort out all of the *emotional* details of the divorce. Counseling can help to minimize the psychological damage associated with the divorce and to prepare the parting couple for new relationships. Predictable emotions surrounding divorce include guilt, anger, fear, anxiety, depression, and loneliness. Counseling can reassure the spouses that their feelings and emotions are normal and not indicative of any emotional illness and that these feelings will decrease with time.

Some physicians and other professionals need to become better acquainted with the divorce process and with strategies for helping people in this situation. Divorcing persons often feel that they have no one to turn to who understands their situation. Many communities have or are developing self-help services for the recently separated and for their children. Every community could benefit from such services.

Children and Divorce

Every year well over a million children under age eighteen are involved in family breakups. And children are the ones most likely to suffer psychological damage in a divorce. Most children respond to divorce with distress, anger, loneliness, sadness, fear, and guilt. (The guilt is caused by the feeling that they in some way caused the divorce.)

While many of these responses are largely unavoidable, their impact on a child can certainly be minimized by the way the parents handle their divorce. Children need to be involved in discussions and planning for the divorce because readjustment for them is at least as difficult as it is for their parents. Even a "civilized" divorce can severely disturb children if conflicts are buried rather than resolved and if mystery and confusion surround the divorce and the new living arrangements.

In no case is it desirable for one or the other parent to simply disappear. Neither is it productive for parents to try to deny the reality of their children's perception of their marital disagreements. There is no point in denying the obvious. Children deserve to be told, preferably by both parents, something about the nature of the marital problems, given assurance that they are not to blame, and given opportunities over a period of time to ask questions and to receive honest answers.

Divorcing parents should never use their children as pawns in custody and visitation disputes. The children's welfare must be considered ahead of the selfish needs of the parents. Usually, one of the parents is better equipped to provide the primary custody for the children. But joint custody (equal time between both parents) is gaining in popularity and may be desirable in some cases ("Why Joint Custody Doesn't Always Work," *Changing Times,* July 1984). It is ideal if both parents can remain in the same geographic area. Children need both parents, and the parents need each other to share parental responsibilities.

Divorced parents also should never compete with each other for their children's love and attention. The children should be free to visit each parent as frequently as they wish. Also, the parent with primary custody should not always be the one who has to set limits for the children while the other parent just takes the kids out for a good time. (In Southern California, this is known as the Disneyland Daddy phenomenon.)

A common factor in children's emotional problems after divorce is their parents' postdivorce depression, which may be severe enough to interfere with parenting functions. A depressed, unhappy parent is an ineffective parent. When depression is severe, the services of a qualified therapist can be engaged, or a community self-help or social support program may be available.

Learning from Experience

Most divorced people do remarry. In fact, U.S. Bureau of Census figures indicate that about 80 percent of those who get divorced will remarry. Further, people don't waste too much time getting into new relationships. Hunt (1974) found that five out of six divorced people (about 83 percent) begin having new sexual relationships within one year after separation from their spouses.

We have mentioned that divorce rates in second and subsequent marriages are higher than in first marriages. This may be a little misleading. Certain individuals—often people with unresolved personality disorders—inflate the statistics by marrying and divorcing repeatedly. The bright side of the story is that many second marriages are extremely successful.

Many people are able to identify the factors that caused conflicts in their first marriage and are able to avoid similar problems in their second marriage. After a first marriage, most people are likely to have a better idea of what traits they want a potential mate to possess. They may be more sensitive to developing conflicts and be able to act more effectively to resolve those conflicts before they damage the relationship. And, of course, they are now "older and wiser" than at the time of their first marriage.

When a divorcing person is unable to pinpoint the problems that destroyed the marriage, a professional counselor can often help to identify these factors and to suggest ways of avoiding the same problems in a future marriage.

1. In today's world, how realistic is the expectation of marrying once and having it last a lifetime?
2. What is your own personal expectation regarding marriage for yourself?
3. A couple who are both close friends of yours are having severe problems with their marriage and each is currently involved with someone else. They are considering divorce and have asked your advice. What are your recommendations for them?

"Good night, Tom! See you in the morning. Don't work too late!"

"I won't. I've got to get home soon or Carol will shoot me!"

Sometimes he wished he could stay all night at the office. Anything was better than going home. He loved his wife, but somewhere along the way their paths had split, and he was having a hard time getting back on the track. He and Carol had once laughed together, taken walks together, snuggled in the dark together, but those times were gone. She belonged to church clubs and bridge clubs, exercise clubs and art clubs; she loved it. He belonged to his desk and to his work, to the challenge of a big deal going down and the risk of gambling on a loser; he too loved the whole darned thing. They were two people married, together, and yet completely alone.

"Have a good time, kids! Oh, and remember, your father and I will be here if you need us, but please don't call if it's not necessary. We need some time together alone for a change."

Carol hoped that Tom wouldn't be too late. She knew that their marriage had become a dry, day-to-day existence, void of love and sharing, but she was bound and determined to mend the rips and hopefully discover her husband again. Her loneliness had finally gotten the best of her, and she had sought help. The advice given to her by her doctor was, "Try to get to know each other all over again. You've become strangers that sleep together in the same bed."

Anxiously awaiting the sound of his car driving up the road, she realized how lonely her marriage had become. It was going to be hard work to share in love that had been put aside for so long. They both enjoyed their separate lives, but it was important that they find a way to share those lives.

"Hi, I'm home. Where is everybody?"

"The kids are staying with my folks tonight. I think it's time we got to know each other again."

He looked into her eyes, "It's not too late?"

"It's never too late."

Summary

1.   The major challenge for young adults is developing intimate relationships with others. Intimacy is characterized by a mutual feeling of caring plus open sharing of feelings and thoughts. The opposite of intimacy of emotional isolation, characteristic of people who are unable or unwilling to establish intimate relationships.

2.   Male and female gender-role concepts are currently in a state of transition; individuals and society are often uncertain what roles are appropriate for each sex. Although both sexes seem to be moving toward less rigid conformity to stereotypical gender roles, many stereotypes linger, such as various sexual double standards of behavior.

3.   Cohabitation (unmarried couples living together) has emerged as a common and widely accepted life-style. Individuals considering cohabitation should engage an attorney to draw up a binding financial agreement to protect the rights of both parties.

4. Living alone is another increasingly popular life-style among people who have never married, are between marriages, or are widowed. The advantage of living alone is freedom; the principal disadvantage is loneliness. For those who view living alone as a positive experience and develop effective ways of dealing with loneliness, living alone can be a highly rewarding life-style.

5. Most people try marriage at some time during their lives, although compared with the past, they marry later, have fewer or no children, and divorce more freely.

6. Readiness for marriage can be assessed in terms of age, emotional maturity, social maturity, and flexibility. The desirability of a potential marriage partner can be evaluated in terms of personality traits, mutual need satisfaction, and communication.

7. When two people marry, each assumes a new role, that of "wife" or "husband." This new role requires a number of personal, social, economic, and sexual adjustments.

8. The sexual success of marriage depends both on the individual characteristics of each partner and how the two partners interact with each other. Potential areas of conflict include frequency of sexual activity, time of sexual activity, choice of sexual activities, and amount of nonsexual attention.

9. Most people still expect sexual exclusiveness in a marriage or committed nonmarital relationship. However, outside affairs are a part of over half of all marriages at one time or another, and the opportunities for having affairs have never been better.

10. Motivations for extramarital affairs include sexual need, the need for novelty and excitement, the need to feel loved, the need for reassurement of sexual attractiveness, the desire to hurt one's marital partner, and all of the complexities of midlife crisis.

11. Infidelity is one of the *results* of marital deterioration, rather than one of the causes. Rather than automatically assuming that the discovery of infidelity must lead to divorce, couples can constructively act to improve the marital relationship, perhaps through marital therapy (counseling).

12. The United States divorce rate is currently over half the marriage rate. Factors contributing to increased divorce rates include liberalized divorce laws, increased expectations for marital and sexual fulfillment, changes in childbearing patterns, and increased life expectancies.

13. Because divorce is almost always painful for all concerned, divorce alternatives should be explored before any irrevocable decision to terminate a marriage is made. Common divorce alternatives include professional marital therapy and periods of trial separation.

14. If, after exploring divorce alternatives, a couple decides that divorce really is the best course of action, the partners should try to carefully plan together the de-

tails of the divorce, including the timing of the divorce, money matters, and child custody. They also might want to consider personal counseling to sort out all of the emotional details of the divorce.

15.   Divorcing parents must take special care that the children involved do not have to suffer any more psychological damage from the divorce than is unavoidable.

16.   Divorcing spouses can prevent problems in future marriages by carefully analyzing the factors that led to their divorce.

14

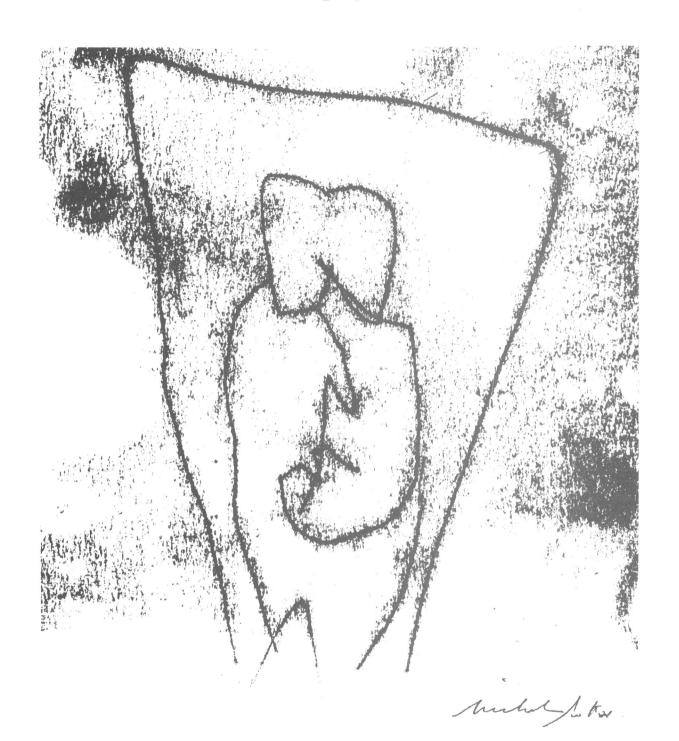

Middle Adulthood
The Climacteric/Midlife Crisis/Sex and Middle Age/Midlife Divorce/Midlife Widowhood

Late Adulthood
The Sexual Response Cycle in Old Age/Continuing Sexual Activity among the Aged

---

"Sue, how was your visit home?"

"OK, I guess. Dad's been acting really weird though. I don't know what it is. The whole time I was there he was grumbling about something. Mom said he's been like that for the past few months."

"Did you talk to your father about it?"

"Yeah, but it didn't do any good. He blamed it all on Mom. Then he said something about getting old and bored. At times, he sounded really depressed."

"How old is he?"

"Oh, I guess he's probably pushing fifty-five or so. Mom thinks he's going through a midlife crisis, whatever that is."

"Sue, have you ever thought about your parents' sex life together?"

"WHAT?"

"I'm serious. Maybe your father is becoming bored or unhappy with sex. I'm sure your mother has been through menopause. Maybe your father is going through a similar phase."

"I've never even thought of my parents having sex. They aren't what I'd call sexy, by any means. Still, I suppose something must be there."

"Listen to yourself! If you think of them as being neuter, think how they must feel. You might want to show a little more understanding the next time you talk to your dad."

We reach our peak of physical development in early adulthood. Decline begins, gradually, in the forties. For example, our height begins to decrease between the ages of forty-five and fifty. Our skin begins to lose some of its elasticity, resulting in facial lines as well as looseness and flabbiness in parts of the body. Our muscular size and strength decreases, and our ability to do hard physical labor steadily declines (Sears and Feldman 1964).

It's no wonder that we may start to worry about how aging is going to affect our sexuality. The fact is, however, we are sexual beings from birth until death and instead of reducing our sexual pleasure, age may even enhance it.

In this chapter, we discuss the two periods of life we pass through after young adulthood, and the physical, emotional, and especially sexual changes we may experience during these periods. The first period is variously known as middle age, middle adulthood, midlife, or adulthood. When does young adulthood end and middle age begin? When does middle age end? We shall see that middle age is not easily defined. The second period of later life is old age, or late adulthood. Old age, as a period of life, has been studied in depth in recent years. It seems better defined by physical changes than by years (Ambron and Brodzinsky 1979).

Middle Adulthood

The terms *middle age, midlife,* or *middle adulthood* are all relative. Any "middle" is created by what comes before and after. With an average life expectancy of about seventy-four years (Population Reference Bureau 1982), middle age statistically begins in the late thirties. Yet, most people define a middle-aged woman or man as between the ages of forty and sixty.

When does a person define himself or herself as middle-aged? Chronological age does not seem to be significant, and people usually do not set boundary dates for themselves. Women tend to perceive middle age in terms of family events, children growing up, and the physical changes that take place during menopause. Men, on the other hand, usually link middle age to work and economic status.

You are only as old as you feel or allow yourself to feel.

The Climacteric

One effect of aging that has been carefully studied is the decrease in the production of the sex hormones *testosterone* from the testes and *estrogen* and *progesterone* from the ovaries. Although the pituitary continues to produce *FSH* (follicle-stimulating hormone) and *LH* (luteinizing hormone), the ovaries and testes simply become less productive in the middle years. These changes affect the overall aging pattern of an individual.

In women, there is the beginning of a *sharp* decline in estrogen and progesterone levels during the late thirties or early forties. Men show a slow, *gradual* de-

climacteric   atherosclerosis   osteoporosis
(kli-mak′ter-ik)   (ath″er-o″skle-ro′sis)   (os″te-o-po-ro′sis)

cline in testosterone starting around the age of twenty. The decline continues until around age sixty, at which time the testosterone level stabilizes. In both sexes, these declines in hormone levels and their effects are called the **climacteric.**

Although the term *climacteric* is generally used to describe changes in the reproductive and sexual organs, other changes also take place. In both sexes, climacteric may result in skin thickening, increased fat deposition, higher blood pressure, and a greater susceptibility to atherosclerosis (deposits of fatty substances in the arteries) and osteoporosis (bone tissue loss). The changes affecting the reproductive and sexual organs of both sexes, however, are more specific and are discussed in the next sections.

Female Climacteric (Menopause)

In women, the changes of the climacteric seem to parallel female adolescent development. A female adolescent clearly becomes a reproductive being with the first menstruation (menarche), although for the first year or so, she may not ovulate every cycle and the menstrual cycles may be irregular. At the climacteric, declining levels of estrogen cause a woman's menstrual cycle to again become irregular, and she is irregularly fertile. This may go on for a year or two before the cessation of menstruation, which is known as **menopause.** A woman is not considered postmenopausal until she has not had a menstrual period for one year. On the average, most women are postmenopausal between the ages of forty-five and fifty (Weideger 1976).

Other specific physiological changes that occur in a woman at climacteric include thinning of the vaginal walls, shortening of the vagina, slowing of the vaginal lubrication response, and atrophy of the ovaries and uterus (Weideger 1976). All of these are caused by declining estrogen levels.

Some women find the climacteric quite uneventful, while others may experience some unpleasant symptoms, such as headaches, insomnia, dizziness, irritability, weight gains, and "hot flashes" or "flushes." These symptoms result from the hormonal imbalances occurring during this time.

For example, hormones influence the dilation and constriction of blood vessels. Because hormone levels fluctuate during menopause, the diameter of the blood vessels may change very rapidly. Rapid dilation of the vessels can cause a momentary rush of blood, producing a "hot flash." These flashes often occur in the face and neck several times a day or during sleep. Sudden rushes of blood to the head can also cause severe headaches. Constriction of blood vessels, on the other hand, reduces blood flow to the head and brain and may influence irritability.

The changes in the vaginal tissues are also hormonally produced. Because of decreasing amounts of estrogen, the vaginal lining becomes thinner and changes to a lighter color. These changes, along with decreased vaginal size and reduced lubrication during sexual response, may result in uncomfortable or painful intercourse at times.

Estrogen Replacement Therapy

One method for treating the sometimes troubling symptoms of menopause is estrogen replacement therapy (ERT). Estrogen replacement therapy has been effective in alleviating two menopausal difficulties—hot flashes and the reduction in vaginal lubrication that causes drying of vaginal tissues. It may also help reduce deterioration in skin tone, osteoporosis, and atherosclerosis. ERT, however, does not delay the natural aging process or other aging changes that take place in a woman.

During estrogen replacement therapy, the menopausal woman takes an estrogen pill daily for three weeks and then stops taking the pill for a week. If the woman wishes to continue menstruation (some women feel that menstruation is a sign of femininity), the estrogen is supplemented with progesterone during the third week. Endometrial bleeding, creating an artificial menstrual flow, then begins during the fourth week.

There are some distinct differences between ERT and oral contraceptive pills. Oral contraceptives usually contain synthetic estrogens, while ERT pills use natural estrogens. Also, much lower dosages of estrogen are administered during ERT than are found in oral contraceptives. In cases where vaginal dryness is the only problem, the estrogen does not even have to be taken orally but can be applied directly to the vaginal area as a salve or cream.

Estrogen replacement therapy is a controversial treatment. ERT proponents feel that estrogen levels should be maintained throughout a woman's life. ERT opponents, however, feel that estrogen is not essential or desirable once a woman's fertility cycles have ended. They argue that most menopausal women need an understanding spouse, reassurance, and education about their changing bodies and that only a few women need estrogen therapy. They also point out that frequent sexual intercourse helps to prevent the reduction in vaginal lubrication that is typical during menopause and that good nutrition, exercise, and maintenance of good health can often alleviate other menopausal symptoms.

There are also questions concerning the safety of estrogen replacement therapy. In the past, ERT was linked with uterine and breast cancer and stroke, but the current use of natural estrogens and the lower dosages may make ERT considerably safer. Only time will tell.

A menopausal woman considering estrogen replacement therapy should carefully evaluate the potential benefits and risks and thoroughly discuss the therapy with her physician before making a decision. If ERT is begun, the woman's physician should monitor it closely. If the therapy is successful in eliminating the woman's troubling menopausal symptoms, ERT can often be discontinued.

Male Climacteric

For men, there is no physiological event, such as menstruation, that tells them that they are fertile. In youth, sperm production gradually increases until there are enough sperm present to produce a pregnancy. The male climacteric also is not signalled by any specific physiological occurrence, such as the cessation of menstruation in women. If experienced at all, male climacteric may be felt as a falling off of sexual desires, with less frequent spontaneous erections or reduced sexual performance.

The slow decline in testosterone levels until around the age of sixty influences certain physiosexual characteristics of males. The size and firmness of the testicles

prostatitis
(pros''tah-ti'tis)

diminish, although these changes in no way impair the ability of the testicles to function. There is also a gradual degeneration of the seminiferous tubules within the testes. The degeneration of the tubules results in a decreasing number of healthy, active sperm. After stabilization of the testosterone level around age sixty, however, the sperm production also stabilizes. Declining testosterone levels also result in a reduction in the force of ejaculation and the volume of ejaculate.

Enlargement of the prostate gland is another common physiosexual change that occurs in the aging male. Inflammation of the prostate gland, called **prostatitis,** is one way in which the prostate can become enlarged. Common symptoms of prostatitis include pain in the pelvic area, discomfort during urination, chills, fever, nausea, and/or a cloudy discharge from the penis. The condition may be treated with antibiotics or prostatic massage, in which the physician inserts a finger into the rectum and rhythmically massages the prostate gland. Enlargement of the prostate in older men can also be the result of benign or malignant tumors of the prostate. These tumors are usually surgically removed.

Middle-aged men also require more time to achieve an erection and a longer period between erections than they did when they were younger (Woodruff and Birren 1975).

Some men do report an increase in insomnia, irritability, headaches, and other "menopausal-like" symptoms in middle life. This has led to speculation as to whether there is a "male menopause." Technically, a male cannot exhibit *menopause,* which is the cessation of menstruation. The general population, however, often uses the word *menopause* to explain or describe male or female irritability in middle life.

---

1. At what age do you think you will be middle-aged? Why? What is your personal definition of middle age?
2. Compare your personal definition of middle age from question 1 to those of others in your class. Do male definitions differ from female definitions? In what ways?
3. Have you ever used the term *menopause* in a derogatory sense, perhaps in reference to a middle-aged person who seemed irritable to you? If so, do you think your use of the term was technically accurate? Why or why not?

Midlife Crisis

In recent years, we have begun to understand a sociological phenomenon with physiological and psychological complications that has become known as the **midlife crisis.** In the past, midlife crisis was linked to climacteric and menopause. But, increasingly, it is now being viewed as a normal developmental period during which life goals are reevaluated. During midlife crisis, a person reflects upon his or her accomplishments, limitations, and life-direction.

Usually, we set some major goals in early adulthood. During the midlife crisis, we often question these goals. If we have achieved our goals, self-questioning may

During the mid-life crisis the children are growing up, the adults see that they are aging, and may seem to have reached a peak in their professions.

go like this: "Is this the goal, life, wife, husband I want?", "Is my anticipated satisfaction now real and meaningful to me?", or "Since I have achieved my goals, what do I do now?" If we have not achieved our goals, the self-questioning can be very disturbing. Reflections might include: "Was the goal, life, wife, husband I wanted realistic for me?", "Am I as adequate and capable as I thought I was?", or "Did I just get bad breaks in life?"

Midlife crisis is usually experienced for two to four years somewhere between the ages of thirty-five and fifty-five. The onset of the crisis is often linked to an occupation or responsibilities that are important in the person's self-concept.

Skilled workers, for example, often experience a midlife crisis between thirty-five and forty years of age because it is at this time that they know whether or not they will become a supervisor or remain at a lower level.

Professionals, business people, or academicians usually experience a midlife crisis between forty and forty-five years of age (Mayer 1978) because, during this period, they find out whether or not they have achieved or can anticipate a desired professional status and economic goal. These people often maintain their positions for about five years and then go through a series of crises in assessing and deciding if they hold a meaningful position in life or what their next goal in life will be.

For professional-level (business, blue-collar, white-collar, academician) women, the midlife crisis may occur early (between the ages of thirty and thirty-five years) (Ambron and Brodzinsky 1979). If married, these women must balance career, marriage, and having a family. The midlife crisis in these women may produce guilt

psychosomatic   arrhythmia
(si''ko-so-mat'ik)   (ah-rith'me-ah)

because the women may not feel that they have done a good enough job in any area. Single, professional-level women experiencing a midlife crisis are often confronted with questions of being different from other women who are married and have children.

The homemaker-wife-mother's midlife crisis is determined by when her children leave home. The women's movement also has heightened these women's self-awareness, causing midlife to bring shifts toward personal independence or conflicts with family, children, and husband needs.

A similar situation occurs when a husband-father-family man decides that his goals are incompatible with his needs. As a result, he may change his goals, life-style, wife, and, often, area of the country in which he lives.

Symptoms of Midlife Crisis
Most individuals going through a midlife crisis experience a variety of symptoms that can be psychosomatic, physiological, sexual, or social in nature.

Psychosomatic Symptoms   People unable to resolve midlife conflicts come to a physician with a wide variety of complaints, many of them psychosomatic (physical symptoms caused by mental or emotional distress). They often complain of undue fatigue or "just not feeling right." Signs of depression are common, including the classic early morning awakening; interrupted sleep and difficulty falling asleep; feelings of irritableness, sadness, and loneliness; crying without provocation; social withdrawal; and an inability to work. Eating disorders are common, such as a lack of appetite or frequent eating, particularly late in the evening or during the night.

Physiological Symptoms   Anxiety or tension created by a midlife crisis can also contribute to a number of actual physiological complaints common at this time, such as heart arrhythmias, chest pain, sensations of dizziness, light-headedness, constipation, and other gastrointestinal disorders.

Sexual Dysfunctions   Changes in sexual behavior are very common during a midlife crisis. The individual experiencing the crisis often feels that his or her partner has a decrease or lack of interest in sexual relationships. This can cause erectile dysfunction or premature ejaculation in the male. Also recurring vaginal infections can cause very painful intercourse in the female, which may lead her to restrict her availability for intercourse.

Social Problems   Individuals experiencing a midlife crisis often have persistent changes in interpersonal relationships that have a negative effect on them or upon the other people in their lives. Changes in personal feelings, attitudes, and behavior invariably have drastic social consequences. The spouse, family, or friends may become either overly protective or withdraw from the individual experiencing the crisis.

Although extramarital affairs may have occurred earlier in life, a new affair may begin that is perceived by the midlife crisis person as different from any previous relationships. Also, the individual may become engaged in a homosexual relationship or admit to previous homosexual relationships for the first time.

Surmounting Midlife Crisis

As a general rule, adults organize their lives with regard to work, recreation, feelings of self, and personal relationships. For an individual to work through and surmount a midlife crisis, there must be a reorganization and reassessment of these aspects of life.

Acceptance of one's financial standing and establishment of a personal gratification in one's work, for example, is crucial to working through a midlife crisis, even if this requires finding a new job or trying a new career.

In addition, the midlife crisis individual must develop enjoyable recreation and hobbies to balance work. Taking time for oneself is very important during this period.

A midlife crisis individual's sense of sexual decline and negative feelings of self may be related to body changes, such as wrinkles, a double chin, sagging breasts, or an increase in and redistribution of weight. What the midlife crisis individual needs to learn, however, is that, regardless of visible body changes, in actuality, midlife usually brings only a limited decline in physical capabilities. When the midlife crisis individual can accept and understand the midlife body changes, a greater acceptance of self and life usually follows. Acceptance of middle age is shown by a greater ability for intimacy and for expressing feelings and a mellowing of anger, indignation, aggressiveness, and ambition. There is also a lessening of petty vanities and envy.

If a midlife individual feels that his or her masculinity or femininity is equated with an ability to bear children, middle age may bring on a midlife crisis requiring reassessment of sexual needs. Satisfaction from a gratifying sexual relationship is a primary way to reestablish self-esteem.

A reorganization of family life also usually occurs during midlife, particularly if the children are leaving home. This reorganization often prompts a reassessment of the reasons for continuing the marriage. The midlife crisis individual may decide that the marriage no longer fills his or her needs or expectations, and the marriage may be terminated. Or the midlife crisis individual may come to see midlife as a time for new relationships with the family. The individual and his or her spouse may renew their prechildren love affair from twenty years ago. Relationships with the children also may change since the children are no longer completely dependent and are becoming adults on their own, which produces conflicting feelings of pride, frustration, envy, and competition in the middle-aged parent. In addition, the mid-life individual may become the "parent" of his or her own parents, who are now dependent.

In summary, a midlife crisis is a time of metamorphosis. Surmounting this crisis demands a transformation of beliefs and a change in attitudes. It requires a revision of definitions of what it means to be a male or a female or an adult. It is a time to redefine reasons for life and to force ourselves to be vulnerable and dependent upon others.

---

1. Have you ever been aware of someone you know going through a midlife crisis? What were the circumstances? How did the person resolve the crisis?
2. Do you think there are ways that you can prevent a personal midlife crisis? Explain.

Sex and Middle Age

In the past, the middle-aged person was believed to experience a decline in sexual desire. Today it is understood that sexuality is a vital part of the lives of most middle-aged adults. Middle-aged women, in particular, often have strong sex drives.

Middle age can bring new sexual satisfaction to some couples for a number of reasons. For one, birth control can be ignored; there is little fear of pregnancy and, after fifty, almost no fear at all. Also, with children leaving home and more money available, privacy increases, and financial fears are often reduced. These changes promote sexual expression and other forms of communication that enhance sexual expression.

Sexual expression in midlife (as at any age) is also influenced by our culture. The sexually relaxed climate dating from the 1960s and 1970s resulted in greater and more varied sexual expression among the middle-aged. The average frequency of marital intercourse from the time of Kinsey's sampling in 1948 to Hunt's sampling in 1974 is shown in table 14.1. Today's thirty-five- to forty-four-year-old age group is more sexually active than the twenty-six- to thirty-five-year-old age group of a generation ago (Hunt and Hunt 1975). Also, the variety of coital positions used and the incidence of oral sex have also increased significantly among the older age groups.

Nevertheless, there are differences between youthful and middle-aged sexuality. Between the ages of forty-six and fifty-five, the majority of men and women become aware of a decline in their sexual responses (Pfeiffer, Verwoerdt, and Davis 1972). Although middle-aged people experience satisfying sexual relationships, sexual response is usually slower, and more imaginative foreplay may be necessary for arousal. While this often enhances the intimacy between partners, the natural slowing of the sexual response can provoke anxiety in either or both partners.

Table 14.1   Frequency of Intercourse Per Week.

Weekly Marital Intercourse Frequency As Estimated by Husbands

1938–1946 Kinsey Surveys			1972–1974 Hunt Survey		
Age	Mean	Median	Age	Mean	Median
16–25	3.3	2.3	18–24	3.7	3.5
26–35	2.5	1.9	25–34	2.8	3.0
36–45	1.8	1.4	35–44	2.2	2.0
46–55	1.3	0.8	45–54	1.5	1.0
56–60	0.8	0.6	55+	1.0	1.0

Weekly Marital Intercourse Frequency As Estimated by Wives

1938–1946 Kinsey Surveys			1972–1974 Hunt Survey		
Age	Mean	Median	Age	Mean	Median
16–25	3.2	2.6	18–24	3.3	3.0
26–35	2.5	2.0	25–34	2.6	2.1
36–45	1.9	1.4	35–44	2.0	2.0
46–55	1.3	0.9	45–54	1.5	1.0
56–60	0.8	0.4	55+	1.0	1.0

Source: Hunt, Morton. *Sexual Behavior in The 1970s*. Chicago: Playboy Press, 1974.

The middle-aged male may begin to fear that he will not be able to perform adequately, and for that reason, he may at times be unable to perform. It is widely recognized that most erectile problems of middle age are the result of anxiety or other psychological problems, rather than an effect of aging. The middle-aged male may be sexually bored, anxious over financial or career decisions, or feeling the effects of overwork and excessive alcohol use. No matter the cause, the result may be periodic erectile problems. Once erectile difficulty appears, some middle-aged males withdraw voluntarily from any coital activity rather than face the ego-shattering experience of periodic sexual inadequacy.

The middle-aged female may also feel anxiety about the natural slowing of the sexual response—especially in her partner. If her partner is having erectile problems, she may identify herself as the cause of those problems and form a negative self-image of herself as undesirable or "past her prime." The facts are, however, that an adult woman can be orgasmic and a satisfying sexual partner at any age, and the sexually experienced middle-aged woman is often more—not less—likely to reach orgasm than a younger woman.

Midlife Divorce

As we discussed in chapter 13, approximately half of all marriages end in divorce. One-fourth of these divorces occur after fifteen years of marriage and, therefore, involve middle-aged or older partners.

Divorce in midlife occurs in response to such stresses as differential growth of partners, midlife career crises, and extramarital affairs. Historical trends may also be at work. Many of today's divorcing middle-aged people married without adequate sexual preparation, since virtually no sex education was available in the schools at that time, and did "what was expected"—married young, had children, and stayed together "for the children" or at all costs. And now, in midlife, these people are finding that divorce has become a more accepted solution to an unpleasant or difficult marriage. Many middle-aged people are seeing their first marriage as a learning experience, and they are basing a remarriage on more stable criteria: mutual interests and goals, less reliance on physical looks, and more reliance on emotional compatibility. Thus, middle-aged remarriages have been more successful than earlier marriages (Hunt and Hunt 1975).

Divorce at any time, however, is painful. It is usually followed by loneliness, self-doubt, mood swings, and the need for many practical adjustments in living. After living with someone for fifteen to twenty years, these adjustments can mean major changes in life-styles. For example, a divorced middle-aged woman may find that she must begin dating at just the time when she begins to experience doubts about her attractiveness. Also, she may be expected to have sexual relations with someone new after fifteen to twenty years of intimacy with one partner.

From a positive outlook, the middle-aged divorce does not carry some of the problems of the young divorce (the anguish of children, economic ruin, and parental disapproval). And, as already mentioned, midlife divorce is frequently followed by successful remarriage.

Midlife Widowhood

The death of one's spouse is probably the greatest emotional and social loss an individual can suffer in the normal course of the life span. It is an emotional emergency that the individual must live through, and then it becomes a social status—widowhood or widowerhood—that she or he must live with, often without adequate emotional preparation.

Most people associate widowhood with old age, but the facts are that approximately one quarter of the women in the United States will lose their husbands before the age of sixty-five (Ambron and Brodzinsky 1979). Nearly half of all women over sixty-five and two-thirds over seventy-five have been widowed. Only about one man in six can expect to outlive his wife.

Some of the problems of the middle-aged widow are unique. (We concentrate on the widow here, rather than the widower, since middle-age widows are much more common than middle-age widowers.) One of these is that the middle-aged widow is probably the first of her friends to lose her husband. The couple's friends are usually all married, and the new middle-aged widow now feels like the "fifth wheel" at any social occasion.

This middle-aged widow is also less willing than older widows to resign herself to a life without male companionship and sexuality. This often makes her married female friends feel threatened, and while exhorting her to socialize, they "forget" to include her in social activities unless they have an eligible male present.

Another problem is that the middle-aged widow is often unable to find single men her age, especially widowed men, who can understand her experience.

1.   Explain why sex in middle life can be extremely satisfying.
2.   If you had to go through a divorce, would you rather experience it as a young adult or as a middle-aged adult? Why?

Late Adulthood

Most of us know very little about the later years of life. We realize at some point that there is the strong likelihood that we will become old—but we don't know when. We are probably less prepared to assume the role of the older person than we are to assume any other role in life. In particular, we don't know what to expect with regard to old-age sexuality.

Many people believe that sexual activity should gradually diminish after middle age and either does not, or should not, occur at all among the old. Sexuality in old people is often frowned upon and considered a moral weakness.

Compounding the problem is the fact that old people themselves sometimes share these attitudes and feel guilty about healthy sexual behavior. They tend to avoid any public displays of sexuality and often go to great lengths to conceal their sexual activity. Most of them grew up during a time when no one discussed sex. For that reason, they are often embarrassed to seek help for a treatable sexual dysfunction.

The sexual stereotypes of old-age sexuality are tied to four facts. First, it is difficult for younger people to acknowledge that their own parents are sexual beings and are engaging in sexual activities.

Second, the Victorian philosophy that sexual activity is primarily a procreative function still exists. Thus, according to this philosophy, those beyond their reproductive years (which, incidently, is lifelong in males) should not engage in sexual activity.

Third, many old and young alike have the idea that sex, love, and romance are feelings only of the young (Troll 1971).

And, fourth, sexuality among the aged is difficult to study, and it is difficult to dispel sexual stereotypes without solid research findings. Elderly people often will not participate in sexual research. Also, researchers are sometimes embarrassed about discussing sexuality with people much older than themselves. (This is often related to the discomfort that children experience when thinking about their parents' sexual activity.) Finally, young researchers have difficulty managing their own aging and often need to deny that aging will happen to them. Therefore, they restrict their research to their own age group.

Often this is as much affection as an older couple are allowed to show by society.

The Sexual Response Cycle in Old Age

In spite of the difficulties inherent in researching sexuality among the aged, in 1966, Masters and Johnson were successful in undertaking a study of the sexual response cycles of older men and women. (See the discussion of the sexual response cycle in chapter 8.) As we will see in the following sections, their findings indicate that while older people's sexual response cycles are not precisely identical to those of young adults, most changes only involve alterations of the *intensity* and *duration* of the sexual response.

Sexual Response of the Older Female

Masters and Johnson's study of the older female involved sixty-one postmenopausal women between the ages of forty-one and seventy-eight. The sexual responses of these women at each stage of the sexual response cycle were observed and measured. The research results follow.

Excitement Phase   Masters and Johnson found that, generally, the vaginal lubrication of the excitement phase begins more slowly in an older woman and that the amount of lubrication is less. Yet, in Masters and Johnson's research group, three older women who had remained sexually active throughout their lives had rapid, full lubrication responses. This indicates that physiological sexual responses remain completely intact when used throughout life. The more sexually active we are, the younger our physiological sexual responses remain.

Masters and Johnson also found that the sex flush and vaginal expansion characteristics of the excitement phase are often less pronounced in postmenopausal women than in premenopausal women, while clitoral sensitivity and nipple erection remain the same.

Plateau Phase   Events of the plateau phase include the development of the vaginal orgasmic platform, the elevation of the uterus, the constriction of the vaginal opening, and the withdrawal of the clitoris under the hood. Masters and Johnson found that in a postmenopausal woman, the orgasmic platform develops more slowly and that the uterus elevates to a somewhat lesser degree. However, the clitoris withdraws and the vaginal opening constricts to the same degree as in the premenopausal woman.

Orgasmic Phase   The contractions of the orgasmic platform and uterus that are typical of the orgasmic phase continue as a woman ages but reduce in number, thereby reducing orgasmic intensity, according to Masters and Johnson's research. Their findings also indicate that, in some older women, uterine orgasmic contractions can be painful because of hormone changes that took place during menopause. This can be corrected by supplementing a woman's estrogen and progesterone through medication.

Resolution Phase   According to Masters and Johnson, the resolution phase seems to occur more rapidly in postmenopausal women than in premenopausal women. The labia, vagina, clitoris, uterus, and nipples all return to normal soon after orgasm.

Sexual Response of the Older Male

Masters and Johnson's study of the older male involved thirty-nine men between the ages of fifty-one and eighty-nine. As with the group of older females, Masters and Johnson observed and measured the sexual responses of this group of older men, and their findings follow.

Excitement Phase   Throughout young adulthood, many males are capable of achieving an erection in a few seconds of emotional or physical stimulation. Masters and Johnson found that, as a male ages, he may require several minutes of stimulation to achieve an erection. This slowed rate of erectile response is a natural occurrence of the aging process and, according to Masters and Johnson, has a positive aspect. After achieving an erection, it is often possible for the older male to maintain this erection for a prolonged period of time. Many older males and their sexual partners enjoy the prolonged sensations that a longer erection provides.

Plateau Phase   Masters and Johnson's research indicates that, during the plateau phase in the older male, the testes may not elevate as close to the perineum, complete penile erection is frequently not obtained until later in the plateau phase, and there is often greater ejaculatory control.

Orgasmic Phase   During orgasm, according to Masters and Johnson, the older male experiences a decline in intensity, a reduction in the sensations of impending ejaculation, and a reduction in the force of ejaculation. Orgasm, however, continues to be a very pleasurable experience.

Resolution Phase   Masters and Johnson found that, as with older females, resolution occurs more rapidly as a male ages. The older male loses his erection much more rapidly following orgasm than does a younger male. Also, the older male's testicles descend immediately after ejaculation.

Masters and Johnson also found that the refractory period between orgasm and the next excitement phase gradually increases as a man ages. By age sixty, in many males, the refractory period may last from several hours to several days.

Continuing Sexual Activity among the Aged

Modern sexual authorities agree that the healthy older person is able and willing to participate in sexual activity with warmth and dignity (Ambron and Brodzinsky 1979). In 1954, Duke University began a study of older people, their sexual potential, and how they remain sexually active. This study continues today as ongoing research. After the first ten years of the study, however, the researchers have found four patterns of sexual activity: (1) some older individuals have become sexually inactive; (2) most older people have sustained regular sexual activity throughout life; (3) some older people have increased their sexual activity; and (4) some older people have decreased their sexual activity.

The Duke study shows that much of the sexual inactivity is among unmarried older women who lack a sexual partner. Yet, over half of the older men and women studied have been sexually active into their eighties. In fact, all of the individuals in the study were interested in sex; the declines in activity were caused mainly by ailing physical health, psychological reasons, or the lack of an acceptable partner. It also appears that most sexual activity among older people is conducted within marriage or a marital-like relationship. Older men fear exposure and failure with an unfamiliar woman, and older women are often unable to engage in aggressive or casual sexual relationships because of their upbringing and the feared negative reactions of their adult children, family, and society (Ambron and Brodzinsky 1979).

Elderly couples who do engage in sexual activity generally tend to be realistic about their sexual capabilities. Many are unable to physiologically perform as well sexually as couples that are sexually active continuously. But sexuality is not limited to physical sex acts; it often involves other aspects of the personality. Sexual goals of elderly couples may include gaining intimacy, friendship, and personal fulfillment from one another, and reestablishing the romantic feelings of a relationship.

All in all, however, given good health, a stable emotional condition, and an acceptable partner, sexual capacity among the aged appears to continue indefinitely. Older people may not engage in intercourse with the same frequency as when they were younger, and, as we saw in the preceding section, their sexual responses may differ in intensity and duration from younger people's responses. But their needs for intimacy and sexual expression continue to grow, and they are quite capable of performing sexually. For those older people who do not participate in sex, the reasons appear to be more psychological and social than biological.

Perhaps the most important element in continuing sexual activity among the aged is that the aged must become more sexually visible to society. In the United States, only the young (or middle-aged people who appear young) are viewed as being sexually attractive. Yet, in European cultures, for example, the older, more mature woman is viewed as being more romantic (Barrow and Smith 1983).

Institutionalization and Sexuality

More than half of the elderly, fourteen out of twenty, live in family settings, typically a husband and wife household with no other relatives. A quarter of the elderly, five out of twenty, live alone or with nonrelatives. The remaining one out of twenty elderly persons live in institutions (Barrow and Smith 1983). Various studies have shown that as many as 20 percent of the elderly are institutionalized at some point.

Studies have also shown that at least 25 percent of those individuals in institutions such as nursing homes don't really need to be there physically but are there because of economics. Even married couples occasionally are forced because of financial difficulties to give up their homes and to admit themselves together to a nursing home.

Most nursing homes are not equipped to handle these individuals who usually are well enough to be sexually active. For example, most nursing homes are based upon the hospital plan of either single- or two-patient rooms. Sometimes, even married couples in nursing homes are separated in an effort to keep the sexes segregated. In addition, many nursing home administrators and personnel, as well as many of the nursing home residents' families, are not comfortable with the idea of elderly sexual activity and thus resist any efforts to validate or encourage old-age sexuality.

Recently, however, some nursing home directors have been making changes to afford the elderly who are sexually active more privacy to form or continue relationships. Innovations have included providing a more homelike atmosphere, allowing spouses to live together, encouraging residents to look upon the nursing home staff as a kind of family, providing private areas where couples can talk or court, and initiating limited self-government so that the elderly have some say over their own lives. Also, individuals who are unmarried or widowed and relatively healthy often are encouraged to find a mate. These couples may then decide to reestablish their own home, if they can afford the cost, or to live as husband and wife within the nursing home.

These kinds of nursing home innovations are especially important in light of research that has shown that old people who consistently have at least one very close relationship can cope better with the severe emotional losses inherent in aging (Rogers 1979). And, as has been stated many times before in this text, our sexuality is an inherent part of us all of our lives. It doesn't cease to exist at age sixty-five. The sooner more nursing homes institute programs and innovations that encourage elderly sexuality, the sooner will nursing home residents be able to lead happier and more fulfilled lives.

Society needs to change some of its values and ways of thinking so that sexual activity and romantic love are not seen as only for the young. Older people are also looking for sex and romance, and they also often have more leisure time to pursue these ambitions. The elderly are sexual beings in as valid a sense as are young people, and when society becomes more open to that fact, there will be greater social acceptance and promotion of sexual activity among older adults.

Quality nursing homes provide for the expression of their residents' social and sexual needs.

1. What are your feelings about old-age sexuality? Can you accept your parents and/ or grandparents as sexual beings? Why or why not?
2. Compare and contrast the sexual responses of older people with the sexual responses of younger people.
3. What factors do you think are important in maintaining sexual activity among the aged?

Dear Dad,

I'm writing this letter to say I love you. You seemed really down and depressed when I visited last week. I was worried about you until I realized you've always been able to handle any problem that arises. I just wanted you to know that I believe in you.

The other day, a friend asked if I thought you were sexy. I just laughed. Then I got out the picture you sent me two years ago, the one of you and Mom on vacation in Hawaii. You really are quite handsome. I never noticed it before, but I can understand why Mom loves you so much. I always figured you were sexy when you were younger, but now I realize that sex doesn't disappear at any age.

I know that this isn't the typical letter you would expect from your college daughter, but I've always prided myself on being an extraordinary offspring!

All My Love,

Sue

Summary

1. Statistically, middle age begins in the late thirties. Women, however, tend to perceive middle age in terms of family events, children growing up, and the physical changes that take place during menopause. Men usually link middle age to work and economic status.

2. In both males and females, declines in sex hormone levels and their effects are called the climacteric.

3. Female climacteric is characterized by menopause, thinning of the vaginal walls, shortening of the vagina, slowing of the vaginal lubrication response, and atrophy of the ovaries and uterus. Some women also experience headaches, insomnia, dizziness, irritability, weight gains, and hot flashes.

4. Male climacteric is characterized by diminished testicle size, decreased sperm production, a reduction in the force of ejaculation and the volume of ejaculate, and enlargement of the prostate gland. Following climacteric, the older male also requires more time to achieve an erection and longer periods between erections.

5.   Midlife crisis is a normal developmental period during which life goals are reevaluated. The onset of the crisis is often linked to an occupation or responsibilities that are important in the person's self-concept, and symptoms can be psychosomatic, physiological, sexual, or social in nature. Surmounting midlife crisis requires a reorganization and reassessment of one's life with regard to work, recreation, feelings of self, and personal relationships.

6.   Sexuality is a vital part of the lives of most middle-aged adults. Although sexual response is usually slower during middle age and more imaginative foreplay may be necessary for arousal, many couples find sex to be more intimate and satisfying during middle age.

7.   Midlife divorce is usually in response to such stresses as differential growth of partners, midlife career crises, and extramarital affairs and requires the separating spouses to make major adjustments in their life-styles. Remarriage in midlife is frequently successful.

8.   The death of one's spouse is probably the greatest emotional and social loss an individual can suffer in the normal course of the life span. Middle-aged widows are much more common than middle-aged widowers and must deal with some unique problems if they are not willing to resign themselves to a life without male companionship and sexuality.

9.   Many people, including many of the elderly, believe that sexual activity either does not, or should not, occur at all among the old. This taboo against old-age sexuality is one of the primary remaining barriers against a fuller social understanding of human sexuality.

10.   Masters and Johnson's study of the sexual responses of older men and women indicated that older people's sexual responses differed mostly in intensity and duration from younger people's responses.

11.   The facts are that, given good health, a stable emotional condition, and an acceptable partner, sexual capacity among the aged appears to continue indefinitely. Older people may not engage in intercourse with the same frequency as when they were younger and their sexual responses may differ in intensity and duration from younger people's responses, but their needs for intimacy and sexual expression continue to grow. For those older people who do not participate in sex, the reasons appear to be more psychological and social than biological.

4

REPRODUCTIVE
SEXUALITY

15

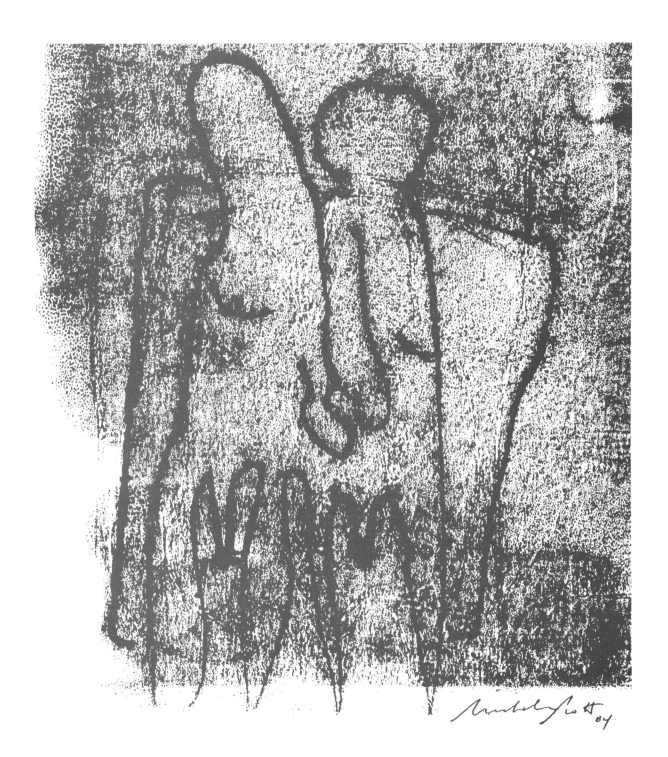

My name is Julie. I am twenty-four, female, somewhat sexually active—not overly so—and sick and tired of being the one solely responsible for contraception in a relationship.

I lost my virginity when I was seventeen. I was in love with the boy I had been dating in high school for two years. One night, the petting got heavy, and we got carried away. Neither of us thought about contraception. I guess we figured it was impossible to get pregnant the first time. We were lucky—nothing happened. We continued having sex for a few months until I had a pregnancy scare. He said I should have been on the pill or something. I told him *he* should have been using something. All the while neither of us was really thinking. Well, once again I was lucky. I got my period a week and a half late.

We broke up shortly after that, but I still dated. I had another relationship in my freshman year of college. He pressured me to go on the pill. He said everyone was on it. I finally did try the pill. I was nervous about some of the risks that I'd heard were connected to the pill, but I went ahead. I gained ten pounds and started bleeding only three weeks after I started. I dropped the pill, and he dropped me.

I abstained from sex for two years after my experience on the pill. Sexual intercourse is a two-person encounter, and I feel that responsibility for the outcome of the act should be taken by both persons involved. I refuse to allow a man to pressure me into the full risk taking of sex. I am bound and determined not to have sex again until I find a man who will share, up front, with the responsibility of contraception.

Sexual intercourse provides one of the most profound and gratifying ways of expressing our sexuality. While immensely pleasurable, however, every act of intercourse may carry with it the chance of pregnancy. The age, marital status, and life goals of each of the sexual partners may determine whether this chance of pregnancy is a positive or negative aspect of sexual intercourse.

In this chapter, we discuss how conception and birth control can provide women and men with the means of planning the pregnancies they desire while expressing their sexuality through intercourse as often as they wish. We examine both the nonsurgical and surgical methods of preventing and terminating pregnancy.

Nonsurgical methods of preventing conception and birth include contraception and abstinence. The term *contraception* ("against conception") is widely used to identify nonsurgical methods of conception and birth control that may be mechanical (blocking of fertilization), spermicidal (killing sperm on contact), or hormonal (averting the production and release of mature sex cells). Contraceptive methods usually involve the blocking of ovulation, spermatogenesis, fertilization, or implantation. Nonsurgical methods of preventing conception also include abstaining from all or any part of sexual intercourse. This would include celibacy (avoiding intercourse entirely), rhythm (avoiding intercourse entirely on those days conception is most likely), and withdrawal (terminating intercourse prior to the male ejaculating). Surgical methods of conception control include sterilization and induced abortion.

As we examine in this chapter these methods of conception control and their respective pros and cons, effectiveness levels, and side effects, it is important to keep in mind that very few methods of conception control are guaranteed, under any and all circumstances, to prevent conception. In addition, human error in the form of inconsistent or incorrect usage of conception control methods can also make the chosen method less effective.

Reasons for and against Conception Control

It is estimated that among married people in the United States who are at risk of pregnancy, nine out of ten couples use some form of conception control (Tietze 1979). Yet, while the control of conception is not the issue it once was, it still remains a controversial matter.

Reasons for Conception Control

Reasons for conception control include preventing unwanted pregnancy, spacing pregnancies, limiting family size, giving a couple time for marital adjustment, protecting a woman's health, avoiding inherited diseases, and allowing the woman more independence.

Preventing Unwanted Pregnancy

The avoidance of unwanted pregnancy is important for all women. About 14 percent of all births are unwanted at the time of or after conception. The percentage of unwantedness is lowest for mothers in their twenties (about 8 percent), is higher for teenage mothers, and is highest (about 18 percent) for mothers in their forties (National Center for Health Statistics 1980).

Many of the unwanted pregnancies are among teenagers. More than a third of teenage mothers are unmarried. The unwantedness of teenage pregnancies is indicated by the fact that, among unmarried teenagers, there are three live births for every five abortions.

Many teenagers are unable to connect sexual intercourse with the personal risk of pregnancy. Only about 14 percent of teenagers seek birth control advice prior to their first intercourse (National Center for Health Statistics 1980).

Spacing Pregnancies

With no conception control, many women are physically able to bear a child every year. But the mother's (and couple's) resources—physical, emotional, and monetary—need protection against pregnancies coming too frequently to properly provide for the welfare of existing children and of the parents.

Limiting Family Size

Couples today have an expectation of the family size they desire. With the effectiveness of modern conception control methods, couples have a good possibility of limiting their family size to a preplanned number, whether that be none, one, or several children.

Aiding Marital Adjustment

Prior to effective conception control methods, it was not uncommon for young couples to be faced with a pregnancy as soon as they became sexually active. This added a heavy financial and emotional burden to the psychological adjustments required for living together, such as developing effective interpersonal skills, good communication, and a feeling of comfort with the stability of the marriage. The use of conception control methods helps to avert pregnancy and thus provides time for such marital adjustments.

Protecting the Health of the Mother

Pregnancy makes especially heavy physical demands on the mother, and any health risk or disease the mother is facing may adversely affect the embryo or fetus. For some women, the health risks of pregnancy are so high that physicians advise them to use conception control methods to avoid pregnancy entirely.

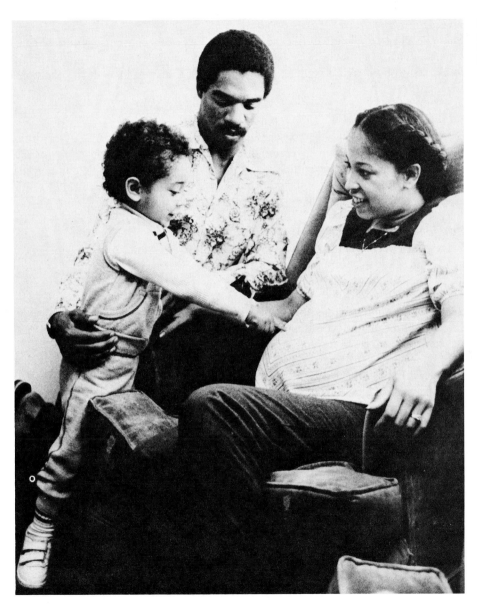

Modern contraceptive methods allow couples to regulate the number and timing of their children.

Avoiding Inherited Diseases

Some people are unfortunately affected by or are carriers of adverse inherited conditions, such as Tay-Sachs disease and sickle-cell anemia. These people may choose to use conception control methods to avoid genetic transmission of such conditions to offspring.

Allowing Women More Independence

Some women wish to pursue their chosen careers and to plan the arrival of children, if desired, around the timing of certain life goals. They may wish to delay pregnancy until they are married, settled into a career, or until they have completed their education. The use of conception control methods allows many women today to successfully integrate education and a career with motherhood.

Reasons against Conception Control

Some people feel strongly against their personal use of certain forms of conception control or against conception controls entirely.

Religious Viewpoints

Some major religious groups, such as the Roman Catholic Church, view the use of chemical or mechanical conception control techniques as immoral. They reason that the control of conception counters a divine natural order.

Minority Viewpoints

Some people fear that the use of conception control techniques is primarily directed against their minority, racial, or ethnic group. They construe such use as a method of population control in which majority groups force birth control upon minority groups who might be able to become competitive if allowed to gain in population balance.

Health Risks

Most methods of conception control carry side effects, some of which are merely inconvenient or bothersome, others of which are serious. Yet, pregnancy itself carries its own health risks which, for the great majority of women, can be far more adverse than the risks involved in using any of the methods of conception control. Mortality among pregnant women, for example, is approximately seven times higher than mortality among women using the birth control pill (National Center for Health Statistics 1980).

Selecting an Appropriate Method of Conception Control

No one method of conception control is best for everyone. In choosing a preferable method of conception control, the individual should weigh several criteria relating to the physical and emotional side effects, usability, and convenience of the particular method being considered.

The two most important factors in choosing a method of conception control are *safety* and *effectiveness.* The ideal conception control method would neither harm one's health nor reduce the capacity for future parenthood. It would be free from harmful or bothersome side effects, both for the person using the method and for the partner. It would also be effective in preventing pregnancy. Unfortunately, the ideal conception control method has yet to be developed, but the individual should strive to choose the method that is personally safest and most effective.

Another factor to be considered in choosing a conception control method is *ease of use.* Some devices, such as the intrauterine device (IUD), are placed into the body by a professional and left there for an extended period of time. Other devices must be applied with each intercourse. Many people prefer a contraceptive they can apply before, rather than during, the lovemaking leading to intercourse.

The chosen conception control method also should be *acceptable* to the user in terms of the person's medical history, physical comfort, religious viewpoints, and personal preferences. Many users of conception control methods prefer one that is *reversible,* which means that, when its use is discontinued, the user's prior fertility is restored. Many couples wish to retain the option of having a pregnancy sometime in the future.

The chosen conception control method should be *easily available* at a *cost* the user can afford. Some contraceptive devices (such as pills and diaphragms) are available only by prescription from a physician, whereas others (such as condoms, foam, and suppositories) are available over the counter (without prescription) from a pharmacy.

Finally, the preferred conception control method should have no inhibiting effect on the user's *sex drive.* Sexual intercourse can be highly pleasurable, and the gratification a person receives from it should not be reduced due to physical discomfort, fears, or guilt arising from use of the conception control method.

Effectiveness of Conception Control Methods

The effectiveness of conception control methods is expressed in terms of pregnancies per one hundred woman years, which means the number of women out of one hundred who would become pregnant in one year when using the method. This is more easily

Table 15.1 Failure Rates of Common Conception Control Methods.

Method	Theoretical Failure Rate	Actual Use Failure Rate	Cost Per Year*	Advantages	Disadvantages
Abstinence (celibacy)	0%	0%	None	No chance of pregnancy	May require much motivation
Abortion	0	0	$1,000	Can terminate a pregnancy after positive pregnancy tests	Surgical risk; possible medical/psychological complications; may reduce cervical competency to retain a pregnancy until term
Hysterectomy	0.0001	0.000	$4,000 (one time)	Permanent relief from pregnancy worries	Major surgery required; possible hormonal complications if ovaries removed
Tubal ligation	0.04	0.04	$1,300 (one time)	Permanent relief from pregnancy worries	Low success of surgical reversal; possible surgical/medical/psychological complications
Vasectomy	0.15	0.15	$650 (one time)	Permanent relief from pregnancy worries	Low success of surgical reversal; possible surgical/medical/psychological complications
Combination birth control pills	0.5	2	$120	Highly effective; easy to use	Continuing cost; slight medical risk; side effects
IUD	1.5	5	$60	Needs little attention; no expense after insertion	Side effects; possible expulsion; some forms need replacement every one or two years

*Will vary in different localities.

expressed as a percentage rate of failure. It is estimated, for instance, that if no conception control method is used, about 90 percent of women will become pregnant within a year (Hatcher et al. 1984). This represents a 10 percent effectiveness rate of avoiding pregnancy.

The *theoretical effectiveness* of a method is its effectiveness when used consistently, under correct conditions, and without human error—in other words, how it *should* work. The *actual use effectiveness* is a method's effectiveness when used under everyday conditions, perhaps inconsistently and incorrectly. Such "user failure," plus "method failure," contributes to the actual use effectiveness.

Table 15.1 shows the theoretical failure rate and the actual use failure rate of the different conception control methods discussed in this chapter.

Method	Theoretical Failure Rate	Actual Use Failure Rate	Cost Per Year*	Advantages	Disadvantages
Foams, creams, sponges, jellies, and vaginal suppositories	3–5	18	$60	Easy to use; no prescription; easy to obtain	Continuing expense; requires high motivation to use it consistently and correctly with every act of intercourse
Diaphragm and cervical cap (with jelly or cream)	2	19	$70	No side effects; minor cost for spermicide and initial diaphragm purchase	Requires high motivation to use it consistently and correctly with every act of intercourse
Condom	2	10	$30	No side effects; easy to use; helps prevent disease; easy to obtain	Continuing expense; some feel that condoms reduce penile sensation; must use every time; may interrupt continuity of lovemaking
Withdrawal (coitus interruptus)	16	23	None	No preparation or cost	May be frustrating; low effectiveness
Rhythm methods	2–20	24	None	Acceptable to Roman Catholic Church	Requires much motivation and cooperation; low effectiveness
Chance (no protection)	90	90	None	No preparation	High risk of pregnancy

1. What are the three most important reasons to you personally for using conception controls?
2. In talking to people who have reservations against using any form of conception control, what arguments might you use in persuading them to change their mind?
3. In selecting a method of conception control, what factors (criteria) would be most important to you?
4. Would the fact that a conception control method was or was not reversible be of significance to you? Why?
5. Explain why the actual use effectiveness of a conception control method might have more meaning than the theoretical effectiveness of that method.

prophylactic
(pro''fi-lak'tik)

Accepting Responsibility

For many couples, the burden of total responsibility of conception control is placed on the woman. It is often reasoned that, since women bear the children, they have more than a passing interest in preventing pregnancy.

Yet, taking total responsibility is burdensome to a woman. She must have the examinations, must be fitted for the device, have the prescription filled, or buy the supply. She must remember to take the pill daily, to be sure the cervical cap, diaphragm, or foam is in place, or to keep correct count of her menstrual days. She may wish to avoid the health hazards the pill or IUD imposes on her. She may find that having to shoulder total responsibility for preventing pregnancy creates feelings that get in the way of her loving feelings (Boston Women's Health Book Collective 1976).

Among some couples, each partner assumes that the other partner has taken the responsibility for conception control and feels embarrassed to ask if the other has. For these couples, no communication may mean no conception control.

For highly motivated couples, conception control can be a shared responsibility of both partners. Some couples share responsibility by each using a conception control device (he the condom, she the diaphragm or foam, for example) and significantly improving method effectiveness. More often (as with the pill, IUD, diaphragm, or sterilization), however, one partner actually uses the conception control device, while both partners share in the sense of responsibility. They may also take turns, periodically, in taking the primary responsibility for conception control.

Contraceptive Methods for the Male

There are few male contraceptives relative to the number of female contraceptives, but research continues in developing more ways in which men can control conception. For example, ultrasound is being tested in the blocking of sperm production. Drugs that block FSH production by the pituitary and vaccines to impair the ability of sperm to penetrate the egg are also being investigated.

The two primary male contraceptives discussed in this section are the condom and the male pill.

Condom

The **condom** has been variously known as the rubber, the prophylactic, the safe, or the French letter. It is a synthetic (latex rubber) or skin (from sheep intestine) sheath worn rather tightly over the erect penis. It is fitted with a rubber ring at the open end to keep it from slipping off the penis. The function of the condom is to prevent sperm from reaching the vagina.

Used for more than a century in the United States to prevent pregnancy and the transmission of sexually transmitted diseases, the condom is second only to the

(a)

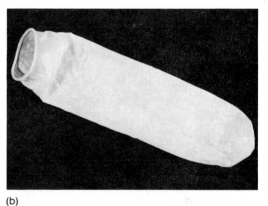

(b)

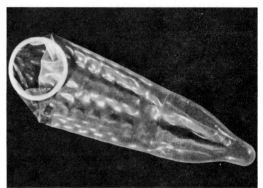

(c)

Figure 15.1 (a) Many reliable brands of condoms are readily available today. (b) Unrolled condom with plain end. (c) Unrolled condom with reservoir tip.

female pill in usage (Castleman 1980). Today, about 15 percent of all couples using contraceptives use the condom exclusively (National Center for Health Statistics 1978).

Condoms vary in shape, texture, and color but usually come in only one length and circumference. While some are tinted, most are a neutral color. They may have either reservoir or plain ends (figure 15.1). Reservoir ends have a nipplelike extension on the tip to hold the ejaculated semen. Some condoms are contoured, with a slight constriction just behind the glans of the penis to help hold the condom more snugly in place. Others have textured surfaces, with dots, ribs, or projections to "increase sensation" for the female.

Since condoms are extremely thin, they cause little or no loss of sensation to the penis. The skin condoms may give greater feeling of sensitivity because of their ability to conduct heat better than latex condoms.

Use and Effectiveness
The condom is unrolled over the erect penis shortly before intercourse. It must be handled carefully to prevent tearing (from fingernails, rings, etc.). Condoms with plain ends should be unrolled about one-half inch before being placed on the penis to create a reservoir at the tip for the ejaculate. Lubricated condoms ease the entry of the erect penis into the vagina. Unlubricated condoms may be used with a water-soluble lubricant, such as K-Y jelly or a contraceptive cream or jelly ("Condoms," *Consumer Reports* 1979).

After ejaculation, the penis should be promptly withdrawn before it shrinks enough for the condom to slip off or for semen to leak out the open end. Pinching the open end of the condom against the penis will help to prevent the condom from slipping off during withdrawal. If the condom does slip off, it should be removed from the vagina immediately, with the open end held tightly closed.

It is wise to check a condom immediately after use to make sure it is still intact. If it has burst during use, or if semen has been allowed to enter the vagina, contraceptive foam should be applied into the vagina immediately to help avoid conception.

The condom has a theoretical failure rate of around 2 percent, while its actual use failure rate is around 10 percent (see table 15.1). When used with vaginal foam, the theoretical failure rate drops to 1 percent and the actual use failure rate to 5 percent.

Pros and Cons of the Condom
The advantages of condom use include cost, safety to one's health, availability, convenience, protection, and reversibility. Commonly purchased in packages of three, twelve, or thirty-six, condoms can cost from well under a dollar to several dollars each. (Skin condoms cost more.) They are safe to use and have no side effects, except for the few persons who are allergic to latex. Condoms are easily available at any drugstore, and there is no need to consult a physician beforehand for an examination, prescription, or fitting. The convenience aspect of condoms is that they can be used right at the time of intercourse; the only planning necessary is to have one on hand. In addition to protecting against conception, condoms also provide some protection against the transmission of sexually transmitted diseases. Another important advantage of condoms is that condom usage is completely reversible. The use of the condom does not affect fertility (*Consumer Reports* 1979).

The disadvantages of condom use vary depending on the couple using the condom. Some couples object to the use of condoms because placing the condom on

gossypol
(gos'ĭ-pol)

the erect penis interrupts the continuity of lovemaking. (Other couples, however, make this a part of their lovemaking ritual.) Some men contend that the condom dulls tactile sensation and that the person wearing it is always aware of its presence. Others object to having to promptly withdraw the penis to avoid spillage or feel inhibited during vigorous lovemaking for fear the condom may come off.

Male Pill

For more than a decade, there have been efforts in the United States to develop a male contraceptive pill. Many substances have been investigated to date. While successful in lowering sperm counts, most of the drugs researched have been viewed as unacceptable due to their lowering of testosterone levels, and thus, reduced sex drive.

One of the more promising male contraceptive substances, currently undergoing clinical testing for safety and efficiency by the Food and Drug Administration, was discovered about twenty years ago in China. The Chinese noticed that men ingesting large amounts of cottonseed cooking oil were having infertility problems. A derivative of cottonseed, **gossypol,** has now been used among Chinese men as a contraceptive for more than a decade and, according to Chinese studies, is 99 percent effective. Gossypol works directly on the testes, impairing their ability to produce sperm. Because it is not a hormone, gossypol causes no reduction in testosterone levels. A gossypol pill must be taken daily for two months before infertility occurs. Sperm counts generally return to normal shortly after use of the pill is discontinued, although in 15 to 20 percent of the cases, fertility has *not* returned a year after use of the drug is stopped (Gregg 1981).

---

1. Have you or a sexual partner ever used a condom as a method of conception control? What were your reactions to the condom?
2. What steps might be taken to increase people's willingness to use condoms?
3. What might be some reasons for the significant difference between the theoretical and actual use failure rates of the condom?
4. Why is there more hope for gossypol, as an acceptable male birth control pill, than for other male birth control drugs that have been previously researched?

Contraceptive Methods for the Female

To allow for intercourse without conception, women have experimented with various contraceptive devices for centuries. In past decades, these devices have included douches, suppositories, foams, and diaphragms. The big breakthroughs came with the introduction of the birth control pill and improved intrauterine devices. Along with being more effective, these newer methods could be taken or applied at a time other than during coitus.

In this section, we examine current female contraceptives, including birth control pills and other hormones (which interfere with ovulation and ovum transport), mechanical barriers (which block the movement of sperm or prevent the implantation of fertilized ova), and spermicides (chemicals that kill sperm).

Birth Control Pills

Introduced over twenty years ago, birth control pills (or oral contraceptives) are used today by between fifty and eighty million women worldwide and by ten million women in the United States (Djerassi 1981). Today, about one out of every two women in the United States using contraceptives uses the pill (National Center for Health Statistics 1978). The pill has had immeasurable impact on sexual practices, couple relations, and population control.

The most commonly used birth control pill is called the *combination* pill because it contains both synthetic estrogen and progesterone. Many different brands of birth control pills are available today, and these brands vary in the specific kinds and amounts of hormones present and in the schedule by which the pills are taken (figure 15.2).

How the Pill Works

The synthetic estrogen and progesterone in birth control pills interfere with the release of follicle-stimulating hormone (FSH) and luteinizing hormone (LH), which are necessary for the development and release of the mature ovum by the ovary. The progesterone in the pill also causes the mucus within the cervical canal to become thick, so that sperm have greater difficulty entering the uterus, and upsets the growth pattern of the endometrium, so that even if an ovum is fertilized, it cannot easily implant itself (Pritchard and MacDonald 1984).

Use and Effectiveness

Birth control pills are usually taken daily, starting with the fifth day after the start of menstruation and continuing for three weeks. During the fourth week, the pill is omitted, and menstruation is allowed to occur, usually beginning two or three days after the last pill is taken.

Some brands of pills come with twenty-eight pills per pack. The first twenty-one pills contain active hormone ingredients, while the last seven pills may contain replacement iron for that lost during the period. Thus, a woman takes a pill every day and does not have to worry about remembering when to start a new pill pack.

When a woman first starts taking the pill, she is not protected from pregnancy until she has taken fourteen pills over a period of fourteen consecutive days. Other birth control methods should be used if intercourse is desired during this fourteen-day period. When a woman who has been using the pill wishes to become pregnant, she finishes her pill pack and does not start another pack. It is recommended that

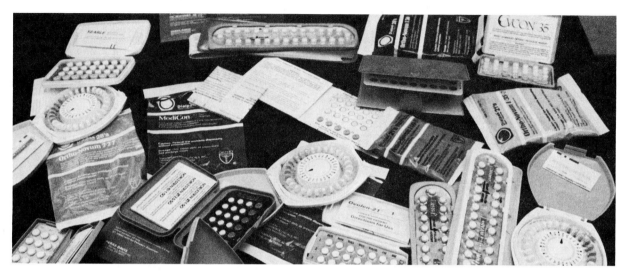

Figure 15.2 Oral contraceptives. Several of the many types of pills now available.

she be off the pill for at least six or seven cycles while using some other form of protection before becoming pregnant. Sixty to 75 percent of women who stop taking the pill have become pregnant within three months after last taking the pill. The pregnancy rate for women who once used the pill is the same as it is for women who have never used it (Cherniak and Feingold 1975).

A complete medical history must be taken before a woman starts taking the pill, and a medical examination, including a gynecological examination and Pap smear for cervical cancer, should be performed. Blood pressure and weight must be recorded. The physician then selects the brand of birth control pill best suited to the woman on the basis of her medical history, age, and physical characteristics.

A woman should take only the type of birth control pill that her physician prescribed since one type may affect her differently than another. Pills should not be accepted from a physician who has not examined a woman, nor should a woman ever supply her pills to a friend.

Since the pill is given only by prescription, regular visits to the physician are necessary for prescription renewal. Most women taking the pill must have a complete checkup once a year.

The theoretical failure rate for oral contraceptives overall is 0.5 percent, while the actual use failure rate is 2 percent (see table 15.1).

Pros and Cons of the Pill

An important advantage of birth control pills is that they are the most effective nonsurgical method of contraception. Another advantage of the pill is that there are no inconvenient devices to bother with at the time of intercourse. Taking the pill each day is a simple matter; there is no mess, no difficulty, no doubts about whether it has been properly inserted and placed (such as there are with diaphrams and IUDs). In addition, many women report that their menstrual cycles are more regular when they use the pill, with less cramping and reduced menstrual flow. Skin problems such as acne also may become less intense.

The drawbacks of birth control pills have attracted wide interest. The least of these is that they require the motivation to obtain them by prescription and to take them daily exactly as prescribed. The greater drawbacks of birth control pills are their various medical side effects.

Lesser Side Effects   Some women report nausea, headaches, fluid retention, and breast enlargement during the first few menstrual cycles while adjusting to the pill. Virtually all of these reactions disappear with the passage of time.

Breakthrough bleeding (bleeding or spotting between menstrual periods) also is common during the first two cycles after starting on the pill. Despite such bleeding, a woman is still protected from pregnancy. Bleeding is abnormal only if it persists after the second cycle of pills or is heavy in amount.

If these or other symptoms are especially bothersome, the woman's physician may change the prescription to a different brand of pill or recommend that the woman alter the time of day the pill is taken.

Serious Side Effects   The use of birth control pills may cause serious complications. Although rare, such complications can be compounded by other factors, including smoking, age, weight, diabetes, high blood pressure, and elevated cholesterol.

Of all of the pill complications, the most serious disorders are those of the circulatory system. While the incidence of death from circulatory problems is higher among users than among nonusers of the pill, only one woman in every 27,000 using the pill dies each year from this cause (Ory, Rosenfeld, and Landman 1980). The most critical circulatory problem related to use of the pill is the formation of blood clots that may damage the brain or lungs.

There is no clear evidence that women taking the pill are at greater risk of cancer than those not taking it ("Contraception: Comparing the Options," *FDA Consumer* 1977). While slightly raising a woman's risk of developing some forms of cancer (cervical and skin), the pill may lower her risk of developing other forms (ovarian and endometrial). The pill's effect on breast cancer is unknown ("The Pill's Vindication: How Solid?" *Medical World News* 1980).

Another serious side effect of the use of birth control pills is increased risk of defect in the fetus if the mother takes the pill after becoming pregnant (*FDA Consumer* July/August 1977). Thus, a woman who believes she may be pregnant should not take the pill.

diethylstilbestrol
(di-eth''il-stil-bes'trol)

Despite all of the side effects of birth control pills, the mortality risk of term pregnancy is considerably higher (seven deaths per every 100,000 pregnant women) than is the risk from the use of the pill (one to three deaths per 100,000 users). Also, the adverse side effects of the pill have been reduced in recent years through the use of lower-dose estrogen pills.

Other Hormone Contraceptives

Hormone methods other than the combination birth control pill that are being researched include the minipill, the morning-after pill, and injectable hormone contraceptives.

Minipill

The **minipill** is a low-dose progesterone pill containing no estrogen. It is available in packets of thirty-five to forty-two pills. One pill is taken daily, without break, for as long as conception control is desired. Often, a woman does not experience menstruation at all while taking the minipill, although spot bleeding may occur. The progesterone in the minipill changes the mucus in the cervical canal, impeding entry of sperm, and changes the inner lining of the uterus, interfering with the implantation of a fertilized ovum (Pritchard and MacDonald 1984). The long-term effects of the minipill are under study. Its theoretical failure rate is 1 percent, with an actual use failure rate of 2.5 percent.

Morning-After Pill

Approved by the Food and Drug Administration for use in emergency situations, the **morning-after pill** is sometimes used after a woman has been placed at risk of pregnancy from sexual intercourse arising from rape or incest, or when a woman's emotional and physical condition is such that a possible pregnancy may have grave results.

The morning-after pill contains twenty-five milligrams of the synthetic estrogen **diethylstilbestrol (DES).** The pill is given in a five-day series of two pills each day, starting within twenty-four hours and no later than seventy-two hours after unprotected intercourse (Pritchard and MacDonald 1984). The pill causes contraction of the uterus and the expulsion of the contents of the uterus. If used as recommended, the morning-after pill produces a pregnancy rate of less than 1 percent (Rinehart 1976).

Aside from its tendency to produce severe nausea, there has been much concern over the cancer-producing potential of DES. The drug has been linked to scores of cases of vaginal and cervical cancer in young women, and testicular cancer in young men, whose mothers took it in the 1940s and 1950s during pregnancy to prevent miscarriage. Such use was later disapproved by the Food and Drug Administration (Hatcher et al. 1984). DES daughters also show a higher incidence of withered

ectopic   intrauterine
(ek-top'ik)   (in''trah-u'ter-in)

fallopian tubes, leading to more **ectopic pregnancies,** in which the embryo implants in the fallopian tube. And ectopic pregnancies are the second leading cause of maternal death ("Some DES Daughters Have Withered Tubes," *Medical World News* 1981).

In continuing to approve the use of DES as a morning-after pill, the Food and Drug Administration argues that there is no significant risk to women under prescribed dosages if the pill is not taken for prolonged periods.

Injectable Hormone Contraceptives

Long-lasting, injectable progesterone, called Depo-Provera, has been used by great numbers of women in various South American countries. The Food and Drug Administration has not approved it for contraceptive use in the United States. Depo-Provera is injected into a woman two to four times a year and prevents pregnancy between injections. During this time, the woman either has no menstrual periods or irregular ones (Pritchard and MacDonald 1984).

Although some women become pregnant as desired when stopping the use of Depo-Provera, others report a six- to eighteen-month delay in regaining fertility. Some report permanent sterility. Other side effects include nausea and weight gain. Animal studies have linked Depo-Provera to breast and cervical cancer, although these results have not been substantiated among humans.

---

1. Why do you think there is a greater number of usable conception control devices available for women than for men?
2. What is the significance of a woman receiving a complete medical examination before being given a prescription for birth control pills?
3. Have you or a sexual partner ever used birth control pills as a method of conception control? What personal advantages and disadvantages do you attribute to use of the pill?
4. What arguments might you give a person who contends that oral contraceptives are too dangerous for the average woman to take?
5. How do the minipill, morning-after pill, and injectable hormones differ in action and content from the combination pill?

Intrauterine Device

The **intrauterine device,** or **IUD,** is a soft, plastic object one to one and one-half inches long and varies in shape. The IUD is inserted through the cervical canal and positioned in the uterus, where it stays in place for several years. IUDs allow sperm to fertilize the ovum but prevent implantation of the fertilized egg into the uterine lining. How the IUD actually works is not precisely known.

Actively experimented with in Europe during the early 1900s, the IUD was not rediscovered until 1959. Since then, a number of different types have been developed. Today, IUDs account for about 12 percent of all contraceptives used in the United States (National Center for Health Statistics 1978).

Types and Actions

There are three types of IUDs, and the devices can be categorized based on their shape and the material from which they are made (figure 15.3).

The *open plastic* IUDs are known by trade names as the Lippes Loop and Saf-T-Coil. These devices are designed in an open configuration and can be straightened out and placed in an applicator for insertion into the uterus, where the devices return to their original shape.

The *copper* IUDs are made of plastic but have a covering of fine copper wire. Two of the more common types are the Copper T and the Copper 7. The copper on these devices dissolves very slowly into the fluids of the uterus and interferes with certain protein substances in the uterus that are necessary for fertilization and embryo implantation. The copper also adversely affects the sperm. The copper in the wire completely dissolves within two years, at which time the IUD should be replaced so that the added protection that the copper provides is not lost (Cherniak and Feingold 1975).

A *medicated* IUD is the Progestasert T. This type of IUD contains a supply of progesterone in the stem of the T that is gradually released into the uterus due to body heat. The progesterone not only inhibits implantation but also reduces cramping. Since the progesterone reservoir is emptied within a year, the device needs to be replaced at the end of this time to renew the action of the medication ("The Second-Generation IUDs . . . Progestasert," *Current Prescribing* 1976).

Use and Effectiveness

IUDs are usually placed into the uterus by a physician or specially trained nurse during the menstrual period when the cervix is dilated (figure 15.4). Insertion at this time also averts the chances of the woman being pregnant; if she is pregnant, the insertion of an IUD can cause an abortion.

Prior to insertion, the physician usually performs a Pap smear to check for uterine cancer and a pelvic examination to determine the position and size of the uterus so that the IUD can be safely inserted. Insertion may cause cramping and spot-bleeding for a few days or weeks, and may cause longer, heavier periods. The physician may want to check in a month or so to be sure insertion was performed correctly (Connell 1977).

Once inserted, the IUD may be left in place for several years, during which time no other contraceptive protection is necessary. The device is equipped with a nylon thread that protrudes from the cervix to allow the woman to confirm the presence of the IUD. Prior to intercourse, a woman should feel with her finger to be certain the device has not been inadvertently expelled. If she cannot feel the thread,

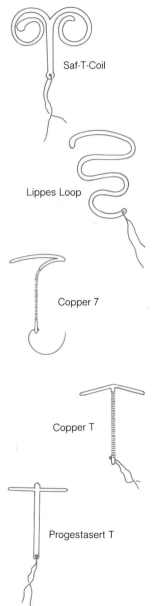

Figure 15.3 Types of IUDs.

Figure 15.4 Insertion of the Copper 7 IUD.

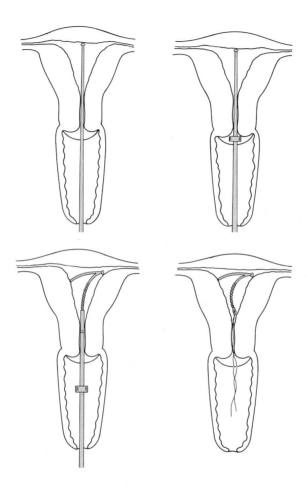

she should return to her physician. In the meantime, she and her partner should use some other form of protection, such as the condom and/or vaginal foam.

The action of the IUD is completely reversible. When the woman wishes to become pregnant, she returns to her physician for the removal of the IUD. Within one month to a year, the uterus is again functioning in a normal way, and most women are able to become pregnant. An occasional pregnancy may occur with the device in place. If pregnancy is confirmed, the Food and Drug Administration advises the immediate removal of the IUD (Connell 1977).

On the average, IUDs have a theoretical failure rate of 1.5 percent and an actual use failure rate of about 5 percent (see table 15.1) (Hatcher et al. 1984). Even though the IUD has a low failure rate, women who must not become pregnant should not rely on the IUD.

Pros and Cons of the IUD

A primary advantage of the IUD is that, once inserted, it requires little attention. There is nothing to place into the vagina before intercourse nor anything to remove afterwards. Also, after the expense of the initial insertion, IUD use requires no additional cost. Another advantage is that the IUD does not affect hormone levels, and its contraceptive action is usually completely reversible upon removal.

Most women using the IUD experience no adverse reactions other than very minor ones for a brief period of time. The most common side effects are heavier bleeding and cramping during a woman's period, and cramping and spot-bleeding between periods. Complaints of cramping, bleeding, and expulsion have lessened, however, with the introduction of smaller, better-shaped devices.

A more serious disadvantage of the IUD is that the IUD may perforate the wall of the uterus. Although this occurs in only about one out of every one thousand insertions, perforation is, nonetheless, a relatively dangerous complication. Surgery is commonly necessary to avert damage to the intestines.

1. Some people object to the IUD on the basis that its action, in principle, is similar to an abortion. What are your feelings on this issue?
2. Of all of the pros and cons of the IUD, which ones are most significant to you?

Diaphragm

The vaginal **diaphragm** is a shallow, round dome of soft latex rubber two to four inches in diameter. Its rim is sealed over a flexible metal spring or coil to hold it in place. The diaphragm is placed inside the vagina and is designed to completely cover the cervix of the uterus. It is held in place by the pressure of its rim against the vaginal wall.

The diaphragm prevents pregnancy by blocking sperm from entering the cervix and by holding spermicidal (sperm-killing) jelly or cream up to the cervix. Since the diaphragm may not always reliably block the cervical canal, the spermicide kills sperm that may have moved across the rim of the diaphragm.

Until the birth control pill and IUD became popular in the early 1960s, the diaphragm was the safest contraceptive method to which women had access. Today, about 6 percent of all couples using contraceptives use the diaphragm (National Center for Health Statistics 1978).

Use and Effectiveness

Women's vaginas vary in length and width. While such size variations have no bearing on one's enjoyment of sexual intercourse, they do affect the snug fitting of the diaphragm. Since a diaphragm of the wrong size may slip out of place or be discharged during intercourse, a woman must be fitted for a diaphragm by a physician.

Women should have the size and fit of their diaphragms checked by a physician every two or three years, after childbirth or miscarriage, or after any significant weight loss or gain. A woman can be fitted as a virgin, but since sexual intercourse stretches the vagina, she should be checked for size after a few weeks of intercourse. Properly fitted and inserted, the diaphragm is usually not felt by the woman or her sexual partner (Boston Women's Health Book Collective 1976).

Prior to insertion of the diaphragm, the diaphragm should be checked for holes and cracks by filling it with water or by holding it up to the light since eventually the latex rubber will deteriorate and leak. Then the woman should cover the inside surface of the diaphragm dome and its rim with spermicide, which is available at drugstores without prescription.

The diaphragm is most easily inserted if the woman stands with one foot raised, squats, lies down with knees raised, or crouches. With the dome directed downward, the woman squeezes the diaphragm into a long, oval shape between her thumb and first or second finger. Holding the vaginal lips apart with the other hand, she slides the diaphragm into place. Once the diaphragm is in place, the woman checks to see that the cervix is completely covered (figure 15.5).

The diaphragm can be inserted up to four hours in advance of intercourse. Since sperm can survive in the vagina for several hours, even in the presence of a spermicide, the diaphragm must be left in place for six to eight hours *after* intercourse. If intercourse is repeated before this time is up, the woman should first insert an applicator full of vaginal foam.

After removal, the diaphragm should be washed with warm water and mild soap, rinsed, dried, and stored in its plastic container away from light and heat.

When used with a spermicide, the theoretical failure rate of the diaphragm is 2 percent. In actual use, its failure rate may be as high as 19 percent (see table 15.1). Among highly motivated women who have been fitted for the correct size and who know how to properly insert the diaphragm, Planned Parenthood reports an actual failure rate of only 2 percent (Vessey and Wiggins 1974).

Pros and Cons of the Diaphragm

For many women, the diaphragm is the contraceptive method of choice. It can be inserted prior to the beginning of sex play (which then does not need to be interrupted). The device cannot get lost in the vagina, nor can its presence injure the woman in any manner. Also, its use involves no hormones to affect the general system of the woman. Another advantage is that, once fitted, a woman can generally use her diaphragm for several years on her own without returning to see her physician. The only cost involved in the use of a diaphragm is the physician's consultation, the purchase of the diaphragm, and the modest cost of the spermicide. Use of the diaphragm is also completely reversible since the diaphragm does not affect fertility.

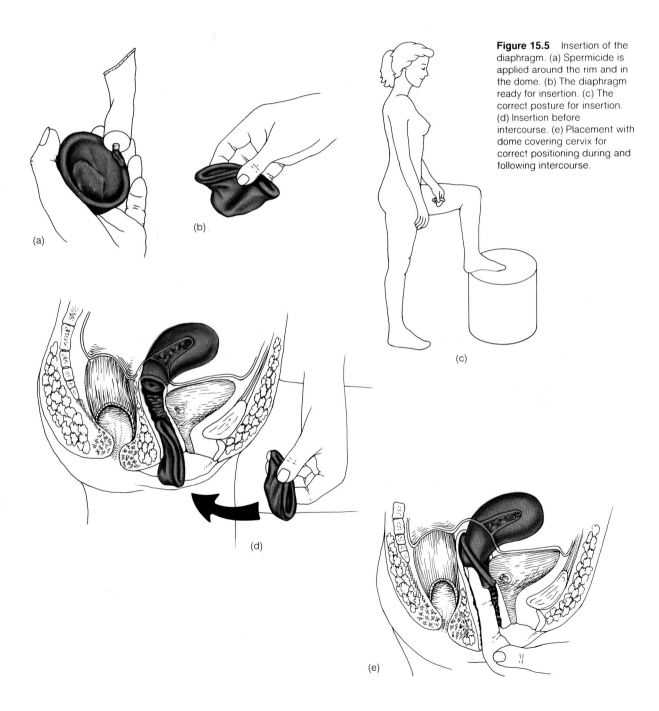

Figure 15.5 Insertion of the diaphragm. (a) Spermicide is applied around the rim and in the dome. (b) The diaphragm ready for insertion. (c) The correct posture for insertion. (d) Insertion before intercourse. (e) Placement with dome covering cervix for correct positioning during and following intercourse.

(a)

(b)

(c)

(d)

(e)

Prentif® Cavity Rim
Cervical Cap

Vimule® Cap

Dumas Cap

Figure 15.6   Three types of
cervical caps.

The primary disadvantage of the diaphragm is that it requires the motivation to use it consistently and correctly with every act of intercourse. Also, some women (and men) find that they are allergic to either the latex or the spermicide being used. If so, they can use a diaphragm made of some other material or shift to another brand of spermicide.

Cervical Cap

The **cervical cap** is a small, thimble-shaped, plastic or rubber device that fits snugly over the cervix and can be left in place for up to several weeks at a time (McBride 1980; Gregg 1981) (figure 15.6). A groove on the inner lip of the cap helps to form an airtight seal around the cervix that holds the cap in place through suction. One type of cervical cap now has a valve to allow secretion of menstrual fluids so that the cap can be left in place for several months (Wills 1981).

Long used in Europe, the cervical cap has recently been imported into the United States by private physicians and clinics. The Food and Drug Administration is now studying its effectiveness. Although manufactured in the United States, the cap is not yet approved for use here. It is being marketed only as an aid in artificial insemination and for collection of menstrual fluid. While some have criticized the government for delaying approval of the cervical cap as a contraceptive device, the recent experience with an IUD—the Dalkon Shield—which was marketed without sufficient testing and with very adverse user experience, helps to underline the need for adequate testing of any such device before approval is given for public use.

Use and Effectiveness

The cervical cap is used with a spermicidal cream or jelly but with much less spermicide than is needed with the diaphragm. The cap is filled one-third full with spermicide before insertion, and no more spermicide need be added for several days, regardless of sexual activity. Some physicians recommend leaving the cap in no longer than twenty-four hours at a time in order to avoid inflammation of the cervix. Some physicians also believe that, if properly fitted, the cap can be used without spermicidal creams or jellies (Wills 1981).

Insertion of the cervical cap takes some practice. The woman grasps the spermicide-containing cap, dome down, between two fingers of one hand and compresses the cap's rim. The cap is then pushed back as far as it will go along the vaginal canal. The rim is pressed around the cervix until it forms a seal (figure 15.7). To remove the cap, the rim is tilted away from the cervix, thus breaking the suction, or the cap can be grasped between two fingers and pulled downward. Both insertion and removal require knowledge of the vaginal tract and the woman feeling confident in her ability to work with the device.

From the available data, the theoretical failure rate of the cervical cap is 2 percent, while its actual use failure rate is 13 percent.

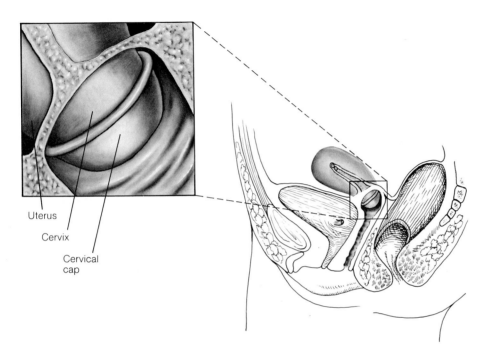

Uterus

Cervix

Cervical
cap

Figure 15.7   The cervical
cap encircles the cervix.

Pros and Cons of the Cervical Cap

Most of the advantages of the diaphragm also hold true for the cervical cap. In addition, some women using the cervical cap prefer it because it is smaller than the diaphragm and more comfortable to wear. As with the diaphragm, women appreciate the control they have over the use of the cervical cap.

The primary disadvantage of the cervical cap at the present time is its limited availability since Food and Drug Administration approval is pending. Also, some physicians do not recommend the cervical cap if there are cervical infections, cysts, or lacerations. Other physicians will not use the cap for fear that it may cause damage to the cervix (Seaman and Seaman 1978).

Spermicidal Agents

A vaginal **spermicide** is a chemical contraceptive carried in an inert base (foam, jelly, cream, sponge, or suppository) that is inserted into the vagina prior to intercourse to prevent pregnancy. Spermicides have been used for centuries.

Spermicides work in two ways. First, the foam, jelly, or cream (the inert base) provides a mechanical barrier that blocks the movement of sperm into the cervical canal of the uterus. Second, the active chemical agent is *spermicidal* within the vagina.

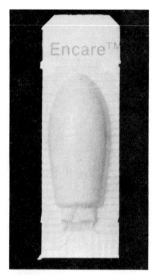

Figure 15.8 A vaginal suppository. The suppository is removed from its wrapping and inserted deep into the vagina fifteen minutes before coitus.

Figure 15.9 The contraceptive sponge and the method of its placement high in the vagina.

Use and Effectiveness

Of the spermicides, the foams are the most effective and the simplest to use. The foam is placed high into the vagina either by an applicator or in the form of foaming tablets that melt at body temperature. The foam spreads quickly and evenly over the cervical opening and forms a relatively good barrier. Jellies and creams are placed high into the vagina with an applicator but often fail to spread uniformly and are more likely to fail as contraceptives. The suppository is a glycerine base, spermicide-containing cylinder about an inch or so long that is placed high into the vagina at the cervix (figure 15.8). The glycerin liquifies at body temperatures, spreading spermicide around the upper vagina. The contraceptive effect of all of the vaginal spermicides—especially the creams and jellies—can be considerably enhanced by the male use of a condom or the female use of a diaphragm in conjunction with the use of the spermicide.

In 1983, the Food and Drug Administration approved a vaginal contraceptive sponge for marketing in the United States (figure 15.9). It is a small, pillow-shaped polyurethane pad of synthetic sponge containing a spermicide. Contoured with a concave dimple on the side intended to be fitted over the cervix, the sponge is moistened and inserted deep into the vagina. Once in place, the sponge provides protection for up to twenty-four hours.

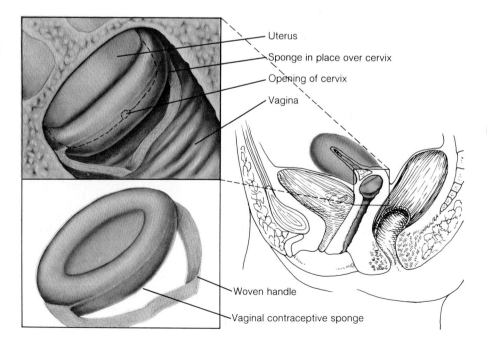

- Uterus
- Sponge in place over cervix
- Opening of cervix
- Vagina
- Woven handle
- Vaginal contraceptive sponge

Effective Uses of Vaginal Aerosol Foams

For best protection, a vaginal aerosol foam must be inserted in two applications no more than thirty minutes before the beginning of actual intercourse. The woman should shake the can or vial and fill the plastic applicator according to the instructions on the can (box figure 15.1a). Prefilled disposable applicators are also available.

To insert the foam, the woman lies on her back, and the applicator is gently pushed into the vagina as far as it will go (box figure 15.1b). With the first application, the applicator is tilted forward before pressing the plunger. This covers the front part of the cervix. The applicator is then filled a second time, inserted, and tilted backward toward the rectum. This covers the back part of the cervix. If the woman gets up from a lying position after the foam is inserted, but before intercourse occurs, *another* application of foam is needed. Each subsequent act of intercourse should be preceded by another two full applications of foam.

While the woman can get up after intercourse without affecting the action of the foam, she should not douche, go swimming, or take a bath for eight hours after intercourse. This would dilute and weaken the spermicidal factor.

Box Figure 15.1 Foam insertion. (a) The applicator is filled. (b) The applicator is then inserted deep into the vagina, and the foam, which kills the sperm, is deposited.

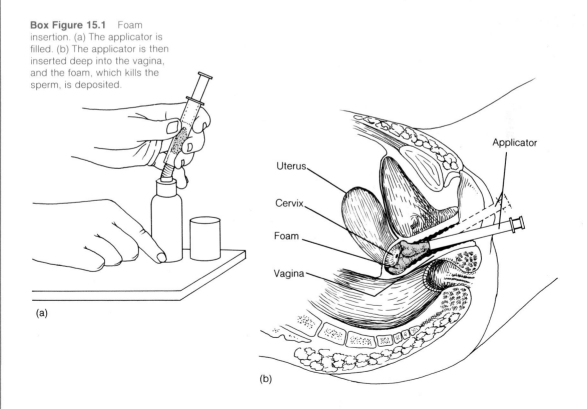

(a)

Uterus

Cervix

Foam

Vagina

Applicator

(b)

In using any spermicide, it is important that the spermicide is inserted into the vagina within the allowable time before intercourse and that a second insertion of spermicide is made before second coitus. Some physicians routinely recommend two insertions of vaginal spermicide before each act of intercourse to give added contraceptive protection.

Since the vaginal lining absorbs most of the spermicidal material, there is little or no reason for vaginal douching to wash out the vagina after using a spermicide. Douching increases the chances of vaginal infection and is not recommended.

The theoretical failure rate for the spermicides is 3 to 5 percent, while the actual use failure rate is 18 percent (see table 15.1).

Pros and Cons of Spermicides

Today, about 6 percent of all women using contraceptives use spermicides for conception control (National Center for Health Statistics 1978). The advantages of the spermicides are that they are harmless to the woman, they do not cause cancer or any other disease, and their effect on pregnancy is fully reversible. In addition, the spermicides are easy to use, their use does not require a physician's visit, and they are readily obtained from any drugstore without prescription. They can be inserted before sex play begins or as a backup method if a birth control pill is missed. They are especially useful for couples having infrequent or unexpected coitus.

Some women dislike the spermicides because they require preplanning and high motivation to use them consistently and correctly before each act of intercourse. Also, some women and men are allergic to some brands of spermicide, in which case the brand may be changed or the woman's physician consulted.

1. Why might Planned Parenthood be recommending the diaphragm for women concerned over their continued use of the pill and the IUD?
2. Contrast the action of the cervical cap to that of the diaphragm.
3. Of all the spermicides, the foam has the lowest failure rate. Why?

Shared Methods of Conception Control

Each of the methods of conception control discussed in the preceding sections can be practiced alone by either the male or the female, even though the interest in using any of these methods is enhanced by the cooperation and involvement of both partners. Other methods of conception control *require* the active cooperation of both partners to be effective in preventing pregnancy. These include the rhythm methods, withdrawal, and abstinence.

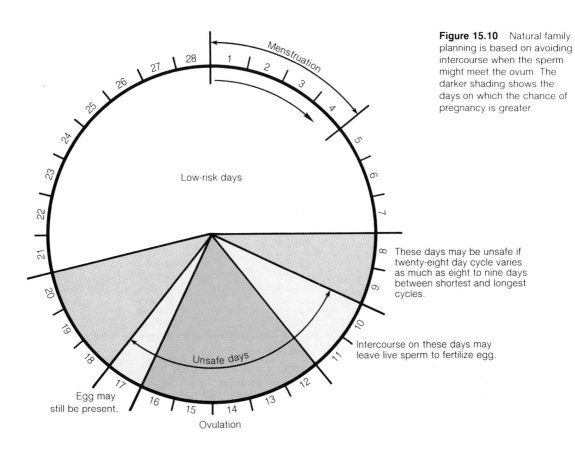

Figure 15.10 Natural family planning is based on avoiding intercourse when the sperm might meet the ovum. The darker shading shows the days on which the chance of pregnancy is greater.

These days may be unsafe if twenty-eight day cycle varies as much as eight to nine days between shortest and longest cycles.

Intercourse on these days may leave live sperm to fertilize egg.

Egg may still be present.

Low-risk days

Unsafe days

Menstruation

Ovulation

Rhythm Methods

The **rhythm methods,** or **natural family planning,** are based upon the fact that a woman usually produces a mature ovum once a month with some predictability, often fourteen days *before* the beginning of the next menstrual flow (although it may occur a day or two earlier than this). If the ovum fails to be fertilized by sperm within twenty-four hours after its release from the ovary, it begins to degenerate. The rhythm methods also take into account that sperm inseminated into the woman's body and kept at normal body temperatures can remain alive for up to seventy-two hours after intercourse and still fertilize the ovum. Thus, conception can occur only if intercourse takes place several days before or during the time in which the ovum is alive. This is called the *fertile* ("unsafe") *period* (figure 15.10). The fertile period can be calculated in several ways.

Table 15.2   How to Figure the "Safe" and "Unsafe" Days for the Calendar Method of Rhythm.

Length of Shortest Period	First Unsafe Day After Start of Any Period	Length of Longest Period	Last Unsafe Day After Start of Any Period
21 days	3rd day	21 days	10th day
22 days	4th day	22 days	11th day
23 days	5th day	23 days	12th day
24 days	6th day	24 days	13th day
25 days	7th day	25 days	14th day
26 days	8th day	26 days	15th day
27 days	9th day	27 days	16th day
28 days	10th day	28 days	17th day
29 days	11th day	29 days	18th day
30 days	12th day	30 days	19th day
31 days	13th day	31 days	20th day
32 days	14th day	32 days	21st day
33 days	15th day	33 days	22nd day
34 days	16th day	34 days	23rd day
35 days	17th day	35 days	24th day
36 days	18th day	36 days	25th day
37 days	19th day	37 days	26th day
38 days	20th day	38 days	27th day

Calendar Method

The simplest technique of calculating the fertile period—the **calendar method**— is based on the length of the woman's shortest and longest menstrual cycles. If five days are allowed during which ovulation may occur and another three prior days are added during which previously deposited sperm may remain alive, at least eight days of abstinence are required in the middle of each cycle. When these unsafe days occur depends on the length of the cycle.

To use this method effectively, a woman needs to record the length of at least eight menstrual cycles on a calendar. She can then calculate the fertile period of the ninth cycle as follows: subtract eighteen days from the length of the shortest cycle to find the first unsafe day and eleven days from the length of the longest cycle to find the last unsafe day (table 15.2). The woman must not have sexual intercourse from the first to the last unsafe day *every month*. If, for instance, her shortest cycle was twenty-five days and her longest cycle was thirty-one days during the eight months of recording, she must refrain from intercourse beginning on day seven $(25 - 18 = 7)$ through day twenty $(31 - 11 = 20)$. Thus, for fourteen days each month she must not engage in intercourse.

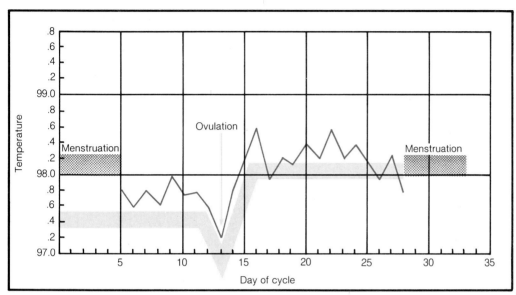

Figure 15.11 Basal body temperature method. Resting, or basal, temperature is taken each morning and recorded for several months. A woman then times intercourse to avoid the days of ovulation each month.

Temperature Method

Another technique for determining ovulation is the **basal body temperature (BBT) method.** The female hormone progesterone, which is released from the ovaries, causes a noticeable shift in BBT (the woman's lowest body temperature at rest) near the time of ovulation (figure 15.11).

A woman using this method should take her temperature every day immediately upon waking. It is best taken with a rectal thermometer of 0.1 degree intervals from 96 to 100 degrees F. Shortly before ovulation, a woman's BBT usually drops slightly, then rises sharply, marking the beginning of ovulation. Her temperature stays high the rest of the cycle. Intercourse is unsafe from the day her temperature drops until three days after it rises. This method, however, does not *predict* unsafe days. It is best used along with the calendar method.

Ovulation Method

Women using the **ovulation method** are taught to recognize when they are ovulating by watching for changes in their vaginal mucus secretions. "Dry" days—days when women notice no vaginal mucus secretions—are times of infertility, while "wet" days are times of possible fertility.

Vaginal mucus secretions are normally cloudy, but during ovulation they become clear and slippery and stretch between the fingers. Vulva moistness or wetness also marks ovulation. The third consecutive day after "peak" slippery mucus, the fertile period usually ends, and the mucus once again becomes cloudy.

Individual variations among women do occur, with each woman having her own pattern, but the "peak" slippery mucus marks ovulation (Boston Women's Health Book Collective 1976).

Symptothermal Method

The **symptothermal method** combines the BBT and the ovulation method. Women are instructed to take their temperature at the same time each day, watching for the temperature rise indicating ovulation. Intercourse is avoided until the end of the third day after the temperature rise or the fourth day after "peak" mucus, whichever is later.

Effectiveness of Rhythm Methods

Overall, the theoretical failure rate of natural family planning is 2 to 20 percent, while the actual use failure rate is about 24 percent (see table 15.1). Actual use failure rate is 21 percent for the calendar method only, 20 percent for the BBT method only, and 25 percent for the ovulation method only (Hatcher et al. 1984). The symptothermal method may have an actual failure rate of only 11 percent ("Natural Birth Control: 1% Pregnancy Rate—or 27%?" *Medical World News* 1980).

Pros and Cons of Rhythm Methods

Unfortunately, various factors affect the rhythm methods. For example, an average woman may vary as much as eight to nine days between her shortest and longest cycles. Following childbirth, the cycles may be upset for several months, and timing ovulation may be impossible. The lengths of cycles also vary with age, health, stress, and drugs being taken. As many as fifteen out of every one hundred women have menstrual cycles so irregular that they cannot use rhythm methods at all.

A major advantage of rhythm methods is that no drugs or devices are needed. Another is that rhythm methods may satisfy those women with strong religious convictions against using mechanical or hormonal methods of contraception.

The disadvantages of rhythm methods are that they require careful record keeping and estimating the time each month during which there can be no intercourse. A physician's guidance is needed, at least at the outset. Some find the methods unsatisfactory because of the extended time each month during which sexual intercourse must be avoided. Many women experience heightened sex drive around the time of ovulation, or during the time, according to the rhythm methods, they must abstain from coitus.

Today, about 7 percent of women practicing conception control use a rhythm method (National Center for Health Statistics 1978).

Withdrawal

Also known as **coitus interruptus, withdrawal** consists of removing the penis from the vagina just prior to ejaculation. If sperm cannot reach the vagina, the woman cannot become pregnant. Withdrawal is still practiced by about 4 percent of all couples concerned with conception control (National Center for Health Statistics 1978).

Use and Effectiveness

For withdrawal to be effective, the man must be alert to the first signs of ejaculation and be prepared to terminate intercourse at the first moment he feels himself "coming." For some couples, this disruption of intercourse just before the moment of greatest satisfaction does not seem to carry any ill effects; for others, it disturbs the entire sexual relationship.

Not only is timing crucial, but distance is essential. Sperm can move on their own, and if deposited between the labia may be able to continue moving up the vagina. Due to sperm mobility, it is essential that sperm contact no part of the woman's genitals. Reassurances by the man that he will be careful may mean little to the woman who knows that if he makes a mistake, intended or not, it is she rather than her partner who must bear the consequences of that miscalculation.

The theoretical failure rate for withdrawal is 16 percent; however, its actual use failure rate is 23 percent (see table 15.1). This is not sufficient for protection.

Pros and Cons of Withdrawal

Withdrawal has certain advantages. It takes no preparation, costs nothing, and is always available. The man assumes the primary responsibility, although the woman's cooperation is necessary.

But there are some significant disadvantages to withdrawal. First, not all men can accurately predict the beginning of ejaculation. Some men do not experience one powerful "gush" of ejaculate. Rather, the semen flows out of the penis in small amounts both before and after climax. These men are usually not aware of the moment when semen first begins to be released (Boston Women's Health Book Collective 1976).

Beyond this, some men and women have difficulty in maintaining self-control as they approach orgasm. They may simply abandon themselves in their passion, and the man may forget to withdraw in time before he ejaculates into the vagina. Even before ejaculation, the few drops of Cowper's fluid that collect at the tip of the penis and may be carrying sperm may enter the vagina. One drop can cause pregnancy, especially since the first drops of semen are the most potent.

For couples desiring success in limiting their family size, withdrawal should be used only in an emergency or as a last resort. It can no longer be considered a significant birth control alternative.

chorionic gonadotropin
(ko''re-on'ik
gon''ah-do-tro'pin)

Abstinence

Abstinence is the voluntary avoiding of coitus and obviously eliminates the chances of a pregnancy. Abstinence may be temporary or permanent.

Some couples choose to temporarily abstain from intercourse to increase their desire for each other. Engaging in "demand" intercourse (rather than responding to an inherent sex drive) can deplete the act of some of its anticipation. Some couples find that through planned, temporary abstinence they increase the yearning for each other that can intensify their pleasure of coital union (Aguilar 1980).

This kind of abstinence does not need to preclude sexual activity. It can be practiced along with self- or partner sexual arousal through the use of the mouth, fingers, or a vibrator. Such arousal need have no physical side effects as long as it includes orgasm to relieve pelvic vasocongestion. Sex play to orgasm through oral and manual stimulation can be pleasurable and satisfying.

Another form of temporary abstinence is when a person takes time out of a sexual relationship. As satisfying as sexual relations with someone else may be, a person may for a time wish to totally focus on himself or herself, children, friends, or work. An intense, intimate relationship may prevent a person from knowing more about his or her needs, potentials, and talents.

Permanent abstinence, called **celibacy,** is expected by some religious groups of their clergy. Some people practice celibacy as a matter of preference.

A person who practices abstinence, whether temporarily or permanently, may encounter loneliness and feel the absence of physical affection and contact from another adult human who can provide for sexual needs. Some in our society find it difficult to accept the idea of refraining from sexual activity. They unnecessarily see intimacy as being synonymous with sexual intercourse, and vice versa. Abstinence, however, whether temporary or permanent, can be satisfying for the person who is able to find other ways of meeting his or her needs for companionship.

Experimental Methods of Contraception

Various other contraceptive techniques are being investigated.

The vaginal ring, resembling the rim of a diaphragm, is infiltrated with both progesterone and estrogen, which it slowly releases from its inserted position high in the vagina. Removed for one week each month to allow a menstrual period, the ring needs replacement every six months. Both its side effects and effectiveness are thought to be similar to that of the pill (Gregg 1981).

A nasal spray containing an analogue (a similar, but not identical form) of luteinizing-releasing hormones that prevent ovulation is also being researched. Some predict that this same analogue may be used to stop sperm production in men.

An antipregnancy vaccine that produces antibodies against **human chorionic gonadotropin (HCG)** is also being tested (Gregg 1981). HCG is a hormone secreted by cells of the implanted embryo in the uterine wall. This hormone has properties similar to LH, the usual inhibition of which would lead to menstrual discharge and loss of the implanted embryo. HCG causes the corpus luteum to be maintained and to continue secreting high levels of estrogen and progesterone. Continued high levels of estrogen and progesterone suppress the release of FSH and LH from the pituitary gland so that normal menstrual cycles are inhibited. Thus, the uterine wall continues to grow and develop, as does the embryo within the uterus.

Research is also being conducted on subdermal (under-the-skin) implants of progesterone. Six implanted capsules provide contraception for six years, replacing 2,500 ordinary contraceptive pills. During this time, the released hormone concentration is approximately 20 percent of that received from daily oral pills taken for the same period of time. Researchers report a pregnancy rate of 0.4 percent, with no ectopic pregnancies (Gregg 1981).

1. Why is the day of the month a woman ovulates so difficult to detect?
2. If the actual use failure rate of the rhythm method is so high, why would anyone choose to use it?
3. Give some possible reasons for the wide difference between the theoretical failure rate and the actual use failure rate of withdrawal.
4. What advice might you give to a person who is using only withdrawal as a means of avoiding pregnancy?
5. Would you expect some manner of abstinence from intercourse to dull or intensify a couple's sexual yearning for each other?

Sterilization

Sterilization is the most effective method of conception control, aside from total abstinence. Sterilization is the surgical interruption of the reproductive tracts of either the male or female, preventing the discharge of sex cells and, thus, fertilization. Not only is this method safe, it is also generally considered permanent. It has great appeal to couples who desire no additional pregnancies or none at all. In almost one-third of couples in which the wife is of childbearing age, one of the partners has undergone surgical sterilization (National Center for Health Statistics 1978).

The permanence of sterilization can be both blessing and curse for some couples. Some persons who have undergone sterilization have later wished, for one of several reasons, to regain their reproductive ability. While sometimes successful, restoration of fertility is far from guaranteed. For this reason, it is important that the consequences of sterilization be carefully considered before seeking it as a replacement for more conventional, less effective, but reversible methods.

oophorectomy
(o"of-o-rek'to-me)

ovariectomy
(o"va-re-ek'to-me)

hysterectomy
(his"tĕ-rek'to-me)

laparotomy
(lap-ah-rot'o-me)

laparoscope
(lap'ah-ro-skop")

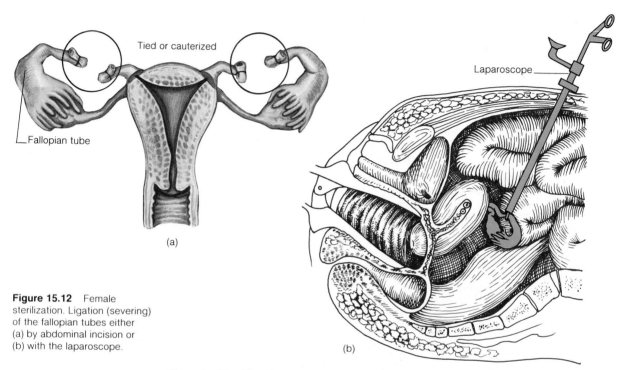

Figure 15.12 Female sterilization. Ligation (severing) of the fallopian tubes either (a) by abdominal incision or (b) with the laparoscope.

Female Sterilization

A woman could be sterilized by removing the ovaries, removing the uterus, or by interrupting the fallopian tubes through which the ova are discharged.

Removal of the ovaries (**oophorectomy, ovariectomy**) is undesirable since the ovaries also produce important sex hormones. The removal of the ovaries may be recommended in cases of malignancies, cysts, or other nonreversible complications (Pritchard and MacDonald 1984).

Removal of the uterus is called a **hysterectomy** and is sometimes necessary due to cancer or other uterine disease. Because of its risk of surgical complication, hysterectomy also is not an acceptable method of sterilization.

The most common method of female sterilization is **tubal ligation** ("tying the tubes"). Until recent years, this was usually performed by **laparotomy,** a surgical procedure consisting of a four- to five-inch incision in the abdominal wall, with a cutting and tying off of the ends of the fallopian tubes (figure 15.12a). With the tubes sealed, the ova are unable to pass from the ovaries into the uterus.

A newer tubal ligation procedure is the endoscopic method, which is often performed under local anesthesia. A lighted, telescopelike tubal instrument, the **laparoscope,** is inserted through a tiny incision into the abdomen (figure 15.12b). The fallopian tubes are located and are cauterized (burned), clipped, sutured, or tied off. When done through the navel, no scar is visible.

laparoscopy
(lap''ah-ros'ko-pe)

hysteroscopy
(his''ter-os'ko-pe)

vasectomy
(vah-sek'to-me)

culdoscopy
(kul-dos'ko-pe)

Endoscopic methods vary depending on where the surgical instrument enters the body: a **laparoscopy** involves entry through an abdominal incision; a **culdoscopy** involves entry through the dome of the vagina; and a **hysteroscopy** involves entry through the vagina and uterus. Because the incision may be closed through a single stitch, the procedure is often referred to as "Band-Aid" sterilization. The woman is usually discharged from the hospital a few hours later (Pritchard and MacDonald 1984; Boston Women's Health Book Collective 1976).

Overall, the success rate of tubal ligation is almost 100 percent. Studies have shown the failure rate to be 0.04 percent (Boston Women's Health Book Collective 1976; Hatcher et al. 1984).

The advantage of tubal ligation is that it is a one-time procedure with no long-term side effects. Also, women who have had tubal ligations are able to enjoy sexual intercourse without any preparation or without fear of pregnancy.

A disadvantage of tubal ligation is that, as with any surgery, there is some risk, although minimal. Another disadvantage is that the procedure is generally nonreversible. A woman should not use this method if she might want to bear children at some future time. About one in one hundred sterilized women request reversal, of which half may be turned down for various medical-psychological reasons. About half of those who undergo restoration surgery actually become pregnant (Gregg 1981).

Another disadvantage is that tubal ligation may involve some psychological complications for some women. Some women, for example, equate fertility with personal worth. This may be especially true for the woman who has enjoyed having children. Other women may fear that their infertility from tubal ligation may prevent their husband from viewing them as a real woman anymore and that he might leave for a fertile woman. Others worry that there might be physical consequences, such as dried up and wrinkled skin. Some women may feel angry at their having to undergo sterilization, rather than their husband consenting to a vasectomy. The power to reproduce is a deep-felt emotion in many women.

Male Sterilization

Male sterilization can be accomplished either by castration or vasectomy. **Castration** (the removal of both testes) is not performed on healthy males since, in addition to producing sperm, the testes are the primary source of male sex hormones. A man who lacked these hormones would lose sexual desire and potency. Today, castration is reserved for treatment of certain diseases, such as cancer of the testes.

Vasectomy is minor surgery that consists of severing the vas deferens, the tubule through which sperm travel from each testis to the genital passage. Requiring only small cuts on each side of the scrotum, vasectomy can be performed in a physician's office under local anesthesia (figure 15.13).

Figure 15.13 Male sterilization, or vasectomy. The vas deferens is severed, and the ends are either tied or cauterized, preventing sperm from being ejaculated.

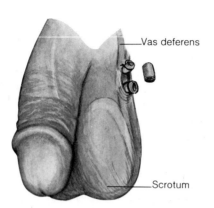

Vas deferens

Scrotum

The procedure does not affect the man's ability to gain erection, to produce ejaculate, or to enjoy orgasm. The ejaculate simply contains no sperm. Sperm cells remain in the testes and epididymis, disintegrate, and are absorbed by blood vessels. Since the bulk of semen comes from the prostate gland and seminal vesicles (neither of which are affected by the surgery) and since sperm cells make up only about 3 percent of a man's semen, the total volume of ejaculate is virtually unchanged.

Sperm do not disappear from the semen immediately after a vasectomy. Many sperm are stored in the vas deferens above the site of surgery, and only some of these sperm leave the vas deferens with each ejaculation. Thus, another method of conception control must be used for six to eight weeks after vasectomy. Only after a man's semen has been shown to contain no sperm can he be considered sterile.

Overall, the success rate of vasectomy is better than 99 percent, with a failure rate of 0.15 percent (Boston Women's Health Book Collective 1976). Failure is due to the two cut ends of the vas deferens growing back together again, incomplete closure of the vas deferens, or unprotected intercourse before all sperm have disappeared from the ejaculate.

The advantages of male sterilization are that it is a one-time procedure, does not require hospitalization, and permits the man to resume normal activity almost immediately. Surgical complications are very uncommon, minor, and treatable. Sterilization allows the man to have intercourse without using any other method or preparation and has no effect on his sexual desire or ability.

The primary disadvantage of male sterilization is that it is generally irreversible. Over half of all vasectomized men develop sperm antibodies that destroy any sperm the men may produce. Only about 30 to 50 percent of sterilized men can be restored to fertility, although some physicians cite higher success rates. It is believed that the longer the period of time between vasectomy and the attempted reversal, the lower the success rate. A man should not use this method if he might wish to someday father children.

Another disadvantage of a vasectomy for some men are psychological consequences. Some men, even though informed, are still anxious about the possible effects of a vasectomy on their sexual performance. Some men view their genitals as central to their anatomy and see the ability to create pregnancy as a sign of their masculinity. A vasectomy, then, may be considered an attack on their manhood. Some men equate virility with fertility and fear becoming impotent. Men who have had past sexual problems may not be good candidates for vasectomy due to their being more apt to develop psychological impotence or other sexual dysfunctions after surgery. Some marriage relationships may be affected if the man, after vasectomy, expects special gratitude from the wife for his sacrificial surgery and feels he does not receive it.

---

1. Compare sterilization with contraception (the pill, condom, IUD, diaphragm, cervical cap, spermicides) in terms of reversibility, effectiveness, and adverse physical factors.
2. If you and your partner were considering sterilization, which partner would you prefer seeing sterilized? Why?
3. Can you list some reasons why sterilization is as popular a method as it is?
4. If you and your partner were considering sterilization, what might be your feelings about the outside chances of wanting a child sometime in the future?

Abortion

The removal or expulsion of a growing embryo or fetus from a pregnant woman's uterus early in pregnancy, before the fetus can survive on its own, is called an **abortion.** A natural abortion, commonly called a **miscarriage,** or **spontaneous abortion,** is a spontaneous termination of pregnancy by the body. An estimated 15 percent of all pregnancies between the fourth and twentieth weeks of gestation (embryo/fetal development) end in spontaneous abortion (Pritchard and MacDonald 1984). An **induced abortion** is the expulsion of the embryo or fetus by artificial means. More than 30 percent of all pregnancies in the United States are now terminated by legal, induced abortions (National Center for Health Statistics 1981).

To whom the decision to abort a pregnancy should be given has been historically debated. In 1973, the United States Supreme Court ruled that the fetus is "potential life" and not a "person" and that, as such, the fetus does not have a "right to life." The Court stated that the Constitution gives a woman the right to have an

Pro-Choice Versus Pro-Life

Whether or not a woman has the right to abort the embryo or fetus she is carrying is a highly controversial issue. Adding to the heat of the debate has been the use of emotionally loaded labels, such as pro-choice and pro-life.

Those who favor a woman retaining this right of choice are generally identified as *pro-choice*. Pro-choice individuals believe that abortion should be a strictly personal matter and that a pregnant woman has the right to decide for herself whether or not to have an abortion because she has an undeniable right to control her own body. They contend that this right entitles her to the support and advice of trusted friends and professionals. They also believe that the woman should be subject to no interference from the state, church, or any other self-appointed guardian of public morality. In addition, they argue that a pregnant woman has a right to easy access to a qualified physician who is an expert at performing abortion, regardless of the woman's ability to pay for the procedure.

Pro-life, or right-to-life, proponents hold that from the moment a sperm cell fertilizes an egg, new life has been created. They contend that the developing embryo or fetus is a separate growing organism, and as such cannot be considered an integral part of the mother's body. They hold that this developing embryo is not only human but that it also has legal rights, including the right to life, at any stage of its development. Rejecting abortion-on-demand as a method of curtailing population increases, pro-life individuals argue that abortion not only poses physical and emotional hazards to a woman but that it constitutes a denial of basic moral and religious principles. They view the "quality of life" ethic, in which a person decides that the quality of his or her life takes precedence over the quality of someone else's life, as discriminatory. Such an ethic, they contend, contrasts with the "absolute value of life" ethic as characterized by Hippocratic, Jewish, and Christian philosophy.

abortion during the first six months of pregnancy, the same right she would have to any other minor surgery. The Court ruled that during the first three months of pregnancy (first trimester), the abortion decision is left to the woman and the medical judgment of her attending physician. During the second three months of pregnancy (second trimester, months four to six), due to the greater danger of complications, the state may specifically control the conditions under which an abortion is performed. During the third three months (third trimester, or months seven to nine), the state may, if it wishes, restrict performance of abortion to those cases in which the life or health of the mother is endangered since, by this time, the fetus often has developed enough to survive on its own if born.

The United States Supreme Court also has held that a woman's right to privacy overrides any state interest in using abortion statutes to regulate sexual conduct.

Abortion Methods

There are several widely used methods of medically performed abortion. Which method is used is determined somewhat by how far along the pregnancy has advanced.

endometrial aspiration
(en''do-me'tre-al
as''pī-ra'-shun)

curettage
(ku''rĕ-tahzh')

Endometrial Aspiration

Often known as menstrual regulation, **endometrial aspiration** involves a small suction tube that is used to remove the uterine lining and any uterine contents. Because of the small caliber of the suction tube, it is usually not necessary to dilate the cervical canal.

Offered in some women's clinics, endometrial aspiration is performed anytime the menstrual flow is due up until pregnancy has been confirmed. A woman on whom this method is used thus may or may not be pregnant. For this reason, some clinicians refuse to practice it (Boston's Women Health Book Collective 1976).

Very Early Abortion

Also called early uterine evacuation, very early abortion is performed *after* a positive pregnancy test until seven to eight weeks from the beginning of the last menstrual period (LMP). Very early abortion is a procedure similar to an endometrial aspiration, but it is more costly and is performed in a physician's office (Boston Women's Health Book Collective 1976).

Vacuum Aspiration

Vacuum aspiration, or vacuum curettage (surgical scraping or cleaning), is the most commonly used method of first trimester abortion. Commonly performed from the seventh through the twelfth weeks LMP, vacuum aspiration accounts for almost 95 percent of all abortions performed in the United States (Centers for Disease Control 1980). Once the woman has been pregnant for more than twelve weeks, the fetus becomes too large and the uterus too soft for vacuum aspiration to be performed safely. Although vacuum aspiration is one of the safest of all surgical operations, frequent side effects include light bleeding and menstruallike cramps.

The vacuum aspiration procedure involves dilating the woman's cervical canal and inserting a small, plastic tube-type curette attached to a suction pump through the cervical opening into the cavity of the uterus. The contents of the uterus are then sucked out (figure 15.14).

Dilation and Curettage

Dilation and curettage (D and C) is a surgical procedure in which the physician first dilates the cervical canal and then inserts a small metal spoon-shaped curette into the cavity of the uterus (figure 15.15). With it, the fetus and placenta are scraped loose, and the fetal tissue is removed with forceps. A D and C is performed under local or general anesthesia, and hospitalization usually is required since there is risk of uterine perforation, bleeding, and infection. A D and C can be safely performed through the fifteenth week LMP (Boston Women's Health Book Collective 1976).

D and Cs are also routinely used to scrape the inside of the uterus in cases of spontaneous abortion and suspected uterine malignancies.

Figure 15.14 Vacuum aspiration, or suction abortion. (a) Removal of fetal material. (b and c) As fetal material is removed, the uterus contracts back to its original size.

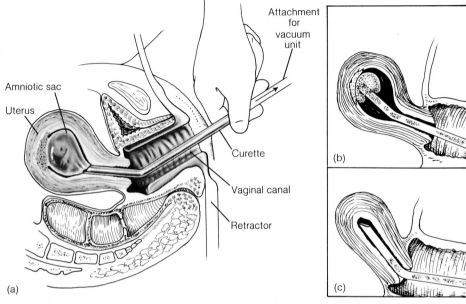

Amniotic sac

Uterus

Attachment for vacuum unit

Curette

Vaginal canal

Retractor

(a)

(b)

(c)

Figure 15.15 Dilation and curettage (D and C). Side view showing dilator opening the cervix through which a curette is inserted to scrape the uterine lining.

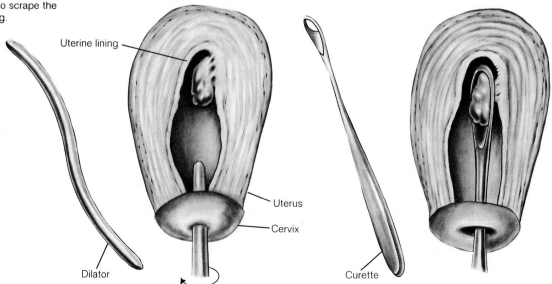

Uterine lining

Uterus

Cervix

Dilator

Curette

instillation
(in''stil-la'shun)

Instillation Abortions

After the twelfth week LMP, the fetus becomes too large to be removed by vacuum aspiration. The safest way to perform an abortion during the second trimester is to induce uterine contractions that stimulate the uterus to expel the fetus and placenta (induce a miscarriage). Contractions may be induced either by the administration of saline (salt) or prostaglandin **instillations.**

In the *saline* method of abortion, the concentrated salt solution is injected (instilled) through the abdominal wall into the amniotic sac surrounding the fetus. This induces uterine contractions, and hours later, the fetus is expelled. Since the risks of saline injection are comparable to those of natural childbirth, the woman must be hospitalized during the entire time between the injection and the passing of the fetus.

The naturally occurring hormonelike substances called **prostaglandins** can also be used to induce abortion. Injected into the abdomen in the same manner as saline, these hormones induce contractions of smooth muscle organs, such as the uterus, which causes the expulsion of the fetus. This method, as with the saline method, requires a hospital stay. Prostaglandin instillation sometimes has such side effects as nausea, vomiting, and diarrhea.

Instillation abortions involve such risky complications as hemorrhaging, retained placentas, and infection. Since pregnancy can be confirmed at six weeks LMP, and since vacuum aspiration is generally possible up through twelve weeks LMP, it is seldom necessary to resort to instillation abortion. Only about 4 percent of all abortions in the United States are performed this way (Centers for Disease Control 1980).

Dilation and Evacuation

Dilation and evacuation (D and E) is an alternate to instillation abortion. As with instillation, a D and E is a second-trimester method used between the thirteenth and twentieth weeks LMP. The procedure is performed under general anesthesia and in a hospital.

A D and E first involves dilation of the cervix. Then, depending on its size and the exact stage of its development, the fetus is removed by a combination of vacuum aspiration and the use of forceps to remove tissue the aspirator has been unable to extract. This may be followed by a scraping of the uterine wall with a metal curette.

Although the woman usually is hospitalized for two days, a D and E usually is less time consuming than instillation abortions and involves fewer complications. A disadvantage, however, is that the risk of cervical injury and inadvertent uterine perforation is increased among D and E patients.

hysterotomy
(his"ter-ot'o-me)

Hysterotomy

Hysterotomy is the surgical cutting into the uterus to remove its contents and is similar to a cesarean section delivery. Performed from sixteen through twenty-four weeks LMP, this method comprises major surgery and involves higher risks than abortion methods already discussed. The hysterotomy procedure involves making an incision into the abdominal and uterine walls and removing the fetus and placenta. A hysterotomy may be performed when an instillation fails to induce labor, but hysterotomies generally are infrequent. Less than 1 percent of all abortions are performed by hysterotomy (Centers for Disease Control 1980).

Incidence of Induced Abortion

The incidence of induced abortion in the United States is around thirty-six abortions per every one hundred live births (or more than one abortion for every three live births). Women who obtain abortions are most often young (about two-thirds are under twenty-five years of age), white (over two-thirds), unmarried (about 75 percent), and have had no live births (almost 60 percent). Almost one-third are teenagers. Also, nearly three-fourths of the women who have abortions have had no previous abortion (Centers for Disease Control 1980).

Curettage procedures, the most common abortion methods, are almost entirely performed during the first trimester (less than twelve weeks of pregnancy). Over half of all women seeking abortions do so at less than eight weeks of pregnancy (Centers for Disease Control 1980).

Abortion Complications

Abortions are not without possible complications. These may be both medical (physical) and psychological.

The medical complications of an abortion may include perforation of the uterine wall by instruments used in curettage and vacuum abortions, damage to the cervix that reduces its ability (competency) to retain the fetus until term in the uterus in a subsequent pregnancy, hemorrhaging, infections, and peritonitis (inflammation of the lining of the abdominal cavity).

In terms of the danger of induced abortion to a woman's life, legal abortions are relatively safe. The rate of mortality (death) from such abortion procedures is about 0.6 per 100,000 abortions, compared with a mortality rate from natural childbirth of 7 per 100,000. The risk is least when the abortion is performed by vacuum aspiration at less than eight weeks of pregnancy. It rises noticeably when the abortion is delayed until the second trimester (Centers for Disease Control 1980).

Because an abortion is a more highly emotional experience than other methods of controlling birth, it may present more than the usual risk to the woman's psychological well-being. The longer a woman is pregnant before the abortion has a bearing on possible effects. Early abortions tend to cause less emotional stress than abortions performed later in pregnancy.

Personal factors relate to a woman's reactions to the abortion: her values about life, her religious points of view, whether she is being pressured into the abortion, the nature of her relationship to the man who impregnated her, the support she feels from family and friends, or whether she is married or single.

A woman may have some very negative feelings. She may need to counter fears of abandonment by her partner, of whether she will be able to have a later pregnancy if desired, or of having another unwanted pregnancy. She may feel anger at her partner who impregnated her or at her parents or her physician for not informing her of the risks of intercourse. She may feel sadness, loneliness, and guilt.

Not all of these reactions are exclusive to the woman; the male partner may feel some of the same feelings. He may want the child, may not be consulted over the abortion decision, and may feel guilty over the burden the abortion places on the woman or over having abandoned the woman once her pregnancy became known to him.

It is very important that a woman considering an abortion receive counseling so that she has an opportunity to process her values, feelings, and needs. The man also should receive counseling if he is willing. There should be opportunity for open communication between the partners if at all possible. This can aid in the decision making and may serve to provide some of the added support the woman will need both during and following the abortion. The input of both partners is needed if they are interested in continuing their relationship.

---

1. How do you view the merits of abortion, pro and con? Give some examples.
2. If a close friend of yours asked your advice because she was unmarried and pregnant and considering an abortion, what would you say to her?

Conception Control among Teenagers and Young Adults

Knowing about conception control and having access to contraceptives is thought by some to be ample motivation for young people to protect themselves against unwanted pregnancy. Yet, a 1979 national survey of teenagers indicates that they are having more sexual intercourse with less protection and that more pregnancies are resulting (Zelnick and Kantner 1980; Green and Poteteiger 1978).

Phases of Conception Control
In an analysis of sexually active young women, Miller (1980) found that they passed through four phases of conception control: abstinence, risk taking, use of nonprescription methods, and finally, use of prescription methods.

The first phase, *abstinence,* does not require contraception since there is no risk of conception.

The second phase marks the beginning of intercourse, or *risk taking.* Even with pregnancy as a definite risk, many young people begin having intercourse without using any birth control method. Zelnick and Kantner (1980) found that about half of fifteen- and sixteen-year-olds having intercourse for the first time did not use any method. There is evidence that such nonuse of contraceptives by a significant percentage of young people continues into their college years (Maxwell et al. 1977). Confirming the risk is the fact that 50 percent of all first premarital teenage pregnancies occur within six months of first sexual intercourse. Of those who use no contraception at all, two-thirds become pregnant by the end of two years following first coitus (Zabin 1980). Further, an estimated 70 percent of all teenage conceptions appear to be unintended (Centers for Disease Control 1980).

There are various reasons behind such nonuse of contraceptives. Some teenagers engage in a series of denials: they deny that intercourse will occur, that they know when it will take place, that pregnancy can result, that contraceptives work, or that they are personally responsible for using contraceptives (Kantner and Zelnick 1973; Maxwell et al. 1977). Some young people fear the shame and embarrassment they would feel if someone else discovered their use of contraceptives and the resulting implication that they were having intercourse (Lindemann 1974). Some run the risk of pregnancy to demonstrate their fertility and to thereby prove their womanhood or manhood. Other teenagers are unwilling to delay their desire for sexual gratification until proper contraceptive methods can be used. Some believe that nonuse of contraceptives will demonstrate their love for their partner or that an unplanned pregnancy will force their partner into commitment. Another reason why some young people risk pregnancy is that they refuse to acknowledge themselves as being sexual and thus see no need of using the protection that sexually active people are expected to use. These individuals, who tend to be more anxious and negative about sex, are the ones who are more likely to risk an unwanted pregnancy (Byrne 1977). Taking risks because they believe that it might attract the kind of supportive attention they have been seeking from their parents is another reason given by some young persons for nonuse of contraceptives.

Miller (1980) describes the third phase as one in which the couple—perhaps after a pregnancy scare—begins seriously using contraceptives for the first time. The couple usually starts by trying nonprescription methods—condoms, withdrawal, foam, or the rhythm method. Out of a hesitancy to assert her sexuality, the female relies more upon the male at this phase to employ a male method. Even so, the couple may find birth control difficult to stick with consistently at this phase because some young people tend to be impulsive, oriented to the present, and able to rationalize their sexual activities (Connolly 1978).

According to Miller, young people then tend to move into a fourth phase in which they switch to prescribed methods designed for females. This step seems to come within the context of commitment and availability to each other within a long-term relationship.

In one study, the gender roles the partners assumed had an effect on the conception control responsibility they took. Fox (1977) found that university men with traditional gender-role attitudes assumed a greater sense of responsibility, while women who held nontraditional gender-role attitudes assumed a greater sense of responsibility over what happened to them.

Parental Consent to Conception Control

The majority of minors who visit family planning clinics or medical facilities for contraceptives do so with their parents' knowledge and consent, according to a recent national study conducted by the Alan Guttmacher Institute (Torres, Forest, and Eisman 1980). At the same time, however, about a fourth of the minors surveyed said that they would not seek contraceptives from facilities that required parental notification and consent. Only 2 percent of those surveyed said that they would stop having sex if it became more difficult to obtain birth control. The researchers concluded that parental involvement in a minor's decision-making process regarding birth control can be encouraged without instituting requirements.

Some states have sought to institute or impose parental-consent requirements on contraceptive use by minors. The Guttmacher study revealed that 40 percent of abortion-providing facilities and 20 percent of family-planning agencies that dispense contraceptives have parental notification or consent requirements, despite United States Supreme Court decisions upholding the rights of mature minors to obtain contraceptive and abortion services.

1. How might a college education have any bearing on the four phases of teenage contraceptive use?
2. What do you think would happen to the incidence of teenage pregnancies if birth controls became harder for teenagers to obtain?
3. If you are sexually active, what kind of conception control do you use? For what reasons have you (or your partner) chosen to use this particular method?
4. How has the reading of this chapter affected your views on conception control?

Julie and I have been living together for almost a year now. When we first started dating, there was very little importance placed on sex. We really enjoyed just being together. After awhile, though, a problem did emerge. She would get really paranoid when our loving would get too close to the actual act of making love. I was worried that maybe she had been hurt by some idiot in the past. I loved her, and I wanted to be understanding. It turned out that she was worried about contraception—not any more than I! We talked about it for a long time. She couldn't go on the pill, so I volunteered to use condoms. Together, we checked out every method of contraception possible. Someday, we may want to marry and have children, but for now we are working together to keep our lovemaking as guilt- and risk-free as possible.

Summary

1. Of couples who are at risk of pregnancy in the United States, about 90 percent use some form of conception control. Reasons for conception control include preventing unwanted pregnancy, spacing pregnancies, limiting family size, giving a couple time for marital adjustment, protecting a woman's health, avoiding inherited diseases, and allowing the woman more independence.

    Some people oppose conception control on religious, racial, or ethnic grounds, while others point out the health risks of some of the conception control methods.

2. No one form of conception control is best for all persons. A method should be safe to the user, effective, easy to use, acceptable (medically, philosophically, and aesthetically), reversible, readily available at reasonable cost, and free from adverse effects on sex drive.

3. The effectiveness of any method is rated both in terms of its theoretical failure rate (when the device is used as it should be) and the actual use failure rate (when human error is added to device error).

4. The only male-designed contraceptive method available in the United States today is the condom. The condom is a sheath worn over the erect penis that prevents sperm from reaching the vagina. Condoms are inexpensive, safe, easily available, and convenient. Added advantages are their protection against sexually transmitted diseases and their reversibility with regard to male fertility.

5. One of the more promising male contraceptive substances, currently undergoing testing by the Food and Drug Administration, is the male pill that contains gossypol, a cottonseed meal extract.

6. Female-designed contraceptive methods include hormones (both oral and injectible), the intrauterine device (IUD), the diaphragm, the cervical cap, and spermicides.

7. The birth control pill consists of a combination of synthetic estrogen and progesterone. It is taken for twenty-one days each menstrual month and prevents ovulation.

8.   The intrauterine device (IUD) is a plastic object that may be wrapped in copper wire or may contain a progesterone-filled reservoir. When inserted into the uterus, the IUD prevents implantation.

9.   The diaphragm is a shallow, round dome of latex rubber surrounded by a spring rim. Fitted high in the vagina over the cervix, it prevents passage of sperm into the uterus.

10.   A cervical cap fits snugly over the cervix, where it blocks sperm passage into the uterus.

11.   Spermicidal agents (in foams, jellies, creams, sponges, and suppositories) kill sperm. When inserted into the vagina, they form a barrier against sperm.

12.   Methods of conception control shared by both partners include the rhythm methods, withdrawal, and abstinence.

13.   The rhythm methods are based on the fertile period (avoiding intercourse when a fertile ovum is present). The fertile period can be calculated by using the calendar, recording basal body temperature, and observing vaginal mucus secretions.

14.   Withdrawal is the removal of the penis from the vagina just prior to ejaculation to prevent sperm from reaching the uterus.

15.   Abstinence is the voluntary avoiding of coitus, thereby eliminating the chances of a pregnancy.

16.   Sterilization, or surgical interruption of the reproductive tract so that sex cells cannot be discharged, is the most effective method of conception control. Sterilization is done by tubal ligation or hysterectomy in the female and by vasectomy in the male.

17.   Abortion is the removal or expulsion of a growing embryo or fetus from the uterus. Spontaneous abortion (miscarriage) occurs in about 15 percent of all pregnancies, while more than 30 percent of all pregnancies in the United States today are terminated by induced abortion. During the first trimester, abortion may be done by endometrial aspiration, vacuum aspiration, or dilation and curettage (D and C). During the second trimester, abortion may be induced by instillations, or may be done by dilation and evacuation (D and E) or hysterotomy.

18.   Young people tend to pass through four phases of conception control: abstinence, risk taking (no protection), use of nonprescription methods, and use of prescription methods. The majority of teenage contraceptive users do so with their parents' knowledge and consent.

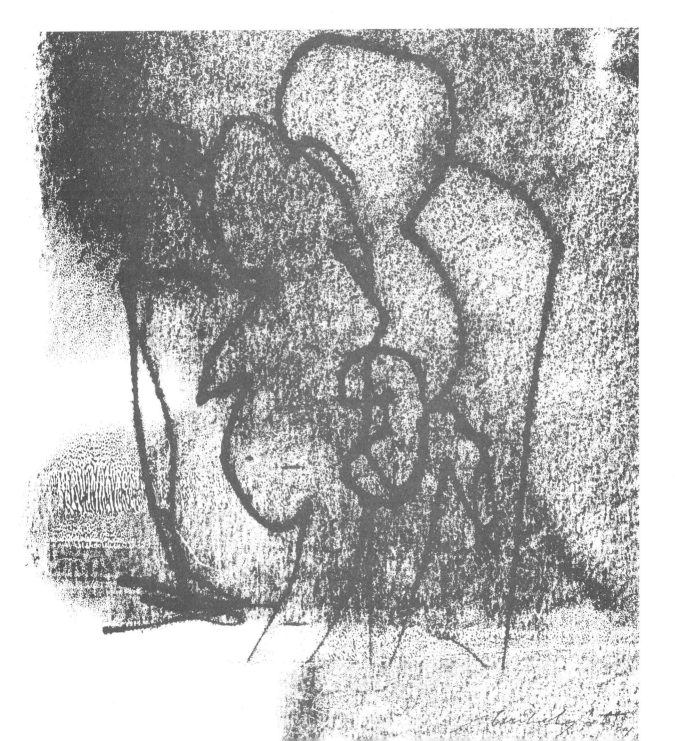

It seems like years since the doctor walked into the office and said, "Congratulations, Mrs. Miller. You're going to have a baby!" That was really only eight short months ago. I was happy and slim—now I'm happy and huge. I was so scared. I didn't know what to do or who to see. . . . I have never even changed a diaper, and now I'm about to become a mother!

I scoured the books on pregnancy, listened faithfully to my obstetrician, and laughed at the warnings of friends who'd been through it. I remember being so tired all the time during the first three months, and *sick!* The constant nausea really got to me, but I didn't want to take anything. Thank God that only lasted a few months. Then came the thrill of the baby's first movement. I still love to feel it move inside me.

Well, after studying hard and going to the childbirth classes, I feel like I'm finally prepared. I'm still scared, but with Joe at my side coaching all the way, I know we are going to have a beautiful baby.

Well, it's almost time. God, I'm scared. Jane's been so good during her pregnancy. I still remember when she came flying in the door, throwing her bottle of prenatal vitamins at me giggling, "Guess what? We're pregnant!" What a nut.

I felt so helpless in the beginning when she was always so nauseous. Then things got better. I love to feel the way her tummy wiggles beneath my hands as our child stretches and kicks inside of her.

We've worked hard in preparing for this baby. The childbirth classes have brought Jane and I closer together. Now we are about to put it all together and have us the best darn baby ever! I'm excited, but scared, too. I know what I'm supposed to do during the birth, but I don't think anything can really prepare me for what's to come after . . . being a father.

zona pellucida
(zo'nah pel-lu'sid-ah)

Earlier chapters have pointed out that most sexual activity is motivated by our desire for personal pleasure rather than our intent to initiate pregnancy. But many people do become parents at some time in their lives. In this chapter, we look at conception, pregnancy, birth, and the early part of infancy. Our emphasis is on producing a healthy, happy, wanted baby.

Of course, one brief chapter cannot serve as a complete guide to pregnancy, and any woman planning a pregnancy will want to work closely with a qualified physician.

Conception and Fetal Development

Pregnancy is the condition of having an offspring developing within the uterus of a female. It results from the fertilization of an ovum by a sperm, a process called **conception.**

Physiology of Conception

Before fertilization can occur, an ovum must be released from the ovary by ovulation and be carried into the fallopian tube. This ovum must then come into contact with a sperm. During sexual intercourse, semen containing sperm is usually deposited by ejaculation in the vagina near the cervix of the uterus. To reach the ovum, the sperm are transported upward through the uterus and fallopian tubes (figure 16.1).

The sperm transport mechanism is relatively inefficient. Of the 300 to 500 million sperm deposited in the vagina by a single ejaculation, only several hundred sperm ever reach the ovum.

The first sperm reach the upper portions of the fallopian tubes within an hour following sexual intercourse, but sperm must remain in the female reproductive tract for four to six hours to become capable of fertilizing an ovum. This is called **capacitation** and is a chemical adaptation of the sperm to the fluids of the female reproductive tract. Inability of a man's sperm to capacitate to a specific female can cause infertility between them.

Fertilization is the union of the sperm cell nucleus with the nucleus of the ovum. This occurs when one sperm penetrates the zona pellucida (the jellylike coating surrounding the ovum) with the aid of an enzyme released from the sperm head.

Normally, although hundreds of sperm may reach an ovum, only one will fertilize it (figure 16.2). This is because once a sperm nucleus has penetrated an ovum, the ovum's membrane and surrounding coat of cells undergo rapid chemical changes and produce a fertilization membrane that is impermeable to the entrance of other sperm.

After the nucleus of a sperm enters an ovum, it fuses with the nucleus of the ovum and forms the nucleus of the first cell of the new embryo (zygote), and fertilization is complete.

Figure 16.1 Paths of ovum and sperm through female reproductive tract.

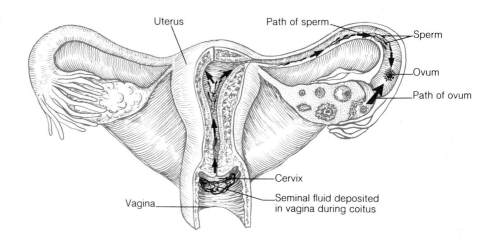

Uterus

Path of sperm

Sperm

Ovum

Path of ovum

Cervix

Seminal fluid deposited in vagina during coitus

Vagina

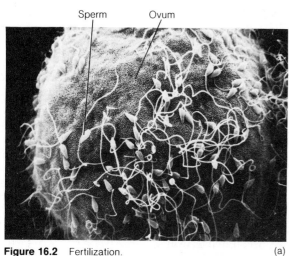

Sperm   Ovum

(a)

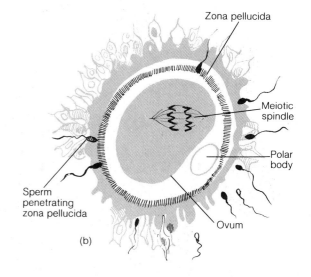

Zona pellucida

Meiotic spindle

Polar body

Sperm penetrating zona pellucida

Ovum

(b)

Figure 16.2 Fertilization. (a) Although many sperm reach an ovum, only one sperm will fertilize it. (b) One sperm penetrates the zona pellucida surrounding an ovum with the aid of an enzyme released from the sperm head.

Fertilization normally occurs when the ovum is in the upper one-third of the fallopian tube within eight to twelve hours after ovulation (Silber 1981).

Implantation

Immediately after fertilization, as the zygote is being transported down the fallopian tube toward the uterus, rapid cell division begins (see figure 16.3). This type of cell division is unique because the cells being produced do not grow or increase in size between divisions. Consequently, the cells become smaller and smaller; this allows the developing mass of cells to pass down through the very small fallopian tube. This type of cell division is termed **cleavage** and results in a hollow ball of cells, the **blastocyst.** Three to four days after fertilization, the newly formed blastocyst enters the uterus.

After entering the uterus, the blastocyst floats around for another three or four days before attaching to the endometrium of the uterus (about seven to eight days after conception). The process of attachment is called **implantation.** At the time of implantation, the endometrium is in its postovulatory phase and is soft and spongy.

Figure 16.3 Fertilization, cleavage, and implantation. Fertilization takes place in the upper third of the fallopian tube. Cleavage occurs in the fallopian tube while the fertilized ovum travels to the uterus. Then the embryo implants into the lining of the uterus.

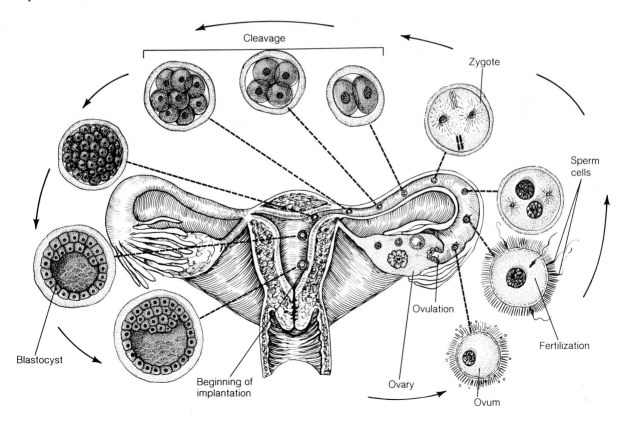

Cleavage

Zygote

Sperm cells

Ovulation

Fertilization

Blastocyst

Beginning of implantation

Ovary

Ovum

ectopic
(ek-top'ik)

Figure 16.4 Structures of the placenta. The mother's blood flows through the maternal blood vessels. The fetal blood flows through the fetal blood vessels that are within the intervillous spaces where the exchanges of oxygen, carbon dioxide, and food take place between the mother's blood in the spaces and the fetal blood in the vessels.

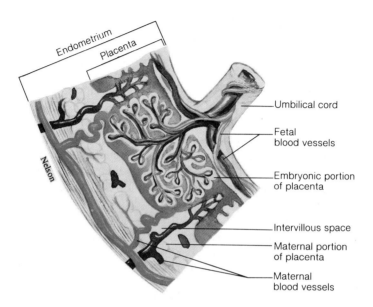

This spongy condition allows cells of the implanting blastocyst to release an enzyme that literally "eats a hole" into the tissue. The blastocyst then becomes completely buried in the endometrial wall of the uterus.

The implanted blastocyst grows in and among the maternal tissues to form a complex structure called the **placenta,** which allows the exchange of materials between the blood of the mother and the blood of the embryo. In time, the placenta attaches the embryo to the uterine wall; exchanges nutrients, gases, and wastes between the maternal blood and the embryonic blood; and secretes hormones important in maintaining the pregnancy to birth (figure 16.4).

Implantation of the blastocyst anywhere other than in the uterus is called an **ectopic pregnancy.** Almost all ectopic pregnancies occur in the fallopian tubes.

Ectopic pregnancy is believed to be caused by conditions that slow the movement of the ovum down the tube or by increased receptivity of the tubal lining to the fertilized ovum. The embryo in an ectopic pregnancy usually dies. The mother may feel severe abdominal pains and, if hemorrhaging occurs, will show vaginal bleeding. In any event, the affected fallopian tube must be removed. This does not preclude later pregnancies, however, since another fallopian tube is still available for ovum transport.

Fetal Development

The first seven to eight weeks of development are considered the *embryonic period,* and the developing human is called an **embryo.** After the second month (seven to eight weeks), the term for the developing human changes from embryo to **fetus.** Medically, the nine-month (thirty-eight weeks or 266 days) span of pregnancy is divided into three, three-month segments called *trimesters.*

First Trimester

After implantation of the blastocyst in the uterus, growth progresses steadily. By the fourth week of development (end of the first month), the mother's menstrual period is one week overdue. Even though the mother may not yet know that she is pregnant, the embryo's heart and circulation have begun to function. The embryo's body is elongated, tapering off into a small, pointed tail. The nervous system and spine, with vertebrae, have begun to form, as have the throat and face. The embryo has grown to about one-fifth of an inch by the thirtieth day of its existence.

During the second month, development accelerates, and the embryo grows about a quarter of an inch a week and looks more and more human every day. The rudimentary arms and legs form. The tissues that will become the ribs move into place, muscles begin forming, and just below the surface the skin is developing. By the sixth week, the arms, legs, body, and face have taken shape, and the embryo is about one-half inch long.

By the third month, all of the fetus's internal organs, such as the liver, kidneys, and intestines, have begun limited functioning. The fetus is now about three inches in length.

Second Trimester

The second trimester begins with the start of the fourth month of pregnancy. At this point, all body structures are complete; everything is present that will be found in the full-term baby. During the second trimester, the fetus grows, details are refined, and functions are exercised. External body parts, including fingernails, eyebrows, and eyelashes become clearly visible. The skin is covered by a fine, downlike hair (baby hair). The fetus now has a human face with eyelids half closed, as in someone who is just about to fall asleep. Hands begin to grip, and feet try their first gentle kicks. Usually, the mother can feel fetal movements (termed **quickening**) by the end of the fourth month.

During the fifth month, the rate of growth decreases somewhat because fat begins to be deposited. The legs achieve their final relative proportions.

By the sixth month, the fetus's outline becomes more rounded, suggesting the chubbiness of a newborn. Weight has increased to over one pound by the end of the sixth month. Occasionally, a fetus of this weight and age survives if born, but most succumb to respiratory problems.

Table 16.1 Monthly Embryonic and Fetal Growth Changes.

End of Month	Approximate Size and Weight	Representative Changes
First Trimester		
1	3/16 inch	Backbone and vertebral canal form; leg and arm buds begin; heart forms and starts beating; body systems start to form.
2	1¼ inches 1/30 ounce	Eyes form far apart; eyelids fuse and nose is flat; ossification of bones begins; limbs become distinct as arms and legs; fingers form; major blood vessels form; internal body systems continue to develop.
3	3 inches 1 ounce	Eyes develop underneath fused eyelids; nose bridge forms; external parts of ears form; arms and legs are fully formed; nails start to develop; heartbeat can be detected.
Second Trimester		
4	6½ to 7 inches 4 ounces	Head is much larger than rest of body; face takes on human features; hair appears on head; joints begin to form between bones.
5	10 to 12 inches ½ to 1 pound	Head becomes less disproportionate to rest of body; fine baby hair is found all over body; body systems show rapid development.
6	11 to 14 inches 1¼ to 1½ pounds	Head becomes birth size; eyelids separate and eyelashes form; skin is still wrinkled and pink.
Third Trimester		
7	13 to 17 inches 2½ to 3 pounds	Head and body become more proportionate; premature baby is now capable of survival.
8	16½ to 18 inches 4½ to 5 pounds	Fat is deposited under the skin; skin is less wrinkled; testes descend into scrotum in male; bones in head are still soft; five-and-a-half-pound fetus is considered full term.
9	20 inches 7–7½ pounds	Additional fat accumulates under skin; baby hair is shed; nails extend to tips of fingers or beyond; further time in uterus will mainly just cause the baby to be heavier.

Third Trimester

The third trimester begins with the start of the seventh month of pregnancy. The fetus's skin is now becoming smoother as fat is deposited. The eyelids, which fused together earlier, reopen. The testes of males descend into the scrotum. A fetus born during the third trimester commonly survives, given the proper medical care and facilities.

melanin
(mel'ah-nin)

Predicting the Birth Date

The ideal way to estimate the date on which a baby will be born is to know the date the baby was conceived. Of course, this is not always possible. However, a good approximation of conception and birth can be calculated. If fourteen days are added to the date of the *onset* of the last menstrual period, this date can be used as the approximate date of conception. The expected date of birth can be estimated by adding 266 days to this date of conception.

The average pregnancy lasts 280 days (266 + 14), calculated from the first day of the last menstrual period. Ninety-five percent of all babies are born between the 266th and 294th day. Thus, most babies are born on this date or not more than fourteen days in either direction. Women who usually have menstrual cycles of more than twenty-eight days also have longer pregnancies.

As the mother is now finding out, the fetus is not always asleep while waiting to be born. Rest periods alternate with periods of intense activity. The baby exercises its arms and legs, bends and stretches its body, sucks, swallows, and makes respiratory movements now and then. As the fetus grows, the space around it becomes smaller and smaller, so the baby feels every motion its mother makes. The baby falls asleep when rocked and wakes up when everything is quiet. It is startled by sudden noises but calms down again when its mother and father talk softly to one another.

During the ninth month, the fetus reaches eighteen to twenty inches in length. Its skin is smooth, and the body appears chubby because of the accumulation of fat under the skin. The reddishness of the skin fades to a bluish pink. This is also true of fetuses of even the darkest-skinned parents, because melanin (the pigment that produces skin color) is not produced until the skin is exposed to light. Thus, it is often difficult to determine the race of a newborn child by its skin color.

At the end of the ninth month, the fetus is said to be full term. The skin has lost its baby hair, the scalp is usually covered with hair, and the fingers and toes have well-developed nails. The fetus usually is positioned upside down (**vertex position**) and is ready to be born.

Table 16.1 summarizes the monthly embryonic and fetal changes that occur during pregnancy.

1. Why can only one sperm fertilize an ovum? Why is this important?
2. Why do you think that the expectant mother's abstention from harmful drugs would be especially crucial during the first trimester?

Pregnancy

Most women find pregnancy to be one of the most special experiences of their lives. To help ensure that the pregnancy reaches a successful conclusion—the delivery of a healthy baby—it is important that the pregnancy be detected early and that the mother initiates a program of careful prenatal care.

Detecting a Pregnancy

For the vast majority of women, the first indication that they may be pregnant is the absence of the menstrual period at the expected time. If a woman has relatively regular menstrual periods, absence of a period for one week or more is considered presumptive evidence of pregnancy. Other women will have either a very light menstrual flow or just experience "spotting" (irregular bleeding) as an indication of pregnancy. Other symptoms that help in diagnosing pregnancy include breast tenderness, nausea, vomiting, or feelings of tiredness and changes in appetite (may increase or decrease).

A gynecologist can usually detect pregnancy by an internal (pelvic) examination within two weeks of the first missed menstrual period. The internal examination is helpful since the mouth of the uterus becomes soft and takes on a bluish-color when a woman is pregnant. Also, the uterus itself expands, is rounder, and becomes softer.

If the pelvic examination is not conclusive, the physician can conduct any one of a number of pregnancy tests. Table 16.2 outlines some of the more common pregnancy tests. A number of these tests show the presence of **human chorionic gonadotropin** (HCG) hormone, which is secreted by the tissues of the implanted embryo. HCG is detectable in a testing solution from about ten days to about a month after conception.

Besides the professionally administered tests, there are pregnancy testing kits available in pharmacies or drugstores. These kits usually show when a woman is *not* pregnant—*if the kit directions are followed exactly.* However, they may be unreliable in showing if a woman *is* pregnant, and the woman should still see a physician to substantiate the kit's findings. Most physicians feel that it is much better for the woman to see her physician or clinic and have a professional examination and test administered by a laboratory rather than relying on these kits.

Prenatal Care

Prenatal care is essential for promoting the health of both the mother and the fetus. The prenatal care of a physician is important for detecting or forecasting potential problems in a pregnancy, but the ultimate welfare of the developing fetus depends upon the prenatal care that the mother gives to herself in observing good nutrition, maintaining good health, and getting adequate rest, routine health care, exercise, and childbirth education.

Table 16.2   Pregnancy Tests.

Name of Test	Description
Antitrypsin tests (Bergmann-Meyer test, Fuld-Goss test, or Muller-Jockmann test)	The ability of the blood serum to inhibit the action of trypsin (an enzyme that digests proteins) is increased with pregnancy. A woman's blood is tested to see if trypsin is unable to digest protein, showing that she is pregnant.
Ascheim-Zondek test (AZT or A-Z test)	The urine of a woman is injected under the skin of an immature female mouse. If the woman is pregnant, the HCG in her urine causes the ovaries of the mouse to swell, congest, hemorrhage, and produce a premature maturation of the ovarian follicles. The mouse is dissected to observe the ovaries and confirm the pregnancy.
Early pregnancy test (EPT or home pregnancy test)	Three drops of urine from the woman are added to a test tube containing a mixture of HCG antiserum from rabbits and HCG-coated red blood cells from sheep. Purified water is added and the mixture shaken for ten seconds and then allowed to stand for two hours. A brown donut-shaped ring with a hole in the center forms at the bottom of the test tube if the woman is pregnant. A reddish-brown residue will settle to the bottom of the test tube if the woman is not pregnant.
Friedman's test (Friedman-Lapham test, rabbit test)	The urine of a woman is injected into a female rabbit. If the woman is pregnant, the HCG in the urine causes the formation of corpus lutea and corpora hemorrhagica in the ovaries of a nonestrus rabbit. The rabbit is then dissected to observe the ovaries and confirm the test.
Galli Mainine test (frog test)	Urine from a woman is injected into a normal male frog or toad. If the woman is pregnant, the HCG in the urine causes the frog to produce sperm, which can be detected in the frog's urine.
Radioimmunoassay test	This test can be modified to determine any number of substances in the blood or urine, and is probably the most sensitive and earliest pregnancy test that can be performed. Blood, or urine, from a woman is mixed with radioactive materials that bind to the HCG hormone. The material is then mixed with an antibody that shows whether or not the woman is pregnant.

Source: From *Dorland's Medical Dictionary*, 26th ed. © 1981 W. B. Saunders Co., Philadelphia, PA. Reprinted by permission.

Multiple Pregnancies

A **multiple pregnancy** is one in which the uterus contains two or more embryos. Twins occur in about one out of every 89 births, and triplets in about one out of every 7,921 (89 × 89). Twins occur more commonly among blacks than among whites (Scheinfeld 1965).

Twins result from the fertilization of either two separate ova or a single ovum (see box figure 16.1). Twins that develop from two separate ova are called *fraternal twins*. Since they come from two separate ova, fertilized by two separate sperm, they are no more alike than any other brother-sister, sister-sister, or brother-brother siblings. They may or may not share the same placenta.

In about one out of every three cases of twins (one in two hundred births), one mature ovum, fertilized by a single sperm, completely separates into two embryos during development (Annis 1978).

Since both developing embryos are from the same ovum and were fertilized by the same sperm, they are identical embryos and develop into *identical twins*. If these two developing embryos do not completely separate, the babies will be *conjoined* (Siamese twins).

Triplets may arise from one, two, or three ova. One embryo may divide into three embryos before implanting, in which case the triplets are identical. If the triplets come from one embryo dividing into two embryos and one ovum developing normally, then there are two identical triplets and one fraternal triplet. This same procedure holds true for quadruplets, quintuplets, and all other kinds of multiple pregnancies. In one case (the Dionne quintuplets), it is believed that all five girls developed from a single ovum fertilized by a single sperm. Thus, all five girls were identical.

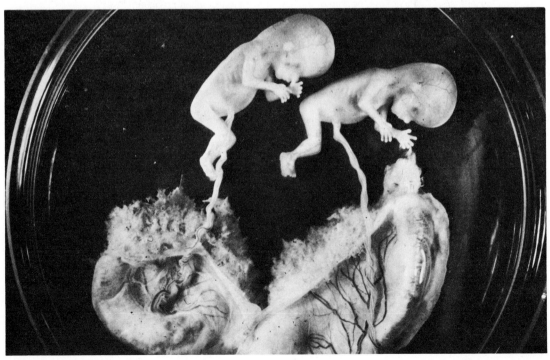

(a)

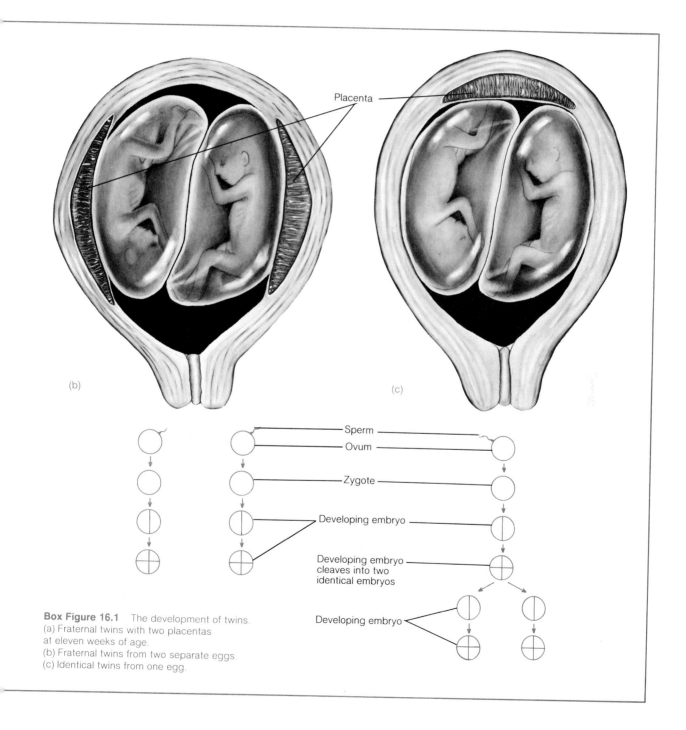

Box Figure 16.1 The development of twins.
(a) Fraternal twins with two placentas
at eleven weeks of age.
(b) Fraternal twins from two separate eggs.
(c) Identical twins from one egg.

Prenatal Doctor Visits

A woman who suspects that she is pregnant should make an appointment to see her doctor as soon as possible to have the pregnancy confirmed. Then the woman usually is scheduled for a series of doctor appointments over the nine months of the pregnancy. Normally, a prospective mother sees her doctor at least once a month for the first seven or eight months of the pregnancy and then biweekly or weekly until birth.

During the first visit to the doctor, the physician will want to know about previous illnesses and diet and may take a short genetic history of the prospective parents. It is important that the doctor be informed of any heart and kidney ailments and diseases such as tuberculosis and diabetes since these problems make pregnancies dangerous to a woman. The doctor will also need to know whether the mother has been exposed to rubella (German measles) or certain sexually transmitted diseases since these diseases can cause congenital defects or the death of the child. The woman should inform the physician about previous miscarriages and full-term pregnancies. All of this information is important in handling the present pregnancy.

The physician also will do a general physical examination, a pelvic examination, a possible cervical smear to detect cancer of the uterus, and a number of blood and urine tests to determine the general health of the prospective mother.

Follow-up doctor visits during the pregnancy are important so that the health of the expectant mother and the development of the fetus can be monitored. Usually, the mother's weight and blood pressure are checked, blood and urine tests are repeated periodically, and the doctor listens to the fetal heartbeat and assesses fetal growth.

Diet

A pregnant woman needs a balanced, nutritious diet. While essentially a pregnant woman really is "eating for two," she must not interpret this too literally and gain large amounts of weight because obesity complicates pregnancy and the delivery of the baby. Normally, a pregnant woman should gradually gain twenty to twenty-five pounds. Her diet should provide sufficient amounts of all types of foods, such as poultry, fish, eggs, low-fat cuts of red meats, fruits, and vegetables. Milk is important because of all of the nutrients it contains. The pregnant woman can drink fresh milk (low-fat) or buttermilk or eat yogurt or cottage cheese. Foods high in sugar, such as rolls, cakes, and pies, should be avoided. Also, during pregnancy, there is an increased need for the B vitamins. Liver, wholegrain breads, egg yolks, and brewer's yeast provide good supplies of these vitamins.

Life As Usual

A pregnant woman can do anything she did before she was pregnant until late in the pregnancy. Thus, it is life as usual. She should continue her normal routine,

toxemia   albumin
(tok-se'me-ah)   (al-bu'min)

including any sports she enjoys. The only caution is to not overdo it. If the woman is not involved in a regular exercise program, her physician can help her to design one. Women who regularly exercise during their pregnancy have easier and more successful deliveries than those who don't (Gersh and Gersh 1981).

Toxemia

Toxemia is the most common complication during pregnancy, and is marked by such symptoms as weight gain and swelling of the hands, feet, and face from water retention; the appearance of albumin (a blood protein important in salt and water balance in the body) in the urine, indicating possible kidney problems; and a rise in blood pressure. In severe cases, convulsions can occur, which are equally dangerous to mother and child.

Toxemia usually appears after the twenty-fourth week of the pregnancy, and an expectant mother and her physician should be on the watch for toxemia symptoms. The appearance of any of the symptoms is a warning signal. Rest and restriction of salt (and other sources of sodium) are important in the treatment of toxemia to reduce water retention and to maintain proper kidney functioning. Also, the pregnant woman with toxemia symptoms may need a change in diet, possibly a short stay in a hospital, or additional help at home.

Sexual Intercourse during Pregnancy

Couples are often concerned about whether or not to have sexual intercourse during pregnancy. For most couples, sexual intercourse can continue until the onset of labor, although if toward the end of the pregnancy there is spotting or vaginal or abdominal pain, or if the woman's water breaks (rupture of the amniotic sac), the couple should abstain.

Women who have had previous miscarriages might be wise to temporarily avoid intercourse at the time when their menstrual period would normally occur if they were not pregnant. Because the body is accustomed to the hormonal changes producing a menstrual flow during certain days of the month, there is a greater chance of a miscarriage at this time.

As the pregnancy progresses, couples may need to modify their intercourse positions. The side-by-side, female-superior, and rear-entry positions become more comfortable than the male-superior position (see chapter 9). Other sexual interactions can continue as usual.

Also, a woman may experience changes in her sexual interest and responsiveness during her pregnancy. Masters and Johnson (1966) found that, during the first trimester, a pregnant woman experiences little change in her sexual interest, and that if there is a change, it is usually a decrease in interest and responsiveness often brought on by nausea, breast tenderness, and fatigue. During the second trimester, according to Masters and Johnson, most women experience an increase in sexual interest and responsiveness because of hormonal changes taking place at this time. Because of these changes, some women may experience orgasm or multiple orgasm for the first time. Masters and Johnson found that, during the third trimester, pregnant women usually experience a decrease in sexual interest.

Premature Terminations of Pregnancy

A pregnancy can be prematurely terminated in one of three ways: induced abortion, spontaneous abortion, or premature birth. Induced abortion is discussed in detail in chapter 15, so we will examine spontaneous abortion and premature birth here.

Spontaneous Abortion (Miscarriage)

As explained in chapter 15, a **spontaneous abortion** or **miscarriage** is a spontaneous termination of the pregnancy by the body. A number of complications may prevent the full-term development of a fetus. Miscarriages between the first and third month usually involve immature ova and severe malformations that have made it impossible for the embryo to survive. An early miscarriage may appear as a heavier than usual menstrual flow. Miscarriage later in pregnancy may produce uncomfortable cramping and profuse bleeding and can usually be traced to a specific situation and corrected in subsequent pregnancies. Whenever a woman has a miscarriage, she should see her physician to avoid complications in later pregnancies.

Spontaneous abortions are not unusual. It is estimated that between 10 and 15 percent of pregnancies end in miscarriage (Ambron and Brodzinsky 1979).

Premature Birth (Low Birthweight Children)

If a newborn weighs less than five and a half pounds at birth, it is considered premature. Today, these children are often called *low birthweight children*. About 8 percent of the children born in the United States are of low birthweight.

A child born weighing less than one pound (end of fifth month) has a very poor chance of survival. Children weighing over three pounds (seventh month) have fairly good chances of survival. However, any low birthweight child has a decreased chance of survival.

Low birthweight babies are placed in an incubator immediately after delivery. The incubator controls oxygen, temperature, and humidity, creating an ideal environment. This greatly increases the babies' chances of survival.

Approximately half of all low birthweight children are unexplainable. The several known causes include maternal disease (toxemia, diabetes, and syphilis), poor nutritional practices, fetal abnormalities, smoking, and multiple pregnancies. Also, teenage women often have low birthweight children because they may not be physically mature enough to carry a pregnancy to term.

parturition
(par″tu-rish′un)

1. Have you or anyone you know been pregnant? How was the pregnancy first detected and confirmed?
2. Do you feel that the state of pregnancy and pregnant women are more accepted in society today than they were twenty years ago? On what do you base your opinion?
3. New medical technology makes it possible to sometimes save even babies that weigh less than one pound, even though these babies may sometimes suffer from severe physical complications and mental retardation for the rest of their lives. Do you think that intensive efforts should continue to be made to save these children? Why or why not?

Childbirth

Parturition is the medical term for childbirth. Birth is preceded by a sequence of events commonly called **labor.**

Labor
The onset of labor is felt as uterine contractions occurring in waves that start at the top of the uterus and move downward. These waves eventually will expel the fetus. *True labor* begins with uterine contractions occurring at regular intervals. As the intervals between contractions shorten, the contractions intensify, as does the woman's discomfort. In true labor, the contractions seem to be localized in the back and are intensified by walking. In contrast, in *false labor,* the contractions are felt in the abdomen at long, irregular intervals. Also, they do not intensify and are not altered significantly by walking.

The final indication of true labor is the "bloody show" and dilation of the cervix. The "show" is the discharge of the blood-containing mucous plug that blocked the cervical canal during the pregnancy. Also, during labor the amniotic sac may rupture, an occurrence called "breaking of the bag of waters."

A woman about to give birth goes through three stages of labor: complete dilation of the cervix, expulsion of the fetus, and expulsion of the placenta.

First Stage of Labor
The first stage of labor (*stage of dilation*) is the period of time from the onset of labor to the complete dilation of the cervix (see figure 16.5, a, b and c). This stage of labor is the longest stage and usually lasts ten to sixteen hours for the first birth and four to eight hours with subsequent deliveries.

Second Stage of Labor
The *stage of expulsion* is the second stage of labor and is the period of time from complete cervical dilation to delivery (figure 16.5 d). During delivery, a woman who

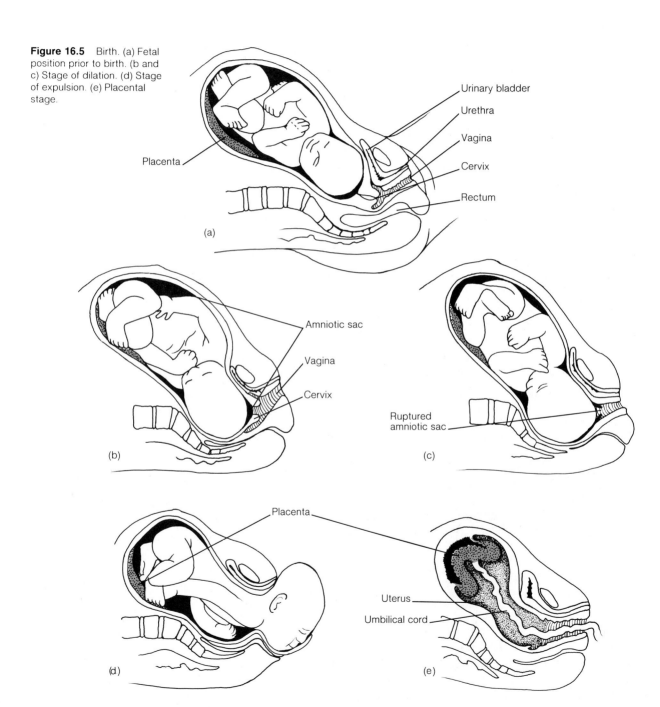

Figure 16.5 Birth. (a) Fetal position prior to birth. (b and c) Stage of dilation. (d) Stage of expulsion. (e) Placental stage.

episiotomy
(ĕ-piz″e-ot′o-me)

cephalic
(sĕ-fal′ik)

cesarean
(se-sa′re-an)

isn't under an anesthetic can actively push with her abdominal muscles and help the baby to be delivered. Many women feel that their active role in delivery is most satisfying.

Third Stage of Labor

The third stage of labor is called the *placental stage*. This is the expulsion of the placenta or "afterbirth" (figure 16.5 e). A few minutes after delivery of the baby, powerful uterine contractions expel the placenta. These contractions also constrict blood vessels during delivery and reduce the possibility of hemorrhage.

Episiotomies

During the second stage of labor, when the mother has pushed to the point where the infant's head is "crowning" at the mouth of the vagina, the attending physician often makes an incision across the perineum from the vagina toward the anus. This is called an **episiotomy.** Episiotomies reduce the pressure on the infant's head and prevent vaginal tearing during delivery. Torn tissue is more difficult to suture than a straight incision and often takes longer to heal. Episiotomies (because they reduce stretching) are believed to help pelvic muscle tone, and the suturing returns the vaginal opening to its original size.

While episiotomies are performed routinely by some physicians, many obstetricians believe that the advantages of episiotomy are not sufficient to warrant such routine use. Healing of the incision is painful, and if the vaginal opening is repaired and left too small, chronic, painful intercourse can result. These physicians feel that if the perineum is manually stretched and that if the mother can relax and engage in proper breathing and pushing, the routine episiotomy often is not necessary.

Forceps

As shown in figure 16.6, **forceps** are shaped like salad tongs. They fit alongside the baby's head and sometimes are used to pull the baby from the vagina if the uterine contractions are not strong enough to expel the baby. Obstetricians use forceps only in cases of emergency. They are not used routinely because they can cause damage to the baby and the mother.

Cesarean Section

About 90 percent of fetuses enter the birth canal with their heads in the cervix and their arms and legs crossed. This is called the *cephalic position* and is ideal for birth. In other pregnancies, the baby has its buttocks in the cervix (breech position), is crossways, or has one leg (leglet position) or one arm (armlet position) lodged in the cervix. Usually, the physician can rotate the fetus into the headfirst position during the last month of pregnancy. Many fetuses develop up to the third trimester in the breech position and make an unassisted 180-degree turn before the last month of pregnancy.

Figure 16.6 Forceps-
assisted delivery.

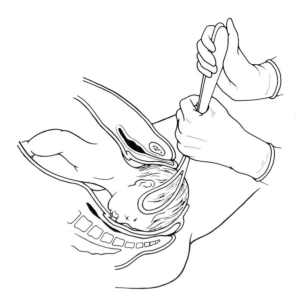

But if the time of birth is approaching and the baby is awkwardly lodged in the cervix, or if the mother's pelvis is too small to accommodate delivery, or in other cases of fetal or maternal distress, a **cesarean section** may be necessary. In this operation, the infant is removed through an incision into the uterus through the abdominal wall.

A cesarean section does not necessarily mean that future births will have to be cesarean sections. If the section was done because the woman's pelvic opening was too small to accommodate delivery, future births will require this procedure. However, if the section was performed because of the position of the fetus or because of an unforeseen emergency, then future births can generally be delivered normally.

Drugs and Childbirth

The value of anesthesia for complicated deliveries (particularly cesarean sections) is indisputable. However, many women and physicians are questioning the routine use of drugs to eliminate the sensations of labor, delivery, and after delivery.

Most drugs given to the woman during childbirth cross the placental barrier and therefore affect not only the mother but also the fetus during delivery and often after delivery for varying lengths of time.

General anesthetics are often given during the second stage of labor. They produce unconsciousness. Some are inhaled (nitrous oxide, halothane, and ether), while others are injected (sodium pentothal). General anesthetics can cause a woman's heart to stop, nausea and vomiting (inhalation of which can cause suffocation), and massive blood loss. They pass across the placenta and into the fetus. Children

epidural
(ep''i-du'ral)

catheter
(kath'ē-ter)

born to women under general anesthesia score lower on **Apgar tests** (a series of tests rating vital physical and mental activities of a newborn) than infants delivered with any other type of drug.

Spinal anesthetics are injected directly into the spinal column. A spinal numbs the body but does not produce unconsciousness. The woman can be selectively numbed from the shoulders to the feet, depending on where the spinal is injected and how much is used. Headaches and low back pain are common following delivery with spinal anesthetics. Also, the activities of infants born to mothers who had spinal anesthetics are depressed for a short time after delivery.

An *epidural injection or infusion* is the injection of an anesthetic near, but outside, the spinal cord. In this procedure, the anesthetic is continuously administered with a catheter (a flexible tube used for introducing fluids into the blood) from late in the first stage of labor throughout the second stage. The woman does not feel her uterine contractions, but she can bear down and assist in the delivery. This is currently one of the most popular techniques among physicians and mothers who have compared it with other methods of anesthetic use and is widely used for cesarean sections. However, infants delivered by the epidural method still have low Apgar scores.

A number of *narcotics* also may be used during delivery. All of them relieve pain; some of them dull the senses and induce sleep. They are often injected toward the end of the first stage of labor, as the cervix stretches to maximum dilation and uterine contractions are the strongest. To relieve the pain, the woman sacrifices awareness and her ability to actively participate in the delivery process. With narcotics, the mother can suffer nausea, vomiting, or hallucinations, while fetal breathing and heart rate are depressed.

Tranquilizers such as Valium and Librium are often used to relax tension and to cause drowsiness during delivery. They also cross the placental barrier, but their effect upon the fetus is relatively slight.

Barbiturates such as Nembutal, Luminal, and Seconal are used in labor to sedate the mother and to induce sleep after delivery. When used in labor, they slow the breathing and depress the mental activity of both mother and child. Barbiturates are selectively stored by the tissue of the brain and have been found to affect a baby's physical activities for more than a week after birth.

Prepared Childbirth

For the normal delivery, several alternatives to routine hospital delivery have been used to increase the involvement of the parents and the individuals performing the delivery. These alternatives are the Dick-Read and Lamaze "natural" childbirth procedures and the LeBoyer birth technique.

Although often referred to as "natural" childbirth, the Dick-Read and Lamaze birthing methods should be more appropriately labeled "prepared" childbirth. In both methods, the woman and her partner "prepare" themselves, through education, for the eventual delivery. Some couples feel that the intense emotional experience of prepared childbirth strengthens their entire relationship. Both procedures have been practiced since the late 1930s and the early 1940s.

Dick-Read believes that most pain during childbirth stems from the muscle tension caused by the fear of delivery. In his book *Childbirth without Fear* (first published in 1940), he explains techniques to help a woman in labor relieve tension. He also advises the woman to surround herself with people (including her partner) she knows during delivery. According to Dick-Read, this procedure helps to reduce the woman's tension, anxiety, and pain, making childbirth a more fulfilling experience.

In the 1950s, French physician Bernard Lamaze began teaching people a more complex series of physical and mental techniques to alleviate the pain of labor and delivery. In the Lamaze method, a woman learns to respond to the accelerating rushes of uterine contractions with a prelearned set of physical postures and breathing techniques. The Lamaze method also stresses the value of surrounding the pregnant woman with participants, including her partner and the physician, who are supportive.

In 1975, Frederick LeBoyer, another French physician, introduced a birthing technique focusing primarily on the birth experience of the infant. His basic philosophy is that the newborn's birth be made as nontraumatic as possible. LeBoyer suggests that the lights in the delivery room be lowered and that people talk in hushed voices. Immediately after delivery, the baby is put onto the mother's belly. Also, the umbilical cord is not cut until it stops pulsating (a sign that the placenta has stopped functioning and the child is on its own). The child is then put into a body-temperature bath to further soothe its sense receptors.

Birthing Alternatives

Expectant parents today have several alternatives to consider with regard to the birth experience, including where they want their child to be born and who they want present at the birth. Each of the birthing alternatives has its respective advantages and disadvantages.

Hospital Births

Hospital births have declined slightly in popularity as birthing clinics and home births have become more common, but childbirth in a hospital setting still provides one major advantage—on-the-spot life-saving emergency equipment and personnel.

When a hospitalized woman is about to give birth, an obstetrician (a physician who specializes in births) and a team of health professionals assist with the birth in a sanitized delivery room that is equipped with various instruments and machines (figure 16.7). The technical advantages of the delivery room are helpful—and often

previa
pre-vi'ah

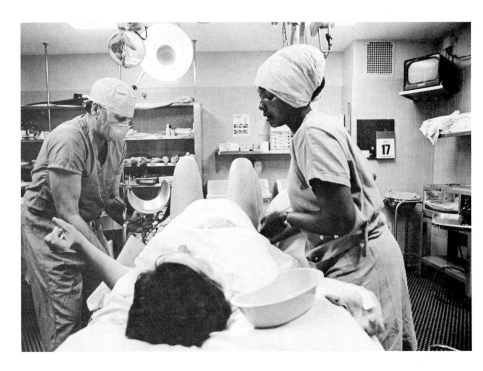

Figure 16.7 Hospital delivery room. The equipment is available for any delivery emergency.

life-saving—in problem births, as are the professionals who work in the delivery room. But the delivery room environment is often "sterile" and emotionally detached, which is a hospital birth's primary disadvantage.

Competent prenatal care will detect most complications requiring a hospital delivery room. High-risk pregnancies requiring the facilities of a hospital delivery room include premature labor (labor contractions in advance of the predicted date of delivery); blood incompatibility (Rh incompatibility) between the mother and fetus; the infant delivering in other than a headfirst presentation; **placenta previa** (a condition where the placenta is over the cervical canal prior to birth); toxemia; four previous births; multiple births; pelvic difficulties; illness; or a mother who is over thirty-five years of age.

Birthing Clinics and Birthing Rooms
Independent birthing clinics and hospital-adjoined birthing rooms are becoming more common and more popular in the United States. These allow a woman to experience labor and delivery in the same room and in the same bed. The rooms are furnished more like a home than a hospital but usually are well-equipped with discreetly hidden emergency equipment (figure 16.8). Family members and friends generally are allowed to be present during the delivery.

Figure 16.8 A birthing clinic room is furnished more like a home than a hospital, but emergency equipment is always available.

Birthing clinics and birthing rooms offer a safe alternative to the sterile setting of a hospital delivery room. They combine the freedom and comfort of a home delivery with the safety of adequate emergency equipment.

In many birthing clinics, the actual delivery is performed by a **midwife.** Today's midwife (the term should not be taken to imply that all midwives are female; there are many male midwives) is a *certified nurse-midwife* (CNM) and has the knowledge needed to perform an adequate delivery. If a woman is at all apprehensive about a midwife, she should ask if the midwife belongs to the American College of Nurse-Midwives (ACNM). This organization requires that its members have adequate training and be licensed within the state.

Home Birthing

An increasing number of prospective couples are deciding that the birth of their child is a very special event that should occur at home within familiar surroundings (figure 16.9). Also, a woman generally is more at ease, less tense, and delivers more easily in a familiar environment where she can be surrounded by family and friends.

Other advantages of home birthing include decreased cost (hospital deliveries are becoming more expensive), freedom from hospital policies and routines, and the immediate family interaction possible with the newborn.

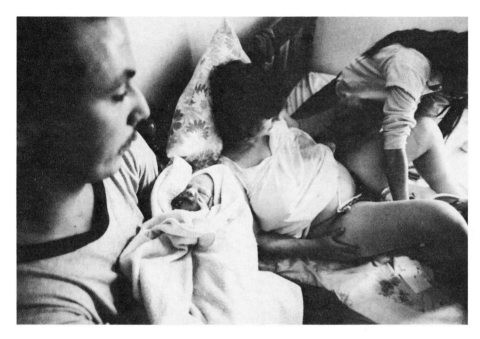

Figure 16.9 Home births can be safe if there is careful prenatal screening, a trained attendant, and rapid access to a hospital or emergency equipment.

Whether a couple chooses home birthing should depend on careful prenatal screening to identify possible fetal or delivery complications, whether or not a skilled attendant can be present to actually perform the delivery (midwives are illegal in some states, and many physicians are opposed to home births), and the ready availability of emergency equipment or access to a hospital. Ninety percent of all pregnancies, however, are delivered normally without medical intervention (Arms 1977).

1. What are the three stages of labor? Which stage do you think is the hardest? The most fulfilling?
2. If you were pregnant and about to deliver, would you want to be given any drugs during labor and delivery to mute any discomfort? If so, what type of anesthetic would you want? Even if you wouldn't want to be given any drugs, do you think it would be a good idea to discuss different anesthetic possibilities with your doctor prior to going into labor? Why or why not?
3. If you or your partner was pregnant, would you be interested in participating in prepared childbirth? Why or why not?
4. If you were an expectant parent, what birthing alternative—hospital, birthing clinic or birthing room, or home—would you prefer? Why?

Parent-Child Bonding

It is now believed that the first few minutes and days after birth are extremely important in parent-child **bonding** (the strong emotional attachment between parents and child) and that bonding has lasting effects on the child's well-being and development.

For this reason, some hospitals are changing the traditional postpartum separation of infant and mother, beginning with the first few minutes after birth. In these hospitals, the newborn is placed on the mother's abdomen immediately after birth, if there are no delivery complications or newborn distress, and the parents are able to talk to, touch, and interact with the infant during its first moments of life. The newborn already knows the voices of its parents, and some believe that it is important to parent-child bonding that the voices the child hears immediately after birth and the other characteristics of the mother and father (such as smell, touch, and skin texture) correspond.

In many hospitals, new mothers can elect to take full-time care of their child while in the hospital. This practice not only strengthens the mother-child bond—it also provides the mother with practical childcare experience in a setting where help and advice is always available if necessary.

One study (Klaus and Kennel 1976) compared groups of infant-mother pairs. Some mothers were given full care of their child until leaving the hospital. These extended-care mothers engaged in more holding, fondling, kissing, eye contact, talking, and breast-feeding. The fathers also were involved in the study and dressed the children twice a day during the hospital stay. Over time, these infants cried less and smiled and laughed more. After five years, the extended-care group of children had significantly higher IQs, performance, and language scores than the other group.

Postpartum "Blues"

The first days and weeks after giving birth are referred to as the **postpartum** period. Postpartum is a time of physical and psychological stabilization for the mother and a time of emotional adjustment for other family members.

The new mother finds herself with a new, demanding, around-the-clock schedule. At times, she may feel that it is more than she can handle. Some women experience moods of discouragement and weepiness—a "down" feeling—as they become adjusted to the enormous demands of motherhood. Some of these emotional highs and lows are produced by the dramatically changing hormone levels in the woman's body as it struggles to return to a prepregnancy state. Fatigue and nervousness about new responsibilities may also be partially responsible. In most cases, these postpartum "blues" disappear within several weeks.

Other family members also find that the new baby requires emotional adjustments and understanding on their parts. The new father may feel a new closeness to the mother and a strong sense of love and nurturance toward his child yet feel displaced because the baby comes first and gets all of the mother's attention. Other children in the family also may have ambiguous feelings about the new little family member and feel protective one minute and jealous the next.

Most of the negative feelings tend to lessen over time as all family members adjust to their new roles and expectations.

Breast-feeding

A complete discussion of the physiology of breast-feeding is found in chapter 6. In this section, we discuss breast-feeding as an advisable process taking place between mother and child.

The trend away from breast-feeding in the United States reversed significantly in the early 1970s. Today, one-third to one-half of all newborns are being breast-fed. The American Academy of Pediatrics and other organizations are actively urging mothers to breast-feed.

During the last few weeks of pregnancy and for the first few days after childbirth, a pregnant woman's breasts secrete **colostrum,** a thin, yellowish fluid that has twice the protein of mature breastmilk and is rich in vitamins A and E. Colostrum is all that a newborn needs for sustenance during the first several days of life. On the third or fourth day after delivery a new mother's breasts stop producing colostrum and become engorged with milk. At first, the breasts may feel uncomfortable, but within several days the discomfort disappears as the amount of milk production becomes regulated to the baby's intake.

There are a number of advantages to breast-feeding. First, breastmilk is the best food for infants. It is superior to cow's milk in its fatty acid content, protein content, and the calories it supplies. Breastmilk also may contain enzymes that help to lead to less obesity in adulthood. In addition, breast-feeding both passively protects against disease and triggers the infant's own disease defenses. For the healthy, full-term baby, breastmilk is the only food necessary until the baby shows signs of wanting solids halfway through its first year. Another advantage of breast-feeding is its convenience. There are no bottles to clean and sterilize, no milk or formula to warm. Breastmilk is always ready, available, and self-replenishing.

Breast-feeding also has disadvantages, however. The primary disadvantage is that breast-feeding makes the mother the sole source of her baby's food, and thus significantly restricts the mother's activities since she must always be available for a feeding. Breast-feeding also prevents others (such as the father) from enjoying the special closeness that comes from feeding an infant. Another disadvantage is that the mother's breasts and nipples may become tender and sore, although this usually disappears within several weeks. Also, her milk may leak out at other than feeding times and be a source of embarrassment.

Some mothers feel that breast-feeding provides special visual, tactile, and olfactory contact between the mother and the baby, and a psychological closeness not found between bottle-fed babies and their mothers. Long-term studies have found, however, that the way a baby is fed (bottle or breast) is not important emotionally if the babies are handled in the same way (Papalia and Olds 1979). The quality of the relationship is more important than the feeding method. The woman who breast-feeds her child because she feels she *should* probably does more emotional harm to her baby by communicating her feelings of resentment and unhappiness than she would if she were a relaxed, loving, bottle-feeding mother.

If a woman is going to breast-feed, she should start to make plans during the last few months of the pregnancy by reading some good, supportive books on the subject. A few of the better books on breast-feeding include *The Complete Book of Breast-feeding* by Eiger and Olds (1972), *Please Breast-feed Your Baby* by Gerrard (1971), *Nursing Your Baby* by Pryor (1963), and *The Womanly Art of Breast-feeding* by the LaLeche League (1973).

If a mother chooses not to nurse her baby, milk production can be stopped by medications that suppress the output of milk-producing hormones.

Sexual Activity after Childbirth

Most physicians recommend abstention from intercourse for several weeks after childbirth to allow episiotomy incisions to heal and the uterus and vagina to return to prepregnancy states. Usually, intercourse is physically safe by three or four weeks after delivery.

Women usually become fertile again within a few months after giving birth to a baby. Women who are breast-feeding usually remain infertile longer than those who are not breast-feeding because the hormonal activity causing lactation (milk production) suppresses the menstrual cycle. But breast-feeding or the absence of menstrual bleeding should not be taken as an indication that ovulation has yet to begin.

If another pregnancy is not immediately desired, some method of conception control should be used. The only problem is that, in the period immediately following birth, most methods of conception control cannot be used. Oral contraceptives cannot be taken by the breast-feeding mother because the hormones (estrogen and progesterone) are transferred to the baby and may be harmful. An IUD cannot be inserted until the uterus contracts to a stable size. The diaphragm used prior to pregnancy will no longer fit, and a new one will need to be obtained. Also, the rhythm

fetology   teratology
(fe-tol'o-je)   (ter''ah-tol'o-je)

methods of conception control are unreliable until predictable cycles of menstrual bleeding are reestablished, which usually takes several months.

Condoms, foams, and jellies are the only safe and effective methods of conception control during the postpartum period. The condom in combination with foam gives almost 100 percent protection from pregnancy.

---

1. Do you think that parent-child bonding in the first few minutes and days after delivery is important? Why or why not?
2. Have you ever had to deal with postpartum adjustments—either as a mother, father, or family member? How long did it take for things to get back to normal?
3. If you are a woman, would you consider breast-feeding your baby? Why or why not? If you are a man, would you want your partner to breast-feed? Why or why not?

Prenatal Abnormalities

Normal embryonic and fetal development occur in most pregnancies. But things can go wrong and the fetus can develop abnormally, or the pregnancy may terminate early in a **spontaneous abortion (miscarriage)**. Prenatal abnormalities can be caused by genetic factors, the general health of the mother, and the actions, life-style, and environment of the mother during the pregnancy.

Fetology is a new area of medicine that is concerned with perfecting techniques for diagnosing and treating fetal illnesses and defects. **Teratology** is a special area of fetology that is concerned with the prevention, diagnosis, and treatment of birth defects.

More than seventeen hundred kinds of abnormalities resulting in birth defects have been identified, and approximately 250,000 abnormal babies are born annually in the United States (Annis 1978).

Hereditary Birth Defects
Hereditary birth defects are those that the fetus inherits from the parental genes or chromosomes and that can be passed on to future children.

As explained in chapter 7, within the nucleus of every cell in the body are located the actual bearers of genetic information, the chromosomes. Chromosomes contain *deoxyribonucleic acid* (DNA), which is the carrier of the genes. Genes express themselves as the many traits we possess. Because each human body cell contains two sets of twenty-three chromosomes (one set from each parent), each cell possesses two genes for each trait.

polydactylism
(pol-e-dak′til-izm)

cystic fibrosis
(sis′tik fi-bro′sis)

Tay-Sachs
(ta saks′)

phenylketonuria
(fen″il-ke″to-nu′re-ah)

Genes are often spoken of as being either *dominant* or *recessive*. A child who receives a dominant gene from one parent and the recessive gene from the other parent *always* exhibits the dominant trait. This child will, in turn, pass the dominant gene to one-half of his or her children and the recessive gene to the other half. If a person receives a dominant gene from both parents, he or she will exhibit the trait and will pass it on to all children. A dominant trait will always be exhibited every generation. If a child is to exhibit a recessive trait, the recessive gene must have been received from both parents.

A person who has one recessive gene for a detrimental condition is called a **carrier** and usually does not exhibit the adverse effects of the condition. It has been estimated that every normal human carries from three to eight potentially harmful recessive genes that could result in a defective child if two carriers were the parents of a child (Annis 1978).

It would be well at this point to clear up some common misconceptions about heredity. First, it is a common belief that recessive genes are always undesirable. A glance at the list of some inherited human traits in table 16.3 shows that, in many instances, the recessive condition is the normal condition and the dominant condition is abnormal. For example, the gene producing six fingers on each hand (*polydactylism*) is dominant over the gene for five fingers, yet the possession of five fingers on each hand is considered by most to be the preferred condition. The same example points out another common misconception: that recessive genes occur less commonly than dominant genes. Obviously, the recessive condition of five fingers per hand is much more common than the dominant condition of six fingers per hand.

Some defects of genetic origin arise as the result of a "genetic accident" during the formation of sperm or ova. The resulting ovum or sperm may deviate from the normal chromosome number of twenty-three, and the resulting offspring may show a corresponding deviation from the usual forty-six chromosomes. Chromosome counts made of cells of living persons have revealed chromosome numbers ranging from forty-five to forty-nine. Such abnormal chromosome numbers and associated conditions are shown in table 7.1 in chapter 7.

The incidence of some genetic defects is quite small, while the incidence of others is of major importance. **Cystic fibrosis,** a disease that causes the secretory glands to not function properly, occurs once in every two thousand births in the United States. **Phenylketonuria (PKU)** causes a deterioration of mental abilities and occurs once in every ten thousand births. Often, genetic diseases and conditions are tied to specific groups. **Sickle-cell anemia** is found mainly among blacks from central Africa, **Tay-Sachs disease** appears among Jews of Eastern European origin, and **Down's syndrome (mongolism)** is a genetic accident that markedly increases with the age of the mother. A forty-year-old pregnant woman is twenty times more likely to have a Down's syndrome child than a twenty-five-year-old woman (Annis 1978).

Table 16.3 Some Inherited Human Traits.

Dominant Condition	Recessive Condition
Hair and skin	
Dark hair	Blond hair
Nonred hair	Red hair
Curly hair	Straight hair
Early baldness (dominant in males)	Normal (recessive in males)
Normal (dominant in females)	Early baldness (recessive in females)
Pigmentation of skin, hair, and eyes	Albinism
Normal	Absence of sweat glands
Eyes	
Brown	Blue or gray
Hazel or green	Blue or gray
Congenital cataract	Normal
Nearsightedness	Normal vision
Farsightedness	Normal vision
Astigmatism	Normal vision
Glaucoma	Normal
Features	
Broad lips	Thin lips
Large eyes	Small eyes
Long eyelashes	Short eyelashes
Broad nostrils	Narrow nostrils
"Roman nose"	Straight nose
Skeleton and muscles	
Short height (many genes involved)	Tall height
Midget	Normal short to tall height
Webbed fingers and/or toes	Normal
Six fingers and/or toes	Five fingers and/or toes
Circulatory system	
Blood groups A, B, and AB	Blood group O
High blood pressure (hypertension)	Normal
Normal	Hemophilia (sex-linked)
Normal	Sickle-cell anemia
Rh factor present (positive)	Rh factor absent (negative)
Hormones	
Normal	Diabetes mellitus
Nervous system	
Normal	Congenital deafness
Huntington's chorea	Normal
Migraine headaches	Normal
Normal	Phenylketonuria (PKU)

Source: Adapted Table 13.3, "Some human traits inherited according to dominance and recessiveness," from page 402 of *Health Science,* Fourth Edition by Kenneth L. Jones, Louis W. Shainberg, and Curtis O. Byer. Courtesy of Harper & Row Publishers, Inc.

rubella
(roo-bel'ah)

microcephaly
(mi''kro-sef'ah-le)

Other Birth Defects

Birth defects that are not hereditary usually are caused by drugs, diseases, or exposure to X rays after conception, and the defect is present at birth. These defects cannot be passed on to the next generation because they are not carried in the genes or chromosomes.

The most critical period in the formation of these birth defects is the first month of the pregnancy. This is often before a woman is certain she is pregnant. Thus, any woman anticipating pregnancy should maintain the best possible health and nutrition before conception and abstain from harmful substances. A complete physical also is appropriate, as is a blood test to determine whether the woman is immune to rubella (German measles).

Communicable Diseases

Diseases that a woman is afflicted with during pregnancy are easily transmitted from the mother to the fetus and in some cases cause birth defects. Because of the critical periods of embryonic and fetal development, the timing of the disease seems to be more crucial than the degree to which the mother has the disease. A mild case of German measles (rubella) in the mother can be as damaging to a fetus as a severe case if it occurs during a sensitive developmental period. Also, a woman's natural immunity is lowered during pregnancy (Thong et al. 1973). Reduced immunity during pregnancy may be a desirable maternal response to protect the fetus from rejection, but it exposes both the mother and the fetus to a greater risk of infection. Thus, a pregnant woman should stay away from crowds, especially during the first three months of the pregnancy, when the fetus is most susceptible to damage.

Sexually transmitted diseases that can affect a fetus are discussed in chapter 17. Therefore, in this chapter, we discuss German measles, which is probably the best-known example of a nonsexually transmitted maternal disease that can seriously damage the fetus, since the rubella virus appears to concentrate in growing embryonic tissue. Besides congenital cataracts, other birth defects caused by rubella include deafness, heart disease, microcephaly (abnormal smallness of the head that is usually associated with mental deficiencies), and stunted growth. Rubella's threat to the developing fetus is greatest during the first six months of pregnancy.

A highly effective rubella vaccine is available and should be given to all children. Also, any female of childbearing age should receive this vaccine if she has not been previously immunized or experienced the actual disease. As the vaccine may present a very slight risk to a developing fetus, it should not be administered during pregnancy, and women are counseled not to become pregnant for three months after receiving this vaccine. However, the risk of vaccine-caused birth defects is so small that the administration of rubella vaccine during pregnancy, as in a case where the woman does not yet know that she is pregnant, is not considered a reason to consider aborting the pregnancy (Centers for Disease Control, 8 June 1984).

thalidomide   phocomelia
(thal-lid'o-mīd)   (fo''ko-me'le-ah)

Drugs

Maternal drug taking may produce birth defects in the developing fetus in three ways. First, the drug dosage that a 120-pound pregnant woman may take is an extreme overdose for a fetus weighing two pounds or less. Second, the fetal liver is incapable of breaking down drugs in the same way as the adult liver. Newborns do not begin developing liver enzymes until the first week after birth. Third, drugs often affect developing tissues in a completely different manner than they affect adult tissues.

The term *drug* has very broad implications. Besides the classical chemicals identified as drugs, any lotions and ointments (especially those containing hormones) absorbed through the skin, vaginal douches, suppositories and jellies, medicated nose drops, cold and headache preparations, and vitamin tablets are all drugs. Compounds such as alcohol, caffeine, and nicotine also are considered drugs. If a woman is pregnant or suspects she may be pregnant, she should tell her physician before any drug is prescribed.

Thalidomide   Thalidomide provides a clear example of the effects of drugs on prenatal development. During the early 1960s, thalidomide was considered in Europe to be an excellent nonbarbiturate tranquilizer and sedative that helped to relieve the symptoms of morning sickness typical of early pregnancy. By the time thalidomide was isolated as a problem drug, over ten thousand babies had been born with **phocomelia** (lacking limbs, or with limbs in an embryonic stage of development). When thalidomide was taken during the critical period for formation of limbs (twenty-seven to forty days after conception), it interfered with the growth of the long bones of the arms and the legs, resulting in children being born with fetal hands appearing almost directly below the shoulders and/or feet attached to the pelvis. Approximately five-thousand of these thalidomide-affected individuals are still alive.

Thalidomide was never sold in the United States because Dr. Francis Kelsey of the United States Food and Drug Administration felt that the drug had not been sufficiently tested when it was put on the market in Europe.

Other Drugs   A woman should stop using any hormone supplements, including birth-control pills, as soon as she suspects that she is pregnant. One study, performed by Janerich, Piper, and Glebatis in 1974, links birth-control pills with limb malformations in fetuses exposed to these hormones during the critical limb formation period.

When it comes to the effects of aspirin on the developing fetus, researchers have obtained mixed results. Studies in the United States have never linked aspirin with any fetal defects. But studies conducted in Europe indicated that there were some links between daily aspirin usage and spontaneous abortion. Also, it is recommended that aspirin not be used during the final three months of pregnancy except on the advice of a physician since aspirin can prolong labor and cause bleeding and clotting problems for both the mother and baby during delivery (Annis 1978).

Zimmerman (1976) reports that several tranquilizers may cause cleft palate in the newborn if the tranquilizers are taken by the mother during the first three months of prenatal development.

Babies born to heroin-addicted mothers are usually smaller than average, and there is a high incidence of maternal complications (toxemia, premature separation of the placenta, retained placenta requiring surgical removal, hemorrhaging after birth, and breech deliveries). Also, the newborns are addicted to heroin as well and usually are not strong enough to survive the withdrawal syndrome. Methadone-addicted babies also suffer withdrawal but are stronger and usually better able to survive.

Existing evidence regarding the effects of marijuana on prenatal development presents a mixed picture, and additional research is needed before definite statements can be made. This is also true regarding the effects of LSD on prenatal development.

Smoking and Fetal Development

Women who smoke during a pregnancy affect two lives: their own and that of the developing child. When a pregnant woman smokes, harmful gases and poisonous chemicals in the smoke cross the placenta into the fetal blood. One of the gases found in smoke is *carbon monoxide* (CO). This chemical replaces oxygen in the red blood cells, greatly reducing the amount of oxygen available to the fetus. *Nicotine* further reduces the oxygen available to a fetus by narrowing the blood vessels in the placenta and the developing baby.

The lack of oxygen caused by the carbon monoxide and the nicotine reduces the fetus's growth rate. Thus, the unborn babies of the over two million mothers who smoke during pregnancy do not develop as fast and are more likely to have a low weight at birth. These smaller babies also have a greater chance of dying soon after birth. Studies have shown that women who smoke during pregnancy also produce more stillbirths and miscarriages (spontaneous abortions) than nonsmoking women.

Caffeine and Fetal Development

The United States Food and Drug Administration has cautioned pregnant women against drinking coffee, tea, and other caffeine-containing products because caffeine may cause birth defects. Experiments in 1979 and 1980 showed that even modest caffeine consumption (equivalent to two cups of coffee a day) by pregnant rats can retard bone growth in developing rat fetuses. Heavy caffeine consumption (equivalent to twelve or twenty-four cups of coffee a day) resulted in rat offspring with missing toes. Other studies of the effects of caffeine on prenatal development are now underway, but, until proven otherwise, pregnant women should drink caffeine-free soft drinks, decaffeinated coffee, milk, fruit juices, or just water.

Fetal Alcohol Syndrome

In 1973, two physicians discovered that they could diagnose a mother's alcoholism from the facial characteristics, growth deficiencies, and psychomotor disturbances in their children (Jones and Smith 1973). They termed the condition in the children **fetal alcohol syndrome** (**FAS**). Other researchers have since been able to diagnose FAS in adults as well.

Mental retardation, learning problems, hyperactivity, and perception and attention problems are common in FAS children. FAS children are small, grow slowly, and show certain facial characteristics (figure 16.10). FAS has been observed in children of all ethnic backgrounds.

The mechanisms that produce FAS effects remain unclear. Alcohol passes freely across the placenta from mother to fetus, making concentrations of alcohol in the fetus at least as high as in the mother. But the question of whether FAS is the direct effect of alcohol or the effect of a breakdown product is not known. It is established, however, that the more alcohol the expectant mother consumes, the greater the damage to the developing fetus.

A safe level of alcohol consumption during pregnancy has not been determined. Recent studies have revealed that even moderate alcohol consumption during pregnancy can have less dramatic, but nevertheless deleterious, effects on the development of a fetus. Some researchers believe that hyperactivity and learning disabilities not apparent until later in childhood may result from the mother's moderate alcohol consumption during pregnancy.

Prenatal Diagnosis of Birth Defects

Prenatal photography, amniocentesis, and the fetoscope greatly increase a physician's ability to diagnose fetal problems.

Prenatal Photography

Great strides in prenatal care have been achieved because of a photographic process that enables physicians to photograph a fetus before it is born. The procedure involves projecting ultrahigh frequency sound waves into body tissues. The echo returning from tissues of differing densities forms a picture. The picture, called a *B-scan*, appears on a televisionlike screen and can be photographed.

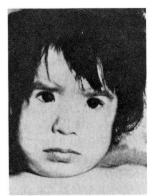
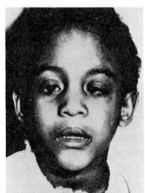
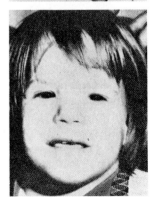

Figure 16.10 Fetal alcohol syndrome. Note shortened (narrowed) eye openings, short nose, reduced central groove on upper lip, thinned vermillion on upper lip, and flattened midface.

hydrocephalus
(hi-dro-sef'ah-lus)

amniocentesis
(am''ne-o-sen-te'sis)

fetoscope
(fe'to-skōp)

Visible in most B-scan photos are the placenta, the amniotic fluid, and a general outline of the fetus's trunk and limbs. The head appears as a solid line. The value of this type of photo is considerable. If an initial B-scan showed an enlarged head, for example, other tests could then be used to look at the brain for signs of **hydrocephalus** (an abnormal accumulation of fluid within the cranium). Also, physicians can use B-scan photos to determine approximate fetal age, fetal growth, many fetal abnormalities, and fetal position.

Prenatal photography is painless and completely safe to the fetus and the mother. The only discomfort the pregnant woman experiences is when a cold gel is applied to her abdomen to enhance the conduction of the sound waves.

Amniocentesis

If there is any reason to believe that a woman is carrying an abnormal child, a procedure known as **amniocentesis** may be performed. This procedure often can confirm whether the developing fetus is normal or abnormal.

First the position of the fetus is determined by a B-scan. This reduces the chance of damage to the fetus or the placenta. After the position of the fetus is determined, a very thin needle is inserted through the maternal abdominal and uterine walls into the amniotic sac surrounding the developing fetus, and a small amount of amniotic fluid is withdrawn. This part of the amniocentesis is performed without anesthetics and takes about five minutes.

The amniotic fluid contains living cells from the fetus and waste products from fetal cellular metabolism. Tests of the cells and the fluid can confirm the presence of about sixty genetic and nongenetic birth defects (Laurence 1974).

Fetoscope

With a **fetoscope** (or endoscope), a physician can look directly at the developing fetus within the uterus to check for defects that would not show up in an analysis of amniotic fluid from amniocentesis. The fetoscope also is sometimes used to perform intrauterine surgery on fetuses.

Use of the fetoscope requires that the uterine wall be punctured as in amniocentesis, but on the end of the needle is a fiberoptic instrument (a flexible, plastic fiber capable of transmitting an optical image) through which a physician can look at the fetus. The fetoscope also contains a side arm that can be manipulated by the physician. The side arm can be used in a number of ways. For example, it can hold a needle to take a fetal blood sample that will determine if the fetus has sickle-cell anemia, which cannot be diagnosed by amniocentesis.

1. Why would it be important to know whether a birth defect was genetically produced?
2. If you and your partner had produced a child with a genetically induced birth defect and had a one in four chance of producing another child with the same defect, would you attempt another pregnancy? On what factors would you base your decision?
3. If you were pregnant and you or your partner was a heavy smoker, could or would either of you quit smoking? Why or why not?
4. If early in the pregnancy your child was prenatally diagnosed as having a birth defect and you and your partner were faced with the agonizing decision of whether or not to terminate the pregnancy, what factors would you have to consider before making your decision?

Infertility

The concept of family planning to most couples implies limiting the number of pregnancies and spacing those pregnancies to suit the needs and resources of the family. This is because the majority of couples who want children have little trouble in producing them. Approximately 50 percent of all fertile couples can achieve pregnancy within the first four months of intercourse using no birth control methods, and 85 percent are successful by the end of twelve months (Silber 1980).

Yet, for an important minority, the problem is just the opposite. Some couples wish for more children than they are able to have, while other couples wanting children have none at all.

Primary infertility is the condition of never having conceived or induced a pregnancy. This is also referred to as **sterility. Secondary infertility** is the condition of having previously conceived but being unable to again conceive. It is estimated that about 15 percent of all couples are classified under these two definitions (Silber 1980).

Causes of Infertility

In general, infertility is due to physical defects, emotional stresses, a mistiming of ovulation, or a sperm allergy. Infertility may be a problem of either partner or of both. In about 50 percent of all infertility cases, the woman is unable to conceive. The man is unable to induce conception in about 30 to 35 percent of the cases. Both partners are infertile in 15 to 20 percent of the cases (Silber 1980).

Medical counsel for problems of infertility may be handled by a family physician or by a fertility clinic in a medical school or larger city. Help in locating such a clinic can be obtained from the local Planned Parenthood clinic or by writing to Planned Parenthood, 810 Seventh Avenue, New York, New York, 10014.

varicocele
(var'ĭ-ko-sēl'')

Male Infertility

The problem in the male is his inability to discharge enough active sperm to reach and fertilize the ovum. Since the male sex hormones and the sperm are produced by different cells, infertility has no bearing on a man's masculinity. A man can be sterile yet achieve erection and have normal sexual relations.

The initial test for determining a couple's infertility problem is a male's *sperm count*. No other test of a couple's infertility is as simple. For a sperm count to be of any value, it must be repeated at least three times over the course of several months. Since intercourse depletes the male temporarily of sperm and since the average American couple has intercourse two to three times a week, it is arbitrarily suggested that a couple abstain from intercourse two to three days prior to a sperm count so that the count will reflect accurately how many sperm are usually delivered to the woman at the time of intercourse.

The sperm are obtained by the male masturbating and collecting the ejaculate in a wide-mouthed, clean collection jar that can be obtained from the laboratory doing the count. The specimen must be taken to the laboratory immediately for a good count to take place. While sperm will live in the female reproductive tract for two to four days, they can live in the specimen collection jar for only an hour or two. Thus, the count must be made within these two hours. Besides counting the number of sperm, the laboratory also determines the mobility of the sperm, the shape of the sperm, and the ability of the sperm to penetrate the vaginal mucus of the female partner.

Sperm production can be adversely affected by illnesses (mumps and other diseases), occupational hazards (exposure to X rays, radioactive substances, certain metals or chemicals, gasoline fumes and carbon monoxide, or excessive heat), infrequent intercourse, excesses in life-style (tobacco, alcohol, and other drugs), poor nutrition, emotional stress, and generally poor health.

A man may have normal sperm production but be unable to discharge the sperm due to blocked ducts (birth defect or infection) or **varicocele** (swelling of the veins on the vas deferens), both of which are easily corrected through surgery. Some males produce and ejaculate normal sperm but have sperm counts that are too low. Too frequent ejaculation (once to several times daily) may prevent the buildup of a sufficient number of sperm. Males bothered by low sperm counts may be advised to wait thirty-six hours or more between acts of coitus.

Techniques have been devised to increase the sperm concentration of the ejaculate. Since the first drops of ejaculate contain a far greater number of sperm than the last drops, some men are advised to withdraw the penis after the first portions of ejaculated sperm have entered the vagina to prevent the dilution of the first drops. Some physicians collect the first drops of ejaculate from several ejaculations of a male, combine them, and then artificially inseminate the sperm into the uterus of the partner.

endometriosis
(en''do-me''tre-o'sis)

Normal Semen

There are various measurements for normal semen. However, it is commonly accepted that semen should amount to:

A minimum volume of three milliliters of ejaculate (one milliliter is approximately one-fourth teaspoon)

At least sixty million sperm per milliliter of semen

At least 60 percent of all sperm normally formed

At least 60 percent of ejaculated sperm motile two hours *after* ejaculation

If the sperm count falls below ten million per milliliter of semen or if the percentage of normal sperm falls below 60 percent of the total sperm, the male is considered functionally sterile.

Female Infertility

Infertility in a woman can be caused by an inability to ovulate, diseases of the fallopian tubes, **endometriosis** (abnormalities of the uterine lining), undersecretion of gonadotropic hormones, or production of vaginal fluids that kill sperm or impede their mobility.

If a woman is not ovulating, sometimes she will begin ovulating after taking an oral contraceptive for several months and then stopping. Other times, ovulation can be started through surgery or with medications. Excess weight loss, resulting in extreme thinness, can also cause a woman to stop ovulating. This may be brought on both by a woman losing weight to fit the image of high-fashion figures or by extreme exercise, such as running. With reasonable weight gain, fertility may be restored ("Women Superdieters and Runners May Lose the Fertility Stakes," *Medical World News,* 27 April 1981).

Fallopian tubes may be opened through very complicated microsurgery.

If a woman has endometriosis, the ovum may be fertilized properly and migrate to the uterus but be unable to attach to the abnormal uterine wall. This can be due to a hormonal imbalance that alters the nature of the uterine lining. Hormonal imbalances can be determined through blood tests and corrected by medications.

Some women produce secretions from the vagina or cervix that inactivate sperm. Certain antibodies or antibodylike substances, induced by the presence of semen, may be responsible. In these women, the chances of conception appear to improve if they can be removed from contact with sperm for a period of time, either through abstinence or through the use of a condom.

Shared Infertility

One cause of infertility shared by both partners is their reaction to emotional stress. Emotional tension may inhibit ovum production and movement. It can also interfere with the production of sperm by the male. Annoying environments, professional and family pressures, nervous exhaustion from overwork, pressure on college students during final examinations, or other stresses can affect people hormonally and may lead to temporary infertility. A leisurely vacation, a change of jobs, or some alteration of life-style may relieve the emotional stresses and result in conception.

Assisted Fertilization

In some cases of infertility, there are procedures that can assist the union of sperm and ovum or the successful implantation of an embryo into the uterus to produce a pregnancy. At present, it is easier to deal with male infertility than to deal with malfunctions of the female reproductive system. However, rapid advances are continuously taking place.

Artificial Insemination

Artificial insemination is the placing of healthy sperm in the vagina of the female through means other than sexual intercourse. Usually, the semen is placed in a cervical cup (a small diaphragm that fits over the cervix), inserted into place, and left for twenty-four hours. The sperm may be from the woman's partner or from a donor. In recent years, artificial insemination has become so acceptable that it results in from 10,000 to 20,000 of the 3,600,000 births each year in the United States (Annis 1978).

The primary reason for artificial insemination is male infertility. Male infertility accounts for 95 percent of all cases of artificial insemination. Often, male infertility is caused by a low sperm count; that is, the male does not produce enough sperm at one time to produce a pregnancy. Artificial insemination with his sperm can be accomplished by pooling the sperm from several ejaculations over a period of time. Such a "sperm pool" is produced by freezing the sperm until enough have been accumulated to guarantee a pregnancy. If a male produces no sperm, then sperm from an anonymous donor can be artificially inseminated into a female to produce a pregnancy.

Another reason for artificial insemination is that a male who has undergone a vasectomy (see chapter 15) may now desire to impregnate his female partner. In a vasectomized male, sperm are still being produced by the testis and stored in the epididymis. These sperm can be taken from the epididymis, by syringe, and artificially inseminated, along with the male's seminal fluids, into the vagina of his female partner. Also, if the vasectomized male had the foresight before the vasectomy to have a sample of his semen frozen and stored at one of the sperm banks located in hospitals throughout the United States, he can later have his sperm thawed, added to his seminal fluid, and artificially inseminated into his female partner.

In a recent survey, physicians performing artificial insemination reported that the third most common reason for artificial insemination was to provide women

surrogate
(sur'o-gāt)

without male partners a chance to conceive a child (Curie-Cohen, Luttrell, and Shapiro 1979). Another reason for artificial insemination is that the couple may fear the transfer to the offspring of genetic diseases found in the male. In both of these cases, donor sperm are inseminated into the female.

The biggest problem with artificial insemination is the legal implications of donors. For example, many states do not recognize the husband of a woman who conceives a child by a donor as being the legal father. Thus, adoption proceedings are a necessity.

In Vitro Fertilization

In 1978, British scientists Dr. Patrick Steptoe and Robert Edwards announced that they had successfully fertilized a human ovum in a laboratory culture dish, outside the human body (*in vitro*—"in glass") and implanted the resulting embryo in the uterus of the woman from whom the ovum was taken. Their procedure, which became known as *in vitro fertilization,* is outlined in figure 16.11.

The first clinic in the United States to perform in vitro fertilization opened in 1980.

Surrogate Mothers

A **surrogate mother** is a woman who is fertilized by the male partner of an infertile couple, carries the child until birth, and then gives the child to the infertile couple. The woman can be fertilized by artificial insemination or may consent to sexual intercourse with the man. Advertisements for surrogate mothers can be found in major newspapers. There are also attorneys who specialize in putting potential surrogate mothers and couples together for a fee.

Some women are surrogate mothers for the money. Often, a woman is paid between three and ten thousand dollars, plus expenses, for carrying the baby for nine months. Other women do it because they enjoy children and want infertile couples to experience the joys of raising children.

Any couple hoping to make use of a surrogate mother should know that the practice is legal, provided that the couple complies with local and state laws. No uniform, comprehensive law covers surrogate motherhood; three sets of laws are involved. These are the laws governing artificial insemination, payment of fees for services, and rights of adoption. Since these laws differ from state to state, prospective parents should become familiar with their state laws or retain an attorney familiar with these laws.

Recently, a New York surrogate mother went to court against a California couple to retain the child she had borne. The surrogate mother won and was able to keep the child, the court's reasoning being that she was the child's natural mother. Thus, surrogates and the prospective parents must trust one another wholeheartedly. Otherwise, they may find themselves trapped in a complicated and painful legal quagmire.

Ad for surrogate mother.

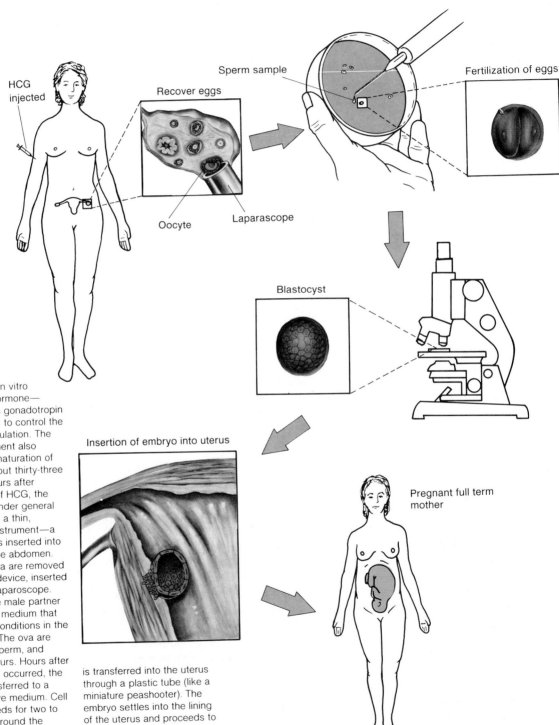

HCG
injected

Recover eggs

Sperm sample

Fertilization of eggs

Oocyte

Laparascope

Blastocyst

Insertion of embryo into uterus

Pregnant full term
mother

Figure 16.11 In vitro
fertilization. A hormone—
human chorionic gonadotropin
(HCG)—is given to control the
exact time of ovulation. The
hormonal treatment also
stimulates the maturation of
several ova. About thirty-three
to thirty-four hours after
administration of HCG, the
woman is put under general
anesthesia, and a thin,
periscopelike instrument—a
laparoscope—is inserted into
an incision in the abdomen.
One or more ova are removed
with a suction device, inserted
alongside the laparoscope.
Sperm from the male partner
are placed in a medium that
simulates the conditions in the
fallopian tube. The ova are
added to the sperm, and
fertilization occurs. Hours after
fertilization has occurred, the
embryo is transferred to a
more supportive medium. Cell
division proceeds for two to
four days. At around the
blastocyst stage, the embryo
is transferred into the uterus
through a plastic tube (like a
miniature peashooter). The
embryo settles into the lining
of the uterus and proceeds to
develop.

1. Have you or anyone you know had infertility problems? Can you elaborate on the painful emotional consequences of infertility?
2. Do you think that diagnosed infertility is harder for a man to accept or a woman? Why?
3. If you and your partner were infertile, would you consider an assisted fertilization procedure? If so, which one and why?
4. How do you think a diagnosis of infertility would affect the sexual activity and satisfaction of a couple?

"How do you feel?"

"Tired."

"Me, too. I love you."

"I love you, too. . . . You were terrific in there."

"Me? You did all the work."

"She really is beautiful, isn't she?"

"She's gorgeous, just like her mother."

"Right now I'm afraid we both look like we've been through World War III."

"Well, she was just squeezed through a rather small tunnel headfirst. How do you think she's going to look? And you just got done pushing an 8½ pound baby out of your body. That's a lot of work!"

"Do you want to hold her?"

"Of course I do. Hello, Princess, remember me? . . . Daddy? We're going to be seeing a lot of each other. Over there is your mommy. You don't know it yet, but we love you very, very much."

Summary

1. Pregnancy is the condition of having an offspring developing within the uterus of the female. Pregnancy results from the fertilization of an ovum by a sperm, a process called conception. Normally, only one sperm fertilizes an ovum.

2. Immediately after fertilization, the zygote is transported down the fallopian tube and implants in the endometrium of the uterus, where it begins to form the placenta.

3. The nine-month span of pregnancy is divided into three, three-month segments called trimesters. By the end of the first trimester, the fetus's internal organs have begun limited functioning, and the fetus is about three inches long. During the second trimester, the fetus grows, details are refined, functions are exercised, and weight increases to over one pound. At the end of the third trimester, the fetus is said to be full term.

4. For most women, the first indication that they may be pregnant is the absence of the menstrual period. Pregnancy can be confirmed by an internal (pelvic) examination and a variety of pregnancy tests.

5.   Prenatal care is essential for promoting the health of both the mother and the fetus. Good prenatal care includes regular visits to the doctor; a balanced, nutritious diet; exercise; and awareness of the symptoms of toxemia.

6.   For most couples, sexual intercourse during pregnancy can continue until the onset of labor, although, as the pregnancy progresses, couples may need to modify their intercourse positions. Also, a woman may experience changes in her sexual interest and responsiveness during pregnancy.

7.   A pregnancy can be prematurely terminated by induced abortion, spontaneous abortion, or premature birth. Spontaneous abortion, or miscarriage, is a spontaneous termination of the pregnancy by the body. Premature births are those that result in low birthweight children (children weighing less than five and a half pounds).

8.   A woman about to give birth goes through three stages of labor: complete dilation of the cervix, expulsion of the fetus, and expulsion of the placenta.

9.   During labor, when the baby's head is "crowning" at the mouth of the vagina, the attending physician often makes an incision across the perineum from the vagina toward the anus. This is called an episiotomy. In emergencies, forceps are sometimes used to pull the baby from the vagina.

10.   If the baby is awkwardly lodged in the cervix, if the mother's pelvis is too small to accommodate delivery, or in other cases of fetal or maternal distress, the infant may be removed through an incision into the uterus through the abdominal wall, a procedure called cesarean section.

11.   Most drugs given to women during childbirth cross the placental barrier and therefore affect not only the mother but also the fetus during delivery and often after delivery for varying lengths of time. Many women and physicians are now questioning the routine use of drugs during childbirth.

12.   The Dick-Read and Lamaze prepared childbirth procedures and the LeBoyer birth technique increase the involvement of the parents and the individuals performing the delivery.

13.   Birthing alternatives currently available to expectant parents include hospital births, birthing clinics or birthing room births, and home births.

14.   It is now believed that the first few minutes and days after birth are extremely important in parent-child bonding and that bonding has lasting effects on the child's well-being and development.

15.   The first days and weeks after giving birth are referred to as the postpartum period. Postpartum is a time of physical and psychological stabilization for the mother and a time of emotional adjustment for other family members.

16.   Today, one-third to one-half of all newborns are being breast-fed. Advantages of breast-feeding include breastmilk's superior nutritional value and the convenience of breast-feeding. Disadvantages include restriction of the mother's activities, tender nipples, and involuntary milk leakage.

17.   Most physicians recommend abstention from intercourse for three or four weeks after childbirth to allow episiotomy incisions to heal and the uterus and vagina to return to prepregnancy states.

18.   Normal embryonic and fetal development occurs in most pregnancies, but the embryo or fetus can develop abnormally, producing prenatal abnormalities, or birth defects. Birth defects can be caused by genetic factors, communicable diseases, drugs, smoking, caffeine, and alcohol.

19.   Three procedures give a physician the ability to diagnose fetal problems before the fetus is born. Prenatal photography enables physicians to photograph a fetus before it is born. Amniocentesis allows amniotic fluid to be withdrawn from around the fetus and tested. With a fetoscope, a physician can look directly at the developing fetus within the uterus to check for defects that would not show up through photography or amniocentesis.

20.   In general, infertility is due to physical defects, emotional stresses, a mistiming of ovulation, or a sperm allergy. In some cases of infertility, there are procedures that can assist fertilization or implantation. In artificial insemination, healthy sperm can be placed in the vagina without sexual intercourse. In in vitro fertilization, the ovum is fertilized in a laboratory culture dish, and the embryo is implanted in the uterus after fertilization. A surrogate mother is a woman who is fertilized by the male partner of an infertile couple, carries the child until birth, and then gives the child to the infertile couple.

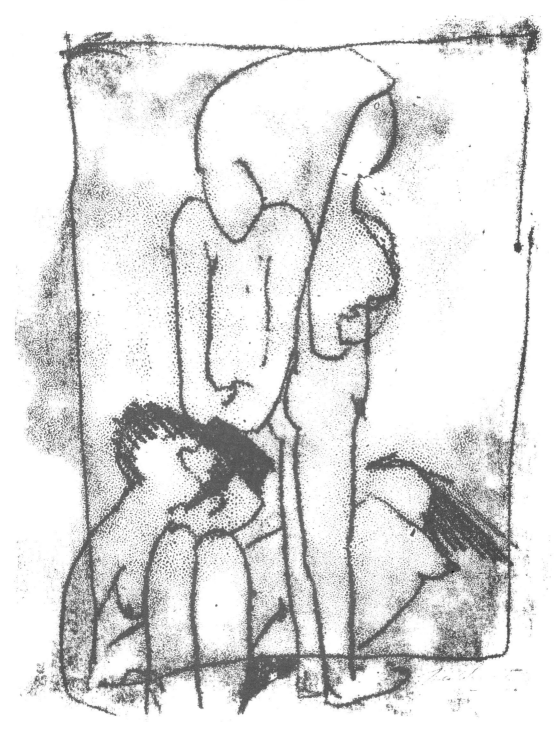

"Debbie, could you come over? There's something I need to discuss with you."

"I'm kind of busy, Jim. Is it important?"

"Very. I'll be expecting you in twenty minutes."

"Could you give me an idea as to what this is about?"

"I'd rather not discuss it over the phone."

"OK, I'll be right over."

". . . That's impossible! I couldn't have given you gonorrhea!"

"Deb, I haven't been with anyone else."

"Are you sure that's what it is?"

"Quite sure. The doctor at the clinic asked me to contact you right away. If you didn't know you had it, you could eventually get really sick. Also, he wants to prevent it from being spread around."

"But where did I get it?"

"I don't know, but it wasn't from me! Try to think back. Who were you seeing before we started dating?"

"The only one I've slept with is . . . oh no! It was that night I got drunk after the frat party! It had to be. Oh God, what am I gonna do? I can't go up to that creep I was with!"

"Well, you're going to have to do something. If he doesn't get treated, it could spread all over campus."

Direct person-to-person contact of warm, moist body surfaces is an ideal means of transmitting certain disease-causing agents. It is not surprising, therefore, that some diseases can be transmitted primarily by sexual contact. These diseases are called **sexually transmitted diseases** or **STDs.**

An older term for these diseases, still in common use, is venereal disease or VD. This name, derived from "Venus," the goddess of love, is not entirely realistic because love often plays little or no role in the transmission of such diseases. The term is a carryover from the Victorian era, when people did not even want to mention words like *sex* or *sexual.* Another phrase used for STDs was "social disease."

Other than their having similar methods of transmission, the various STDs are quite different. They do have in common an affinity for the mucous membranes, such as those lining the reproductive organs. They also tend to have relatively weak resistance to adverse environmental conditions, such as dryness and cold. This is why their transmission generally requires the direct contact of genital or other moist body surfaces, and they are seldom transmitted by means of contaminated, inanimate objects.

In this chapter, we examine the various STDs—their symptoms, their prevalence, and their treatment.

Some Background Information

Sexually transmitted diseases all fall into the general category of communicable diseases—those that can be transmitted from one person to another. As such, there are various general concepts that apply to all of these diseases. A brief review of some of these concepts may be helpful.

Pathogens
Communicable diseases are caused by infectious agents called **pathogens** (table 17.1). Pathogens include microscopic living organisms, such as bacteria, fungi, yeasts, and protozoa (one-celled animallike organisms), and larger parasites, such as worms and certain insects. Other important pathogens are viruses, which are extremely small and are usually considered to be semiliving particles. Sexually transmitted diseases are communicable diseases caused by pathogens in all of these groups.

Transmission
Transmission is the transfer of a pathogen from one person to another. It can be accomplished in many ways, including direct contact, or through contaminated objects (indirect contact), airborne dust or droplets, insect bites, and contaminated food and water. A disease that can be transmitted directly from person to person is

Table 17.1   Pathogen Groups Causing Sexually Transmitted Diseases.

Photo	Name of Group and Size	Sexually Transmitted Examples	Description	Comments
	Viruses (10–250 nanometers)	Herpes simplex, possibly hepatitis B, genital warts	Minute particles of nucleic acid and protein	Smallest known pathogens; not controlled by antibiotics
	Bacteria (1–10 micrometers)	Gonorrhea, syphilis, *Chlamydia*	Microscopic cells in rodlike, spherical, or spiral shapes	Produce toxins and enzymes that damage human cells; most are controllable with antibiotic drugs
	Yeasts (a few micrometers)	*Candida*	Microscopic oval cells; reproduce by budding	Release enzymes that damage human cells; controllable with special antibiotic drugs
	Protozoa (a few to 250 micrometers)	*Trichomonas,* amoebiasis	Microscopic single-celled animals	Release enzymes and toxins that destroy human cells

said to be *contagious.* Sexually transmitted diseases are transmitted almost exclusively through direct contact and are highly contagious.

Incubation Period
Following exposure to a communicable disease, a period of time passes before symptoms appear. This is the **incubation period.** During this time, the pathogen is increasing in numbers and commencing the process of disease production. The incubation period for different diseases ranges from hours to years but is usually a matter of days or weeks. During the latter part of the incubation period, many diseases become contagious to other people, even though no symptoms are apparent.

Communicable Period
Every disease has its own particular time during which it may be transmitted to other people. As we have mentioned, this **communicable period** often begins before the appearance of symptoms. Also, for some diseases, a recovering patient continues to be a source of infection after symptoms have disappeared.

Symptomless Carriers
For many diseases, it is possible to be a source of infection to others even though symptoms have never been apparent. The pathogen colonizes some part of the body and can infect other people, but the carrier individual experiences no discomfort. At some later date, however, the symptomless infection may erupt into the disease.

Body Defenses
Our bodies have many built-in mechanisms for protection against pathogens. The unbroken skin and mucous membranes, for example, form a barrier against many pathogens. In addition, white blood cells are often able to engulf and destroy pathogens that do enter the body.

The body's immune mechanism offers effective protection against a wide range of pathogens. Immunity is developed against specific pathogens upon exposure to each pathogen or upon exposure to a vaccine derived from the pathogen. Lifelong immunity often results from a single experience with a disease or immunization against it. However, some diseases do not stimulate an effective immune response and may be experienced repeatedly. Unfortunately, most sexually transmitted diseases are in this category.

Treatment
Effective drugs are now available to combat most categories of pathogens. Bacteria, fungi, yeasts, and protozoa, for example, all respond well to drug therapy. Viruses, however, present a greater challenge. None of the antibiotics or sulfa drugs is effective against viruses. Specific antiviral drugs have been developed, and some are

gonorrhea   syphilis
(gon''o-re'ah)   (sif'ĭ-lis)

available for use. However, as this is written, the situions in which antiviral drugs perform both safely and effectively are still quite limited. For the majority of viral infections, at this time, we are basically limited to treatment of symptoms, rather than a direct attack on the virus. With time, better antiviral drugs will probably become available.

For any disease, prevention is preferable to treatment, and the most effective prevention is usually through immunization. With the exception of hepatitis B, vaccines are not yet available for any of the major sexually transmitted diseases, although efforts to develop them are underway.

---

1. Why is sexual contact an ideal way to transmit certain pathogens?
2. What is an incubation period?
3. Suppose research efforts succeed in developing effective vaccines against the major STDs. Who would you recommend to receive these immunizations? Would you arrange to be immunized? Would you have your children immunized?
4. What group of pathogens currently presents the greatest challenge in treatment? Why?

History of STDs

The early history of most diseases is clouded by the confusion and lack of scientific knowledge that surrounded diseases until fairly recently. However, diseases fitting the descriptions of various STDs can be traced back for thousands of years. Hippocrates wrote of gonorrhea in 460 B.C. Descriptions of symptoms that strongly resemble syphilis appear in several chapters of the Bible (Lev. 21:18; Num. 31:2–23; Deut. 28:27–29).

Surprisingly, syphilis seems to have disappeared from Europe somewhere around 1000 A.D. and to have reappeared shortly before 1500 A.D. (Chiappa and Forish 1976). At that time, it is believed to have been brought back from the New World by Columbus's crews. The first great recorded epidemic of syphilis broke out in Naples (Italy) two years after Columbus's first return. There was widespread death and disfigurement throughout Italy, France, Spain, Switzerland, Germany, England, Scotland, Hungary, Russia, and other countries by the year 1500. While no exact records were kept at that time, it is believed that millions of people died. The first effective treatment for syphilis was still four hundred years away.

For many years, gonorrhea and syphilis were thought to be the same disease. This erroneous idea was corrected in 1879 by the German bacteriologist Neisser, who identified the pathogen causing gonorrhea.

Both syphilis and gonorrhea have been known by a variety of names. Gonorrhea has been called "clap," "dose," "strain," and "GC." Syphilis has been called "pox," "scab," "French pox," "Spanish sickness," "German pox," "lues," and "syph." Syphilis received its present name in 1530 in a poem by a physician named Fracastoro about an afflicted Greek shepherd boy named Syphilus who had offended the sun-god.

Neither syphilis nor gonorrhea were first contracted by people through sexual activity with animals, as is commonly believed. In fact, no known animal is a natural host for either of these diseases. The pathogens causing STDs apparently evolved over a long period of time from nonpathogenic ancestors or organisms causing different types of diseases.

Genital herpes infection also has a long history of inflicting misery on people. The ancient Greeks knew about herpes. Their physicians gave it the name herpes, derived from the Greek word meaning "to creep," because the sores seem to creep over the surface of the skin. References to herpes appear throughout medical history. For example, in 1921, a Dr. B. Kipschütz, working in Germany, published a complete review of herpes in which he suggested that the oral and genital forms were probably caused by different viruses (Hamilton 1980).

In more recent history, the incidence of STDs declined to a low point in the early 1950s, presumably due to intensive public health efforts and the prevailing conservative sexual mores of that era. However, in about 1957, the number of cases of syphilis and gonorrhea started to rise. While we can only speculate as to the cause of this increase, it seems to have coincided with the beginning of a trend toward more casual sexual relationships. While no government records are kept on genital herpes, its incidence apparently started to increase during the late 1960s. Now let's look at the current situation.

Today's Incidence of STDs

Sexually transmitted diseases now occur at epidemic levels (figure 17.1). The United States Public Health Service keeps incidence records for over forty diseases. By law, every case of these diseases must be reported to health authorities. In recent years, the number of cases of gonorrhea and syphilis together has exceeded the combined total for all other diseases. That includes such common or formerly common diseases as measles, rubella (German measles), mumps, chicken pox, hepatitis, and tuberculosis.

There are now about a million new cases of gonorrhea officially reported each year. But it is estimated that only one case out of every four actual infections is reported. Many cases treated by private physicians are not reported, and many other cases are not even treated. Thus, the actual incidence is probably three to four million cases per year. Over 33,000 cases of primary and secondary syphilis are reported each year. Like gonorrhea, this is probably considerably less than the actual

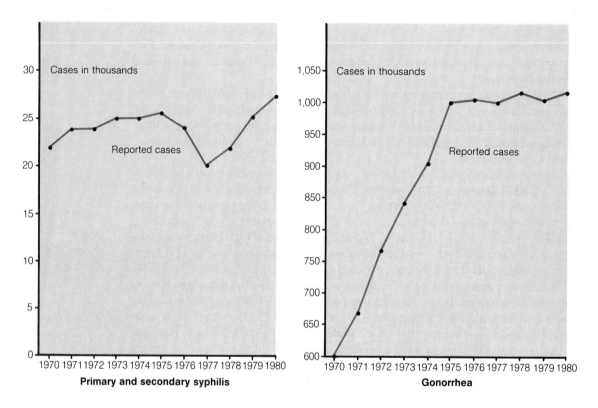

Figure 17.1 Reported cases of syphilis and gonorrhea between 1970 and 1980 (in thousands).

number of cases that occur. New cases of genital herpes simplex, not a reportable disease, are estimated to number at least half a million each year (McKean 1981).

Who Gets STDs?

STDs have permeated all social levels. Infections cross all lines of age, income, and ethnic group. According to the World Health Organization, certain groups are particularly susceptible to these diseases. For example, military personnel, highly mobile businesspeople and vacationers, sexually active young people, and homosexually oriented males are more likely, statistically, to encounter this epidemic health problem (Judson 1981). This is presumed to relate to the multiple sexual partners of some members of these groups.

But what must be emphasized is that *any* sexually active person can acquire an STD. Awareness of the possibility of STD and frank communication between sexual partners concerning this possibility is appropriate for all of us. If anything positive can be said about the current genital herpes outbreak, it is that it has increased our awareness of the threat of STD and has encouraged communication on the subject.

Neisseria
(nis-se're-ah)

gonococcus
(gon''o-kok'us)

Why So Much STD?

According to some authorities, one important factor in the current STD epidemic is the birth control pill. The pill has largely eliminated fear of pregnancy, thus encouraging greater freedom of sexual activity. Furthermore, it has reduced the use of condoms, a birth control method that is also of value in preventing the transmission of some STDs. More than this, the pill increases the alkalinity and moisture of the female genital tract, which encourages the rapid growth of gonorrhea organisms and other pathogens. Other contraceptive aids for females, such as vaginal jelly and foam, are acidic. They thus provide an environment antagonistic to the growth of infectious organisms.

The life-styles of people today have incorporated greater sexual freedom and increased personal mobility, both of which are favorable to the spread of infections. Other changes in sexual behavior that may have contributed to the increased incidence of sexually transmitted diseases include sexual relationships beginning at earlier ages and greater variety in sexual partners.

Attitudes may also contribute to the problem. The belief that an STD is a disgrace or a punishment for "sin" can discourage an individual from seeking treatment or from discussing the possibility or prevention of STD with sexual partners. Such attitudes probably have slowed efforts to produce effective vaccines or other preventive methods. Some people feel that government support of research on STD vaccines is an endorsement of "immorality" and that STDs serve to enforce standards of sexual behavior. This is speculation, of course, but there hasn't been the outcry for government action to control STDs that there has been for some much less significant diseases.

1. Would you describe STDs as a recent problem?
2. What groups of people have statistically high STD rates?
3. What factors are thought to contribute to today's high rates of certain STDs?

Gonorrhea

Gonorrhea is caused by a bacterium called *Neisseria gonorrhoeae,* also called the *gonococcus* (figure 17.2). *Neisseria gonorrhoeae* is extremely selective about where it grows, requiring just the right temperature, humidity, and nutrients. It dies or is inactivated when exposed to cold or dryness. For this reason, the transmission of gonorrhea requires contact between warm, moist body surfaces. Inanimate objects such as toilet seats can harbor the gonococcus for a few seconds, but they account for very few cases of gonorrhea.

urethritis
(u''rē-thri'tis)

Source and Transmission

Humans are the only natural source of gonorrhea. The organism occurs in the moist mucous membranes of infected persons. The gonococcus may be transmitted through various kinds of sexual contact—heterosexual or homosexual—including genital, oral-genital, and anal-genital contact.

Nature of the Disease

The gonococcus has an affinity for various body membranes. It most commonly infects the mucous membranes of the genitals, throat, rectum, or the eye and is usually a local infection of one or more of these areas. However, if the organism enters the blood, it can infect the membranes lining the heart or the joints.

Gonorrhea in a Male

In most males, symptoms of gonorrhea appear in two days to a week after exposure. At least 10 percent of males, however, remain free of obvious symptoms, becoming symptomless carriers (Davis et al 1980).

When there are symptoms in a male, the disease begins with a painful inflammation of the urethra *(urethritis)*. This causes a scalding pain during urination. The inflammation begins at the tip of the penis and works up the urethra. The result is a "drip" of pus from the penis. In early infection, this discharge tends to be watery or milky. Later, it becomes thick greenish yellow and is often tinged with blood.

The burning sensation upon urination may subside after two or three weeks. By this time, the infection may have reached the prostate gland and testicles, as well as the bladder and kidneys. Permanent damage can include urinary obstruction, inflammation and abscesses of the prostate, and sterility. Sterility is caused by blockage of the vas deferens and epididymis. Infection of the throat occasionally occurs following oral-genital contact, usually fellatio. It feels much like any sore throat. Rectal gonorrhea, which can be painful or symptomless, may follow anal-genital intercourse.

Gonorrhea in a Female

The early symptoms of gonorrhea in females are often so slight that they may be ignored. In fact, at least 50 percent of infected women do not realize they have the disease until their male partners discover their own infections (Davis et al 1980). The prevalence of long-term female carriers is an important part of the history of the gonorrhea epidemic. Public Health Service studies show that about 4.7 percent of all women in the United States may be carriers of the gonococcus (Centers for Disease Control, 29 June 1979).

The symptoms of gonorrhea in a female are different from those in a male. The usual symptom of a woman is irritation or "smarting" of the vagina, accompanied by a discharge. Unfortunately, such discharge is an unreliable sign in a fe-

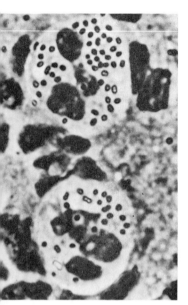

Figure 17.2 *Neisseria gonorrhoeae,* commonly called the gonococcus. Occurring as pairs of tiny spherical bacteria, this organism is the cause of gonorrhea.

male, since she may ordinarily experience vaginal discharges unrelated to gonorrhea. In a female, the gonococcus prefers the cervix and fallopian tubes. Cervical infection can cause pain during sexual intercourse. The infection can also occur in the rectum or throat.

Gonorrhea in a woman becomes a more serious matter as it moves up through the genital tract. As it reaches the uterus and fallopian tubes, the pus discharge may increase. Sterility or ectopic pregnancy (see chapter 16) often results because of scar tissue left in the fallopian tubes following gonorrhea. The infection also can spread out of the fallopian tubes into the abdominal cavity, causing a massive infection called **pelvic inflammatory disease (PID).** PID's symptoms include abdominal pain, fever, and nausea, and may be mistaken for appendicitis. About 40 percent of PID cases are gonorrhea; the remainder are caused by other pathogens.

Gonorrhea in Newborns
When a woman with gonorrhea gives birth, there is a chance of the baby's eyes becoming infected during the delivery process. Unless promptly treated, a gonorrheal eye infection can lead to blindness. To prevent this infection, laws require that silver nitrate or another effective antiseptic be placed in the eyes of every newborn infant. Infants may also acquire genital infections during birth.

Systemic Gonorrhea
Gonorrhea occasionally progresses into a serious, even fatal, systemic (blood-borne) infection. Systemic gonorrhea may attack the joints (causing a form of arthritis), heart lining (endocardium), heart muscle, brain, membranes covering the brain (meninges), lungs, kidneys, veins, and skin. A common group of symptoms of systemic gonorrhea includes fever, arthritis, and sores on the skin. Even though the gonococcus is fragile outside the human body, its potential for tissue destruction within the body is great.

Diagnosis of Gonorrhea
The most reliable tests for gonorrhea are cultures and stained microscope slides. For either cultures or slides, swabs are rubbed over the possibly infected tissue (urethra, cervix, throat, etc.). The swab is then rubbed over agar (the culture medium) or a glass microscope slide.

Agar cultures, which are considered the most reliable method of diagnosing gonorrhea, require twelve to sixteen hours of incubation before the gonococcus can be detected (Tortora, Funke, and Case 1982). This is a real problem in public health clinics, where many patients fail to return for treatment.

While microscope slides can be stained and viewed in a matter of minutes, they are less reliable, especially in detecting long-term (chronic) cases of gonorrhea.

tetracycline	Vibramycin	*Treponema pallidum*
(tet″rah-si′klen)	(vi-brah-mi′sin)	(trep″o-ne′mah pal′ĭ-dum)
	spectinomycin	
	(spek″tĭ-no-mi′sin)	

Treatment of Gonorrhea

The gonococcus has a long history of developing resistance to everything that has been used for its treatment. Some of the drugs that have gradually lost their effectiveness are potassium salts, silver compounds, sulfa drugs, and most recently, penicillin. An ever-increasing percentage of cases of gonorrhea are caused by strains of the gonococcus that produce an enzyme (penicillinase) that has the ability to break down penicillin into an ineffective form. Such organisms, called PPNG (penicillinase-producing *Neisseria gonorrhoeae),* accounted for about 1,910 cases of gonorrhea in the United States in the first nine months of 1981 (Centers for Disease Control, 22 January 1982).

Tetracycline drugs such as Vibramycin or spectinomycin are now being recommended for most cases of gonorrhea. It has been found that many people who have gonorrhea also carry one or more other genital infections. Tetracycline drugs are more effective than penicillin in curing these other infections, while at the same time curing gonorrhea.

It must be emphasized that there is no effective home remedy for gonorrhea. Nothing can be mixed up or bought from a drugstore or by mail that will cure this or any other sexually transmitted disease. The infected person must see a private physician or his or her local public health department for effective treatment. Gonorrhea must be treated promptly before any permanent damage, such as sterility, can occur.

There is still no vaccine available to the public that will prevent gonorrhea, although research efforts to create such a vaccine continue. Also, no immunity results from having had gonorrhea; repeated infections are possible.

---

1. Have you or anyone you know had gonorrhea? Describe the symptoms. How was the disease treated?
2. Is a male or female more likely to be aware of having gonorrhea? Why?
3. What are the major hazards of untreated gonorrhea?

Syphilis

While less common than gonorrhea, **syphilis** is a more serious disease because it always spreads to the bloodstream and is thus a systemic infection. The main similarity between syphilis and gonorrhea is that both are transmitted primarily by sexual contact.

The pathogen causing syphilis is the **spirochete** (spiral bacterium) *Treponema pallidum* (figure 17.3). This organism is very frail and cannot survive drying or chilling. Since it is killed within a few seconds after exposure to air, it is easy to see

spirochete
(spi′ro-kēt)

chancre
(shang′ker)

why syphilis must be transmitted by sexual intercourse, kissing, or other intimate body contact. The germ requires warm, moist skin or mucous membrane surfaces for its penetration into the body.

After the spirochetes burrow through the skin or mucous membrane and enter the blood, they are carried throughout the body. Because its symptoms are so varied that they can resemble any one of many other diseases, syphilis has been called the "great imitator." It progresses through definite stages.

Primary Syphilis

After infection with syphilis, there is a symptomless incubation period of ten to ninety days. During this time, the spirochetes multiply and migrate through the body.

The first symptom that appears is the primary lesion or **chancre** (figure 17.4). This is a sore that appears at the exact spot where infection took place. There may be one or several. The typical chancre is pink to red in color, raised, firm, and painless. It is usually the size of a dime, but it may be so small that it resembles a pimple. *The chancre is swarming with spirochetes.* Any contact with it is likely to result in another infection.

The usual location of the chancre is on or near the sex organs, but it can be on the lip, tongue, finger, or any part of the body. In females, the chancre is often within the vagina and, since it is painless, goes unnoticed.

Even if primary syphilis is not treated (which it definitely should be), the chancre will disappear spontaneously in three to six weeks. But disappearance of the chancre does not mean that the disease is cured. It is just progressing to the next stage. At about the time the chancre disappears, blood tests for syphilis become positive.

Secondary Syphilis

In secondary syphilis, the true systemic nature of syphilis becomes obvious. Symptoms may appear throughout the body, starting one to six months after the appearance of the chancre. (In many cases, this stage is skipped over, especially if the person is taking antibiotics.).

The most common symptom of secondary syphilis is a rash that does not itch (figure 17.5). This rash is variable in appearance and may cover the entire body or any part of it. Common sites of this rash are on the palms of the hands or the soles of the feet. Large, moist sores may develop on or around the sex organs or in the mouth. Such sores are loaded with spirochetes and contact with them, through sexual intercourse or even kissing, may cause infections. Secondary syphilis is, therefore, extremely contagious. Other symptoms of secondary syphilis may include a sore throat, headache, slight fever, red eyes, pain in the joints, and patches of hair falling out.

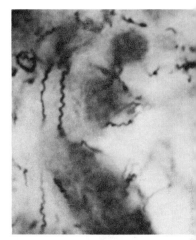

Figure 17.3 *Treponema pallidum,* the spirochete that causes syphilis.

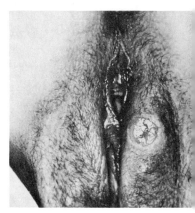

Figure 17.4 Chancre of primary syphilis. The first symptom of syphilis is usually a chancre like this. It may be anywhere on the body, and there may be more than one of them.

aneurysm
(an'u-rizm)

paresis
(pah-re'sis)

Anyone who has these symptoms and who may have been exposed to syphilis should explain this fact to a physician. Because syphilis can easily be mistaken for many other diseases, it is difficult to diagnose and may not be properly treated. Syphilis at this secondary stage is best diagnosed by means of a specific blood test.

The symptoms of secondary syphilis last from several days to several months. Then, like the chancre of primary syphilis, they disappear even without treatment. Syphilis has then entered the latent stage.

Latent Syphilis

Latent (dormant) syphilis begins with the disappearance of untreated secondary symptoms. If the disease remains untreated, there may be periodic reoccurrences of the secondary lesions (sores) for several years. Contact with these sores can transmit syphilis. When sores no longer appear, sexual transmission is no longer possible.

Now symptomless, latent syphilis can last from a few months to a lifetime. A blood test will show that the individual has syphilis, but there will be no visible signs of the disease. In this latent stage, progressive degeneration of the brain, spinal cord, hearing, sight, or bones may be occurring unnoticed. When the symptoms of this degeneration appear, the individual has reached the last and most destructive stage of syphilis.

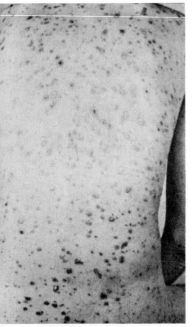

Figure 17.5 Rash of secondary syphilis. The rash of secondary syphilis is extremely variable, ranging from slight to severe. It may cover the entire body or any part of it.

Late (Tertiary) Syphilis

Late or tertiary syphilis is characterized by permanent damage to vital organs. Although almost any part of the body may be affected, the most common manifestations occur in the circulatory system and the nervous system.

Circulatory System

In the circulatory system, the damage from syphilis in most cases is located in the aorta, the large artery carrying blood from the heart to the body. The elastic tissue is destroyed, and the aorta stretches, producing an **aneurysm** (saclike bulge). The infection may also involve the aortic heart valve, causing an insufficient flow of blood.

Nervous System

In the nervous system, widespread destruction of the tissues of the brain and spinal cord is inflicted by large numbers of spirochetes. The term **paresis** encompasses all of the mental and physical effects of syphilitic degeneration of the nervous system.

Mental changes vary but most commonly include gradual changes of personality, decreased ability to work, and impairment of concentration and judgment. These changes produce abnormal behavior, including delusions, loss of memory, lack of insight, apathy or violent rages, convulsions, and disorientation.

Some Frequently Asked Questions about Syphilis

Can a Person Have Syphilis and Gonorrhea at the Same Time?

Yes. In fact, early research on both of these diseases was often confused by concurrent infections. In an effort to distinguish between syphilis and gonorrhea, the celebrated English physician John Hunter (1728–1793) inoculated himself with the urethral discharge of a patient with gonorrhea (early disease researchers often used themselves as "guinea pigs"). Unfortunately, the donor had a double infection. Hunter erroneously concluded that syphilis and gonorrhea were the same disease, publishing his results in 1786. He suffered from the complications of both diseases, and the syphilis probably contributed to his death in 1793. It was not until the mid-nineteenth century that syphilis and gonorrhea were clearly differentiated (Sigerst 1958; Davis et al 1980).

Does a Syphilis Infection Confer Immunity on a Person?

Many people develop immunity against syphilis if they are not treated during the primary or secondary stages. In fact, some people spontaneously recover without treatment and are subsequently immune (Benenson 1980). However, delaying treatment to allow development of immunity is very foolish since permanent damage to the brain and other organs could occur in the process.

Are Some People Naturally Immune to Syphilis?

Benenson (1980) states that there is no natural immunity to syphilis. Susceptibility is universal, although only about 10 percent of exposures (intercourse with infected persons) result in infection.

The most common outcome of the progressive destruction of the spinal cord is impaired muscle control. Occasionally, all reflexes may be lost, including the ability to vary pupil size (affecting vision), a general sense of balance, and muscular co-ordination. Considerable paralysis may eventually result from untreated syphilis.

Syphilis can also cause degeneration of the optic nerve, usually first noticed as a loss of peripheral vision. Central vision may be lost in advanced cases, leaving the individual completely blind.

In treated cases, life can be prolonged, but permanent institutional care may be necessary because of extreme degeneration prior to treatment. Syphilis is responsible for placing many people in chronic-care institutions as well as for causing about 190 deaths per year in the United States (National Center for Health Statistics, 20 December 1982).

Congenital Syphilis

If a woman has syphilis during a pregnancy, infection of the fetus takes place when the spirochetes cross the placental membranes. This fetal infection apparently does not occur before the fifth month of development. Consequently, adequate treatment of an infected pregnant woman before the fifth fetal month should ensure the child's safety. Treatment given the mother after the fifth month may also cure the syphilitic fetus. All pregnant women should receive blood tests for detection of syphilis.

Syphilis is a common cause of stillbirth. Among the infants born alive to untreated syphilitic mothers, approximately 50 percent have syphilis at birth (congenital syphilis). A syphilitic infant may show damage at birth, or it may appear normal at birth and develop damage within a few months. Or, it may remain without symptoms until adolescence, when the symptoms of late syphilis may appear. As a rule, the earlier the symptoms appear, the more severe the infection. Syphilis is capable of producing many different types of damage in an infant.

Diagnosis of Syphilis

Early diagnosis followed by prompt and adequate treatment can completely cure syphilis. Diagnosis can be made through microscopic examinations or blood tests.

Microscopic Examination

The lesions of primary and secondary syphilis are swarming with spirochetes. Tissue taken from these lesions and viewed under a microscope will reveal many spirochetes.

Blood Tests

Several types of blood tests for syphilis are in use. The blood tests become positive at about the time the chancre of primary syphilis disappears, and remain positive until after successful treatment. Blood tests are the standard screening device for syphilis. They are commonly required before obtaining a marriage license. They are also performed during pregnancy and as a part of some routine physical examinations. Anyone who has a variety of sex partners is wise to have a blood test for syphilis done annually. Some cases of syphilis develop with little or no outward indication and can only be detected through a blood test.

The Venereal Disease Research Lab (VDRL) blood test, and a number of similar tests, are commonly used for preliminary screening for syphilis. While these tests are reliable in detecting syphilis, producing few *false negative* results, they do produce a fair percentage of *false positive* results (Tortora, Funke, and Case 1982). A number of physical conditions other than syphilis can cause false positive results. For this reason, a positive VDRL-type result is usually followed up with a more specific test, such as a FTA-ABS (fluorescent treponema antibody absorption) test. These highly accurate tests are less used in preliminary screening because of their greater difficulty and higher cost.

Treatment of Syphilis

The purposes of syphilis treatment are to destroy all spirochetes and to prevent further damage to the body. Treatment of syphilis also serves to prevent the spread of the disease to others.

After many years of use, penicillin remains the most common treatment for syphilis. Larger doses of penicillin are needed to treat syphilis than for most other diseases. Also, a more prolonged period of treatment is required for syphilis than for gonorrhea (Tortora, Funke, and Case 1982). Thus, the treatment normally given for gonorrhea is not likely to simultaneously cure an undetected coincidental case of syphilis.

The earlier syphilis is treated, the easier a cure is achieved. The ideal time to begin syphilis treatment is during primary syphilis.

When a patient is allergic to penicillin, other antibiotics may be effectively used. As with gonorrhea, there is no home remedy, mail-order cure, or nonprescription drugstore product that will cure syphilis.

1. Have you or anyone you know had syphilis? Describe the symptoms. How was the disease treated?
2. How does the general nature of syphilis differ from that of gonorrhea? Which is more dangerous?
3. What are the possible results of long-term untreated syphilis?

Genital Herpes Virus Infections

Making the cover of *Time* magazine has long been considered some kind of badge of importance. **Genital herpes** received that honor (2 August 1982) in connection with an interesting article emphasizing the emotional and behavioral implications of genital herpes infection. With over twenty million Americans already carrying lifelong infections, and another half million being infected each year, genital herpes is influencing the sexual decisions of a great many people, infected or not.

At least three characterisics set herpes apart from most other STDs: it is caused by viruses; it is often a lifelong infection; and there is currently no real cure.

Two types of herpes viruses have been identified to date: herpes simplex virus type 1 (HSV-1) and herpes simplex virus type 2 (HSV-2) (figure 17.6). HSV-1 more typically attacks the upper parts of the body and causes most so-called cold sores and fever blisters. HSV-2 causes most genital herpes infections. However, there are many exceptions to these generalizations. Freely transmitted by oral sex, either virus may attack either the oral or genital region. Laboratories can distinguish between the two viruses on the basis of the greater damage done to cells by HSV-2, as well as through blood tests.

In addition to oral and genital lesions (sores), herpes viruses are associated with skin lesions, corneal infection, infection of the membranes covering the brain

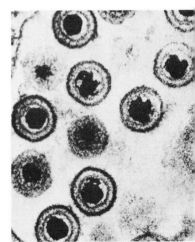

Figure 17.6 Herpes simplex virus. Too small to be seen even with the light microscope but visible with the electron microscope, these tiny particles cause persistent genital infections.

meningitis
(men''in-ji'tis)

encephalitis
(en''sef-ah-li'tis)

Plague of the Upper Middle Class?

According to many experts, if you are healthy, well-educated, have a good income, and enjoy a variety of sexual partners, the only communicable disease that is likely to give you any real problem is genital herpes (Leo 1982). The Herpes Resource Center (P.O. Box 100, Palo Alto, CA 94302) is a national organization of herpes sufferers, having (as of 1983) over forty thousand members and over fifty local chapters. The purposes of the organization are to provide up-to-date herpes information to members and the public and to support research on genital herpes. The profile of the members of this group is:

Sex: 51 percent are female.

Ethnicity: 95 percent are Caucasian.

Age: 80 percent are twenty to thirty-nine years old.

Education: 53 percent completed at least four years of college.

Income: 56 percent earn $20,000 a year or more.

---

and spinal cord (meningitis), brain infection (encephalitis, especially in newborns), and possibly cervical cancer. It is these latter two possibilities that lead to the greatest concern over genital herpes.

Long-Term Infection

Following initial infection, herpes simplex viruses apparently remain as lifelong infections in most cases, although they spend most of the time in a state of latency (dormancy). Infected people carry antibodies against the viruses, as indicated by blood tests, but these antibodies do not prevent occasional reactivation of the virus. Some 70 to 90 percent of adults carry antibodies against HSV-1, and over 20 percent carry antibodies against HSV-2.

Between active attacks, the herpes virus stays in the nerves serving the site of infection. This is why people tend to have repeated infections at the same site. In the case of genital herpes, the virus travels clear up to the sacral ganglia, nerve bundles located just outside of the spinal cord in the lower back (Hamilton 1980).The immune mechanism is apparently unable to reach the virus at this site.

Following the first attack of either oral or genital herpes lesions, one-third of all infected people experience no further attacks, and another third have attacks only very rarely. The unfortunate other third are subject to periodic, repeated attacks (Hamilton 1980). They may have four or five recurrences in the first year after initial infection and two or three in each subsequent year.

The virus seems to be reactivated by various stimuli, such as mechanical irritation, stress, hormonal changes, and certain foods. The infection is contagious whenever lesions are present. Some authorities suspect that the virus may be transmitted to others even when no symptoms are visible. This is especially true when infection is on the cervix of the uterus.

Symptoms of Herpes

Genital herpes sores may occur on the labia or within the vagina in females, or on the penis or within the urethra in males. They may also occur on the inside of the thighs or on the buttocks in either sex.

In someone not already carrying the virus, the symptoms of genital herpes usually appear about six days after sexual contact with an infected person. Subsequent attacks are caused by reactivation of the virus.

The first sign of a developing herpes attack that most people notice is a tingling, itching, or burning sensation near the site of the developing infection. Usually within hours, small red marks appear which, within a few more hours, develop into fluid-filled blisters that are red around the edges (figure 17.7). The entire area around the sores may be swollen and inflamed. The pain may be quite sharp, radiating out to adjacent areas. Many people will also experience more general symptoms, including swollen lymph nodes, aching muscles, fever, and a generally unwell feeling (Hamilton 1980).

Over the next two to ten days, the blisters break and begin to "weep." Before a scab forms, the sores may appear ulcerlike (depressed or cratered). Scab formation indicates that healing is under way. A person's first herpes attack may take as long as four weeks to completely heal, while subsequent attacks usually heal within two weeks. The scabs simply fall off, and no scar usually remains.

Figure 17.7 An attack of herpes simplex begins with the appearance of one to many small blisters, which in two to ten days will perforate and leave painful open lesions.

Herpes in Infants

If a pregnant woman has active herpes lesions at the time of the birth of her baby, there is a good chance that the infant will contract the disease during the birth process. Because the immune system of an infant is poorly developed, it is unable to fight the virus, which may spread throughout its body. The affinity of herpes virus for nerve tissue often leads to brain infection (encephalitis) in the infant with severe brain damage.

According to Hamilton (1980), when infants are infected at birth, about two-thirds suffer systemic (bodywide) infection, while about one-third have more localized infections, usually involving sores around the mouth or infection of the eyes. Of those with systemic infection, about 40 percent die, even with aggressive treatment with newly developed antiviral drugs (McKean 1981). Most of the survivors exhibit permanent brain damage. When the eyes are infected, there is danger of partial or complete loss of sight.

Because of the extreme risk to infants born when active herpes lesions are present in the mother, physicians almost always recommend cesarean deliveries for these cases.

dysplasia   *in situ*
(dis-pla′se-ah)   (in si′tu)

Cervical Cancer—A Sexually Transmitted Disease?

The cervix is the most common portion of the female reproductive system in which cancer appears. Considerable research has focused on a possible relationship of herpes simplex virus type 2 to cervical cancer. This research has demonstrated that women with genital herpes infections experience a doubling in the frequency of cervical **dysplasia**—abnormal changes in the tissue covering the cervix (Bettoli 1982). These changes often precede the appearance of cervical cancer. Even more alarming is the finding that women with genital herpes infections have an increase in actual carcinoma *in situ* (the first stage in cervical cancer). This increase is variously reported in women with genital herpes at anywhere from four times (McKean 1981) to eight times (Bettoli 1982) the rate of women who don't have genital herpes.

The American Cancer Society (1981) reports that the incidence of cervical cancer may be statistically related to a patient's sexual history. Apparently, the incidence of cervical cancer is higher among women who begin sexual intercourse at younger ages and among those with a history of many sexual partners. Conversely, the incidence of cervical cancer has been reported to be low among virgins, women experiencing intercourse at a later date, and women with a history of few sexual partners (Christopherson 1981; Gusberg 1981; Bettoli 1982). This statistical correlation may be related to the correlation between genital herpes and cervical cancer in that early intercourse and multiple sexual partners increases one's chances of being infected by the herpes virus.

It is important to emphasize that no cause-and-effect relationship between herpes virus and cervical cancer has been demonstrated; only a statistical correlation has been found. It is not known if the virus causes the cancer or if its presence is just coincidental. Other factors might also account for an association between herpes virus and cancer. For example, early intercourse and multiple sexual partners would also increase the possibility of being infected by other sexually transmitted pathogens that might contribute to cancer development.

In any case, it seems advisable for women carrying herpes simplex virus type 2 to obtain periodic Pap smears. As cervical cancer usually remains in the tiny *in situ* stage for several (perhaps five) years before starting to invade other tissue, routine Pap smears detect these tiny spots while they can still be easily and successfully removed.

Living with Herpes

Herpes can create a heavy emotional burden. Sores on the lips or face are unattractive. A genital outbreak causes worry for the victim as well as for his or her sexual partners. The apparently increased risk of cervical cancer among women with genital herpes is a special source of anxiety. Some infected people view themselves as "sexual lepers" and withdraw entirely from the sexual arena (Leo 1982). However, this seems to be an overreaction to the problem.

End of the Sexual Revolution?

According to Leo (1982), genital herpes may be bringing a reluctant, grudging chastity back into fashion. Millions of those who carry the virus fear transmitting it to others, and millions who don't yet have herpes fear picking it up from a casual sexual partner. At least for some people, herpes has tipped the balance away from casual sex for pleasure toward sex only in a committed relationship.

For many, the psychological effects of having herpes overshadow its physical discomfort. Leo (1982) reports that many people who contract herpes go through stages similar to those of mourning for the death of a loved one: shock, emotional numbing, isolation and loneliness, serious depression, and sexual dysfunctions such as impotence. As time goes on, some people come to see themselves as ugly, contaminated, and dangerous.

How, when, and whether to tell potential sexual partners that one has herpes is a thorny matter. If one reveals this information too soon, there is a good chance that no relationship will develop. On the other hand, withholding this information from a sex partner doesn't seem very fair. Many herpes sufferers think that it is not necessary to tell early in a relationship or on one-night stands (Leo 1982). Among sufferers, there is a feeling that women are more honest than men about telling about the disease.

Certainly, those not already infected need to be pretty cautious about their sexual activity. It is not at all improper to ask a potential sexual partner whether he or she has genital herpes.

During an active outbreak and perhaps when symptoms are just starting, oral and genital herpes are quite contagious. Yet, according to Hamilton (1980), a few common-sense precautions can reduce the risk of spread and lessen the risks of herpes complications:

1. Individuals should avoid direct contact with oral or genital herpes lesions by not kissing or having sexual intercourse with someone who is in the midst of an attack. The infected person shouldn't kiss or have sexual intercourse with others until his or her sores are completely gone. Some authorities recommend the use of condoms if either partner has genital herpes but is between attacks, although it is not known whether latex is an effective barrier to the virus (Bettoli 1982).

2. The infected area should be dried thoroughly to prevent secondary infections, and the virus should not be carried to the eyes by hands, towels, or similar means.

3. Individuals with herpes should maintain general good health and nutrition and avoid physical irritation of the genitals as this seems to precipitate repeated attacks. Emotional stress is also thought to stimulate new attacks in some people.

4. Women with genital herpes should have semiannual Pap smears to ensure early detection of cervical cancer, should it develop. (The risk of cervical cancer is increased by an estimated four to eight times.)

A diagnosis of herpes is no reason to abandon hope. Understanding how herpes infections are transmitted and how symptoms can be successfully treated can help reduce both the pain and the anxiety that can accompany the disease.

Tzanck
(tsank)

Zovirax
(Zo'vir-aks)

acyclovir
(a-si'klo-vir)

Diagnosis of Herpes

Herpes is diagnosed by the Tzanck test. A small amount of tissue is scraped from the suspected herpetic lesions and smeared on a glass microscope slide. After a stain (methylene blue, for example) is applied, microscopic examination reveals unusually large tissue cells with multiple nuclei. Diagnosis is confirmed by specific blood tests (Benenson 1980).

Treatment of Herpes

As this is written, there is only limited relief of genital herpes available through drugs. One prescription drug, Zovirax (acyclovir), was approved in 1982 for treating genital herpes. It effectively reduces the severity and speeds the healing of a first attack of genital herpes, which is generally a person's most severe attack. However, it does not really eradicate the infection. Reactivation attacks may still occur, and this drug is not effective against such attacks. Drugs are also being used for herpes infection of the cornea of the eye and for the severe brain infection that develops in infants infected at birth.

For now, treatment of recurring attacks of genital herpes centers on the relief of pain, itching, and burning. Astringent and drying agents, such as Burow's solution or Epsom salts, may help. Some physicians recommend use of local pain relievers and antiseptic solutions, such as Betadine, to prevent bacterial infection of the open lesions. Fortunately, however, such bacterial infection seldom occurs.

There is little documented evidence that the virus is affected by special diets, vitamins, or nonprescription remedies. As in any disorder, unproven remedies should be avoided.

The fact that genital herpes lesions clear up with the passage of time even if untreated tends to make any form of treatment appear to work at least part of the time. What is really needed is an effective herpes vaccine. Several laboratories are working on such a vaccine, but its successful development appears to be several years in the future (Wallis 1982).

---

1. Do you or anyone you know have genital herpes? Are prospective sexual partners told about the disease? If so, how and when? If not, why not?
2. In terms of the type of pathogen, what distinguishes genital herpes from most other STDs? What are the current implications of this difference?
3. Do you think that the threat of herpes infection will alter or is already altering the more casual sexual relationships typical of the 1970s and early 1980s? Why or why not?
4. If you have herpes, explain how you cope with it on a day-to-day basis.

Candida albicans
(kan'di-dah al'bi-kanz)

candidiasis
(kan''di-di'ah-sis)

Vaginitis

Vaginitis is inflammation of the vagina. It can be caused by infectious organisms or by chemical or other irritations. The pathogens that cause vaginitis may be sexually transmitted, although they are often present in the healthy vagina and vaginitis is not necessarily related to sexual intercourse.

Many beneficial bacteria grow in the vagina of a healthy woman. Some of these bacteria help to keep the vagina acidic, and the acidity keeps potential pathogens under control. Thus, vaginitis often relates to something harming the beneficial bacteria or reducing the vagina's acidity, rather than being something that is "caught." Some of the factors known to promote vaginitis are: general lowered resistance (from stress, bad diet, fatigue, illness, or other factors), diabetes or pre-diabetic conditions, hormonal changes from pregnancy or birth control pills, antibiotics harming the beneficial bacteria, douching too often or with harmful products, wearing nylon or other clothing that does not "breathe," or mechanical irritation from intercourse without enough lubrication or masturbation with unclean or irritating objects.

Symptoms of vaginitis include an itching or burning sensation, pain, and vaginal discharge. Two of the more common causes of vaginitis are pathogens called *Candida* and *Trichomonas*.

Candida (Yeast Infection)

Some of the more troublesome infections of the sexual organs, especially the vagina, are caused by a yeastlike organism called *Candida albicans* (figure 17.8). This organism is a normal inhabitant of the mouth, digestive tract, and vagina. It is usually held in check by the other organisms present and by the body's natural defenses. *Candida* infection is technically called **candidiasis,** and is commonly called a "yeast infection."

Characteristic symptoms of vaginal candidiasis include burning and itching and a thick, whitish discharge that can be quite abundant. There may be patches of white pseudomembrane (false membrane) on the vaginal lining.

In treating vaginal candidiasis, there are several considerations. The vaginal area should be kept dry, and any contributing conditions, such as poor nutrition, should be corrected. Also, a variety of effective oral and vaginal medications are available by prescription. Male sex partners should use condoms during the period of the female's infection. This avoids "Ping-Pong" infections in which the male is infected and later reinfects the female.

Figure 17.8 *Candida albicans,* a common cause of vaginitis. This organism is a yeast.

Trichomonas
(trik"o-mo'nas)

trichomoniasis
(trik"o-mo-ni'ah-sis)

Flagyl
(flag"l)

metronidazole
(me"tro-ni'dah-zōl)

Trichomonas

Another common cause of vaginitis is infection by the protozoan (a one-celled organism) ***Trichomonas vaginalis*** (figure 17.9). *Trichomonas* lives in the vaginas of at least half of all women without producing noticeable symptoms (Boston Women's Health Book Collective 1976; Tortora, Funke and Case 1982). Symptomless infections of the male prostate gland, urethra, and seminal vesicles are also common. Under certain conditions, however, such as modification of the protozoan's environment by antibiotic therapy or by hormonal changes associated with birth control pills or pregnancy, *Trichomonas* can multiply enormously in either the male or female reproductive organs. Symptoms in the female can include intense itching and burning of the vagina and small rashlike spots on its lining. There is a profuse discharge of a thin, foamy, yellowish substance that may have a foul odor. Symptoms in the male, though they rarely occur, include urethritis or, even more rarely, inflammation of the prostate or seminal vesicles.

Trichomoniasis, as it is technically known, is a common infection among women throughout the world. The organism is transmitted from person to person by contact with vaginal and urethral discharges of infected persons during sexual contact, during birth, and possibly by contact with infected articles.

Trichomoniasis can be successfully treated by medically prescribed oral or vaginal medications. Simultaneous treatment of sexual partners is important in preventing reinfection. Even though a partner may by symptomless, he or she may be carrying the organism.

One drug commonly prescribed to treat trichomoniasis—Flagyl (metronidazole)—has several possible side effects that its users should be aware of. Most significantly, it has been shown to cause cancers (lung, breast, and lymphatic) in laboratory animals. For this reason, any unnecessary use should be avoided. Further, Flagyl should not be used in the first trimester of pregnancy because of the possibility of its causing congenital defects in the infant. Nursing mothers should use an alternative method of feeding their infants if Flagyl must be used. Finally, alcohol should not be consumed when Flagyl is being taken since the combination causes cramps, vomiting, and headaches.

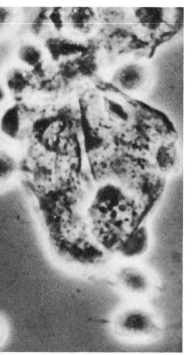

Figure 17.9 *Trichomonas vaginalis.* This microscopic, one-celled organism produces vaginitis and can colonize the male reproductive organs.

1. If you are a woman, have you ever had vaginitis? What do you think caused the vaginitis in your case? How was it treated?
2. Is vaginitis usually the result of sexual indiscretion? Why or why not?
3. What factors commonly contribute to the development of vaginitis?

cystitis
(sis-ti'tis)

Preventing Vaginitis

Since much vaginitis is caused by organisms already present in the vagina, rather than being "caught" from a partner, there are many things a woman can do to help prevent vaginitis. These suggestions are from *Our Bodies, Ourselves* by the Boston Women's Health Book Collective (1976) and other sources.

1. In general, douching is not recommended. Douching may actually contribute to the development of vaginitis by damaging the vagina's protective mucous layer and harming the beneficial, acid-forming bacteria. If you feel that you simply must douche, the less frequently you do so, the better. Further, an acidic solution, such as one or two tablespoons of vinegar or a small amount of unflavored yogurt in a quart of warm water, is preferable to most commercial douching products.
2. Wash your genital and anal region thoroughly every day and dry the area carefully. Don't use other people's towels or washcloths. Wash from front to back to avoid carrying rectal bacteria to the genital area. Avoid irritating soaps or sprays.
3. Wear cotton panties. Avoid nylon panties or panty hose. If purchasing panty hose with a cotton crotch, be sure it is really a cotton inset and not just cotton sewn over the nylon.
4. Avoid pants that fit so tightly in the crotch that they "cut" or irritate the genitals.
5. Make sure your sexual partners are clean. It is a good idea for a man to wash his penis before intercourse.
6. If lubrication is needed for intercourse, use a water-soluble jelly rather than petroleum jelly.
7. Avoid any sexual practice that is painful or abrasive to your vagina.
8. Try to eat a proper diet. The body's defenses against infection work much more effectively with adequate nutrition.

Cystitis

Cystitis is inflammation of the urinary bladder. Any of a variety of pathogens can cause this problem. The symptoms include frequent, burning, or painful urination; chills; fever; fatigue; and, infrequently, blood in the urine. Bladder infections occur more often in females than in males because the shorter urethra of the female makes it easier for bacteria to reach the bladder.

Cystitis should be treated promptly with medically prescribed drugs. Untreated, it may become a chronic problem or spread to the kidneys. Cleanliness, frequent urination, and drinking adequate water help to prevent this infection. Cystitis may or may not be related to sexual activity. Vigorous sexual activity tends to force bacteria through the urethra to the bladder, especially in women. Urinating immediately following intercourse helps to prevent cystitis arising from this cause. Also, females should cleanse the genital area from front to back to avoid carrying intestinal bacteria from the anus to the urethra. Some people report that drinking cranberry juice, which acidifies the urine, helps to prevent cystitis.

Chlamydia trachomatis   trachoma
(klah-mid'e-ah trah-   (trah-ko'mah)
ko'mah-tis)

Chlamydia Infection

Nonspecific urethritis (NSU), also called nongonorrheal or nongonococcal urethritis (NGU), is a term often applied to any inflammation of the urethra caused by something other than gonorrhea. Numerous pathogens have been associated with urethral infections, but the most common appears to be ***Chlamydia trachomatis***. (The same organism causes the eye infection *trachoma* [Saltz 1981].) *Chlamydia* are extremely small bacteria that live within host cells.

Symptoms of *Chlamydia* urethritis include pain during urination and a watery urethral discharge, often of a chronic nature. Since the symptoms are often mild in males, and females are usually without symptoms, many cases go untreated. In time, males may develop inflammation of the epididymis. In females, inflammation may cause sterility because of blockage of the cervix or fallopian tubes (Tortora, Funke, and Case 1982). As in gonorrhea, the bacteria can pass from mother to infant during childbirth, infecting the baby's eyes. Untreated, this eye infection leads to blindness because of the formation of scar tissue on the cornea. *Chlamydia* are the leading cause of blindness in the world today.

Chlamydia trachomatis has emerged as one of the most prevalent STDs among both adolescents and adults. Saltz (1981) found that 22 percent of sexually active adolescent females were infected, often on the cervix, while only 3 percent had gonorrhea.

Chlamydia is transmitted through sexual contact and is more common among people having a variety of sexual partners. Most cases can be cleared up with the combination of prescribed medication, avoidance of alcohol and caffeine, and moderation in sexual activity until the infection is healed. Partners should be treated simultaneously.

Pubic Lice

Commonly called "crab lice" or "crabs" because of their crablike appearance, pubic lice are small, gray insects (1/16 inch long) that live as external parasites on the body (figure 17.10). They live in body hair, holding onto the shaft of the hair with their crablike pincers. They prefer pubic hair but will also live in underarm hair and in eyebrows, eyelashes, and beards; they rarely live in scalp hair (which is too fine in texture).

Crab lice do not really pinch with their claws. But they do feed on human blood, causing an intense itching and discoloration of the skin. They often remain attached for days, with their sucking mouth-parts inserted into the skin of an unfortunate person.

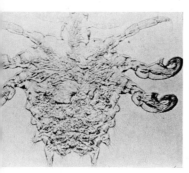

Figure 17.10   Pubic louse (crab louse). These small, gray insects live in body hair (preferably pubic hair) and feed on human blood. Actual size is only about one-sixteenth of an inch.

scabies
(ska'bēz)

Female lice attach eggs, called *nits,* to the body hair. These eggs hatch in six to eight days. Since the sexual maturity of pubic lice is reached in only fourteen to twenty-one days and each female lays up to fifty eggs, a crab louse infection can grow to alarming proportions in just a short time. Heavy infestations may result in fever and other disorders caused by toxins injected by the feeding lice.

Pubic lice may be transmitted through sexual intercourse. They can also be spread through other physical contact with infested people or by use of contaminated clothing, toilet seats, bedding, or other materials.

Crabs can usually be killed by washing the affected body parts with a special insecticide-containing shampoo, such as Kwell. Several applications are required. Contrary to popular belief, infested hair need not be shaved. Also, exposed clothing need not be thrown away, but it should not be worn until it is thoroughly washed in hot water.

Genital Warts

Genital warts may develop on, in, or around the sex organs. They commonly appear on the penis, labia, vaginal wall, or cervix. They are also common in and around the anus in homosexual males. Like other warts, genital warts are caused by a virus. This virus is usually transmitted by direct contact. Sixty percent of sexual partners of infected persons will develop genital warts (Dretler 1981).

Genital warts begin as tiny, soft, pink or red swellings. They grow rapidly, often developing a cauliflower appearance. They are usually diagnosed by their appearance, although sometimes a biopsy is done if the warts resemble cancer.

Genital warts seldom do any serious damage and usually disappear in time, even without treatment. They may be effectively treated or removed by a physician. People afflicted with genital warts should never try to treat the warts by themselves because the delicate surrounding tissues can be damaged in the process.

Scabies

Scabies is infection of the skin by tiny burrowing mites (figure 17.11). Scabies is highly contagious from person to person, usually by direct contact, and is often sexually transmitted. Scabies is not spread by clothing or bedding.

Symptoms include burrows that appear as discolored lines on the skin, welts, and water- or pus-filled blisters. Extreme itching is typical. In addition to the genital areas, scabies may appear under the breasts, in the armpits, between the fingers, and elsewhere. Scabies do *not* occur above the neck.

Scabies may be easily cured using Kwell or other insecticide-containing soaps, lotions, or ointments.

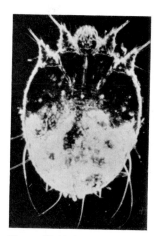

Figure 17.11 Scabies mite or itch mite. These tiny mites burrow through the skin, causing intense itching. They are spread from person to person by sexual or other contact. Actual size is about 0.3 mm.

STDs in the Gay Male Community

"Traditional" STDs, such as gonorrhea and syphilis, have long been recognized as being more prevalent among gay males than among heterosexual males or females or among lesbians.

Several explanations have been proposed for the major STD problem among gay males. Part of the answer seems to lie in the great variety of partners experienced by some, although not all, gay males. Possibly because of society's response to homosexuality, there is a tendency among some gay males to engage in impersonal, even anonymous, relationships that are extremely transient.

Specific sexual practices are also believed to be involved in the STD problem in the gay male community. In particular, oral and anal intercourse and anilingus (oral stimulation of the anus) are well suited for transmitting certain diseases. For example, dysenteries (diarrhea-producing intestinal infections) are easily transmitted through anilingus or fellatio following anal intercourse and are much more prevalent in the gay male population than in comparable heterosexual groups (Ismach 1981).

Hepatitis B (a viral infection of the liver) is another major problem in the gay male community (Centers for Disease Control, 4 June 1982). It is present in 38 percent of homosexual men who report having had twenty or more partners in a six-month period (Marwick 1981). Hepatitis B virus may remain in the blood for years following infection and is often transmitted by exposure to blood or blood products. The virus is also thought to be present in the semen of infected males. A relatively new vaccine effectively prevents hepatitis B and is highly recommended for gay males who have multiple sexual partners.

Of greatest concern has been the emergence among gay males and certain other high-risk groups of **acquired immune deficiency syndrome (AIDS).** (A syndrome is a group of characteristic symptoms of a particular condition.) Other groups experiencing high AIDS rates have been Haitian immigrants (4 percent of the cases), intravenous drug abusers (17 percent of the cases), and recipients of blood transfusions (1 percent of the cases). Most cases (72 percent) have occurred in gay males (Centers for Disease Control, 22 June 1984). The same source reports that 45 percent of all known patients have died and that 76 percent of people diagnosed as long as two years previously had died. As of mid-1984, about 5,000 cases had been diagnosed.

AIDS involves a disruption in the functioning of the immune mechanism, greatly reducing one's immunity to infectious diseases and increasing the risk of certain cancers. In 1984, several research groups reported finding an apparent cause—a virus infecting the lymphocytes (blood cells that produce immunity). This virus is seemingly transmitted in much the same way as the hepatitis B virus, including some sexual practices (especially anal intercourse) as well as exposure to blood or blood products.

Pneumocystic carinii
(nu''mo-sis'tik kah-ri'ne)

Most AIDS deaths have been from two causes. Foremost is a type of pneumonia caused by the protozoan *Pneumocystis carinii*. Second is a form of cancer called Kaposi's sarcoma. Both of these conditions are quite rare except in AIDS patients. Needless to say, AIDS is a major concern within the gay community and among public health workers.

---

1. Is cystitis more common in men or women? Why?
2. *Chlamydia trachomatis* has emerged as one of the most prevalent STDs among both adolescents and adults. Had you ever heard of it before? Would you recognize its symptoms?
3. Why can a pubic lice infestation grow so quickly?
4. What happens to genital warts if they are not treated?
5. Several types of infections have become prevalent in the gay male community. What are they, and what sexual practices do they seem to relate to?

Preventing Sexually Transmitted Diseases

So far, our discussion of STDs has emphasized recognition of their symptoms and the importance of obtaining prompt treatment if infection occurs. But from both personal and public health standpoints, it is always more desirable to prevent any disease than to treat it. The prevention of STDs requires action by both the individual and public health personnel.

Personal Prevention

As with most other diseases, the ultimate responsibility for the prevention of STDs lies with the individual. The most important personal preventive measure is the avoidance of sexual contact with anyone who is likely to be infected. Considering today's high incidence of sexually transmitted diseases, that would include anyone who has a variety of partners. It would also include someone who has one regular partner who, in turn, has many partners. It is important to remember that STDs can be transmitted through either heterosexual or homosexual contact. Also, they can be transmitted through either genital-genital, oral-genital, or anal-genital activities.

The prime mechanism for prevention of sexually transmitted diseases, then, is selective sexual behavior. Unfortunately for the public as a whole, this mechanism has failed because it has never been widely practiced. The current STD incidence is glaring evidence of this failure. Thus, for the person who chooses to be somewhat less discriminating in his or her choice of sexual partners, it becomes important to make maximum use of other personal preventive methods to reduce the chances of infection. We use the word *reduce* rather than *eliminate,* since even the best of the currently available preventive methods is far from totally effective.

During precoital sex play, individuals should be alert to any signs of possible infection in their partner, such as a urethral discharge or genital sores of any kind. If any such signs are present, further sexual activity with that partner should be avoided. Incidentally, while a shower before coitus is very pleasant and may also help prevent disease transmission, it is not the best place to hold "inspection," as any urethral discharge that might be present is washed away.

During intercourse, the use of a condom by the male is considered very helpful in preventing disease transmission, especially gonorrhea. A condom helps to prevent the transmission of gonorrhea in either direction—from male to female or from female to male. To be effective, however, the condom must be applied onto the erect penis at the very start of any sexual activity, before any genital contact is made.

Even when a condom is used, it is still important to wash with soap and water immediately after contact because the condom covers only the penis. Several of the diseases, especially syphilis, can enter the body through the skin at any point. The condom thus affords only limited protection against syphilis. In its favor, however, it should be noted that the condom is the only commonly used device that is effective both as a preventive measure against gonorrhea and as a contraceptive. Carefully and consistently used, it can be reasonably effective for both purposes. Although it has traditionally been a male responsibility to provide condoms, a woman might want to keep a supply available to protect herself against STD and, if she is not otherwise protected, against pregnancy as well.

As we have mentioned, it is important to wash with soap and water immediately after sexual contact even if a condom has been used. The pathogens of the diseases that enter the body through the skin can sometimes be killed or removed in this manner.

Urination immediately after sexual contact may help to reduce the chance of infection by gonorrhea. It also helps to prevent urethritis as well as bladder infections (cystitis).

A special precaution suggested for gay males is to avoid oral-anal stimulation except in an exclusively monogamous relationship (Ismach 1981). The incidence of amoebic and other dysenteries is very high among gay males having many partners.

Antibiotics have been used on a preventive basis, administered either before or after possible exposure to STD. However, this practice cannot be recommended for routine use because it tends to breed antibiotic-resistant strains of pathogens. It also tends to build allergies to the antibiotics in those who receive them.

The ideal personal preventive would, of course, be a vaccine for each disease. Few communicable diseases have ever really been controlled until effective vaccines have been developed against them. Smallpox, for example, was totally eradicated through immunization.

Public Health Measures

Many methods are used by public health agencies in their fight against STDs. And while STD is still rampant, it seems likely that the incidence would be even greater than it is without the efforts of public health workers.

Most public health departments sponsor education programs concerned with prevention and symptoms of sexually transmitted diseases and the importance of prompt treatment. Some public health departments assist local schools in their STD education programs.

Clinics for the diagnosis and treatment of STD are also common functions of public health departments. The services of clinics are usually offered at little or no cost to the individual. Laws in most states have been revised to allow the treatment of minors, often as young as twelve years of age, without obtaining permission from their parents or otherwise notifying them. It has been found that when parental permission must be obtained prior to treatment, many young people will avoid treatment out of fear of reprisal from parents, thus tragically risking permanent damage from infection.

Another important public health function in STD control is *case finding.* In many localities, each patient treated for a sexually transmitted disease, especially for syphilis, is interviewed to determine from whom the disease might have been caught and to whom it may have been transmitted. These people can then be contacted, notified that they may be infected, and asked to visit the public health department or their private physician for STD testing. Since so many cases of STD are symptomless, this is the only way in which many infected people can learn of their disease before serious damage is done.

While it may seem obvious, the STD patient should be warned to refrain from sexual contact with previous partners until they have been tested and, if necessary, treated. It is common in STD clinics to find that a newly cured patient has gone back to the same partner and become reinfected.

A public health technique that has revealed thousands of cases of syphilis is compulsory blood testing for certain people, such as applicants for marriage licenses, pregnant women, military personnel, hospital patients, and new employees of many corporations. Most of the cases so detected are in the symptomless latent period, and without detection and treatment, many would progress into late syphilis, with its irreversible damage to vital organs and even death. However, some of this testing, such as that required for obtaining a marriage license, has been challenged as being too expensive in terms of the number of cases revealed.

In summary, while public health departments are making great efforts to control STDs, syphilis, gonorrhea, and genital herpes still occur in epidemic proportions. It is imperative for individuals to take reasonable precautions against infection, to know the symptoms of these diseases, to seek prompt treatment if symptoms develop, and to notify recent sexual partners of the possibility of their being infected.

1.   If you were about to engage in sexual activity with someone you only recently met but were highly attracted to, what precautions relative to the STDs would you take?

"Did you talk to the guy?"

"No, but I did go to see the doctor at the clinic. He said he would call him, said he would explain the situation without using my name."

"Did you get taken care of?"

"Yeah, the doctor said I was lucky that you told me. It could have stayed undetected for a long time. Then I'd really have been in trouble."

"Good, I'm glad that's over."

"Jim, where do we go from here?"

"I don't know, Deb. Let's just take it easy for awhile. I don't think either one of us wants to pick up *exactly* where we left off. Let's just take it one step at a time."

Summary

1.   Some pathogens have an affinity for mucous membranes and limited survival away from the body. Thus, sexual contact is ideal for their transmission.

2.   Some general concepts of communicable diseases are: pathogens are the infectious agents; transmission is the transfer of a pathogen from one person to another; the incubation period is the time between exposure and appearance of symptoms; the communicable period is when the disease can be transmitted to other people; symptomless carriers are those people who are able to infect others even though they themselves experience no symptoms; body defenses are able to protect us against many pathogens; and drugs can control most types of pathogens but are of limited value against viruses.

3.   Diseases fitting the descriptions of various STDs can be traced back for thousands of years. The incidence of STDs declined to a low point in the early 1950s, but in 1957, the incidence began increasing, apparently coinciding with the beginning of a trend toward more casual sexual relationships.

4.   The current incidence of gonorrhea is estimated at three to four million cases per year; over 33,000 cases of syphilis are reported each year; and new cases of genital herpes are estimated at over half a million each year.

5.   STDs affect all age, income, and ethnic groups. Contributing to high STD rates are birth control pills (greater sexual freedom, less use of condoms, reduced vaginal acidity), life-styles incorporating greater sexual freedom and mobility, sexual

relationships at earlier ages, greater variety in sexual partners, and attitudes that inhibit discussion, prevention, or treatment of STDs.

6.   Gonorrhea begins as a local infection of the membranes of the genitals, throat, rectum, or the eye. If not promptly treated, it may enter the blood and infect the membranes lining the heart or the joints. In males, genital gonorrhea begins as painful urethritis. In females, early symptoms include slight vaginal irritation and discharge and often are ignored. In either sex, untreated gonorrhea may lead to sterility. Untreated females also may develop massive abdominal infection. Gonorrhea is diagnosed by stained microscope slides and cultures. Tetracycline drugs are replacing penicillin in treating gonorrhea.

7.   Syphilis is always a systemic infection with definite stages. Primary syphilis consists of one or more chancres. Secondary syphilis may include a variable rash, oral and genital sores, and other symptoms. Latent syphilis, which has no symptoms, may last for many years. Tertiary (late) syphilis involves permanent damage to vital organs. Congenital syphilis can cause a stillborn or damaged infant. Syphilis is diagnosed by blood tests and microscope slides and treated with penicillin.

8.   Genital herpes virus infections present special problems because they are often lifelong and cannot yet be cured with drugs. The primary symptoms of genital herpes are small blisters that appear and then break to leave raw, sore spots. Attacks recur, although the first is usually the worst. If a pregnant woman has active herpes lesions at the time of the birth of her baby, there is great likelihood that the child will contract the disease and die or have permanent brain damage. Women carrying herpes simplex virus type 2 appear to have four to eight times increased risk of cervical cancer. Herpes is diagnosed by the Tzanck test and blood tests.

9.   Vaginitis is very common and may or may not relate to sexual activity. Symptoms include an itching or burning sensation, pain, and vaginal discharge. *Candida* (a yeast) and *Trichomonas* (a protozoan) are among the most common causes. Either may be found in the healthy vagina but usually are held in control by acid-forming bacteria. Vaginitis can be successfully treated with a variety of oral and vaginal medications.

10.   Cystitis (bladder inflammation) can be caused by a variety of pathogens and should be treated promptly. It can often be prevented by drinking plenty of water, urinating frequently, urinating after sexual intercourse, and cleansing the female genitals from front to rear.

11.   *Chlamydia* infection of the urethra, also called nonspecific or nongonococcal urethritis, is a term often applied to any inflammation of the urethra caused by something other than gonorrhea. Symptoms include painful urination and a watery urethral discharge. It is sexually transmitted and can be cured with antibiotics.

12.   Pubic lice (crabs) are blood-sucking insects that live in body hair and that are often transmitted during sexual contact. Crabs are controlled by special shampoos.

13.   Genital warts are caused by a sexually transmitted virus. They seldom do any serious damage and usually disappear in time, even without treatment.

14.   Scabies is infection of the skin by tiny burrowing mites. Often sexually transmitted, scabies is easily cured with insecticide-containing products.

15.   Other diseases may be sexually transmitted and present special problems in the gay male community. Hepatitis B virus is thought to be transmitted in semen, while intestinal infections are transmitted through anilingus or fellatio following anal intercourse. Acquired immune deficiency syndrome (AIDS) is believed to be caused by a virus and to be transmitted in the same ways as hepatitis B. It results in infections and cancers that are often fatal.

16.   Prevention of STDs is a personal responsibility. It involves selective sexual behavior, examining a prospective sexual partner for signs of disease, showering before and after contact, using a condom during intercourse, and urinating after intercourse. Public health measures of preventing STDs include educational programs, clinics for STD diagnosis and treatment, case-finding efforts, and compulsory blood testing for certain people.

5

PATTERNS IN SEXUALITY

18

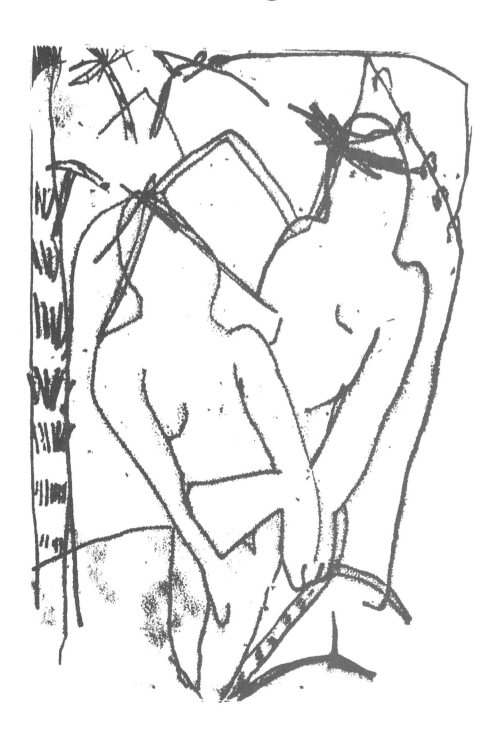

Dear Frank,

I know that this will come as a complete surprise and shock to you, but I am filing for a divorce. It is true that we have always gotten along very well, but there is something that you must know. Over the past several years, I have gradually become aware that I actually prefer the love of other women. Frank, I am a lesbian.

Believe me, I didn't know this when we got married; I would not have deceived you in that way. As you know, you were my first lover. Very early, I wondered why sex didn't seem the same for me as it apparently does for other women. I hope you haven't interpreted my lack of sexual enthusiasm as meaning that I don't love you, because, Frank, I really do love you. But, sexually, I am just not very excited by men. Please don't take this personally—you are the nicest man I have ever known. It is really hard for me to write this letter.

You know that it was a long time before I ever climaxed when we made love. But you don't know how I finally did it. One day at work a new woman was hired, and I felt some kind of instant attraction to her. At the time, I didn't even know it was sexual. But one morning while you and I were making love I started thinking about her. And that was the first time I ever came with you. I still remember how happy you were and how guilty I felt because, Frank, in my mind, you were her as I was coming.

For about the next year, I always thought about women while you and I made love. But it still hadn't really occurred to me to try a relationship with a woman. Then one day some of the women from work were planning a party for after work and invited me. It was the biggest shock of my life when I saw them starting to kiss each other at that party. At that time, I thought that lesbians must be really different from other women, and these women seemed so normal. But after my shock, what I felt was excitement—sexual excitement. And that evening was my initiation to the lovemaking of another woman.

Our preference for sexual partners of the same or opposite gender, or both genders, is our sexual orientation. Being attracted mainly to people of the opposite sex is **heterosexuality.** Being attracted primarily to people of our own sex is **homosexuality.** Feeling attraction to people of both sexes is **bisexuality.**

Marmor (1980) defines a homosexual person as one who is motivated in adult life by a definite preferential erotic attraction to members of the same sex and who usually (but not necessarily) engages in overt sexual relations with them. Such a definition does not include patterns of homosexual behavior such as adolescent experimentation or homosexual activity among those who are deprived of heterosexual partners. It does include, however, people who have intense sexual longing for members of the same sex, yet are prohibited by fears or moral training from actually indulging in homsexual activity. We should also note that the definition does not exclude the capacity for *heterosexual* arousal and activity. Many primarily homosexual individuals are to some degree involved in heterosexual activity.

In this chapter, we use the term **straight** for a person who is primarily heterosexual. The term **gay** is applied to a primarily homosexual person of either sex, while **lesbian** is another term for a homosexually oriented female. The word *lesbian* derives from the Greek island of Lesbos, where, in the seventh century B.C., the poetess Sappho lived and wrote about her love for other women. Some homosexual women would rather be referred to as lesbian, in preference to gay, while others feel that either of the terms is acceptable.

It is common among poorly informed people to stereotype individuals on the basis of their sexual orientation. But there is no such thing as *the* homosexual, any more than there is *the* heterosexual. Each one of us is a unique individual, regardless of our sexual orientation. Our sexual orientation is just one of many aspects of our personality. Thus, any statements we make about people on the basis of their sexual orientations must be highly qualified.

Continuum of Sexual Orientations

Homosexuality-heterosexuality is not an either-or proposition. Sexual orientation lies along a **sexual continuum**—a wide range with infinite degrees of balance in sexual attraction falling between the two extremes of exclusive homosexual attraction and exclusive heterosexual desire (figure 18.1).

In placing individuals along the continuum of orientation, it may be argued whether it is more meaningful to emphasize each person's perceived attractions or his or her actual sexual partners, since there may be quite a discrepancy between the sex of the partners a person would really prefer and the sex of a person's actual partners. Some people, for example, would prefer partners of their own sex, but for reasons of social acceptability or perhaps as a result of religious training, they con-

Figure 18.1 People are not necessarily either homosexual or heterosexual, but may feel any degree of relative attraction to people of each sex. People who are about equally attracted to both sexes are said to be bisexual. The numbers 0 to 6 refer to Kinsey's system of classification.

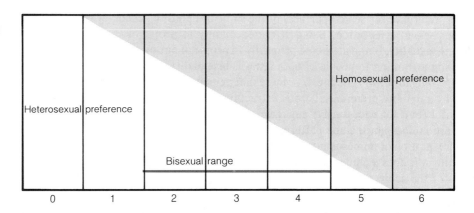

fine themselves to relationships with people of the opposite sex. Some married men and women fall into this latter category. Conversely, people who prefer partners of the opposite sex may, in a restrictive environment such as a prison, have relationships with persons of the same sex. Thus, it appears that the attractions a person *feels* are more significant in classifying that person's sexual orientation than is the sex of any of that person's sexual partners.

Alfred Kinsey (1948), who was so often a pioneer in sexual research, recognized that sexual orientation fell along a continuum, even though most people at that time thought only in terms of homosexuality *or* heterosexuality. Kinsey classified people at seven points along the continuum, ranging from exclusive heterosexuality (0) to exclusive homosexuality (6) (tables 18.1, 18.2, and 18.3). Kinsey's seven categories were:

0. Exclusively heterosexual attraction or experience
1. Minimal homosexual attraction or experience
2. Some homosexual attraction or experience
3. Truly bisexual; equal homosexual and heterosexual attraction or experience
4. Some heterosexual attraction or experience
5. Minimal heterosexual attraction or experience
6. Exclusively homosexual attraction or experience

The estimates in tables 18.1 and 18.2 are for the entire white male U.S. population, for current sexual activity. This is very old data, but there is no similar survey of this magnitude (over twelve thousand interviews) that has assessed sexual orientation in this manner more recently. The estimates in table 18.3 are based on interviews of over eight thousand white U.S. females. Combined figures for all females (married and unmarried) were not published.

Table 18.1 Kinsey's Sexual Orientation Ratings for All Males Surveyed.

	Ratings							
	0	1	2	3	4	5	6	X
Age								
15	48.5%	3.6%	6.0%	4.7%	3.7%	2.6%	7.4%	23.6%
20	69.3	4.4	7.4	4.4	2.9	3.4	4.9	3.3
25	79.2	3.9	5.1	3.2	2.4	2.3	2.9	1.0
30	83.1	4.0	3.4	2.1	3.0	1.3	2.6	0.5
35	86.7	2.4	3.4	1.9	1.7	0.9	2.6	0.4
40	86.8	3.0	3.6	2.0	0.7	0.3	2.3	1.3

Source: Kinsey, Alfred C., Wardell B. Pomeroy, and Clyde E. Martin. *Sexual Behavior in the Human Male.* Philadelphia: Saunders, 1948.
Note: X indicates no sexual contacts or desire for contacts.

Table 18.2 Kinsey's Sexual Orientation Ratings for Married Males.

	Ratings							
	0	1	2	3	4	5	6	Total of 1–6
Age	*Education level: Some high school completed*							
20	83.2%	4.8%	4.8%	4.8%	1.2%	1.2%	0.0%	16.8%
25	92.5	1.9	4.7	0.9	0.0	0.0	0.0	7.5
30	88.7	3.8	2.5	0.0	5.0	0.0	0.0	11.3
35	91.5	3.4	0.0	1.7	3.4	0.0	0.0	8.5
Age	*Education level: Some college completed*							
20	96.6%	0.0%	3.4%	0.0%	0.0%	0.0%	0.0%	3.4%
25	91.3	4.8	1.8	0.9	0.6	0.3	0.3	8.7
30	89.9	7.3	1.0	0.8	0.5	0.5	0.0	10.1
35	90.2	5.7	2.7	0.7	0.7	0.0	0.0	9.8

Source: Kinsey, Alfred C., Wardell B. Pomeroy, and Clyde E. Martin. *Sexual Behavior in the Human Male.* Philadelphia: Saunders, 1948.

Table 18.3 Kinsey's Sexual Orientation Ratings for Females.

	Ratings							
	0	1	2	3	4	5	6	X
Age	*Single females*							
15	34%	2%	1%	1%	—	—	2%	60%
20	72	5	2	1	1	1	1	17
25	72	4	3	1	3	1	2	14
30	67	5	4	2	3	2	2	15
35	61	6	3	3	2	3	3	19
Age	*Married females*							
17	80%	9%	1%	0%	0%	0%	1%	9%
20	89	5	1	1	—	—	—	3
25	90	6	1	—	—	—	—	2
50	88	4	3	0	0	1	0	4

Source: Kinsey, Alfred C., Wardell B. Pomeroy, Clyde E. Martin. *Sexual Behavior in the Human Female.* Philadelphia: Saunders, 1953.
Note: X indicates no sexual contacts or desire for contacts.

Incidence of Homosexuality

Various figures are quoted on the incidence of homosexuality in the United States. Much of this variation relates to different survey techniques used and the continuing reluctance of some homosexual people to reveal their sexual preferences. But another variable is in where the line is drawn in defining homosexuality. As we have already discussed, sexual orientation falls along a continuum, with all degrees of relative attraction to one's own or opposite sex.

On the basis of various studies, Marmor (1980) concluded that the incidence of more or less exclusively homosexual behavior in the United States and other Western cultures ranges from 5 to 10 percent for adult males and from 3 to 5 percent for adult females. If bisexual behavior is included, the incidence may easily be twice these figures.

In any event, it adds up to perhaps as many as sixteen million gay Americans. The exact number is not really that important, except to illustrate that gay people make up a sizable group that can represent a significant economic and political force in our society. For this reason, gay rights organizations emphasize the large number of gay people. The National Gay Task Force, for example, estimates that one out of every four families has a gay family member.

1. Where would you place yourself on Kinsey's continuum of sexual orientation?
2. Were you surprised to learn of the number of homosexual and bisexual people in the United States? If so, why do you think you were surprised?
3. Does your college or university have organizations of gay and/or lesbian people?

Origins of Homosexuality

At this time, little can be said with any certainty regarding the development of homosexuality, or any other sexual orientation for that matter. Over the years, many theories have been proposed to explain a homosexual orientation. Some have been conclusively disproven, but none has been conclusively proven. Theories on sexual orientation can be categorized as biological, psychological, and cultural, although this compartmentalization is somewhat unrealistic. Each of these categories influences the others, and all seem to influence our choice of sexual partners. A valid theory will explain the development of heterosexual orientation as well as homosexual orientation.

Before examining any specific theories, it should be noted that many forces are believed to influence the development of sexual orientation. No single theory is ever likely to adequately explain how everyone's sexual orientation develops or even how one specific individual's preference in sexual partners has developed. Human emotions and behavior are far too complex to be explained by simplistic theories.

Biological Theories

Biological theories on the development of sexual orientation usually revolve around chromosomes, genes, hormones, and/or various prenatal influences. The possibility of variations in the numbers of sex chromosomes (X and Y) or other chromosomes influencing sexual orientation can be rather quickly dismissed, however. The fact is that the chromosomes of homosexual or bisexual people are no different in number or structure than those of heterosexual individuals (Money 1980a). When people have irregular chromosomes, they may have physical abnormalities and may exhibit deficient intellect, but they are not necessarily homosexual.

The possible role of other genetic factors in influencing sexual orientation is less clearly understood at this time. Certainly, no definite genes for homosexuality, bisexuality, or heterosexuality have been identified. If any yet-to-be-detected genes do influence sexual orientation, they probably act through influencing the prenatal hormonal conditioning of the brain, which *may* destine our ultimate adult sexual orientation to be heterosexual, bisexual, or homosexual (Money 1980a). Meanwhile, most available evidence favors a nongenetic basis for the development of sexual orientation.

The role of sex hormones in influencing sexual orientation has been researched, but much conflicting information has been published (see table 18.4). Given

Table 18.4 Hormone Levels of Homosexual vs. Heterosexual People, Survey of the Literature.

Hormone	Total Number of Studies	Number of Studies Showing		
		Increase	Decrease	No Difference
Homosexual Males				
Testosterone	12	4	3	5
Estrogens	6	5 (in blood)	1 (in urine)	
Luteinizing hormone	7	3		4
Follicle-stimulating hormone	5	2		3
Homosexual Females				
Estrogens	2		1	1
Testosterone	3	2		1
Luteinizing hormone	1	1		

Source: Tourney, Garfield. "Hormones and Homosexuality." In *Homosexual Behavior*, edited by Judd Marmor. New York: Basic Books, 1980.

narcissism
(nar'si-sizm)

all of this conflicting information, it is difficult to draw any valid conclusions. Future studies using more refined methods of recording hormone levels and based upon more carefully selected and controlled population groups may settle the question of the relationship, if any, of hormones to homosexuality.

Considerable research in recent years also has focused on the possibility of prenatal (before birth) sexual differentiation of the brain having an influence on adult sexual orientation. Many researchers (Tourney 1980; Bell, Weinberg, and Hammersmith 1981) feel that if hormones do influence the development of heterosexuality, bisexuality, and homosexuality, they are more likely to exert this action prenatally rather than at puberty or in adulthood. Again, though, we will have to wait for the results of painstaking future research for the possible confirmation of this theory.

Psychological Theories

Most authorities now favor psychological theories on the development of sexual orientation. Unfortunately, they do not all agree on any one particular theory. And, perhaps, it is unrealistic to expect that a single mechanism could account for so complex a phenomenon as human sexual orientation.

Before we describe any of the psychological theories, we should mention one criticism that is leveled at much of the research done in this area. The problem is that many of the research subjects are people who are involved in therapy for emotional problems or conflicts. Many research projects thus fail to reflect a true cross section of either the homosexual or the heterosexual populations. In particular, studies on homosexual orientation tend to ignore the fact that a majority of gay people are quite happy (Riess 1980) and, thus, do not come to the attention of psychologists.

One of the earlier psychological theories, and an example of those derived from studies of patients in therapy, is the psychoanalytic, or Freudian, theory. This theory holds that a homosexual orientation is the result of unresolved Oedipus conflicts (Socarides 1978). In brief, the idea is that every child goes through a phase of sexual attraction for the parent of the opposite sex. But this attraction must be suppressed for fear of reprisal from the parent of the same sex. Most people grow up to transfer their heterosexual feelings to people other than their parent. But, in some, any attraction to a person of the opposite sex calls forth all of the anxieties, fears, and guilts once elicited by attraction to the parent of the opposite sex. Thus, heterosexual relationships are difficult or impossible for these people. Homosexual relationships are preferred because they produce less anxiety.

Another early theory (Solomon and Patch 1971) relates to narcissism, the love of one's own self or body. According to this theory, partners of one's same sex are preferred because they more closely resemble one's own beloved self.

Some of the more widely accepted theories on the psychological development of sexual orientation relate to early childhood family experiences—how parents relate to a child and to each other. One such theory on male homosexuality (Bieber 1962; Saghir and Robins 1973) holds that the mother transfers her love to her son while at the same time being overprotective. She is seen as being seductive with her son and as communicating her contempt of the male role. The father in this situation is seen as being withdrawn and resentful of or hostile to his son. However, many homosexual males come from very different home situations, and many people from parents fitting this description grow up to be heterosexual.

Most of these theories presume that the "normal" pattern of development is toward a heterosexual orientation and that a homosexual orientation is assumed to result from something going astray in that development. Not all authorities, however, accept the idea that we are naturally destined to be heterosexual. Instead, they feel that we are born **pansexual** or **omnisexual.** Either term means that we will respond to anything that feels good, whether those good feelings come from our hand, some object, or a person of either sex. But we learn to restrict our sexual responses to those stimuli toward which our culture directs us. In our culture, that generally means people of the opposite sex. But, in some cultures, homosexual relationships are encouraged, especially in youth. That enjoyment of homosexual activity is nearly universal in such cultures tends to contradict the notion that heterosexual attraction is "normal" and that homosexual relationships are the result of flawed psychosexual development.

Cultural Factors

Information on homosexual behavior in most of the world's past or present societies is scarce and often unreliable. This lack of knowledge stems from fear and prejudice surrounding the study of human sexual behavior and from the difficulties associated with the collection of information on a subject that is regarded as personal in most societies (Carrier 1980).

Cross-cultural data on homosexual behavior also have been complicated by the prejudice of some observers (especially in the past) who have considered homosexuality to be unnatural or immoral. Also, in many of the societies studied, homosexuality has been stigmatized (condemned) and thus not openly practiced or discussed. Thus, information of this kind must be interpreted cautiously.

Different expectations for females and males are present in every known society (Carrier 1980). Although the behavioral boundaries between the sexes vary considerably from culture to culture, there is a general expectation in every society that most adult men and women will cohabit (live together) and produce the next generation. Social pressure is thus applied in the direction of heterosexuality. The general rule is that one should have a mate of the opposite sex and produce children.

Carrier (1980) reports three major types of societies with regard to the type of response made to homosexual behavior: those that basically accept homosexual behavior, those that outlaw such behavior as scandalous and/or criminal, and those that neither accept nor outlaw homosexual behavior but have a cultural formulation that tries to ensure that homosexuality does not occur.

In a study of seventy-six societies, Ford and Beach (1952) found that, in 64 percent of them, homosexual activities were considered either "normal" or "socially acceptable" for at least certain members of the community. In some societies (Keraki of New Guinea, Aranda of Australia, and Siwans of North Africa), male homosexual activities were universal but did not preclude the more predominant heterosexual activities. Even among the 36 percent of societies in which homosexual practices were either condemned or prohibited, there was evidence, at least in some, that such practices continued covertly.

Those behaviors that are considered to be homosexual vary from culture to culture. What is considered homosexuality in one culture may be considered appropriate behavior within gender roles in another culture. For example, in the United States, fellatio and anal intercourse between two males is generally (unless force is involved) considered homosexual behavior for both parties. However, in some cultures, such as those of Mexico, Brazil, Greece, Turkey, and Morocco, only the passive recipient (insertee) is considered homosexual while the active insertor is not (Carrier 1980). Further, some societies, such as those in the highlands of New Guinea, have incorporated what in many cultures are considered homosexual acts into their male rituals. For example, the swallowing of semen through fellation by young males is considered essential for proper growth, strength, and masculinity.

Finally, few cultures (and few people in our own culture) perceive the distinction between gender-role behavior and sexual orientation. Gender-role behavior is how closely one conforms to his or her culture's stereotyped concepts of appropriate male or female behavior. It includes one's choice of career, one's mannerisms, and one's general life-style. It does *not* include one's preference in sexual partners; that is one's sexual orientation.

In most cultures, however, people assume that someone who behaves in *nonsexual* ways that are more characteristic of the opposite sex must also prefer homosexual relationships over heterosexual activities (Carrier 1980). Because of this assumption, many people who would prefer heterosexual partners find limited acceptance in heterosexual society. Conversely, in many societies, there are individuals who would prefer to have exclusively homosexual relationships but who are prevented or inhibited from doing so by cultural edicts.

Regardless of whatever biological and/or psychological factors may eventually be proved to influence sexual orientation, culture provides another dimension that cannot be ignored.

homophobic
(ho″mo-fo′bik)

---

1. Briefly summarize current biological, psychological, and cultural theories on the origins of homosexuality. Which theory or theories do you believe to be most valid?
2. Can you (and do you) personally distinguish between gender-role behavior and sexual orientation? Give an example.

Emergence of Homosexual Orientation

How and when does a person become aware of his or her sexual orientation? When does one know whether one is straight or gay? What are the signs? What is the evidence?

Most authorities agree that a person's ultimate adult sexual orientation is determined early in childhood, probably by age three or four (Green 1978; Marmor 1980). However, people differ greatly in when and how they become aware of their orientation.

Some gay people report that throughout their childhood they felt that they were somehow "different" from most other people, although they were for a time unsure just what the difference was. For others, the awareness came later, perhaps even in adult life.

In our homophobic (fearing homosexuality) society, many heterosexual people worry well into their adult lives that perhaps they are really homosexual. Conversely, some homosexual people refuse for many years to consciously accept the obvious evidence of their homosexual reactions and desires and desperately keep trying to feel and act straight.

Sooner or later, most of these uncertain people arrive at a time when they recognize what their true feelings are and feel certain that they are either heterosexual or homosexual. But until that time, they wonder about things like:

Most authorities agree that a person's ultimate adult sexual orientation is determined early in childhood, probably by age three or four. According to this theory, the eventual sexual preference of each of these children is already determined.

> If a person who, when awake, feels attracted to the other sex occasionally has a homosexual dream, does that mean that he or she is really homosexual? (*Not at all;* heterosexual people commonly experience homosexual dreams [Salzman 1980]. Such dreams can even arise from one's concern about the possibility of being homosexual [Klinger 1979].)
>
> If a male has a slender build, is he certain to have a homosexual orientation? (*No.* Many homosexual men rate as very masculine according to our cultural stereotype of masculinity.)
>
> If a female is muscular, is she certain to be lesbian? (*No.* Many homosexual women rate as extremely feminine by our cultural concept of femininity.)
>
> If a male prefers reading or cooking to playing football, does that mean that he's gay? (*No.*)

If two adolescent males manually stimulate each other or engage in other sexual experiments, are they really homosexual, even though they stop doing these things after a few months? (*No.* Kinsey (1948) reported that about 37 percent of all males have such experiences.)

If two adolescent females kiss each other and sexually stimulate each other, perhaps to orgasm, aren't they certain to be lesbians in their adult lives? (*No.* As with males, passing homosexual attractions and activities are quite common in girls.)

If none of the "obvious" signs are reliable, just how and when does a person know if he or she is straight, gay, or bisexual? Let us look at some of the issues raised in the preceding questions in a little more detail.

"Sissies" and "Tomboys"

Most retrospective (looking back) studies of the relationship, if any, between adult sexual orientation and childhood gender-role behaviors have indicated some correlation of these behaviors (Bell, Weinberg, and Hammersmith 1981). For example, Saghir and Robins (1973) reported that of a group of about ninety homosexual males surveyed, most of whom were enjoying good emotional health (they were not in therapy), about two-thirds recalled "sissylike" behavior during boyhood. This included a preference for so-called "girls' " toys and games, a preference for female playmates, and an avoidance of rough, aggressive play. This percentage was considerably higher than that recalled by a heterosexually oriented comparison group.

Saghir and Robins also studied females. They found that about two-thirds of adult homosexual females recalled "tomboyish" behavior during their preteen years, compared with less than 20 percent of the heterosexual adult comparison group.

Whitam (1977) questioned 107 homosexual and 68 heterosexual males about their childhood interests and whether they had been regarded by other boys as "sissies." Twenty-nine percent of the homosexual men recalled being regarded as a "sissy," compared with 1.5 percent of the heterosexuals. Further, about 80 percent of the gay males had preferred childhood sex play with other boys, while a similar percentage of straight males had preferred childhood sex play with girls. Obviously, data such as these can be interpreted in many ways, but the study would seem to support the belief that homosexuality develops quite early in life.

Still, Bell, Weinberg, and Hammersmith (1981) emphasize the frequent lack of correlation between childhood behaviors and later adult sexual orientation. They remind us that there is, at present, no reliable way to predict whether a "sissy" or "tomboy" will exhibit a homosexual or heterosexual orientation as an adult. Also, Pattison (1982b) reminds us that "tomboy" or "sissy" behavior may be quite healthy and appropriate, or it may reflect developmental difficulty. If the "tomboy" or "sissy" behavior is prolonged and extreme, it may reflect major stress in gender identity development and may predict adult transsexuality. But it is surely not a reliable indicator of homosexuality.

Early Homosexual Experiences

Most people are familiar with the *heterosexual* experiments of children and adolescents, but what is not nearly as well known is the amount of *homosexual* experimenting in which children and adolescents engage. During and following puberty, about a quarter to a third of all males have some homosexual experiences (37 percent, according to Kinsey [1948]). But most of them do so only a few times or for a short period. They stop, sometimes out of fear or guilt, but often because they find that they are more interested in heterosexual activity. Much the same pattern is followed by females, although apparently fewer females than males have adolescent homosexual experiences. Kinsey (1953) found that, by age twenty, about 9 percent of females have had actual homosexual experiences, although 17 percent experience homosexual arousal. Like the males, many females abandon homosexual activity after a few times and engage in primarily heterosexual pairings.

By age twenty, about 25–33 percent of males have had homosexual experiences, though many abandon homosexual activity after a few times.

But what about those whose orientation is primarily homosexual? It may be harder for them to accept their orientation than it is for heterosexuals, because they have been exposed to our culture's overtly negative attitude toward homosexuality. Yet, the homosexual feelings are strong and persistent. Generally, these young people feel guilty and are afraid of being found out by their parents or others, but that does not stop their homosexual activity.

Most adolescents whose orientation is primarily homosexual also have some heterosexual experiences. They date the opposite sex, and about half of all primarily homosexual males and females try heterosexual intercourse. And even though they find their own sex far more exciting than the opposite sex, they often go through a period of reluctance before accepting themselves as homosexual.

Fighting the Feeling

Many primarily homosexual males and females fight their homosexual orientation, often with no real awareness of what is going on. Some examples (Saghir and Robins 1973; Humphreys and Miller 1980) include:

Dating people of the opposite sex and often developing romantic or caring feelings about some of them and having sexual interaction with them.

Permitting themselves to have homosexual relationships only when under the influence of alcohol or other drugs. They can then tell themselves that they did not realize what was happening.

Homosexuality and Heterosexual Marriage

It is commonly assumed that someone who is heterosexually married, and especially someone who has children, must be heterosexually oriented. Few people seem to be aware that it is not uncommon for homosexual or bisexual people to marry.

A 1978 study by the Kinsey Institute investigated the lives of professed homosexual men and women in the San Francisco area (Maddox 1982). Among the findings were that one-fifth of the men interviewed and one-third of the women had been married at some time in their lives. Kinsey's (1948) interviews of married males revealed considerable extramarital homosexual activity in this group.

Why do people who are primarily homosexual marry? Some people, especially women, do not become fully conscious of their sexual orientation until after they are married, according to Maddox (1982). If a young woman has not had extensive premarital sexual experience, she may learn, only after marriage, that she is just not very highly aroused by males. Some women are married for years before they become fully aware that their primary erotic attraction is to other women.

Sometimes, love is the force that motivates homosexual people to marry. In our preoccupation with the sexual aspects of love, we sometimes forget that a very strong love relationship can exist in the absence of sexual attraction. This could easily be strong enough to motivate someone to marry.

External pressure is another possible motivation for marriage. Parents and other relatives sometimes pressure a person to marry if they suspect that he or she may be gay. Some people apparently still hold the belief that marriage can "cure" homosexuality.

The desire for children is another reason for marriage. Just because a man or woman is gay or lesbian does not mean that he or she does not love and desire children. Incidentally, most research to date supports the gay activists' assertion that gay people can be good parents (Maddox 1982). Apparently, homosexuality is not "contagious" from parent to child, as Maddox found that children of homosexual parents do not have an unusually high incidence of homosexuality.

Society's attitude toward homosexuality motivates some homosexual people to marry (Dank

Using the mental mechanism of denial: "I can't be gay because . . . (I'm a football player, I'm a homecoming princess, I'm a truck driver, I date lots of men, etc.)."

Keeping homosexual relationships at an impersonal level. The lack of emotional involvement is viewed as meaning that it is not really homosexual.

Getting married. In the United States today, perhaps a million married women and two to three million married men have homosexual experiences outside of their marriage (Maddox 1982). Most of these people, however, do not think of themselves as having a homosexual orientation. They view their marriage as proof of their heterosexuality or at least of their bisexuality.

1972). In some regions of the United States, and in some occupations, homosexual people still face resentment, hostility, and barriers to their personal and career fulfillment. In these situations, people may marry for "appearances," knowing that most people assume married people to be heterosexual.

The spouses of these individuals may or may not know of their partner's homosexuality. People who marry without telling their prospective spouses of their homosexuality could be accused of playing a "dirty trick." The discovery of a spouse's secret homosexual activity can be very difficult to deal with. "I can compete with other women, but there is just no way I can compete with men," was the comment of one depressed wife who had recently accidentally observed her husband in a homosexual relationship.

Maddox (1982) identified certain types of women who are likely to unknowingly marry gay men. They are women with little basis of comparison and little experience in sexual situations. They tend to be shy, are often virgins, and may be low in self-esteem. Their prospective husbands may perceive them as women who will make few sexual demands. These women initially feel pleased with

their good luck in attracting a handsome, single man.

Once the "secret" of one spouse's homosexuality is out, the tensions on a marriage are formidable, and the outlook for such marriages is not good (Maddox 1982). The straight partner may be forced into the unwanted role of pseudoparent (loving care, but no sexual activity). The thought of a spouse's ongoing homosexual activities may cause discomfort and anxiety, as well as resentment and anger.

At the same time, being married and gay is not the easiest way to live, whether one's spouse knows or not. Living with any deception is anxiety provoking—there is always the fear of being "caught." Further, some married gay people find that they are not well received in the single gay or lesbian world, their married status causing scorn and resentment (Maddox 1982). Thus, straddling two worlds is not easy. But many homosexual people perceive it as the only way they can satisfy their needs for economic security, children, and/or family life (Humphreys and Miller 1980).

Coming Out

Eventually, most homosexually oriented people begin to think of themselves as homosexuals. It happens to some as early as childhood; it happens to a few as late as middle age. But on the average, for males, the moment of self-recognition comes in the late teens, after about four to six years of homosexual feelings and experiences. For females, on the average, it comes a little later (Dank 1971).

The expression "coming out" has two meanings. The first is the recognition, within one's self, that one is homosexual. The other is when one becomes part of homosexual society, perhaps visiting a gay bar, baths, or private party. Often, the second of these "coming outs" precedes and leads to the first. For example, a gay man who is not fully aware of his homosexuality or who has been denying it may be taken to a gay party by a friend and suddenly feel that he is one of these people and that he has finally found his own kind.

Part of a gay person's coming out is entering into homosexual society. Often, the first view of gay society is both exciting and reassuring.

Often, the first interaction with the gay community is both exciting and reassuring. For a gay person who is still struggling with a negative view of homosexuality, it can be quite a revelation to see that gay people are not so terrible after all.

Coming out makes life much easier for the gay person. He or she no longer feels alone. There is a thriving gay social structure to fit into. And coming out ends the internal battle to deny one's gay desires and to force oneself to appear heterosexual. It usually results in a distinct increase in personal happiness and self-esteem.

Out of the Closet

For some gay people, one final step in coming out is "coming out of the closet." This is giving up all pretense of heterosexuality. It is showing all the world that one is gay and proud of it. To come out of the closet, to give up hiding, pretending, and lying, to no longer fear being exposed, is the dream of most gay people, but currently a reality for relatively few. The majority of gay people still perceive that, for themselves, the cost of coming out of the closet would outweigh the benefits (Warren 1980). And in many cases, they are probably right.

In many parts of the United States, and especially in certain occupations, to be publicly known as gay is to be stigmatized and discriminated against. In terms of location, the East and West Coasts are, in general, the most tolerant toward homosexuals. Certain large cities, such as San Francisco, Los Angeles, and New York,

Gay People and Their Parents

A dilemma many young gay people face is how, or whether, they should explain their sexual orientation to their parents. To most people of any sexual preference, having the approval of their parents seems quite important. Certainly, parental approval and understanding are no less important to homosexual people than to heterosexuals.

Deisher (1982) offers some suggestions for gay people who wish to tell their parents of their sexual orientation:

1. Plan your presentation and prepare your parents to understand your homosexuality.
2. If possible, provide books or other sources of factual information for them to read.
3. If there are friends or acquaintances who are homosexual, especially those whom your parents like, having them talk with your parents may be a means of calming some parental fears about homosexuality in general.
4. When informing parents of your homosexuality, stress your hope that it does not in any way change your relationship with them. Explain that you want to share this important information about yourself with them so that they can understand you better.
5. Give your parents time to absorb this information.
6. If one parent seems better able to accept the fact, it may be preferable to talk first to that parent and to have him or her tell the other parent.
7. Remember that accepting is not necessarily approving, and that the value systems of some parents may prevent them from really approving of homosexuality—yours or anyone else's.

8. If there is a partner whom you would like to introduce to your parents, do so, even though this may not be easy for you. Parents often find that it is easier to accept a real person than their fantasies of what that person might be like.

Deisher offers further advice to parents who learn of their child's homosexual orientation:

1. Your child is not really any different than he or she has been all along and has not suddenly become homosexual. Sexual orientation develops early in childhood; only your awareness of your child's orientation is new.
2. There are many homosexual people in our society, and the majority are successful, productive people who are no different from anyone else except in their sexual preference. Homosexuality is not considered an illness.
3. You need not feel guilty about your child's homosexuality. The causes of homosexuality are still unclear, but it appears unlikely that anything you did or did not do caused a homosexual orientation.
4. Homosexual people have to deal with many stresses, and parental help and understanding can be very important.
5. Some communities have organizations such as Parents and Friends of Gays that can provide much helpful information and support to parents who are having trouble accepting the homosexuality of their child. You might check your phone book or a community referral service for such organizations.

are especially favorable environments, with well-developed gay social structures and little interference from straight society. Conversely, the central and southern states, and particularly small towns, represent a more hostile environment in which an "out of the closet" gay person can usually expect various forms of social and economic discrimination.

In terms of career choices, openly gay people find acceptance in some fields but still face discrimination in others. Despite the great need for qualified military personnel, gay people still face discharge from the U.S. armed forces. And in most localities, police and fire departments do not hire or retain openly homosexual people.

Inflicting perhaps the greatest hurt of all, many families reject their openly gay members. Perhaps they place a greater value on their social status than on the welfare of their own family members. Perhaps they are so strongly homophobic (threatened by homosexuality) that they are unable to tolerate the homosexuality of even their own son or daughter, brother or sister.

Heterosexual friends, especially those of the same sex, may also become uncomfortable with the gay person who has come out of the closet. They may fear that their gay friend will make advances toward them or that other people will think that they are gay themselves.

Despite all of these (and other) difficulties the openly gay may face, many still feel that the freedom to live their lives honestly is worth the price. It is a choice every gay person must individually make.

---

1. When did you first become aware of the various sexual orientations people may have?
2. When did you first become aware of your own sexual orientation? Was this a gradual or a sudden awareness? Do you still hold some uncertainty about your orientation?
3. In your childhood, there were probably some friends who were known as "sissies" or "tomboys." What seems to be their current sexual orientation?
4. What may be the advantages to a gay person of being open about his or her sexual orientation? The disadvantages?

Homosexual Pleasuring

One of the least discussed aspects of homosexuality is what gay people actually do together sexually. For many centuries, the sex acts of homosexual people were considered so disgusting in some societies that they were never talked about or mentioned in print. In fact, in many states that have or had laws prohibiting homosexual acts, the lawmakers could not bring themselves to specify the acts that they were forbidding. Instead, homosexual acts were alluded to in such vague terms as "unnatural carnal copulation," "unnatural and lascivious acts," or "crimes against nature."

But actually there is very little that is unusual about homosexual acts except that they are performed by two persons of the same sex. Most of the same physical

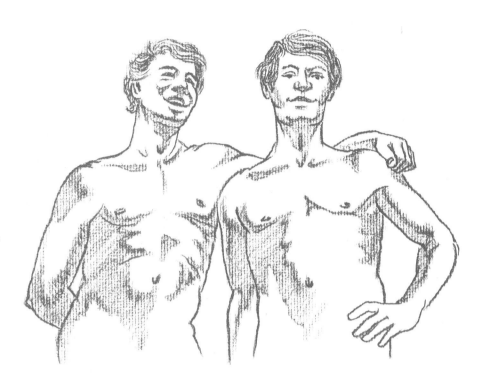

acts are also enjoyed by the majority of heterosexual people, either as preliminaries for vaginal intercourse or as sources of orgasm in themselves. In fact, in many states the "sodomy" laws make it just as much a crime for a married heterosexual couple to enjoy these sexual acts as for a homosexual couple.

Body Contact

The simplest homosexual pleasuring consists of hugging, kissing, and rubbing the bodies together. Pelvic areas may be pressed and rubbed together for genital stimulation. This type of contact is more favored by lesbians than by gay males.

Manual Stimulation

A large majority of gay males use manual stimulation, either as a source of orgasm or as a preliminary to other activities (Masters and Johnson 1979). Each partner stimulates the penis of the other by hand, just as he would stimulate himself, either in turn or at the same time.

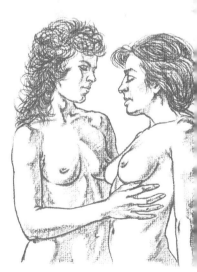

For most lesbians, manual stimulation is the most important sexual technique. Genital stimulation is generally preceded by kissing and by fondling of the breasts.

dildos
(dil'dōz)

sadist
(sad'ist)

fetishism
(fet'ish-izm)

masochist
(mas'o-kist)

(Incidentally, according to many sources, lesbian women spend considerably more time stimulating their partners' breasts before commencing genital stimulation than do heterosexual males. Can it be that women are better judges of what women enjoy?) Each partner then manually stimulates the labia and clitoris of the other, just as she would stimulate herself. Many lesbians find that manual stimulation to orgasm is extremely satisfying.

Oral Stimulation

Oral sex is of particular importance to homosexual people. Just as most heterosexual people find oral stimulation to be extremely intense and pleasurable, so do gay men and lesbian women. Fellatio is practiced and enjoyed by almost all gay males and cunnilingus by almost all lesbians. Most homosexual people find that both giving and receiving oral stimulation is highly pleasurable.

Anal Intercourse

Among gay males, anal intercourse is the second most widely used technique after fellatio (Masters and Johnson 1979). Some gay males prefer to be the inserter (the one who enters), while others prefer to be the insertee (the one who is entered), although most actually do both at times. The one who enters almost always achieves orgasm. The one who is entered also often experiences orgasm from the combination of the psychic stimulation and the intense stimulation of the prostate gland that is characteristic of anal penetration.

Other Practices

Contrary to popular belief, lesbians rarely use dildos (artificial penises) for stimulation. For one thing, if the penis was sexually important to them, they probably would not be lesbians. For another, even straight females rarely masturbate using dildos (Hite 1976).

While some homosexual people, like some heterosexual people, are **sadists** (sexually aroused by hurting others) and **masochists** (sexually aroused by being hurt), there is no evidence that sadomasochism is more prevalent among gay people than among straights.

Fetishism—the use of special clothing or other items to enhance sexual arousal—is believed to be somewhat more prevalent among gay males than among heterosexual males. It is not at all common among either lesbian or straight females (Hunt 1977).

Group sex is definitely more common among gay males than among either heterosexuals or lesbians (Saghir and Robins 1973). Part of this may be due to the tendency of some gay males to seek a variety of sexual partners. It may also relate to the fact that any time three or more people engage in sex together, there will

Lessons for Heterosexual People

In their laboratory studies of sexual activity, Masters and Johnson (1979) observed significant differences in how a lesbian stimulates her partner as compared with how a heterosexual male stimulates his female partner. Since it seems reasonable to assume that a woman knows what a woman enjoys, there may be lessons here for heterosexual males.

First, Masters and Johnson found that lesbians spent considerably more time in kissing and overall body stimulation prior to breast or genital stimulation than did heterosexual males. Then, when lesbians did begin breast stimulation, it was continued for a much longer time than was similar heterosexual male behavior. The full breast was stimulated manually and orally, with particular concentration focused on the nipples. Care was taken to spend an equal time with each breast.

Masters and Johnson also found that the focus of lesbian breast play was the pleasure of the recipient, while heterosexual breast stimulation seemed more for the pleasure of the male stimulator. While the lesbian recipient of breast stimulation typically experienced copious vaginal lubrication and sometimes experienced orgasms from breast stimulation alone, the heterosexual recipient tended to lubricate moderately at most and in no case was observed to orgasm during breast stimulation by a male partner.

In addition, lesbian couples that Masters and Johnson observed seemed much more aware than did heterosexual males that at some times in the menstrual cycle a woman's breasts are tender and that breast play may not be pleasurable for the woman at these times.

Differences in genital stimulation were observed as well. Lesbians tended to concentrate their stimulation more externally on the labia, thighs, clitoris, and vaginal opening, while males were more likely to penetrate the vagina through finger insertion.

Perhaps the greatest difference found by Masters and Johnson involved the general approach to sexual activity. Heterosexual couples seemed much more goal-oriented, rushing first to arousal and then to orgasm. Lesbian couples tended to approach lovemaking in a more leisurely way, enjoying the moment, rather than working toward some goal. Pehaps this is the most important lesson of all for the heterosexual population.

automatically be some homosexual interaction. Thus, group sex may be more ideally suited for gay rather than straight people. Male group activity usually includes oral, anal, and manual stimulation.

Finally, the belief that in every homosexual relationship one partner is always dominant and the other passive is a misconception. While some gay males and females do consistently prefer to play a mainly dominant or passive role and some gay couples do consist of one more dominant and one more passive member, this is certainly not always the case. Most male or female gay couples consist of two individuals who relate to each other as equals, sexually and otherwise.

1.   What is your personal reaction to the specifics of homosexual pleasuring?

dystonic
(dis-ton′ik)

Professional Opinions on Homosexuality

Like so many other questions on homosexuality, the question of how or whether homosexuality should be professionally "treated" draws different answers from different authorities. The concept of treatment of a condition carries the implication that the condition is a disorder. And mental health professionals are certainly not all in agreement that homosexuality should be labeled as such.

The *Diagnostic and Statistical Manual of Mental Disorders,* 3d ed. (DSM-III), published by the American Psychiatric Association (1980), takes a workable approach to homosexuality. Homosexuality itself is not considered a disorder. A homosexual person who is satisfied with his or her sexual orientation and general life adjustment is not viewed as a candidate for therapy.

However, a disorder termed **ego-dystonic homosexuality,** described in DSM-III, is reserved for homosexual individuals who have internalized negative societal values toward homosexuality. As a result, they are dissatisfied with their own homosexuality, and the desire to change sexual orientations is a "persistent concern."

Essential features of ego-dystonic homosexuality are a desire to acquire or increase heterosexual arousal so that heterosexual relationships can be initiated or maintained. Individuals with ego-dystonic homosexuality are often unable to fully enjoy their homosexual relationships because of their strong negative feelings about homosexuality. In some cases, the negative feelings are so strong that the homosexual arousal has been confined to fantasy. Since heterosexual relationships are also difficult or impossible, individuals with ego-dystonic homosexuality may be forced to forego all sexual partnerships. Thus, loneliness is particularly common among these people. They may also feel guilt, shame, anxiety, and depression.

Another controversy relates to how professionals can best help individuals with ego-dystonic homosexuality. One school of thought, characterized by Masters and Johnson (1979), is that efforts should be made to convert dissatisfied homosexuals to heterosexual life.

Masters and Johnson (1979) report considerable success in converting (or reverting) to heterosexuality selected homosexual individuals who are dissatisfied with their homosexuality. There are two requirements of such individuals to achieve treatment success. First, there must be a high degree of motivation for alteration of sexual preference. Second, there must be available an understanding opposite-sex partner who can be a source of support during the therapy. This second requirement is so essential that Masters and Johnson report that no homosexual man or woman has been treated for conversion or reversion to heterosexuality without a heterosexual partner. The approach used in this therapy is a variation of the intensive two-week program outlined in chapter 10.

Masters and Johnson emphasize that successful therapy requires a therapist who takes an objective approach to homosexuality. They see little point in trying to deal with basic causes of homosexuality, since such causes have yet to be proven. Instead, their approach is to identify, evaluate, and then openly discuss with the client (patient) the positive and/or negative contributions that the client's homosexuality is making to his or her life-style.

The therapist first concentrates on neutralizing or removing the psychosexual barriers to effective heterosexual interaction. As in other Masters and Johnson sex therapies, every effort is made to avoid or eliminate performance anxieties. No pressure is placed on the homosexual individual to change his or her preference in partners. Rather, the possibility of enjoyable heterosexual activity is demonstrated, leaving the individual to make his or her own choice of sexual orientation.

Masters and Johnson (1979) found that far fewer lesbians than gay males applied to their clinic for possible conversion to heterosexuality. In fact, only sixteen lesbians applied (and thirteen were accepted) over a ten-year period, about one-fourth the number of gay males applying. Possible explanations for this difference are that lesbians are less interested in changing their sexual orientation than are gay males, that lesbians are more reluctant to seek therapy, or that lesbians are more often able to initiate heterosexual involvement without the need for professional assistance. Masters and Johnson speculated that the latter was probably the case.

Following rather rigid screening and selection of clients for conversion therapy, Masters and Johnson reported that about 80 percent of those clients accepted for therapy were at least temporarily successful in conversion or reversion to heterosexuality. In five-year follow-up studies, about 65 percent of the males continued heterosexual activity, while most of the remainder had reverted to homosexual activity. The number of lesbians in conversion therapy was too small to allow any conclusions regarding the effectiveness of the programs. In any case, Masters and Johnson concluded that the general belief that homosexually oriented males and females cannot be converted to heterosexuality is just not valid.

Other authorities, however, such as Marmor (1980) and Silber (1981), emphatically state that a person's sexual preference is so deeply ingrained that it can seldom be changed by any form of therapy. These authorities feel that it is more productive to assist unhappy homosexual people in becoming more comfortable with their homosexuality than to try to change their basic orientation.

Reflecting his psychoanalytic approach, in contrast to the behaviorism of Masters and Johnson, Marmor (1980) expressed the opinion that Masters and Johnson's claim of converting or reverting 65 percent of homosexual males to heterosexuality with fourteen days of treatment was misleading. Marmor pointed out that the majority of subjects were bisexual, rather than strictly homosexual, and that there was

Some Common Myths about Homosexuality

Each of the following common myths about homosexuality is partly correct but is partly, or even mostly, incorrect. Each is true of some homosexual individuals but is not true of some or most others.

Myth: *You can always tell homosexual people by the way they look and act. Gay men always dress, talk, walk, and act in an effeminate way. Men who seem feminine must be gay. Gay women always have short haircuts, deep voices, and act like men. Masculine-seeming women must be lesbians.*

Facts: These stereotypes may sometimes prove accurate, but they do not apply to the majority of gay people (Krajeski 1981). There are gay men and lesbian women who do fit the stereotypes in terms of mannerisms, and there are also many heterosexuals who fit these stereotypes. Appearances are often unreliable in judging a person's sexual orientation.

In some communities, some of the gay people conform to a particular manner of dress and hairstyle. Such fashions vary from place to place and constantly change in any one given place. For example, among males in San Francisco in 1981, if one had short hair, a moustache, and wore blue jeans, work boots, and a leather jacket, one was presumed to be gay and very likely was gay. However, in a Midwestern farm town in 1981, a male with the same appearance was presumed to be heterosexual.

For individuals who are not secure with their own masculinity or femininity, it may seem important to be as unlike a homosexual person as possible. To accomplish this, these insecure individuals may maintain in their minds the stereotype of the effeminate gay male or masculine lesbian and thus view themselves as more sexually adequate in contrast (Krajeski 1981). Such individuals are very disturbed and threatened when they encounter gay people who fail to fit their stereotyped concept.

Myth: *Homosexual people never marry. People who never marry are probably gay. People who marry and have children can be presumed to be heterosexual.*

Facts: Many homosexual people do marry and have children, and many people who never marry

---

no evidence that their homosexual fantasies or arousal was altered. Finally, Marmor argued that there was a fundamental error in Masters and Johnson's assumption that a homosexual preference is attributable to anxiety about heterosexual performance (Masters and Johnson's approach to conversion therapy was to reduce such anxiety).

---

1.   Describe the controversy over how a therapist might best assist an unhappy homosexual person. Where do you stand on this issue?

are strictly heterosexual. Hunt (1977) and Maddox (1982) estimate that about one out of every five gay men and one out of every three lesbians enter into heterosexual marriage at some time. Hunt further estimates that at least 2 to 3 percent of currently married American men are bisexual and have sex with other men at least once in a while in addition to having sex with their wives.

Myth: *Homosexual people are all undersexed. Or, homosexual people are all oversexed. (It's heard both ways.)*

Facts: Like heterosexuals, gay people represent a broad range of sexual desire. A few gay males are extremely sexually active, exceeding the sexual capacities of almost all straight men (Hunt 1977), but they are the exception rather than the rule. The sexual activity level of most gay people is not significantly different from that of most heterosexual people.

Myth: *The number of gay people has increased tremendously in the past few years. Gay people are constantly trying to convert straight people to homosexuality.*

Facts: First, the incidence of homosexuality has remained fairly constant for at least thirty years (Kinsey 1948; Marmor 1980). However, homosexual individuals are more visible now than in the past. Many have stopped keeping their sexual preferences secret and have come out in the open, one very beneficial result of the gay liberation movement. But apparently the percentage of people of primarily homosexual orientation has changed little.

As to trying to seduce straight people, a few homosexual individuals do try to seduce straights, just as a few heterosexual people enjoy trying to seduce gays. But the great majority of gay people do not. They just are not attracted to people who are not attracted to them. And since, as we have seen, sexual orientation is apparently determined quite early in life, any efforts to convert straight people to homosexuality (or vice versa) are highly unlikely to succeed.

Homophobia

Many of the difficulties homosexual people experience in dealing with straight society arise from a condition called **homophobia,** an unrealistic fear of homosexuality experienced by many heterosexual individuals. Homophobia may have many different causes. One is simply fear of the unknown. It may be part of our basic human nature to feel threatened by anything we do not fully understand. And few straight people take the time or interest to become knowledgeable about homosexuality.

In particular, some people believe that homosexuality is a behavior pattern that is chosen by a conscious act of will or that is "caught" from others, perhaps by modeling oneself after homosexual individuals to whom one has been exposed.

Neither of these beliefs is valid. People do not "choose" to be homosexual any more than they "choose" to be heterosexual. It is believed that, in almost all cases, the ultimate adult sexual orientation of a person is established before the school years begin (Green 1978). Thus, exposure to homosexual people in positions such as teaching is not going to influence a person's sexual orientation. In any event, that modeling is not a relevant factor is demonstrated by the facts that virtually all homosexual people come from heterosexual parents (certainly our most important models) and that the overwhelming majority of "models" we are exposed to as our cultural heroes and heroines are heterosexual.

Another factor that may be partially responsible for homophobia is childhood conditioning. Many of us, as children, were warned by our parents to be wary of homosexual child molesters. Our fears were then reinforced by the fears and misconceptions of our peers. In some cases, even our religious training may have instilled prejudice against homosexuality. Even though as adults we may better understand homosexuality at a conscious level, our unconscious minds may carry residual fears of homosexual people.

Another problem contributing to homophobia is that homosexual people so seldom conform to our stereotypes about them. The only thing that is true of all homosexuals is that they are sexually attracted to people of their own sex. Almost everything else that is commonly said about gay people is true of only some of them and not true of many or most others.

The fact that most homosexual people do not conform to stereotypes is one of the main reasons homosexuality is so alarming to some people. They hear much about what homosexuality is like, but they also meet or hear about homosexual people who do not fit the picture. They begin to wonder whether friends, neighbors, and others who look and seem straight are actually homosexual. They even begin to wonder about themselves. If they have ever felt any attraction to someone of the same sex or played adolescent sex games with friends of the same sex, they fear that they themselves may be homosexual, with all the negative implications they have learned to associate with homosexuality (Marmor 1980).

It is the latter group who often express the greatest hostility toward homosexual people. They are likely to use derogatory names for gay people (faggot, queer, dyke, fairy, and so on) and to tell jokes about gay people. Their hostility toward homosexuality is thinly disguised, if at all. It can even reach the point of seeking out gay people and physically assaulting them. Such extreme behavior is usually interpreted as an effort to deny or suppress the possibility of homosexual feelings in the assailants.

Another result of homophobia can be conformity to rigid sex-role stereotypes. In other words, homophobic people tend to restrict their lives unnecessarily, out of fear of appearing to be homosexual. Clothing may be chosen carefully to express "masculinity" or "femininity." Career choices may be influenced by the same concern. For example, a male who might really enjoy being a nurse or secretary might avoid these options for fear of being labeled gay. Even heterosexual lovemaking can be influenced by homophobia. A male may not allow himself to take a passive role or a female may deny herself the pleasure of a more sexually assertive role because they associate these roles with their stereotyped concepts of homosexuality. It is possible that some heterosexual people may be even greater victims of their homophobia than are gay people.

1. If you found out that your seven-year-old son's male teacher was gay, how would you react?
2. Can you recall any early learning about homosexuality and homosexual people from your parents or peers? Was the information you received positive or negative, accurate or inaccurate?
3. Do you feel that you can always tell a gay or lesbian person by his or her appearance or mannerisms? Have you ever misjudged someone's sexual orientation?
4. How could homophobia adversely influence a straight person's life?

Gay Rights

Homosexual people have been persecuted for thousands of years. It is only in recent years that gay liberation groups have been able to instigate changes that are increasing gay people's civil and social rights.

Persecution of Homosexuals

Persecution of homosexual people goes back to the ancient Hebrews, whose attitudes toward homosexuality are set down in the earliest books of the Old Testament. In Genesis 13:13, we read that the men of the city of Sodom were "wicked and sinners before the Lord exceedingly" because they practiced homosexuality. (This is why the term *sodomy* is sometimes used in reference to homosexual acts. Sodomy may also mean oral or anal heterosexual acts or coitus with animals.) Leviticus 20:13 makes homosexual acts illegal and sets a harsh penalty:

> If a man also lie with mankind, as he lieth with a woman, both of them have committed an abomination: they shall surely be put to death; their blood shall be upon them.

Interestingly, the Old Testament says nothing directly about lesbianism. Perhaps in a strongly patriarchal society, the behavior of women seemed unimportant to the ancient Jews. Indeed, throughout Western history, female homosexuality has been less harshly condemned than male homosexuality (Tannahill 1980).

One possible explanation of the unequal treatment of homosexuality in men and women lies in the old belief that sperm carried miniature people; therefore, wasting sperm in anything other than reproductive intercourse was a great sin. Women were just a fertile environment for the male "seed" to grow in, so their homosexuality was less significant.

In the early days of Christianity, the approach to male homosexuality was less extreme than was the Hebrew stand. The Christians were living under Roman law, which was far more tolerant of sexual variations. But the Church fathers did preach that homosexuality was a grave sin and that homosexual males could not enter heaven and would surely be punished in hell.

Several of the Christian emperors of Rome passed laws against homosexuality, but it remained for Emperor Justinian in A.D. 538 to set the legal standard that held for the next thirteen centuries in Europe (Hunt 1977; Tannahill 1980). Justinian decreed that homosexual people were to be tortured, castrated, paraded in public, and then burned alive. Later on, the Church also resorted to violence against homosexuals. Allegedly homosexual people were tortured until they confessed. Then, having confessed, they were burned at the stake.

During the nineteenth century, homosexual people came to be treated less severely, although homosexuality remained a crime in most European countries as well as in the United States. Even as late as 1980, homosexual acts remained illegal in the states of Alabama, Arizona, Arkansas, Florida, Georgia, Idaho, Kansas, Kentucky, Louisiana, Maryland, Michigan, Minnesota, Mississippi, Missouri, Montana, Nevada, New Jersey, New York, North Carolina, Oklahoma, Rhode Island, South Carolina, Tennessee, Texas, Utah, Vermont, Virginia, Wisconsin, and the District of Columbia (Curry and Clifford 1980).

Harsh laws, and the public attitudes that went with them, never succeeded in eradicating homosexuality at any time in history. They did, however, cause homosexual people to live in constant fear and to keep their homosexuality a guarded secret. For many centuries, gay people were forced to live a double life, having one set of desires and behaviors but pretending to have another.

Worst of all, most homosexual people accepted the prevailing public view of homosexuality. Like others, they believed that the real person inside them was sinful, criminal, and shameful. Many came to despise themselves, and the suicide rate for homosexual people was far in excess of that for the straight population (Solomon and Patch 1971).

Not until late in the nineteenth century did the ancient antihomosexual tradition start to show any signs of moderation. At that time, some physicians (first Baron Richard von Krafft-Ebing in 1887 and later Sigmund Freud) began to think of homosexuality as a disease rather than as a sin or crime. The implication was that one should not be punished for an illness. As a result, legal penalties for homosexuality were eased in some European countries and in some states in the United States.

By the 1940s, most better-educated people in the United States had come to think of homosexuality as a disease or abnormality beyond the control of the individual. The less-educated majority of Americans, however, still considered homosexuality to be sinful or criminal or both (Hunt 1977).

Then Kinsey (1948, 1953) reported the results of his massive surveys of American sexual behavior, revealing homosexual acts to be far more prevalent than most people had imagined. (He reported that about a third of all American men and a fifth of all women had experienced at least some homosexual activity in their lives, if transient adolescent experiences were included.) This information was widely publicized, and more people came to believe that, if homosexual activity was so common, then perhaps it was not as abnormal as they had thought.

Next, in the 1960s, some physicians and psychologists began to see that calling homosexuality an illness rather than a sin or a crime was not as liberal an idea as it had once seemed. It was merely a different way of condemning homosexual behavior. Also, there was the problem that no clear cause of this "disease" could be demonstrated. Maybe it was not an illness at all; perhaps it was just a variation in behavior. Authorities were beginning to suspect that the emotional problems that seemed prevalent among homosexual people were not associated with the homosexuality in any direct cause-and-effect relationship but were the result of society's intolerance of gay people. And, in the 1960s, people in general were still quite hostile toward homosexuality. It was in this atmosphere that the gay liberation movement began.

Gay Liberation

As late as the 1960s, homosexuals were still a highly persecuted minority. Even the police seemed to take special delight in harassing homosexuals. Open homosexuality meant job discrimination, beatings, and arrests. Public opinion polls revealed that at least 80 percent of Americans were quite hostile toward homosexual people (Weinberg and Williams 1974). But the militancy of other minority groups was starting to pay off with improved civil rights, and this fact did not go unnoticed by gay people. The stage was set for gay liberation.

Christopher Street

A name now synonymous with gay rights, Christopher Street in New York City's Greenwich Village was the site of the first major display of gay militancy (Humphreys 1972). On June 28, 1969, the police raided the Stonewall, a gay bar. The raid was not unusual at that time, but the response of the patrons was. Without any advance planning, the customers began to fight back. They threw cans and rocks at the police, locked them in the bar and set it on fire, and then fought with other police in the street for hours (Hunt 1977). The outgrowth of the "Stonewall Rebellion" was the formation of militant gay rights groups all over the United States. By 1975, there were over eight hundred such groups.

The emergence of gay militancy is often traced to June 28, 1969, when the patrons of the Stonewall, a gay bar on Christopher Street in New York City's Greenwich Village, vigorously resisted a police raid.

Changes Brought about by Gay Liberation

Gay rights groups have used most of the techniques characteristic of other civil rights organizations. They have marched, picketed, boycotted certain products, sent lobbyists to Washington and state capitols, taken legal actions against discrimination in employment, published books, appeared on television talk shows, and held press conferences.

Some of the changes since the 1960s include:

More realistic portrayal of gay people in films, books, on television, and on the stage.

Some, though not all, organized religions have modified their positions on homosexuality as a sin and on homosexual individuals as clergy or other leaders.

In many parts of the country, gay people feel much more free to be open about their homosexuality without fear of losing jobs or suffering social recrimination.

The American Psychiatric Society voted in 1973 to stop classifying homosexuality as a psychiatric disorder.

Many cities have passed homosexual rights laws assuring gay people of equal rights to jobs, housing, and public accommodations such as restaurants.

In 1975, the U.S. Civil Service Commission dropped its long-established policy of not hiring homosexual people for government jobs.

Many states have repealed "sodomy" laws, legalizing any form of private sexual behavior between consenting adults.

The goal of full civil and social rights for gay people is still far from a reality. But gay people today feel much better about themselves than was typical in the past. And the straight world is becoming increasingly accepting of homosexuality. The day will come when people will no longer be discriminated against on the basis of their sexual orientation and when the millions of people who are erotically responsive to their own sex will live lives of dignity and self-respect.

1. Can you cite any examples in your own community of unfair treatment of homosexual people?
2. Has your study of human sexuality led to your having any greater concern regarding the civil and social rights of gay people? Why or why not?

Frank, that was about two years ago. Since then, I have had serious relationships with two women and one or two more casual affairs. I have always been very discreet, so the only people who know are those who were involved. But now I'm tired of living a lie. It isn't fair to keep on deceiving you. And it's not the life I want for myself. I even talked to a counselor to see what I should do. She said that some therapists try to convert lesbians to be turned on to men, but that she didn't recommend it.

The big question now is the children. To be honest, right now I just want to be on my own, to find myself and my place in the world. But I don't want to close the door on some day having one or both of them live with me. Some of my lesbian friends have children, and they are good parents.

For now, I hope that you won't mind taking care of the kids. They love you, and they are old enough to be able to pretty much take care of themselves.

I'm sorry I had to tell you all of this in a letter. I would rather have told you in person, but I just couldn't do it. I hope that we can still be friends. You are a great person. You were a good husband. I just can't handle it any more. Please understand.

Love,

Jan

1.   Being attracted mainly to people of the opposite sex is heterosexuality. Being attracted primarily to people of our own sex is homosexuality. Feeling attraction to people of both sexes is bisexuality.

2.   Sexual orientation lies along a continuum of infinite degrees of balance between exclusive homosexuality and exclusive heterosexuality.

3.   It is estimated that from 5 to 10 percent of adult males and from 3 to 5 percent of adult females in the United States are more or less exclusively homosexual. If bisexual behavior is included, the incidence may be twice these figures.

4.   The development of sexual orientation is poorly understood at this time. There are biological, psychological, and cultural theories on the subject.

5.   A review of the biological theories shows that chromosomes of homosexual and heterosexual people are not different; that there are no known genes for homosexuality or heterosexuality; that hormonal studies of homosexual vs. heterosexual people have yielded conflicting information; and that current research involves possible hormonal effects on the brain prior to birth.

6.   There are many diverse psychological theories for the development of sexual orientation. Most of the more widely accepted theories relate to early childhood family experiences.

7.   Cultural attitudes about homosexual activity range from strict prohibition to incorporation into mandatory rituals of behavior. Not all cultures agree on what is homosexual behavior.

8.   Most authorities agree that sexual orientation is determined early in childhood (by whatever means) but that people differ in when they become aware of their orientation. Some become aware as children, some as adolescents, and some as adults.

9.   "Sissy" and "tomboy" childhood behaviors are statistically associated with adult homosexuality but do not reliably predict adult sexual orientation.

10.   Many young people (perhaps 37 percent of males and 9 percent of females) engage in some homosexual experimentation as adolescents.

11.   Some primarily homosexual people resist accepting themselves as such for a time. Resistance may even include marrying and having children.

12.   "Coming out" can have two meanings: recognizing one's self as homosexual and becoming part of homosexual society.

13.   "Coming out of the closet" is giving up all pretense of heterosexuality—letting the world know that one is gay and proud of it.

14.   Homosexual pleasuring is quite similar to heterosexual activity and includes kissing, body contact, manual stimulation, oral stimulation and anal intercourse. Lesbians rarely use dildos. Sadomasochism is no more common among homosexual people than it is among heterosexual people. Group sex and fetishism are believed to be more common among gay males than among lesbians or heterosexual people.

15.   Mental health professionals are not in agreement on how to best help a dissatisfied homosexual person. Some would try to convert that person to heterosexuality; others would try to help the person to accept his or her homosexuality and
to deal effectively with straight society.

16.   Homophobia is an unrealistic fear of homosexuality experienced by many heterosexual individuals. It is based on misconceptions about homosexuality and sometimes on one's own fear of being homosexual.

17.   Persecution of homosexual people goes back thousands of years. Punishment
for homosexuality has been harsh, and even today, straight society is often intolerant
of gay people.

18.   Gay militancy is usually traced to 1969 and Christopher Street in Greenwich
Village. Despite many advances, the goal of full civil and social rights for gay people
is still far from a reality.

19

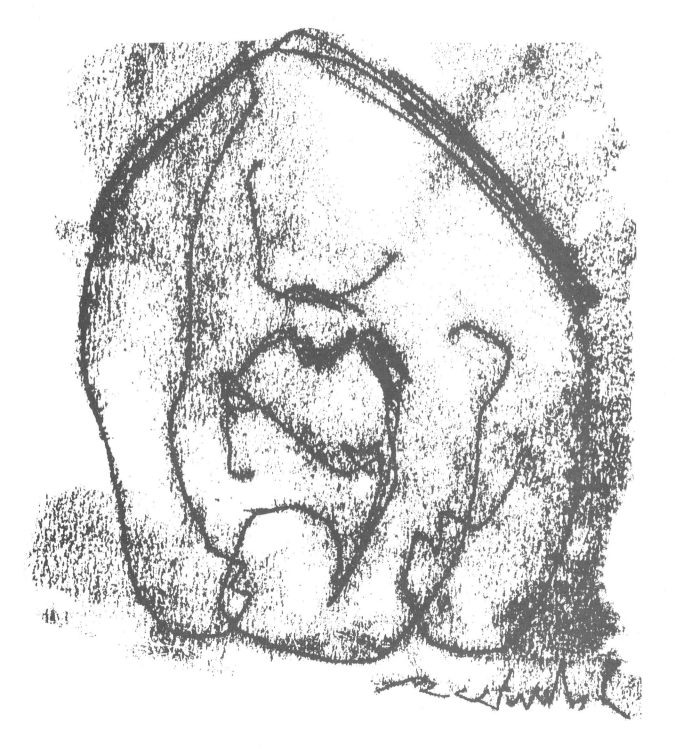

It's not something I like to talk about, but if I remain silent, others may feel the same shame and pain that I felt and never know that they should scream out for help. That is why I talk at schools, so that students know that someone does care, that others have been through it, that they need not be ashamed.

I was sexually abused as a child. I was about nine when my older brother (who was eighteen) first started coming into my room. At first, he would just stand at the foot of my bed and stare at me as I pretended to sleep. Then he began touching me. He told me that he loved me and that we should love each other if we wanted a happy family.

I wasn't sure what was going on until he forced these night raids into sexual acts. I knew then that what he was forcing on me was wrong, but he said he would blame it all on me if I told anyone. I felt so alone. I couldn't tell anyone for fear I was the one that was doing wrong. It got worse. He started to come into my room every night. Sometimes, he became violent. I wanted to scream out, but I was afraid of what would happen.

Then, one day I saw a way out. I couldn't tell my folks, or anyone at school, or anyone in my family, but I knew that God would understand if I went to Him.

I waited one day until everyone was out of the house. I went into the bathroom and took every pill I could find in the medicine cupboard. Then I went into my room, laid down on my bed, and waited to die. . . .

Most adults enjoy affectionate heterosexual practices with another consenting adult. Some persons, however, engage in unusual forms of sexual behavior, either occasionally or exclusively.

People react in various ways to sexual behavior they view as different from the norm. They may be tolerant of certain acts, but respond with gossip, ridicule, or persecution to others. Some individuals practicing "other" forms of sexual behavior are regarded as eccentric and harmless; others are seen as being emotionally sick and dangerous.

In this chapter, we examine the various forms that unusual sexual behavior can take. Before we begin, however, we need to determine just what sexual behavior is normal and what is abnormal.

What Is Normal?

There is no simple way to arrive at a consensus on which sexual behavior is to be considered normal. One person may call behavior normal on quite different grounds than the next person. When people speak of normal behavior, they may have one or more of the following standards in mind (Pomeroy 1966):

1. *Social.* To be socially normal, an act harms neither society nor another person. The act occurs only between consenting adults, is voluntary, and is done in private.
2. *Statistical.* That behavior which is engaged in by the majority is viewed as being statistically normal. According to this measurement, nonmarital intercourse, oral-genital sex, and masturbation would be considered normal. Chastity before marriage would be abnormal.
3. *Psychological.* Any act that creates positive feelings, raises self-esteem, and contributes to feelings of well-being is viewed as being psychologically normal. A given act might at times lead to positive feelings and at other times, under other circumstances, lead to negative feelings. For example, sexual intercourse with affection can be psychologically normal, but with exploitation can be psychologically abnormal.
4. *Legal.* Any sexual behavior that violates a law is, by legal definition, abnormal. The legal statutes, in most instances, closely resemble the moral code, although legal changes often lag behind changes in public opinion. Thus, in some states, cunnilingus, fellatio, and nonmarital coitus are, by legal definition, abnormal behavior.
5. *Moral.* Moral codes are based on various religious or philosophical viewpoints. For any particular moral code, sexual acts are judged normal or abnormal in terms of whether they violate that code.

phylogenetic
(fi''lo-jĕ-net'ik)

paraphilia
(par''ah-fil'e-ah)

6.   *Phylogenetic.* A phylogenetic definition is based on whether any given sexual behavior is practiced among mammals other than humans. Some religious groups view any behavior that is found among other mammals as part of the "natural law." Any other sexual practice is viewed as abnormal and as a violation of the natural law.

7.   *Cultural.* Sexual behavior that conforms to accepted cultural practice is viewed as normal. Since our society is multi-cultural, the practices of one culture do not conform to those of others in all regards. Yet, within the larger cultural context, there are many sexual practices on which there is general consensus. On this basis, incest, for example, is viewed as abnormal in most cultural contexts in this country.

Marmor (1977) has suggested a psychiatric model to contrast normal, healthy behavior to abnormal, pathological behavior. According to Marmor, *normal sexual behavior* is motivated primarily by feelings of affection and tenderness, seeks to give and receive pleasure, tends to be discriminating as to partner choice, and is motivated by recurring erotic sexual tensions in the context of physical attraction and affection. *Abnormal sexual behavior,* says Marmor, is used as a means of discharging anxiety, hostility, and guilt; tends to primarily seek to receive sexual pleasure; tends to be nondiscriminating as to partner choice; and is triggered by nonerotic sexual tensions that are often compulsive.

Since sexual variations are psychosexual phenomena, in this chapter, we use the psychiatric model for discriminating between normal and abnormal sexual behavior.

Sexual Paraphilias

As discussed in chapter 10, sexual disorders can be separated into two categories: the dysfunctions and the paraphilias.

Sexual **dysfunctions** are disorders that make it impossible for a person to have or enjoy sexual intercourse. The person does not respond adequately to arousal and does not find sex pleasurable (Kaplan 1974). The causes of, types of, and therapies for sexual dysfunctions are examined in chapter 10.

Sexual **paraphilias** (variations) are psychosexual disorders typified by sexual actions that are pleasurable, yet whose object and/or aim deviates from the norm. The term *paraphilia* means "aside from, or beyond love," which stresses that these sex acts are not based on the usual affectionate love relationship with a sexual partner.

Paraphilias contrast with usual sexual behavior in that the paraphiliac requires some extraordinary or bizarre sexual experience to bring on sexual excitement (American Psychiatric Association 1980; Kaplan 1974). Without such distortions, sexual excitement or orgasm cannot be attained, and the person's tensions go unrelieved. The act or imagery may be harmless or playful, and may be performed with a mutually consenting partner. More often, however, the partner does not share the gratification and feels erotically excluded or unnecessary. In more extreme cases, the imagery may be acted out with a partner who is nonconsenting, who views the act as highly offensive, or who is subject to injury or bodily harm. While anyone who is not disordered may often be sexually excited by such unusual images (as during masturbation or sexual intercourse), for the paraphiliac, these images are *necessary* for him or her to become sexually excited.

Often, paraphiliacs feel that their behavior should cause no one distress. Their only problem, as they see it, is the reaction of others to their behavior. Many do not see themselves as ill and may become known to the professionals (legal, social, medical, psychological) only when their behavior has resulted in some public incident, legal or social. Others acknowledge guilt, depression, and shame over behavior that they realize is unacceptable socially.

Some paraphiliacs are married, but they may be emotionally immature and unable to give affection to their partner. If their partner learns of their unusual sexual behavior, the relationship may suffer. Some partners allow for the unusual sexual behavior as an insignificant trade-off in an otherwise acceptable relationship. Others find a paraphiliac partner unacceptable and use the behavior as a basis to terminate the partnership.

In the great majority of reported cases, the paraphiliacs have been males (American Psychiatric Association 1980; Money 1980b).

Some of the paraphilias described in this chapter are rather common; others are rare. Some are of legal or social importance because they are performed with nonconsenting partners. While there is interest in all paraphilias, of particular concern are those in which the behavior is viewed by society as sufficiently offensive to call for therapy and/or legal intervention. Of special concern are those behaviors that become usual or exclusive and that may not be easily modified (American Psychiatric Association 1980).

Sexual paraphilias may take one of two forms. The first group includes paraphilias that deviate in choice of sexual *object* (with whom or what one has intercourse). The second group includes those that deviate in choice of sexual *aim* (a goal other than seeking intercourse) (Kaplan 1974).

---

1. What criteria would you use to characterize abnormal sexual behavior?
2. Why do you think that the term *paraphilias* is preferable to explain unusual sexual practices than the older terms *sexual deviations* and *sexual perversions*?
3. What distinguishes the manner in which the paraphiliac attains sexual arousal from the manner in which a more normal person becomes sexually excited?

Misconceptions about Sexual Abuse of Children

There are several popular misconceptions about child sexual abuse and abusive adults:

1. ***Abusive parents are invariably disadvantaged.*** While there are external stresses in poverty (low incomes, poor housing, and overcrowded neighborhoods), the most crucial stresses—the internal stresses—are very similar for rich and poor parents alike.

2. ***Abusive parents are fundamentally abnormal, psychotic, criminal, or retarded.*** The majority of abusing parents are normal intellectually and psychologically but have trouble handling stresses and fulfilling their own emotional needs.

3. ***Child sexual abuse is very rare.*** It is estimated that there are as many as 336,200 sexual offenses against children committed each year in this country (Sarafino 1979).

4. ***The abusive father is the victim of a provocative and seductive child.*** While some fathers tend to rationalize incest by emphasizing their daughters' physical maturity and provocative behavior, adult motives cannot be ascribed to children engaged in "affection-seeking" behavior with their fathers. Rather, it is nearly always the father who introduces specific sexual behaviors (Peters 1976).

Variations in Choice of Sexual Object

The first group of paraphilias discussed are those that vary in terms of with whom or what one has intercourse. Instead of having a mature, interpersonal relationship with an adult partner, individuals with these paraphilias choose to sexually abuse a child (either through pedophilia or incest), or they engage in a sexual relationship with an adolescent female (unlawful sex), an inanimate object (fetishism), or an animal (zoophilia).

Sexual Abuse of Minors

Sexual abuse of children and adolescents can be defined as forced, pressured, or stressful sexual behavior engaged in with a person under the age of seventeen (Burgess et al. 1978). Such sexual exploitation involves a dependent child or adolescent in sexual activities that he or she does not fully comprehend, to which he or she is unable to give informed consent, or that violate the social taboos of family roles (Kempe and Kempe 1978).

Dealing with the sexual abuse of children has become a national priority (Burgess et al. 1978). The concern is based partly upon the prevalence of such abuse. It is estimated, for instance, that 20 percent of all female children and 9 percent of all male children in this country are victims of sexual abuse (Finkelhor 1979). No less important is the profoundly damaging effect of the assault upon the victims. Evidence of this is seen in higher victim incidence of promiscuity, prostitution, and

pedophilia
(pe''do-fil'e-ah)

sexual dysfunction, and also in the sexual abuse of victims' children (Meiselman 1979; Tsai and Wagner 1979; Geiser 1979; Masters and Johnson 1970).

Forms of sexual abuse of children and adolescents discussed here include pedophilia and incest.

Pedophilia

Meaning "love of children," **pedophilia** (child molestation) describes a behavioral pattern in which an adult is sexually attracted to and sexually aroused by prepubertal children.

Pedophilia is one of the most common, yet most abhorent, of the sexual offenses (about one-third of *all* reported sexual offenses are acts of child molestation) (Finkelhor 1979). Public response to pedophilic acts is related to the age of the child victim; often, the younger the child and the older the adult, the greater the public rage (Kempe and Kempe 1978). Much of the strong public reaction centers on possible effects on the child. Such reaction is due in part to the belief in the sexual innocence of the child, to the emphasis put on a child's virginity, and to a child's need for protection.

The great majority of pedophilic contacts involve casual touching or fondling, often of the child's genitals. About 85 percent of child molestation cases, according to Jaffe (1976), involve indecent exposure, genital manipulation, obscene language, and physical advances. In about 11 percent of the cases, vaginal intercourse, anal penetration, and rape are involved. While many people have a mental image of violence being done to the child, in only about 15 percent of the cases is there coercion or threats of any sort. Severe physical violence occurs in no more than 3 percent of the cases.

Isolated sexual acts with children are not viewed as a basis for a diagnosis of pedophilia. Such acts may be caused by marital discord, recent loss, or intense loneliness (American Psychiatric Association 1980).

A potential child molestation. Has this child been taught how to recognize and deal with this situation?

The Offenders Almost all pedophiles are adult males, although there are cases of females having repeated sexual contact with children (Tollison and Adams 1979). Most offenders are teenagers and young and middle-aged adults. The over-fifty males ("dirty old men") make up a very small percentage of offenders (Finkelhor 1979; Groth 1979). Twice as many offenders prefer children of the opposite sex as children of the same sex. Thus, about two-thirds of all victims are girls, most often between the ages of eight and ten (American Psychiatric Association 1980).

Almost all (about 85 percent) of child molesters are family friends, relatives, or acquaintances (Jaffe 1976). The great majority of contacts occur in homes; they infrequently occur in parks, school yards, or automobiles. The advance may be made in the offender's home or in the child's home, where the offender may be staying as a boarder or visitor (Sauzier 1981). About one-fourth of the offenders are drunk at the time of the offense (Finkelhor 1979).

Adolescent offenders are most often related to the victim and engage in touching the victim; older offenders are more often nonrelatives and are more exhibitionistic (Finkelhor 1979).

Offenders tend to be moralistic. They show considerable immaturity, strong dependency needs, much overall regression, and harbor feelings of inadequate sexual performance as males. Offenders often act impulsively, as though not in control of themselves, and often report feeling compelled in their sexual acts.

Some pedophiles have always been sexually attracted to children; others substitute sexual contacts with children for contacts they are unable to manage with adults (Groth 1979). Not infrequently, the offender feels rejected by his wife or girlfriend and approaches a less threatening sexual object. The child molester has a need to exercise authority and to avoid rejection; thus, children become appealing victims. Generally avoiding violence, the molester who is rebuffed by a child may turn to another one. He is interested in a consenting relationship and often chooses a child he knows, if only slightly. He tends to identify with the child, whom he sees as loving, open, warm, and innocent. If he does inflict harm, it is usually inadvertently or out of panic (Geiser 1979).

The Victims   Between thirty and forty percent of girls are exposed to a molester at some time (Herjanic 1980). Often traumatized, the girl may feel guilty (blaming herself for the incident), worthless, depressed, and distrustful of all males. She may speculate on why she was singled out to be a victim. Some girls who are molested develop feelings of isolation when they become sexually active; others end up sexually nonresponsive (Tsai and Wagner 1979).

While many girls resist these sexual advances, some do not, often because of the authority position of the adult over the child. The child who has been taught to passively obey adults and to do as she is told often complies with the wishes of the offender. The offender may rationalize such obedience as cooperation or encouragement.

With boy victims, pedophilic acts involve more exhibitionism, oral sex, and mutual masturbation. Boys are more apt to cooperate with the offender. The majority of boy victims, especially of adolescent offenders, say that they were interested and felt pleasure. Because adult offenders may be careful to obtain the affection of the boy before becoming sexually active with him, they are infrequently reported to the authorities by their victims.

Parental Response   Many who study cases of child molestation believe that the incident itself has less potential for damaging the child than the response of the

Counseling Children After Molestation

While many children are instructed on how to avoid contact with child molesters, few parents know how to respond after their child has been molested. Here are some pointers from Barbara Herjanic (1980):

1. *Allow the expression of feelings.* Some children are hurt and disappointed that someone they loved and trusted has let them down. Encourage the child to verbally express the hurt and angry feelings, and help the child to work through the grief and disappointment. Explain to the child that the offender is sick and needs treatment.

2. *Reassure the child of your protection.* Some children are very fearful after a molesting incident. The offender may have threatened to kill them. Along with your verbal reassurances, the child needs to understand the steps that have been taken to provide him or her with protection. If the offender was a member of the household, the offender's removal from the home and from the child is usually necessary, at least temporarily.

3. *Help to reduce the child's feelings of guilt.* If the child willingly participated with the offender, you must help the child to understand that he or she is not to blame or is not "bad." The child, however, needs to know why the behavior was inappropriate. If the molester was from the home, the child may need help in not feeling guilty over breaking up the home.

4. *Provide professional help.* You and your child may need outside help to resolve the molestation incident. Some parents doubt the child's story. For the child to be first molested and then viewed as a liar is a double victimization, the resolution of which may require referral to a professional counselor or psychiatrist. Some parents feel guilty about not being able to prevent the molestation, and they may feel extreme anger or rage toward the molester. These parents may require professional advice on how to best resolve these feelings.

child's parents, who may find it difficult to control their alarm and who may involve the child in their great fears over the incident.

After an experience of molestation, it is critical that the child receive proper counseling either from his or her parents and/or a professional. Professional help may be necessary since some children do not feel free to talk to their parents about *any* sexual matters. Others are reluctant to talk about the incident for fear that they may be viewed as being guilty for what happened (DeVine 1980).

1. If you were a parent, what would be your greatest apprehension over your child encountering a pedophile?
2. If your child had been sexually molested, what steps would you take to reduce the adverse effects as much as possible?
3. If your child has been sexually molested, would you report the offense to the police? Why or why not?

Incest

Another common form of sexual abuse that frequently involves children is **incest.** Although incest is highly tabooed, recent evidence is showing that its incidence is far greater than previously believed.

By definition, incest is sexual intercourse between persons so closely related that they are forbidden by law to marry. The majority of cases involve parent-child and sibling relations. Some states also forbid intercourse between other closely related family members: step-relatives, in-laws, grandparents, uncles, aunts, nephews, nieces, and cousins. The type of sexual contact involved in incest may be sexual propositioning, exhibitionism, sexual fondling, hand-genital or oral-genital contact, mutual masturbation, or sexual intercourse.

Incest does not occur in emotionally stable families (Poznanski and Blos 1975). It is a strong indicator of an estrangement and breakdown in the marital relationship in the home.

Taboos Against Incest   Incest is a near-universal taboo in most societies today. Reinforcing the taboo in this country are laws in each of the states penalizing incestuous behavior (Giarretto 1980).

There are several bases for the incest taboo. A valid biological argument is that incest may lead to defective offspring (Parker 1976; Sagarin 1977). Another basis for the incest taboo is that, psychologically and legally, the child is viewed as a powerless individual, as dependent upon the family, and as unable to give full and informed consent. Coercing children into a sexual relationship to which they may not give consent and the effects against which they do not have full protection is a form of child abuse. Women who as children have experienced incest report feelings of guilt, fear, and complicity (Tsai and Wagner 1979).

Prevalence of Incest   The exact extent of the incest problem is difficult to ascertain. Some estimate that as many as twenty million (one in ten) Americans may have been involved in an incestuous experience (Geiser 1979). Surveys indicate that of all sex abuse of minors, almost one-half of that which occurs with females and one-fifth of that which occurs with males is incestuous (Finkelhor 1979). Ninety-two percent of the victims of incest are females, and 97 percent of the offenders are males. The median age of the child at first encounter is nine to eleven years. Three-fourths of the cases occur before age twelve and one-fourth before age nine. However, victims range in age from several months to the late teenage years (Geiser 1979).

The most common types of incestuous relations involve father-daughter, step-father-stepdaughter, sibling, and mother-son. Of these, the most frequently reported, and potentially the most damaging, is father-daughter incest.

Myths about Incest

The following are some common myths about incest, along with the facts that dispel each myth (Geiser 1979):

Myth: *Incest is limited to Appalachia or other poor rural sections of the country.*

Facts: Incest is not, in fact, limited by geography, socioeconomic class, religion, or ethnic factors.

Myth: *The incest offender is psychotic.*

Facts: Actually, very few incest offenders are psychotic.

Myth: *Incest is a one- or two-time affair.*

Facts: This myth is discredited by the finding that, on the average, individual cases of incest have been going on for years prior to discovery. Nor is incest usually limited to a single child in the family.

Myth: *Incest is merely another harmless deviation of a normal varied sex life.*

Facts: This does not fit with the fact that incest often leaves its victims psychologically devastated and almost always indicates family pathology and breakdown.

Myth: *Incest is less traumatic to the child victim than a sexual assault by a stranger.*

The child frequently ends up in more psychological turmoil and is more often scarred after an incident of incest (in which the child is betrayed by a trusted adult) than after molestation by a stranger.

Myth: *The child victim of incest is responsible for the adult's actions because of the child's seductive behavior.*

Facts: Regardless of whether or not the child was seductive, or how the adult may have interpreted the action, the final responsibility in the encounter lies with the adult, who is older, more experienced, more mature, and more knowledgeable than the child.

Father-Daughter Incest Incestuous fathers are generally weak and ineffective, both within and outside the family. Many have come from troubled childhood homes, in some of which there were poor father relations, father desertion, and economic poverty (Meiselman 1979).

In many cases, the incestuous father, as a child, was deprived of an affectionate mother relationship. As an adult, he may expect his wife to "mother" him. When such expectations are unmet, the marital relationship may become strained and cause the partners to drift apart both emotionally and sexually (Geiser 1979).

The mother in an incestuous family usually has some problems of her own. She may have been deprived of a normal family life as a child; in fact, she may have been abused emotionally and sexually (Geiser 1979; Gottlieb 1980). When she eventually has her own daughter, the mother may find it hard to relate well to her. She may not provide her daughter with strong role modeling as a mother, and she may load up the daughter with undue responsibilities for the home.

In short, in the incestuous family, everyone is searching for the mother they did or do not have. The basic anxiety in incestuous families revolves around abandonment by the mothering adult (Geiser 1979).

Fearing or realizing rejection from his wife, the father is confident that the daughter will not reject him. The sexually inexperienced daughter is viewed as being available and vulnerable (Finkelhor 1979; Geiser 1979). Alcohol often deadens the father's moral constraints and allows the first act of incest to occur. Between 20 and 50 percent of incestuous fathers are alcoholics (Meiselman, 1979).

The mother may be an active nonparticipant in the incestuous affair between the father and daughter in that she may provide opportunities for the father and daughter to be together. She may do so explicitly or tacitly by not "seeing" and avoiding acknowledgement of what is going on. While the mother may see herself as a nonparticipant, her "permission" is required. Incestuous acts cannot occur without some degree of awareness of them by the mother.

The oldest daughter is the most vulnerable to the father's incestuous actions (Meiselman 1979). While "appearing" mature and sexually seductive to the father, the daughter may be quite the opposite in reality. She may feel anxious and confused over the secretiveness of the sexual contact and the erotic pleasure she may derive from the contact.

If and when the daughter reports the incestuous relationship to a social services agency, she is often taken out of her home and placed in a foster home for her protection. The daughter may feel that this confirms that the sexual contact with her father was her fault, adding to any sense of guilt she may already be feeling over having disrupted the family by exposing the incest (Geiser 1979).

Because she feels betrayed by those who, for her, should have been most trustworthy, the daughter learns to distrust adults in general, and men in particular. Perceiving her body as her only value, she may become promiscuous or turn to prostitution (Herman and Hirschman 1981). As many as 90 percent of the apprehended runaways in some major cities are from incestuous homes (Hatcher 1980). The daughter may come to see adult expressions of caring as dangerous and harmful. Her rage may become secretly internalized, only to erupt years later. Divorce, inability to respond sexually, and inability to develop intimacies with men are a common heritage (Masters and Johnson 1970; McGuire and Wagner 1978; Geiser 1978).

Stepfather-Stepdaughter Incest There is some evidence that stepfather-stepdaughter incest is actually as much as five times (on a percentage basis) more common than father-daughter incest (Finkelhor 1979). The stepdaughter is viewed as being more vulnerable because she and the stepfather are not blood relatives; thus, the biological taboo is bypassed. Also, stepfathers, if they have not known their stepdaughters as young children, may have fewer paternal, protective instincts that act to "shield" the natural fathers from incest (Finkelhor 1979).

Sibling Incest Sexual contact between siblings (brother-sister, brother-brother, sister-sister) is generally held to have a higher actual incidence than father-daughter incest. Sibling incest is believed to account for at least one-half of all incest and for

Prevention of Incest

Central to preventing incest is the development of strong feelings of unity within the nuclear family. There needs to be a strong, romantic, sexual bonding between the parents. The parents must understand and work together to fulfill each other's needs. When children are in the home, the parents need time alone (weekends, short vacation periods). The parents also need to develop a strong loyalty toward their children. If the parents and children spend time together and the parents recognize the needs of the children, a parental sense of protectiveness for the children is created. If one of the parents is estranged or absent (desertion, separation, divorce, death), the remaining parent needs to maintain strong feelings of relatedness with the children. In newly restructured families, new loyalties need to be created. Stepfathers need to develop genuine fatherly feelings toward stepdaughters, particularly if the relationship starts during or past puberty (Meiselman 1979). Formal adoption of children by stepparents, equal participation by step- and natural parents in family discipline, and use of the words *mother* and *father* by children help to emphasize the parental role of new stepparents. All of these elements are basic to a strong, unified nuclear family, and with a strong, unified nuclear family comes a markedly decreased possibility of incest.

In addition, all of us, and especially educators, family physicians, counselors, and religious advisors, need to be aware of the *high risk factors* for incest, so that, in any given family, the possibility of incest as a source of family discord can be, if not prevented, at least identified and treated. These high-risk factors include:

An alcoholic or violent father; a mother who is absent from home, chronically ill, or passive; or an eldest daughter who has been forced to play a "little mother" role in household duties and care of younger children

Any condition that impairs self-control in the parent (low intelligence, psychosis, unusual stresses) or a hostile, apprehensive attitude by the family (especially the father) toward outsiders

Failure of parents to develop and maintain a mutually gratifying sexual relationship

Circumstances that cause the father and daughter to be alone together for long periods of time, or to share a bed together

A father and daughter who seem to be developing a special, romantic relationship or who engage in an unusual amount of physical contact; a father who seems extremely interested in the daughter's sexual activities with boyfriends; or a father who picks out one daughter for special gifts or favors

A child who evidences a sudden change in basic emotions

A previous occurrence of incest in the nuclear family or in the parents' extended families

Under any of these circumstances, the need for counseling should be apparent (Meiselman 1979).

94 percent of all the incest within the nuclear family. It accounts for 39 percent of all incest reported by girls and 21 percent reported by boys, whereas only 4 percent of involved girls report father incest (Finkelhor 1979). Ninety percent of the boys and 80 percent of the girls were under age twelve at the time of the experience, most commonly around the ages of nine or ten (Finkelhor 1979). About 30 percent of the sibling incest takes place for the girls under force or threat of force (Finkelhor 1979). There is greater concern as to effect upon the siblings if there is a wide age gap, forced contact, pregnancy, infection, or trauma (Geiser 1979).

Most vulnerable to sibling incest appears to be the youngest sister from the large family in which there are several older brothers (Meiselman 1979). Also at greater risk is the young teenage male who is seduced by the older sister. Such a relationship may take on a semimaternal aspect and may eventually result in the boy developing impotence as an adult (Geiser 1979).

Overall, the effect of brother-sister incest is believed to be less traumatic to the participants than parent-child incest because of the closer age of the two individuals. Sisters appear less traumatized than daughters by the incest itself, particularly if there has been no exploitation of a younger sister by an older brother or of a younger brother by an older sister (Meiselman 1979).

Sibling incest is less often discovered than other forms of incest. When it is discovered, it may be less offensive, both to the partners and to family members. It also is more easily dealt with within the family (Finkelhor 1979).

Other Forms of Incest   Incestuous relations between mother and son are very uncommon, and few cases are reported or prosecuted. Many view this type of incest as the most traumatic and the most destructive to the relationship of the family (Geiser 1979). It occurs only in a context of psychosis or extreme family disorganization (Finkelhor 1979), and the person initiating the incest is typically very disturbed (Meiselman 1979).

If the son is a child, the incestuous activity would typically involve a fondling of the child's genitals without intercourse. With postpubertal sons, however, sexual intercourse is most common.

Other forms of reported incest include father-son and mother-daughter incest. Information on either of these forms of incestuous behavior is so scant that very little is understood as to the dynamics of either type (Geiser 1979).

---

1. Why do you suppose that father-daugher incest, which is considerably less common than stepfather-stepdaughter incest or sibling incest, is the most frequently reported?
2. What points would you make to refute any argument that father-daughter incest is a healthy sexual learning experience for a child? (Answer in terms of the father, mother, and daughter.)
3. List some factors that might indicate a stronger chance of incest occurring in a family.

Unlawful Intercourse

Known as statutory rape in some states, **unlawful intercourse** is voluntary intercourse between an adult and a minor (under the age of consent), who are not married to each other. One of the oldest crimes, it is based on the premise that the minor is not sufficiently experienced, responsible, or mature to give informed consent to sexual intercourse. It is assumed that since the minor is unable to comprehend the significance of pregnancy, risk of disease, and affected reputation, the consent he or she might give for intercourse is immaterial (Rush 1980).

Under the age of consent concept, such permission for intercourse could be legally given only by a parent or guardian. The age of consent, determined by state law, generally varies betwen sixteen and twenty-one years of age. Legally, in many states, all that is required to convict a man of statutory rape is proof of entry of the penis and the age of the female.

New Jersey has enacted a law that is more realistic in terms of the widespread sexual activities today by teenagers. In 1979, it lowered its age of consent for sexual intercourse to thirteen years, except for intercourse with relatives, guardians, and school or business personnel.

While many teenage females engage in sex voluntarily, and without knowledge of (or concern about) matters of age of consent, they place an adult sexual partner at risk of being trapped. Some adolescent females are able, with the aid of cosmetics, appropriate clothing, and conduct, to appear years older than they are, and they may easily mislead an unwary man. Although it may sound ridiculously outmoded, in most states, adult males are well advised to know something about the age of a young female sex partner. Otherwise, they may run the risk, slim though it admittedly is, of being charged with statutory rape by an offended parent or guardian.

Fetishism

In **fetishism**, sexual arousal is induced mainly through the use of some nonliving object or body part that most people would not regard as being sexual in nature. The fetish object becomes a sexual symbol that replaces a partner as a source of sexual arousal.

Fetishes tend to be articles of clothing, such as female underclothing, high-heeled shoes, boots, hats, and handkerchiefs, since fetishism occurs almost entirely in men. Other fetishes may be parts of the body of the opposite sex, such as hair, hands, thighs, feet, ears, eyes, and breasts. In fact, any body part or object can be endowed with fetishistic meaning.

During masturbation, some fetishists fondle, manipulate, smell, or kiss the fetish object to produce arousal and orgasm. Others may look at the object to stimulate a fantasy scenario (American Psychiatric Association 1980). During sexual activity with a partner, the fetish object may be required to provide sufficient sexual excitement.

The fetish object is often associated with someone with whom the individual was intimately involved during childhood, such as a mother, nurse, or teacher (American Psychiatric Association 1980). The object may be preferred by the fetishist because it is nonthreatening and can be harmed or destroyed without con-

Fetishism. Some stores specialize in the sale of fetishistic items.

sequence (Stoller 1977). Usually, the disorder begins in adolescence, although the fetish may have taken on special significance earlier in childhood. Once established, the disorder tends to be chronic, or unusual.

A continuum of fetishistic behavior has been suggested by Gebhard (1976). At one end of the continuum are those who express a *slight preference* for a fetish object; next are those holding a *strong preference;* next are those who *must have* the fetish object to function sexually; and finally, at the other end of the continuum, are those who *substitute* the fetish for a human sexual partner. Gebhard suggests that normalcy ends and fetish deviance begins at about the point where a strong preference for the fetish object is expressed.

Many persons have some degree of preference for a particular item of lingerie or body part as an aid in sexual arousal. A male may masturbate with the help of female lingerie because the items boost his fantasies in the absence of a female partner. This behavior is not necessarily fetishistic. For the fetishist, the use of the object becomes *compelling*. The fetish item is focused on to the exclusion of everything else (Stoller 1977). The key to fetishism is whether the object of choice is the repeatedly preferred or exclusive method of becoming sexually excited, or whether it is resorted to only in the absence of a female partner's company.

kleptomaniac
(klep''to-ma'ne-ak)

pyromaniac
(pi''ro-ma'ne-ak)

zoophilia
(zo''o-fil'e-ah)

bestiality
(bes-te-al'i-te)

Besides serving to sexually arouse an individual, some fetishes become associated with other practices. A **kleptomaniac,** or compulsive stealer, may steal an object of no value to him or her except for its significance in sexual gratification. In fact, the very act of stealing and the danger associated with it may become a source of sexual excitement. Often, a kleptomaniac is a female who is emotionally disturbed over a perception of being unloved and unwanted (Alexander 1965).

The **pyromaniac,** or compulsive fire setter, may receive sexual gratification from the "heat" of the fire or from watching the inferno. He or she may stand in the shadows of the fire and masturbate. Having achieved orgasm, the pyromaniac may feel guilty and actually become one of the volunteers helping to extinguish the fire (Coleman 1972).

Or the male fetishist may combine his object preferences with **masochism,** in which he insists on being whipped or beaten by a woman wearing black lace hose or some other fetish object.

There is a thriving business in the manufacture and sale of fetish items. Usually found in adult stores or advertised in the sex tabloids, there are inflatable life-size dolls, pubic fur, imitation vaginas and dildos. It is also not uncommon to find advertisements of fetishists seeking out sexual partners for a wide array of practices involving the use of fetishes.

Zoophilia

In **zoophilia** ("love of animals"), also called **bestiality,** sexual arousal is induced through repeated or exclusive sexual contact with animals. While many different types of animals may be used, the most common ones are those found on farms and in homes. The animal may be used for intercourse or may be trained to sexually excite the person by licking or rubbing. Usually, the preferred animal is one with which the individual had contact during childhood. In zoophilia, the animal is preferred regardless of what other forms of sexual outlets are available (American Psychiatric Association 1980).

Zoophilia is very uncommon in comparison with other sexual practices. Kinsey (1948) found that while 8 percent of adult males and 3 percent of females reported such contacts, these activities accounted for a fraction of only 1 percent of their total sexual outlets. The males involved were mostly from rural areas, and their contact was usually with farm animals during their adolescence (ages ten to fourteen). The females tended to be involved with household pets. About half of them reported contacts before the age of twenty and the rest later in life. The female contacts tended to be of somewhat shorter duration and lesser frequency than the male contacts.

Reasons for sexual contacts with animals vary. Some individuals engage in zoophilia simply out of curiosity, out of an interest in experimentation, or because of a need for sexual release when a human partner is unavailable (Tollison and Adams 1979). Sexual contact with animals may be the male's method of avoiding distress because of his belief that sex relations with any woman may suggest incest with his mother. Or it may be a method of showing hostility or contempt toward women by attempting to identify them with animals or by choosing animals in preference to women. Most adolescents, both male and female, go on from experimenting with zoophilia into the usual heterosexual experiences. Only those with deeper problems persist in animal sexual contacts.

Most states have laws prohibiting sex relations between humans and animals. In many states, the violation is a felony. Damage to the animal involved is not relevant to the violation of this law. One of the legal reasons behind the prohibition against zoophilia is that one partner is involved without its consent, even though no force is used.

---

1. Do you think that New Jersey's new law that lowers the age of consent for sexual intercourse to thirteen years is a good idea? Why or why not?
2. Distinguish between harmless fetishistic sexual behavior and that which is viewed as a paraphilia.
3. Explain the basis for laws against the practice of sex with animals.

Variations in Choice of Sexual Aim

The second group of paraphilias discussed are those that vary in terms of a goal other than seeking intercourse. Paraphiliac replacements for intercourse include exposing one's genitals (exhibitionism), secretly watching others nude or in sexual activities (voyeurism), cross-dressing (transvestism), using anonymous lewd language (making obscene telephone calls), and engaging in a group of additional atypical paraphilias. Two others, inflicting pain (sexual sadism) and suffering pain (sexual masochism), are discussed in chapter 21.

Exhibitionism

In **exhibitionism,** sexual arousal is induced from exposing the genitals to an unsuspecting and unconsenting stranger, who is often a woman or a child. Some people show off their bodies in a manner society considers reasonably appropriate for the situation because they want to be admired for their attractiveness. In contrast, the exhibitionist exposes the genitals in a manner considered quite inappropriate for the purposes of personal sexual arousal.

The victim who reacts coolly and pays little attention disappoints the offender and provides him little gratification. The victim's best approach is to calmly ignore the act and to suggest that the exhibitionist would do well to receive psychotherapy.

The exhibitionist may expose himself while sitting in a parked car, riding a bus or subway, or standing in a park or on a beach. The wish of the exhibitionist is to surprise, frighten, or humiliate the victim. He may have an erection at the time and be pleased to view the shocked reaction of a victim. He may ejaculate right there or may masturbate to orgasm shortly afterwards (Stoller 1977).

Exhibitionists are most often males. While some are females, the public has a more tolerant attitude toward the exposed bodies of females, and the chances of a female exhibitionist being reported by the viewer are believed to be somewhat less.

Exhibitionism.

Some exhibitionists expose themselves due to some transitory life stress or sexual deprivation. The anger felt because of the life stress or sexual deprivation is often directed toward strangers perceived as uncaring. The exhibitionist attempts to reaffirm his potency and to overcome feelings of insignificance and inadequacy by gaining some attention. If the victim reacts strongly, the exhibitionist interprets this as a compliment to his virility. Usually, when the life stress is removed or when the man is no longer sexually deprived, the exhibitionist stops exhibiting. Most exhibitionists practice genital exposure for short periods of time only, and most are not arrested (Gagnon 1977).

Studies of those arrested suggest that the exhibitionist is a shy, inhibited man who has had little sexual experience. He is usually timid and submissive, lacks normal aggressiveness, and doubts his own masculinity. He has feelings of inadequacy and insecurity.

Few exhibitionists are dangerous or a menace. More of a nuisance, they rarely become involved with more serious crime, except for those few who also molest children (Tollison and Adams 1979; American Psychiatric Association 1980). The child molester is much more likely to become an exhibitionist than the exhibitionist is likely to become a molester (Gagnon 1977). Victim's fears of rape or physical harm from the exhibitionist are mostly unsubstantiated since the offender is rarely violent or aggressive. Most exhibitionists "flash" at some distance—usually six to sixty feet from their victim (Gebhard et al. 1965).

The vice of exhibitionism lies partly in the fact that the element of choice is taken away from the victim. Looking at another's genitals is not offensive if that is what a person wants to do. But with exhibitionism, the victim is unwillingly used for the sexual excitement of the offender. The law seeks to protect people against their being used sexually without their consent. Often, exhibitionism is not reported because children and parents do not take it seriously enough to bother.

A long-term decline in exhibitionism is thought to be related to an increasing social acceptance of sexuality. As people become more and more blasé about sexual matters, exhibitionists can no longer count on their past levels of success at shocking people. And, as our sexual attitudes become more healthful, fewer people may feel the need to become exhibitionistic.

voyeurism
(voi'yer-izm)

Voyeurism

Many people in our society find looking at nude or skimpily attired people a pleasant and acceptable diversion. Men may attend a striptease show or topless bar or page through the photos of nude females in magazines. Not to be outdone, women today have female-only clubs in many cities that feature G-string clad or totally nude male dancers. Also, *Cosmopolitan* and *Playgirl* magazines feature photos of nude males. Many people find looking at the bodies of the opposite sex (or the same sex) pleasurable and incidental. But for some it represents a paraphilia.

Voyeurism is the need to secretively view unsuspecting people, usually strangers, in the act of disrobing, when they are naked, or when they are engaging in sexual activity, to become sexually aroused.

The voyeur is also known as a "peeping Tom." According to legend, in the eleventh century, the Lord Leofric of Coventry proposed to raise his tenants' taxes. His wife, Lady Godiva, agreed to ride through the streets naked on a white horse, covered only by her long hair, if he would rescind the tax. Out of gratitude and respect, everyone in town stayed inside their closed houses and shuttered windows and did not look at her, except for one man, Tom the tailor. He, according to the legend, peeped and went blind.

For most people, sexual activity includes becoming sexually aroused from watching each other undressing and looking at each other nude. Such looking usually is a prelude to further sexual activity and is done with a partner who is willingly in view. Also, many of us enjoy looking at commercialized nudity, filmed or live. Such tendencies are not voyeuristic. Viewing becomes the paraphilia of voyeurism when the looking is done secretly—watching people in what they believe is the privacy of their own homes, cars, or hotel rooms. To the voyeur, such acts of looking are compulsive, are consistently preferred to intercourse, and are the voyeur's exclusive means of gaining sexual arousal.

Voyeurs are usually male, single, and relatively young (usually in their twenties); few women are arrested on charges of peeping. The first voyeuristic act is likely to occur in early adulthood. Most voyeurs typically have had a slowed heterosexual development (Tollison and Adams 1979); most of them attempt their first intercourse at a later date than most other males (Gebhard et al. 1965). Voyeurism is a transient activity for many; for others, it may become usual and continue for years. Few voyeurs, however, show serious mental disorder or use alcohol or drugs prior to their voyeuristic acts.

Looking, for the peeper, fulfills a sense of adventure and participation he fails to find in real life. Because he feels that his self-worth is threatened, his looking protects him against personal failure in sexual activity. It gives him a sense of superiority over the victim who is being secretly viewed. Orgasm, usually produced by masturbation, may occur during the peeping or later, in response to the memory

Voyeurism, or "peeping Tomism."

of what he has seen. Often, a voyeur enjoys thinking about his victim's helplessness and the feelings of humiliation the victim would experience if he or she knew of the voyeur (American Psychiatric Association 1980).

Voyeurs are heterogeneous in terms of intelligence, occupation, and family background. They are more often the youngest children in their families. The one common thread running between most voyeurs is a history of very deficient social relationships with the opposite sex.

Most voyeurs are reported to police by passersby or neighbors rather than by the victims themselves. While some states have special laws against voyeurs, others prosecute voyeurism under disorderly conduct statutes. In most states, it is a misdemeanor.

1. Why do you think that female exhibitionism is viewed with less alarm than male exhibitionism?
2. How would you be able to tell whether your interest in viewing live or portrayed nudity represented normal or unusual sexual behavior?
3. With nudity so prevalent in the media and in live entertainment, what factors might cause a person to practice "peeping Tomism"?

Transvestism

Transvestism is cross-dressing in the clothing of the opposite sex for the purpose of obtaining sexual excitement. Recurrent and persistent, the cross-dressing is almost always by a heterosexual male (American Psychiatric Association 1980). While some women may dress in masculine clothing, they do not seem to be sexually excited by the act (Stoller 1971).

Transvestite acts range from secretly wearing female lingerie, to occasionally dressing up in female clothing, to cross-dressing permanently. A small percentage of transvestites eventually choose to dress and live permanently as women. The cross-dressing typically begins in childhood or early adolescence but may not be done in public until adulthood.

A parent's rejection of a child's biological sex may underlie the development of transvestism. According to some, the punishment of humiliating a boy by dressing him in girls' clothes ("petticoat punishment") is common in the history of individuals who later develop this disorder. While genetically and hormonally normal for their sex, they develop gender-role problems.

More commonly, transvestites believe that they are, in fact, two personalities. They see themselves as both male and female within one body, with the female personality appearing when they cross-dress and the male personality appearing the rest of the time. Some even make a clear-cut division between the two personalities by having a separate name for each.

Transvestites are usually male and heterosexual but are sexually aroused by wearing women's clothing.

Most transvestites, when not cross-dressing, are typically masculine. They work in typically masculine occupations, and when in men's clothing, they do not act effeminate. They may have working arrangements with their families that they may cross-dress at home daily or on occasion. Their identity discomfort is satisfied by creating two distinct worlds and two distinct selves (Gagnon 1977). If their cross-dressing is interfered with, intense frustration results.

Transvestites are distinct both from male homosexuals who masquerade in theatrical fashion as women ("drag queens") and from female impersonators such as those performing in nightclubs. Neither of these types relies on cross-dressing for sexual arousal or for relief from tension.

Very few transvestites are **transsexual** (see chapter 11). The true transsexual dislikes his or her genitals and sees himself or herself as a person locked in the wrong body. Wishing to be rid of their natural genitals, transsexuals may undergo sex reassignment surgery and live as a member of the opposite sex. Only in a few cases has transvestism evolved into transsexualism (American Psychiatric Association 1980; Stoller 1977).

Obscene Telephone Calls

Obscene telephone calls are anonymous telephone communications involving lewd language. Primarily males are engaged in this activity. Intent on annoying another person, the caller often masturbates while calling, needing the stimulation of the call to enable him to ejaculate. The obscene telephone caller usually feels sexually inadequate and seeks sexual arousal and gratification through this anonymous and safely remote manner. As with the exhibitionist, his pleasure is enhanced by the shock and embarrassment of the person receiving the call, but, unlike the exhibitionist, the obscene phone caller can act out his paraphilia without the fear of actually facing the other person.

The content of the calls may vary. The caller may verbally threaten the woman with bodily harm, may vividly describe the masturbation he is engaged in, or may solicit revealing details of the sexual life of the woman.

Victims of the obscene telephone caller are virtually all females, and most of them interpret the calls as more than just an offensive nuisance. They may wonder what will happen if the caller comes around. Many females listed in a telephone directory are unmarried, and these women are most often the target of the lewd caller.

Obscene telephone callers come from homes in which they appear to have good relationships with parents, siblings, and partners. They seem to have adequate heterosexual sexual activity in terms of number of partners and frequency. Homosexuality appears to be no significant element (Gebhard et al. 1965), and the use of alcohol and other drugs appears to play little part in the reduced inhibitions of

frottage	klismaphilia	coprophilia
(fro-tahzh′)	(klis″mah-fil′e-ah)	(kop″ro-fe′le-ah)
troilism	coprolalia	necrophilia
(troi′lizm)	(kop″ro-la′le-ah)	(nek″ro-fil′e-ah)

obscene telephone callers. The compulsive nature of the act is underlined by the fact that obscene telephone callers often continue their activities even after having been once or repeatedly arrested for prior obscene behavior.

Telephone companies often recommend that women receiving obscene telephone calls hang up promptly. Or in the event another person and another telephone is available, it may be possible to alert an operator, who may have the facilities to trace the source of the call.

Other Paraphilias

Some paraphilias, such as frottage, troilism, klismaphilia, coprophilia, coprolalia, and necrophilia, occur very uncommonly, and little is known about their causes.

Frottage is sexual arousal from rubbing or pressing against the body of a fully clothed person in a crowded situation, such as in a crowded corridor, in an elevator, or on a sidewalk.

Troilism is the sharing of a sexual partner or close relative (such as a daughter) with a third person, while the first person looks on. Troilists are able to become sexually aroused only as they are actively "sharing" through watching the sexual act.

Obtaining sexual excitement from receiving an enema is known as **klismaphilia.** After discovering this pleasure in childhood while receiving an enema from a loving parent, the child may continue to associate pleasure when receiving enemas from someone else.

Coprophilia is obtaining sexual excitement from viewing or perceiving the odor of feces.

Coprolalia, or scatologia, is deriving sexual arousal from using or hearing lewd or filthy language. Coprolalia does not include lovers who enhance sexual arousal during lovemaking with the use of language that some might consider inappropriately lewd. Coprolalia, by distinction, is the need to use or hear such language to become sexually excited. Coprolalia also includes scribbling sexual graffiti and writing lewd letters if the person carrying out these acts receives sexual pleasure from them.

Obtaining sexual excitement from looking at a corpse or from having intercourse with a corpse is called **necrophilia.** The sexual contact may be followed by the offender mutilating the corpse. To provide themselves with a corpse, necrophiles may kill or may remove corpses from cemeteries or morgues (Tollison and Adams 1979). Some necrophiles derive erotic pleasure from contact with simulated corpses. It is reported that some prostitutes cater to such a preference: they powder themselves, dress in shroud, and lie very still during intercourse to simulate a corpse. Exceedingly rare, necrophilia indicates a serious psychological disturbance or a psychotic person.

nymphomania
(nim″fo-ma′ne-ah)

satyriasis
(sat″ĭ-ri′ah-sis)

1. Compare the motives of a "drag queen" with that of the true transvestite in the practice of cross-dressing.
2. Contrast transvestism and transsexualism.
3. Aside from hanging up, what other effective measures have you heard of for discouraging obscene phone calls?
4. Contrast frottage with exhibitionism.
5. Why is necrophilia an indication of serious psychological disturbance?

Hypersexuality

An unusually intense sex drive that leads to little or no sexual gratification despite numerous sex acts with numerous partners is known as **hypersexuality.** The hypersexual person experiences more or less continual sexual desire and arousal yet is unable to establish satisfying interpersonal relationships because of this sexual compulsion (Tollison and Adams 1979). While sex and the thoughts of sexual conquest direct the hypersexual's life, his or her sexual experiences are disappointing and shallow. In women who feel such constant sexual hunger and tenseness, the condition may be called **nymphomania;** in men, **satyriasis** ("Don Juanism").

Hypersexuality may be caused by disease in or injury to parts of the brain. Although not fully researched, it may also have a psychological explanation. Some individuals have a strong, unfulfilled need for love and intimacy yet may be unwilling or unable to make the emotional investment necessary for true intimacy. A severely socially abnormal person may have the need to use others sexually in an attempt to satisfy his or her own needs while maintaining emotional detachment. In some cases, a person may not even have a strong sex drive yet may try to relieve anxiety and tenseness by having sex (Kaplan 1979).

Stereotyping "Nymphs" and "Satyrs"
Some people use the terms *nymphomania* and *satyriasis* disparagingly to ridicule anyone whose sex drive and desire for frequency of sex is greater than their own. There is a commonly accepted stereotype of a woman "normally" having a low sex drive and a man a high one. In terms of this myth, any woman who has a high sex drive is abnormal and a "nymph," while the man who has a high sex drive is normal. Thus, few men are called "satyrs."

Calling a woman a nymphomaniac or a man a "Don Juan" simply because they want more sex than someone else is meaningless. By branding someone else's desire as abnormal, we are, by implication, trying to identify ourselves as the norm. Most men are quite satisfied with a single orgasm, while the sexually mature woman, who may have the capacity and desire for multiple orgasms, may not find one orgasm as fully gratifying (Masters and Johnson 1966). Not understanding this, some men may honestly believe that any woman desiring intercourse more often or for longer duration than themselves is truly a nymphomaniac.

What constitutes "too much" or "too little" is often defined by the sex partners. Some men think it is excessive for their partner to want intercourse once a day, once every other day, or perhaps once a week. Other men feel just the opposite and wish their partners would want intercourse more often. Some women experience the same differences of opinion with their male sex partners. As seen in chapter 9, there is a wide range of frequencies with which people engage in sexual intercourse, and it becomes virtually meaningless to try to define "normal" in terms of sexual desire and frequency of intercourse.

Promiscuity

Any higher-than-average frequency of sexual activity may raise the charge of a person being promiscuous in his or her sexual behavior. By definition, however, **promiscuity** is indiscriminate, transient, sexual intercourse with many persons for the relief of sexual tensions rather than for any feelings of affection (Hettlinger 1974). Finding relief from sexual tensions distinguishes the promiscuous person from the one who is truly hypersexual. Also, promiscuous sexual behavior is not, in fact, due to sex drives that are stronger or different than those of the average person.

Some might insist that, by this definition, few people could be said to be truly promiscuous since few persons would have sex with just anyone under any circumstance. Some people see promiscuity as meaning too many sex partners, whatever that number might be. For some, this number would be one, while for others it might be more than five. Some people feel that people are promiscuous if they have any sex partner other than the one they are married to. Thus, the word *promiscuous* can easily be used in a subjective fashion to give a derogatory label to anyone whose life-style is different from one's own.

The word *promiscuous* can, however, be legitimately used to mean any sexual activity outside of a caring, affectionate relationship, or any sexual activity to gain attention or to cope with emotional problems. This behavior arises from feelings of inadequacy, personality problems, and emotional conflicts. Promiscuous individuals may tend not to accept responsibility for their own behavior but blame friends, partners, and parents for their limitations. Through counseling, they can gain a sense of self-worth and resolve the cause of their promiscuity.

---

1. On what basis might a person who enjoys frequent coitus feel confident that he or she is not hypersexual?
2. Contrast promiscuity to both normal affectionate relations and to hypersexuality.

The next thing I remember I was laying in a hospital bed, with my mother on one side and our minister on the other. At nine years old, I had tried to commit suicide. I had seen no alternatives, but my family, with the help of our minister and a family counselor, helped me to find a way out of my nightmare.

It took me a long time to find the courage to tell of my brother's attacks against me. I didn't know if they would believe me, but they did. Our whole family went into therapy. I couldn't even look at my brother when we first started. We are still working out our problems. My brother doesn't live at home anymore. I don't know when or if I'll ever be able to forgive him.

The most important point I want to make to you is that I almost died to hide the shame that I felt, and it would have been such a waste. My parents and friends have helped me put my life back together. I want you to know that holding it inside helps no one. Please, if you or anyone you know is being abused sexually, physically, or mentally, please seek help. If you can't talk to your parents, talk to your priest or minister, a teacher, anyone! Don't hold it inside. You may not wake up in time. . . .

Summary

1.   Not everyone agrees at what point sexual behavior may be considered unusual or variant. Definitions for *normal* sexual behavior often include one or more of the following standards:
   a. Social: Acts that harm neither society nor another person
   b. Statistical: Acts that are engaged in by the majority
   c. Psychological: Acts that lead to positive feelings and that do not exploit another person
   d. Legal: Acts that violate no laws
   e. Moral: Acts that conform to a given religious or philosophical viewpoint
   f. Phylogenetic: Acts that are natural, as practiced by other mammals
   g. Cultural: Acts that conform to accepted cultural practice

2.   Normal sexual behavior is motivated by feelings of affection, seeks to give and receive pleasure, tends to be discriminating in partner choice, and is motivated by erotic sexual tensions.

3.   Sexual disorders can be separated into two categories: sexual dysfunctions, which prevent a person from having or enjoying sex, and sexual paraphilias, which are typified by sexual actions that are pleasurable, yet whose object and/or aim deviates from the norm. Sexual paraphilias require some unusual or bizarre acts or images to bring on sexual arousal.

4.   The sexual paraphilias may take one of two forms: paraphilias that deviate in choice of sexual object (with whom or what one has intercourse) and paraphilias that deviate in choice of sexual aim (a goal other than seeking intercourse).

5. Paraphilias in which there is variation in choice of sexual object include sexual abuse of children (pedophilia and incest), and sex with an adolescent female (unlawful sex), with inanimate objects or body parts (fetishism), and with animals (zoophilia).

6. Sexual abuse of minors is forced, pressured, or stressful sexual behavior engaged in with a person under the age of seventeen. There is concern over its prevalence and its effect on its victims since children are dependent, immature persons, involved in sexual activities they do not fully comprehend, to which informed consent is not given, and which violate cultural taboos. Forms of sexual abuse of children include pedophilia and incest.

7. Pedophilia describes a behavioral pattern in which an adult is sexually attracted to and sexually aroused by prepubertal children. Offenders are most often younger males who approach young girls to look at or touch, usually in the home of the victim or offender.

8. Incest is sexual intercourse between persons so closely related that they are forbidden by law to marry. Incest is a strong indicator of an estrangement and breakdown in the marital relationship in the home. Most often reported is father-daughter incest, although stepfather-stepdaughter is more prevalent on a percentage basis. Sibling incest is thought to be highest in actual incidence.

9. Unlawful sexual intercourse (statutory rape) is voluntary sexual intercourse between an adult male and a minor female (who is under the age of consent), who are not married to each other.

10. Sexual arousal induced mainly through the use of nonliving objects or body parts, in which the object or body part replaces the partner as a stimulus to sexual arousal, is fetishism. While many people enjoy certain objects as aids in sexual arousal, the use of the objects becomes compelling for the fetishist. Kleptomania (compulsive stealing) and pyromania (compulsive fire setting) are variant fetishes.

11. Zoophilia is sexual arousal induced through repeated or exclusive sexual contact with animals. It is a felony in most states.

12. Paraphilias in which there is variation in choice of sexual aim include exhibitionism, voyeurism, transvestism, obscene telephone calls, and several additional unusual paraphilias.

13. Sexual arousal induced from exposing the genitals to an unsuspecting or unconsenting stranger is exhibitionism. Exhibitionists are most often males, and the victims are usually women or children. The exhibitionist is rarely dangerous to the victim.

14. Voyeurism (peeping Tomism) is secretively viewing unsuspecting people in the act of disrobing, when they are naked, or when they are engaging in sexual activity to become sexually aroused. While many people have voyeuristic tendencies, to the voyeur, the act is compulsive.

15.   Transvestism is cross-dressing in the clothing of the opposite sex to attain sexual arousal and to relieve sexual tensions. Transvestism is distinguished from transsexualism, in which the person dislikes his or her genitals.

16.   Obscene telephone calls are anonymous telephone communications involving lewd language. The acts are compulsive in nature, and the caller may masturbate while calling.

17.   Unusual paraphilias include frottage (arousal from rubbing against the body of a fully clothed person in a crowded situation), troilism (arousal from watching one's partner have sex with someone else), klismaphilia (arousal from taking an enema), coprophilia (arousal from viewing or perceiving the odor of feces), coprolalia (arousal from using or hearing lewd or filthy language, and necrophilia (arousal through sexual activity with a corpse).

18.   Hypersexuality is an uncommon psychiatric disorder in which the person feels constant and compelling sexual desire yet finds little or no sexual gratification, despite numerous sex acts with numerous partners. Hypersexuality is called nymphomania in females and satyriasis ("Don Juanism") in males. By contrast, the promiscuous person finds sexual gratification, although the sexual activity is indiscriminate and without feelings of affection.

Prostitution
*Female Prostitutes/Male Prostitutes/Recruiting of Female
Prostitutes/Why Men Visit Prostitutes/Laws Regarding
Prostitution*

Pornography
*Cultural Sadism/Pornographic Fantasies/Child
Pornography/Pornography in the Media/Effects of
Exposure to Pornography/Pornography and the Law/
Public Protest against Pornography*

Sex in Advertising
*Television Advertising/Printed Advertising/Sexual
Symbolization/Subliminal Advertising/Public Reaction to
Sex in Advertising*

"C'mon, honey, smile for the camera. Good, now toss back your hair and really grab that fishing pole!
Now hug it . . . closer . . . in tight . . . now run your lips down it. Good!"

"Good Lord, Terry, this is an ad layout for fishing gear, not some girlie magazine. Give me a break!
Nobody buys a fishing pole because it's sexy. They buy it because it catches fish. Why don't you find a fish to
run its lips down the thing?"

"Listen, the agency rep said sex, so sex is what we are going to give him. It's sex that sells and
everyone knows it. Even the dumb idiot who buys this stuff knows why we advertise the way we do. Sex sells.
Now, can we please get back to work?"

"But this is so . . . well . . . tacky!"

"Look, you're getting paid good money, so when I say more cleavage, I mean *now*! OK, Look into the
camera, bend down . . . c'mon, a little more thigh . . . lick your lips and think of all the money you're
making off those poor fishermen."

Sex is closely tied to money and commerce. The history of people paying money in return for sex is as old as written records. Its survival in the face of the "behavioral enlightenment" of our society is a commentary to the precedence of money over our own and other people's sexual dignity.

Prostitution, pornography, and the use of sex in the mass media is money, and big money at that. The monetary rewards are reaped by the respectable and criminal alike. Prostitution profits not only the pimp, but also the hotel owners, bellhops, defense attorneys, bailspeople, medical doctors, and news reporters. Pornography is profitable to the underworld, as well as to the newsstand owner, television advertiser, and movie producer. The eroticization of the media produces exceptional return on the advertising investments of respectable people, who use sex to sell goods in the marketplace.

To satisfy their own sexual obsession or curiosity, the purchasers are willing to pay, even though it means the debasement of persons (usually women) to the level of mere objects. On the other hand, the willingness of people (often women) to demean themselves and others in return for payment addresses their failure to see the more rewarding aspects of sexuality.

This chapter is concerned not only with the commercialization of sex but with the distortion of sexuality. It addresses the life-styles of those persons whose bodies are being merchandised and used.

Prostitution

The only sex offense more often charged against women than men is prostitution. Prostitution also is the only sexual offense in which women are prosecuted to any significant extent.

Prostitution may be defined as a "profession" of persons who perform sexual acts with others for pay. The word comes from the Latin *prostituere,* which means "to expose" or "to offer for sale." The definition includes the elements of indiscriminate sex relations, largely without affection, in return for money or gifts. The payment, usually beforehand, for the service is immediate and is limited to that specific occurrence.

The commercialization of prostitution is centuries old. In ancient Greece and Mesopotamia, prostitution was part of temple worship, required of all females before marriage as a religious ritual. In some temples, there were female prostitutes who provided sexual services for male worshippers.

In spite of attempts to eliminate it, the "profession" has continued in virtually all cultures and during all periods of social and religious enlightenment. Condemned by most cultures, it has nevertheless either been tolerated or has been tacitly provided for.

Because prostitution generally is illegal, prostitutes are easily victimized. There grows up around prostitutes a large number of people, mostly men and male-dominated institutions, who live off prostitutes' incomes. The industry, whether syndicated or loosely organized, recruits prostitutes, promotes their services, manages them, guides people to them, and operates as a link with law enforcement. The "system" includes the **panderer,** who procures or recruits prostitutes; the **pimp,** who lives off the earnings of prostitutes, manages their time and money, pretends to protect their interests, and keeps them in line and working; the **madam,** who may manage prostitutes' apartments or a house of prostitution; and the bellhop, cabdriver, or bartender who supplies information to potential customers. It also includes the criminal justice system (bailspeople, attorneys, police, prosecutors, judges, bailiffs, jailers) and the owners of the places in which prostitution occurs (hotels, convention centers, casinos, and apartment houses).

Prostitution's criminal status and its identification with degraded sex shapes the "profession" and the life of the prostitute. The prostitution subculture has its own language, training procedures for new members, values for members to adhere to, and human relationships (Gagnon 1977).

Usually, prostitutes are women who offer their services to men. Because this is by far the most common prostitute relationship, we will be concerned mainly with female prostitutes in this chapter, although we will also briefly discuss different forms of male prostitution.

Female Prostitutes

Female prostitutes solicit male customers and practice their trade in various ways; there is no reliable stereotype. Because they are opportunists, prostitutes adapt to each situation to provide the sexual services their client is willing to pay for. The following are some of the primary ways in which prostitutes perform their work.

Call Girls

The **call girl,** or "pony girl," is a prostitute who keeps individual dates with clients. The location is a place that both the call girl and the client agree on, usually either his apartment or hers. The client makes the appointment for each date either with the woman herself, often with the help of an answering service, or through a third party.

Usually, the most highly paid of the female prostitutes, the call girl is expected to be well dressed and attractive. Since her fees are higher, she normally spends more time with her clients than do other types of prostitutes. She may be his social date for the evening or accompany him on weekend trips. If a call girl has past knowledge of her client, she will generally try to cater to his preferences in attire and/or food. Several call girls may entertain a group of men for a private party or as part of a corporate meeting.

It is important for a call girl to develop a substantial clientele. She may need to depend upon referrals from other call girls or a madam, with whom she will need to split her fees.

A call girl usually goes through an apprenticeship before becoming a full member of the profession. Often introduced into her apprenticeship by another call girl or by a pimp, she may share an apartment with another call girl who instructs her in the use of the telephone and in handling and exploiting her clients. The apprenticeship often lasts for two to three months and terminates either when her accumulated clientele is sufficient or a misunderstanding develops with her trainer.

Because she has little legal protection, a call girl must always be concerned with her own protection. She must determine whether her client is an authentic customer or a police officer, and whether or not he is safe and nonviolent.

Streetwalkers

Walking the street is a very common method used by certain prostitutes to solicit business. Called **streetwalkers,** these prostitutes solicit clients walking by, driving past in cars, or sitting in bars.

Sometimes called the "queen" of the prostitutes, the streetwalker must learn to successfully manage the rigors of the street. First, she must be aggressive in attracting her client ("trick" or "John"). More significant than her attractiveness, however, is how capable she is at convincing him to buy her services. The more competent she is at flattering and pleasing him, the more money she will earn. Once she has a client, the streetwalker must find a suitable location for their sexual activity, collect the money, perform her sex act ("turn the trick"), protect herself from disease and injury, and all the while avoid the police (James 1977a).

Because streetwalking is a career of relatively short duration, most streetwalkers are relatively young. Few are older than their midthirties.

Streetwalkers may or may not be under the surveillance and protection of a pimp. Since they are often exposed to muggings and other street violence, streetwalkers may ply the street in twos or threes. In addition, in one study, 67 percent of the prostitutes interviewed had been seriously injured by their clients (James et al. 1975).

Streetwalkers have the most difficult lives of all prostitutes. They must be skilled in protecting themselves, attracting and persuading clients, and collecting money, all while avoiding arrest.

House Prostitutes

During the first half of this century, the most typical settings for prostitution were the **brothels** ("whorehouses," "houses of ill repute," "disorderly houses," or "bordellos"). Often located in "red light districts," the houses were usually large and luxurious. Many such houses were closed with the ending of World War I and the advent of women's suffrage.

While houses of prostitution continue to exist, they are not as luxurious as in the past because such an investment is too easily confiscated by the law. Those who

masseuse
(mah-suhz')

masseur
(mah-ser')

Profile of a Female Prostitute

Their average age was twenty-two. They began prostitution at an average age of seventeen after completing the tenth grade. Most of the women were white (67 percent), single (60 percent), and childless (63 percent). Most had been runaways (63 percent). Eighty percent had been victims of physical or sexual abuse (37 percent incest/sexual abuse in the home, 55 percent physical abuse, 60 percent rape). Eighty percent of the women had pimps, which explains why 83 percent reported no savings, even though they earned an average of $140 per day.

Source: Neckes, Marilyn and Theresa Lynch. "Cost Analysis of the Enforcement of Prostitution Laws in San Francisco." Women's Jail Project. Research sponsored by the Unitarian Universalist Service Committee, 1978. (As cited by Barry, Kathleen. *Female Sexual Slavery*. Englewood Cliffs, N.J.: Prentice-Hall, 1979, p. 101.)

---

operate houses of prostitution today or who contribute to them in any way are subject to prosecution. In Nevada, however, where prostitution is legal, brothels openly exist.

While some brothels still occupy large houses, they more commonly are a set of house trailers or one- or two-bedroom apartments occupied by a few prostitutes. Often, there is a central room with sofas and sometimes a bar, where **house prostitutes** meet the clients. After a client has been introduced to the women, he makes his selection and is taken to the woman's room. The services she performs for him determine the charges, which he pays in advance. Sometimes the brothel is supervised by a madam who introduces the clients, pays the bills, provides protection, and manages the women (James 1977b).

Some brothels operate today under the "cover" of massage parlors, "nude photography" studios, "nude counseling" centers, escort services, and other commercial disguises.

Masseuses

Some prostitutes work "pseudomassage" parlors. The customer pretends to go into the parlor for a massage, which is conducted in a private room. In the privacy of the room, the **masseuse** (female **masseur**) is able to sell her services to the client. These services may range from "discussions only" to fellatio, anilingus, and intercourse. (Intercourse, however, may not be that convenient due to the absence of a bed.) The sliding scale of fees of the masseuse will be based on the services she is asked to provide.

Legitimate massage parlors are legal in most states and are not centers for prostitution. In fact, in some localities, it is illegal for a masseuse to massage a person of the opposite sex, except by a physician's prescription (Winick and Kinsie 1971). The legal status of massage parlors, however, makes them a tempting locale for the "pseudomasseuse."

Mistresses

Defining the **mistress** or "kept woman" as a prostitute may not seem to conform to the classic view of the prostitute since there is no "cash on the barrel" for the mistress's services. But in many cases, a mistress is "paid" in other ways. The man may set her up in an apartment, give her gifts, and pay her bills, all so that she will be readily available to him primarily for sexual purposes.

In other cases, however, a mistress could not be considered a prostitute. She may herself be in a marriage and living with a husband who does not provide her with the same sexual gratification and emotional satisfaction her mistress association does. Or she may be a woman who has formed and maintained a lasting, intimate relationship with a man to whom she is not legally married and with whom she has no expectations of marriage. In either of these cases, the mistress would be distinguished from the prostitute because in prostitution the client purchases only or primarily the sexual act.

Lesbian Prostitutes

While homosexual women may be drawn into prostitution out of a need for money, the incidence of prostitution among lesbians does not appear to be high. In Gebhard's (1969) sample, over 60 percent of the female prostitutes surveyed had had no homosexual experience whatsoever, and fewer than 25 percent had had pleasurable lesbian contacts ten times or more. Some lesbian prostitutes aggressively solicit clients ("Janes") from all-female bars; others strike up acquaintances at parties. Some may live together, with the one having the greater financial assets paying for the keep of the poorer one. Aside from these general observations, very little is known of the profile of lesbian prostitutes.

---

1. Describe ways in which prostitutes can be victimized and by whom.
2. Compare the types of female prostitutes, the conditions under which they work, and how their clientele might differ.

Male Prostitutes

While not as common as female prostitution, male prostitution exists, particularly in certain sections of larger cities.

gigolo
(jig'o-lo)

Male Heterosexual Prostitutes

The name **"gigolo"** is often used to describe a male heterosexual prostitute. His role is often similar to that of the call girl in that many gigolos provide social companionship as well as sexual services for their clients. Since money or gifts are the medium of exchange, the clients are usually well-to-do, middle-aged females who are lonely, looking for sexual opportunity, or who are concerned about retaining their physical beauty. The young, handsome gigolo provides his clients with flattery, attention, and social companionship. Some males provide such services through escort services, massage parlors, boutiques, saunas, and dance studios. Others frequent resorts, spas, and vacation spots popular with well-to-do, middle-aged women.

In contrast to the female who is able to "perform" sexually even though not sexually aroused, the male prostitute must be aroused. He is paid for his erection, and perhaps, ejaculation. Physiologically, such sex on demand may prevent him from functioning sexually under pressure or stress. It may also limit the number of sexual contacts he can have in one evening.

Male Homosexual Prostitutes

Male prostitutes who perform their sexual acts for pay with homosexuals are known as **"hustlers."** Usually younger males, hustlers hang around certain street corners, doorways, hotel lobbies, gay bars, and coffee shops, where they solicit openly. They often stand in a provocative pose, eye a prospective client's genitals, or try to make eye contact with him. Some try to enhance their masculine image by wearing tight clothing, leather, or boots (Ginsburg 1977).

Other hustlers work out of massage parlors (masseurs) and modeling agencies, or in male steam bath houses, where the client may also have access to orgy rooms, bars, and Turkish baths. Some hustlers are "kept boys," housed by older, wealthy men with primary or occasional homosexual desires. Such an "in-house" prostitute may be given a title, such as "auto mechanic," "chauffeur," "gardener," or "private secretary."

The hustler may have his own sexual routine—he may allow the client to perform fellatio and/or anal intercourse on him or he performs them on the client.

Clients of hustlers are usually older men. Some hustlers charge higher fees for older clients and lower fees for younger, more attractive ones.

Boy Prostitutes

Teenage boys who sell themselves as prostitutes are known as **"chickens."** They usually are attracted to the trade out of a need for money and/or affection. Some of the boys have run away from poor, uncaring, or abusive families; others have left homes in which there has been drunkenness, separation, or divorce (Ritter and Weinstein 1979). Many of the boys have had brushes with juvenile courts and schools for various offenses.

The Victimization of Child Prostitutes

Child prostitutes—both male and female—are victimized by their pimps and their clients, but they are especially vulnerable to this victimization because of the lack of public attention to their plight. Beyond all of the jurisdictions providing for the custody of children, there are few good programs for helping child prostitutes. The usual practice of finding them and sending them home may return them to the intolerable neglect and abuse from which they were running (Prager and Claflin 1976).

Some cities are now sending minor-age prostitutes to rehabilitation homes, although there are too few of these available. Providing public shelters where minors can walk in for food and housing and protection from pimps, rather than forcing them to turn to prostitution for survival, is another choice. Government programs for homeless children, however, continue to draw little funding.

Arriving in a strange city with little money and no connections, these run-aways often are easily recruited into hustling by pimps because they need a place to stay, or money for food or drugs, or because they are lonely.

The adult customers are called "chickenhawks." They contact the boy prostitutes on the streets, and the two complete their sexual acts in a nearby hotel, darkened theater, car, or alley. The boy may fellate the adult client, or the client may have anal sex with the boy. While some of the homosexual clients are single, many are family men.

The concern with boy prostitution is not only with the deep aversion many people feel toward sex between a boy and an adult, but with the prospects of violence and other criminal activities that may surround the boy. Also, some of the boys are recruited into posing for the "chicken" magazines of the pornography industry. Boy prostitution is a reflection of troubled families and a problem society (Lloyd 1976).

---

1. In terms of sexual arousal, how would the sexual performance of the male prostitute differ from that of the female prostitute?
2. Compare the types of male prostitutes, the conditions under which they work, and how their clientele might differ.

Recruiting of Female Prostitutes

Women are brought into prostitution through various kinds of enticements. *Procuring,* or *pandering,* is a strategy for acquiring women and turning them into prostitution; *pimping* keeps the women there. As we shall see, procuring almost always involves some degree of cunning, fraud, intimidation, and/or coercion. A woman who is procured is "convinced" against her will or knowledge to enter prostitution.

This will most likely amount to being *talked* into working for a pimp, rather than being physically forced to do so.

Patterns of Procuring

Kathleen Barry (1979) outlined several different ways in which young women are procured into prostitution:

1. ***Befriending.*** According to Barry, one pattern of procurement involves befriending. A runaway teenage girl or young woman is befriended by a procurer and is set up in a romantic connection to fit her dependencies. Professing love for her, the man initiates sexual activity with her. Then, using the "if you love me, you'll do anything for me" line, he coerces her to have sex with someone else. "Hooked," she is made to believe she is a "slut." The man then takes her earnings, breaks her will, reduces her ego, and separates her from her previous life, establishing ownership of her mind as well as of her body.

2. ***Pseudoemployment Agencies.*** Pseudoemployment agencies offering "exciting" jobs abroad also are effective in procuring young women, according to Barry. Women who are bored, frustrated, and unemployed may take the job, only to find upon arrival at their destination that the job is nonexistent or the situation quite different. Unable to pay return airfare, they may settle for work in a bar where their duties go well beyond serving drinks.

3. ***Purchase.*** Barry states that, in some countries, teenage girls are purchased with cash from parents in poor areas and are forced into prostitution.

4. ***Kidnapping.*** Some young girls in the United States are abducted and then forced into prostitution, according to Barry. Runaways and bar dancers are easy prey for sex slave procurers. These girls fear the police as much as their abductors, which makes it difficult to prosecute their captors.

Reasons Women Become and Remain Prostitutes

Few women are prostitutes because they actually enjoy their sexual experiences as prostitutes. Many are seeking emotional and financial reassurances of their personal worth as desirable women and see the opportunity to earn substantial amounts of money as proof of that worth. Nonroutine work, the chance for glamour and important clients, and the excitement of an illegal profession attract them. Some are unemployed and so desperate that they will consent to any kind of work. They may have a child or family to support, or may need the money to maintain a drug habit. Others, according to one study (Wallace 1978), come from families in which the fathers and mothers either were no longer or had never been married to each other. Unconsciously, these women may attempt to act out the destruction of the family by having sex with other women's husbands. This eases the pain of their own loss of family.

The relationship between the prostitute and the pimp is also important in explaining why women remain prostitutes. The relationship is only superficially voluntary. The prostitute who attempts to sever relations is often threatened or intimidated so that she changes her mind. Pimps have two ways of holding on to their women. One is verbal and psychological abuse wherein the woman is made to feel worthless; the other is through creating fear. If the prostitute still wants to leave, the pimp may insist on some form of settlement. The prostitute may pay off or disappear by moving out of town.

Others who can leave, do not. They passively stay, especially if they have had a history of sexual and physical abuse. A young woman who has been sexually abused by her father, beaten by her husband, called a "whore" by her mother when the daughter tells her of the father's sexual abuse, or accused by her husband of infidelity when she tries to tell him of her rape may eventually believe them. A woman's self-image is at least partly derived from the opinions of those closest to her, and she may eventually think she deserves the abuse she is getting. For such a woman, to resist being a prostitute is inconsistent with the way she may have seen herself while growing up.

---

1. How might the recruiting of a woman into prostitution through befriending be interpreted as a "victimization" of her?
2. If the prostitute is the "victim," who is the offender?
3. As a parent, what steps could you take to reduce the chances of your child (male or female) becoming a prostitute?

Why Men Visit Prostitutes

Men visit prostitutes for a variety of reasons. Some men, lonely and away from home, want sociability with women without the usual dating. Escort services or call girls may give them pleasant company for the evening along with automatic sex.

Other men are shy or inept and lack the social skills necessary to carry on a normal relationship with a woman. Or they may be physically deformed, ugly, or mentally deficient. Fearing rejection by other women, these men seek out the prostitute, knowing that she will refuse no one who can pay.

Some men visit prostitutes because contact with a prostitute reduces a man's obligation to the woman. Most heterosexual relationships require a certain personal or emotional commitment, but a man can walk away from an evening with a prostitute without any sense of responsibility (Stein 1974).

Men who want sexual variety they cannot find otherwise may also come to the prostitute. Some wives are not willing to perform any sex acts they think of as repugnant or perverted, or the man may not be able to accept his wife doing such an act even if she is willing. The prostitute, who is the "bad" woman, can be expected to provide "kinky" sex. Some men seek the chance to experience sexual excitement in a context of humiliation, degradation, beatings, and torture (Barry 1979). Payment of money eliminates the embarrassment connected with such activities.

Since most prostitutes are usually young, the older man may seek out a prostitute to supply the youth the man does not otherwise have access to (unless he is wealthy or powerful).

Finally, some men visit prostitutes because their wives would rather that they have a transient encounter with a prostitute than become emotionally involved in an extramarital affair, believing that there is less chance of a divorce.

Laws Regarding Prostitution

Prostitution is illegal everywhere in the United States, except in some of the counties of Nevada. There, houses of prostitution may be established or maintained as long as they are not on primary business streets or within four hundred yards of a schoolhouse or church, and do not disturb the peace of the neighborhood. Cities and counties in Nevada may regulate, prohibit, license, tax, and suppress houses of prostitution. Thus, prostitution is legal in fifteen of Nevada's seventeen counties, the exceptions being Washoe (Reno) and Clark (Las Vegas).

Many state and federal laws deal with prostitution. These laws relate to various sorts of behavior and are directed at various individuals, in addition to the prostitute, connected with organized prostitution. In some states, such as California, prostitution *per se* is not against the law. That is, it is not illegal to be a prostitute. A person caught soliciting, however, may be prosecuted as a vagrant under the disorderly conduct statute. The penalty for this as well as for that for patronizing a prostitute is a misdemeanor.

Prosecuting the Prostitute

Prosecution of prostitution most commonly involves prosecuting the prostitute. Streetwalkers, because of their visibility, are more frequently arrested than any other type of prostitute. Prostitutes who do not seek clients in public places are less often apprehended. Officials often have difficulty obtaining sufficient evidence against call girls (Winick and Kinsie 1971).

If convicted, the prostitute may be fined and/or jailed for a few days. Some cities increase the severity of the sentence for subsequent convictions; others may fine the prostitute and release her to resume her occupation.

Such a scenario amounts to a "tax" on prostitution rather than to a stopping of it. Street prostitutes, for example, are hassled and fined but never to the point of eliminating them from the streets. Containment by vice squads is a way of assuring the community that local morality is being upheld (Barry 1979), and it also is an attempt to move prostitution to parts of the city where it does not damage business (and may even improve others). The police also may use the prostitute as an information source on the underworld or as a source of illicit money.

Laws governing prostitution promote the isolation of prostitutes, setting them apart from the rest of society. The legal and/or social status they are placed in aids their exploitation and often prevents them from leaving the "profession."

Prosecuting the Client

Only a few states have laws against the clients of prostitutes, and the clients are rarely arrested. In most states, using the services of a prostitute is not a specific crime, although it may fall under provisions of more general statutes, such as those relating to adultery. In 1977 in San Francisco, 2,938 persons were arrested for prostitution, while 325 persons were arrested as clients (although it is estimated that there are ten times as many clients as prostitutes in San Francisco). Of the prostitutes, 419 served time; of the clients, none.

Women who engage in prostitution are punished, while the men who derive pleasure from it are largely ignored. It is inexplicable that in a social system that encourages prostitution, the "victim" is the only person who is prosecuted and incarcerated (Wallace 1978).

Prosecuting the Pimp and/or Panderer

In some states, it is a felony to engage in pandering, pimping, operating a house of prostitution, or inducting a minor into the "profession." But until prostitutes turn in their pimps, the prosecution of pimps is virtually impossible.

Bringing women into the country or transporting them across state lines for the purpose of prostitution is a federal offense under certain provisions of the Immigration and Nationality Act and of the Mann (White Slave) Act (1910). The Mann Act provides for prosecution even though prostitution is not involved.

Proposals for Changing the Laws

There are two major proposals for changing the legal status of prostitution. The first option is the *legalization* of prostitution through licensing or some other form of regulation. The state would license, tax, and control. This option is already being used in various places (South Korea, West Germany, Amsterdam, and Nevada), and its success has been mixed. In some German cities, it is estimated that only half of the prostitutes are registered and that most still use pimps. In Nevada, prostitutes are taxed by the state but are not given Social Security or other benefits normally given to other taxpayers.

The second option is *decriminalization* of prostitution, which would make any sex between consenting adults legal, whether the sex was paid for or not. While not removing the social stigma of prostitution nor getting the prostitutes off the street, decriminalization might make the prostitute less vulnerable to the criminal operation, would not further encumber the criminal justice system, and would not lead to further unnecessary disrespect for law. Because there is no real experience with this option, it is not known how successfully it would work.

Sex Is Power

Kathleen Barry, author of *Female Sexual Slavery* (1979), writes with insight into the nature of the male sex drive and sex violence. According to Barry, in Western society, the sex drive is considered synonymous with male sexuality. It is viewed as being overwhelming and out of control, yet demanding a fitting object of release. A female, by contrast, states Barry, is thought to not possess a strong sex drive. Her sexual feelings are believed to be diffuse and subtle. She learns that the focus of sexual power is in the male. His sex drive becomes a context for her developing sexual feelings. Her feelings assume a secondary role as she learns to respond to the male's needs and their primary role.

Kinsey saw the sex drive as *learned* behavior, rather than as an uncontrollable instinct. According to Kinsey, boys readily learn, first, that their sex drive is one that must be fulfilled because it cannot be contained; and second, that they have the implicit right to take girls and women as objects to gratify that drive.

The male's culture, at the same time, expects him to live up to the pornographic models of sex. Males experiment with sex as they grow up, sexually free from both restraints and responsibility. Some males, according to Barry, learn that sex is power. They learn that they must find the most desirable route of expression for something they are never expected to control, something they have learned they cannot control. They learn that the female object they choose cannot say no, or that saying no really means yes. Therein emerges the adult male sex power behavior. Learned, impulsive, uncontrollable, the adolescent male sex drive becomes for many men the ideal of their adult sexual behavior.

Actually, this type of male sex power behavior reflects an arrested sexual development that has not grown beyond what was acted out at age twelve, thirteen, or fourteen. Self-centered, exploitative, bullying behavior, it characterizes violent men (pimps, procurers, rapists, wife-beaters, and child-abusers). These men, states Barry, learn to expect immediate sexual gratification, and ultimately any other form of gratification, in whatever way they choose.

Some men do not need to act out of that power. Rather than aggressively coercing another, they learn to expect a mutually pleasurable sexual encounter. For example, an increasing number of men, feeling it is important for a woman to have an orgasm and self-critical if their partner does not fully respond sexually, are making a conscious effort to delay their orgasms as long as possible.

The *sex-is-power* ethic, according to Barry, denies (or demands) female response and replaces mutuality with domination. Such a sexual domination acted out in one-to-one relationships is the basis for the cultural domination of women by men and for female sexual slavery. Because this domination is usually expressed in separate, personal, private sexual experiences, the abuse of women from the sex-is-power ethic is seen only as individual acts. Unfortunately, concludes Barry, much of this female sexual "slavery" is accepted by many as normal social intercourse.

There may be slim chance for either legalization or decriminalization of prostitution in the near future. The American Law Institute (ALI), composed of law professors, judges, and practicing lawyers, through its Model Penal Code (1962), has recommended that prostitution be continued as a criminal offense. The ALI attempts to protect what it sees as legitimate concerns of society—rape, unlawful sex, prostitution, obscenity, open lewdness, and indecent exposure.

The legalization or decriminalization of prostitution represents a complicated issue for the women's movement. On one hand, prostitution is the commercial use by men of a woman's body. The system particularly recruits troubled, minority, and poor women into a criminal life-style. On the other hand, laws against prostitution limit the control that women have over their own bodies. The problem is how to be opposed to prostitution without being opposed to the prostitute (Gagnon 1977).

1. Why might some cities not work to eliminate entirely the practice of prostitution in their areas?
2. Why is there less prosecution of the client of the prostitute than of the prostitute?
3. Why is prostitution described as the only sex crime in which the "victim" becomes the criminal?
4. Would you like to see prostitution legalized? Decriminalized? Why or why not?

Pornography

Humans, among all animals, are the only ones that can use sex for both procreative and nonprocreative purposes. They have the capacity of separating sexuality for pleasure from the act of conception. Humans can use sexuality as a primary way of bonding, of communicating emotions, and of giving and receiving pleasure.

Yet, not all nonprocreative sex is good. Sexual communication can also be used to humiliate, to debase, to assert power over another, and to place distance (psychologically, at least) between the two partners.

The common definition of the word *pornography* is the depiction through the written word and pictures of erotic behavior with the intent of causing sexual excitement. This definition does not distinguish between nonprocreative sex that provides pleasure to both partners and sex that debases and separates.

Steinem (1978) makes the point that pornography is sex used for dominance and conquest over the less powerful—mostly women and children. It may even be used as a weapon of violence. Such communication, Steinem contends, depicts a person (usually a woman) as being lewd or "dirty," and protrays such debasing as the real pleasure of sex.

But nonprocreative sexual communication can also be used for the pleasure of *both* partners. Steinem makes an interesting distinction between pornography and **erotica.** Erotica, coming from the root word *eros* ("sexual love"), is defined by Steinem as a "mutually pleasurable expression between people who have enough power to be there by positive choice." This definition carries the meaning of sensuous love, freely expressed. It does not require the viewer to identify with a conqueror or a victim.

Pornographic books and magazines are widely available and openly displayed today. Movies during the 1960s and 1970s openly portrayed nudity, coital embraces, and other explicit sex activities.

In short, erotica is about sexuality, while pornography is about power and sex as a weapon. While there may be personal differences about what is and is not erotica, much of the depicting of sex in written and pictorial material debases and humiliates (usually, again) women.

The pornography industry is larger than the record and film industries combined and is estimated to take in well over $4 billion a year. The Adult Filmmakers Association claimed an average weekly audience of 2.5 million people paying an approximate total of $455 million to see hard-core films in 1978. That same year, the association estimated that there were 400,000 X-rated videotape cassettes sold for private consumption.

It is believed that organized crime holds a virtual free hand in the distribution of pornography, controlling better than 80 percent of hard-core magazine, book, and newspaper publishing. Much of this is believed to have occurred since the 1967 Supreme Court decision lifting restrictions on pornography (Barry 1979).

Cultural Sadism

The word *pornography* is derived from the words *porne* and *graphos*, meaning "the graphic depiction of prostitutes or female captives." Pornography today, however, is not only the depiction of the sexual activities between prostitutes and their clients. It is increasingly developing into a culturewide **sadism** (receiving sexual gratification by imposing pain on someone else). Its content portrays women being raped, wives being battered, and children being molested. It has been evolving from what one can do to a prostitute to what one can do with a lover, spouse, and even child.

The scenario of distortion often includes a setting of **seduction** (luring a victim into coitus without the use of force) or abduction (the use of force for same). The victim is expected to offer initial resistance but then turn "willing collaborator." Her loss of virginity merely unleashes her overwhelming desire for sex. When pain is afflicted, the victim disclaims any concern over it. Nor does she respond with hostility toward her captor. Inherent in this scenario is the supersexed male with the supersized penis and the sexually insatiable nymphomaniac female who likes nothing better than endless intercourse (Barry 1979).

Such pornography distorts reality and, according to Barry (1979) implies:

1. That sadism—beatings, rape, humiliation, and pain—is a source of pleasure for women. (On the contrary, most women find mutual tenderness and affection central to their human needs.)
2. That **sadomasochism** (receiving sexual gratification from both giving and receiving pain) is typical of human nature—the one being abused holds equal power with the abuser, leaving the abuser guilt-free. (On the contrary, sadomasochism is a disguise for the act of sexually forcing a woman against her will.)
3. That the whippings and beatings of sadism, while resulting in cuts and bruises, leave no visible blood or marks on the woman's body. (This is untrue.)

These distortions become cultural symbols and images that are part of the successes of advertising and selling merchandise. They are woven into the modern tales of love and romance. Women and their sexuality are taken out of the context of the real world and given fantasy images consistent with the way men see them and want to use them.

Pornographic Fantasies

Fantasy serves to expand, distort, and exaggerate reality, and is neither positive nor negative in and of itself. The way in which fantasy is used, however, determines whether its effect on our attitudes and behavior is positive or negative.

For example, when a person replaces a sexual experience with another person with fantasy, the social-sexual reality and needs of the other person may also be replaced by fantasy. Thus, pornographic movies, books, and pictures, when used as erotic stimulants, reduce the need for people to relate to each other (Barry 1979). In this respect, then, pornographic fantasy can be negative.

Content of Pornographic Fantasies

The most common sexual fantasy in pornography is one in which men sadistically dominate women and children sexually. Some men like to believe that all women wish to be raped. Women, on the contrary, find it difficult, if not impossible, to be sexually aroused by fantasizing sadistic sexual aggression toward men. Nor does sadistic sexual aggression toward a man by other men appeal to women (Geiser 1979).

Most heterosexual men find pornography in which the male is the object of sadistic sexual aggression by other men anxiety producing, rather than sexually arousing. This is due to the man being placed in the devalued role. Such pornography may be directed toward certain homosexuals (Geiser 1979).

Functions of Pornographic Fantasies

By identifying with sexually active and satisfied men in pornographic fantasies, some men are able to deny their fears about sexual inadequacy, sexual fatigue, or failing sexual interest.

Some believe that male pornographic sexual fantasies are a way of denying, absorbing, or containing male aggression toward other men. Male sexual aggression upon the bodies of women allows men to associate with other men without the danger of male aggression against them. "Women absorb male aggression sexually so that men are safe from each other" (Dworkin 1981). In this way, women become "sexual sponges" for male hostility.

Pornographic sexual fantasies can also serve to ward off submerged desires for heterosexual incest. Few male fantasies involve older women. They usually involve female objects much younger than themselves (Geiser 1979).

Responding to Pornographic Fantasies

The purchasers of sexual pornography commonly respond to the pornography by masturbating while viewing or reading. The male is not apt to share his pornographic experience with anyone else; he is not likely to check it out with friends to help determine where the lines between reality and fantasy are blurred. Such a check with reality usually is neither desired nor available. Self-perpetuating, the distortion stimulates a sexual response which, in turn, reinforces the enjoyment of the distortion. In sorting through the experiences, the consumer selects what to believe as reality and what to choose as fantasy. Stored in the memory, the pornographic experience may later be recalled for future fantasies or to be acted upon. However, it may never be acted upon.

Whether ever acted upon or not, the pornographic experience remains as part of one's experience and contributes toward defining values, molding personality, and shaping behavior (Barry 1979).

Child Pornography

Known as **"chicken porn"** or "kiddie porn," child pornography involves children of both sexes, although most of it concentrates on young boys between eight and ten years of age. The publications carry such wholesome-sounding titles as *Lillitots, More Lillitots,* and *Moppets.* They feature poses showing vaginal and anal orifices, miniorgies between minipartners, sex between adults and children, and sex with animals (Dudar 1977).

While some child pornography comes from overseas, a great deal comes from our own large cities. Here, young runaways can find adults willing to provide food and shelter in exchange for "services" demanded. Many of the more than one million runaways in the United States come from intolerable homes, often where there has been child abuse. Lacking working skills, these youngsters learn to survive on the streets by thieving, seducing, being seduced, and hustling (Ritter and Weinstein 1979). Many, both boys and girls, become prostitutes and child pornography subjects. Others are from homes where parents, some of whom are prostitutes, knowingly rent them out. Some child pornography occurs at the hands of daytime supervisors of children, without the parents' knowledge or permission.

For the child, there is always a payment: a gift, money, affection, or a drug fix. For some children, the filming confers an illusion of importance.

Most of the children in "chicken porn" look scared, as if they are forced to participate. If knowledge is a requirement for sexual consent and if maturity is necessary for sexual knowledge then the use of children in pornography is by definition forced (Barry 1979). Dr. Judianne Densen-Gerber, psychiatrist, lawyer, and founder of Odyssey drug treatment centers, contends that we still class our young as property over which parents have rights, including the right to damage what they own (Dudar 1977). The using of children who are still dependent on an exploiting adult for protection, money, or approval is an abuse of the powerless.

The average customer for child pornography is white, male, middle-class, middle-aged, and usually married. Child pornography publications, says Densen-Gerber, are "primers" for the seduction of children and an inducement to incest. The male whose fantasy life is stimulated through adult pornography should be able to find a consenting female, either for money or companionship. But there is no way a man, whose fantasy life is stimulated by a five-year-old, can find a legitimate and healthy outlet for that stimulation (Dudar 1977).

Giving the states broad authority to combat child pornography, the U.S. Supreme Court (*New York v. Ferber,* 1982) ruled that the production, sale, or distribution of child pornography can be banned by states. In so doing, the Court supported a crucial distinction between ordinary obscene materials and child pornography: Obscenity laws are designed to protect the audience that sees sexual conduct, while child pornography laws are aimed at protecting children who participate in sexual conduct.

---

1. How would you distinguish between material that is erotic from material that is pornographic?
2. Explain the basis on which pornography is viewed as *cultural sadism.*
3. How is fantasy essential in the transferring of pornography from the printed/pictorial page into human experience?
4. On what grounds is child pornography emotionally damaging to a child?

Pornography in the Media

Since the mid-1960s, the media have become more sexually explicit in themes and characterizations, and they now serve as a primary source of explicit sex information in our society. This media eroticization has occurred in three main areas: magazines, movies, and television.

Magazines

Magazines with stories about sex have been available for more than a century but only recently have they become so widely available and openly displayed. An early magazine from the 1930s, setting a new precedent for sophistication in erotic magazines, was *Esquire: The Magazine for Men.* In the early 1950s, *Playboy* attempted to strike a balance between offering advice on male attire and an open philosophy toward sex with photos of nude women and titillating fiction. As women's and men's magazines came closer and closer in their content to erotic picture magazines, *Cosmopolitan* and *Playgirl* began printing photos of nude men and stories with special erotic appeal for women. *Penthouse* and *Oui* were some of the first magazines to deal openly with sex. Then came the explicitly graphic sex glossies—*Screw, Smut, Hustler, Ball, Stud,* and *Hot Stuff.* They not only portrayed male and female nudes showing pubic hair and genitals, but nude couples in sexual embraces, kinky sex, and classified ads advertising sex services and requesting sexual partners for all sorts of sexual activity.

Movies

Movies during the first half century of the industry were almost totally lacking in explicit sex. While there were innuendos, what people did together sexually was left to the viewer's imagination. Female actresses on the screen never wore less than bathing suits, and men and women were never shown together in bed.

Then in the mid-1960s, bare female breasts were seen in the *Pawnbroker*. Overt erotic themes appeared—a male prostitute (*Midnight Cowboy*), a female prostitute (*Klute*), a sexual spree between a young man and an older woman (*The Graduate*), swinging couples, group sex, and sex-change operations. Also in the 1960s, nude films began to appear in selected theaters, followed by ones showing couples in coital embraces. The 1970s brought some of the pornographic classics (*Deep Throat, The Devil in Miss Jones*), depicting a variety of explicit sexual activities. In the early 1980s, sex films became less explicit and dealt with more social issues.

The movie industry has attempted to enforce standards of sexual explicitness through its rating system. R-rated films are restricted primarily to adults; X-rated films clearly have erotic content. The rating system, enforced by responsible theater owners, has helped to control who can view films in theaters. The prevailing attitude seems to be that erotic films ought to be available for those adults willing to pay to see them, provided that young people can be excluded.

Many, however, feel that the line between these ratings has eroded and that sexual themes of various sorts, nudity, and soft-core pornography are now common in theatrical releases with an R-rating.

Hard-core pornography is widely available on film. Its main purpose is to show ten- to twenty-minute scenes of genitals and/or persons engaged in any form of sexual activity. Greatly overpriced, these 8-mm and 16-mm films are known as "blue movies" in England and as "stag films" in the United States. Sold for private use, they are available through mail order or in shops selling pornographic items. Some pornographic arcades provide private booths in which coin-operated projectors show a few minutes of explicit sex (heterosexual coitus, sex with children, sadomasochism, and fetishes). Some of the sadomasochistic films that are appearing end with the simulated but graphic murder of the woman.

Television

Sex themes shown on television are subject to more debate than sex in films because television comes into the home and is difficult to impossible for many parents to completely control. Some children are allowed to watch any television program aired. Balancing new attitudes toward sexuality on television against what the viewing public wants or will tolerate is a major problem for television networks and federal regulatory agencies.

Generally, television has evolved toward more sexual explicitness. This is particularly evident in the content of the midday soap operas ("General Hospital," "All My Children"), situation comedies ("M*A*S*H," "Soap"), and talk shows ("Phil Donahue Show"). Yet, United States television programming has not reached the explicitness of movies shown in theaters. Frontal nudity, sadomasochism, incest, masturbation, and oral-genital sex are still rarely or not seen on television.

Many television programs with sexual themes are preceded by suggestions to parents that they use their discretion in allowing children to view the program. If movies originally made for theaters are shown on television, sexually explicit dialogue and scenes usually are cut before airing. Some sexually explicit films are now being carried on cable television and are also available through the home use of video machines.

Certain citizen's groups are calling for more governmental control and censorship over television programming. The position of the Federal Communications Commission has been that local stations and parents should exercise their own controls.

1. Give your impressions on the accuracy of the movie industry in rating the sexual explicitness of their films (GP-, R-, and X-ratings).
2. Describe your feelings on the appropriateness of children viewing the midday soap operas. Is there any basis for the concern that some express over the sexual explicitness of some of the scripting and scenes of these soaps?

Effects of Exposure to Pornography

One of the more common social debates has to do with the impact pornography has on a person's behavior. Although the research is far from completed, some of the findings to date have been interesting.

One such finding has to do with the similarity of men and women in their response to pornography. Kinsey's research (1948, 1953) led him to believe that women were less aroused by explicit materials than men. More recently, however, Julia Heiman (1975), in her study of sexually experienced college students, confirmed a more similar response between men and women to erotic materials. Heiman measured genital blood-volume changes of men and women when exposed to erotic tapes and found that women often responded physically to the tapes, although they were not always aware that vaginal changes were occurring. Aside from the fact that a woman's response to sexual arousal is less public than a man's, Heiman concluded that social cues may influence whether a woman recognizes her arousal (such as her being taught to suppress sensual responsiveness). Further supporting the arousability of women, Heiman found that sexual fantasies of women are as vivid and self-arousing as those of men.

Other interesting research findings on the effects of exposure to pornography were reported by the Commission on Obscenity and Pornography (1970), whose members were appointed by President Lyndon Johnson. The conclusions of the commission, after a three-year study, have been controversial.

The commission's findings indicate that most Americans are first exposed to explicit sex materials during adolescence. More than 50 percent of boys are exposed to explicit sex materials by age fifteen; 50 percent of girls are exposed a year or two later. By age eighteen, 80 percent of boys and 70 percent of girls have read descriptions of coitus and have seen pictures of it. The commission reported that, while exposure to erotica among adolescents is more than casual, such exposure does not indicate an obsession.

The commission also reported that more men than women, more young adults than older ones, and more better-educated than less-educated persons are apt to be *exposed* to explicit materials. The same is true for those more widely read than less and more socially and politically active than less active.

Arousal to erotica, reported the commission, is more often reported by persons who are young, college-educated, and sexually experienced than by those who are older, less well-educated, more religiously active, and less sexually experienced. Also, people are more apt to judge erotica as obscene where they are older, less well-educated and religiously active, with little experience with erotica.

The commission also reported that explicit sexual materials have been used by people for years with no apparent harmful effects on themselves or on others. The commission stated that convicted sex offenders generally have had significantly less experience with explicit sex materials in adolescence than the average person. The commission also reported that there was no evidence to suggest that exposure of youngsters to pornography had a detrimental impact upon their moral character, sexual orientation, or attitudes.

The commission concluded that its analyses

> do not support the thesis of a causal connection between the availability of erotica and sex crime among either juveniles or adults.

Its conclusion, it said,

> is stated with due and perhaps excessive caution since it is obviously not possible, and never would be possible, to state that, never, on any occasion, under any conditions, did any erotic material ever contribute in any way to the likelihood of any individual committing a sex crime.

As a result, the majority of the commission members recommended the repeal of legislation prohibiting the sale, exhibition, or distribution of sex materials to consenting adults.

The 1970 Report of the Commission on Obscenity and Pornography was not, however, unanimous. The conclusion that pornography was socially harmless has been disputed by a minority of the commission members and by some women's

prurient
(proo'ri-ent)

groups. Both the Congress and the then-President Richard Nixon rejected the commission's advice and opted, instead, for laws restricting the sale of erotic materials viewed as being unacceptable by local standards.

While many people think of pornography in terms of sexual material, some believe that the real villain may be violent sex, and ultimately, just plain violence. Some parents carefully guard their children from sexual materials, while exposing them to an unabated flood of violence on television and in the movies. Studies have shown that exposure to violence on television increases children's level of violence in real life (Liebert, Neale, and Davidson 1973). Studies also show that children already having trouble handling their sexual-aggressive feelings are the most likely to imitate such media violence (Geiser 1979). It is paradoxical that the laws are directed more at prohibiting sexual stimulation than at prohibiting the stimulation of aggressive and violent behavior (Katchadourian and Lunde 1980).

1. Would you support or reject the conclusion of the Commission on Obscenity and Pornography that pornography is socially harmless?
2. Do you agree that exposure to violence on television might be a greater damage to the thinking and behavior of children than viewing sexual materials? Why or why not?

Pornography and the Law

The legal interpretation of pornography introduces the word *obscenity*. While pornography is "the graphic depiction of prostitutes" and is concrete and evident, to be **obscene,** there must be a *judgment of value* that the material is not fit to be shown or displayed (Dworkin 1981).

It has not always been clear what is obscene. Some authorities have distinguished between erotic works of art, literature, and cinema and those works produced purely for commercial exploitation and utterly without redeeming social value (hard-core).

In *Roth v. United States* (1957), however, the United States Supreme Court determined that, to be obscene, pornographic material must meet three criteria: (1) the dominant theme of the material must appeal to a "prurient" interest in sex, (2) the material must be "patently offensive to contemporary community standards," and (3) the material must lack "redeeming social value." **Prurient interest** was defined as "shameful and morbid interest in nudity, sex, or excretion, and which goes beyond customary limits of candor."

This case also addressed itself to the Comstock Act. The Comstock Act (1873) makes it a felony to knowingly deposit in the United States mails any obscene, lewd, or lascivious book, pamphlet, picture, writing, paper, or other publication of an "indecent character." In *Roth v. United States,* the question was whether or not the Comstock Act violates the First Amendment ("Congress shall make no law . . .

abridging the freedom of speech, or of the press"). In this regard, the Court declared that "obscenity is not within the area of consitutionally protected speech or press."

In *Miller v. California* (1973), the Court further clarified the limits of obscenity by laying out four essential guidelines: (1) the material must be viewed in terms of its potential appeal to the average person; (2) contemporary community standards are to be applied; (3) the dominant theme of the material and its content must be taken as a whole, rather than out of context; and (4) its appeal must be to prurient interest, a requirement applicable to its content as well as to the intentions of its authors or publishers. On this basis, the Court ruled that state legislatures themselves may adopt their own limits on commerce in pornography, thereby placing added responsibility for judgments against pornography on local governments. Since then, most U.S. attorneys have been satisfied to leave the prosecution of pornography to local district attorneys.

Because the definitions for judging obscenity have tended to be vague and subjective, and because the Court has shifted some of its definitions, enforcement of obscenity laws (whether on the federal, state, or local levels) has proven difficult, expensive, time-consuming, and frequently unsuccessful. Some view this as the reason for the expanding production of pornographic books, films, magazines, and newspapers, and for the proliferation of "adult book stores."

Public Protest against Pornography

The increase in exploitative and violent pornography has prompted groups, such as Women Against Porn (WAP) and Women Against Violence Against Women (WAVAW), to protest the commercial degradation of women. These groups demand that sexually explicit material be free of violence. They insist that pornography showing women in bondage to men with whips and chains and pornography that expresses an obsessive need to control women's sexual choices is dehumanizing and obscene.

Some engaged in the struggle over control of pornography advocate legal curbs through censorship. By qualifying the First Amendment, censorship would thereby place legal restraints on the publishing of any materials the government deemed exceeding stated standards. Others, however, feel that any restraints through censorship might eventually backfire and at some other time be used to restrict their own messages in attempts to correct other controversial social processes.

---

1. How would you contrast obscenity and pornography?
2. How has the U.S. Supreme Court addressed the question of First Amendment rights versus freedom of speech in matters of obscenity? Who today generally has the responsibility for deciding whether or not any given material is obscene?
3. How do you react to the protests against pornography and violence? Compare your feelings with those of others in your class.

Feminist groups are increasingly visible in their protest against the commercial degradation of women.

Sex in Advertising

Sex has been an extremely marketable commodity from the day it evolved. And in the last decade, the use of sex to sell products has become increasingly intentional. Sex in media commercials is being used to push everything from traveler's checks to tea. While sex has always moved merchandise, it has never before been so explicit. What is being done today would not have been tried even five years ago (Bronson 1980). There has been a massive proliferation of sexual advertising on television, in magazines, and on billboards.

Television Advertising

Jean designers started the "flood" of sexual advertising by turning prime-time television into a bombardment of sexy commercials. Advertisers of designer jeans (Gloria Vanderbilt, Calvin Klein, Jordache, and Sassoon) have focused mainly on denim-clad behinds, and children's jeans feature preteens in coy, sexy poses. Other commercials, however, have been equally "creative."

"Advertisers are looking for a new stimulant on the subconscious level, and sex is the last taboo," says the director from the advertising agency of Weiss and Geller, Inc. (Bronson 1980). He goes on to say that the newly explicit ads are targeted to reach what are perceived as a jaded, turned-off populace, who feel dead and pessimistic about the future. Advertisers believe that the shock value of sexy

commercials is needed to penetrate the "clutter" of competing television messages bombarding us.

As to the magnitude of that bombardment, it is estimated that the average television viewer sees over five hundred television commercials a week. By the time the average person graduates from high school, he or she has seen 350,000 commercials (Kilbourne 1977).

The particularly upsetting aspect of sexy commercials to some people is that, while television programs may appear once or twice, often with an advance warning of any sexy content, a sexy commercial can come into the home unannounced over and over again.

Printed Advertising

While sex in television advertising is already blatant, the print campaigns are often even more explicit. In an ad for Paco Rabanne men's cologne, which appeared in *Vogue,* and *Esquire,* a woman tells her nude artist-lover, "I'm going to take some (Paco Rabanne cologne) and rub it on my body when I go to bed tonight. And then I am going to remember every little thing about you . . . and last night." An ad advertising electronic hand games shows a partly exposed nude couple lying in bed, with the man in front of the woman, playing his electronic hand game. Meanwhile, she whispers in his ear, "Like enticing challenges? Try curling up with one of these little electronic teasers."

Such practices have even invaded food advertising. The California Avocado Commission has used Angie Dickinson, sprawling across two pages in national magazines, to promote the avocado's nutritional value. The copy line reads, "Would this body lie to you?" In a recent ad in *Vogue*, sex is used to help boost travel to Alaska. The ad pictures a bikini-clad girl looking up adoringly at her bundled-up companion, with the copy reading, "Summit conquered . . . here we are, half naked on an ice field, and loving it. It's called Ruth Glacier (loving name for an ice dream)." Elsewhere in the ad spread is a picture of a couple in a cabin along with the copy, "Sultry . . . in the Far North; there's a reason for the long nights."

Objects associated with the genitals—condoms, douches, vibrators, and menstrual products—while found only in magazines such as *Esquire* and *Playboy* a decade ago, are now common in newsweekly (*Time* and *Newsweek*), women's, and family magazines.

Sexual Symbolization

Beyond the obvious seminudity and sexual innuendo in television and print advertising, the media have advanced to the use of sexual symbolization. Ad copy may use phallic symbols (lipsticks, cigarettes, candles, pencils) and vaginal symbols (round or elliptical shapes—lips, eyes, apples, oranges, balls, cherries, eggs). Symbols of the union of male and female also can be represented by a key inserted into a lock, a nut being screwed on a bolt, or a beer glass foaming at the top as it is being filled from a bottle (Key 1976).

One of the more daring examples of this sexual symbolization is a Macho cologne bottle shaped like a stylized set of testicles with a penis. The ad caption tells its readers that Macho cologne is a "powerful new scent for men by Faberge. Macho is b-a-a-a-d. And that's good."

Subliminal Advertising

Meaning "below the threshold of consciousness," the word *subliminal* is a synonym for the unconscious or deep mind. This is the part of the human brain that retains information and operates without our conscious awareness.

Coined by public relations executive James Vicary in 1956, the term *subliminal advertising* refers to commercial ads and messages that are flashed onto a screen so rapidly that a person's mind is not conscious of seeing them. According to Vicary, when messages such as "Drink Coke" and "Eat popcorn" were momentarily flashed on a theater screen so fast that people were not consciously aware of them, there were significant increases in the subsequent sales of Coca-Cola and popcorn in the lobby. It would seem that the people exposed to this subliminal advertising purchased these products because their conscious minds could not resist what their unconscious minds told them to do (McConnell 1980). Some believe that the usual defense mechanisms (repression, denial, etc.) can be circumvented at the subliminal level (Key 1976). There has been no confirmation by behavioral scientists, however, that subliminal advertising can affect what people buy or do (McConnell 1980).

Subliminal Stimuli—Do They Really Work?

Psychological experiments have so far failed to prove the effect of subliminal stimuli on behavior. According to McConnell (1980), sensory input into the mind from the outside must pass at least two neural thresholds (barriers) before a person becomes conscious of the stimulus, and must pass a third threshold before the person responds to the input. First, a stimulus must have enough strength to cross the *sensory threshold* (and cause a person's sensory receptors to fire). Second, the stimulus must still be strong enough to cross the *perceptual threshold* and pass into conscious awareness. Subliminal stimuli are believed to pass the sensory threshold but not the perceptual. And third, before a person responds to the stimulus in a measurable way, the stimulus must still be strong enough to pass the *action threshold*. An "Eat popcorn" message flashed across the screen may pass the sensory threshold, but not the perceptual one. And even if the person is aware of the instruction to "eat popcorn," he or she might choose not to respond. Certain other messages, such as "This building is on fire!" however, would undoubtedly pass all three thresholds without delay.

Regardless of the questionable success of subliminal advertising, advertisers continue to insert hidden sexual messages into their ad copy in an attempt to manipulate human behavior. One such technique is embedding, a technique in which sexual words or symbols are implanted in print so lightly or subtly that the person viewing the material perceives the symbols only unconsciously. Embedding can be done through photoengraving (in which the word or symbol is lightly etched on the surface of the photographic plate), through airbrushing (in which the word or symbol is very lightly airbrushed onto a drawing or photograph), or through the use of a transparent overlay for a photograph or drawing (which is then double-exposed over an art layout for a fraction of a second) (Key 1972). Much national advertising includes such embedding. *Sex* is the most frequently embedded word, although such words as *fuck, cunt, ass,* and *whore* are also frequently used as "subliminal triggers" in an attempt to influence purchasing behavior (Key 1976).

Public Reaction to Sex in Advertising

Sex seems to be selling. Viewers are attracted to well-endowed women and virile-looking men who use sexual innuendos and nudity in their endorsements of designer jeans, shampoos, and shaving creams. Even a Citicorp subsidiary boasts that its market share for traveler's checks has grown significantly since it shifted from ads portraying bank tellers to one showing a naked American couple and a naked Japanese man meeting each other in a communal Japanese bath.

Others point out that, because of the billions of dollars invested in advertising, marketing research, and psychological persuasion, the customer does not really have all that much choice, like it or not. In his definitive analysis of consumer manipulation by the advertising industry, Key (1980) observes that

> U.S. consumers are not more naive than anyone else but that they have not been informed that they pay dearly for the torrent of [sexual advertising]. The more than $50 billion invested in advertising during 1979 was added to the prices for virtually everything consumers bought. . . . A substantial proportion of each retail dollar spent pays for media advertising, even though the cost is hidden . . . the cost being added on to the price of food, clothing, housing, medicine, and so on. With many products today, the cost of *packaging* and *selling* actually exceeds the value of the merchandise.

Yet, with some people, sexy ads just don't work. Some people, while fond of sex, believe that it is a private affair, something personal between two individuals. Such people are not likely to be turned on by a sexy ad. For other people, religious convictions rule out the promiscuous playing around that goes on in such ads. By offending people like these, advertisers may lose business; some potential customers refuse to buy sexily advertised products (O'Connor 1979).

Sex in advertising is not the only option open to the advertising industry. Another option is using ads that work on customers by telling them what the product will do for them in saving time and money, in cutting down on waste, and in giving them greater pleasure. Such ads, states the magazine *Sales Management,* are harder to put together and require more product knowledge (Trytten 1973). Such ads get fewer laughs but can still move merchandise.

1. Give your reaction to the sexual content of the advertising of designer jeans. Is such advertising demeaning to the self-esteem of a woman or a man? Compare your feelings with someone of the opposite sex.
2. Should there be limits to the sexual explicitness allowed in printed and television advertising? Why or why not?
3. What has been your reaction to sexual symbols used in the merchandising of products?
4. How do you react to the suggestion that advertisers may try to manipulate you subliminally?
5. Do you respond positively to honesty in advertising?

"I hate doing those stupid photo sessions!"

"Which ones?"

"Oh, I had a session today for some fishing gear. They gave me a pair of cutoffs that were cut up to the hip and a halter that barely covered anything. Then the photographer wanted me to turn on to a fishing pole and tackle box."

"Well, what did you do?"

"I did it, of course. That's what I'm paid for, but I don't like it, and I told him so."

"Look, most of the stuff you do involves using sex to sell a product. You get paid a fortune to look sexy for advertising cologne, jeans, shampoo, and even washing machines! Why should using your body to sell fishing tackle be any different?"

"Well, at least some of the products I model for have some sexual appeal. I just wonder if other models feel this way when they have to make compromises."

"If it bothers you, quit. If not, put the money in the bank and forget it. Society isn't going to change the way it buys and sells products simply because one little model feels dirty about the system."

Summary

1. Prostitution is a "profession" of persons, many of whom are women, who perform sex acts with others for pay. The prostitute support system may include the panderer (procurer), pimp (manager), police, bartenders, bailspeople, and judges.

2. Female prostitutes may perform their work as call girls, streetwalkers, house prostitutes, masseuses, mistresses, or lesbian prostitutes.

3. Male prostitutes may ply their trade as male heterosexual prostitutes, male homosexual prostitutes, or boy prostitutes.

4.   Recruiting, or procuring, of prospective prostitutes may be done through befriending of lonely teenage girls or young women, through false employment agencies, by purchasing young women from parents, or by abducting women through kidnapping.

5.   Women become prostitutes due to troubled homes and the need for reassurances of worth. Women remain prostitutes out of fear, drug use, low self-esteem, or the need for a pimp's management.

6.   Reasons why men visit prostitutes include a need for sociability, a need for sex, a fear of sexual rejection by women other than prostitutes, loneliness, or a desire for unusual sexual activities.

7.   Laws regarding prostitution exist in every state. In Nevada, however, prostitution is legal in most counties. Laws against prostitution may be directed at prosecuting the prostitute (this is the most common), prosecuting the client, or prosecuting the pimp and/or panderer. Proposals for changing the laws regarding prostitution include proposals for legalization or decriminalization of prostitution.

8.   Pornography is the depiction through the written word and pictures of erotic behavior with the intent of causing sexual excitement. Pornography usually portrays the debasement of a woman or child as the real pleasure of sex. Erotica is distinct from pornography in that erotica involves people present by positive choice in a mutually pleasurable expression.

9.   A culturewide sadism, in which women are raped or battered or children are molested, is developing in some pornography. This pornography distorts reality, implying that sadism is a source of pleasure for women, that sadomasochism is typical, and that sadistic abuse leaves no visible scars on victims.

10.   Pornographic fantasies influence the defining of values, the molding of personality, and the shaping of behavior.

11.   Child pornography ("chicken porn" or "kiddie porn") involves children of both sexes—most of them runaways—who pose in return for payment.

12.   The mass media are becoming increasingly pornographic through magazines (both soft-core and hard-core), movies (both R- and X-rated), and television (through sex themes that are more sexually explicit).

13.   Research shows that both men and women respond similarly to erotic materials. The presidential Commission on Obscenity and Pornography concluded that there is no causal connection between the availability of pornography and sex crime among either juveniles or adults.

14.   A charge of obscenity requires a value judgment that material is not fit to be shown or displayed. The U.S. Supreme Court has legally defined obscenity, has set limits for obscene material, and now allows communities to set their own standards of obscenity.

15. Public protest against pornography has come primarily from feminist groups, who protest the commercial degradation of women.

16. Increasingly explicit sex is being used to sell merchandise on television, in magazines, and on billboards. Symbols with sexual innuendos, such as phallic symbols, vaginal symbols, and symbols of the union of male and female, are now sometimes used to advertise and package products.

17. Subliminal advertising that supposedly enters a person's unconscious mind (without conscious awareness) and affects conscious behavior is used by some advertisers, but the success of such advertising is questionable.

18. Public reaction to obvious sexual advertising may be negative. Ads without sexual messages can be effective in selling merchandise.

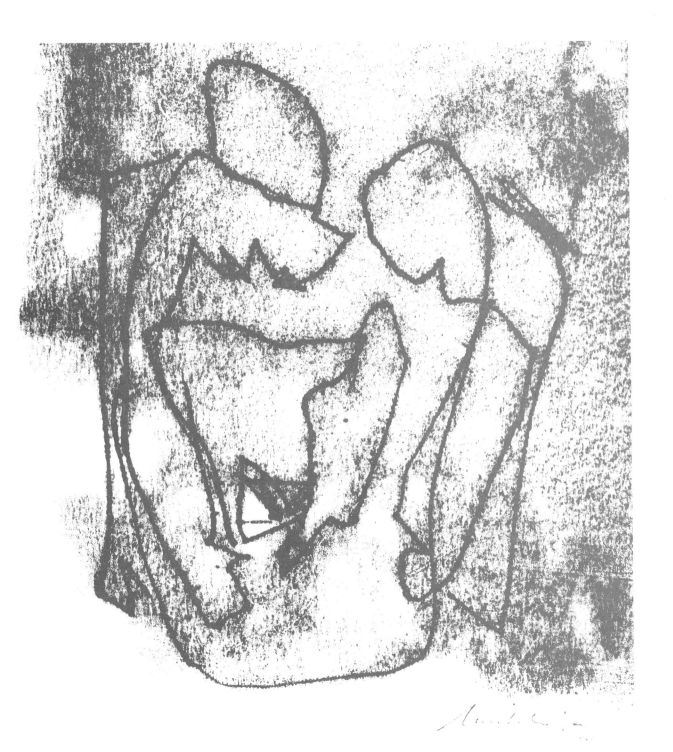

Powerless. Dave felt totally powerless. His wife Joanne had been raped while he was out of town for the weekend. Now he had to try to pick up the pieces of his life and the pieces of their marriage. He wondered if their marriage was strong enough.

"Mr. Thorpe, this is the Pleasantville police department. Your wife has been raped. Could you fly back?" Anger surged through him. What?? How did it happen?? Where did Joanne go that she had left herself open? Why didn't she scream or run or fight? Rage ran through his veins. Who was the man who did it? Did they catch the guy? He wanted to see the man dead. If the courts wouldn't do it, then he would.

As he walked through the hospital corridors, he tried to collect himself. If ever there was a time that his wife needed him, it was now. Grief, anger, and deep frustration nearly overcame him as he walked up to her. "Come on, Jo, we're going home." To what, he thought. What would they talk about? How many hours of tears would need to be shed before she would be able to smile again. He didn't know. She needed him to help her get over the whole ordeal, but who was going to help him?

In part 5, we have been focusing to some extent on the sexual paraphilias, those sexual alternatives sometimes called deviant. While some of this variant behavior is passive, other forms are violent or motivated by power. In this chapter, we deal with that sexual behavior which is most often violent or motivated by power demands, including sexual harassment, sadomasochism, and rape.

During this discussion, it will become apparent that the person who exhibits violent sexual behavior or uses sex as a source of power is usually male. We do not want to imply, however, that only males exhibit such behavior. For some violent behavior (such as rape), this generally is true. But, for other types of behavior, such as sadomasochism, this may not be true. The tendency to assume that males are predominately involved in violent sexual behavior may be influenced solely by their involvement in rape or by a somewhat biased nature of research, reporting, and prosecution of violent individuals.

Sexual Harassment on the Job

As yet, there is no clear definition of **sexual harassment.** It can take many forms. An unwanted pinch, hug, look, profanity, or any unwanted attention of a sexual nature that makes a person uncomfortable may be interpreted as sexual harassment. If a sexual harassment charge reaches a court, it is usually as sexual discrimination on the job, under Title VII of the 1964 Civil Rights Act. To claim sexual harassment under this law, there must be a direct relationship between the individual being abused and the one being charged. Also, the person being harassed must have suffered a monetary loss, such as loss of a job, a pay raise, or a promotion.

The Power Aspect of Sexual Harassment

Most experts agree that the real issue in sexual harassment is not sex, but power (the ability of one person to control another). The one in control (usually the supervisor or boss) uses this power to obtain sexual favors from the one being abused (usually the subordinate or employee). The ability to exercise power over the other person is more important than any actual sex obtained.

Often the harassers may feel that they are just being friendly, but the people suffering the harassment know that the harassers can fire them. Thus, for example, if a man's "friendly" advances are rejected by a woman employee, this rejection can consciously or unconsciously become the reason for the woman losing her job or not receiving a pay raise or promotion.

Women list the commonplace "pat on the fanny" as one of the most frequent forms of sexual harassment on the job. Often, if this advance is not rejected, the male then makes more suggestive advances. Being touched "by accident" and being forced to listen to sexual jokes and conquests are also very common forms of sexual

Sexual harassment on the job is a daily problem for millions of people, most of them women.

harassment. Since more women have attained positions of power within organizations, an increasing number of men are claiming sexual harassment by their female bosses.

Sexual harassment seems to be mainly a problem of lower management. Often, the aggressor has not obtained a position in the company equal to his or her expectations. The ability to control someone through sexual harassment fulfills achievement needs that are unfulfilled by the position the aggressor has obtained.

Fighting Sexual Harassment

Anyone who must put up with sexual advances to keep a job or to receive deserved promotions or raises is a victim of sexual harassment. Sexual harassment on the job is illegal. One can accept the advances, quit and walk away, or fight back. The fighting back alternative, however, is not easy. Taking a case to court is costly, and sexual harassment is often hard to prove. People who want to fight back, however, should keep the following points in mind:

1.   The individual being harassed should keep a diary, listing the time, date, and place of each incident of harassment and whether or not there were any witnesses. Physical or emotional stresses caused by the incident should be noted. The individual should also list any professional person (psychologist, physician, counselor) that has been consulted.

A diary can help to put the situation into perspective, especially if the harassed individual worries that perhaps the harassment is simply his or her imagination. A diary can also help the harassed individual to decide if he or she is sexually interested in the offender and whether he or she is sending out unconscious messages to which the offender is reacting. If the harassment comes to the attention of management, a diary may help management to decide what actions to take.

2.   The individual being harassed should ask the offender to stop the harassment in as polite, unemotional, and clear way as possible. The harassed individual should not give the aggressor any information or emotions that could be used against the victim later.

3.   If the harassment continues, the individual being harassed should complain to the union, a grievance committee, the personnel department, or members of higher management who are sympathetic and willing to listen.

4.   Also, if the harassment continues, the harassment victim should write a low-key, polite, short letter to the aggressor. Experts recommend that the letter be divided into the following three parts:

Part 1: The harassed individual should give a detailed statement of the facts as he or she sees them. This information can be taken from the diary. The letter could start out something like: *"This is what I think happened . . ."*

Part 2: The harassed individual should describe his or her feelings and what personal damage the harassment has caused to him or her. The individual should state any perceived or actual costs and damages, along with his or her feelings of distrust, misery, anger, fear, etc. The letter could include a statement similar to: *"Your actions made me feel terrible. You have caused me to quit, transfer to another department, take excessive time off, etc."*

Part 3: Finally, the letter should include a short statement of what actions the individual being harassed would like the offender to take. The victim should ask that the harassment end, that the victim be reinstated in his or her former position, or that the objection to the victim's advancement be withdrawn. The statement could start out something like: *"I would like our relationship to be on a purely professional basis . . ." "Please withdraw your objections to my advancement until we can work out a fair evaluation . . ."* Also, the harassment victim should explain his or her implication in any actions that were part of the harassment, such as: *We were once quite happy dating, but now I think our relationship should only be on a professional basis . . ."*

The individual being harassed should hand deliver the letter to the offender and take a witness. Also, the victim should keep a copy of the letter since this will be valuable legal evidence if the victim has to go to court.

Usually, the offender simply accepts the letter, says nothing, and the harassment stops. Once in a while, there is an apology, a discussion of perception of sexual harassment, or a denial. At any rate, a letter is a peaceable attempt to settle the problem.

5. The harassment victim should talk to other people on the job. Often, these people have been victims of sexual harassment by the same person. Collaborative testimony will help the victim in pursuing the charge and also will make the victim feel better about complaining. Talking with other people about the harassment also puts the victim's concern on record with someone else.

6. If the harassment victim quits because of the situation, he or she should send a letter to the head of the personnel department. The letter should be a very detailed account of the sexual harassment and should be compiled from the victim's diary.

7. If the harassment victim is fired because he or she turned down sexual advances, the victim should talk to an attorney. The victim may have to prove his or her complaint just to collect unemployment benefits. The victim should try to find an attorney familiar with sexual harassment cases.

8. To sue under the sexual discrimination act, Title VII of the 1964 Civil Rights Act, the victim must file a complaint with the local office of the Equal Employment Opportunity Commission within 180 days of leaving the company. To collect, the victim will need to sue the company, the offender, or both.

The Stress of Sexual Harassment

While undergoing sexual harassment and for years afterward, victims can suffer from physical symptoms of stress and the loss of self-esteem and self-confidence. Symptoms often include headaches, sleeplessness, weight gain or loss, and difficult sexual relationships with their partners.

If the harassment incident is not resolved, the emotional stress for the victim can be severe enough to cause some victims to talk to a psychologist, psychiatrist, employee assistance person, social worker, or company counselor. People who feel victimized should do whatever possible to talk to others who will understand. Rape hot lines are excellent sources of information. Also, compassionate and responsible organizations available to the sexually harassed include the Alliance Against Sexual Coercion, the Working Women's Institute, and the National Commission of Working Women. These organizations will also support a victim through the courts.

After a harassment incident has been resolved, both persons are likely to feel much better about themselves and others. The sexual harasser may now seek help, which may have been needed for years. This help can increase his or her self-esteem and may prevent future harassment of others.

Teacher/Student Sexual Harassment

The great majority of sexual involvements between students and their teachers are initiated by the teachers, and the involvements usually consist of dating. But the transition from the classroom to the bedroom can be perilous. The teacher faces the possiblity of sexual harassment charges, blackmail, disapproval from colleagues and administrators responsible for faculty promotions, and the other students feeling that the professor's lover is receiving favoritism in grading or letters of recommendation for graduate schools, assistantships, or jobs.

The percentage of faculty who frequently or occasionally date their students is very difficult to determine. A 1978 national survey of one thousand faculty members by Kenneth Pope, an assistant professor of clinical psychology at UCLA, found that 19 percent of the men and 8 percent of the women teachers reported sexual contact with their students.

Criticism of faculty-student sexual relationships generally centers on the inequality in status and power between the individuals. Teachers are admired and in positions of leadership, and power can be exciting and attractive. Many professors are probably able to date individuals that they would be unable to date if they were not in a position of authority.

Colleges and universities are adopting policies prohibiting the sexual harassment of students by teachers. The complaints against professors are similar to any other professional relationship: from unwanted physical advances to lascivious looks and remarks. But few guidelines or procedures have been established regarding dating between consenting adults.

1. Have you or anyone you know been the victim of sexual harassment? How was the situation handled? What was the outcome?
2. If you were being sexually harassed, would you accept the harassment to save your job, quit, or fight back? On what factors would you base your decision?
3. If, as you were handing in a final exam, your professor asked you out, would you accept the invitation? On what would your decision be based? Attraction? Fear? Explain.

Sadomasochism

Sadomasochism (SM) is receiving sexual arousal and pleasure by inflicting or receiving physical or emotional pain. **Sadists** obtain their pleasure by inflicting pain. **Masochists** obtain their pleasure by receiving pain.

The word *sadism* is derived from the name of the Marquis de Sade (1740–1814), a French nobleman and writer, who was imprisoned because of his writing. While in prison, he wrote several novels about his sexual fantasies. In these novels, he showed that wickedness was rewarded and that virtue was always punished. De Sade felt that sadistic acts were normal and natural. He wrote that sex was the ultimate expression of nature and that sexual pleasure demanded the total subjection of a sexual partner to any impulse, even if these impulses were destructive to life. Feelings in France, at this time, were so strong against the Marquis de Sade that, when the Bastile was stormed in 1789 (the beginning of the French Revolution), de Sade was the only prisoner not freed.

A century later, Leopold Von Sacher-Masoch (1836–1895) wrote a novel entitled *Venus in Furs*. R. A. Krafft-Ebing coined the term *masochism* to describe the practices in the book that stimulated sexual excitement from receiving pain. The book focused on erotic degradation of men by women.

Sadomasochism is currently enjoying a great popularity. In its milder forms it can safely enhance the sexual pleasure of those who enjoy such practices. Extreme forms reflect neurosis or psychosis and may severely injure participants.

Forms of Sadomasochism

Sadomasochism can take several forms. It may be enjoyed safely by sexual partners as a sexual variation and a living out of fantasies. Or it can reflect a severe neurosis or psychosis, making sexual activities a nightmare.

Some degree of domination and submission is present in all sexual relationships. This point is important to understand because of the mistaken belief that many forms of sexual stimulation are perversions. "Love-bites" and a certain amount of rough love-play are common. The infliction of pain in the heat of passion may be either involuntary or a deliberate application of technique for arousal.

Sadomasochistic feelings are also widespread on a fantasy level. Sadomasochistic fantasies are deeply rooted in our culture because they are the traditional male and female stereotypical roles taken to their ultimate sexual expression.

While many people have sadomasochistic fantasies, however, few act them out, beyond minor pain inflicted during sexual play. Kinsey's 1953 study (findings similar to a later study by Hunt in 1974) revealed that approximately 20 percent of men and 12 percent of women were sexually aroused by stories of rape, bondage (tying up your sex partner), punishment, whips, and chains. But, in Hunt's 1974 study, only 10 percent of the males and 8 percent of the females reported that they actually obtained sexual pleasure from either inflicting or receiving pain during sexual play, and the feelings of aggressive interaction that were expressed during sex were usually very mild forms of sadomasochistic behavior. They included "love-bites," hair pulling, scratching, violent thrusting of the male during intercourse, and enjoyment of some unusual intercourse positions.

Sadomasochism only really becomes a dangerous threat if an individual cannot control his or her sadomasochistic tendencies and the acts become criminal sadism. It is difficult to find a partner willing to suffer pain, even for a price. Thus, extreme sadists assault unwilling victims, and often an orgasmic release is produced by the homicidal violence. In these cases of extreme sadism, aggression is stronger than sex and serves as a substitute. A sadist is considered a psychopath when his or her behavior becomes antisocial in the form of rape, violent assault, or murder.

Causes of Sadomasochism

The causes of sadomasochism are not well understood. Some feel that sadists may have been taught to have contempt and disgust for any sexual activity or feeling and that, thus, sadists are punishing their partner for their partner's sexual indulgence. Another theory is that sadists have vast feelings of inferiority, and that because they fail to dominate in other parts of their lives, they need to dominate a sexual partner to obtain pleasure. Others feel that sadism is rooted in a deep hostility toward parents.

Masochism may find its root in the parental teaching of disgust of sexuality. Punishing individuals during childhood and adolescence for sexual activities easily establishes an association between sex and pain. As adults, masochists receive pleasure at the same time that they receive punishment, thereby releasing all guilt. Or, they feel that they have the right to feel sexual pleasure, having first experienced the pain.

Some psychologists believe that sadomasochistic behavior can be traced to many childhood experiences that function in the subconscious to bring about sadomasochistic behavior in adulthood (Chesser 1971). For example, if a young boy is spanked by his dearly loved mother, who is wearing a fur-lined dressing gown at the time, and if the experience makes enough of an impression upon the child, he may, when he grows up, desire to recreate the incident with a woman who plays the part of his mother by spanking him. Because of the fur on the dressing gown, he may also develop a fetish for furs.

Reasons for Sadomasochism

Studies show that individuals who participate in sadomasochism tend to be conservative and fairly stable, and a West German survey found that most lead well-adjusted, inconspicuous lives (Greene and Greene 1974). So why are they drawn to sadomasochism as a form of sexual expression?

One reason, according to some therapists, is that in this advanced age of sexual liberation, the bored are looking for new taboos to break. Sex manuals, such as Alex Comfort's *The Joy of Sex* (1972), approve "bondage games" and treat "loving" sadomasochism as just another sexual variation. Michael Evans, a psychologist at the Berkeley Therapy Institute, estimates that a third of all couples have tried spanking at least once and that perhaps as many have tied up a sexual partner (McNeil 1974).

Couples who dabble in sadomasochism, according to one view, are expressing resentments and anger under the guise of a game. Psychologist C. A. Tripp (1975) thinks that resistance, tension, or some sort of problem between the partners always enhances sex and that sadomasochism is just an extreme version of this ordinary principle.

Sadomasochism also may provide individuals with an escape from the routine, restrictive behavior required in everyday life. Some men, for example, tend to use the bedroom to reverse roles played in outside life: meek, mild men may want to be powerful and dominant, while powerful, aggressive men may prefer to be submissive and overpowered by their partner.

---

1. Have you ever had fantasies involving sadomasochism? Have you ever acted out any of these fantasies?
2. Have you ever had a sexual partner who was interested in experimenting with sadomasochism? How did you know? What was your reaction?
3. How would you describe abnormal sadomasochism?

Rape

Although the legal definition of rape varies from state to state, in most states, **rape** is defined as a sexual assault with penile penetration of the vagina under the use or threat of force that overcomes the earnest resistance of the victim.

Rape and the other actions that usually accompany rape, are all acts of violence. Doctor Dorothy J. Hicks (1978), medical director of a rape treatment center in Miami, places rape in its proper perspective in the following statement:

> Rape is not a sex act. It is a violent crime that has nothing to do with sex except that sex organs are involved. Rape is an attempt to humiliate a victim who happens to be vulnerable and handy at the time. It's really the ultimate invasion of privacy and terribly misunderstood.

Sexual intercourse, as we usually think of it, has very little to do with rape. The ultimate feeling behind rape is not sex, but dominance and power. In rape, the weapon is the penis, or a foreign object, such as a gun barrel, stick, or wrench, which is used as a spear to attack, subordinate, and humiliate the victim. There is often no orgasm for the attacker. Rapists, by placing their victim in an inferior and degraded position, satisfy their hostile feelings toward women, and sometimes men, by forcing submission. Often, the sadistic impulses are compensation for feelings of sexual or social inadequacy.

Most rape victims are women, but homosexual rapes of males are being reported more frequently.

Rape Myths

Many men today, as in the past, believe that women *want* to be raped and that women want a man to prove his masculinity by overcoming their resistance. They also tend to believe that, after the woman yields, she enjoys the rape. In addition, many people, both men and women, feel that women often "ask" to be raped by the type of clothes they wear and that a "woman can't get raped if she doesn't want to." These are all myths.

Ruth Hershberger (1948) explains that the threat of being raped, the actual act of being raped, and the emotional outcome after someone has been raped are all complicated by the many myths surrounding rape. Rape is an assault—an act of violence—there is nothing erogenous about it. The previously mentioned myths about rape often cause a woman to not take the threat of being raped as seriously as she should and also may keep her from reporting an assault.

Another rape myth is that many men are falsely accused of rape. FBI statistics, however, show that false accusations for rape are the same as for any other felony—about 5 percent (Brownmiller 1975).

Rape Statistics

In 1981, 7,133 rapes were reported in the United States (*Statistical Abstracts* 1982). The number of rapes that actually occur, however, can only be estimated since rape is one of the most underreported crimes in the United States. A study by Amir (1971) indicated that only one in five rapes is reported to the police, while a study by Bode (1978) indicated that this number is closer to one in eight or ten.

Rapist and rape victim profiles can be obtained from two classic studies of rape: John McDonald's *Rape Offenders and Their Victims* (1971) and Susan Brownmiller's *Against Our Will* (1975).

According to these studies, 64 percent of rapists are between the ages of fifteen and twenty-four, with a median age of twenty-three. Forty-seven percent of rapists are black, while 51 percent are white. Regardless of their race, nearly all convicted rapists come from the lower socioeconomic levels and are highly aggressive, have

Date Rape

Date rape occurs when a sexual relationship is forced upon an unwilling partner during a date. Sexual advances may be accompanied by enough coercion that a woman fears violence or other retribution if she refuses to cooperate. (Males may occasionally find themselves in similar heterosexual situations, but we confine this discussion to the more likely case of the female as victim.)

With the possible exception of spousal rape, date rapes are the least reported of all rapes (L. Schultz 1975). Women fail to report such rapes for a variety of reasons. They may not view such incidents as rape, believing that unwanted sex is the chance they take when dating. They may not want to report someone who is part of their own peer group or social set. They may feel that reporting such an incident is not worth the time and embarrassment. Young women may not want their parents to know that they allowed themselves to get into such a position. And some may feel that they were perhaps responsible for what took place.

Men who force their attentions on their dates can find all kinds of rationalizations for their rapes. Some feel that a woman "owes" them sex after they have picked up the tab for the evening. Some may (quite erroneously) believe that women really want to be raped or taken by force. Some rationalize that the woman "led them on" or was a "tease" or that the fact that a woman has had sex with other men makes her available to them as well.

Rape authorities (see Brownmiller 1975) feel that if women were more likely to report date rape, and if legal authorities were more likely to view it as a serious offense, the incidence of this act could be sharply reduced.

very low incomes and little education, and probably are unemployed. Seventy percent of all rapists have previous arrest records, and 85 percent of rapists go on to repeat rape or to be arrested for other crimes.

These studies also show that 60 percent of rapes are performed by strangers, while 17 percent are performed by casual acquaintances (with about half of these being individuals the woman met that day—often in a bar). When a woman knows her attacker well, he is a stepfather or a mother's boyfriend (4 percent); a neighbor (1 percent); a brother-in-law (1 percent); or an ex-husband, future father-in-law, fellow employee, or fellow tenant in an apartment building (1 percent).

Women of all ages and from all socioeconomic groups are victims of rape. Rape victims, however, are usually between the ages of ten and twenty-nine, and up to 90 percent of them are of the same socioeconomic class, racial background, and age group as the man that attacks them.

1. Have you or anyone you know ever been raped? What were the circumstances? Was the rapist prosecuted or convicted? How did the victim personally resolve the incident?
2. Why do you think that rape is one of the most underreported crimes in the United States?

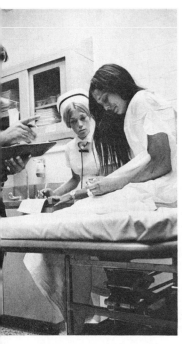

Medical and legal procedures for handling rape victims are improving in most areas.

Rape and the Medical, Law Enforcement, and Legal Communities

In the past, if a rape victim expected her assailant to be punished, she had to be sober, homely, hysterical at the time of the rape, and either be a virgin or have had only one relationship with someone other than the rapist. If the rape victim had an active sex life, did not have *severe* injuries, or was acquainted with her attacker, the rapist would never be found guilty. In addition, the rape victim often faced massive insensitivity from the medical, law-enforcement, and legal communities.

Medical attention for the rape victim up until now has tended to be inadequate and unsupportive. Many hospitals have turned rape victims away because they were reluctant to become involved in situations in which legal implications could absorb a great deal of time. Private physicians have felt the same way. Rape victims have often ended up in an emergency room of a public hospital facing a long wait for treatment (since rape is not considered life threatening), with little privacy, and without rape-crisis trained personnel to give support and guidance.

Police, in the past, have often been unsympathetic and more interested in the details of the rape than in the collection of evidence to arrest the rapist. Since most police officers are male, they may feel—like many in our society—that women who are raped have put themselves into positions where they could be raped. When the officers handling a rape have been male, only about half of all reported rapists have ever been apprehended, and only 10 to 20 percent have ever been convicted (Bode 1978).

If the rapist is apprehended, the criminal justice system has seemed in the past to favor the rapist over the victim. Until now, rape laws have been based on the concept of male ownership of women, and, thus, the intent of rape laws has been the protection of men: fathers from the loss of a daughter's virginity, husbands from the loss of a wife's chastity, and other men from false accusations. Also, until recently, most states restricted the definition of rape to include only forced vaginal intercourse, and there had to be proof that the male ejaculated in, or on, the female.

Fortunately, medical, law enforcement, and legal procedures for handling rape victims are changing. Many hospitals now provide a private waiting room for the rape victim and personnel trained in the collection of physical evidence and in providing emotional support for the victim. An increasing number of police departments are establishing rape investigation units that are staffed by female officers. When staffed by female officers, these units have a rapist conviction rate of up to 90 percent. Also, from the legal standpoint, since 1975, rape laws and the intent of protection have been changing to protect women from the power and violence of rape. Many states also are changing their legal definition of rape to include all forced sexual activity, including oral and anal contact and the use of objects to commit rape.

Reducing the Chances of Rape

To keep from being a victim of any crime, especially rape:

1. Use only secure locks on your doors and windows. Have dead-bolt locks installed on all exterior doors and windows on the ground floor. Install screens on all windows. Change locks whenever moving or after losing a key.

2. Know who you are opening a door for. Install and use a peephole in the front door, and never open a door to a stranger. Install chain-locks to limit openings whenever talking to someone. Always ask for proper identification and check it out with a phone call before allowing someone to enter an apartment or home.

3. Keep your car in good repair to avoid car trouble on the highway. Always keep at least a quarter of a tank of gas in the car. Lock your car whenever it is parked. When you return to your car, always have your keys in your hand and ready to unlock your car door before you leave a store or your home. (Keys also make a good weapon if you are attacked.)

Check the backseat of your car before entering to make sure no one is hiding there. When in the car, keep all the doors locked, the windows rolled up as far as possible, and your purse or valuables out of sight. Do not put your name on your car license plate or frame, or do not respond to your name if you have it on your license plate.

4. When walking, plan your route and avoid dark streets, high shrubbery, and dark hallways. Be extra careful when approaching alleys, recessed doorways, parks, and open fields. Walk with authority; this makes an attacker shy away. Know where you are at all times. Knowledge of the area you are in may help if you need to escape from someone.

5. Leave lights on in your apartment or home if you plan on returning after dark.

6. Take precautions not to be alone in isolated places, such as public or apartment Laundromats.

7. Always remember to think ahead, take precautions, use common sense, and remain calm.

Self-Defense against Rape

There is no single best way to deal with a sexual assault situation because every woman, rapist, and situation is different. Betty W. Brooks (1980), however, offers the following seven tips on self-defense that can help to increase awareness and readiness when confronted with a possible sexual assault:

1. The woman should be aware of her space and of danger signals in the environment.

2. If approached or attacked, a woman should *Yell*. It will frighten the attacker, counteract the woman's tendency to "freeze" and not do anything, and give more power to any striking and kicking the woman does.

3. A woman should keep thinking while acting: *Turn-Fear-into-Anger-into-Action*. The woman should remember that the common reaction is: *Fear-Paralysis-Hiding* (the woman often feels that the assault is not happening to her; or that if she does anything, the attacker will kill her; or that if she is nice to the attacker, he will not hurt her). To change this into the Fear-into-Anger-into-Action reaction, the woman can yell to mobilize her anger: How dare you!! Who said you have the right to attack me!! I am a survivor!!

Women are urged to learn how to protect themselves from rapists.

4.   The woman should aim her kicks and blows at the vulnerable areas of the attacker's body. Hitting and jabbing the eyes, nose, and throat and kicking the groin, knees, and toes can immobilize and incapacitate an attacker. Kicks to the knees are very effective because they are unexpected, powerful, and can disable. Jabs to the eyes or jabbing the palm up into the nose also is very effective. Jabs to the throat can get an attacker to release an individual and give the victim time to run or to plan the next move.

5.   A woman should do all hitting and kicking by surprise to keep the attacker off guard. Speed and power in combination with surprise are the keys to a successful defense.

6.   A woman should always run away from an assailant if possible. And while running, she should yell, "Fire!" Help will come more quickly if she yells "Fire," and it forces people to get involved. The woman should not be afraid to break windows or otherwise damage property to get attention.

7.   Talking to the attacker may or may not work. But a woman should *never beg or plead*. She should always be prepared to use physical force if words do not work. She should never count on being able to reason with the attacker.

These tips can make a woman aware of ways to handle an attacker, but the woman is the one being attacked and she must use her best judgment, at the time of the attack, about how to protect herself. There is no right or wrong way to handle an attacker. Whatever a woman does is probably the best she could do in that situation. The woman should always feel she did the best that she could to prevent the attack or to survive the attack.

What to Do after an Assault

A woman who has been sexually assaulted would probably be best advised:

1.   To contact a rape-crisis hot line. These hot lines operate in most larger cities twenty-four hours a day. Contacting the hot line will connect the woman with professional and competent rape-crisis groups that will act as advocates for the victim when dealing with police, health care professionals, family, friends, and spouse. (Often, the victim's family, friends, and spouse may need help to understand the situation.)

2.   Not to shower, bathe, douche, change or destroy clothing, or straighten up the area where she was raped (if the rape occurred indoors) since this could destroy important evidence.

3.   To go to the nearest hospital that is "sensitive" to the needs of someone who has been assaulted. The woman's bruises and lacerations can be treated, and preventives for sexually transmitted diseases can be administered. Many women do not seek this emergency care because they fear disclosure of the rape or being forced to file legal charges against the rapist. A hospital is required to report a rape to the police, but a woman is not required to make any official report. On the other hand,

if the woman decides to file rape charges, a record of the physical damage she sustained is absolutely necessary to convict a rapist.

4. To call the police and to write down every detail she can remember about the rape and the rapist as soon as possible if the woman is going to report the assault. Any delay makes it harder to find and convict a rapist.

5. To seek immediate professional counseling. While women may suffer physical damage at the hands of a rapist, the emotional scars of a rape are usually more serious and longer lasting. Rape victims often experience feelings of shock, fear, disbelief, guilt, shame, anger, and depression. These feelings are hard to cope with and need to be worked out, usually with a professional counselor, over a period of time.

The emotional scars of rape are usually more severe than the physical damage. Immediate and ongoing counseling of a rape victim can help her deal with the many difficult emotions that follow rape.

Homosexual Rape

Homosexual rapes in society are increasing, but reliable statistics are not available. Most homosexual rapes occur in prisons. As with other forcible rapes, homosexual rapes are not usually motivated by true homosexual feelings. Rather, they are done to show dominance in the prison population and humiliation of the victim. Brownmiller (1975) states:

> Prison rape is generally seen today for what it is: an acting out of power roles within an all-male, authoritarian environment in which the younger, weaker inmate, usually a first offender, is forced to play the role that in the outside would be assigned to women.

Marital Rape Exemption

In most states today, a husband cannot be prosecuted for forcing his wife to have sex with him. Legally, this is known as the **marital rape exemption.** It has its beginnings in a seventeenth-century statement in Sir Matthew Hale's famous book on the foundations of English law, *The History of Pleas of the Crown* (1778). The statement reads:

> The husband cannot be guilty of a rape committed by himself upon his lawful wife, for by their mutual matrimonial consent and contract the wife hath given up herself in his kind unto her husband, which she cannot retract.

On the basis of this statement, the first marital rape exemption law was passed in Massachusetts in 1857. All states followed, and most of these laws still are in force today. In these states, the only way to convict a husband of an offense connected with rape is if he forces his wife to have sexual intercourse with a third person.

An interesting aspect of the marital rape exemption is that, from state to state, there is a wide variation in the legal definition of a "husband." In some states, he must be legally married to the woman, while in other states, a husband can be "anyone cohabitating with a woman at the time the rape is committed." Also, in some states, a woman can file rape charges if she and her husband were living apart at the time of the rape. In other states (such as Nevada, Michigan, and Minnesota), the man and woman must not only be living apart, but they must have filed for divorce or separate maintenance before the man can be prosecuted for rape.

The marital rape exemption laws, however, are beginning to change. Some states (such as Oregon and South Dakota) have eliminated their marital rape exemption laws altogether and will prosecute the husband for rape. The State of Delaware has classified rape into two degrees. Rape "in the first degree" is charged if the victim is *not* the defendant's voluntary companion on the occasion of the rape and had not previously permitted him sexual contact. If the victim is the defendant's voluntary companion, the rapist can be charged with rape in the "second degree." A married woman is considered a "voluntary companion" if her husband rapes her.

The courts in some states hold that allowing a husband to be prosecuted for rape causes a number of problems, including increased risk of fabricated accusations; invasion of the sanctity of marriage; increased ability on the part of the wife to obtain a larger property settlement in a divorce, the rape being used as a weapon of vengeance by a spurned wife; and the possibility that accusations of rape would lessen the likelihood of reconciliation if divorce charges were filed.

Feminist groups, however, feel that these courts have overlooked some simple logic. They argue that the sanctity of the marriage is not invaded since there is seldom a witness to a marital rape. The accusation of rape disintegrates into his word against hers unless there is physical evidence such as bruises. So, the word of neither the husband nor the wife would be significant to either prove or disprove a rape. Feminists also point out that there are already a number of charges that can be falsely brought against a husband *or wife* by a vengeful spouse. Assault and battery, larceny, and fraud are examples of such charges.

Lastly, feminists believe that if a relationship has deteriorated to the point of forcible sexual advances by the husband, a reconciliation is already highly unlikely.

Using these points as the basis of their arguments, many feminist groups are currently lobbying the state legislatures of many states to remove the marital rape exemption from their laws.

1. Explain the intent of rape laws in the past. How has this changed today? How do you think it will change in the future?
2. Should rape be defined without reference to marital status? Should sex on demand be a marital obligation, enforceable by strength? Give your opinions.

The rapist was set free, due to some police officer's error—the man who had destroyed Dave and Joanne Thorpe's lives was walking the streets. He was free to perhaps attack another innocent victim.

Dave and Joanne underwent counseling. The pain was beginning to subside, but dull hatred had set in. They still had each other though. Dave hoped that in time their lives would begin to take a turn for the better. Until then, there was nothing he could do but to hope and pray and love his wife and put away his pain.

Summary

1. Any unwanted attention of a sexual nature that makes a person uncomfortable may be interpreted as sexual harassment. The real issue in sexual harassment is not sex, but power. The ability to exercise power over another individual is more important than any actual sex obtained. Sexual harassment seems to be mainly a problem of lower management.

2. Fighting sexual harassment may involve keeping a diary, talking personally with the aggressor, complaining to anyone in a position to help, writing a letter to the aggressor, seeking collaborative testimony from others, and, perhaps, retaining an attorney for advice on suing.

3. Victims of sexual harassment can suffer from physical symptoms of stress and a loss of self-esteem and self-confidence.

4. Colleges and universities are adopting policies prohibiting the sexual harassment of students by teachers. But few procedures have been established regarding dating between teachers and consenting students.

5. Sadomasochism is receiving sexual arousal and pleasure by inflicting or receiving physical or emotional pain.

6. Sadomasochism can take several forms. It may be enjoyed safely by sexual partners as a sexual variation and a living out of fantasies. Or it can reflect a severe neurosis or psychosis, making sexual activities a nightmare. Sadomasochism only really becomes a dangerous threat if an individual cannot control his or her sadomasochistic tendencies and the acts become criminal sadism.

7. The causes of sadomasochism are not well understood, but many believe that sadomasochistic behavior can be traced to childhood experiences that function in the subconscious to bring about sadomasochistic behavior in adulthood.

8. Individuals may be drawn to sadomasochism as a form of sexual expression because they are bored and looking for new taboos to break, because it is a way to express resentment and anger under the guise of a game, and because it may provide an escape from the routine, restrictive behavior required in everyday life.

9.   In most states, rape is defined as a sexual assault with penile penetration of the vagina under the use or threat of force that overcomes the earnest resistance of the victim. Rape, and the other actions that usually accompany rape, are all acts of violence.

10.   Rape myths, such as "women want to be raped," "women enjoy being raped," and "women ask to be raped by the type of clothes they wear," often cause a woman to not take the threat of being raped as seriously as she should and also may keep her from reporting an assault.

11.   Rape is one of the most underreported crimes in the United States, with only an estimated one in five or one in eight rape victims ever seeking prosecution. Nearly all convicted rapists come from the lower socioeconomic levels, are highly aggressive, have very low incomes and little education, and probably are unemployed. Women of all ages and from all socioeconomic groups have been victims of rape.

12.   In the past, the rape victim has often faced massive insensitivity from the medical, law enforcement, and legal communities. Fortunately, however, medical, law enforcement, and legal procedures for handling rape victims are changing to protect women as much as possible from the power and violence of rape.

13.   There is no single best way to deal with a sexual assault situation because every woman, rapist, and situation is different, but becoming familiar with self-defense tips can help to increase a woman's awareness and readiness when confronted with possible sexual assault.

14.   A woman who has been sexually assaulted should contact a rape-crisis center for help in dealing with the police, health care professionals, family, friends, and spouse. She should also seek medical treatment and professional counseling.

15.   Homosexual rapes are increasing and usually occur in prisons. Prison rape, like other acts of rape, is an acting out of power roles.

16.   In most states today, a husband cannot be prosecuted for forcing his wife to have sex with him (marital rape exemption), but this is slowly beginning to change.

GLOSSARY

abortion Expulsion or removal of an embryo or fetus from a pregnant woman's uterus early in pregnancy, before the fetus can survive on its own.

abstinence The voluntary avoidance of coitus.

acquired immune deficiency syndrome (AIDS) A disruption of the body's immune mechanism; probably caused by viral infection of the lymphocytes, a type of white blood cell.

acrosome A caplike structure in the head of a sperm that contains chemicals that "digest" a hole into the ovum, allowing penetration by the sperm.

adolescence The period of life extending from puberty to adulthood.

adultery Sexual intercourse between a married person and an individual other than the married person's legal spouse.

amniocentesis The surgical penetration of the abdomen to the uterus to obtain amniotic fluid; used to assist in the diagnosis of prenatal disease.

anal intercourse Sexual intercourse by inserting the penis into the anus.

anaphrodisiac A chemical agent or substance that diminishes or depresses sexual desire or function.

anatomy Relating to the structure of the body.

androgens Hormones that promote the development of male or malelike sexual structures and characteristics.

androgyny Showing some characteristics of both sexes.

aneurysm A bulge in the wall of a blood vessel.

anilingus Oral stimulation of the anus.

anorgasmia *See* orgasmic dysfunction.

anovulatory Without ovulation.

Apgar test (score) A numerical rating of the condition of a newborn infant; the sum of points gained on assessment of the heart rate, respiratory effort, muscle tone, reflex irritability, and color; usually determined sixty seconds after birth.

aphrodisiac A chemical agent or substance that is supposed to increase or stimulate sexual desire.

areola The area surrounding the nipple of the breast.

arousability The speed with which a person can be sexually aroused.

artificial insemination The introduction of semen into the vagina of a woman by means other than sexual intercourse.

aural sensations Perception, or awareness, of sound.

autoerotic activities Activities that produce sexual gratification in one's own body through self-stimulation of the genitals or other body parts.

autosomes The numbered chromosomes; chromosomes other than the sex chromosomes X and Y.

Bartholin's glands Small glands lying on either side of the vaginal opening that secrete mainly mucus; correspond to the Cowper's glands of the male.

basal body temperature method (BBT) A technique for determining female ovulation by observing changes in body temperature upon awakening each morning.

bestiality *See* zoophilia.

bisexuality Being sexually attracted to people of both sexes.

blastocyst An early stage in embryonic development in which the embryo is a hollow ball of cells.

bonding The strong emotional attachment between parent and child.

brothel A house of prostitution; also known as "whorehouses," "houses of ill repute," "disorderly houses," or "bordellos."

calendar method A technique of calculating a woman's monthly fertile period by counting the number of days in menstrual cycles.

call girl A prostitute whose primary method of soliciting clients is by making telephone appointments.

Candida albicans A species of yeastlike pathogenic fungus that causes vaginitis.

candidiasis Infection by *Candida albicans;* a yeast infection.

cantharidin Dried insects of the beetle species *Cantharis vesicatoria;* sometimes taken as a sexual aphrodisiac.

capacitation The process by which a sperm becomes capable of fertilizing an ovum after the sperm reaches the fallopian tube.

carpopedal spasms Spastic contractions of the muscles of the hands and feet, as occurs during sexual excitement.

carrier A person who has a certain gene but does not show the effects of it.

case study Studying in detail one individual or situation rather than numerous individuals or situations.

castration The surgical removal of the testes.

cavernous bodies The two upper cylinders of erectile tissue that extend the length of the shaft of the penis.

celibacy Abstention from sexual activity.

cell The basic biological unit of living organisms; consists of a circumscribed mass of protoplasm containing a variety of organelles and a nucleus.

cervical cap A small plastic or rubber contraceptive device positioned on the cervix to serve as a barrier to sperm.

cervix The narrow lower third of the uterus that connects the vagina to the body of the uterus.

cesarean section Delivery of a child through a surgical incision in the abdominal and uterine walls.

chancre The lesion of primary syphilis.

"chicken" A teenage male prostitute.

"chicken porn" The pornographic portrayal of prepubescent children; also known as "kiddie porn."

child molestation See pedophilia.

Chlamydia trachomatis A species of bacteria that causes genital infections and the eye disease called trachoma.

chromosomes Rodlike DNA-containing structures in the nucleus of cells; transmit genetic information from generation to generation.

circumcision The surgical removal of all or part of the prepuce (foreskin) of the penis.

cleavage Division of the cells of the zygote from fertilization until implantation into the uterus.

climacteric The syndrome of changes that occur during middle age as a result of declining hormone levels.

climax *See* orgasm.

clitoral hood The fold of the labia minora covering the clitoral shaft; sometimes known as the female prepuce or foreskin.

clitoral orgasm According to Freudian theory, an orgasm attained exclusively through direct clitoral stimulation.

clitoridectomy Excision, or removal, of the clitoris.

clitoris A small, sensitive, erectile projection situated at the anterior end of the vestibule; homologous with the male penis.

cohabitation In general, living together; usually refers to unmarried sexual partners sharing housing.

coitus Heterosexual intercourse by inserting the penis into the vagina; sexual intercourse.

coitus interruptus A method of conception control in which the male removes the penis from the vagina prior to ejaculation.

colostrum The thin, yellow, milky fluid secreted through the mammary glands a few days before and after the birth of a baby.

communicable period Period during which a disease is contagious from one person to another.

companionate love A form of love characteristic of long-term relationships, involving friendly affection and deep attachment; less emotionally intense than passionate love.

conception The moment of fertilization of an ovum by a sperm.

condom A thin sheath of rubber or skin worn over the penis during coitus to prevent sperm from entering the vagina; also known as a safe, prophylactic, or French letter.

congenital syphilis Syphilis that is present in a baby at birth.

contraception Preventing conception by the nonsurgical use of various devices, drugs, and techniques.

coprolalia Sexual arousal through using or hearing lewd or "filthy" language; also known as scatologia.

coprophilia Sexual excitement from viewing or perceiving the odor of feces.

corona The rim of tissue surrounding the base of the penile glans.

corpus albicans White, connective tissue that replaces the regressing corpus luteum in the human ovary in the latter half of pregnancy, or soon after ovulation if pregnancy has not taken place.

corpus luteum The yellow mass that forms in an ovarian follicle after ovulation; secretes the hormone progesterone.

Cowper's (bulbourethral) glands Two glands located beneath the prostate gland on either side of the male urethra; secrete pre-ejaculatory fluid.

culdoscopy Examination of the pelvic cavity through the introduction of an endoscope through the posterior cavity of the vagina.

cunnilingus Oral stimulation of the female genitals.

cystic fibrosis Hereditary disorder in which there is widespread dysfunction of the secretory glands.

cystitis Inflammation of the urinary bladder.

diaphragm A soft, shallow, dome-shaped contraceptive device that is positioned inside the vagina over the cervix during coitus to serve as a barrier to sperm.

diethylstilbestrol (DES) A synthetic estrogen. (*See* morning-after pill.)

dilation and curettage (D and C) Surgical procedure in which the cervix is dilated and the uterine lining is then gently scraped with a metal instrument (curette); sometimes used as a form of abortion during the first trimester.

dilation and evacuation (D and E) A second trimester abortion procedure in which the cervix is dilated and the fetus removed through a combination of vacuum aspiration and use of forceps.

dildo An artificial penis.

DNA (deoxyribonucleic acid) A self-replicating molecule that controls inheritance and protein synthesis.

douching Use of a liquid to flush the vagina.

Down's syndrome A type of moderate to severe mental retardation accompanied by a variable series of physical traits; usually associated with a chromosomal imbalance.

dysfunctions In a sexual sense, disorders that make it impossible for a person to have or to enjoy sexual intercourse.

dysmenorrhea Painful menstrual flow.

dyspareunia Painful intercourse.

dysphoria The condition of feeling ill at ease; gender dysphoria refers to any degree of difficulty in gender identity.

dysplasia Abnormal development of tissue.

ectopic pregnancy Any pregnancy that occurs when a fertilized ovum implants itself outside the lining of the uterus; virtually all such implants occur in the fallopian tubes.

ego-dystonic homosexuality Homosexuality that is perceived by the individual as unacceptable and undesirable; the desire to change sexual orientation is a persistent concern.

ejaculation The sudden expulsion of semen from the erect penis.

ejaculatory incompetence *See* retarded ejaculation.

embryo The unborn child during the first eight weeks of development after conception.

emission Discharge of seminal fluid from the fluid-producing glands of the reproductive system.

encephalitis Inflammation of the brain.

endocrine glands Body glands that secrete hormones into the blood or lymph.

endometrial aspiration Removal of the uterine lining through the use of a suction instrument called an aspirator; sometimes used for menstrual extraction.

endometriosis Abnormalities of the uterine lining.

endometrium The mucous membrane of the uterus; thickness and structure varies with the phases of the menstrual cycle.

epididymis The tightly coiled, cordlike structure along the posterior border of the testis; stores sperm.

episiotomy Surgical incision of the perineum for delivery of a baby.

erectile dysfunction The inability to have or to maintain penile erection of sufficient firmness for coitus; also known as inhibited sexual excitement.

erectile tissue Tissue that is capable of erection.

erection The condition of being made rigid and elevated.

erogenous zones Areas of the body that are especially sensitive to sexual stimulation.

erotica The graphic depiction of nudes in a manner that is a mutually pleasurable expression between people and not a debasing of the individual.

erotic sensations Those sensory perceptions that are sexually gratifying.

estrogen A group of hormones that produce a recurrent period in which a female becomes sexually receptive to males; these hormones also promote development of the female reproductive tract and bodily characteristics.

excitement phase The first phase of the sexual response cycle in which engorgement of the sexual organs and an increase in muscle tension, heart rate, and blood pressure occurs.

exhibitionism Deriving sexual gratification from repeatedly exposing the genitals to unsuspecting and unconsenting strangers.

fallopian tube The tube or duct that connects the ovary to the uterus; serves to convey the ovum from the ovary to the uterus and the sperm from the uterus toward the ovary.

fantasy Any daydream with an elaborate script; known as sexual fantasies when associated with sexual scenarios.

fellatio Oral stimulation of the male genitals.

female adrenogenital syndrome Masculinization of the external female genitals; caused by exposure of a female fetus to testosterone.

fertilization The union of the sperm cell nucleus with the nucleus of the ovum.

fetal alcohol syndrome A variable series of psychomotor disturbances, facial characteristics, and growth deficiencies found in the children of women who drank alcohol during their pregnancy.

fetishism The use of specific inanimate objects or body parts for sexual arousal.

fetology Scientific and medical study of the developing child until birth.

fetoscope An instrument that allows direct visual observation of the developing fetus.

fetus The developing child from about the eighth week after conception until birth.

fimbriae Fingerlike projections that form a fringe around the entrance to a fallopian tube.

follicle The small sac or cavity enclosing an ovum in the ovary.

follicle-stimulating hormone (FSH) A gonadotropin secreted by the pituitary gland that stimulates the development of an ovarian follicle in a female or the production of sperm in a male.

forceps An instrument shaped like a salad tongs for grasping an infant's head during the delivery process.

foreplay Any type of sex play that precedes coitus.

fornication Sexual intercourse between unmarried heterosexual adults; a violation of the law in some states.

frenulum A highly sensitive thin strip of skin connecting the penile glans to the foreskin.

frequency Rate of recurrence; the number of times regularly recurring events take place.

frottage Sexual arousal from rubbing or pressing against the body of a fully clothed person in a crowded situation.

gamete A mature male or female reproductive cell; the sperm or ovum.

gay Homosexual; applied to both sexes or to males only.

gender Strictly speaking, the social and behavioral aspects of being male or female; also used for the physical fact of being male or female.

gene The functional unit of heredity; genes "tell" our cells how to construct the many chemicals needed for all of the functions that occur in our cells and our body.

general sexual dysfunction A sexual problem in which the female arouses little, if at all, when sexually stimulated.

genital herpes Infection of the male or female genital area by herpes simplex virus.

genital warts Infection of the genital area by the common wart virus.

gigolo A heterosexual male prostitute.

gonadotropin-releasing factor (GnRF) A hypothalamic hormone that acts upon the pituitary gland, causing it to secrete follicle-stimulating hormone (FSH) and luteinizing hormone (LH).

gonadotropins Hormones secreted by the pituitary that stimulate activity only in the male testes and the female ovaries (gonads).

gonads Male and female sex glands: the testes in the male and the ovaries in the female.

gonorrhea Infection by the gonococcus *Neisseria gonorrhoeae*.

gossypol A cottonseed derivative taken as a pill to inhibit sperm production.

Graafian follicle The primary follicle; the follicle that contains the ovum that will be ovulated that month.

G-spot A theoretical spot on the front wall of the vagina that, in some women, is highly sensitive to stimulation; stimulation of this spot may lead to orgasm.

guilt The act or fact of having committed an offense or done a wrong.

gustatory sensations Perceptions, or awareness, of taste.

gynecomastia Enlargement of the male mammary glands (breasts); common developmental event during male puberty.

halo effect The tendency to judge a likable, attractive, or intelligent person as being "good" in other respects as well and to overlook his or her undesirable traits.

hetairae A special class of early Greek prostitutes who were sought by men because of their beauty and education.

heterosexuality Being sexually attracted to members of the opposite sex.

homophobia The fear of homosexuality.

homosexuality Being sexually attracted to members of one's own sex.

hormones Chemicals originating in an organ, or gland, that are conveyed through the blood to another part of the body, affecting it by chemical action to increased or decreased functional activity.

house prostitutes Those who perform sex for pay in brothels ("houses of prostitution").

human chorionic gonadotropin (HCG) A gonadotropic hormone produced by the chorionic tissues of the embryo and fetus.

"hustler" A male prostitute who performs sexual acts for pay with homosexuals.

hydrocephalus Increased accumulation of cerebrospinal fluid within the ventricles of the brain; head is unusually large.

hymen A membrane that normally partially covers the entrance to the vagina.

hypersexuality Having an unusually intense sex drive which, despite numerous sex acts, leads to little or no sexual gratification.

hypertension An increase in blood pressure above the normal, as occurs during sexual excitement.

hyperventilation Increased rate or depth of breathing, as occurs during sexual excitement.

hypothalamus Floor of the third ventricle of the brain; secretes a series of substances that help to regulate some body processes.

hypothesis The proposed explanation for the occurrence of some specified group of phenomena.

hysterectomy Partial or total removal of the uterus.

hysteroscopy Examination of the uterus by the use of an endoscope.

hysterotomy Incision into the uterus; used for a cesarean section childbirth and as an abortion technique during the second trimester.

immunoglobulin A family of proteins capable of acting as antibodies.

imperforate hymen Unusually thick hymen completely covering the entrance to the vagina.

implantation Embedding of the blastocyst in the uterus seven or eight days after conception.

incest Sexual intercourse between persons so closely related that they are forbidden by law to marry.

incidence The range of occurrence of events; from the least frequent to the most frequent.

incubation period The period of time between exposure to an infectious disease and the appearance of its symptoms.

induced abortion Abortion intentionally brought on through the use of drugs or instruments.

infanticide The killing of an infant.

infatuation An attraction based on similarity to an idealized partner.

infundibulum The funnel-shaped structure at the end of each fallopian tube that lies very close to an ovary.

inhibin A protein that may be a hormone and that may inhibit secretion of follicle-stimulating hormone from the pituitary gland.

inhibited male orgasm *See* retarded ejaculation.

inhibited sexual excitement *See* erectile dysfunction.

instillation Introduction of a liquid into a cavity; instillation of saline or prostaglandins sometimes used to induce abortion during the second trimester.

interstitial (Leydig) cells The testosterone-secreting cells located between the seminiferous tubules of the testes.

interstitial cell-stimulating hormone (ICSH) Pituitary hormone that stimulates the interstitial cells of the testes to secrete testosterone.

intimacy A state of warm friendship and the sharing of innermost feelings and emotions; develops through long association.

intrauterine device A plastic birth control device that is placed inside the uterus and left there; believed to interfere with implantation of the fertilized ovum.

in vitro fertilization The fertilization of a human ovum by a sperm within a glass container outside the body.

jealousy Fear of the loss of someone's exclusive devotion; excessive possessiveness.

karyotype A systematic arrangement of the chromosomes of a single cell in the metaphase stage of mitosis.

kleptomania A fetish that involves obtaining sexual gratification from compulsive stealing of objects that usually have no value to the person other than as a source of sexual arousal.

Klinefelter's syndrome Chromosomal abnormality resulting from the presence of two X chromosomes and one Y chromosome (XXY) in a human cell; individuals with Klinefelter's syndrome have male internal and external genitals, but their testes are very small and nonfunctional.

klismaphilia Sexual arousal through receiving of enemas.

labia The covering, or lips, of the vulva.

labor The process of giving birth.

lactation The secreting of milk by the mammary glands of the breasts.

laparoscope Endoscopic device; in sterilization, used to locate the fallopian tubes; in vitro fertilization, used to locate the ovary.

laparoscopy Abdominal exploration through the use of an endoscope called a laparoscope.

laparotomy A surgical procedure involving an incision through the abdominal wall; a common procedure in female sterilization in the past.

lesbian A homosexual female.

libido The sexual drive, urge, or desire for pleasure or satisfaction; also a term used to denote sexual motivation.

luteinizing hormone (LH) Pituitary hormone that stimulates the release of ovarian hormones and ova in the female or testicular hormones and sperm in the male; also called interstitial cell-stimulating hormone (ICSH) in the male.

luteinizing hormone-releasing factor A chemical factor secreted by the hypothalamus that stimulates the pituitary gland to produce luteinizing hormone.

madam   A woman who manages prostitutes.

mammary glands   Glands in the breast that secrete milk when an infant is nursing.

marital rape exemption   A law that exempts a husband from being prosecuted for raping his wife.

masochist   One who obtains sexual pleasure from being physically or mentally abused or dominated.

masseur   A man whose work is massaging.

masseuse   A woman whose work is massaging.

masturbation   Stimulation of one's own genitals to create sexual pleasure.

mean   An average; midway between two extremes.

median   The plane or point that is the middle in a given sequence.

meiosis   The process of cell division by which ovum and sperm cells are formed.

menarche   The first menstrual period of a female during puberty.

menopause   That period which marks the permanent cessation of menstrual activity.

menstrual cycle   The monthly reproductive cycle in women; each cycle terminates with menstruation.

menstruation   The monthly flow of bloody fluid from the uterine lining tissue.

midlife crisis   A normal developmental period that usually occurs between the ages of thirty-five and fifty-five during which life goals are reevaluated; may be complicated by physiological, psychological, and social changes occurring in the individual at this time.

midwife   A trained individual who assists in childbirth but is not a physician.

milk ducts   Ducts within the breast that conduct milk from the mammary glands to the nursing infant.

minipill   A contraceptive pill containing only progesterone in a low dosage.

miscarriage   Interruption of pregnancy by spontaneous expulsion of the embryo or fetus during the first or second trimester.

mistress   A woman whose life-style as a sex partner is maintained by a man to whom she is not married and who does not provide her with immediate payment for her services.

mitochondria   Slender, filamentlike rods found in cells; the source of cellular energy.

mitosis   The process by which all body cells of multicellular organisms multiply.

mittelschmerz   Pain felt by some women at ovulation; caused by the ovum breaking out of the follicle.

mode   The value having the greatest frequency.

monogamy   Being married to only one person at a time.

mons veneris   Fatty, hair-covered pad over the pubic bone in the female.

moral values   Those values that relate to a person's behavior or conduct with, and treatment of, other people.

morning-after pill   A high dosage of diethylstilbestrol (DES) taken orally after unprotected coitus that prevents implantation.

Müllerian ducts   Ducts in the embryo that develop into the fallopian tubes, the uterus, the cervix, and possibly the upper part of the vagina in the female.

Müllerian inhibiting hormone   A hormone produced by the testes that stops formation of female internal genitals.

multiple orgasm   The experience of more than one orgasm within a short period of time and without dropping below the plateau level of sexual arousal.

multiple pregnancy   Having more than one developing embryo or fetus in the body at the same time.

myotonia   Increased muscle tension.

narcissism   Love of or sexual desire for one's self.

natural family planning   *See* rhythm methods.

necrophilia   Arousal through sexual activity with a corpse.

New Morality   A system of ethics which states that people's attitudes or intentions in a certain situation determine whether their behavior in that situation is right or wrong.

nipple   The conical protuberance in each breast of the female from which milk is discharged during lactation.

nocturnal emissions   Involuntary male orgasms and ejaculations that occur during sleep and that are usually associated with sexual dreams; also called "wet dreams."

nocturnal orgasms   Orgasms in both females and males that occur during sleep and that are usually associated with a sexual dream.

nuclear family   Parents and their children as a group.

nymphomania   Compulsive sexual activity in females without the relief of sexual tensions; the affected person is sometimes called a "nymph."

obscenity   That which is offensive to modesty or decency; by legal distinction, the graphic depiction of nudity that is judged unfit to be shown or displayed.

olfactory sensations Perception, or awareness, of smell.

omnisexual *See* pansexual.

oogenesis The formation and development of ova.

oophorectomy Surgical removal of the ovaries.

oral-genital sex Mouth to genital contact between partners to create sexual pleasure.

orgasm A highly pleasurable series of muscular contractions of the pelvic floor muscles occurring at the peak of sexual arousal; involves the sudden discharge of accumulated sexual tension.

orgasmic dysfunction An inhibition of the orgasmic reflex in women; also known as anorgasmia and inhibited female orgasm.

orgasmic platform The narrowing of the vagina due to vasocongestion of the surrounding tissue during sexual excitement.

orgasm phase The third phase of the sexual response cycle in which rhythmic muscle contractions of the pelvic area occur.

ovariectomy Surgical removal of the ovaries.

ovary One of a pair of female reproductive glands in which ova and female hormones are produced.

ovulation The periodic ripening, rupture, and discharge of ova from the ovary.

ovulation method A technique for determining female ovulation by observing changes in the cervical mucus.

ovum The female reproductive cell, or gamete.

oxytocin A hypothalamic hormone released through the pituitary gland; performs a number of sex-related functions, one of which is causing milk ejection (or letdown) from the mammary glands.

panderer A person, usually a man, who procures and recruits women into prostitution.

pansexual Responding to all forms of sexual stimuli.

Pap smear (Pap test) A screening test for the detection and diagnosis of premalignant and malignant conditions of the female genital tract (cancer of the vagina, cervix, and endometrium).

paraphilias Those sexual actions that are pleasurable and gratifying, yet whose object (with whom or what one has intercourse) and/or aim (a goal other than seeking intercourse) deviate from the norm.

paresis Paralysis and mental symptoms resulting from damage to the brain and spinal cord by the spirochetes of syphilis.

parturition The act or process of giving birth to a child.

passionate love A strongly emotional state occurring early in relationships; the loved person is idealized and is intensely sexually exciting.

pathogen A disease-causing agent.

pedophilia A sexual paraphilia in which an adult is sexually attracted to and sexually aroused by prepubertal children.

"peeping Tom: *See* voyeurism.

pelvic inflammatory disease A uterine and pelvic cavity infection.

penile chordee Painful downward curvature of the penis on erection.

penile glans The tip, or head, of the penis. The urethral orifice, or opening, is at the center of the glans.

penile prosthesis An implant of a mechanical device within the penis to aid in erection.

penis External male reproductive organ through which urine and sperm pass from the male; erects during sexual excitement.

perineum The area between the anus and scrotum in the male, and between the anus and the vaginal opening in the female.

personhood A person's highest fulfillment.

petting Noncoital sexual activity, such as stimulation of the breasts and genitals.

Peyronie's disease Hardening of the cavernous bodies of the penis, causing a distortion or deflection of the penis, especially when erect.

phenylketonuria (PKU) A disease caused by the body's failure to properly metabolize the amino acid phenylalanine; if not treated early, brain damage occurs.

pheromones Chemical odors produced by certain female animals during their fertile periods that communicate reproductive readiness.

phocomelia A congenital malformation wherein the long bones of the arms and/or legs are poorly developed or absent; thus, the hands and/or feet are attached to the trunk directly or by means of poorly formed bones.

physiology Relating to the functioning of the body.

pimp A man who lives off the earnings of prostitutes, manages their time and money, pretends to protect their interests, and keeps them in line and working.

pituitary gland An endocrine gland attached to the base of the brain; secretes a number of hormones regulating many body processes.

placenta The organ that unites a fetus to its mother's uterus; it facilitates gas exchange, nutrition, and waste removal, and it secretes hormones.

placenta previa A placenta that develops in the lower segment of the uterus; it covers or adjoins the internal opening of the cervix.

plateau phase The second phase of the sexual response cycle in which vasocongestion, muscle tension, heart rate and blood pressure increase.

population The total number of individuals under consideration; the total group of individuals affected by the outcome.

pornae Early Greek women who were hired to provide sexual gratification; prostitutes.

pornography The depiction through material such as books, photographs, or films of erotic behavior with the intent to cause sexual excitement.

postpartum The days and weeks following childbirth.

postpubescent stage The stage following puberty when the secondary sex characteristics are well developed and the sex organs are capable of adult functioning.

premature ejaculation A sexual problem in which a male cannot maintain voluntary control over the ejaculatory reflex and may ejaculate early and unintentionally.

premenstrual syndrome The physical discomforts and/or emotional mood swings that some women experience before menstruation.

prepubescent stage The stage before puberty when the secondary sex characteristics begin to appear.

prepuce The fold of skin (foreskin) over the penile glans in the male; the fold of the labia minora that covers the clitoris in the female (*see* clitoral hood).

priapism Prolonged and uncomfortable penile erection without sexual desire.

primary infertility The condition of never having conceived or induced a pregnancy.

procreation Sexual intercourse entirely for the purpose of reproduction.

progesterone A hormone secreted by the ovaries and placenta that promotes the growth and maintenance of the uterine endometrium, mammary glands, and placenta.

projection The attribution of one's own thoughts, feelings, or actions to others.

prolactin Pituitary hormone that directs the synthesis of milk in the mammary glands of nursing mothers.

prolactin-inhibiting factor (PIF) Hypothalamic hormone that blocks the release of prolactin, keeping the mammary glands milk-free; the stimulus of nursing reflexively blocks the release of prolactin-inhibiting factor, allowing prolactin to be secreted and the mammary glands to synthesize milk.

proliferative phase The period of growth of the uterine endometrium during the early part of the menstrual cycle (approximately days 6 through 14).

promiscuity Indiscriminate, transient, sexual intercourse with many persons for the relief of sexual tensions, rather than for feelings of affection.

prophylactic *See* condom.

prostaglandin One of a group of fatty acid derivatives produced by the body that is extremely active biologically, including affecting the contraction of the uterus.

prostate A gland that surrounds the neck of the bladder and urethra in the male; secretes the fluid that initiates the movement of sperm.

prostatectomy Surgical removal of all or part of the prostate gland.

prostatitis Inflammation of the prostate gland.

prostitution The profession of performing sexual acts with others for pay.

prurient interest Extraordinary concern with nudity, sex, or excretion that goes beyond normal curiosity.

psychosexual Pertaining to the emotional or mental aspects of sexuality.

puberty The period in life during which one becomes functionally capable of reproduction.

pubescent stage The stage during puberty when the reproductive organs become capable of producing mature eggs and sperm.

pubic lice Small insects that infect the pubic and other coarse body hair; commonly called crabs.

pyromania A fetish that involves obtaining sexual gratification from compulsive fire setting.

quickening The first fetal movements detected by the mother; usually occurs in the fourth month of pregnancy.

random assignment A sample in which every individual in the population being studied has an equal chance of being selected.

range The extent of variation possible; the difference between the least frequent and the most frequent.

rape A sexual assault with penile penetration of the vagina under the use or threat of force that overcomes the earnest resistance of the victim.

receptor site A point on a target cell that binds a chemical molecule, permitting the molecule to exert its biological effect.

refractory period The period in the male immediately following ejaculation during which further orgasm is physiologically impossible; there is no such period in the female response cycle.

research design The plan to be followed during a research project.

resolution phase The fourth phase of the sexual response cycle, in which the sexual systems return to their nonexcited state.

retarded ejaculation The delay or absence of ejaculation following an adequate period of sexual excitement; also known as ejaculatory incompetence and inhibited male orgasm.

rete testis A network of ducts in each testis that receive sperm from the seminiferous tubules and convey the sperm to the epididymis.

retrograde ejaculation A condition in the male in which orgasm is not accompanied by an external ejaculation of semen; instead, the ejaculate goes into the urinary bladder.

rhythm methods Methods of conception control based on the abstinence from coitus during the calendar days of highest female fertility.

sadist One who derives sexual pleasure from hurting another person.

sadomasochism A variant sexual behavior in which the infliction of pain (sadism) and the submission to pain and humiliation (masochism) occur simultaneously and voluntarily between partners to achieve sexual arousal or gratification.

sample group The individuals within a population being studied.

satyriasis Compulsive sexual activity in males without the relief of sexual tensions; also called "Don Juanism"; the affected person is sometimes called a "satyr."

scabies Infection of the skin by itch mites.

scatologia *See* coprolalia.

scripts Behavioral scenarios that serve as guides to what we have done in the past, what we are presently doing, and what we plan to do.

scrotum The thin, loose pouch of skin in the male that contains the testes and the spermatic cord.

sebaceous glands The oil-secreting glands of the skin.

secondary infertility The inability to produce further offspring after having conceived or induced a pregnancy.

secretory phase The period of the menstrual cycle following ovulation when the corpus luteum secretes both progesterone and estrogen (approximately days 15 through 28).

seduction Luring, or inducing on the promise of a reward, a female or male into coitus without the use of force.

self-actualization The process of making full use of one's human potential.

semen A grayish-white, sticky mixture discharged from the urethra of the male during ejaculation; contains the sperm and seminal fluid.

seminal fluid The fluid portion of semen from the seminal vesicles, the prostate gland, and Cowper's glands.

seminal vesicles Two saclike glands in the male, lying behind the bladder and connected to the vas deferens on each side; secrete a fluid that forms a part of the semen.

seminiferous tubules Highly coiled tubules in the testes that produce sperm.

sensate focus A series of touching exercises for couples undergoing sex therapy to teach nonverbal communication and to reduce anxiety.

sensation Perception, or awareness, of conditions within or without the body resulting from stimulation of sensory receptors.

sensual sensations Those sensory perceptions that are gratifying or pleasurable.

Sertoli cells Cells of seminiferous tubules that nourish developing sperm.

sex chromosomes The X and Y chromosomes.

sex flush A temporary, reddish, spotty, rashlike color change that may develop on certain body parts during sexual excitement.

sex therapy The treatment of sexual dysfunctions.

sexual anesthesia A condition in which some people feel nothing from sexual stimulation.

sexual continuum A range of sexual attraction with infinite degrees falling between the two extremes of exclusive homosexual attraction and exclusive heterosexual desire.

sexual harassment Someone using their position or power to obtain sexual favors from someone else.

sexual intercourse Heterosexual intercourse by inserting the penis into the vagina; coitus.

sexuality The sum of a person's sexual characteristics, behavior, and tendencies; includes biological, psychological, and cultural attributes.

sexually transmitted diseases Diseases that may be transmitted by sexual contact.

sexual moral values The worth assigned to those behaviors or relationships dealing with proper sexual conduct.

sexual orientation One's attraction to persons of the same, opposite, or both sexes; one's placement on the continuum ranging from homosexuality to heterosexuality.

sexual reproduction Reproduction by fusion of a female ovum with a male sperm.

sexual response cycle The series of physiological and psychological events the human body goes through as it gains and then loses sexual arousal.

shared humanity The feelings and emotions of an individual conducting a survey that affect the answers of the person being surveyed.

sickle-cell anemia A severe inherited disease in which the red blood cells become sickle- or crescent-shaped when the person is low in oxygen; such cells are destroyed in large numbers by the body and produce numerous complications from a lack of oxygen in the body.

Skene's glands Glands situated on either side of the female urethra that secrete mucus.

smegma Thick, cheesy, ill-smelling secretion from sebaceous glands that accumulates under the clitoral hood in the female and under the prepuce of the male.

sodomy Oral or anal copulation with a member of the same or opposite sex or any copulation with an animal.

spectatoring A psychological process wherein a person becomes a "spectator" to his or her own sexual performance, monitoring and evaluating the performance; a common cause of sexual dysfunctioning.

sperm The male sex cell, or gamete.

spermatic cord Cord extending from abdominal cavity to each testis; contains the vas deferens and various blood vessels and nerves; helps to suspend testes within scrotum.

spermatogenesis The formation of mature, functional sperm by the testes.

spermicide A chemical agent that kills or immobilizes sperm and is carried in an inert base (foam, cream, jelly, sponge, or suppository).

spirochete A long, slender, spiral bacterium.

spongy body The lower cylinder of erectile tissue in the penis; extends the length of the penile shaft and forms the penile glans.

spontaneous abortion Abortion occurring naturally, without having been induced.

squeeze technique A method for reducing the tendency for premature ejaculation; technique consists of squeezing the penis at the base of the glans.

statutory rape *See* unlawful intercourse.

sterility The inability to produce offspring.

sterilization The surgical interruption of the reproductive tracts of either the male or female, preventing the discharge of sex cells, and, thus, fertilization.

straight Heterosexual.

streetwalker A prostitute whose primary method of soliciting clients is by walking the streets.

subliminal Below the threshold of sensation, or normal consciousness.

surrogate mother A woman who is fertilized by the male partner of an infertile couple, carries the child until birth, and then gives the child to the infertile couple.

symptothermal method A rhythm method that combines the techniques of observing basal body temperature and cervical mucus to determine when a woman ovulates.

syphilis Systemic infection by the spirochete *Treponema pallidum.*

tachycardia Increased rapidity of heart action, as occurs during sexual excitement.

tactile sensations Perception, or awareness, of touch.

target tissue A tissue stimulated or inhibited by a hormone.

Tay-Sachs disease Hereditary enzyme deficiency that results in brain deterioration and death usually within the first eighteen months of life.

temperature method *See* basal body temperature method.

teratology The study of congenitally deformed children.

testicular feminization Feminization of the external male genitals; caused by the suppression of testosterone in a male fetus.

testis One of a pair of male reproductive glands in which sperm, inhibin, and testosterone are produced.

testosterone The most important hormone in sexual functioning; present in both sexes; sometimes called the major male hormone; secreted by the testes and adrenals in the male and the ovaries and adrenals in the female.

touch spots Clusters, or groups, of tactile receptors that occur throughout the skin.

toxemia A dangerous condition that may occur during pregnancy; symptoms include sudden weight gain and swelling of the hands, feet, and face; the appearance of albumin in the urine, and a rise in blood pressure.

transmission The transfer of infectious disease from one person to another.

transsexualism A persistent sense of discomfort with one's biological gender accompanied by the desire to change the anatomy to the gender of the opposite sex and to live as a member of that sex.

transvestism Deriving sexual gratification from dressing in the clothing of the opposite sex.

Trichomonas vaginalis A pathogenic species of protozoan that may cause vaginitis.

trichomoniasis Infection by *Trichomonas vaginalis*.

troilism Sexual excitement through sharing of a sex partner or close relative (such as a daughter) with a third person while the first person observes.

tubal ligation Surgical procedure for the sterilization of the female by cutting and cauterizing each fallopian tube.

Turner's syndrome Chromosomal abnormality resulting from the presence of only one X chromosome and no Y chromosome (XO) in a human cell; individuals with Turner's syndrome have normal female external genitals but lack functional ovaries.

unlawful intercourse Voluntary sexual intercourse between an adult and a minor (under the age of consent), who are not married to each other; also known as statutory rape.

urethra A duct for the discharge of urine from the bladder to the outside.

urethritis Inflammation of the urethra.

uterus The female organ for containing and nourishing the embryo and fetus from implantation to birth.

vacuum aspiration Abortion method in which the cervix is dilated and the contents of the uterus are removed through a plastic tube (curette) connected to a vacuum pump.

vacuum curettage *See* vacuum aspiration.

vagina The tubular, muscular organ that forms the passageway between the uterus and the vulva.

vaginal introitus The opening, or entrance, to the vagina.

vaginal orgasm According to Freudian theory, an orgasm attained exclusively through vaginal stimulation.

vaginismus Involuntary spasms of the muscles around the lower third of the vagina when penetration of the penis is attempted.

vaginitis Inflammation of the vagina.

value indicator Any behavioral expression that has not yet developed into a true value.

values Those expressions, relationships, or items to which we attach the greatest worth; guides that give direction to life.

variocostocele Swelling of the veins on the vas deferens.

vascular spaces Cavities within erectile tissue that fill with blood during the erection process.

vas deferens Small, muscular tube that carries sperm upward from each epididymis to the ejaculatory duct.

vasectomy Surgical procedure for the sterilization of the male by cutting and tying each vas deferens.

vasocongestion The engorgement of blood vessels in body tissues, especially the genitals and female breasts, during sexual arousal.

vasodilation Dilation of blood vessels.

vertex position When the head of the child is presented for delivery and the long axis of the body is transverse to the mother's body.

vestibule The area between the labia minora.

volunteer bias The strong inclination of a person to have a preconceived opinion about something.

voyeurism Obtaining sexual gratification from secretly viewing unsuspecting people in the act of disrobing, when they are naked, or when they are engaging in sexual activity.

vulva The external genitals of the female.

"wet dreams" *See* nocturnal emissions.

withdrawal *See* coitus interruptus.

Wolffian ducts Ducts in the embryo that develop into some of the internal male genitals.

zoophilia Obtaining sexual arousal through repeated or exclusive sexual contact with animals; also known as bestiality.

zygote The fertilized ovum.

REFERENCES

Abrahams, Jesse. "Azoospermia before Puberty." *Medical Aspects of Human Sexuality* 1(1982):13.

Abramson, Paul. "The Relationship of the Frequency of Masturbation to Several Aspects of Personality and Behavior." *Journal of Sex Research* 2(1973):132–42.

Ackroyd, Peter. *Dressing Up, Transvestism and Drags— The History of an Obsession.* New York: Simon & Schuster, 1979.

Adams, Jane. *Sex and the Single Parent.* New York: Coward, McCann & Geoghegan, 1978.

Adams, Virginia. "Sex Therapies in Perspective." *Psychology Today* 3(1980):35–36.

Aguilar, Nona. "Post-Pill Couples Discover the Joy of Abstinence." *Los Angeles Times,* 16 November 1980, p. 28.

Alexander, M. "Sex and Stealing." *Sexology* (April 1965):636–40.

Ambron, Susann, and David Brodzinsky. *Lifespan Human Development.* 2d ed. New York: Holt, Rinehart & Winston, 1979.

American Cancer Society. *Cancer Facts and Figures.* New York: American Cancer Society, 1981.

American Psychiatric Association. *Diagnostic and Statistical Manual of Mental Disorders* (DSM-III). 3d ed. Washington, D.C.: American Psychiatric Association, 1980.

Amir, Menachem. *Patterns of Forcible Rape.* Chicago: University of Chicago Press, 1971.

Anderson, T. P., and T. M. Cole. "Sexual Counseling of the Physically Disabled." *Postgraduate Medicine* 1(1975):117–23.

Annis, L. F. *The Child before Birth.* Ithaca, N.Y.: Cornell University Press, 1978.

Annon, Jack. *The Behavioral Treatment of Sexual Problems, Volume 1: Brief Therapy.* New York: Harper & Row, 1974.

Appleton, William. "Counseling a Couple after Infidelity." *Medical Aspects of Human Sexuality* 12(1981):104–13.

Arafat, Ibtihaj, and Wayne Cotton. "Masturbation Practices of Males and Females." *Journal of Sex Research* 4(1974):293–307.

Arms, Suzanne. *Immaculate Deception.* New York: Bantam, 1977.

Athanasiou, R. "Pornography: A Review of Research." In *Handbook of Human Sexuality,* edited by Benjamin B. Wolman and John Money. Englewood Cliffs, N.J.: Prentice-Hall, 1980.

Bailey, Derrick. *Sex Relations in Religious Thought.* New York: Harper, 1959.

Bakwin, Harry. "Erotic Feelings in Infants and Young Children." *Medical Aspects of Human Sexuality* 10(1974):200.

Barclay, Andrew M. "Sexual Fantasies in Men and Women." *Medical Aspects of Human Sexuality* 7(1973):205–16.

Bardwick, Judith. *Psychology of Women: A Study of Biocultural Conflicts.* New York: Harper & Row, 1971.

Barr, M. L., and E. G. Bertram. "A Morphological Distinction between Neurones of the Male and Female, and the Behavior of the Nuclear Satellite during Accelerated Nucleoprotein Synthesis." *Nature* 163(1949):676–77.

Barrow, Georgia M., and Patricia A. Smith. *Aging: The Individual and Society.* 2d ed. St. Paul, Minn.: West Publishing, 1983.

Barry, Kathleen. *Female Sexual Slavery.* Englewood Cliffs, N.J.: Prentice-Hall, 1979.

Beach, Frank A., ed. *Human Sexuality in Four Perspectives.* Baltimore: Johns Hopkins Press, 1977.

Bell, Alan, and Martin Weinberg. *Homosexualities.* New York: Simon & Schuster, 1978.

Bell, Alan, Martin Weinberg, and Sue Hammersmith. *Sexual Preference.* Bloomington, Ind.: Indiana University Press, 1981.

Bell, Ruth. *Changing Bodies, Changing Lives.* New York: Random House, 1981.

Bem, Sandra. "Androgyny Versus the Tight Little Lives of Fluffy Women and Chesty Men." *Psychology Today* 4(1975a):58.

———. "Sex-Role Adaptability, One Consequence of Psychological Androgyny." *Journal of Personality and Social Psychology* (1975b):634–43.

Benenson, Abram. *Control of Communicable Diseases in Man.* 13th ed. Washington: American Public Health Association, 1980.

Bermant, G., and J. Davidson. *Biological Bases of Sexual Behavior.* New York: Harper & Row, 1974.

Berscheid, Ellen, and Elaine Walster. "Physical Attractiveness." In *Advances in Experimental Social Psychology,* edited by Leonard Berkowitz. New York: Academic Press, 1974.

———. *Interpersonal Attraction.* 2d ed. Reading, Mass.: Addison-Wesley, 1978.

Bettoli, E. "Herpes: Facts and Fallacies." *American Journal of Nursing* 6(1982):924–29.

Bieber, Irving. *Homosexuality: A Psychoanalytic Study.* New York: Basic Books, 1962.

Bloom, Mark. "Impotence in the Era of Sex Therapy." *Medical World News* 5(1977):37–50.

Bode, Janet. *Rape: Preventing It: Coping with the Legal, Medical, and Emotional Aftermath.* New York: Watts, 1978.

Boston Women's Health Book Collective. *Our Bodies, Ourselves.* 2d ed. New York: Simon & Schuster, 1976.

Botwin, Carol. *The Love Crisis.* New York: Bantam, 1980.

Brecher, Edward. *Sex Researchers.* Boston: Little, Brown, 1969.

Brenna, B., and J. R. Heilman. *The Complete Guide to Midwifery.* New York: Dutton, 1977.

Brennecke, John, and Robert Amick. *The Struggle for Significance.* Beverly Hills, Calif.: Glencoe Press, 1971.

Briddell, Dan, David Rimm, Glenn Caddy, Gil Krawitz, David Sholis, and Robert Wunderlin. "Effects of Alcohol and Cognitive Set on Sexual Arousal to Deviant Stimuli." *Journal of Abnormal Psychology* 4(1978):480–92.

Broderick, Carlfred. "The Case for Sexual Fidelity." *Medical Aspects of Human Sexuality* 9(1976):16–25.

Bronson, Gail. "King Leer, Sexual Pitches in Ads Becoming More Explicit and More Pervasive." *Wall Street Journal* 18 November 1980, p. 1.

Brooks, Betty W. *Self Defense and Rape* (pamphlet). Los Angeles County, 1980.

Brooks-Gunn, Jeanne, and Wendy S. Matthews. *He and She: How Children Develop Their Sex-Role Identity.* Englewood Cliffs, N.J.: Prentice-Hall, 1979.

Brownmiller, Susan. *Against Our Will.* New York: Random House, 1975.

Bruce, F. F. *Paul: Apostle of the Heart Set Free.* Grand Rapids, Minn.: Eerdmans, 1977.

Bullough, Verne L. *Sexual Variance in Society and History.* New York: John Wiley & Sons, 1976.

Burgess, Ann W., A. Nicholas Groth, Lynda Lytle Holmstrom, and Suzanne M. Sgroi. *Sexual Assault of Children and Adolescents.* Lexington, Mass.: D.C. Heath, 1978.

Bush, Patricia. *Drugs, Alcohol, and Sex.* New York: Robert March Publishers, 1980.

Byrne, Donn. "A Pregnant Pause in the Sexual Revolution." *Psychology Today* 7(1977):67–68.

Carrera, Michael. *Sex: The Facts, the Acts, and Your Feelings.* New York: Crown, 1981.

Carrier, J. M. "Homosexual Behavior in Cross-Cultural Perspective." In *Homosexual Behavior,* edited by Judd Marmor. New York: Basic Books, 1980.

Castleman, Michael. "The Condom Comeback." *New Roots* (January/February 1980): 21–24.

Centers for Disease Control. *Morbidity and Mortality Weekly Report.* Washington, D.C.: U.S. Department of Health and Human Services, 29 June 1979.

———. "Teenage Childbearing and Abortion Patterns— United States, 1977." *Current Trends* 14(11 April 1980). Washington, D.C.: U.S. Department of Health and Human Services.

———. *Abortion Surveillance, Annual Summary, 1978.* Washington, D.C.: U.S. Department of Health and Human Services, November 1980.

———. *Annual Summary, 1980, Morbidity and Mortality Weekly Report.* Washington, D.C.: U.S. Department of Health and Human Services, September 1981.

———. *Morbidity and Mortality Weekly Report.* Washington, D.C.: U.S. Department of Health and Human Services, 22 January 1982.

———. *Morbidity and Mortality Weekly Report.* Washington, D.C.: U.S. Department of Health and Human Services, 4 June 1982.

———. *Morbidity and Mortality Weekly Report.* Washington, D.C.: U.S. Department of Health and Human Services, 30 July 1982.

———. "Rubella Prevention." *Morbidity and Mortality Weekly Report.* Washington, D.C.: U.S. Department of Health and Human Services, 8 June 1984.

———. *Morbidity and Mortality Weekly Report.* Washington, D.C.: U.S. Department of Health and Human Services, 22 June 1984.

Chamberlin, Robert. "Counseling Parents about Children's Sex Games." *Medical Aspects of Human Sexuality* 12(1974):4–5.

Cheetham, Juliet. *Unwanted Pregnancy and Counseling.* London: Routledge & Kegan Paul, 1977.

Cherniak, Donna, and Allan Feingold. *Birth Control Handbook.* 12th ed. Montreal: Montreal Health Press, 1975.

Chesser, E. *Love without Fear.* New York: New American Library, 1971.

Chiappa, Joseph, and Joseph Forish. *The VD Book.* New York: Holt, Rinehart & Winston, 1976.

Chiazze, L. et al. "The Length and Variability of the Human Menstrual Cycle." *Journal of the American Medical Association* 203(1968):377–80.

Child Welfare League of America. *Standards for Services for Unmarried Parents.* New York: Child Welfare League of America, 1976.

Christopherson, William. "Effect of Earlier Coitus on Cervical Cancer." *Medical Aspects of Human Sexuality* 8(1981):94.

Cline, V. B., ed. *Where Do You Draw the Line? An Exploration into Media Violence, Pornography, and Censorship.* Provo, Utah: Brigham Young University Press, 1974.

Cohen, Monroe. *Growing Free.* Washington, D.C.: Association for Childhood Education International, 1976.

Cohn, Michael, David Raphling, and Phillip Green. "Psychological Aspects of the Maltreatment Syndrome of Childhood." *Journal of Pediatrics* 2(1966):279–84.

Coldsmith, Don. "My Most Unusual Sexual Case: Extreme Sexual Innocence." *Medical Aspects of Human Sexuality* 11(1979):126.

Cole, William. *Sex and Love in the Bible.* Chicago: Association (Follett), 1957.

Coleman, J. C. *Abnormal Psychology and Modern Life.* 4th ed. Chicago: Scott, 1972.

Coleman, S., and P. Piotrow. "Spermicides: Simplicity and Safety Are Major Assets." *Population Reports,* September 1979.

Comarr, A. Estin. "Sex among Patients with Spinal Cord and/or Cauda Equina Injuries." *Medical Aspects of Human Sexuality* 3(1973):222–38.

Comfort, Alex. *The Joy of Sex.* New York: Simon & Schuster, 1972.

Commission on Obscenity and Pornography. *The Report of the Commission on Obscenity and Pornography.* New York: Bantam, 1970.

"Condoms." *Consumer Reports* 10(1979):583–89.

Connell, Elizabeth B. "Various Types of Intrauterine Devices." *Medical Aspects of Human Sexuality* 10(1977):15–24.

Connolly, Lisa. "Boy Fathers." *Human Behavior* 1(1978):40–43.

"Contraception: Comparing the Options." *FDA Consumer* 6(1977):7–15.

Cottrell, Thomas. "Sexual Problems of the Paraplegic." *Medical Aspects of Human Sexuality* 5(1975):167–68.

Criswell, Howard. "Why Do They Beat Their Child?" *Human Needs* 9(1973):5–9.

Cuber, John. "Sex in the Upper Middle Class." *Medical Aspects of Human Sexuality* 7(1974):8–34.

Curie-Cohen, M., M. L. Luttrell, and S. Shapiro. "Current Practice of Artificial Insemination by Donor in the United States." *New England Journal of Medicine* 306 (15 July 1979): 721–22.

Curry, Hayden, and Denis Clifford. *A Legal Guide for Lesbian and Gay Couples.* Reading, Mass.: Addison-Wesley, 1980.

Curry, Judith, and Kathryn Peppe. *Mental Retardation.* St. Louis: Mosby, 1978.

Dalton, Katherina. *Premenstrual Syndrome and Progesterone Therapy.* Chicago: Year Book Medical Publications, 1977.

Dank, Barry. "Coming Out in the Gay World." *Psychiatry* 34(1971):180–97.

————. "Why Homosexuals Marry Women." *Medical Aspects of Human Sexuality* 8(1972):14–23.

Davis, Bernard, Renato Dulbecco, Herman Eisen, and Harold Ginsberg. *Microbiology.* 3d ed. New York: Harper & Row, 1980.

Davis, E. G. *The First Sex.* Baltimore: Penguin Books, 1972.

Davis, Kingsley. "Extreme Social Isolation of a Child." *American Journal of Sociology* 3(1940):554–64.

Deisher, Robert. "Boys with Effeminate Mannerisms." *Medical Aspects of Human Sexuality* 12(1981):17–20.

————. "When Parents Learn Their Child Is Homosexual." *Medical Aspects of Human Sexuality* 6(1982):16U–16V.

Delp, H. "Sex Education for the Handicapped." *Journal of Special Education* 4(1971):363–64.

Deutsch, M., and L. Solomon. "Reactions to Evaluations by Others As Influenced by Self-Evaluations." *Sociometry* 22(1959):93–112.

DeVine, Raylene. "Discovering and Treating Sexual Abuse of Children." *Medical Aspects of Human Sexuality* 10(1980):25–26.

Dickes, R. "Psychodynamics of Fetishism." *Medical Aspects of Human Sexuality* 1(1970):39–52.

Dick-Read, G. *Childbirth without Fear.* 2d ed. New York: Harper & Row, 1959.

Disbrow, Mildred. "Parents Who Abuse Their Children." *Washington State Journal of Nursing* 13(1972):5–9.

Djerassi, Carl. *The Politics of Contraception.* New York: Norton, 1979.

Dolan, J. *Child Abuse.* New York: Watts, 1980.

Dorland's Medical Dictionary. 26th ed. Philadelphia: W. B. Saunders, 1981.

Douthwaite, Graham. *Unmarried Couples and the Law.* Indianapolis, Ind.: Allen Smith, 1979.

Dowling, Colette. *The Cinderella Complex, Women's Hidden Fear of Independence.* New York: Summit, 1981.

Dretler, Stephen. "Venereal Warts." *Medical Aspects of Human Sexuality* 15(July 1981):52b–52h.

Dudar, Helen. "America Discovers Child Pornography." *Ms.* 2(1977):45–47.

Dutton, Donald, and Arthur Aron. "Some Evidence for Heightened Sexual Attraction under Conditions of High Anxiety." *Journal of Personality and Social Psychology* 4(1974):510–17.

Dworkin, Andrea. *Pornography, Men Possessing Women.* New York: Perigee, 1981.

Dyer, Wayne W. *Your Erroneous Zones.* New York: Funk & Wagnalls, 1976.

———. *Pulling Your Own Strings.* New York: Funk & Wagnalls, 1978.

———. *The Sky's the Limit.* New York: Simon & Schuster, 1980.

Earls, Felton. "Problems of Adolescent Fathers." *Medical Aspects of Human Sexuality* 7(1981):14.

Ehrhardt, Anke. *Genetic Mechanisms of Sexual Development.* New York: Academic Press, 1979.

Ehrhardt, Anke, and Heino Meyer-Bahlburg. "Effects of Prenatal Sex Hormones on Gender-Related Behavior." *Science* 4488(1981):1312–13.

Eiger, Marian S., and Sally W. Olds. *The Complete Book of Breastfeeding.* New York: Workman Publishing, 1972.

Eller, Vernard. *Private Communication.* LaVerne, Calif.: University of LaVerne, 1982.

Ellis, Albert. *Growth through Reason.* Palo Alto, Calif.: Science & Behavior Books, 1971.

Ellis, Havelock. *Studies in the Psychology of Sex.* 2 vols. New York: Random House, 1942.

Epstein, Louis M. *Sex Laws and Customs of Judaism.* New York: Bloch Publishing, 1948. Reprint. New York: Ktav Publishing House, 1967.

Erikson, Erik. *Childhood and Society.* New York: Norton, 1950.

Farkas, Gary M., and Raymond C. Rosen. "Effect of Alcohol on Elicited Male Sexual Response." *Journal of Studies on Alcohol* 3(1976):265–71.

Farley, Margaret. "Sexual Ethics." In *Encyclopedia of Bioethics,* vol. 4, edited by Warren Reich. New York: Free Press (Macmillan), 1978.

Fawcett, J. W., ed. *Psychological Perspectives on Population.* New York: Basic Books, 1973.

Federation of Feminist Women's Health Centers. *A New View of a Woman's Body.* Touchstone Book. New York: Simon & Schuster, 1981.

Feldman, Philip M. "Extramarital Sex As a Substitute for Communication." *Medical Aspects of Human Sexuality* 4(1981):52k–52x.

Finch, Stuart. "Viewing Other-Sex Genitals." *Medical Aspects of Human Sexuality* 1(1982):72.

Finkelhor, David. *Sexually Victimized Children.* New York: Free Press, 1979.

Fisher, S. *The Female Orgasm.* New York: Basic Books, 1973.

Fisher, William A., and Donn Byrne. "Sex Differences in Response to Erotica? Love Versus Lust." *Journal of Personality and Social Psychology* 2(1978):117–25.

Fletcher, Joseph. *Situation Ethics: The New Morality.* Philadelphia: Westminster Press, 1966.

Fogarty, Thomas. "Sexual Estrangement in Marriage." *Medical Aspects of Human Sexuality* 4(1977):122–35.

Ford, C. S., and F. A. Beach. *Patterns of Sexual Behavior.* New York: Harper & Brothers, 1952.

Forward, Susan, and Craig Buck. *Betrayal of Innocence, Incest and Its Devastation.* Los Angeles: J. P. Tarcher, 1978.

Fox, Lynn. *Women and Mathematics.* Washington: National Institute of Education, 1977.

Fraker, S. "Crackdown on Porn." *Newsweek* 9(1977):21–27.

Freud, Sigmund. *Three Essays on the Theory of Sexuality.* London: Hogarth, 1905.

———. *Selected Papers on Hysteria and Other Psychoneurosis.* Reprint. New York: Harcourt Brace Jovanovich, 1912.

———. *The Ego and the Id.* London: Hogarth, 1927.

———. *The Standard Edition of the Complete Psychological Works.* Edited by J. Strachey. London: Hogarth, 1953.

Friedmann, T. "Prenatal Diagnosis of Genetic Disease." *Scientific American* 225(1971):34–42.

Fromm, Erich. *The Art of Loving.* New York: Harper & Row, 1956.

Fromme, Allan. *The Ability to Love.* New York: Pocket Books, 1965.

Gagnon, John. "Sex Research and Social Change." *Archives of Sexual Behavior* 4(1975):111–41.

———. *Human Sexualities.* Glenview, Ill.: Scott, Foresman, 1977.

Gagnon, John, and William Simon. *Sexual Conduct: The Social Sources of Human Sexuality.* Chicago: Aldine, 1973.

Ganzfield, Solomon, ed. *Code of Jewish Law.* Revised edition translated by Hyman E. Goldbin. New York: Hebrew Publishing Co., 1961.

Gardner, Ernest. *Fundamentals of Neurology.* 6th ed. Philadelphia: W. B. Saunders, 1975.

Gardner, Richard A. "Exposing Children to Parental Nudity." *Medical Aspects of Human Sexuality* 6(1975):99.

Garrison, R. J., V. E. Anderson, and S. C. Reed. "Assortative Marriage." *Eugenics Quarterly* 15(1968):113–27.

Gay, George R., and Charles W. Sheppard. "Sex in the 'Drug Culture.' " *Medical Aspects of Human Sexuality* 10(1972):28–50.

Gay, George R. et al. "Drug-Sex Practice in the Haight-Ashbury or 'The Sensuous Hippie.' " In *Sexual Behavior: Pharmacology and Bio-chemistry,* edited by M. Sandler and G. L. Gessa. New York: Raven Press, 1975.

Gebhard, Paul H. "Misconceptions about Female Prostitutes." *Medical Aspects of Human Sexuality* 3(1969):24–30.

———. "Fetishism and Sadomasochism." In *Sex Research: Studies from the Kinsey Institute,* edited by M. Weinberg. New York: Oxford University Press, 1976.

Gebhard, Paul H., John H. Gagnon, Wardell B. Pomeroy, and Cornelia V. Christenson. *Sex Offenders.* New York: Harper & Row, 1965.

Geiser, Robert. *Hidden Victims, The Sexual Abuse of Children.* Boston: Beacon Press, 1979.

Gelman, David et al. "Just How the Sexes Differ." *Newsweek* 20(1981):72–83.

Gerrard, Alice. *Please Breastfeed Your Baby.* New York: New American Library, 1971.

Gersh, Eileen S., and Isadore Gersh. *Biology of Women.* Baltimore: University Park Press, 1981.

Giarretto, Henry. "Humanistic Treatment of Father-Daughter Incest." In *The Sexual Victimology of Youth,* edited by Leroy Schultz. Springfield, Ill.: Charles C. Thomas, 1980.

Ginsburg, Kenneth N. "The 'Meat-Rack': A Study of the Male Homosexual Prostitute." In *Sexual Deviancy in Social Context,* edited by Clifton Bryant. New York: New Viewpoints/Franklin Watts, 1977.

Glenn, N. D. et al. "Has There Been a Resurgence of Fidelity?" *Medical Aspects of Human Sexuality* 4(1981):53–61.

Goldberg, Martin. "Counseling Couples after Infidelity." *Medical Aspects of Human Sexuality* 3(1981):33–39.

Goldstein, Bernard. *Human Sexuality.* New York: McGraw-Hill, 1976.

Gordon, Sol. *The Teenage Survival Book.* New York: Times Books, 1981.

Gottlieb, B. "Incest: Therapeutic Intervention in a Unique Form of Sexual Abuse." In *Rape and Sexual Assault,* edited by C. Warner. Germantown, Md.: Aspen Systems Corp., 1980.

Gould, R. A. *Living Archaeology.* New York: Cambridge University Press, 1980.

Gould, Robert et al. "Do Men Like Women to Be Sexually Assertive?" *Medical Aspects of Human Sexuality* 3(1977):36–51.

Green, C. P., and K. Poteteiger. "A Major Problem for Minors." *Society* 4(1978):8, 10–13.

Green, Richard. "Sexual Identity of 37 Children Raised by Homosexual or Transsexual Parents." *American Journal of Psychiatry* 135(June 1978):692–97.

Greenburg, Jerold S., and Francis X. Archamabault. "Masturbation and Self-Esteem." *Journal of Sex Research* 1(1973):41–51.

Greene, Gerald, and Caroline Greene. *Sado-Masochism: The Last Taboo.* New York: Ballantine, 1974.

Gregg, Sandra R. "Tailoring Contraceptives to Patients." *Medical World News* 4 (16 February 1981):47–61.

Gross, Leonard H., and Robert D. Hershberger. "Sexual Dysfunction, Sorting Out the Body-Mind Mix." *Medical World News* 21(12 October 1981):56–71.

Groth, A. Nicholas. *Men Who Rape.* New York: Plenum, 1979.

Gunderson, M. P. "The Effects of Sex Education on Sex Information, Sexual Attitudes, and Behavior." Master's thesis, University of Houston, 1976.

Gusberg, Saul. "Promiscuity and Cervical Cancer." *Medical Aspects of Human Sexuality* 9(1981):44.

Haeberle, Erwin J. *The Sex Atlas.* New York: Seabury Press, 1978.

Halas, Celia. *Why Can't a Woman Be More Like a Man?* New York: Macmillan, 1981.

Halleck, Charles et al. "Viewpoints: Should Prostitution Be Legalized?" *Medical Aspects of Human Sexuality* 4(1974):54–83.

Hamilton, Richard. *The Herpes Book.* Los Angeles, Calif.: J. P. Tarcher, 1980.

Handy, Willowdean. *Forever the Land of Men.* New York: Dodd, Mead, 1965.

Hannan, Thomas, and Michael Fulks. *A Basic Handbook on Birth Control and Reproductive Physiology.* Davis, Calif.: University of California, Davis, 1976.

Harlow, H., M. Harlow, and S. Suomi. "From Thought to Therapy, Lessons from a Primate Laboratory." *American Scientist* 5(1971):539–49.

Harrison, Saul. "Children's Exposure to Parental Intercourse." *Medical Aspects of Human Sexuality* 9(1976):115.

Hass, Aaron. *Teenage Sexuality.* New York: Macmillan, 1979.

Hatcher, Geri. Supervisor, Child Sexual Abuse Project, Los Angeles County, Department of Public Social Services. Public lecture. Mount San Antonio College, Walnut, California, 12 May 1980.

Hatcher, Robert, Felicia Guest, Felicia Stewart, Gary Stewart, James Trussell, and Erica Frank. *Contraceptive Technology, 1982–1983.* 11th ed. New York: Irvington, 1982.

———. *Contraceptive Technology, 1984–1985.* 12th ed. New York: Irvington, 1984.

Hatterer, Lawrence. *The Pleasure Addicts.* New York: A. S. Barnes, 1980.

Hecht, Annabel. "Vaginal Contraceptives: Available But—." *FDA Consumer* 1(1980):29–30.

Heiman, Julia R. "Women's Sexual Arousal—The Physiology of Erotica." *Psychology Today* 11(1975):91–94.

Herjanic, Barbara. "Advising Children about Child Molesters." *Medical Aspects of Human Sexuality* 6(1980):51–52.

Herman, Judith, and Lisa Hirschman. *Father-Daughter Incest.* Cambridge, Mass.: Harvard University Press, 1981.

Hershberger, Ruth. *Adam's Rib.* New York: Pellegrini and Cudahy, 1948.

Heston, L., and J. Shields. "Homosexuality in Twins." *Archives of General Psychiatry* 18(1968):149–60.

Hetherington, E. Mavis, and Ross D. Parke. *Child Psychology: A Contemporary View.* 2d ed. New York: McGraw-Hill, 1979.

Hettlinger, Richard. *Human Sexuality, A Psychosocial Perspective.* Belmont, Calif.: Wadsworth, 1974.

Hicks, Dorothy J. "Viewpoints—What Should a Woman Do When Threatened with Rape?" *Medical Aspects of Human Sexuality* 10(April 1978):136.

Hite, Shere. *The Hite Report.* New York: Macmillan, 1976.

———. *The Hite Report on Male Sexuality.* New York: Alfred A. Knopf, 1981.

Hofmann, Adele. "Guiding the Adolescent Female toward Her Yes or No Decision." *Medical Aspects of Human Sexuality* 7(1981):56–65.

Hole, John W., Jr. *Human Anatomy and Physiology.* 2d ed. Dubuque, Iowa: William C. Brown, 1981.

Hooper, Judith. "Feminism and the Brain." *OMNI* 10(1981):35.

Hoyt, Michael. "Children's Accidental Exposure to Parental Coitus." *Medical Aspects of Human Sexuality* 1(1982):64–65.

Humphreys, Laud. *Out of the Closets.* Englewood Cliffs, N.J.: Prentice-Hall, 1972.

Humphreys, Laud, and Brian Miller. "Identities in the Emerging Gay Culture." In *Homosexual Behavior,* edited by Judd Marmor. New York: Basic Books, 1980.

Hunt, B., and M. Hunt. *Prime Time: A Guide to the Pleasure and Opportunities of the New Middle Age.* New York: Stein & Day, 1975.

Hunt, C. *Males and Females.* Baltimore: Penguin Books, 1972.

Hunt, Morton. *Sexual Behavior in the 1970s.* Chicago: Playboy Press, 1974.

———. *Gay.* New York: Farrar, Straus & Giroux, 1977.

Hutchison, J. B. *Biological Determinants of Sexual Behavior.* New York: John Wiley & Sons, 1978.

Ismach, Judy. "Health Hazards of Homosexuals." *Medical World News* 24(23 November 1981):56–57.

Jaffe, A. C. "Child Molestation." *Medical Aspects of Human Sexuality* 4(1976):73, 96.

James, Jennifer. "Prostitute-Pimp Relationship." *Medical Aspects of Human Sexuality* 11(1973):147–63.

———. "Answers to the 20 Questions Most Frequently Asked about Prostitutes." In *The Politics of Prostitution.* Seattle, Wash.: Social Research Associates, 1977a.

———. "Women As Sexual Criminals and Victims." In *Sexual Scripts,* edited by Judith Laws and Pepper Schwartz. Hinsdale, Ill.: Dryden Press, 1977b.

James J., J. Withers, M. Haft, S. Theiss, and M. Own. *The Politics of Prostitution.* Seattle, Wash.: Social Research Associates, 1975.

Janerich, D. T., J. M. Piper, and D. M. Glebatis. "Oral Contraceptives and Congenital Limb-Reduction Defects." *New England Journal of Medicine* 291(1974):697–700.

Jensen, Gordon D. "Teenagers' Fears That They Are Homosexual." *Medical Aspects of Human Sexuality* 5(1981):47–48.

Johnson, Martin H., and Barry J. Everitt. *Essential Reproduction.* Boston: Blackwell Scientific Publications, 1980.

Jones, Hardin B., and Helen C. Jones. *Sensual Drugs.* New York: Cambridge University Press, 1977.

Jones, Kenneth L., Louis W. Shainberg, and Curtis O. Byer. *Health Science.* 4th ed. New York: Harper & Row, 1978.

Jones, Kenneth L., and D. W. Smith. "Recognition of the Fetal Alcohol Syndrome in Early Infancy." *Lancet* 2(3 November 1973):999–1001.

Judson, Franklin. "Prevalence of Gonorrhea among Homosexuals." *Medical Aspects of Human Sexuality* 8(1981):91.

Kallman, Franz. "Comparative Twin Study on the Genetic Aspects of Male Homosexuality." *Journal of Nervous and Mental Disease* 4(1952):283–98.

Kaminer, Wendy. "A Woman's Guide to Porno and the Law." *The Nation* 24(21 June 1980):754–56.

Kantner, J. F., and M. Zelnick. "Contraception and Pregnancy: Experience of Young Unmarried Women in the U.S." *Family Planning Perspectives* 1(1973):21–35.

Kaplan, A. *The Conduct of Inquiry: Methodology for Behavioral Science.* San Francisco: Chandler, 1964.

Kaplan, Helen. *The New Sex Therapy.* New York: Times Books, 1974.

———. As quoted by Mark Bloom in "Impotence in the Era of Sex Therapy." *Medical World News* 5 (7 March 1977):37–50.

———. *Disorders of Sexual Desire.* New York: Simon & Schuster, 1979.

Karacan, Ismet. "Advances in the Diagnosis of Erectile Impotence." *Medical Aspects of Human Sexuality* 5(1978):85–97.

Katchadourian, H. A., and D. T. Lunde. *Fundamentals of Human Sexuality.* 3d ed. New York: Holt, Rinehart & Winston, 1980.

Kelly, Gary E. *Sexuality: The Human Perspective.* Woodbury, N.Y.: Barrons, 1980.

Kempe, Ruth S., and C. Henry Kempe. *Child Abuse.* Cambridge, Mass.: Harvard University Press, 1978.

Kempton, Winifred. *Guidelines for Planning a Training Course on the Subject of Human Sexuality and the Retarded.* Philadelphia: Planned Parenthood Association, 1974.

Kestenbaum, Clarice. "Sex Among Very Young Middle-Class Adolescents." *Medical Aspects of Human Sexuality* 2(1978):164–77.

Key, Wilson Bryan. *Subliminal Seduction.* New York: Signet, 1972.

———. *Media Sexploitation.* New York: Signet, 1976.

———. *The Clam-Plate Orgy: And Other Subliminal Techniques for Manipulating Your Behavior.* New York: Signet, 1980.

Kilbourne, Jean. "Images of Women in TV Commercials." In *TV Book,* edited by Judy Fireman. New York: Workman, 1977.

Kinsey, Alfred C., W. Pomeroy, and C. Martin. *Sexual Behavior in the Human Male.* Philadelphia: W. B. Saunders, 1948.

———. *Sexual Behavior in the Human Female.* Philadelphia: W. B. Saunders, 1953.

Kirkendall, Lester. *Sex Education* (SIECUS study guide no. 1). New York: Sex Information and Education Council of the United States, 1965.

Klaus, M., and J. Kennel. *Journal of Maternal Infant Bonding.* St. Louis: Mosby, 1976.

Klinger, Eric. *Structure and Function of Fantasy.* New York: Wiley-Interscience, 1979.

Koff, Wayne C. "Marijuana and Sexual Activity." *Journal of Sex Research* 3(1974):194–204.

Kohlberg, Lawrence. "Development of Moral Character and Moral Ideology." In *Review of Child Development Research,* vol. I, edited by M. L. Hoffman and L. W. Hoffman. New York: Russell Sage Foundation, 1964.

———. "Continuities in Childhood and Adult Moral Development Revisited." In *Lifespan Developmental Psychology: Personality and Socialization,* edited by P. B. Baltes and K. W. Schaie. New York: Academy Press, 1973.

Komisaruk, Richard. "Clinical Evaluation of Child Abuse-Scarred Families." *Juvenile Court Judges Journal* 2(1966):66–70.

Krajeski, James. "Identifying Homosexuals by Mannerisms." *Medical Aspects of Human Sexuality* 7(1981):52.

Kreitler, Peter. *Affair Prevention.* New York: Macmillan, 1981.

Kroop, Merle. "Are Frigid Women Capable of Love?" *Medical Aspects of Human Sexuality* 12(1977):41–50.

Kuiper, B. K. *The Church in History.* Grand Rapids, Minn.: Eerdmans, 1952.

LaLeche International. *The Womanly Art of Breastfeeding.* Franklin Park, Ill.: LaLeche International, 1973.

Langmyhr, George J. "Varieties of Coital Positions: Advantages and Disadvantages." *Medical Aspects of Human Sexuality* 6(1976):128–39.

———. "Reciprocity in Sexual Problems." *Medical Aspects of Human Sexuality* 9(1977):7–21.

Laurence, K. M. "Fetal Malformations and Abnormalities." *The Lancet* 6(1974):939–42.

Lein, Allen. *The Cycling Female, Her Menstrual Rhythm.* San Francisco: Freeman, 1979.

Lemere, Frederick, and James E. Smith. "Alcohol-Induced Sexual Impotence." *American Journal of Psychiatry* 2(1973):212–13.

Leo, John. "The New Scarlet Letter." *Time* 5(2 August 1982):62–66.

Levin, Robert, and Amy Levin. "Sexual Pleasure: The Surprising Preferences of 100,000 Women." *Redbook Magazine* 9(1975):51–58.

Levinger, C. "Husbands' and Wives' Estimates of Coital Frequency." *Medical Aspects of Human Sexuality* 9(1970):42–57.

Liebert, Robert, John Neale, and Emily Davidson. *The Early Window: Effects of Television on Children and Youth.* New York: Pergamon Press, 1973.

Lief, Harold. "Controversies over Female Orgasm." *Medical Aspects of Human Sexuality* 4(1977):136–38.

Lincoln, G. A. "Luteinizing Hormone and Testosterone in Man." *Nature* 252(1974):232–33.

Lindemann, Constance. *Birth Control and Unmarried Young Women.* New York: Springer, 1974.

Lipman, Timothy. "Sexual Transmission of Enteric Disease." *Medical Aspects of Human Sexuality* 9(1981):44–45.

Lloyd, Robin. *For Money or Love: Boy Prostitution.* New York: Vanguard Press, 1976.

Lobsenz, Norman M. "What You Can—and Can't—Learn from the New Hite Report." *Family Circle* (22 September 1981):12.

London, Perry. "Sexual Behavior." In *Encyclopedia of Bioethics,* vol. 4, edited by Warren Reich. New York: Free Press (Macmillan), 1978.

LoPiccolo, Joseph, and Leslie LoPiccolo, eds. *Handbook of Sex Therapy.* New York: Plenum, 1978.

Lyons, M. F. "Sex Chromatin and Gene Action in the Mammalian X-Chromosome." *American Journal of Human Genetics* 14(1962):135–48.

McBride, Gail. "Putting a Better Cap on the Cervix." *Journal of the American Medical Association* 16 (25 April 1980):1617–18.

McCarthy, Barry. "First Intercourse Experiences." *Medical Aspects of Human Sexuality* 10(1979):6–18.

McCarthy, Michelle. *Relating.* Dubuque, Iowa: William C. Brown, 1981.

McCary, James, and Stephen McCary. *McCary's Human Sexuality.* 4th ed. Belmont, Calif.: Wadsworth, 1982.

Maccoby, E. E., and C. N. Jacklin. *The Psychology of Sex Differences.* Stanford, Calif.: Stanford University Press, 1974.

McConnell, James V. *Understanding Human Behavior.* 3d ed. New York: Holt, Rinehart & Winston, 1980.

MacDonald, John. *Rape Offenders and Their Victims.* Springfield, Ill.: Charles C. Thomas, 1971.

McDonald, Paula, and Dick McDonald. *Loving Free.* New York: Grosset & Dunlap, 1973.

McGuire, L., and N. Wagner. "Sexual Dysfunction in Women Who Were Molested As Children: One Response Pattern and Suggestions for Treatment." *Journal of Sex and Marital Therapy* 4(1978):11–15.

McKean, Kevin. "Closing in on the Herpes Virus." *Discover* 10(1981):75–78.

MacLusky, Neil, and Frederick Naftolin. "Sexual Differentiation of the Central Nervous System." *Science* 4488(20 March 1981):1294–1303.

McNeil, Elton B. *The Psychology of Being Human.* New York: Harper & Row, 1974.

Maddox, Brenda. *Married and Gay.* New York: Harcourt Brace Jovanovich, 1982.

Maletzky, Barry. "Why Homosexuals Marry." *Medical Aspects of Human Sexuality* 6(1982):16–17.

Marmor, Judd. "Some Considerations Concerning Orgasm in the Female." *Psychosomatic Medicine* 16(1954):240–45.

Marmor, Judd, ed. *Homosexual Behavior.* New York: Basic Books, 1980.

Marmor, Judd et al. "What Distinguishes 'Healthy' from 'Sick' Sexual Behavior." *Medical Aspects of Human Sexuality* 10(1977):67–77.

Marwick, Charles. "The Epic of Hepatitis B." *Medical World News* 22(26 October 1981):50–62.

Maslow, A. H. *Motivation and Personality.* New York: Harper & Row, 1954.

Masters, William. "First Night Disasters." *Playboy* 7(1978).

Masters, William, and Virginia Johnson. *Human Sexual Response.* Boston: Little, Brown, 1966.

———. *Human Sexual Inadequacy.* Boston: Little, Brown, 1970.

———. *The Pleasure Bond.* Boston: Little, Brown, 1975.

———. *Homosexuality in Perspective.* Boston: Little, Brown, 1979.

Masters, William, Virginia Johnson, and Robert Kolodny. *Human Sexuality.* Boston: Little, Brown, 1982.

Mattinson, J. *Marriage and Mental Handicap.* Pittsburgh: University of Pittsburgh Press, 1970.

Maxwell, J. W., A. R. Sack, R. B. Frary, and J. F. Keller. "Factors Influencing Contraceptive Behavior of Single College Students." *Journal of Sex and Marital Therapy* 4(Winter 1977):265–73.

May, Rollo. *Love and Will.* New York: Norton, 1969.

Mayer, Nancy. *The Male Mid-Life Crisis.* Garden City, N.Y.: Doubleday, 1978.

Mayle, Peter. *Where Did I Come From?* New York: Lyle Stuart, 1973.

Mead, Margaret. *Male and Female.* New York: Morrow, 1949.

———. *Jealousy: Primitive and Civilized.* In *The Anatomy of Love,* edited by A. M. Krich. New York: Dell, 1960.

———. *Sex and Temperament in Three Primitive Societies.* New York: Morrow, 1963.

Meiselman, Karin C. *Incest, A Psychological Study of Causes and Effects with Treatment Recommendations.* San Francisco: Jossey-Bass, 1979.

Menninger, Karl. *Love Against Hate.* New York: Harcourt Brace and World, 1942.

Michael, R., R. Bonsall, and P. Warner. "Human Vaginal Secretions: Volatile Fatty Content." *Science* 186(1974):1217–19.

Miller, Howard L., and Paul S. Siegel. *Loving: A Psychological Approach.* New York: John Wiley & Sons, 1972.

Miller, Warren B. "Sexual and Contraceptive Behavior in Young Unmarried Women." In *Psychomatic Obstetrics and Gynecology,* edited by David B. Youngs and Anke A. Ehrhardt. New York: Appleton-Century-Crofts, 1980.

Money, John. "Genetic and Chromosomal Aspects of Homosexual Etiology." In *Homosexual Behavior,* edited by Judd Marmor. New York: Basic Books, 1980a.

————. *Love and Lovesickness.* Baltimore: Johns Hopkins Press, 1980b.

Money, John, and Anke Ehrhardt. *Man and Woman, Boy and Girl.* Baltimore: Johns Hopkins Press, 1972.

Moody, Paul Amos. *Genetics of Man.* New York: Norton, 1975.

Mooney, T. O., T. M. Cole, and R. A. Chilgren. *Sexual Options for Paraplegics and Quadriplegics.* Boston: Little, Brown, 1975.

Morris, Jan. *Conundrum.* New York: New American Library, 1974.

Mourad, Mahmoud, and Wu Shung Chiu. "Marital-Sexual Adjustment of Amputees." *Medical Aspects of Human Sexuality* 2(1974):47–57.

Murstein, Bernard I. "The Relationship of Mental Health to Marital Choice and Courtship Progress." *Journal of Marriage and Family* 29(1967):447–51.

————. *Love, Sex, and Marriage through the Ages.* New York: Springer, 1974.

Myers, Wayne A. "The Primal Scene: Exposure to Parental Intercourse." *Medical Aspects of Human Sexuality* 9(1974):156.

National Center for Health Statistics. "Contraceptive Utilization in the United States: 1973 and 1976." *Advancedata.* U.S. Department of Health and Human Services, no. 36, 18 August 1978.

————. "Wanted and Unwanted Births Reported by Mothers 15–44 Years of Age: United States, 1976." *Advancedata.* U.S. Department of Health and Human Services, no. 56, 24 January 1980.

————. "Induced Terminations of Pregnancy: Reporting States, 1977 and 1978." *Monthly Vital Statistics Report.* U.S. Department of Health and Human Services, vol. 30, no. 6, supplement 1, 28 September 1981.

————. *Monthly Vital Statistics Report.* U.S. Department of Health and Human Services, vol. 30, no. 13, 20 December 1982.

————. "Final Marriage Statistics for 1981." *Monthly Vital Statistics Report.* U.S. Department of Health and Human Services, vol. 32, no. 11, 29 February 1984.

"Natural Birth Control: 1% Pregnancy Rate—or 27%?" *Medical World News* 24(24 November 1980):13.

Neckes, Marilyn, and Theresa Lynch. "Cost Analysis of the Enforcement of Prostitution Laws in San Francisco." Women's Jail Project, Unitarian Universalist Service Committee, 1978. (As cited by Kathleen Barry in *Female Sexual Slavery.* Englewood Cliffs, N.J.: Prentice-Hall, 1979.)

Neier, Aryeh. "The First Amendment, Freedom of Speech Versus Censorship." *Current* 225(1980):45–49.

Newton, N. "Interrelationships between Sexual Responsiveness, Birth, and Breastfeeding." In *Contemporary Sexual Behavior—Critical Issues in the 1970s,* edited by J. Zubin and J. Money. Baltimore: Johns Hopkins Press, 1973.

Oakley, Ann. *Sex, Gender, and Society.* London: Maurice Temple Smith, 1972.

————. *The Sociology of Housework.* New York: Pantheon Books, 1974a.

————. *Woman's Work.* New York: Pantheon Books, 1974b.

O'Connor, John J. "Sex Roles in Advertising Draw Hisses and Boos." *Advertising Age* 11(12 March 1979):48.

Oettinger, Katherine. *Not My Daughter.* Englewood Cliffs, N.J.: Prentice-Hall, 1979.

Offit, Avodah. "Common Causes of Female Orgasm Problems." *Medical Aspects of Human Sexuality* 8(1977):40–48.

Olds, Linda. *Fully Human.* Englewood Cliffs, N.J.: Prentice-Hall, 1981.

Orr, Donald. "Child's Sex Play." *Medical Aspects of Human Sexuality* 12(1981):28.

Orvin, George. "Discussing Sex with Teenagers." *Medical Aspects of Human Sexuality* 11(1981):13.

Ory, H. W., A. Rosenfeld, and L. Landman. "The Pill at 20: An Assessment." *Family Planning Perspectives* 12(1980):278–83.

Packard, Vance. *The Sexual Wilderness.* New York: David McKay, 1968.

Paddack, Charles. "Children's Possession of Pornography." *Medical Aspects of Human Sexuality* 7(1981):19.

Paige, K. E. "The Ritual of Circumcision." *Human Nature* (May 1978):40–48.

Paluszny, Maria. "Fear of Homosexuality As a Cause of Marriage." *Medical Aspects of Human Sexuality* 5(1982):63.

Papalia, Diane E., and Sally W. Olds. *A Child's World: Infancy through Adolescence.* 2d ed. New York: McGraw-Hill, 1979.

Parker, S. "The Precultural Basis of the Incest Taboo." *American Anthropologist* 2(1976):285–305.

Pattison, E. Mansell. "Effeminate Boys." *Medical Aspects of Human Sexuality* 2(1982a):19.

———. "Sissies and Tomboys." *Medical Aspects of Human Sexuality* 3(1982b):95.

Peele, Stanton. *Love and Addiction.* New York: Signet, 1976.

Pepmiller, Earl. "How the Handicapped Make Love." *Sexology Today* 9(1980):30–34.

Perry, John, and Beverly Whipple. "Diagnostic, Therapeutic, and Research Applications of the Vaginal Myograph." Presentation at the meeting of the American Association of Sex Educators, Counselors, and Therapists, Washington, D.C., 6 March 1980.

Peters, Joseph. "Children Who Are Victims of Sexual Assault and the Psychology of Offenders." *American Journal of Psychotherapy* 30(1976):398–421.

Peters, Joseph, and Robert Sadoff. "Clinical Observations on Child Molesters." *Medical Aspects of Human Sexuality* 4(1970):20–32.

Petersen, James R., Kevin Cook, Arthur Kretchmer, Barbara Nellis, Janet Lever, and Rosanna Hertz. "The Playboy Readers' Sex Survey." Parts I-III. *Playboy* 2(1983):108–250; 3(1983):90–184; 5(1983):126–220.

Pfeiffer, E., A. Verwoerdt, and G. C. Davis. "Sexual Behavior in Middle Life." *American Journal of Psychiatry* 128(1972):10, 82–87.

Phillips, Debora. *How to Fall Out of Love.* New York: Fawcett, 1980.

"The Pill's Vindication: How Solid?" *Medical World News* 24(24 November 1980): 10–12.

Pogrebin, Letty Cottin. *Growing Up Free.* New York: McGraw-Hill, 1980.

———. "Good-bye to Sissies and Tomboys." *Next* 1(1981):96–100.

———. "Big Changes in Parenting." *Ms.* 8(1982):41–46.

Pomeroy, Wardell. "Normal Versus Abnormal Sex." *Sexology* 32(1966):436–39.

———. *Dr. Kinsey and the Institute for Sex Research.* New York: Harper & Row, 1972.

———. *Your Child and Sex.* New York: Dell, 1976.

Pope, Kenneth S. *On Love and Loving.* New York: Jossey-Bass, 1980.

Population Reference Bureau. "Teen Pregnancy #1 U.S. Health Problem." *Intercom* 10(October 1976):2.

———. *World Population Data Sheet, 1982.* Washington, D.C.: Population Reference Bureau, 1982.

Powell, Barbara. *How to Raise a Successful Daughter.* Chicago: Nelson-Hall, 1979.

Powell, John. *Why Am I Afraid to Tell You Who I Am?* Niles, Ill.: Argus Communications, 1969.

Poznanski, Elva, and Peter Blos. "Incest." *Medical Aspects of Human Sexuality* 10(1975):46–76.

Prager, Emily, and Edward Chaflin. "Prostitution: Conversations with People in 'The Life'." *Viva* 11(1976):9–10.

Pritchard, Jack A., and Paul C. MacDonald. *Williams Obstetrics.* 16th ed. New York: Appleton-Century-Crofts, 1984.

Pryor, Karen. *Nursing Your Baby.* New York: Harper & Row, 1963.

Purtilo, David T. *A Survey of Human Diseases.* Menlo Park, Calif.: Addison-Wesley, 1978.

Racy, John. "Ten Misuses of Sex." *Medical Aspects of Human Sexuality* 2(1971):136–45.

Raths, Louis, Merrill Harmin, and Sidney Simon. *Values and Teaching.* 2d ed. Columbus, Ohio: Charles E. Merrill, 1978.

Reich, Warren T., ed. *Encyclopedia of Bioethics.* Vol. 4. New York: Free Press, 1978.

Reichlin, S. Seymour. "Relationships of the Pituitary Gland to Human Sexual Behavior." *Medical Aspects of Human Sexuality* 2(1971):146–54.

Rekers, George. "Childhood Sexual Identity Disorders." *Medical Aspects of Human Sexuality* 3(1981):141–42.

Renshaw, Domeena C. "Sexuality and Depression in Infancy, Childhood, and Adolescence." *Medical Aspects of Human Sexuality* 6(1975):24.

———. "Drugs and Sex." *Nursing Care* 2(1978):16–19.

Renshaw, Domeena C., and Sybil J. Circle. "Escalation of Sexual Problems into Marital Rupture." *Medical Aspects of Human Sexuality* 3(1981):105–16.

Rhymes, Douglas. *No New Morality.* London: Constable, 1964.

Riess, Bernard. "Psychological Tests in Homosexuality." In *Homosexual Behavior,* edited by Judd Marmor. New York: Basic Books, 1980.

Rinehart, W. "Postcoital Contraception: An Appraisal." *Population Reports,* Series J (9), January 1976.

Ritter, Bruce, and Bob Weinstein. "The Tragedy of Teenage Prostitution." *Senior Scholastic* 2 (8 February 1979):20–21.

Robbins, E. S. et al. "Sex and Arson: Is There a Relationship?" *Medical Aspects of Human Sexuality* 10(1969):57–64.

Robertson, Ian. *Sociology.* New York: Worth, 1977.

Rogers, Dorothy. *The Adult Years.* Englewood Cliffs, N.J.: Prentice-Hall, 1979.

Rosenberg, Lynn et al. "Oral Contraceptive Use in Relation to Nonfatal Myocardial Infarction." *American Journal of Epidemiology* 111(1980):59–66.

Rossman, Parker. "The Pederasts." *Society* 10(1973):29.

Rothchild, Ellen. "Answering Young Children's Sex Questions." *Medical Aspects of Human Sexuality* 12(1975):23.

Rubin, Robert, June Reinisch, and Roger Haskett. "Postnatal Gonadal Steroid Effects on Human Behavior." *Science* 4488(20 March 1981):1318–24.

Rush, Florence. *The Best-Kept Secret: Sexual Abuse of Children.* Englewood Cliffs, N.J.: Prentice-Hall, 1980.

Sagarin, Edward. "Incest." *Journal of Sex Research* 2(1977):126–35.

Saghir, Marcel, and Eli Robins. *Male and Female Homosexuality.* Baltimore: Williams & Wilkins, 1973.

Saltz, Glenn. "Cervical Infection by *Chlamydia trachomatis* in Female Adolescents." *Medical Aspects of Human Sexuality* 8(1981):127–28.

Salzman, Leon. "Latent Homosexuality." In *Homosexual Behavior,* edited by Judd Marmor. New York: Basic Books, 1980.

Sarafino, E. P. "An Estimate of Nationwide Incidence of Sexual Offenses against Children." *Child Welfare* 2(1979):127–34.

Sarrel, Philip, and Lorna Sarrel. "The Redbook Report on Sexual Relationships." *Redbook* 10(1980):73–80.

Sauzier, Maria. "Sex Abuse of Tots 'Happens' Everywhere." *Medical World News* 22(13 April 1981):37–38.

Scales, Peter. "Myths about Sex That Mislead Young People." *Medical Aspects of Human Sexuality* 4(1981):132–48.

Scheinfeld, Amram. *Your Heredity and Environment.* New York: Lippincott, 1965.

Schmidt, G., and V. Sigusch. "Sex Differences in Responses to Psychosexual Stimulation by Films and Slides." *Journal of Sex Research* 5(1970):268–83.

Schrotenboer, Kathryn, and Genell J. Subak-Sharpe. *Freedom from Menstrual Cramps.* New York: Bantam, 1981.

Schultz, Donald D. *Critical Issues in Criminal Justice.* St. Louis: Thomas Law Book Co., 1975.

Schultz, Leroy. *Rape Victimology.* Springfield, Ill.: Charles C. Thomas, 1975.

Seaman, Barbara, and Gideon Seaman. *Women and the Crisis in Sex Hormones.* New York: Bantam, 1978.

Sears, R. R., and S. Feldman. *The Seven Ages of Man.* Los Altos, Calif.: William Kaufmann, 1964.

"The Second-Generation IUDs . . . Progestasert." *Current Prescribing* 1(1976):15–16.

Shahan, Lynn. *Living Alone and Liking It.* New York: Stratford Press, 1981.

Sha'ked, Ami. *Human Sexuality in Physical and Mental Illnesses and Disabilities.* Bloomington, Ind.: Indiana University Press, 1978.

Sheehy, Gail. *Hustling.* New York: Delacorte Press, 1973.

Sherfey, M. J. *The Nature and Evolution of Female Sexuality.* New York: Random House, 1972.

Shope, David F. *Interpersonal Sexuality.* Philadelphia: W. B. Saunders, 1975.

Sigerst, Henry. *The Great Doctors.* Garden City, N.Y.: Doubleday, 1958.

Silber, Sherman J. *How to Get Pregnant.* New York: Warner Books, 1980.

———. *The Male from Infancy to Old Age.* New York: Scribners, 1981.

Silverstein, Charles. *A Family Matter.* New York: McGraw-Hill, 1977.

Simenauer, Jacqueline, and David Carroll. *Singles: The New Americans.* New York: Simon & Schuster, 1982.

Singer, I., and J. Singer. "Types of Female Orgasm." *Journal of Sex Research* 11(1972):233–67.

Smith, Selwin, Ruth Hanson, and Shiela Noble. "Parents of Battered Babies: A Controlled Study." *British Medical Journal* 11(1973):388–91.

Socarides, Charles. *Homosexuality.* New York: Jason Aronson, 1978.

Sokolov, J. J., R. T. Harris, and M. R. Hecker. "Isolation of Substances from Human Vaginal Secretions Previously Shown to Be Sex Attractant Pheromones in Higher Primates." *Archives of Sexual Behavior* 5(1976):269–74.

Solomon, Philip, and Vernon Patch. *Handbook of Psychiatry.* 2d ed. Los Altos, Calif.: Lange Medical Publications, 1971.

"Some DES Daughters Have Withered Tubes." *Medical World News* 12(8 June 1981):41–42.

Sorensen, R. C. "Adolescent Sexuality in Contemporary America." In *The Sorensen Report.* New York: World Publishing, 1973.

Spanier, Graham. "Sources of Sex Information and Premarital Sexual Behavior." *Journal of Sex Research* 2(1977):73–88.

Spark, Richard et al. "Impotence Not Always Psychogenic." *Journal of the American Medical Association* 8(22/29 February 1980):750–55.

Sparks, John. *The Sexual Connection—Mating the Wild Way.* New York: McGraw-Hill, 1977.

Stauffer, J., and R. Frost. "Male and Female Interest in Sexually Oriented Magazines." *Journal of Communication* 26(1976):25–30.

Stein, Martha. *Lovers, Friends, Slaves . . . The Nine Male Sexual Types.* New York: Berkley Publishing (Putnam's), 1974.

Steinem, Gloria. "Erotica and Pornography, A Clear and Present Difference." *Ms.* 5(1978):53–57.

Steinhart, J. "What Women Are Learning about Vibrators." *Sexology* 4(1980):17–21.

Stoller, Robert. "The Term 'Transvestism'." *Archives of General Psychiatry* 24(1971):230–37.

———. "Sexual Deviations." In *Human Sexuality in Four Perspectives,* edited by F. Beach. Baltimore: Johns Hopkins Press, 1977.

Strasser, Susan. *Never Done: A History of American Housework.* New York: Pantheon, 1982.

Sue, David. "Erotic Fantasies of College Students During Coitus." *Journal of Sex Research* 4(1979):299–305.

Sullivan, W. "Boys and Girls Are Now Maturing Earlier." *The New York Times,* 24 January 1971.

Surawicz, Frida, and Charles Winick. "Debate: Should Prostitution Be Legalized?" *Medical Aspects of Human Sexuality* 9(1979):120–29.

Symonds, Martin et al. "Viewpoints: Is Prostitution a Victimless Crime?" *Medical Aspects of Human Sexuality* 8(1978):94–109.

Tannahill, Reay. *Sex in History.* New York: Stein & Day, 1980.

Tavris, C., and S. Sadd. *The Redbook Report on Female Sexuality.* New York: Delacorte, 1977.

Taylor, D. L. *Human Sexual Development.* Philadelphia: Davis, 1970.

Thong, Y. H., R. W. Steele, M. M. Vincent, S. A. Hensen, and J. A. Bellanti. "Impaired In Vitro Cell-Mediated Immunity of Rubella Virus during Pregnancy." *New England Journal of Medicine* 19(1973):253–60.

Thornburg, Hershel D. *Development in Adolescence.* Monterey, Calif.: Brooks/Cole, 1975.

Tietze, C. "Unintended Pregnancies in the U.S., 1970–1972." *Family Planning Perspectives* 11(1979):186–88.

Tollison, D., and H. Adams. *Sexual Disorders: Treatment, Theory, Research.* New York: Gardner Press, 1979.

Tomeh, Aida K. *The Family and Sex Roles.* Toronto: Holt, Rinehart & Winston of Canada, 1975.

Torres, Aida, Jacqueline Forest, and Susan Eisman. "Telling Parents: Clinic Policies and Adolescents' Use of Family Planning and Abortion Services." *Family Planning Perspectives* 6(1980):284–92.

Tortora, Gerard, Berdell Funke, and Christine Case. *Microbiology.* Menlo Park, Calif.: Benjamin/Cummings, 1982.

Tourney, Garfield. "Hormones and Homosexuality." In *Homosexual Behavior,* edited by Judd Marmor. New York: Basic Books, 1980.

Tripp, C. A. *Homosexual Matrix.* New York: McGraw-Hill, 1975.

Troll, L. E. "The Family of Later Life: A Decade of Review." *Journal of Marriage and Family* 33(1971):263–90.

Trytten, John. "Sex in Advertising: The Easy Way Out!" *Sales Management* (28 May 1973):36–37.

Tsai, Marvis, and Nathaniel Wagner. "Women Who Were Sexually Molested As Children." *Medical Aspects of Human Sexuality* 8(1979):55–56.

U.S. Bureau of the Census. *Statistical Abstracts 1982.* 100th ed. Washington, D.C.: U.S. Government Printing Office, 1982.

U.S. Vital and Health Statistics. *Divorces and Divorce Rates,* series 21, no. 29, March 1978. Washington, D.C.: U.S. Government Printing Office.

Valente, Mario. "Sexual Advice for the Mentally Retarded and Their Families." *Medical Aspects of Human Sexuality* 10(1975):91–92.

Vandervoot, H. E., and T. McIlvenna. *The Yes Book of Sex. You Can Last Longer.* San Francisco: Multimedia Resource Center, 1972.

Vessey, M., and D. Wiggins. "Use-Effectiveness of the Diaphragm in a Selected Family Planning Clinic Population in the United Kingdom." *Contraception* 9(1974):15–21.

Viscott, David. *Risking.* New York: Pocket Books, 1979.

Walfish, Steven, and Marilyn Myerson. "Sex-Role Identity and Attitudes toward Sexuality." *Archives of Sexual Behavior* 9(1980):199–204.

Wallace, Arla. "Viewpoints: Is Prostitution a Victimless Crime?" *Medical Aspects of Human Sexuality* 8(1978):94–109.

Wallis, Claudia. "Battling an Elusive Invader." *Time* 5 (2 August 1982):68–69.

Walsh, Robert, and Wilbert Leonard. "Usage of Terms for Sexual Intercourse by Men and Women." *Archives of Sexual Behavior* 4(July 1974):373–76.

Walster, Elaine. *Self-Esteem and Romantic Attraction.* Research paper read at American Psychological Association, Miami Beach, Florida, 1970.

Walster, Elaine, and G. William. *A New Look at Love.* Reading, Mass.: Addison-Wesley, 1978.

Warren, Carol. "Homosexuality and Stigma." In *Homosexual Behavior,* edited by Judd Marmor. New York: Basic Books, 1980.

Warren, Michelle. "Onset of Puberty Later in Athletic Girls." *Medical Aspects of Human Sexuality* 4(1982):77–78.

Wassmer, Arthur. *Making Contact.* New York: Fawcett, 1980.

Weideger, P. *Menstruation and Menopause.* New York: Alfred A. Knopf, 1976.

Weinberg, Martin, and Colin Williams. *Male Homosexuals.* New York: Oxford University Press, 1974.

Westman, Jack. "Telling Children about Sexual Molestation." *Medical Aspects of Human Sexuality* 8(1975):53.

Whitam, F. "Childhood Indicators of Male Homosexuality." *Archives of Sexual Behavior* 6(1977):89–96.

"Why Joint Custody Doesn't Always Work." *Changing Times* 38(July 1984):58–60.

Wills, Judith. "Cervical Caps—The Perfect Untested Contraceptive." *FDA Consumer* 3(1981):20–21.

Wilson, E. *On Human Nature.* Cambridge, Mass.: Harvard University Press, 1978.

Wilson, G. Terence, and David M. Lawson. "Expectancies, Alcohol, and Sexual Arousal in Women." *Journal of Abnormal Psychology* 3(1978):358–67.

Wilson, G. Terence, David M. Lawson, and David B. Abrams. "Effects of Alcohol on Sexual Arousal in Male Alcoholics." *Journal of Abnormal Psychology* 6(1978):609–16.

Wilson, W. Cody. "The Distribution of Selected Sexual Attitudes and Behaviors among the Adult Population of the United States." *Journal of Sex Research* 11(1975):46–64.

Winick, Charles, and Paul Kinsie. *The Lively Commerce, Prostitution in the United States.* Chicago: Quadrangle, 1971.

———. "Prostitution." *Sexual Behavior* 1(1973):33–43.

Winter, Ruth. *The Scientific Argument against Smoking.* New York: Crown Publishers, 1980.

Wistreich, George A., and Max D. Lechtman. *Microbiology.* New York: Macmillan, 1984.

Wolfe, Linda. *The Cosmo Report.* New York: Arbor House, 1981.

"Women Superdieters and Runners May Lose the Fertility Stakes." *Medical World News* 22(27 April 1981).

Woodruff, D. S., and J. E. Birren, eds. *Aging: Scientific Perspectives and Social Issues.* New York: Van Nostrand, 1975.

Woods, Nancy F. *Human Sexuality in Health and Illness.* 2d ed. St. Louis: Mosby, 1979.

Yankelovich, Skelly, and White. "The New Morality." *Time* 21(1977):111–16.

Zabin, Laurie. "Nonuse of Birth Control by Teenagers." *Medical Aspects of Human Sexuality* 2(1980):143.

Zelnick, Melvin, and John Kantner. "Sexual Activity, Contraceptive Use, and Pregnancy among Metropolitan-Area Teenagers." *Family Planning Perspectives* 12(1980):230–37.

Zepke, Brent. *Law for Non-Lawyers.* Totowa, N.J.: Littlefield, Adams, 1983.

Zilbergeld, Bernie. "Pursuit of the Grafenberg Spot." *Psychology Today* 10(1982):32–34.

Zilbergeld, Bernie, and Michael Evans. "The Inadequacy of Masters and Johnson." *Psychology Today* 8(1980):28–44.

Zimbardo, Philip G. *Essentials of Psychology and Life.* 10th ed. Glenview, Ill.: Scott, Foresman, 1980.

Zimmerman, D. R. "Your Family's Health." *Ladies' Home Journal* 10(1976):78.

CREDITS

Line Art Credits

Chapter 5

Fig. 5.1: From Mader, Sylvia S., *Inquiry into Life* 3d. ed. © 1976, 1979, 1982 Wm. C. Brown Publishers, Dubuque, Iowa. All Rights Reserved. Reprinted by permission.

Figs. 5.4, 5.6, 5.7, 5.8, 5.9, 5.10, and 5.11: From Hole, John W., Jr., *Human Anatomy and Physiology* 3d. ed. © 1978, 1981, 1984 Wm. C. Brown Publishers, Dubuque, Iowa. All Rights Reserved. Reprinted by permission.

Chapter 6

Figs. 6.1, 6.3, 6.4, 6.8, and 6.9: From Hole, *Human Anatomy and Physiology* 3d. ed. © 1978, 1981, 1984 Wm. C. Brown Publishers, Dubuque, Iowa. All Rights Reserved. Reprinted by permission.

Fig. 6.2: From Mader, Sylvia S., *Inquiry into Life* 3d. ed. © 1976, 1979, 1982 Wm. C. Brown Publishers, Dubuque, Iowa. All Rights Reserved. Reprinted by permission.

Box fig. 6.1: Source: National Cancer Institute.

Fig. 6.7: From Mader, Sylvia S., *Human Reproductive Biology.* © 1980 Wm. C. Brown Publishers, Dubuque, Iowa. All Rights Reserved. Reprinted by permission.

Chapter 7

Figs. 7.6 and 7.7: From Maxson, Linda and Charles Daugherty, *Genetics: A Human Perspective.* © 1985 Wm. C. Brown Publishers, Dubuque, Iowa. All Rights Reserved. Reprinted by permission.

Chapter 8

Figs. 8.1 and 8.2: From Masters, W. H. and Johnson, V. E., *Human Sexual Response.* Boston: Little, Brown, 1966, p. 5

Chapter 15

Fig. 15.13: From Hole, John W., Jr., *Human Anatomy and Physiology* 3d. ed. © 1978, 1981, 1984 Wm. C. Brown Publishers, Dubuque, Iowa. All Rights Reserved. Reprinted by permission.

Chapter 16

Figs. 16.1, 16.2b, 16.3, and 16.4: From Hole, John W., Jr., *Human Anatomy and Physiology* 3d. ed. © 1978, 1981, 1984 Wm. C. Brown Publishers, Dubuque, Iowa. All Rights Reserved. Reprinted by permission.

Fig. 16.11: From Maxson, Linda and Charles Daugherty, *Genetics: A Human Perspective.* © 1985 Wm. C. Brown Publishers, Dubuque, Iowa. All Rights Reserved. Reprinted by permission.

Chapter 17

Fig. 17.1: Source: U.S. Center for Disease Control, Atlanta, GA.

Chapter 18

Fig. 18.1: From Kinsey, A. C., et al, *Sexual Behavior in the Human Male.* W. B. Saunders, 1948, p. 638. Reprinted by permission of the Kinsey Institute for Research in Sex, Gender & Reproduction, Inc.

Illustrator Credits

Chapter 2

Fig. 2.1: McCullough Graphics

Chapter 5

Figs. 5.1c and 5.5: Ruth Krabach

Box fig. 5.1 and fig. 5.12: Rinehart/Sally

Figs. 5.2 and 5.3: Mildred Rinehart

Chapter 6

Fig. 6.3: Ruth Krabach

Fig. 6.5: Mildred Rinehart

Box fig. 6.1: Nancy Sally

Fig. 6.6: McCullough Graphics

Chapter 7

Fig. 7.10: Rinehart/Sally

Chapter 8

Figs. 8.1, 8.2, and 8.8: McCullough Graphics

Figs. 8.3, 8.4, and 8.7: Ruth Krabach

Figs. 8.5 and 8.6: Rinehart/Sally

Chapter 9

Figs. 9.1–9.7, 9.9–9.14: Thomas Bowker

Fig. 9.8: Mildred Rinehart

Chapter 10

Box fig. 10.1 and fig. 10.4: Mildred Rinehart

Figs. 10.1–10.3: Thomas Bowker

Box fig. 10.2: McCullough Graphics

Chapter 13

Box fig. 13.1: McCullough Graphics

Chapter 15

Figs. 15.3, 15.5–15.7, 15.9, 15.12b, 15.14–15.15, and box fig. 15.1: Ruth Krabach

Fig. 15.4: Rinehart/Sally

Figs. 5.10 and 5.11: McCullough Graphics

Chapter 16

Box fig. 16.1 and fig. 16.5: Ruth Krabach

Fig. 16.6: Rinehart/Sally

Chapter 17

Fig. 17.1: McCullough Graphics

Chapter 18

Fig. 18.1: McCullough Graphics

INDEX